IF BY SEA

IF BY SEA

The Forging of the American Navy
—From the American Revolution
to the War of 1812

GEORGE C. DAUGHAN

BASIC
BOOKS

A Member of the Perseus Books Group
New York

Books published by Basic Books are available at special discounts for bulk purchases in the United States by corporations, institutions, and other organizations. For more information, please contact the Special Markets Department at the Perseus Books Group, 2300 Chestnut Street, Suite 200, Philadelphia, PA 19103, or call (800) 810-4145, ex. 5000, or e-mail special.markets@perseusbooks.com.

Designed by Linda Harper

Library of Congress Cataloging-in-Publication Data

Daughan, George C.
If by sea : the forging of the American Navy-- from the American Revolution to the War of 1812 / George C. Daughan.
   p. cm.
Includes bibliographical references and index.
ISBN 978-0-465-01607-5 (alk. paper)
   1. United States. Navy--History--Revolution, 1775-1783. 2. United States. Navy--History--19th century. 3. United States--History, Naval--18th century. 4. United States--History, Naval--19th century. 5. United States--Politics and government--1783-1865. I. Title. II. Title: Forging of the American Navy, from the American Revolution to the War of 1812.

VA56.D38 2008
359.00973'09033--dc22

                                                                    2008001690

10 9 8 7 6 5 4 3 2 1

FOR KAY WITH LOVE

The infant periods of most nations are buried in silence, or veiled in fable, and perhaps the world may have lost but little which it need regret. [But] the origin and outset of the American Republic contains lessons of which posterity ought not to be deprived.

—James Madison

CONTENTS

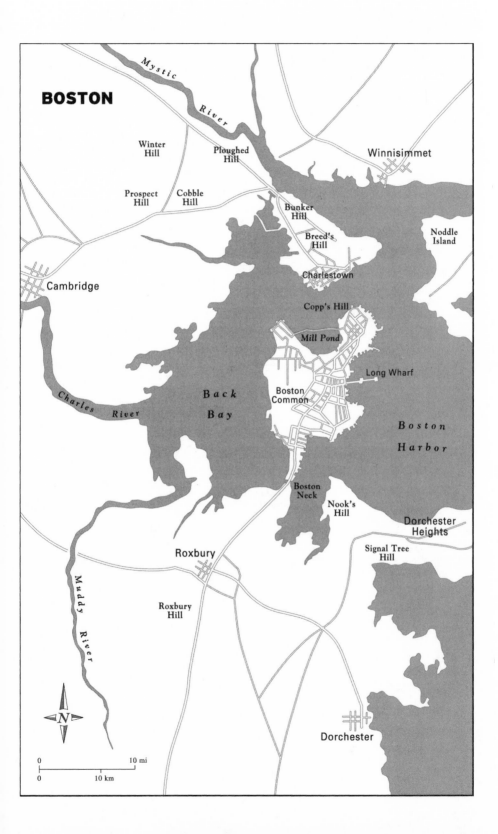

BOSTON

Mystic River

Winter Hill

Ploughed Hill

Winnisimmet

Prospect Hill

Cobble Hill

Bunker Hill

Breed's Hill

Noddle Island

Charlestown

Cambridge

Copp's Hill

Mill Pond

Long Wharf

Charles River

Back Bay

Boston Common

Boston Harbor

Boston Neck

Nook's Hill

Dorchester Heights

Roxbury

Signal Tree Hill

Muddy River

Roxbury Hill

N

Dorchester

0   10 mi

0   10 km

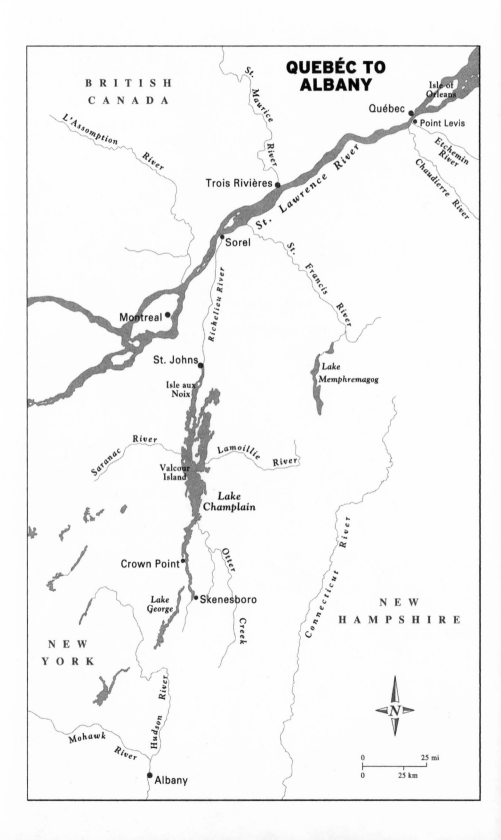

QUEBÉC TO ALBANY

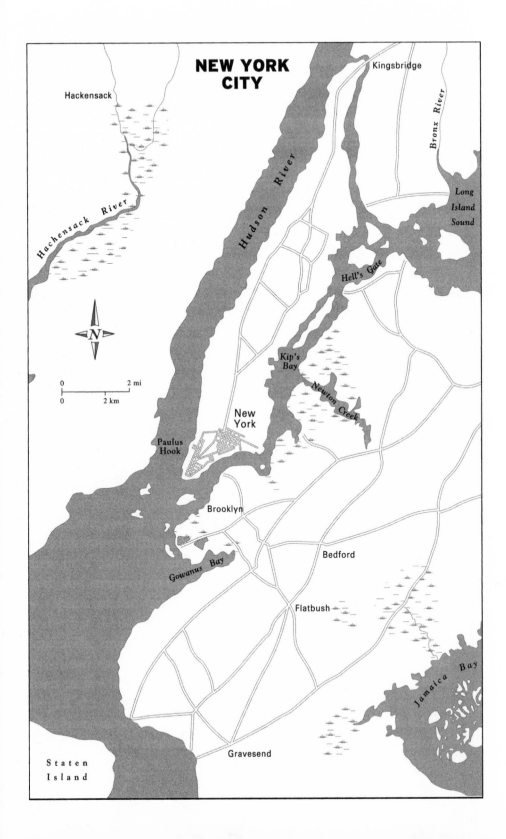

NEW YORK CITY

Kingsbridge

Hackensack

Bronx River

Long Island Sound

Hudson River

Hachensack River

Hell's Gate

N

0   2 mi

0   2 km

Kip's Bay

Newton Creek

New York

Paulus Hook

Brooklyn

Gowanus Bay

Bedford

Flatbush

Jamaica Bay

Gravesend

Staten Island

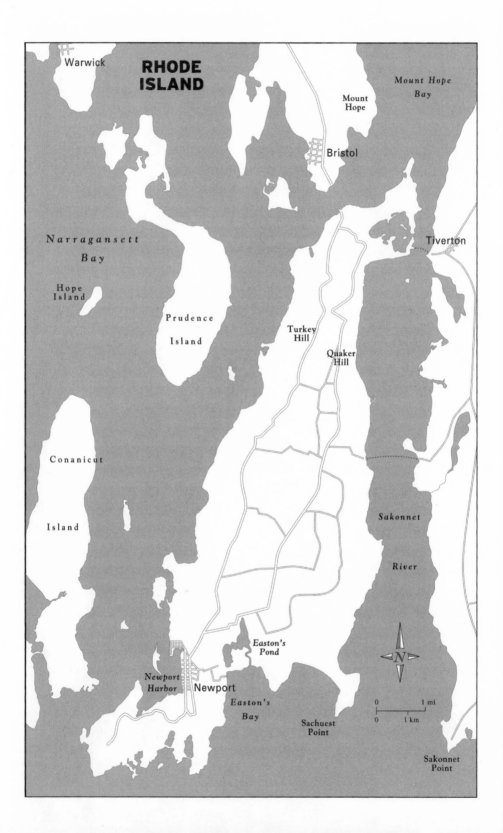

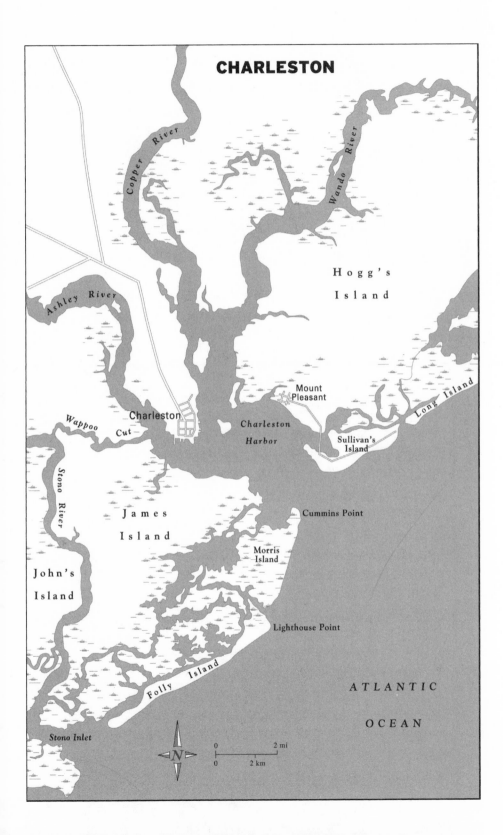

CHARLESTON

Copper River

Wando River

Ashley River

Hogg's Island

Wappoo Cut

Charleston

Mount Pleasant

Charleston Harbor

Sullivan's Island

Long Island

Stono River

James Island

Cummins Point

Morris Island

John's Island

Lighthouse Point

Folly Island

Stono Inlet

ATLANTIC

OCEAN

0   2 mi

0   2 km

N

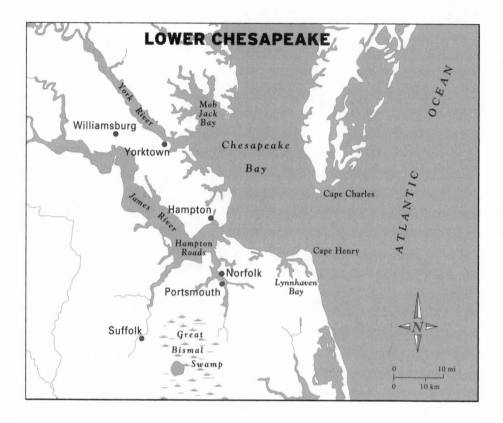

LOWER CHESAPEAKE

York River

Williamsburg

Mob
Jack
Bay

Yorktown

Chesapeake

Bay

Cape Charles

James River

Hampton

Hampton
Roads

Cape Henry

Norfolk

Portsmouth

*Lynnhaven
Bay*

Suffolk

*Great
Bismal
Swamp*

ATLANTIC OCEAN

N

| 0 | 10 mi |
| 0 | 10 km |

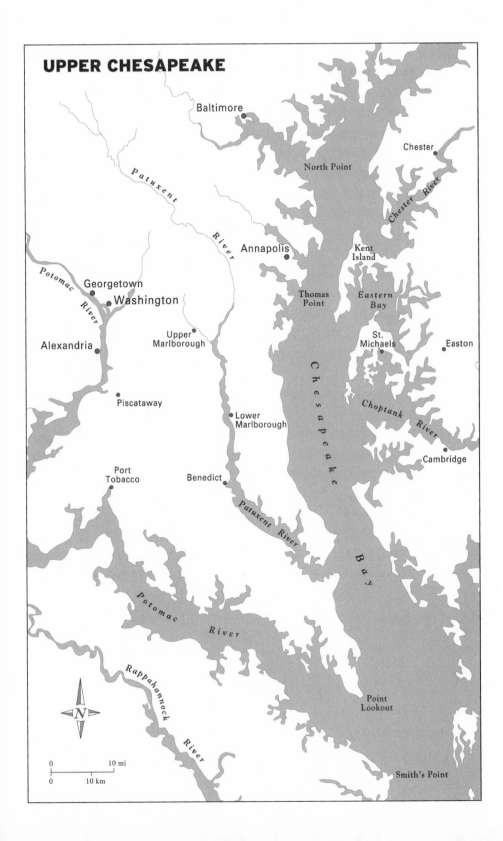

UPPER CHESAPEAKE

Baltimore

Chester

North Point

Patuxent

River

Annapolis

Kent Island

Chester River

Potomac

Georgetown

Washington

River

Thomas Point

Eastern Bay

Upper Marlborough

St. Michaels

Easton

Alexandria

Piscataway

Chesapeake

Choptank River

Lower Marlborough

Port Tobacco

Benedict

Cambridge

Patuxent River

Bay

Potomac

River

Rappahannock

River

N

Point Lookout

0   10 mi

0   10 km

Smith's Point

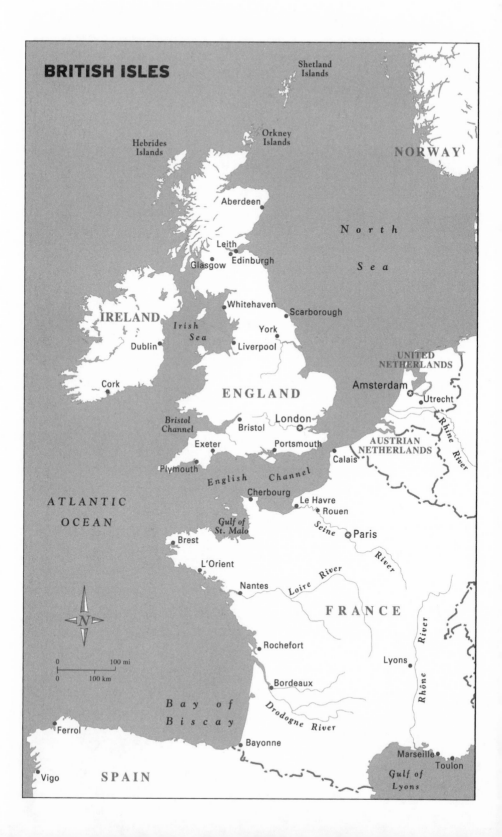

BRITISH ISLES

Shetland
Islands

Orkney
Islands

Hebrides
Islands

NORWAY

Aberdeen

North

Leith

Sea

Glasgow
Edinburgh

Whitehaven
Scarborough

IRELAND
*Irish
Sea*
York

Dublin
Liverpool

UNITED
NETHERLANDS

Cork

ENGLAND

Amsterdam
Utrecht

*Bristol
Channel*
London

Rhine
River

Bristol

AUSTRIAN
NETHERLANDS

Exeter
Portsmouth

Plymouth
Calais

English   Channel

ATLANTIC
Cherbourg

OCEAN
Le Havre
Rouen

*Gulf of
St. Malo*
Seine
Paris

Brest

L'Orient
River

Nantes
Loire River

FRANCE

N

Rochefort

Lyons

0   100 mi

Rhône
River

0   100 km

Bordeaux

*B a y   o f
B i s c a y*

Drodogne   River

Ferrol

Bayonne

Marseille
Toulon

Vigo
SPAIN
*Gulf of
Lyons*

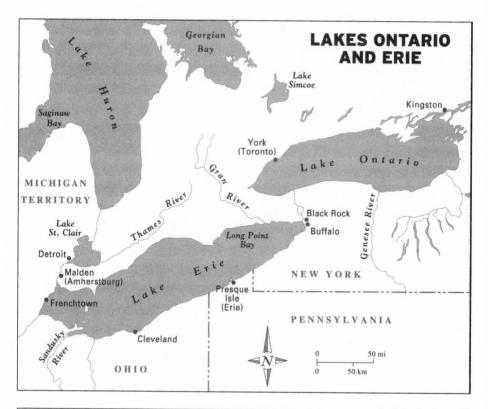

LAKES ONTARIO AND ERIE

Lake Huron

Georgian Bay

Lake Simcoe

Kingston

Saginaw Bay

York (Toronto)

Lake Ontario

Gran River

MICHIGAN TERRITORY

Thames River

Lake St. Clair

Black Rock

Buffalo

Genesee River

Detroit

Malden (Amherstburg)

Long Point Bay

Lake Erie

NEW YORK

Frenchtown

Presque Isle (Erie)

PENNSYLVANIA

Sandusky River

Cleveland

OHIO

N

0   50 mi
0   50 km

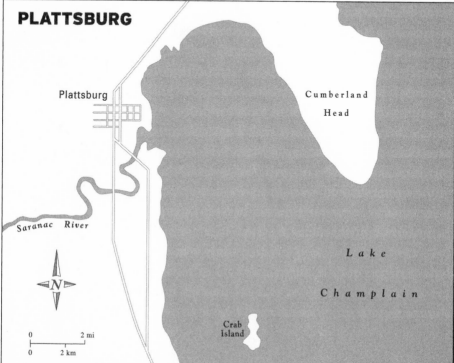

PLATTSBURG

Plattsburg

Cumberland Head

Saranac River

Lake Champlain

N

Crab Island

0   2 mi
0   2 km

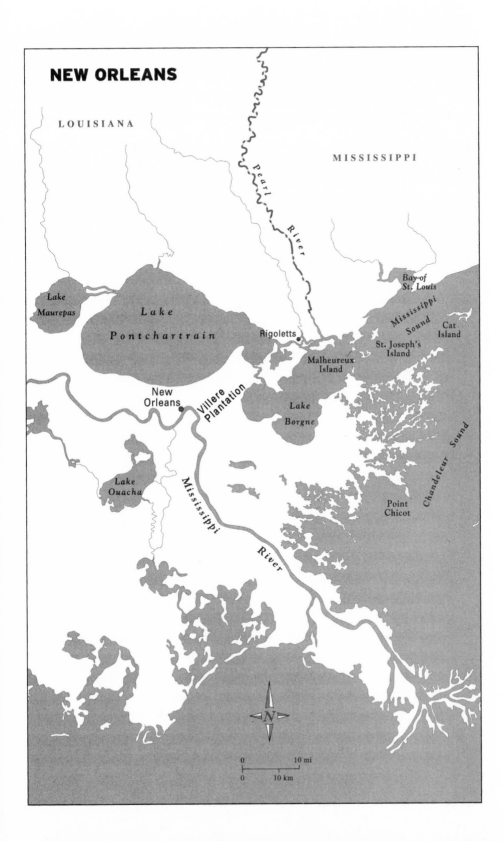

NEW ORLEANS

LOUISIANA

MISSISSIPPI

Pearl

River

Lake
Maurepas

Lake

Pontchartrain

Rigoletts

Bay of
St. Louis

Mississippi

Sound

Cat
Island

St. Joseph's
Island

Malheureux
Island

New
Orleans

Villere
Plantation

Lake
Borgne

Chandeleur Sound

Lake
Ouacha

Mississippi

Point
Chicot

River

N

0   10 mi

0   10 km

Illustration Source: Liber Nauticus, the art of Marine Drawing by Dominick Serres,
Collection of The New-York Historical Society.

THE SAILS OF A SQUARE-RIGGED SHIP

1. Flying jib
2. Jib
3. Fore topmast staysail
4. Fore staysail
5. Foresail, or course
6. Fore topsail
7. Fore topgallant
8. Mainstaysail
9. Maintopmast staysail
10. Middle staysail
11. Main topgallant staysail

12. Mainsail, or course
13. Maintopsail
14. Main topgallant
15. Mizzen staysail
16. Mizzen topmast staysail
17. Mizzen topgallant staysail
18. Mizzen sail
19. Spanker
20. Mizzen topsail
21. Mizzen topgallant

INTRODUCTION

On the Fourth of July 1963, President John F. Kennedy wrote a foreword for the initial volume of *Naval Documents of the American Revolution*. He hoped that publication of these primary sources would "make it amply clear the critical role played by sea power in the achievement of American Independence." He added that "between the lines [these papers] tell the story of the courage and valour which established the high traditions of the American Navy."

I was mulling over these words a dozen years ago while sitting on a huge granite boulder with my wife Kay at Pemaquid Point in Maine. We were looking at twelve miles of spectacular ocean between us and Monhegan Island. Kay and I came often to this place to paint and read. I had spent the last two years immersed in the literature of the American Revolution, something I had been doing, off and on, for most of my life.

President Kennedy would have been surprised, I thought, that he had failed. Despite the publication of many volumes and thousands of pages of documents, the role of the sea in the Revolution was as little appreciated at the end of the twentieth century as it had been in his day. The story of the influence of marine affairs, both naval and commercial, on the War of Independence remained to be told. America's foremost historians acknowledged this state of affairs but had done nothing to remedy it.

By not giving the sea its due, accounts of the Revolution were, as William Bell Clark, the editor of the *Naval Documents of the Revolution*, wrote, "bound to be imperfect." I decided to help fill this gap by focusing on the Continental Navy, which historians had traditionally ignored. In the previous hundred years only two noteworthy books had been written on the subject: Gardner W. Allen, *A Naval History of the Revolution*, published in 1913, and William M. Fowler Jr., *Rebels Under Sail*, published in 1976. Although both books provided valuable information and insights, they told the story of the Continental Navy apart from the overall war. I felt thatit could be told best by integrating it with the general history of the Revolution. I had long believed that the disconnection of naval history from history in general had given a distorted view of both.

Historians might have felt safe ignoring the Continental Navy because it had been an abject failure, playing almost no part in winning independence. When the patriots created their new fleet in 1775, they hoped it would make an important contribution to the war effort, but in the months and years that followed, it proved utterly unable to do so.

It seemed to me that examining why the patriots had created such a force and why it had failed illuminated much about the Revolution that had been hidden. It also showed that patriot efforts on the water were not entirely in vain. Much had been accomplished, so much, in fact, that the true beginning of the modern United States Navy was here, in the patriots' struggle to build what John Adams called a "naval power."

So little research had been done on the Continental Navy that it wasn't clear when it actually began. The generally accepted date was August 26, 1775, when the Rhode Island Assembly instructed its delegates to the Continental Congress to push for "building and equipping an American fleet." This was the view of William Bell Clark, but I came to the conclusion that the Continental Navy really began with the first shots fired at Lexington and Concord in April 1775.

The failure of the Continental fleet had led historians to posit 1794, not 1775, as the date when the modern American navy began. This, it seemed to me, was a serious mistake for a number of reasons, particularly since it minimized the importance of the "courage and valor" of the fighters of the Continental Navy, whom President Kennedy so admired. One of the purposes of this book is to show the clear connection between the revolutionary war fleet and the navy that followed.

When Washington proposed building a new American navy in his second term as president, John Adams supported him, but Thomas Jefferson and James Madison were strongly opposed. All four wanted to keep the country out of the wars of the French Revolution then raging in Europe. They had endured the horrors of the War of Independence and did not want to repeat them. They also agreed that war posed the biggest threat to the fragile republican institutions they were creating and to the nation's prosperity. Peace with honor was their common objective, but they profoundly disagreed about how to achieve it.

The argument over the usefulness and dangers of a blue water fleet lasted through four administrations and kept the navy's existence continually in doubt. It was not until the War of 1812 crystallized the needs of the country that the role of a respectable navy of the kind advocated by Washington and Adams became acknowledged by those who had previously opposed it. By then, forging the United States Navy had taken an improbable forty years.

I

WHALEBOATS
AND MEN-OF-WAR

April 1775–July 1775

At ten o'clock on the moonlit night of April 18, 1775, Paul Revere arrived at Dr. Joseph Warren's elegant residence on Hanover Street in a state of high excitement. He was about to receive his orders. The dapper, Harvard-educated, thirty-four-year-old Dr. Warren was president of the Massachusetts Provincial Congress, the extralegal revolutionary government that had seized power in the Bay Colony in 1774. With Samuel Adams and John Hancock hiding in Lexington, Dr. Warren had become the patriot leader in Boston.

A few blocks away, seven hundred British light infantrymen and grenadiers in full battle gear were embarking from the foot of Boston Common in twenty boats, manned by dozens of seamen from the fleet in the harbor, for a one-mile dash across the Charles River to Lechmere Point in East Cambridge. From there, as Warren and Revere well knew from their spies, the redcoats would be marching west to Concord via Lexington to arrest Adams and Hancock for treason, and to destroy arms and military supplies the Provincial Congress had hidden around Concord.

King George III, who followed events in the colonies closely but with little understanding, believed that removing a few rebel leaders and making a show of force would go a long way toward snuffing out the incipient revolt in Massachusetts. Lieutenant General Thomas Gage, the commander of British forces in North America and the royal governor of Massachusetts, had four thousand regulars in Boston, supported by a fleet of twenty-four men-of-war. Surely, the king reasoned, this was enough to suppress the deluded Massachusetts upstarts, who, as far as he knew, had no army to speak of, and no navy at all. "Once those rebels have felt a smart blow," he wrote, "they will submit."

At this point in British history the king had regained a considerable amount of power, dominating the government in a way George I and George II never had. George Otto Trevelyan described him: "Intent, heart and soul, on his favorite scheme for establishing a system of personal rule, under which all threads of administration should center in the royal closet, he entertained an instinctive antipathy to high-minded and independent men of all political parties, [selecting] his instruments among those who were willing to be subservient."

Major John Pitcairn, leader of the marine regiment in Boston and second in command of the column marching to Lexington and Concord, agreed with the king's approach. He wrote to Lord Sandwich, the first lord of the Admiralty, "Vigorous measures at present would soon put an end to this rebellion. The deluded people are made to believe . . . they are invincible . . . When this army is ordered to act against them, they will soon be convinced that they are very insignificant when opposed to regular troops." In another letter to Sandwich, Pitcairn wrote, "I am satisfied that one active campaign, a smart action, and burning two or three of their towns, will set things to rights." The march to Concord with the arrest of Adams and Hancock was the kind of "smart action" the king wanted.

Boston in those days was a tiny, pear-shaped peninsula tenuously hitched to the mainland by a 120-foot-wide, half-mile-long isthmus called the Neck. With mudflats on either side, it was regularly submerged during the high tides of a full moon, turning the town into a veritable island. For those traveling west, the fastest way out of the city was by boat. The entire British column could be across the river in an hour; by two o'clock the redcoats could be in Lexington, only twelve miles away. Concord was just an hour's march from there.

After leaving Dr. Warren's house, Revere told his young neighbor Robert Newman to hang two lanterns from the belfry of nearby Old North Church, Boston's highest point and most prominent landmark. With the help of vestrymen John Pulling and Thomas Barnard, also Revere's neighbors, the twenty-three-year-old New-man climbed the belfry steps. Working in the dark, he flashed two lanterns from a window above the great bells, signaling Charlestown patriots that the regulars were crossing the Charles River by boat rather than marching overland across the Neck. Revere then col-lected two companions, Joshua Bentley and Thomas Richardson, and hurried down to the mouth of the Charles in North Boston, where his twenty-foot skiff was tucked in a clump of bushes. Less than a mile upstream the regulars continued crawling across the river, their boats looking like giant water bugs. It was now ten-thirty. The three patriots launched the skiff into calm water, and while Bentley and Richardson rowed with muffled oars, Revere sat in the stern sheets searching the dark outline of Charlestown, where a fast horse waited.

The town wharf was only six hundred yards away, but he doubted they would be landing there tonight, for riding at single anchor directly in front of him was HMS *Somerset*, a gigantic, 64-gun sail of the line, her nightlights blazing fore and aft. Revere wasn't surprised by her presence; she'd been in position for several days, taking the place of two smaller warships, *Canceaux* and *Lively*. Admiral Samuel Graves, commander of the British fleet in North America, kept a warship stationed in the ferryway to intimidate Charlestown patriots who might be tempted to set artillery on Bunker Hill or Breed's Hill. He warned that if they did, men-of-war would incinerate the town. Such an action, as he was well aware, would be highly pleasing to the king and his circle in London. Graves directed operations personally from his flagship, the 50-gun *Preston*, which never left the harbor.

Revere assumed the *Somerset* would be on high alert, watching for alarm riders, but he was determined to slip past her. "It was then young flood," he recalled many years later, "the *[Somerset]* was winding [on her single anchor] and the moon was rising." He naturally expected a lookout or, more likely, a tar on a guard boat to spot him. Deserters were a constant problem for the men-of-war, and they patrolled every night. If a guard boat captured Revere, red-coated marines would clap him and his mates in irons and throw them into a cramped wooden brig in the suffocating bowels of the giant battleship. It could be weeks, even months, before he and his friends breathed fresh air again. Admiral Graves might even hang them.

The trio circled the *Somerset* to the east, being careful not to row too far in front of her, lest one of the other sixteen men-of-war in the harbor notice them. If the warships were on alert—which Revere had to assume they would be—it was hard to imagine how they could miss him. This particular night, however, the *Somerset* had no guard boats running. They were all being used downstream to ferry troops across the Charles. In less than thirty minutes Revere's skiff glided unnoticed past the *Somerset*'s bow and brushed up against Charlestown's main wharf near the old battery. After he hopped out, his companions rowed back the very way they had just come, passing once more under the *Somerset*'s nose. And again, she ignored them. Unaccountably, her captain, Edward LeCras, had received no orders from Admiral Graves to stop boat traffic between Boston and Charlestown, or even to be on the lookout for alarm riders, though General Gage had specifically requested Graves to do both.

Not only did Graves not have his warships on alert, but he had also failed to provide enough boats to ferry the infantrymen across the Charles all at once. As a result, a crossing that should have taken an hour became a lengthy expedition, consuming more than three hours. That gave Revere and his compatriot, William Dawes (whom Dr. Warren had sent by land), plenty of time to gallop into the countryside and ignite the alarm riders who would alert every village and town that the regulars were out.

Bells began tolling and alarm muskets firing, as young farmers rushed to village greens where their town militias were assembling. Those immediately adjacent to Boston answered the call first. As word spread, militiamen from the rest of Massachusetts, Connecticut, Rhode Island, and New Hampshire turned out. In a few hours, thousands were marching toward Concord. "A sudden alarm brought them together, animated with the noblest spirit," Dr. Warren later wrote to Sam Adams. "They left their houses, their families, with nothing but the clothes on their backs, without a day's provision, and many without a farthing in their pockets."

The militiamen had been in training for months. The patriots had been organizing since the fall of 1774 to counter an expected British outbreak from Boston. After establishing a separate government in Massachusetts, the Provincial Congress had urged all the towns to begin serious militia training and prepare 25 percent of their toughest members to be ready at a minute's notice.

The patriots had already won the first battle of the Revolution by gaining political control of all the towns in Massachusetts with the exception of Scituate and Marshfield. Elected officers committed to the patriot cause replaced the old Tory leadership in the town militias. Once in power, the new leaders began drilling their men in earnest, creating the building blocks for a revolutionary army.

No attempt, however, was made to organize sea militias or create a revolutionary navy. There were no precedents for such a force in the colonial past. Town militias, in contrast, had existed from the earliest times and were easily applied to the new army. Furthermore, the Royal Navy appeared so dominant that it would have seemed lunacy for anyone to organize a patriot sea force along the lines of its land army. And no one did.

British Lieutenant Colonel Francis Smith, commanding officer of the troops marching to Concord, was determined to carry out his orders no matter what delays or obstacles he encountered. When he reassembled his men after crossing the Charles River, he hoped they could march to Concord and back without opposition. After all, General Gage had given no orders telling him what to do if the patriots attacked him. Gage was hoping that when the farmers saw a large force of regulars dressed in all their finery they would withdraw.

As Smith marched his column toward Lexington, he began hearing the bells ringing and guns firing. He heard so much noise that at three o'clock when he reached Menotomy (now Arlington), the town adjacent to Lexington, he sent for reinforcements. He also ordered Major Pitcairn, his second in command, to march six companies ahead to Lexington as fast as he could to make up for lost time, while Smith followed behind with the rest. At five o'clock, Pitcairn, who was expecting to teach the rebels a lesson, was approaching Lexington Green. There he saw seventy-seven men of the town militia assembled with their muskets.

As Pitcairn's companies approached, Captain John Parker, the elected leader of Lexington's militia and a veteran of the French and Indian War, could see the disparity of forces and ordered his men not to initiate any foolhardy action. He had no intention of fighting against such odds. Parker was not leaving the green, either; he intended to remain and watch the redcoat column as it passed. Although Parker had good control of his men, Pitcairn did not. Without orders or provocation, his redcoats began running wildly toward the patriots, firing their bayonet-tipped muskets as they went. Parker and his men fled before the onslaught, eight being killed and nine wounded before Pitcairn could restore order. Only one of his soldiers had received a scratch.

Lieutenant Colonel Smith now came up with the rest of his men and continued down the road to Concord. As he marched, word of the Lexington massacre spread and the gathering militiamen, their anger raised to a high pitch, prepared for a bloody fight. Smith reached Concord by nine o'clock and spent the next three hours destroying a few supplies and munitions and waiting for reinforcements. Shots were exchanged at North Bridge over the Concord River and some of Smith's men were killed, as the patriot ranks swelled ominously. By noon Smith decided he could wait no longer. Pretending he had accomplished his mission, he began the long trek back to Boston.

Patriot militia units that were well protected by stone walls and trees now guarded key points on the road between Concord and Lexington. The first was at Meriam's Corner, where a pitched battle broke out that staggered Smith. Another occurred at Nelson's Bridge, where Captain Parker and his Lexington men exacted retribution for the surprise attack on them earlier. As Smith's bloodied column stumbled toward Lexington, it was obvious they would never make it back to Boston. Still thinking reinforcements would arrive, Smith refused to surrender. Fortunately for him, General Gage had dispatched, albeit belatedly, twelve hundred men under Brigadier General Lord Percy. They appeared on a hill overlooking Lexington with two brass field pieces just as Smith was about to give up and he raced into their welcoming arms. But the number of armed provincials kept growing, and Percy had to fight his way back to Boston.

At this point Dr. Joseph Warren and patriot Brigadier General William Heath arrived on the scene. Thanks to Graves's lax oversight of the harbor, Warren had crossed over the Charlestown ferryway earlier that morning and galloped to Lexington, arriving shortly after Percy. On the way he met General Heath, one of five general officers of militia appointed by the Massachusetts Provincial Congress. Heath had just reached the outskirts of Lexington. In the fast-moving situation, Warren and Heath gave the patriots what direction they could.

A full-scale battle developed between the equivalent of two brigades of British regulars led by an outstanding general and at least twice that number of patriot militiamen. Although greatly outnumbered, Lord Percy had the advantage of unity of command and experience. With cool courage and monumental determination, he fought his way to Charlestown Neck, arriving just after sunset. General Heath was close on his heels. But lacking firm control of the diverse militias or any artillery, he and Dr. Warren decided not to cross the Neck and fight it out with Percy in the dark.

Admiral Graves used the *Somerset*'s boats to ferry what was left of Percy's exhausted force back to Boston. At the same time, suddenly aware that he might have some explaining to do to the Admiralty, he finally issued orders to the *Somerset's* captain to stop patriot boat traffic moving between Boston and Charlestown. Later Graves told the Admiralty that the whole fracas had taken him by surprise.

By the end of the day fourteen thousand well-drilled, well-led patriot militiamen had answered the call. In the succeeding forty-eight to seventy-two hours their ranks would swell to over twenty thousand—as many men under arms as existed in the whole British army. Seventy-three British regulars were dead from the fighting, one hundred seventy-four wounded, and twenty-six captured. The patriots suffered forty-nine killed, forty-one wounded, and five captured. "From beginning to end," British Lieutenant John Barker lamented, "[this expedition] was [as] ill planned and ill executed as it was possible to be."

As bad as the defeat was, it would have been far worse had the patriots been as organized on the water as they were on land. They might have boarded and captured some of the men-of-war dozing in the harbor that night, including the *Somerset*. Fortunately for Admiral Graves, none of the patriot leaders in Massachusetts had given any thought to creating a navy, though the raw materials for one were readily available. Only when the fighting began did their thoughts turn to the sea. And even then, they failed to recognize where their real naval strength lay.

Admiral Graves, however, saw it clearly. Once he awoke to the fact that a war was on, he became anxious about the safety of his ships. He saw threats coming from two places in particular: hills and whaleboats. If rebel artillery were placed on Dorchester Heights or the high ground in Charlestown, it could force him out of the harbor. As for whaleboats, he wrote to the Admiralty, "[They] lay in abundance in different creeks round this harbor, [and might] in a calm night . . . surprise one of the frigates of the squadron and carry her by suddenly pouring in great numbers." He might have added that if enough whaleboats were so deployed, the entire fleet in Boston, which fluctuated in numbers and was at times quite small, could be in danger.

In the hours and days immediately following the fighting, Dr. Warren, as head of the Provincial Congress's executive body, the Committee of Safety, worked tirelessly from his new headquarters at Jonathan Hastings House in Cambridge. Forty-eight-year-old General Artemus Ward, an honored veteran of the French and Indian War and head of the Massachusetts militia, moved in with him. Warren, as the political leader, was in command, but the two worked smoothly together. With firm support from the full Provincial Congress, they focused on keeping the militiamen from returning to their farms. Warren offered enlistments of eight months and pay from the Provincial Congress if they would join the incipient patriot army. This and their burning patriotism seemed to be enough, as hundreds and then thousands signed on. No one envisaged a long struggle. Everyone assumed there would be an early settlement and the men would be home before Christmas.

But while Warren, Ward, and their associates were organizing the new army, using whaleboats to challenge Admiral Graves never seems to have occurred to them. Dr. Warren knew the essential shape an army would take, but he had no conception of what a successful sea force might look like. Although Warren had no vision of a navy, John Adams, his cousin Sam Adams, and some of their colleagues did. Once the shooting had started—"this glorious crisis" Sam Adams called it—the Adamses and some of their associates turned their thoughts to building a prestigious American navy of large frigates and sail of the line. They took these bold ideas to the Continental Congress, not realizing where the patriots' real naval strength lay—in the humble whaleboats that worried Admiral Graves.

In the midst of organizing an army, Dr. Warren was also working hard to get the true story of Lexington and Concord before the British public. At his urging, the Provincial Congress on April 22 appointed Elbridge Gerry of Marblehead to chair a committee of nine and charged it with collecting eyewitness accounts. With characteristic energy, Gerry and his associates interviewed dozens of spectators and participants, including captured British soldiers. Their research showed unmistakably that General Gage's infantrymen had initiated the bloodshed, massacring the minutemen assembled on Lexington Green.

Well schooled in the importance of propaganda by his mentor Sam Adams, Dr. Warren wanted these facts spread by London's newspapers as soon as possible. Richard Derby, a prominent Salem merchant and solid member of the Provincial Congress, offered his family's yacht-like schooner *Quero* for the job. His son John, an experienced captain, volunteered to sail her. Attentive to every detail, the tireless Dr. Warren had instructed Derby to take a roundabout route to London. "Make for Dublin," he urged, "or any good port in Ireland, and from thence cross to Scotland or England, and hasten to London . . . so that [you] may escape all cruisers that may be found in the chops of the [English] Channel."

The *Quero* set out quietly on the night of April 27, eight days after the battle of Lexington and Concord. As the sleek schooner fell away from Derby wharf with no lanterns lit, she appeared little more than an indistinct shadow in the dim moonlight. Salem Neck was immediately to port, and before passing it, William Carleton, the *Quero*'s master, had all his canvas up, trying to catch every breath of wind. He would need all of the schooner's speed that night. A 20-gun British frigate, HMS *Lively*, was patrolling the waters off nearby Marblehead. While Derby suspected she might be looking for him, he wasn't overly concerned. Even if the warship spotted her, the *Quero* would be hard to catch, unless the *Lively* managed an exceptionally lucky shot in the dark from a distance.

Still, Derby knew the *Quero* was in a race. Four days earlier, the British fast packet *Sukey* had departed Boston with Lieutenant Joseph Nunn aboard, carrying General Gage's official dispatches. Anticipating that London would view Lexington and Concord as a calamity, Gage, the consummate military bureaucrat, had artfully composed an account that minimized the bad news and had it aboard the *Sukey* on April 24, five days after the battle. By the time Derby put to sea, the *Quero* had four days to make up. The tiny schooner was fast, and unlike the *Sukey*, she carried no cargo, only ballast. Nonetheless, Derby would be hard put to beat her to England.

Thinking Warren's instructions unnecessary, Derby ignored them and sailed straight to Portsmouth, England, navigating boldly up the Channel to the Isle of Wight, where Carleton deposited him and then put back out to sea, planning a rendezvous later at Plymouth. Once ashore on the Isle of Wight, Derby rented a pair-oared wherry that carried him to the mainland through Britain's giant naval base at Portsmouth. As he viewed the great warships in the harbor, he clutched Dr. Warren's sensational documents under his surtout. Waiting on the dock as he landed was a post chaise to London, and he hopped aboard, arriving in the capital twenty-nine days after slipping past the *Lively* in Salem Bay. The *Sukey* and her unsuspecting captain, William Brown, along with his most important passenger, Lieutenant Joseph Nunn, were still far out at sea.

Derby hurried directly to Benjamin Franklin's quarters. To his surprise Dr. Franklin, the longtime London agent for Massachusetts, had already left for America. In spite of his unceasing efforts to avoid it, war now appeared inevitable to him. Without hesitating, Derby rushed to the lodgings of Franklin's associate and rival, Arthur Lee, who took Warren's documents to Mansion House, the official residence of the lord mayor of London, John Wilkes. A supporter of the American cause and a bitter foe of the king, Wilkes instantly grasped the significance of the papers and brought them to the antigovernment *London Evening Post*, which printed them immediately. Other newspapers picked up the story, issuing special editions, and in a few days the entire country had the news.

The *Post*'s story stunned the British. While they were enjoying the beautiful spring of 1775, they hadn't been paying attention to the conflict back in Massachusetts. They assumed—as their king did—that General Gage and his four thousand regulars would easily put a stop to the disturbances in Boston. Now there came reports that Gage had suffered a crushing defeat. How could this be? Great Britain was supreme among the world's powers, without rival since her victory over France in the Seven Years War; it was absurd to think that a few undisciplined peasants could withstand the power of His Majesty's armies. The king refused to believe the newspaper accounts, assuming them to be based on rebel sources, though he was greatly agitated that an official report wasn't available to contradict them.

The *Sukey* finally reached London on June 9, thirteen days after Derby landed at Portsmouth. Lieutenant Nunn, still unaware of any urgency, waited until the following morning before delivering the dispatches to Lord Dartmouth at Whitehall. Dartmouth, secretary of state for the colonies, knew of the king's distress and was relieved to see Nunn's dispatches. As he read them, however, they confirmed what the newspapers had been saying, with the exception of Gage's claim that the Americans had been the aggressors. Nor did the sparse, carefully worded paragraphs deny the rebel victory. Dartmouth was crestfallen; the king would be furious.

Dr. Warren had hoped the *Quero*'s mission would lead to negotiations and an end to the bloodshed. Among the papers he had entrusted to Derby was a letter for Arthur Lee. "Lord Chatham and our friends," Warren wrote, "must make up the breach immediately or never. The next news from England must be conciliatory, or the connection between us ends, however fatal the consequences may be." But when Lord Dartmouth presented the dispatches, the king reacted angrily toward both the rebels and his hapless general. Never for a moment did he consider a political compromise. Instead of the conciliatory approach Dr. Warren hoped for, he renewed his commitment to crushing the rebellion, hanging its leaders, and imposing a draconian regime on America that would ensure she never rose up again. The latter part of the plan he kept to himself; it could only be inferred from the unguarded comments of his more belligerent supporters.

The king was convinced that entering into talks with the likes of Dr. Warren would lead to the loss of not only Britain's North American possessions but the rest of the empire as well, including India and Ireland. Even the homeland might become infected with New England's leveling ideas. Speaking for the king, Lord Dartmouth wrote to the Admiralty, "It is His Majesty's firm resolution of which I am directed to acquaint your Lordships, that every measure be pursued for suppressing, by the most vigorous efforts, by land and sea, this unnatural rebellion which menaces the subversion of the present happy constitution. To this end it is His Majesty's pleasure that the Admiral commanding upon the Boston station, do carry on such operations upon the seacoasts of the four governments of New England as he shall judge most effectual for suppressing in conjunction with His Majesty's land forces, the rebellion which is now openly avowed and supported in these colonies."

Thus in spite of the patriots' desire to end the war swiftly through a negotiation, the king's hostile attitude prolonged the fighting. Chief among his instruments would be the Royal Navy. Without its enormous power, he could never have contemplated waging a colonial war three thousand miles away. With it, he could imagine an easy victory.

The overwhelming superiority of Britain's sea force was so obvious that challenging it would appear at first glance to be madness. But in the first days and weeks of the war, important naval activity erupted spontaneously in a number of places that suggested how a successful American navy might be organized. Ironically, leaders like the Adamses, who never lacked the courage to defy the Royal Navy, failed to grasp the lessons of this activity.

During the first week of May, for instance, while on patrol in Buzzards Bay, British Captain John Linzee, commander of the 14-gun sloop-of-war *Falcon,* sent a lieutenant and twenty men in a tender to capture a patriot sloop laden with provisions. The lieutenant completed his mission swiftly enough and was just heading back to the *Falcon* with the sloop in tow when Captain Daniel Egery and thirty patriots from nearby Dartmouth, Massachusetts, in a ragtag squadron of small craft, attacked him. In the ensuing melee, the lieutenant, the gunner, and a doctor's mate were wounded before the British tender finally struck her colors, thereby yielding to the patriots. Captain Egery took the captured vessel back to port and sent thirteen British prisoners off to the Taunton jail.

At the same time, in early May, Lieutenant Colonel Samuel Thompson was contemplating an even bolder action in the busy seaport town of Falmouth (now Portland), in the Maine district of Massachusetts. Admiral Graves had sent the 6-gun *Canceaux* up from Boston to shepherd a large shipment of white pine masts, spars, and yards to England. Colonel Thompson planned to capture it. The giant white pines of Maine and New Hampshire were vital to the Royal Navy. Along with Portsmouth, New Hampshire, Falmouth was a principal mast port. But local patriots, led by Enoch Freeman and Jedediah Preble, had recently blocked the export of all wood products from Falmouth to Britain. Graves expected the *Canceaux* to extradite the embargoed masts.

On the night of May 9, Thompson arrived in Falmouth with fifty armed men, sporting boughs of spruce in their hats and a spruce pole with a green top for a standard. They seized the *Canceaux*'s captain, Lieutenant Henry Mowat, while he was walking on shore with two shipmates. Upon hearing of Mowat's capture, the warship's master, Mr. Hogg, put a spring on her cable and hove it taut, bringing three guns to bear on the town. He then fired two warning shots. Horrified, Freeman and Preble insisted that Thompson abandon his plan and release Mowat. The captain was allowed to return to his ship, but he was unable to get the shipment of masts released. He was forced to sail back to Boston empty-handed, demonstrating that the *Canceaux* alone could not force Falmouth to do anything against its will.

Mowat was aware that if Falmouth's patriot leadership had supported Colonel Thompson, he could have captured the *Canceaux*. Enoch Freeman betrayed the leaders' collective timidity when he wrote to the Provincial Congress the next day, calling Thompson's actions "rash, injudicious, and unjustifiable." He was worried, Freeman said, that Admiral Graves might retaliate by sending a whole squadron against the defenseless town. He neglected to explain why a town of four thousand had no defenses, or why it wasn't preparing any.

Of far greater importance than the activity in Maine and Buzzards Bay was the patriots' capture of Fort Ticonderoga on May 10. Ethan Allen, accompanied by Benedict Arnold and eighty-three Green Mountain roughnecks, crossed Lake Champlain at three o'clock in the morning in a boat and barge, attacking while the fort's forty-eight defenders were asleep. Taken by surprise, Captain William Delaplace surrendered, handing the patriots an important cache of weapons, including eighty heavy artillery pieces, twenty brass guns, a dozen mortars, small arms, powder, and ball.

The next day, patriot Lieutenant Colonel Seth Warner captured nearby Crown Point and its military stores. At the same time, another band of Green Mountain Boys easily took nearby Fort George at the head of Lake George. Worried for months about all three forts, General Gage had sent a warning to General Guy Carleton in Quebec. But the warning came too late; in any case, Carleton, with only a few men, was in no position to act.

Immediately after seizing Ticonderoga, Colonel Arnold set out to add to his luster by capturing Lake Champlain. On May 15 he put seventy men in bateaux (flat-bottomed boats, tapering toward the ends) and headed for St. Jean on the Richelieu River at the outlet of the lake, intent on seizing the only British warship stationed in those waters. On the way, his party stopped a bateau with a British lieutenant carrying mail from Canada. Not only did the cache of letters reveal that a mere seven hundred redcoats were defending the entire country, but they also gave Arnold a general idea of where the soldiers were located—all of which sent his outsize ambition soaring.

The following day a small schooner, which patriots had taken from the notorious local Tory leader Philip Skene at Skenesborough, caught up with Arnold; he climbed aboard and charged down the lake. Thirty miles from St. Jean he lost the wind and was forced to transfer his men back to the bateaux, rowing the rest of the way. When he reached land on the 18th, he hid his men in a bug-infested swamp and sent a spy up to the village. The soldier soon returned with the news that both the town and its schooner were practically defenseless. Breathing more easily, Arnold's men crept into St. Jean, surprising a sergeant and twelve redcoats who surrendered without a fight. Afterward, the crew of the warship, seeing such a large number of armed colonials, surrendered as well "without any loss on either side," Arnold reported.

The captured warship was sixty feet long and carried two brass 6-pounders—enough to dominate the lake. Arnold renamed her *Enterprise*. There were also nine bateaux at St. Jean. Arnold gathered all the munitions and supplies he could find into four of them and burned the remaining five before leaving. With the *Enterprise* and the other captured schooner, as well as the three forts, Arnold now commanded the lake. This achievement was of great strategic importance, since control of Lake Champlain was essential to stopping a British invasion from Canada.

By this time the patriot army that had gathered after Lexington and Concord numbered well over fifteen thousand. It had succeeded in trapping the British within Boston, forcing General Gage to rely on the Royal Navy for sustenance. On May 14, Dr. Warren and his Committee of Safety, hoping to further tighten the patriots' land blockade, planned to remove all livestock and provisions from the many islands dotting Boston harbor. The beleaguered Gage had immediate intelligence of Warren's plans—presumably from the villainous patriot insider, Dr. Benjamin Church—and warned Graves.

The admiral had a particular interest in one of the islands, Noddle's. He had hidden away boards, spars, and other wood products in a storehouse there. He claimed the materials were scheduled to be sent to the repair yards at Halifax, Nova Scotia. But he was probably holding them for sale in Boston later that winter, when supplies would be tight.

Even in that golden age of speculation, the admiral's greed was noteworthy. His "fishing policy" (despite the crying need for fresh fish in the city, no one was permitted to drop a line in the harbor without paying a small bribe) was but one of many examples.

In spite of his interest in Noddle's, the quixotic admiral informed General Gage that he was sending only a single guard boat to watch it and neighboring Hog Island. He also insisted that soldiers would protect the island more effectively than his ships. Graves had no intention of cooperating with the army. As had been the case during the battle of Lexington and Concord, he appeared strangely indifferent to the war.

On May 27 Dr. Warren ordered more than two hundred men under New Hampshire's John Stark to remove the horses, cattle, sheep, hay, and other supplies from Hog, Noddle's, and Snake islands, as well as the nearby Chelsea coast. Stark set out early in the morning and began taking horses and cattle, along with one hundred sheep, from Hog Island. In the early afternoon, a party of about thirty patriots waded across the creek to Noddle's Island. As they slogged through the knee-deep water, a red flag shot up from Graves's flagship, *Preston*. A hundred marines from the warships *Cerberus*, *Glasgow*, *Somerset*, and *Mercury* made for the island to drive the rebels away, even as the armed schooner *Diana*, commanded by the admiral's nephew, Lieutenant Thomas Graves, hurried up Chelsea Creek to cut off Stark's party.

With her four 4-pounders, twelve swivel guns, and thirty men, the *Diana* was a machine to reckon with. Seeing what was coming, the patriots retreated to Hog Island, where they jumped into a ditch and faced the marines, fending them off easily while receiving fire from the *Diana*. Then, at six o'clock in the evening, wind and tide turned against Lieutenant Graves, prompting the admiral to send the *Somerset*'s tender, *Britannia*, and eleven barges armed with swivel guns to rescue his nephew.

It took the barge captains a painfully long time to maneuver into position. The delay gave the patriots time to strengthen Stark on Hog Island. When the barges finally managed to secure lines on the *Diana*, the wind and tide compelled them to tow her slowly down Chelsea Creek, forcing the entire party to pass through a vicious gauntlet of musket fire from patriots on the mainland. Meanwhile, Dr. Warren was directing the battle from his headquarters in Cambridge. With the *Diana* under siege, he had ample time to muster a thousand men under Brigadier General Israel Putnam, a popular hero of the French and Indian War.

The general positioned the bulk of his men on the high ground at Winnisimmet (now Chelsea), where the barges and the *Diana* would have to pass. Around eleven o'clock, a sudden breeze blew the struggling schooner aground near the ferryway at Winnisimmet. Wading into the water, General Putnam shouted to Lieutenant Graves to surrender. The lieutenant answered with a burst of cannon fire. Putnam returned fire with two field pieces. A brisk exchange flared, the hot fire eventually forcing the lightly armed barges to cast off and desert the *Diana*. In spite of his brave crew's willingness to fight on, Lieutenant Graves recognized the hopelessness of his situation. He abandoned ship and fled with his men to the *Britannia*, which was obliged to withdraw.

The victorious patriots boarded the *Diana* and removed everything of value—first and foremost her cannon. Then they stuffed hay through the cabin windows and set her on fire. "I wish we have something of this kind to do every day," General Putnam remarked. "It would teach our men how little they have to fear from cannonballs."

The following morning General Gage dispatched two hundred men to augment the marines on Noddle's, only to withdraw them the next day for fear of a patriot attack. By May 31, Putnam's men were back on the island, burning buildings and stores. Soon afterward they turned their attention to Peddock's Island, removing five hundred sheep and thirty head of cattle without opposition. Next, they advanced to Deer Island, where they took eight hundred sheep and lambs. When a barge from a man-of-war came to investigate, they promptly captured it and took five prisoners.

News of the battle of Chelsea Creek and the capture of the *Diana* soon reached the Continental Congress in Philadelphia, winning a major generalship for "Old Put." But the startling fact that the patriots could operate effectively against the Royal Navy in Boston harbor was lost on both Congress and the patriot leadership in Massachusetts. Had Dr. Warren possessed any kind of naval strategy, he might have kept the *Diana*, rather than burning her, and let the admiral come after her. It would have been interesting to see how Graves reacted to the insult, for his tools in Chelsea Creek, even with the cooperation of General Gage, were limited.

Following the battle of Chelsea Creek, the patriots again exhibited their naval prowess. On May 24, General Gage had requested that Graves dispatch an armed escort for two trading sloops traveling to Machias, Maine, a lumbering town. These sloops were loaded with provisions to exchange for lumber needed in Boston. Graves reluctantly agreed to help, not because he cared a twig about Boston's lumber shortage but because he wanted to retrieve the cannon that Lieutenant Joseph Nunn had lost on February 15, when he had run the armed schooner *Halifax* aground at Machias and abandoned her. Graves suspected that Machias rebels had the guns.

The admiral demonstrated his level of interest in the mission by providing the poorest warship in the fleet, the converted merchant schooner *Margaretta*. Though she boasted four double-fortified 3-pounders and fourteen swivels, she was a dull sailer and generally in such poor shape that exercising her cannon might be enough to rip her apart at the seams. Graves appointed one of his favorites, Midshipman James Moore from the *Preston*, as captain, and supplied him with twenty men from the flagship as a crew. But neither the admiral nor the midshipman had any idea what the *Margaretta* would encounter when she reached her destination. Located 316 miles from Boston, Machias might have been a tiny lumbering village, but its militia, along with those of the surrounding towns, was composed of more than a hundred wilderness-hardened fighters. Were their sympathies to lie with the rebels, the unsuspecting Moore would be heading for trouble.

Unaware of the political situation in the town—or that it mattered—Moore arrived in the Machias River on June 2 with the two seventy-ton merchant sloops, *Unity* and *Polly*, laden with a variety of goods, which, after a long winter, Machias desperately needed. The owner of the sloops, Captain Ichabod Jones, had been bringing supplies from Boston to Machias for ten years, and he knew how badly the townspeople wanted what was stuffed in the holds and strapped to the decks of his ships. Nonetheless, fired up by reports of the fighting at Lexington and Concord, and well aware that their timber would be of great use to General Gage, most of the townspeople refused to trade with him. Annoyed, Jones convinced the inexperienced Moore to position the *Margaretta* closer to town and threaten it with his 3-pounders. When Moore obliged, the frightened townspeople called an emergency meeting with Jones in attendance. After heated debate, they decided by a narrow margin to trade. But Jones wasn't satisfied. Some of the remarks he'd heard were so disparaging he wanted to retaliate. When he edged his sloops over to the town wharf, he refused to sell to anyone who had reproached him at the town house.

This enraged the entire population of the town, and trading came to an abrupt halt. Led by fiery young Jeremiah O'Brien and veteran Captain Benjamin Foster, the townspeople held a secret meeting in the thick woods just outside town on Sunday, June 11. They invited their neighbors from the villages of Mispecka and Pleasant River, many of whom came with their weapons. After wrangling for some time, the assembled townspeople agreed to capture Jones and Moore, who were attending church services in town that day. But the patriots were careless in their movements. Moore spotted them coming, leaped through an open window with his lieutenant, and ran to the *Margaretta*'s gig, tied at the town dock. Jumping in and casting off, Moore managed the tiller, while his men rowed back to the warship as fast as they could. Jones, meanwhile, fearing for his life, fled to the woods and hid, only to be captured a few days later.

After Moore was secure aboard his ship, he delivered an angry message to the town, announcing that he had express orders to protect Captain Jones, that he was "determined to do my duty whilst I have life," and that, if the people presumed to stop Captain Jones's vessels, he would burn the town.

O'Brien, Foster, and their followers responded by attacking the two sloops, *Unity* and *Polly*. The thirty-one-year-old O'Brien—along with his five brothers and thirty-five other men brandishing guns, swords, axes, and pitchforks—boarded the *Unity* and easily overpowered her terrified crew, while Foster with other armed patriots seized the *Polly*. Lieutenant Moore was livid, but he remained calm, weighed anchor, and slipped downstream to within musket shot of the *Polly*, forcing Foster to run her aground and run for cover. Moore then tried to retake her, but patriots on shore, with help from Foster and his men, kept up a steady hail of musket fire. After an hour and a half, they drove Moore off.

He retreated downriver, drifting with the tide. Townsmen on shore and in boats and canoes chased him, keeping up their attack. Moore returned fire. Then, with darkness deepening, he dropped anchor for the night, expecting the attacks to stop. But they continued. It was all his crew could do to beat them off with swivel and musket fire.

Early the next morning, Moore tried to escape. Explaining to Admiral Graves why he had retreated would be difficult, but Moore was now convinced that his force was too small for the mission. Intent on returning to Boston, he took advantage of a favorable wind and tide and stood down the Machias River. The *Margaretta*, however, would not cooperate. In jibing while going downstream before the wind, her main boom and gaff carried away. Minutes later, Moore spotted a sloop at anchor in the river. Maneuvering over to her, he took her boom and gaff for his own before racing once more for the open ocean.

Just as he reached it, he saw two vessels bearing down on him. They were O'Brien in the *Unity* and Foster in the *Falmouth Packet,* a loyalist trading schooner he had appropriated only that morning. Jury-rigging the new boom and gaff on the *Margaretta* had delayed Moore, allowing his pursuers to catch up with him. O'Brien had on every bit of sail, as did Foster. Both sporting breastworks of pine boards, and anything else they could find to screen themselves from the *Margaretta*'s small-arms fire, they were well prepared for a fight.

O'Brien watched as Moore struggled to increase speed by adding sail and cutting away the small boats towing astern. But O'Brien and Foster soon caught the decrepit *Margaretta*, and hot action ensued. Moore fired stern swivels and muskets at the approaching schooners, then luffed and gave them both a broadside with his swivels. But he never fired his cannon. He probably feared that the *Margaretta* would be torn apart if he did.

O'Brien shouted to Moore to strike his colors, but in spite of the three-to-one odds against him, the plucky midshipman continued to fight it out. O'Brien and Foster now closed with the *Margaretta*. As they did, Moore threw hand grenades at them, but to no avail. The patriots swarmed aboard, shooting Moore in the chest and belly. As blood spurted from his wounds, all resistance collapsed. Admiring the midshipman's courage, O'Brien's men brought him below and tried to save him, asking in frustration why he hadn't struck his colors. Moore replied that he'd rather die than "yield to such a set of villains."

O'Brien next took the *Margaretta's* armament into his own schooner, along with the prisoners and the mortally wounded Moore, and sailed back to Machias. The grateful townspeople greeted him as a hero. Later he renamed the *Unity* the *Machias Liberty.* The *Margaretta*, however, was too far gone to be salvaged, so he ran her aground and left her to rot.

Angered and embarrassed by the incident, Admiral Graves dispatched Lieutenant John Knight in the 6-gun schooner *Diligent* and her tender, the *Tapnaquish*, from Halifax, to intercept and destroy the Machias upstarts. But O'Brien, working with Benjamin Foster again in the coasting vessel *Falmouth Packet*, managed to capture both British vessels and their crews, including the luckless Knight, while they were ashore near Machias on July 12. No lives were lost on either side.

Decades later, James Fenimore Cooper, in his *History of the Navy of the United States of America*, called this episode "the Lexington of the sea." Of course there had been earlier battles, but the analogy was well taken. Once again, in their arrogance the British had sent out a ludicrously small force to subdue a far greater number of rebels.

Not long afterward, on the afternoon of June 16, Commodore Abraham Whipple of the newly created Rhode Island state navy was patrolling off the north end of Conanicut Island in Narragansett Bay in the 12-gun *Catey* (sometimes called *Katy*) with a tender when he spotted a small British vessel, one of several attached to the 20-gun frigate HMS *Rose.* The frigate's notoriously anti-American captain, James Wallace, had been wreaking havoc on the local patriots by examining every vessel entering or leaving the bay. Whipple chased the tiny sloop, which turned out to be the *Diana*, under the command of Savage Gardner, a master aboard the *Rose.* Having hailed her and tried to bring her to, Whipple was answered with swivel fire, which his 6-gun tender returned. A brisk exchange followed for half an hour. Then Gardner made a run for it. Greatly outgunned and outnumbered, he ran the *Diana* aground and escaped with all his men. Whipple then landed some sailors who ran after the fleeing British tars but failed to catch them. Gardner and his men returned safely to the *Rose*, leaving the *Diana* to the patriots.

The *Catey*, with twelve 4-pounders, and her tender with six, comprised Rhode Island's only navy at the time. These vessels were converted merchantmen that John Brown, the renowned merchant prince of Providence, had reluctantly sold to the colony, keeping private the rest of his huge fleet so as not to antagonize Captain Wallace. In a bit of irony, the *Diana* was revealed to be a packet that Captain Wallace had appropriated from Thomas Linsey of Providence, and when presented with the evidence, Whipple returned her to her former owner.

Many years later Whipple claimed that this action was "the first shot . . . fired on water in defiance of the British flag." He also stated, with more hyperbole, that he had risked everything "at a time when no other man in the colony would undertake the hazardous business lest he should be destined to the threatened cord," ignoring what General Nathanael Greene's Rhode Island militiamen were, even then, risking every day in Boston.

These various incidents throughout May and June demonstrated that the patriots could hold their own on the water using unorthodox, low-cost, guerrilla-style tactics. If cleverly organized on the larger scale that Admiral Graves feared, they might pose a serious problem for the Royal Navy. They could play an important role in defending Boston, Newport, New York, Philadelphia, Norfolk, Charleston, and Savannah. And they could be used to capture British men-of-war, allowing the patriots to acquire larger warships without having to build them.

2

LAUNCHING THE
CONTINENTAL NAVY

July 1775–June 1776

A month prior to the incidents at Machias and Narragansett Bay, the arch British spy, Dr. Benjamin Church, smuggled a note to General Gage at Province House in Boston. "They intend shortly to fortify Bunker's and Dorchester Hills," he wrote of the patriots. Gage already knew that Dr. Warren had been considering such an action, but he didn't feel his force was strong enough to do anything about it. When Generals William Howe, John Burgoyne, and Henry Clinton arrived in Boston harbor aboard the fast frigate *Cerberus* on May 25, he changed his mind. Even before Lexington and Concord, the king had sent the three generals to infuse more offensive spirit into Gage's operation. Before long, "an absurd and destructive confidence" had spread through the British camp, pushing Gage to preempt Dr. Warren by undertaking an aggressive attack of his own. June 18 was the strike date.

Warren had his own spies, of course, and on June 13 they informed him that the British were planning a lightning attack on Dorchester

Heights, followed by a sweep through Roxbury, over the Charles River, and through the patriot center at Cambridge. From there they intended to push east over Charlestown Neck to Bunker Hill and then Breed's Hill, completing a great campaign arc that would end the rebellion.

During a tense meeting called by Warren, the council decided to fortify Bunker Hill on the night of June 16. The patriots would commit only a part of their army there, fearing that Gage might attack Dorchester Heights or Cambridge while they were concentrated at Charlestown. Warren seems to have given no thought to what part Admiral Graves might play, although he was fully aware of the power of Graves's fleet: his warships, in combination with cannon mounted on barges, could destroy whatever fortification the patriots devised.

When the evening of the 16th arrived, Reverend Samuel Langdon, president of Harvard College, left Hastings House at seven o'clock and walked across the road to Cambridge Common. A large body of troops had gathered there with blankets and one day's provisions. As President Langdon made his way through their ranks, the young men stepped aside respectfully, following him with somber expressions as he mounted a makeshift stage. Once there, he paused a moment and considered them in the dim evening light. Their hats off, hundreds of expectant youths stared back at him, awaiting his benediction. Then, following their commander, Colonel William Prescott of Pepperell, Massachusetts, they bowed their heads as Langdon invoked Almighty God's blessing on their enterprise.

Colonel Prescott waited until dark before giving the order to march. It was nine o'clock. A mile down the Cambridge-Charlestown Road, Connecticut men under Captain Thomas Knowlton Jr. of Ashford joined the column, increasing its number to about a thousand. The soldiers marched in silence, gripping their trenching tools. Then General Putnam appeared unexpectedly, raising everyone's spirits.

To the left on Charlestown Common they passed the mummified body of a black slave who had been hanged from a gallows many years before as a warning to others who might consider killing their masters. The soldiers were fighting for their own rights, and free blacks were numbered among their ranks. But the mummified body and what it stood for remained unremarkable in the young men's eyes. No one seemed to think much about it.

Bunker Hill was 110 feet high. Colonel Prescott had orders to construct a redoubt there, but after consulting with Putnam and others he ordered his engineer, Colonel Richard Gridley, to build on Breed's Hill, which was only sixty-two feet high but closer to Boston, making it far deadlier as an artillery platform. Bunker Hill could then be used as a fallback position as well as a forward staging area.

The soldiers began digging on the summit of Breed's Hill around midnight. The noise was so loud that British sentries in Boston heard it clear across the water. So did the watch aboard the much closer 20-gun frigate, HMS *Lively*, just off shore in the narrow ferryway between North Boston and Charlestown. Normally she was stationed at Marblehead, but Admiral Graves had recently moved her, replacing the much larger and more cumbersome *Somerset*.

The *Lively*'s officer of the watch alerted her captain, Thomas Bishop, to the activity on Breed's Hill, but he did nothing. A court-martial arranged by Graves had recently reprimanded Bishop for failing to rush a chest of the admiral's gold to Boston fast enough. Unwilling to suffer another rebuke, Bishop hesitated to shoot at the diggers without direct orders from the flagship.

The 14-gun miniature frigate *Falcon* was also nearby, off Moulton's Point in Charlestown. Her crew heard the noise, as did those of the 20-gun frigate, *Glasgow*, off Boston's West End, and the armed transport *Symmetry*, stationed just west of Charlestown Village. None of their captains reacted either. They were as inattentive as they had been on the night of April 18, when HMS *Somerset* had allowed Paul Revere to row right past her bow.

Finally, at four o'clock, the *Lively*'s Captain Bishop began shooting at the diggers, even though he had received no orders as yet from the flagship, whose crew had been hearing the strange sounds for four hours.

Meanwhile, General Henry Clinton, reconnoitering in Boston's North End a little after midnight, had also heard the digging. He reported it to Generals Howe and Gage, urging an attack on Charlestown at daybreak. Gage, however, remained idle as the ominous sounds continued.

The *Lively*'s cannon bursts, however, could not be ignored. Gage hastily called a council of war. According to General Howe, they decided to set aside the previous arc scheme. In its place, Gage substituted a reversal of his planned sweep, this time beginning at Charlestown and ending at Dorchester Heights, rather than the other way around. He committed twenty-two hundred men to the task—a third of his force. Each infantryman carried three days' provisions, so that they could exploit their anticipated victory in Charlestown, move on to the patriot center in Cambridge, and then around, in a great arc, to Dorchester. The feeling among the British leaders, General Clinton observed, was that "the hill was open and of easy ascent and, in short, could be easily carried." But Clinton did not agree with them; he proposed taking five hundred men and landing at the old burying ground across from School House Hill, where he could attack the redoubt from the rear while General Howe conducted a frontal assault with the main force. Clinton's suggestion was turned down.

Admiral Graves was not included in the deliberations. While he might well have played a critical role, the generals assumed that this was the army's affair. The navy's role was to support them. But even then, it should have been apparent that there was no need to use infantrymen against the rebel redoubt at all; the navy could have handled the whole business easily. British Lieutenant John Barker noted in his diary, "Yesterday, [June 18] three gondolas (large flat boats, sides raised and musket proof) came up the Mystic River or Mystic Bay, the water on our right, where they still remain; they cover that flank and now and then take a shot at the fellows who come down among the ruins to fire at our men at work; had these boats been with us on Saturday [June 17] at the time of the attack they could have been of great use, as they would have cut off numbers; instead of that they were on the other side and of no manner of use."

In fact, Admiral Graves had several ways he could have driven the patriots from their ground. The *Symmetry* transport, which drew little water and mounted eighteen 9-pounders, could have done the job alone. General Howe made a weak attempt to move artillery into the Mystic River on scows but failed. The largest men-of-war—the 64-gun *Somerset*, the 70-gun *Boyne*, and the 50-gun *Preston*—contributed men and small boats, but otherwise Graves kept them out of the action.

The navy's participation began at noon, when the admiral's flagship signaled twenty-eight longboats to ferry the regulars from Boston to Charlestown. This they accomplished without difficulty. The *Lively*, *Falcon*, and *Spitfire* then covered the landing, "firing," as Graves explained, "so long as they could annoy the enemy without injuring our own troops." During the rest of the battle, the 20-gun *Glasgow*, the 18-gun *Symmetry*, the 6-gun *Spitfire*, and two scows, each with a single 12-pounder, positioned themselves in the Charles River near the mill dam and kept a constant fire on the Charlestown causeway to prevent patriot reinforcements from crossing. Their rounds, although bothersome, proved ineffective.

General Howe, in overall command, personally led the right wing of the attack, and General Pigot the left. Eleven companies of Howe's light infantry were aimed at the rebel flank, which extended down to the Mystic River. Victory seemed assured. In fact, Howe thought it likely he would not have to actually fight. He expected that when the New Englanders saw the full panoply of British regulars—in their splendid uniforms, with muskets, bayonets, and artillery, all supported by a dazzling naval force—they would flee. General Burgoyne too thought that when the peasants saw the redcoats in all their finery, poised to strike, they would throw aside their muskets and run.

Howe did not bother to reconnoiter the rebel positions before embarking his troops from Boston. It was not until he was ashore in Charlestown that he saw "the enemy . . . very strongly posted." The rebels had not only constructed a redoubt on Breed's Hill but "had a breastwork (three hundred yards long) made with strong railing taken from the fences and stuffed with hay." It extended from the redoubt all the way down to the Mystic River. Howe thought the breastwork "effectively secured those behind it from musquettry."

Admiral Graves could have easily moved one of his cruisers into the Mystic River and forced the patriots away from their breastwork. Howe's light infantry could then have proceeded down the beach and outflanked the redoubt, forcing the rebels to retreat or be annihilated. But no British warship of any kind appeared in the mile-wide Mystic that day.

At two o'clock in the afternoon, an hour and a half before the heavy fighting began, Admiral Graves stepped ashore to ask Howe if he wouldn't like Charlestown burned to get rid of the snipers firing on General Pigot's men from there. Graves had kept his eye on Charlestown for some time. He had already asked General Gage if he could burn it after the battle of Lexington and Concord, but Gage had refused. This time Howe accepted, and Graves could not have been more pleased. He arranged his ships, and in concert with the Copp's Hill battery in Boston, they hurled dozens of carcasses—fire bombs—into the old town's four hundred wooden buildings. The "red hot balls had been prepared with that in view," Graves later bragged to the Admiralty. Charlestown's aged timbers caught fire immediately, engulfing the entire town in a giant fireball. In the aftermath Graves sent sailors in small boats to make certain that every structure was consumed.

Graves knew that burning Charlestown would have the double virtue of being popular with the king and giving the appearance that the admiral had been in the thick of things. Nonetheless, since the results of the battle were eventually so disastrous, he thought it politic to explain to their Lordships that he was in no way responsible. "As this affair was sudden and unexpected," he reported immediately after the fighting was over, "there was no time for constructing floating batteries, or rafts of real service, as such would have been the work of some days."

Around three o'clock Howe began his frontal attack with an artillery barrage. Two lines of scarlet-clad infantry, stretching from the Mystic River to smoldering Charlestown, stepped out smartly in the open field and marched toward the rebels. Howe advanced slowly, halting frequently to give the artillery time to fire. But the topography of the peninsula, which he had not bothered to reconnoiter, hindered the progress of his infantrymen. Rail fences, high grass, large stones, and clay pits bedeviled them.

As the redcoats advanced, the patriots held their fire. General Putnam, sword in hand, passed along the lines warning his men not to shoot too soon. Colonels Stark, Knowlton, and Prescott did the same. When the redcoats were within fifty feet, the patriot leaders yelled, "Fire!" A barrage of musket balls from point-blank range hit the British hard. Firing from behind their makeshift barricade on the beach, Colonel Stark's men staggered Howe's light infantrymen. The redcoats stopped and fired back and then withdrew in complete disorder. The patriots remained in their protected positions and did not pursue.

Howe regrouped in fifteen minutes and moved forward in formation as before, except that he abandoned the beach. The patriots held their fire once more and then unloaded a withering fire that sent the redcoats retreating in confusion.

Howe did not easily regroup a third time. His troops had no stomach for more fighting. Their officers argued for withdrawal, but Howe knew that defeat was unthinkable; a patriot victory might mean the end of British rule in North America. He sent for reinforcements and began a new assault. This time he succeeded. The patriots ran out of powder and were forced to retreat. By five o'clock the fighting was over.

Since the British were in possession of the battlefield, Colonel Prescott was under the impression that Howe had won. But the colonel was mistaken; the "victory" had been so dearly bought that another like it would destroy the king's army in Boston. Eleven hundred men—fully 50 percent of Howe's force—were either killed or wounded. And since the patriots had made a point of targeting officers, they accounted for an unusually high percentage of the casualties. Major Pitcairn himself had been shot in the head by Peter Salem, a free black man.

The patriots lost 450 killed or wounded, among them Dr. Warren, who had personally joined the troops in the redoubt on Breed's Hill, staying until the end of the fighting. In the final moments of battle, he was struck by a musket ball on the right side of the head and died instantly. Earlier in the day, just as he was about to leave Hastings House for the front, Elbridge Gerry had tried to stop him, but Warren insisted on going, saying, "Dulce et decorum est pro patria mori" (It is sweet and honorable to die for one's country). His death was anything but sweet for his comrades, who had relied on his inspired leadership.

General Gage was entirely unprepared for the number of wounded who flooded back into Boston. Their excruciating cries could be heard throughout the city for many days and nights, reminding everyone of the price they had paid for the generals' needless dash to Charlestown. With the returning British soldiers were thirty-one captured Americans, nearly all of whom had been taken during the final brutal fight at the redoubt. Embittered British infantrymen hauled them to Long Wharf and left them out in the open overnight. The following day Gage threw them into the ancient stone jail near the Old State House, like so much vermin. The sadistic sheriff, Joshua Loring Jr., and his henchman, prison provost William Cunningham, took over from there, and within a few weeks twenty of the thirty-one had died horrible deaths, mainly from starvation.

When Gage's official report on Bunker Hill reached London on July 25, His Majesty saw immediately that the "victory" was in fact a disaster. He was now faced with the unhappy choice of either negotiating with the Continental Congress—a body he refused to recognize—or applying sufficient military force to crush the rebellion. Without hesitating, he chose the latter course, convinced that he'd triumph in a single season—by Christmas 1776. Nor would he again fail to apply enough force. This time he was determined to raise the largest armada in English history.

His first move was to dismiss Gage. On August 2, Lord Dartmouth ordered "the mild general" home for consultations. As the new commander in chief, the king appointed General William Howe, the man most responsible for the disaster at Breed's Hill. In the ensuing weeks, Britain embarked on a stupendous buildup of her army and navy. She also sought help from Russia and several German princes. However, the new force would not be fully deployed until the summer of 1776—later than the king wished, certainly, but still giving General Howe enough time to succeed.

Overjoyed by these developments, France moved deftly to exploit them without provoking a war she was as yet unprepared to fight. Young King Louis XVI accepted his advisers' counsel to strengthen his armed forces, particularly the navy, while secretly aiding the Americans at a level that would keep them in the fight without forcing Britain to declare war before Paris was ready.

In London, the king's spies kept him well informed of French intentions but he remained unconcerned, convinced that Britain would crush the rebellion long before any involvement by Paris could make a difference. Lord North liked to point out that France would quickly abandon a losing cause.

King George's plan to bring the Americans to heel in a single season contained two essential elements. The first—command of the sea—was so obvious that it ran the risk of being taken for granted. The Royal Navy, even though it had been allowed to deteriorate under Lords Sandwich and North, was expected to be invincible before the Americans. The king never considered that the rebels might produce a navy of their own to challenge the British fleet.

The second of these two elements was a three-pronged invasion. An army would first occupy New York and then push up the Hudson River to meet another force coming down from Canada. The joining of the two armies at Albany would supposedly sever New England from the colonies to the south, mortally wounding the rebellion. At the same time, to ensure a complete, simultaneous victory, the king planned to send an amphibious force—much smaller than the others but still potent—to subdue the south, which he considered the soft underbelly of the Revolution. He was confident that these three armies, acting in concert and supported by the Royal Navy, would crush the rebellion before Christmas 1776.

Since New York City was the logical place from which to direct the invasion, the king ordered General Howe to evacuate Boston and remove himself first to Halifax, where he would be reinforced, and then to New York. There he would rendezvous with his brother, Admiral Lord Richard Howe, who would bring additional warships and troops from England. The force sent to the south was expected to make quick work of the rebellion there and soon become available to General Howe in New York.

Threatened with this massive invasion and unable to discern its full dimensions, the patriots were divided. Many were unconvinced that, even after all the bloodshed, His Majesty was truly unwilling to negotiate a settlement that would protect colonial rights while keeping America within the empire. Some members of Congress, like the Adamses and Benjamin Franklin, were convinced that the king was beyond reach. But others, like John Dickinson of Pennsylvania, continued to hope for compromise. And so, on July 8, 1775, Congress voted unanimously to send His Majesty the Olive Branch Petition written by Dickinson and John Jay of New York.

John Adams voted in favor of the petition for political reasons, but he was certain the king would see the document as a sign of weakness. Rather than bowing and pleading, Adams wanted Congress to "raise a naval power, and open our ports wide; to [arrest] every friend of government on the continent and [hold] them as hostages for the poor victims in Boston, and then [open] the door as wide as possible for peace and reconciliation." His cousin Sam Adams agreed. "It is folly," he wrote, "to supplicate a tyrant."

When the peace petition reached London on August 21, Arthur Lee and Richard Penn rushed it to Lord Dartmouth, who later told the House of Lords that "the softness of the language . . . concealed the most traitorous designs."

Nothing could have been further from the truth, but Dartmouth's words faithfully reflect the views of the king, who refused to receive the petition. On August 23, he issued "A Proclamation for Suppressing Rebellion and Sedition," declaring America to be in a state of rebellion. "All our officers, civil and military," he said, "are obliged to exert their utmost endeavors to suppress such rebellion."

Meanwhile, feeling the weight of the British Empire on them, Dr. Warren and his colleagues in Massachusetts had desperately sought help from the Continental Congress. It responded on June 16 by appointing the most renowned soldier in America, forty-two-year-old George Washington, to take command of the patriot army besieging Boston.

Washington had become famous in his early twenties by distinguishing himself at Fort Necessity and Laurel Hill during the French and Indian War, and by serving General Braddock as his aide-de-camp. At the age of twenty-three he had been appointed commander in chief of Virginia's militia and then directed its complicated affairs for three years. Perhaps as importantly, he had served fifteen years in the House of Burgesses and was a skilled politician with a deep respect for the prerogatives of the legislature. John Adams nominated him and Sam Adams seconded the nomination. Since the army was made up almost exclusively of New Englanders, the Adamses, seeking to bind the country together, wanted a Virginian to lead it.

Two weeks after his appointment Washington, accompanied by General Charles Lee, rode into Cambridge, splendidly attired in a blue and buff uniform with a handsome sword at his side, astride a magnificent white horse. The moment he saw the six-foot three-inch Virginian, James Warren, the replacement for the late Dr. Warren (the two were not related), was overjoyed. Like many patriots, Warren had thought it imprudent to attempt entrenching Breed's Hill and saw the subsequent battle as a defeat. He was anxious for Washington to replace General Artemus Ward.

James Warren was not the only patriot impressed with Washington. Abigail Adams wrote to her husband, "I was struck with General Washington. You had prepared me to entertain a favorable opinion of him, but I thought the one half was not told me. Dignity with ease, and complacency, the gentleman and soldier look agreeably blended in him. Modesty marks every line and feature of his face. Those lines of Dryden instantly occurred to me:

Mark his majestic fabric! He's a temple
Sacred by birth, and built by hands divine
His souls the deity that lodges there.
Nor is the pile unworthy of the God."

Although pleased with his reception, Washington was shocked by the state of the army. A few days later he wrote to John Hancock, the president of the Continental Congress, "We labor under great disadvantages." And to Richard Henry Lee he wrote, "Between you and me I think we are in an exceedingly dangerous situation."

Washington overestimated the danger. General Gage, who would not be informed of his recall until September, had been so stunned by the fight at Charlestown that he had no intention of attacking the rebels until he received further instructions and massive reinforcements from London. He remained on the defensive through the summer, granting Washington plenty of time to shape his militiamen into real soldiers.

When he first arrived, Washington was appalled by the treatment American prisoners were receiving in Boston. He immediately complained to General Gage, expecting a positive response, since he and Gage had served together under Braddock during the French and Indian War. But Gage ignored Washington's protests. General Burgoyne observed that these men were "destined for the cord . . . for I acknowledge no rank that is not derived from the King." Washington replied that their rank "flowed from the uncorrupted choice of a brave and free people."

While Washington was training his army during the summer, important naval activity was taking place in Boston harbor that once again demonstrated how a successful patriot navy might be organized. During the night of July 10, Major Benjamin Tupper, a Rhode Islander serving under Generals Nathanael Greene and John Thomas, left his camp in Roxbury with three hundred men in whaleboats and attacked Long Island in Boston harbor, capturing sheep and cattle, burning hay, and taking thirteen British prisoners. Unaccountably, Admiral Graves appeared indifferent to the loss. But General Gage was irate; he wrote to Lord Dartmouth, complaining of how tight supplies were and how little the Royal Navy was doing to relieve his distressed troops.

Ten days later, on July 20, while a man-of-war patrolled nearby, Major Tupper again led a similar force in whaleboats and burned Boston lighthouse, the oldest beacon in America, sitting ten miles from town at the head of the harbor on rocky Little Brewster Island. "They are more afraid of our whaleboats," James Warren wrote to John Adams, "than we are of their men-of-war." At the same time Tupper was carrying out his raid, other patriots in whaleboats burned the lighthouse on Thatcher Island off Cape Ann, fourteen miles away.

Admiral Graves reacted by sending twelve carpenters and thirty-three marine guards to repair the lighthouse on Little Brewster. But at two o'clock on the morning of July 31, Major Tupper and his men rowed back and struck again, this time killing a subaltern officer and several marines and taking twenty-three prisoners, ten of whom were Tory refugees. Before leaving, Tupper torched all the other buildings on the island.

By coincidence, Captain Jonathan Robinson, the *Preston*'s flag captain, was out in the harbor that same night with a large force in small vessels, seeking to destroy rebel whaleboats. So important was Robinson's mission that General Gage staged a mock attack on patriot lines, firing artillery from Boston Neck and Bunker Hill. General Clinton then led a raiding party against the American sentinels on Boston Neck at one o'clock in the morning, burning the rebels' advance post, the George Tavern.

The unfortunate Robinson never found any whaleboats. He got lost in the dark. Graves blamed the fiasco on Robinson's pilot—a familiar excuse from this admiral. In reality, Graves and Robinson should have known every nook and cranny of the harbor. They had been in Boston since June 1774, after all, without once taking the *Preston* to sea.

On the way back from this embarrassing venture, Robinson heard the commotion at Boston lighthouse and saw Major Tupper's patriots leaving. Hoping to salvage something from the night's endeavors, Robinson gave chase. But another Rhode Islander, patriot Major Crane, was ready with a field piece on nearby Nantasket beach, covering Tupper's approach to the mainland. As Robinson closed in on the retreating whaleboats, Crane fired and sank one of the *Preston*'s boats, allowing Tupper to reach land safely. In the melee the Rhode Islanders lost one young fighter, who was buried later in nearby Braintree.

After the successful patriot raid on Boston lighthouse, Captain Broderick Hartwell, skipper of the largest warship in the harbor, the 70-gun battleship HMS *Boyne*, became so hysterical about whaleboats that he wrote to Graves, "I am obliged to beg that you take into your serious consideration what the consequences may be should the rebels endeavor to burn the *Boyne*, (which I think is far from being improbable) considering that she lies out of the way of any ready assistance from the rest of the squadron." At the time Hartwell had a crew of only 320—half his normal complement—many of whom were disaffected pressed men, little better than prisoners. How hard would they fight for the ship? The captain couldn't be sure.

The day after Tupper's raid on Boston lighthouse, Admiral Graves had another scare. "The *Symmetry* armed transport," he wrote to the Admiralty, "had . . . perceived a great number of whaleboats, [in the Charles River] rowing very softly toward Boston, whereupon she made the private signal, and the rebels, finding they were discovered, retired. These nocturnal movements of the whaleboats about the harbor, and the knowledge of there being some hundreds of them, capable of carrying 10 to 16 men each, with ease, began to cause some apprehensions even in the large men of war." Graves was so concerned, in fact, that he regularly ordered protective booms placed around his warships.

Even as the admiral and his captains worried about the whaleboats, Washington was organizing a tiny fleet of converted merchantmen to attack unarmed British supply vessels entering Boston. He hadn't been a month on the job before he recognized the fundamental need for a navy. "Finding we had no great prospect of coming to close quarters with the ministerial troops in Boston," he wrote later to a Virginia friend, William Ramsay, "I fitted out at the Continental expense several [converted merchantmen], chiefly with a design to intercept their fresh provision vessels from Nova Scotia and Canada."

For help with his naval plans, Washington turned to a forty-two-year-old shipowner, Colonel John Glover of Marblehead. Soon they had converted the merchant vessel *Hannah* (named after Glover's wife) into a man-of-war. Working in Glover's Marblehead shipyard, his men cut four gunports in her bulwarks, strengthened her planking to absorb the shock of firing cannon, and added topsails and a flying jib to give her more speed. She was ready for sea on September 2, under Captain Nicholson Broughton. In his detailed instructions Washington told Broughton, "You are particularly charged to avoid any engagements with any armed vessel of the enemy, though you may be equal in strength, or may have some small advantage; the design of the enterprise being to intercept supplies of the enemy, which will be defeated by you running into unnecessary engagements."

Six more tiny vessels were soon added to the makeshift fleet. Although Captain Broughton and the *Hannah* proved disappointing, the others were remarkably successful. During the fall and winter only eight of the forty supply vessels that left the British Isles bound for Boston ever arrived. Horrendous storms in the North Atlantic accounted for some of the losses, as did the hard luck of a few British captains, who, unfamiliar with New England's treacherous waters, ran aground or found themselves set upon by enterprising Yankees lurking along the coast. But so did Washington's navy. In its short career it made thirty-eight captures, the most spectacular being the seizure of the ordnance brig *Nancy*. Forty-two-year-old John Manley in the *Lee*, a sixty-foot schooner carrying six 3-pounders—the smallest of Washington's fleet—took the *Nancy* on November 28 without firing a shot.

The *Nancy*'s captain, John Hunter, had been fooled into thinking the *Lee* was carrying a Boston pilot to guide him into port. Only when Manley and his crew climbed over the side, brandishing pistols and cutlasses, did Hunter realize his mistake and surrender. Manley was amazed to discover that the *Nancy*'s hold contained some two thousand muskets with bayonets, scabbards, and steel rammers; 100,000 flints; a mountain of musket and round shot; two brass 6-pounders; a 13-inch brass mortar; and much more. The only thing lacking was gunpowder.

Washington was ecstatic.

General Howe was incredulous. Graves should never have let it happen. Howe fired off a letter to London, angrily pointing out that "[Washington was] now furnished with all the requisites for setting the town on fire." In his own defense, Graves insisted to the Admiralty that the *Nancy* had been "lost by the treachery of the Master or Pilot." He also blamed bad weather, for the *Nancy*'s escorts at different stages had been the powerful frigates *Cerberus* and *Mercury*, which had indeed lost her in a storm. "O the glory of the British Navy," an exasperated Tory, Francis Hutcheson, would later write to General Haldimand in New York. "Two flags flying with all the pomp of war, and Yankees can spit in their face." Lord Sandwich, for his part, attributed the capture to the ubiquitous patriot whaleboats Admiral Graves was forever complaining about, and to the "treachery" of the *Nancy*'s master.

Manley's capture of the *Nancy* was just one of several events in the fall of 1775 that persuaded Congress to organize a navy. While encouraged by their own military successes, the delegates were shocked by the king's relentlessly aggressive tactics. One of the most unsettling of these was an attack on Falmouth, Maine, on October 18.

Since August, Admiral Graves had been planning attacks along the New England coast north of Boston, and on September 1 he announced to General Gage that he was finally going to take action by laying "waste such seaport towns in the New England governments as are not likely to be useful to His Majesty's stores and to destroy all the vessels within the harbors. . . . I can no longer delay," he wrote, "using the means in my power to prevent the progress of [this rebellion]."

The king had ordered Graves to assault coastal towns. This directive was issued partly out of sheer malice, but it was also intended to force the towns to keep their militiamen at home. Even more importantly, the king wanted to prevent the patriots from fitting out hundreds of privateers to attack British shipping.

To carry out his grisly project, Graves organized a four-ship squadron—the 6-gun armed vessel *Canceaux*, the 18-gun armed troop transport *Symmetry*, the 6-gun schooner *Halifax*, and the 6-gun sloop *Spitfire*. He put one of his favorites, Lieutenant Henry Mowat, in command. But it took the admiral weeks to prepare the tiny force, so that Lieutenant Mowat did not receive his final instructions until October 6 and did not sail from Boston until October 13. "My design," Graves told him, "is to chastise Marblehead, Salem, Newburyport, Cape Anne Harbor, Portsmouth, Ipswich, Saco, Falmouth in Casco Bay, and particularly Machias, where the *Margaretta* was taken . . . and where the *Diligent* schooner was seized and the officers and crew carried prisoners up the country, and where preparations I am informed are now making to invade the Province of Nova Scotia. . . . You are to go to all or as many of the above named places as you can, and make the most vigorous efforts to burn the towns, and destroy the shipping in the harbors."

Given the limited strength of Mowat's squadron, his orders were preposterous. He had no choice but to ignore them and concentrate instead on only one of the proposed targets. Falmouth, Maine, was a town he knew well from his run-in with Colonel Samuel Thompson back in May, and he seemed to be holding a grudge. The town's moderate leaders, Enoch Freeman and Jedediah Preble, were under the impression that they had done Mowat a favor by persuading Thompson to release him. And so, when Mowat reappeared on October 17, Preble felt that Falmouth had nothing to fear.

He soon changed his mind. The *Canceaux's* lieutenant landed at Falmouth's town pier and announced to a frightened crowd that

Mowat would begin firing on the city in just two hours. Aghast, Preble and two others rushed out to the flagship to plead for more time, which Mowat granted, while also suggesting that a certain amount of room existed for negotiating. He provided so little time for this, however, that Preble had no hope of organizing the town for talks.

At nine-thirty the next morning, while terrorized townspeople clogged the few roads out of town, a thunderous blast announced the start of the bombardment. The fleet then fired salvo after salvo, until by noon, fires raged over the entire southern third of the city. An early afternoon breeze spread the flames to the rest of the town.

This was not enough to satisfy Mowat. At three o'clock he sent Lieutenant Fraser ashore with the *Canceaux*'s senior midshipman, Mr. Larkin, and thirty marines and sailors. They proceeded to fire the buildings that had escaped damage. It was a measure of the contempt Mowat felt for Jedediah Preble and whatever militiamen were scattered about that he thought thirty men would be sufficient. And Fraser's sailors did run through the city unimpeded. No one fired on them or attempted to attack their boats as the wild-eyed tars invaded every part of town, throwing flaming torches into windows, breaking down doors, and setting fires in the hallways of homes. In just over an hour they returned to their boats without a single man lost.

Fraser then shoved off for the *Canceaux*. As he did, Mowat commenced firing again. The entire city became a gigantic ball of flame, rising as if part of some fantastic pagan rite. But Mowat did not cease firing until six o'clock. An hour later he weighed anchor, retiring to the safety of nearby Hog Island Roads in Casco Bay, where he passed the night undisturbed.

Despite the admiral's orders, the following morning Mowat stood out from Casco Bay and returned directly to Boston. He had expended all his ammunition, and his ships were in danger of coming apart at the seams from the constant recoil of cannon. They were in no condition to attack any of the other towns on Graves's list. The most Mowat could do was limp back to port, relieved that no storm or patriot warships were around to threaten his hobbled squadron.

In the end, rather than demonstrating the strength of the Royal Navy, the burning of Falmouth actually revealed its limitations. Nor did it succeed in cowing the patriots. It only served to enrage the country and strengthen the rebellion.

Believing that Mowat would attack only shipping, wharves, and adjoining warehouses, General Howe was dismayed when he heard what had happened. Even Lord George Germain, who had replaced Lord Dartmouth as secretary of state for the colonies and was fiercely anti-American, found Graves's actions excessive; they seemed a grotesque overcompensation for his pitiful lack of activity in previous months.

The news of Falmouth was quickly followed by word of the king's curt dismissal of the Olive Branch Petition. Afterward came disheartening reports of his belligerent speech opening Parliament on October 26. "I have increased my naval establishment," he declared, "and greatly augmented my land forces . . . [and] I have received the most friendly offers of foreign assistance." Following His Majesty's speech that day there was an extensive, soul-baring debate in both the House of Lords and the Commons. The solicitor general, Alexander Wedderburn, reflecting the king's views, thundered, "Relinquish America, and you also relinquish the West Indies, and confine yourself to the narrow insular situation, which once made you hardly discernable on the face of the globe . . . we have too long shown our forbearance . . . faction must be crushed . . . America must be conquered."

Less than a month later, on November 20, 1775, Lord North presented the far-reaching Prohibitory Act to Parliament. The law banned "all trade and intercourse with the . . . colonies . . . during the continuance of the present rebellion." As North told the members, the country was now "at war."

Even as these disturbing events were impressing Congress with the need for an American navy, good news arrived: patriot General Montgomery had captured Montreal on November 13. Congress now expected Montgomery to join forces with Colonel Benedict Arnold shortly. The plan was to put all of Canada into patriot hands by January 1776.

In one of the great gambles for which he would become noted, Washington had dispatched Arnold and twelve hundred of his best soldiers on September 11, with orders to march through the Maine and Canadian wilderness and take Quebec City by surprise. Washington hoped that General Guy Carleton would find it impossible to counter both Montgomery and Arnold at the same time. Washington had his eye on the military stores in the lightly defended fortress at Quebec. During the summer he had searched everywhere to obtain the artillery he needed to drive the British out of Boston. Early in his tenure at Cambridge he had recognized that, for whatever reason, a stalemate had developed. He determined that he could stop worrying about the British attacking him and instead contemplate making a "decisive stroke" against them to end the war. Another pressing issue was that patriot enlistments extended only until Christmas. Washington worried that his men would leave before he could engage in a decisive action.

Sam Adams, whose naive belief in the superiority of American arms was limitless, urged him to make his move, as did a majority in Congress. "I hope," Adams said, "that our troops will before long force their way into Boston." The great fortress at Quebec, Washington thought, could provide the weapons he needed for such a move.

Admiral Graves knew about Arnold's expedition three days before Arnold left Cambridge. Two patriot deserters had told General Gage what was afoot on September 8, and he passed the intelligence on. Graves, then, knew that Arnold planned to march his men to Newburyport, Massachusetts, and from there sail to the Kennebec River in Maine, whence they would begin the long trek to Canada. But he chose to do nothing, even though he could have easily stopped it. Graves informed Gage that if he wanted to prevent Arnold from sailing, he could send troops to Newburyport.

On September 19 Arnold had assembled enough boats to get underway. At sunrise, he dispatched scouting vessels to make certain the coast was clear and then stood out from Newburyport with eleven unarmed schooners and sloop—smany of them fishing boats

stinking from bait. They headed for the swirling waters at the
mouth of the Kennebec. Fog, seasickness, gale winds, and mounting
waves plagued the vessels. Arnold did not reach the river until nine
o'clock the following morning. He feared that British warships
would attack him along the way, but happily he saw none.

Arnold's successful departure contributed to growing optimism
in Congress during October, November, and December of 1775,
when it was organizing the Continental Navy. Delegates like Sam
Adams exuberantly assumed the united colonies would not only
conquer Canada but drive the British out of Boston and build a
prestigious navy, all at the same time.

Ever since the battle of Lexington and Concord, the two
Adamses, along with many other patriot leaders, had dreamed of
building a British-style American navy, and they pushed hard for
one in Congress. But they had met with strong opposition from
delegates who felt that a navy would lead to independence, for
which they were unprepared. All Congress could agree upon on
July 18, 1775, was to leave to the respective colonies "the protection
of their harbors and navigation on their sea coasts."

Five weeks later, however, on August 26, Rhode Island, which
paradoxically had done little about its own sea defenses, urged
Congress "to [build] and [equip] an American fleet as soon as possible." This was far more than what most delegates would accept,
and the proposal was tabled. But as the weeks went by, support for
a Continental Navy grew. And on October 5, after a wrenching
debate, Congress agreed to ask Washington to send two armed
Massachusetts vessels to intercept two powder brigs en route from
England to Quebec, as well as "any other transports laden with
ammunition, clothing or other stores." At the same time Congress
urged Rhode Island and Connecticut to "send armed vessels" of
their own to do likewise.

On October 7 there followed a contentious debate on the
Rhode Island resolution of August. Again the resolution was
tabled, but support for it was growing. By the end of October, the
tide had turned; the momentum for creating a "naval power" had
become irresistible. Unfortunately, the talk in Congress was limited

to the desirability of having a navy. There was little discussion as to what kind of sea force would be most effective, given the enemy's strengths and weaknesses and the patriots' limited resources.

The pro-navy delegates, recognizing that their dreams were about to become reality, moved swiftly to create as extensive a sea force as possible. Taking the Royal Navy as a model, they assumed that the army and navy would have to be segregated into different departments, as the English had done for centuries, even though the negative consequences of this tradition were all too apparent in Boston; indeed, the divisions within His Majesty's sovereign departments would be one of the primary reasons for the loss of the war.

It would have made far more sense for Congress to place an American navy directly under Washington. And since Benedict Arnold had demonstrated extraordinary leadership abilities on the water, it would have been logical to put him on Washington's staff in charge of doing in Boston harbor what he had done on Lake Champlain—capturing British warships. But this idea was anathema to the delegates. The Adamses would have been the first to oppose assigning Washington additional authority over naval matters. Well-versed in Greek and Roman history, they were wary of giving any military leader too much power. "A standing army," Sam Adams wrote, "however necessary it may be at some times, is always dangerous to the liberties of the people. . . . Such a power should be watched with a jealous eye." Adams saw the navy as less of a threat than the army, but he still wanted them strictly separated and kept under tight civilian control.

The Adamses and their allies (most notably Benjamin Franklin) believed that, with her shipbuilding traditions, America could easily construct and man a fleet of frigates, and even sail of the line. "I lament with you the want of a naval force," Franklin had written to Silas Deane, the special American agent in Paris, on August 27. "I hope the next winter will be employed in forming one. When we are no longer fascinated with the idea of reconciliation, we shall exert ourselves to some purpose. 'Till then things will be done by halves."

While Franklin and the Adamses dreamed of building a naval power modeled on the Royal Navy, Admiral Graves worried about guerrilla attacks by whaleboats and row-galleys. Slightly larger than a whaleboat, a row-galley was an inexpensive vessel of forty to fifty feet, with a prow that could accommodate a single cannon of great power—an 18-pounder or larger. Ironically, the Pennsylvania Committee of Public Safety under Franklin's leadership had already deployed thirteen such vessels in the Delaware River for the defense of Philadelphia. And these vessels were greatly admired by John Adams. But, for whatever reason, the big-navy advocates in Congress could not conceive of building hundreds of such craft for deployment in New York, Boston, Rhode Island, Philadelphia, the Chesapeake, Charleston, and Savannah. Instead, when thinking about a Continental Navy, their minds always turned to the frigates and 74s of the British fleet.

Interestingly, on June 7, while John Adams was in Philadelphia, he had written to Elbridge Gerry in Marblehead about discussions he had had with Christopher Gadsden of South Carolina about acquiring a fleet "at a cheap rate—and this would give a great spirit to this continent, as well as a little spirit to the ministry." Having served briefly in the British navy, Gadsden was considered something of an authority. He proposed seizing British sloops, schooners, and cutters, and using them in turn to attack their larger ships. According to Gadsden, the great British men-of-war were populated by pressed men who might not fight against "their fellow subjects."

"He thinks it of great importance," Adams wrote Gerry, "that some experiment should be made on the cutters." Unfortunately, Adams quickly forgot the idea, as did Gadsden himself. The dream of building a British-style navy simply had too firm a grip on their imaginations. Adams considered the Royal Navy "the greatest that ever existed," and it would forever be his model.

On October 30, with the destruction of Falmouth still fresh, Congress created a Naval Committee of seven members—Gadsden, Stephen Hopkins of Rhode Island, John Adams of Massachusetts,

Joseph Hewes of North Carolina, Silas Deane of Connecticut, John Langdon of New Hampshire, and Richard Henry Lee of Virginia— all staunch supporters of a British-style Continental Navy. In the weeks that followed, the committee supervised the creation of an ad hoc fleet of eight converted merchantmen, soon to be followed by three more, bringing the total number of warships in the new American fleet to eleven.

"The pleasantest part of my labors for the four years I spent in Congress," John Adams recalled, ". . . was in this naval committee. Mr. Lee, Mr. Gadsden were sensible men, and very cheerful: but Governor Hopkins of Rhode Island, above seventy years of age, kept us all alive. Upon business his experience and judgment were very useful. But when the business of the evening was over, he kept us in conversation till eleven and sometimes twelve o'clock, in the evening, and then his beverage was Jamaica spirit and water. It gave him wit, humor, anecdotes, science, and learning. He had read Greek, Roman and British history: and was familiar with English poetry particularly Pope, Thomson and Milton. And the flow of his soul made all of his reading our own, and seemed to bring to recollection in all of us all we had ever read. I could neither eat nor drink in those days. The other gentlemen were very temperate. Hopkins never drank to excess, but all he drank was immediately not only converted into wit, sense, knowledge and good humor, but inspired us all with similar qualities."

Converting so many merchantmen to warships in such a short time was a remarkable feat. Wharton & Humphreys, a leading Philadelphia shipyard, played a critical role during November and December. Like other American shipbuilders, Wharton & Humphreys had some experience crafting men-of-war. Twenty-four-year-old Joshua Humphreys had been an apprentice to James Penrose, who built one of the more storied privateers of the French and Indian War, the 24-gun *Hero*. Humphreys now put his experience to work, organizing joiners, sawyers, caulkers, and other specialists, along with ordinary yard hands, to transform merchantmen like the *Black Prince* (owned by Willing & Morris, Philadelphia's prominent merchant house) into the warship *Alfred*.

They pierced the keel, increased stanchions in the waist, cut new gun ports, added new planking, rearranged the standing and running rigging, and strengthened every inch of the ship.

Their most difficult task was finding armament, but that too became available in a remarkably short time. General Washington, observing from a distance, wondered whether the scarce weaponry might not be put to better use in Cambridge. Deferring to Congress, however, as he always did, Washington found other means to solve his problems. He had already sent Arnold to Quebec, and on November 18, as winter settled over the northeast, he dispatched Henry Knox to Fort Ticonderoga to bring its captured cannon and ordnance down to Boston.

John Adams wrote the "Rules for the Regulation of the Navy of the United Colonies of North America," adopted by Congress on November 28. On December 11 Congress appointed a permanent Marine Committee composed of a member from each colony to "devise ways and means for furnishing these colonies with a naval armament."

"A very powerful force is coming from England against us," Franklin warned a friend on December 12. In his mind a strong Continental Navy was urgently needed to combat it. In the same letter he pointed out the successes of Washington's small squadron and added, "This little naval force we are about to augment, and expect it may be more considerable in the next summer."

On December 13, following the committee's recommendation, Congress voted to build thirteen new frigates of between twenty-four and thirty-two guns each, bringing the total number of ships in the infant navy to twenty-five. This was not enough for some of the more enthusiastic delegates. On December 22 Sam Adams wrote from Philadelphia to his cousin John, who was on leave in Massachusetts, "I know it gives you great pleasure to be informed that this Congress have ordered the building of thirteen ships of war, viz five of 32 guns, five of 28 and three of 24—I own that I wished for double or treble the number, but I am taught the rule of Providence, to let the fruit hang until it is ripe."

Congress hoped to have the new frigates ready for action by the spring of 1776, with many more to follow. Congressman Francis Lightfoot Lee, a member of the powerful Lee clan of Virginia, wrote to Colonel Landon Carter, "We . . . are determined to exert the whole force of the continent this winter to fit out as many large ships as possible."

The ad hoc fleet of converted merchantmen was set to sail by year's end under the command of fifty-seven-year-old Esek Hopkins, brother of the chairman of the Naval Committee, Stephen Hopkins. Esek was given the title "Commodore," signaling that he was the head of a fleet, though his actual rank was captain. As with Washington, Congress didn't want to give military leaders exalted titles that might enhance their reputation and power beyond sensible bounds for a republic. Nevertheless, Esek was routinely called "Admiral" and was looked on by many as Washington's naval counterpart. Congress intended Hopkins to be subordinate to Washington but left their relative ranks and their relationship unclear.

The commodore's flagship was the *Alfred*. She carried an impressive arsenal of twenty 9-pounders and ten 6-pounders. Dudley Saltonstall of Connecticut, brother-in-law of Silas Deane, was her captain, and twenty-eight-year-old John Paul Jones, sponsored by Joseph Hewes of North Carolina, was her first lieutenant. Jones had been in Philadelphia since the summer, using his Scottish connections, among others, to obtain a suitable position with the new fleet. Among his duties aboard the *Alfred* was commanding the main battery of 9-pounders on the lower gun deck.

The committee appointed Abraham Whipple of Rhode Island— Commodore Hopkins's brother-in-law—as captain of the second largest ship, *Columbus*. She mounted eighteen 9-pounders and ten 6-pounders. John Hopkins (Stephen Hopkins's son) was named captain of the *Cabot*, a brig with fourteen 6-pounders; Philadelphia's Nicholas Biddle was given command of *Andrew Doria*, a brig with sixteen 6-pounders; Hoysted Hacker was appointed skipper of the *Fly*, a schooner with six 9-pounders; and John Hazard was named captain of the *Providence*, a sloop with twelve 4-pounders. These six were assembled at Philadelphia, and two others in Baltimore—the sloop *Hornet*, mounting ten 6-pounders under William Stone, with sixteen-year-old Joshua Barney as master's mate or second in command; and the *Wasp*, a schooner, with eight 6-pounders under William Hallock.

John Adams wrote that the *Alfred* was named "in honor of the founder of the greatest navy that ever existed. The . . . *Columbus* after the discoverer of this quarter of the globe. The . . . *Cabot* for the discoverer of this northern part of the continent. The . . . *Andrew Doria* in memory of the great Genoese admiral who never saw North America, and the . . . *Providence* for the town where she was purchased, the residence of Governor [Stephen] Hopkins and his brother Esek whom we appointed first Captain."

The three additional converted merchantmen that were soon added to the fleet, although not in time to sail with Hopkins on his maiden voyage, were commanded by some of the finest officers ever to serve America. The *Lexington*, a brig mounting fourteen 4-pounders and two 6-pounders, sailed under Captain John Barry; the *Reprisal*, a ship with eighteen 6-pounders, under Captain Lambert Wickes; and the *Independence*, a sloop carrying ten 4-pounders, under Captain John Young.

As Gadsden assessed "the first American fleet that ever swelled their sails on the Western Ocean," he was justifiably proud, thinking Congress had provided "Admiral" Hopkins with a splendid set of ships and a surprising number of outstanding officers and men.

By year's end the Continental warships were ready to sail. But before Commodore Hopkins could put to sea, the British committed another atrocity, similar to the one they had perpetrated in Falmouth, Maine, back in October—this time in Norfolk, Virginia.

Virginia militiamen led by William Woodford had inflicted a humiliating defeat on Lord Dunmore at Great Bridge, near Norfolk, on December 10, and the hotheaded royal governor was keen to retaliate. After his victory, Woodford had occupied the city, precipitating an exodus of loyalists, many of whom sought refuge aboard

British warships anchored nearby. Governor Dunmore had fled Williamsburg many months before, in June 1775, and was living in cramped quarters aboard HMS *Fowey*.

An uneasy truce developed between the fleet offshore and the rebels in town. At some point the mercurial Dunmore found the situation intolerable and ordered Norfolk incinerated. On New Year's Day at three o'clock in the afternoon, Captain Henry Bellew, standing on the quarterdeck of HMS *Liverpool*, sent up signal flags. Three warships began an intense cannonade of the waterfront. An hour later, a few of Bellew's men landed in small boats and torched any warehouses left standing, as well as any sailing vessels that remained afloat. The wind soon spread the flames to other parts of the doomed town. Once the sailors had returned to their ships, Norfolk patriots torched what remained of the city to deprive the British of a port and supplies. Eight days later, the fires were still burning. The horror of the attack on Norfolk moved Sam Adams to write to James Warren, "This will prevail more than a long train of reasoning to accomplish a confederation, and other matters which I know your heart as well as mine is much set upon."

That same day, the patriots at Quebec City received another brutal shock.

It would have been impossible, sitting in Philadelphia—or Cambridge, for that matter—to conceive of the conditions that Montgomery and his superior as head of the Northern Department, General Schuyler, operated under in Canada. Both men wanted to resign, especially Montgomery. His soldiers were ill clothed, ill supplied, underpaid, disease ridden, unruly, and by now nearly ungovernable. As winter came on, they were scattering into the woods, so that following the victory at Montreal, he had only around eleven hundred left to attack Quebec.

In the wee hours of the morning, during a raging blizzard, Montgomery and Arnold attempted to storm the city walls. As the battle started, Montgomery, one of the finest officers in the patriot army, was killed, and Arnold was seriously wounded. General Guy Carleton captured 426 patriots and killed or wounded another 60.

Arnold, who had barely escaped capture, was left with no more than 600 men. Though badly injured, he remained in command and kept them from scattering.

News of this stunning defeat reached Congress on January 17. But so powerful was the dream of including Canada in the patriot cause—to say nothing of the perceived danger of a British attack from that quarter—that Congress would not give it up. Confidence in patriot arms was still high at the time, and the delegates feared that if Canada were not secured, the British would mount a powerful attack from there that could isolate New England and kill the rebellion. On the 19th, the Congress made a fateful decision—strongly supported by Washington—to reinforce the Canadian army rather than pull it back to defensive positions at Crown Point and Ticonderoga.

Even as the delegates were deciding what to do about the depressing situation in Canada, news arrived that Henry Knox had accomplished the impossible. Using forty-two sleds and eighty yoke of oxen, he had dragged forty-three heavy cannon, ranging in size from 12- to 24-pounders, along with fourteen mortars, a howitzer, and a quantity of lead and flints, all the way from Ticonderoga to Boston. In the harshest conditions of winter, he moved down the Hudson Valley to Kinderhook and then trudged eastward to Great Barrington, Massachusetts, across the blistering-cold, snow-encrusted Berkshire Mountains, all the way to Springfield, where he obtained fresh oxen before moving on to Cambridge. On January 18, after a three-hundred-mile journey, he presented Washington with the weapons the patriots needed for a "decisive stroke" against General Howe.

Despite setbacks at Norfolk and in Canada, the patriots retained high expectations for Commodore Hopkins and his fleet in January. While waiting for him to depart Philadelphia on his first mission, they were cheered by the widespread acclaim for Thomas Paine's fifty-page pamphlet, *Common Sense*, which openly advocated independence. Enthusiasm for the work had spread through the colonies with amazing speed, though on its ultimate aim opinion was still divided. Not yet fully cognizant of the king's policies, many colonists continued to view the war as one for rights within the empire. Paine helped change some minds, but more importantly, he strengthened the convictions of those who were beginning to realize that, given the king's belligerence, independence was inevitable.

Based on intelligence received from Washington, the Naval Committee had given Commodore Hopkins his first orders on January 5, 1776. John Manley in the *Lee* had captured the British armed sloop *Betsey*, which was carrying dispatches from an angry Lord Dunmore to General Howe, describing the aggressive actions he intended to take in Virginia. Washington passed this information on to Congress. To counter Dunmore, the Naval Committee directed Hopkins to take his fleet south to Chesapeake Bay. Upon arriving, he was to send out a small, swift vessel to gather intelligence of enemy forces. If practicable, Hopkins was to destroy or capture them. Then he was to sail for the Carolinas and establish naval supremacy in those waters. After that, he was to proceed north to Newport, Rhode Island, and "attack, take and destroy all the enemy's naval force that you may find there." The committee added, "Notwithstanding these particular orders, which 'tis hoped you will be able to execute, if bad wind or stormy weather, or any other unforeseen accident or disaster disable you so to do, you are then to follow such courses as your best judgment shall suggest to you as most useful to the American cause and to distress the enemy by all means in your power."

By January 18, Hopkins still had not put to sea. The committee passed on the additional intelligence that three southern governors might be gathering at Savannah, Georgia, to reclaim that province for the king. "Should it be your fate to go southward as far as Savannah," they wrote to Hopkins, "it is probable you may have three governors to dine with you on board your own ship— increase your naval strength by the *Tamar, Scorpion & Cherokee*." (The *Tamar* was a sloop-of-war with Lord William Campbell, the new royal governor of South Carolina, aboard; the *Scorpion* a sloop-of-war carrying Governor Martin of North Carolina; and the *Cherokee* an armed vessel accompanying Governor Campbell and his family.) The members urged Hopkins to capture all three.

Delay followed delay, however, and the "admiral" did not put to sea for another month. On February 13 he was still in Delaware Bay when Captain William Stone of the *Hornet*, accompanied by the *Wasp*, joined him. Stone had brought his swift vessels through the narrow entrance to the Chesapeake, into the Atlantic, and around to Delaware Bay, eluding a formidable British task force under Captain Andrew Snape Hamond, one of the more capable officers in the Royal Navy. Hamond was stationed off Cape Henry at the entrance to the Chesapeake with specific orders to stop Captain Stone, but Hamond never saw him.

Four days later, Commodore Hopkins's eight warships finally stood out beyond the Delaware capes into the wintry Atlantic. Convinced that vastly inflated ideas in Congress about the capabilities of the fledgling navy would put it in harm's way prematurely, he ignored his orders. And it was well he did. Had he ventured into the Chesapeake, he would have run smack into Snape Hamond and the 44-gun *Roebuck;* the *Liverpool* of 20 guns, Captain Bellew; the *Otter*, with 16 guns, Captain Squire; the *Kingsfisher*, mounting 16 guns, Captain James Montagu; and the *Fowey*, with 20 guns, Captain George Montagu. It would have been a slaughter.

Thanks to excellent intelligence of the existence and plans of the new American navy, Admiral Graves had sent Hamond to Norfolk to take charge of the Chesapeake squadron with specific orders to destroy Hopkins's fleet. Through his own informants Washington was aware that Graves had issued these orders; he concluded, as he wrote to Joseph Reed, his trusted confidant, that "the destination of the vessels from your port is so generally known, as to defeat the end."

Not only did Commodore Hopkins decide to avoid the Chesapeake, but he steered clear of the Carolinas and Georgia as well, which was fortunate, since a second and much larger British squadron was on the way there.

As part of the king's strategy for conquering America in 1776, he had dispatched two powerful task forces to meet off the coast of North Carolina and attack the southern colonies. The combined groups were expected to accomplish their work in a few weeks and then join General Howe and Admiral Howe in attacking New York later in the year. To this end, the king had ordered General Howe to release fifteen hundred men from his sparse army in Boston for the southern invasion.

Having lived for months surrounded by thousands of inflamed Massachusetts patriots, Howe could not imagine that the rebels in the southern colonies would be so easily subdued. He wrote to Whitehall expressing his misgivings. The royalist governors of these provinces, he thought, were greatly exaggerating their support. Nonetheless, Howe followed orders. On January 20, while Esek Hopkins was in Delaware Bay waiting for the ice to clear enough to allow him to get to sea, General Henry Clinton and fifteen hundred infantrymen departed Boston harbor—the ice apparently not handicapping him—and sailed for North Carolina and a rendezvous with Lord Cornwallis and Admiral Sir Peter Parker, who were scheduled to depart from Cork, Ireland.

In addition to his flagship, the 50-gun *Bristol*, Parker's squadron was composed of the frigates *Actaeon*, *Boreas*, *Solebay*, and *Syren*, each of 28 guns; the *Dealcastle* and *Sphynx*, each of 20 guns; the 10-gun sloop-of-war *Hawke*; and an 8-gun bomb vessel, *Thunder*. In addition, Parker was reinforced by the 50-gun *Experiment*, which Admiral Shuldham (Graves's temporary replacement, pending the arrival of Admiral Howe) had sent from Boston. If the new American fleet had run into Parker, it would have been ripped to pieces.

But there was no danger that Hopkins would run into Parker or Hamond. When he finally stood out from Delaware Bay with a northeast wind, he steered not to Virginia or the Carolinas, but to the warm, pacific waters of New Providence Island in the Bahamas, uncertain what he was going to do when he got there.

Two days into the cruise, the *Hornet* and *Fly* collided during the night in a heavy gale, forcing both to return to port for repairs. Undeterred, Hopkins pressed on with his remaining ships, and the weather soon turned benign. As the fleet approached New Providence, it captured two sloops. According to their captains, there was a large cache of arms in Nassau, and no British warships defending it.

The Continental Navy now had its first mission.

Arriving off Nassau on March 1, the fleet swiftly captured a splendid store of arms: seventy-one cannon, from 9-pounders to 36-pounders; fifteen brass mortars; thousands of shells, balls, and fuses; as well as gun carriages, ordinance tools, and twenty-four casks of gunpowder. Hopkins had hoped for more powder, but, due to his own blunder, his fleet had been spotted by Governor Montfort Browne in time for him to spirit away most of the island's 150 barrels.

It took Hopkins two weeks to load the booty. Then he sailed north into rough seas, arriving off Long Island's Montauk Point on April 3.

While Hopkins had been away, a momentous event had taken place in Boston. Using the weapons Henry Knox had brought from Ticonderoga to good effect, Washington had secretly moved enough cannon onto Dorchester Heights in a single night to force General Howe and the British to evacuate the city. Howe had intended to leave Boston anyway, but in his own good time. Now his long-planned departure looked like a great patriot victory.

Howe was well on his way to Halifax before Commodore Hopkins and the Continental fleet arrived off Montauk Point. There, on April 4, the fleet captured two small British warships, the armed schooner *Hawk* and the bomb brig *Bolton*, which had just left Newport, Rhode Island, where a strong British squadron was anchored under Captain James Wallace.

Two days later, at one o'clock in the morning, lookouts from every ship in the American fleet spotted a stranger who had come about and was heading straight for them. Before Hopkins could organize his scattered ships into a fighting unit, the *Cabot*, the lead vessel under his nephew John Hopkins, suddenly found herself within pistol shot of a 20-gun British frigate, HMS *Glasgow*. Her commander, Tyringham Howe, was carrying dispatches from General Howe to General Clinton, who was sailing south to spearhead the invasion of North Carolina. With admirable presence of mind, Captain Howe threw his dispatches overboard. Then he turned on the tiny 6-gun *Cabot*. Before young Hopkins knew what was happening, Howe had expertly maneuvered across his bow. The *Glasgow*'s ten deadly 9-pounders then raked the *Cabot* mercilessly fore and aft, instantly disabling the much smaller American vessel, which fell off, badly cut up.

Meanwhile, the *Alfred* had come up into position. John Paul Jones was ready on the lower deck with a bank of 9-pounders manned by well-drilled sailors. The two ships closed and traded broadsides. A shot from the *Glasgow* carried away the *Alfred*'s wheel block and ropes, dismantling her steering and causing her to fall off broadside to the wind. The British frigate then raked her fore and aft, just as she had done to the unfortunate *Cabot*.

Avoiding the drifting *Alfred,* Captain Nicholas Biddle in the *Andrew Doria* now maneuvered to engage, as did Captain Whipple in the *Columbia*. At this point, Captain Howe, his sails, masts, and spars badly damaged, made a run for it, laboring toward Newport. As an American prisoner on board later reported, "The *Glasgow* was considerably damaged in her hull, had ten shot through her mainmast, fifty-two through her mizzen staysail, one-hundred and ten through [her] mainsail, and eighty-eight through her foresail; [and] had her spars carried away and her rigging cut to pieces."

Even with a vastly superior fleet, Hopkins failed to catch his crippled opponent, invoking a number of excuses, including being loaded down with armament and fearing the British warships in Newport. At six-thirty he gave up the chase. The 12-gun *Providence*, with eighty men and marines under Captain John Hazard, never entered the action. The cruel, incompetent Hazard had never meant to. On May 8 he would be court-martialed and drummed out of the service.

Nicholas Biddle, who earlier in his life had served as a midshipman with Horatio Nelson in the Royal Navy, called the encounter with the *Glasgow* a "shameful loss. . . . A more imprudent, ill-conducted affair," he wrote in disgust, "never happened. . . . For the action [the commodore] deserved the severest censure." Most members of Congress agreed, regarding the incident as a humiliation. The entire American navy had failed to defeat a 20-gun British frigate.

Afterward, Hopkins sailed his damaged fleet, two prizes, and precious munitions into New London, Connecticut. There, on April 8, he met with General Washington, who was traveling from Boston to Manhattan, preparing for an expected British attack on New York. This was the first meeting of the two supreme commanders, who had to find a way to work together. Washington tried to coordinate his efforts with the navy, but Hopkins had other priorities. However much he protested to the contrary, the "admiral" had no plans to engage in joint operations with the army; his priority was getting his valuable ships and munitions to the safety of Providence. Whatever cooperation he gave Washington at the moment was directed toward that end. As soon as he was able, he took the fleet out of New London and proceeded on April 25 directly to Providence. He remained there, idle, while Washington, forced to improvise on the water in New York just as he had in Boston, fought the British alone, without the support of the Continental Navy.

Needless to say, Commodore Hopkins's first mission was a huge disappointment to the naval enthusiasts in Congress. Of course, blaming Hopkins for the ills of the Continental Navy was patently unfair. It is true that he lacked the ability or experience to be a commodore and that he placed his self-interest above his country's, but the principal blame belonged with Congress for giving Hopkins an impossible assignment. In fact, its whole approach to creating a navy had been misguided. There never should have been a commodore or a navy separate from the army. Nor should Congress have undertaken to build a British-style fleet from scratch in the middle of a war with the world's greatest sea power. The country simply did not have the expertise or resources. Attempting to construct such a navy was, as Samuel Chase had declared to Congress way back on October 7, 1775, "the maddest idea in the world." Washington should have been in charge of a very different sort of navy, with all its resources placed at his command.

Unfortunately, the thirteen new frigates, which were supposed to be ready by the spring of 1776, took far longer to build and were far more expensive than anticipated, straining the limited supplies of iron and other necessary materials, not to mention skilled workers and money. Not one of the warships was at sea before 1777. The delay provided more evidence that attempting to build even this small squadron was beyond America's capacity, and was entirely in keeping with the overblown instructions given to Commodore Hopkins. None of the frigates would prove of any real value during the war. Indeed, six of them were later captured by the British, taken into the Royal Navy, and used against the patriots.

While the new navy was proving such a disappointment on the eastern seaboard, things were going from bad to worse in Canada. After the debacle on New Year's Day, Arnold had expected General Carleton to sally forth from the great fortress at Quebec and attack his much smaller, dispirited force. But Carleton chose instead to await reinforcements. British General John Burgoyne had left Boston on December 6, returning to London aboard the 70-gun battleship *Boyne*. In quiet talks with the king, he had confirmed all of His Majesty's plans to invade America. Now, on May 2, he appeared at the mouth of the St. Lawrence with fifteen ships and six thousand fresh, healthy men—seven Irish regiments, one English regiment, and some two thousand German mercenaries.

That spring the patriots sent thousands of reinforcements to Canada under some of their best officers. But in a decisive battle at Trois Rivières on June 8, the Americans were routed, and their numbers reduced to perhaps twenty-five hundred. Tormented by disease, particularly smallpox, as they had been throughout the Canadian campaign, they fled south. Making matters worse, the vast majority of Canada's population—sixty thousand French habitants—had turned against them. The Congress, after all, had sent the army into Canada with inadequate supplies, forcing it to live off the land, which had infuriated the French. And so the Canadian venture, for which Congress had held such high hopes, was turning into a disaster of the first order. Perhaps as many as five thousand soldiers died in the effort, along with two of America's best generals, Montgomery and Thomas.

By the end of June, the British had pushed the Americans out of Canada and were threatening to march to Albany for the planned rendezvous with General Howe. Infected with sickness and totally demoralized, the remnants of the American army gathering at Crown Point and Ticonderoga could offer no resistance. On June 17, Congress, urged on by the Adamses and other New England members, ordered the ambitious General Horatio Gates to take charge of the Canadian army, creating a dual command with the aristocratic General Schuyler. Though vastly dissimilar in personality, Gates and Schuyler, to their credit, managed a tentative partnership while confronting their desperate situation.

The one element of strength the Americans still possessed was their tiny Lake Champlain fleet. Though it had been allowed to deteriorate during the winter, it still controlled the lake.

Before he could move farther south, General Carleton had to restore British naval supremacy on the lake. At the beginning of July, the patriots' Lake Champlain fleet was the only force standing in Carleton's way. He could have destroyed it easily had he been able to sail his warships straight down the full length of the Richelieu River, but between Chambly and St. Jean, there were ten miles of impassable rapids.

To his chagrin, Carleton soon found that dragging warships on rollers around the rapids didn't work; the soil was too soft. He was forced into the arduous, time-consuming process of dismantling ships at Quebec and Chambly and carting the pieces overland, only to reassemble them at St. Jean. This gave the Americans time to augment their squadron, compounding Carleton's difficulties.

Following Washington's suggestion, General Gates gave Benedict Arnold naval command of Lake Champlain. Arnold threw himself into the daunting task of competing with Carleton and the Royal Navy. General Schuyler and his naval commander, Jacobus Wynkoop, had already begun restoring and adding to the patriots' Champlain fleet in the spring of 1776. Now Arnold breathed new life into the effort. A critical arms race developed. As the British hurried to assemble a fleet at St. Jean large enough to dominate the lake, Arnold worked feverishly to build more warships, knowing that the outcome of the competition could well determine the fate of the Revolution.

The Continental Navy was of no more help to Arnold than it had been to Washington. While Arnold, Gates, and Schuyler were desperately trying to repair and add to the lake fleet for what could be the most important naval battle of the war, the Continental Navy was busy constructing its thirteen frigates in New England, Pennsylvania, Maryland, and New York, consuming resources in men and materials that Arnold desperately needed. Two of the thirteen, the *Congress* and the *Montgomery*, were being constructed close to Arnold at Poughkeepsie, New York.

In the early summer of 1776, patriot prospects looked bleak. General Carleton's success appeared highly probable. The king's mighty force under General Henry Clinton, Lord Cornwallis, and Vice Admiral Sir Peter Parker arrived off Charleston, South Carolina, at the same time that General Howe was making his way toward New York with a force of well-trained professionals that would ultimately reach thirty thousand. Against him stood Washington with nineteen thousand ill-equipped, poorly trained men and no navy to speak of. And the patriot defenders in Charleston were even less prepared to meet the British invaders.

While the Continental Congress wrestled over the precise wording of America's Declaration of Independence, the king's massive, three-pronged invasion appeared certain to succeed, nullifying whatever inspiring language the patriots might adopt.

3

BATTLES IN CHARLESTON, NEW YORK, AND NEW JERSEY

June 1776–January 1777

Occupying the tip of Sullivan's Island, Fort Sullivan guarded the northern entrance to Charleston harbor. On June 1, Colonel William Moultrie stood on the ramparts with a long telescope. The king's dreaded invasion fleet had just hove into view, six leagues offshore. Moultrie counted fifty ships in all, including ten men-of-war. "The sight of these vessels," he later recalled, "alarmed us very much—all was hurry and confusion, the President [patriot Governor John Rutledge] with his council busy in sending expresses to every part of the country to hasten down the militia; men running about the town looking for horses, carriages, and boats to send their families into the country; and as they were going out through the town gates to go into the country, they met the militia from the country marching into the town. Traverses were made in the principal streets; fleches thrown up at every place where troops could land; military works going on everywhere, the lead taken from the windows of the churches and dwelling houses to cast into musket balls, and every preparation to receive an attack which was expected in a few days."

But the attack did not come "in a few days." In fact, not until an entire month had passed would it begin, giving the patriots time to organize. General Clinton and Admiral Parker, although supremely confident in British arms, acted with the caution typical of Clinton. Speed, however, was essential. It was critical to take advantage of the Charleston rebels while they were unprepared, but the entire British operation was months behind schedule.

At least as early as October 1775, His Majesty had decided to invade the southern colonies, but the attack was to have begun in North Carolina, not South Carolina, and in the first week of February, not the beginning of June. The king had hoped to have all four provinces—Georgia, Virginia, and the Carolinas—in loyalist hands by the first of July, so that Clinton and Parker could then sail north to join General William Howe and Admiral Lord Howe for the more difficult task of subduing New York.

Glowing reports from royal governors in all four provinces had fed His Majesty's optimism about conditions in the south. In letter after letter they had described the rebels as a deluded minority manipulated by a handful of demagogues, and they had predicted that as soon as a sufficient British force appeared in the offing, backcountry loyalists would easily dispatch them. Lord William Campbell, the royal governor of South Carolina, argued that Charleston, the most important city in the south, could be held by just two battalions, two frigates, and a detachment of artillery. Lord Dartmouth wrote to Governor Josiah Martin of North Carolina that the king was acting "upon the assurances given by yourself and the rest of His Majesty's Governors in the southern Provinces, that, even upon the appearance of a force much inferior to what is now sent, the Friends of Government would show themselves, and the Rebellion be crushed and subdued."

In any case, by the time His Majesty's fleet arrived off the coast of Charleston, it was so far behind schedule that its original mission appeared hopelessly compromised. General Clinton, starting from Boston in the middle of January with fifteen hundred regulars, had managed to reach the designated rendezvous point, the Cape Fear River in North Carolina, on March 12, but Admiral Parker, sailing from Ireland with the main body of the fleet and twenty-five hundred additional troops under Lord Cornwallis, did not arrive at the river until May 3. Given the delay, Clinton had to decide whether or not to proceed with the original plan. He considered the governors' estimates of nascent loyalist strength exaggerated. After all, when rebels had driven the governors from their capitals the previous year, all of them had sought refuge aboard British warships, instead of fleeing to the backcountry and taking command of the legions of the king's supporters they claimed were waiting to be rallied.

Even more telling, loyalists had already suffered crushing defeats at Great Bridge, Virginia, in December, and at Moore's Creek Bridge, North Carolina, in February. In light of this recent history, as well as the lateness of the season, Clinton might well have set aside his original mission and sailed directly to New York, leaving the south for another day. In fact, just before reaching Charleston, he had received a letter from Lord George Germain, leaving it up to him whether or not to proceed in the Carolinas, or, since the invasion was so far behind schedule, give it up for the time being and concentrate on New York. Germain advised that only if Clinton expected a signal success in the south should he remain there.

Knowing how much London wanted action in the south, however, Admiral Parker urged Clinton to continue with the original mission. After two junior lieutenants reported on May 26 that Sullivan's Island was weakly defended, Parker suggested striking there. Clinton agreed, although neither he nor Parker had a clear idea what they were going to do if they succeeded.

Further complicating matters was Clinton's inability to collaborate with Parker. Throughout the war, Clinton found it impossible to work with any naval commander. For whatever reason, he repeatedly declined Parker's invitations to come aboard the flagship for talks, and instead communicated solely by letter. Both commanders assumed they would have an easy time of it on Sullivan's Island. Parker thought his warships would reduce Colonel Moultrie's unfinished fort to splinters in thirty minutes, and Clinton expected his troops to seize the four-mile-long island a few hours later. Had they pressed their attack on the day they arrived, as someone like Horatio Nelson might have done, they would have stood a good chance of taking Sullivan's, and Charleston as well. But they hesitated and did not begin their assault until June 28. By that time more than sixty-five hundred patriot fighters had gathered in the Charleston area.

As in Boston the year before, the patriots made no attempt to organize a naval force to impede the progress of Parker's warships into Charleston harbor. The entrance had a notoriously tricky bar, especially dangerous for heavy warships to cross. At the very least the British would have to remove all their cannon to cross it. Still, the patriots allowed Parker to work his men-of-war into position against Fort Sullivan without opposition except for the removal of buoys and other markers, which the British easily replaced.

The rabid Charleston patriot and former British naval officer Christopher Gadsden was on the scene and might well have organized a makeshift fleet to oppose Parker. Instead, he had rushed from Philadelphia to assume command of the approximately 380 men of the 1st Regiment of Foot. He was assigned to guard the harbor's southern entrance from Fort Johnson on James Island, and, as it turned out, he played no part in the subsequent action. Once again, the patriots—including even Gadsden—were so awestruck by the Royal Navy that developing a plan to mount a seaborne attack on Parker's warships seemed a dangerous waste of time and resources.

The Continental Navy was of no help, either, as Robert Morris wrote to Silas Deane in Paris on June 5. "Commodore Hopkins has [fallen far] short of expectation," he reported, "and his fleet, which might have performed most signal service under an active vigilant man, have been most useless. He remains with the *Alfred* at Rhode Island and the rest are gone and going on separate cruises after transports [and such]."

On the morning of June 28 Admiral Parker, who had by then worked his warships over the bar, threaded his way northward up the main channel, passing close to the southern tip of Sullivan's Island. A black pilot, a runaway slave by the name of Sampson, helped guide him in. When Parker was within 350 yards of Fort Sullivan—point-blank range—he anchored the 50-gun ships *Bristol* and *Experiment*, the 28-gun *Active,* and the 28-gun *Solebay.* As soon as their hooks were set, he ordered springs pulled taut on their cables, bringing seventy-eight guns to bear on Colonel Moultrie—more than enough firepower to decimate his fort in half an hour. Still, Parker wasn't satisfied. Behind his frontline ships, spaced in the intervals between, he stationed the 28-gun frigates *Syren, Actaeon,* and *Sphinx.* In addition, he placed the bomb vessel *Thunder* a mile and a half away; from that position she could throw her deadly mortar rounds into the tiny fort. He placed the 26-gun *Friendship* beside the *Thunder* to defend her.

Meanwhile General Clinton prepared to land twenty-five hundred infantrymen on the northern tip of Sullivan's Island, four miles from the fort. Since June 15, they had been on adjacent Long Island, separated from Sullivan's by a seventy-five-yard-wide inlet called the Breach. Judging that landing directly on Sullivan's in its heavy surf would be too dangerous, Clinton planned to cross the Breach at a ford, which he understood to be only eighteen inches deep. But in case that proved impracticable, he had small craft available to ferry the men across. With all this arranged, he expected to take Sullivan's northern end quickly and then join Parker to "attack the rebel works" and gain an easy victory by nightfall.

The patriots had grown stronger as Clinton and Parker dithered for a month. But Fort Sullivan, and indeed the whole island, remained vulnerable. Moultrie had the talented, forty-four-year-old Francis Marion as his lieutenant, but he had only four hundred men from the 2nd Carolina Regiment and twenty from the 4th Carolina Artillery Regiment. And his fort, which slaves had been working on since January, was only half finished. Made of soft, sponge-like palmetto logs filled in with earth, and having merlons sixteen feet thick, the fort appeared wholly inadequate to withstand the expected assault. As for weaponry, there were only twenty-six guns—18- and 26-pounders—and a mere twenty-eight rounds for each piece. Even worse, there was little gunpowder. Every shot would have to count.

Patriot General Charles Lee, like Clinton and Parker, considered the fort indefensible, describing it as a "slaughter pen." He would have ordered it abandoned had not strong-minded patriot Governor John Rutledge overruled him. Lee was now in command of the army at Charleston. On March 1, while he had been in New York, shadowing Clinton as he worked his way down the coast, Congress had appointed him head of the newly created Southern Department. And so when General Lee had marched into Charleston on June 4 with three thousand badly needed Continental troops from Virginia and North Carolina, Governor Rutledge happily turned over command to a general regarded by many, including Washington, as the most experienced in the patriot army.

Lee's prowess, however, was a myth. As Washington's biographer, Douglas Freeman, has pointed out, "For all his talk of foreign wars and campaigns, Lee had never had the direction of a battle." His most noteworthy field accomplishment had been under the direction of Burgoyne in Spain at Villa Velha on October 6, 1762. In that action Lee had destroyed a magazine, spiked four cannon, and taken nineteen prisoners and sixty mules. He was, in short, little more than a glib-tongued novice.

Appalled by the amateurish defenses he had found upon his arrival in Charleston, Lee immediately set about reorganizing them, hoping an attack would be delayed. He was particularly annoyed with the patriots' naive reliance on Fort Sullivan, which, given the size of the British fleet, he assumed would be pulverized in the opening minutes of the battle. He removed half the gunpowder from the fort and was about to remove Colonel Moultrie, whom he considered an incompetent rube, when fighting broke out on June 28.

At ten o'clock that morning Parker's warships, expecting a quick surrender, began firing as soon as they were in position. Despite the staggering odds against him, Colonel Moultrie refused to give in. As cannonballs whizzed about his head, he commanded his gunners, "Mind the commodore! Mind the two 50-gun ships."

"It was a clear, fine, but very sultry day," one observer noted, and Moultrie's men dutifully aimed their cannon at the two larger men-of-war. A lucky shot severed the *Bristol*'s mooring hawser, causing her to swing around on her other anchor, presenting her stern, rather than her broadside, to the fort. Moultrie reacted swiftly, concentrating "the fire of all the guns that could bear upon her," turning *her* into a "slaughter pen." A hundred and eleven men fell on the stricken flagship that day, including her captain, John Morris, who was mortally wounded. South Carolina's royalist governor, Lord William Campbell, who had taken an active part in the fight, was also severely injured. Even Admiral Parker was hit, although not seriously. The *Experiment* was knocked about as well, sustaining seventy-nine casualties, and her captain, Alexander Scott, lost a hand.

Meanwhile, the fort, which was supposed to fall easily, continued its slow, deadly fire, while the hundreds of British cannonballs that poured into it were absorbed by the spongy palmetto logs and did little damage.

After the fruitless bombardment continued for more than an hour, Parker ordered the *Actaeon*, *Syren*, and *Sphinx* to break off and move to the western side of the fort, which was still unfinished. From there the three frigates were directed to enfilade the fort and then cut off the rebels' line of retreat to the mainland. Had these frigates succeeded in maneuvering into position, Colonel Moultrie later observed, "they would have enfiladed us in such a manner as to have driven us from our guns." But the three warships never reached their destination.

The *Sphinx*, which was in the van, had no pilot who knew the waters and ran aground on Middle Ground shoal. The *Actaeon*, following about a half cable to the eastward, promptly ran into the *Sphinx*, becoming entangled in her bowsprit and deeply embedded in sand. The *Syren*, following the others, also ran aground close by. Later, at flood tide, the *Sphinx* and *Syren* managed to warp off the sand and withdrew. The *Sphinx* had to cut away her bowsprit in order to break free. But the *Actaeon* was stuck so fast she could not be moved. The next day her captain, Christopher Atkins, burned her to prevent her from falling into rebel hands. *Thunder*, meanwhile, had long since ceased firing, as the excessive powder she was forced to use in order to reach the fort had fouled her beds, forcing her to withdraw.

Throughout the long, steamy Carolina afternoon, Admiral Parker relentlessly pounded the fort, expecting General Clinton to charge to the rescue at any moment. Fortunately for Parker, Colonel Moultrie's powder was running low, forcing the patriots to reduce their rate of fire to ten-minute intervals. Then General Lee brought in another seven hundred pounds of powder, allowing Moultrie to resume firing at a somewhat faster pace.

As darkness approached, both sides slackened their fire, and shortly after nine o'clock the battle stopped. Two hours later, Parker ordered his battered ships to slip their cables and drop down with the tide, out of range of Moultrie's guns.

With great regret the colonel watched the ships stagger away. "If we had had as much powder as we could have expended in the time," he later wrote, "the men-of-war must have struck their colors or they would certainly have been sunk, because they could not retreat, as the wind and tide were against them, and if they had proceeded up to town they would have been in a much worse situation."

Meanwhile, Clinton was trapped on Long Island, unable to cross over to Sullivan's Island. Though he'd been on the scene for nearly two weeks, he had failed to discover that in some places the breach between the islands was too shallow for his boats, while in others it was too deep for his men to wade. When he did attempt a crossing, he met with telling fire from 780 well-positioned Continentals and militiamen under the command of experienced wilderness fighters Lieutenant Colonel William "Old Danger" Thompson and John Peter Muhlenberg of Virginia's Shenandoah Valley. They had two field pieces, one 18-pounder and a brass 6-pounder, which they used to good effect. Reminiscent of the resolute patriot defenders at Breed's Hill, Thompson and Muhlenberg prevented Clinton's twenty-five hundred regulars from crossing, leaving Parker the honor of doing all the fighting.

Afterward, Clinton let his men linger on Long Island for three weeks in sweltering heat, plagued by mosquitoes and the fatal diseases of a lowland summer, while their empty transports idled offshore. Meanwhile, Parker's men worked hellish hours in the same foul atmosphere to repair the battered fleet.

The patriots in Charleston heard reports from deserters describing the terrible conditions aboard the crippled warships, filled with disgruntled sailors, many of whom were pressed men. Although the ships were vulnerable to guerrilla-style assault during fog or dirty weather, General Lee, Colonel Gadsden, and Governor Rutledge never considered attacking them. But then General Lee never gave much thought to naval matters anyway, beyond having an exaggerated view of the power of the Royal Navy. Its reputation often saved the British a world of trouble.

In the end, Colonel Moultrie's remarkable victory appeared largely a matter of luck. Moultrie himself admitted that the three frigates' running aground at the wrong moment saved the patriots in Fort Sullivan. But the stalwart colonel had very nearly captured a number of His Majesty's mightiest warships. At a minimum, he demonstrated that the Royal Navy was vulnerable.

Admiral Alfred Thayer Mahan, in his astute volume *The Major Operations of the Navies in the War of American Independence*, writes, "The fight in Charleston Harbor [was] the first serious contest in which ships took part in this war." Actually, as noted earlier, warships took part from the start of the rebellion, particularly at Bunker Hill, where Admiral Graves was employed ineffectively. It is true, however, that Charleston was the first engagement in which British warships were an integral part of the fighting. And it was the first in which the patriots defeated the Royal Navy's large men-of-war.

The unexpected victory at Charleston was welcome news to Washington in New York, and he immediately announced the outcome of the battle to his troops, as he had after the Declaration of Independence. Like their commander, they needed cheering up. The threat from General Sir Guy Carleton on Lake Champlain and from the Howe brothers in New York was growing increasingly ominous. The British had already crushed the patriot army in Canada. Generals Montgomery, Thompson, and Thomas were dead, and at least five thousand men had been lost.

Washington had taken large numbers of essential troops from the defense of New York and sent them to their deaths in Canada. In April he had dispatched General William Thompson with four battalions, and in May he had sent six more under General John Sullivan, reducing the army at New York to a dangerously low level. Carleton and Burgoyne were now poised to sail down Lake Champlain, take Crown Point and Ticonderoga, and then push on to Albany before winter.

Even as Washington was receiving this alarming intelligence, Congress summoned him to Philadelphia for consultations. After critical discussions, the patriot leaders made the fateful decision to continue disputing every foot of ground along the St. Lawrence River while simultaneously defending New York City and the Hudson River. It was universally believed that the Hudson was "the jugular of America, the severance of which meant death." According to Washington biographer Douglas Freeman, Washington felt that "New York [City] had to be defended, otherwise the British probably would have been able to ascend the Hudson and sever New England. Had that been accomplished, any commander, even one of the very front rank, would have found it exceedingly difficult to keep the American cause alive."

Washington was not alone in this belief. All his military colleagues shared it, as did the Congres. Thomas Jefferson wrote that the loss of the province of New York would "cut off all communication between the Northern and the Southern Colonies and which effected, would ruin America."

The king was also convinced that control of the city and river would split the colonies and lead to the collapse of the rebellion. He fully expected Washington to throw his entire army into the defense of the Hudson, thereby bringing on the decisive battle that would crush him and the revolt.

Contrary to this widely held assumption, at no time did the British have the capacity to control the Hudson. The Royal Navy did not have sufficient resources. The physical impossibility of their possessing the Hudson was demonstrated time and again throughout the war, but the conviction on both sides that it was America's jugular remained.

To the patriots, defending Manhattan appeared impossible. In laying out the city's defenses, Washington's principal adviser, General Lee, contended that the Royal Navy could be expected to have absolute control of the water, making New York Island indefensible. As far as Lee was concerned, the patriots' only hope was to sell it dearly, which he recommended they do.

By July 1776 it was painfully evident that the Continental Navy would be of no help to Washington. The appointment of Commodore Hopkins had been a huge mistake, but who would replace him was unclear. Congress was perplexed about what to do with the "naval power" it had created. For the most part, the Marine Committee employed individual ships or small squadrons of two or three in commerce raiding, carrying important personages to foreign assignments, showing the flag, performing convoy duty, and running arms from French and West Indian ports. All of those activities could have been left to privateers. In carrying out these varying assignments, outstanding individuals emerged, but none were appointed to succeed Commodore Hopkins; instead, Congress chose to direct the navy itself—an impossible job for a legislative body. It was never able to fashion a satisfactory strategy for the Continental fleet, and it never assigned its outstanding captains to places where the real fighting was deciding the outcome of the war. Superb leaders like John Paul Jones, John Barry, Lambert Wickes, Nicholas Biddle, Seth Harding, John Manley, Joshua Barney, and James Mugford, to name just a few, were wasted in largely meaningless, although at times spectacular and heroic, missions.

While the Marine Committee was having difficulty finding a suitable role for the Continental Navy, patriot General Artemus Ward in Boston was continuing to make good use of the little fleet Washington had created in the fall of 1775. When the British had evacuated Boston in March 1776, they left behind a powerful squadron to lie in Nantasket Roads and collect the transports arriving from England who weren't aware that General Howe had left the city. These late arrivals were to be turned around and shepherded to Halifax. The British fleet patrolling off Boston included the 50-gun *Renown*, under Captain Francis Banks; the frigate *Lively*, under Captain Thomas Bishop; the frigate *Milford*, under Captain John Burr; the sloop-of-war *Swan*, under Captain James Ayscough; and the armed brig *Hope*, under Lieutenant George Dawson.

Fearing that Captain Banks might try to burn Boston, General Ward remained on constant alert while he fortified the city. Defying the British warships on patrol nearby, patriot Captain James Mugford in the schooner *Franklin* captured the three-hundred-ton ordinance brig *Hope* under Master Alexander Lumsdale off Boston on May 17. Stuffed in her hold were a thousand carbines, five gun carriages, ten thousand sandbags, and most importantly, fifteen hundred barrels of gunpowder, almost all of which was forwarded to Washington in New York. Adverse winds that day prevented the British patrols from intercepting Mugford, and the arms cache was brought into the city in small boats. By then General Ward had made Boston secure against an attack by water.

Seeking revenge, the British squadron kept a careful eye on Mugford. During the night of May 20, after seeing that he had gone aground in the *Franklin*, they attacked him with thirteen small craft filled with armed men. Though greatly outnumbered, Mugford and his crew put up a stiff fight, driving off the attackers. But Mugford was killed, as General Ward wrote to Washington, "a little before the enemy left his schooner . . . run through with a lance while he was cutting off the hands of the pirates as they were attempting to board him; and it is said that with his own hands he cut off five pair of theirs; no other man was killed or wounded on board the *Franklin*."

On June 8 the armed schooners *Warren* and *Lee* of Ward's tiny fleet captured the *Anne,* a 223-ton transport from Scotland with a light infantry company of Highlanders aboard—about one hundred men—under Captain Hamilton Maxwell. Captain Nicholas Biddle in the Continental naval vessel *Andrew Doria* then took two more transports, the *Oxford* and the *Crawford*, with a total of 210 Highlanders, all part of a three-thousand-man contingent sent to reinforce General Howe for his attack on New York.

In another action on June 17, General Ward's armed schooner *Lee*, under Captain Daniel Waters—in company with the armed schooner *Hancock*, under Captain Samuel Tucker; the *Lynch*, under Captain John Ayres; the *Warren*, under Captain William Burke; and the *Franklin*, under Captain John Skimmer—attacked the British troop transports *George* and *Annabella* just outside Boston harbor. The transports were carrying 322 Highlanders, led by Lieutenant Colonel Archibald Campbell, who had no idea that the British army had already left Boston. Campbell's transports, however, proved too strong for Ward's fleet, and the patriots quit the action. Colonel Campbell then anchored his transports in Nantasket Roads for the night.

Several hours later, just before midnight, patriot Captain Seth Harding attacked Campbell in the 14-gun Connecticut state vessel *Defence*, supported by the *Lee* and her companions.

Captain Harding called out to the *George*. "Strike!"

"I'll strike," came the heavily burred reply from Campbell, followed by a broadside. Harding returned fire, and a hot exchange continued for an hour and a half. Badly injured, the two British transports finally struck their colors.

The following day, Harding and his squadron took yet another troop transport, the *Lord Howe*, without a fight. It too had a company of Highlanders aboard.

In all, the patriots captured around 750 men.

Lieutenant Colonel Campbell later reported to General Howe, "Since our captivity I have the honor to acquaint you that we have experienced the utmost civility and good treatment." He was residing at the time in the Concord, Massachusetts, jail. The "good treatment" he described contrasted markedly with the way Howe handled American prisoners.

By the spring of 1776, six gifted leaders had emerged from the Continental Navy: Nicholas Biddle, John Barry, Lambert Wickes, John Manley, Seth Harding, and John Paul Jones. On May 10, while General Howe was gathering his forces at Halifax to attack New York, Jones was given command of the sloop *Providence*, replacing John Hazard, a slovenly man, cruel and erratic in disciplining his men. The crew hated him. Jones ran a tight ship, but he was fair, and saw to it that the men were well fed and clothed, and treated with respect. Jones was assigned convoy duty and other tasks of little consequence. On August 1, shepherding a few colliers from Boston, skirting all the naval activity in and around New York City, he landed in Philadelphia. Less than a week later, on August 6, the Marine Committee—seemingly oblivious to the massive British invasion aimed at New York—sent him off on an independent cruise with the vaguest of orders to proceed "against our enemies."

A deep, fast sloop, the *Providence* was the former Rhode Island state ship *Katy*, built by the merchant banker, slave trader, and privateer John Brown of Providence. She was seventy feet long, with a huge, thirty-nine-foot bowsprit and flying jib-boom, a twenty-foot beam, an eighty-four-foot mast, and a crew of seventy. For armament she carried twelve 4-pounders. The crew included twenty-five marines. All Continental warships had a large marine contingent; they guarded the officers from the crew, acted as a police force on the ship, and fought when the time came.

Jones departed the Delaware capes on August 21. A week later he came across a fleet of five sail, and while he was trying to figure out who they were, the largest of them tore after him. She turned out to be the 26-gun British frigate *Solebay*. Jones did his best to get away, but, as he reported later, "she sailed fast and pursued us by the wind till after four hours chase, the sea running very cross, she got within musket shot off our lee quarter." With the cool courage that eventually made him famous, Jones put on every sail, turned downwind, and "bore away before the wind," sailing right past the bow of the surprised *Solebay*. "Before her sails could be trimmed," Jones wrote, "and steering sails set I was almost out of reach of grape [shot] and soon after out of reach of cannon shot.

Our hairs breath escape and the saucy manner of making it must have mortified him not a little. Had he foreseen this motion, and been prepared to counteract it he might have fired several broadsides of double headed and grape shot which would have done us very material damage, but he was a bad marksman, and tho' within pistol shot did not touch the *Providence* with one of the many shot[s] which he fir'd."

Jones continued his cruise for another two weeks without seeing any vessels. With his water and wood running low, he sailed north. On the way a terrible storm struck and continued for two days, obliging him to dismount all his guns and take them, and everything else he could, below. Three days later, on September 20, he was off Sable Island when he ran into another British frigate, HMS *Milford*. Jones's men were fishing at the time, and they immediately stowed their poles as the frigate bore down on them. Jones waited until the frigate was almost within cannon shot before making "sail to try his speed." Finding that he was faster, Jones then "shortened sail to give him a wild goose chase and tempt him to throw away powder and shot . . . Accordingly," Jones reported, "a curious mock engagement was maintained between us for eight hours . . . He excited my contempt so much by his continual firing at more than twice the proper distance that when he rounded too to give his broadside I ordered my marine officer to return the salute with only a single musket." Jones's audacity impressed his crew and the Marine Committee.

On October 7, after a forty-nine-day voyage during which he had taken sixteen prizes, Jones sailed into Newport, Rhode Island. Six of his captures had been sent safely into port, while the rest had been either retaken by the British or intentionally destroyed.

Taken on its own merits, Jones's trip was hugely successful. But in his absence, the crucial battles of the Revolution were being fought in New York and on Lake Champlain. Jones had been merely following orders, of course, and the Marine Committee considered his voyage a great triumph, as did his crew, who had prize money to split. But Jones was never used where he could have done the most good.

Meanwhile, Nicholas Biddle also made the most of his questionable assignments. On June 6, he had been transferred from the *Andrew Doria* and appointed captain of the Continental frigate *Randolph* being built at Philadelphia. His primary mission would be commerce raiding.

Biddle's old ship, the Continental brig *Andrew Doria*, was transferred to Captain Isaiah Robinson. In October 1776, Robinson sailed to the Dutch island of St. Eustatius for a shipment of military supplies, arriving on November 17. There the new American flag was saluted. This was the flag's second foreign recognition; three weeks earlier a schooner flying the American colors had been saluted by Danes at St. Croix. On the way home, Robinson and the *Andrew Doria* met the 12-gun British sloop-of-war *Racehorse* off Puerto Rico. After a deadly two-hour battle, he captured her.

John Barry, another star of the Continental Navy, had worked many years for the Willing & Morris Company, skippering their merchant ship *Black Prince* before it was converted to Hopkins's flagship *Alfred*. On March 13, the Marine Committee gave Barry command of the brigantine *Lexington*, a sleek, seventy-foot vessel with sixteen 4-pounders, sixteen oars, and plenty of speed. As soon as she was outfitted in Philadelphia, Barry wanted to put to sea, but Snape Hamond in HMS *Roebuck* was patrolling Delaware Bay. Barry proceeded cautiously, sneaking around the fearsome, deep-draft *Roebuck* at night in shallow, rocky waters. Since the patriots had removed all the markers in the bay and river, Hamond had to be cautious as well. Next morning he spotted Barry's *Lexington* and chased her, but the *Lexington* was too fast. After three hours, Hamond gave up.

On April 7, soon after springing himself loose from Delaware Bay, Barry encountered the armed British sloop *Edward* off the Virginia capes. She was the *Liverpool*'s tender, under Lieutenant Richard Boyer, and mounted six guns and six swivels. When her lookout spotted the oncoming *Lexington*, Boyer delayed for a few anxious moments, fired a useless broadside, and fled. Barry easily overtook him, and a spirited, hourlong battle followed before the intrepid Boyer struck his colors. The *Edward* was taken into the Continental Navy and renamed *Sachem*.

During 1776 another outstanding Philadelphia fighter, Captain Lambert Wickes, and his 16-gun brig *Reprisal* were employed not to defend the city or assist Washington in New York, but to ferry important personages to their posts. On June 10, Congress ordered him to convey the new American agent, William Bingham, to the French island of Martinique. Wickes did not get underway from Philadelphia for nearly a month. In the interim he participated in an action with John Barry against two British men-of-war and their tenders—the 6-gun armed sloop *Kingsfisher*, under Captain Alexander Graeme, and the 6-gun armed sloop *Orpheus*, under Captain Charles Hudson.

On July 6 the *Kingsfisher* and *Orpheus* chased the patriot munitions brig *Nancy* off Cape May. Her captain, Hugh Montgomery, made for shore and anchored close to the beach. The two British sloops approached as close as they could and then sent longboats filled with men to claim their prize. The *Nancy* carried a treasure trove: four hundred barrels of gunpowder and sixty small arms. As the longboats drew near, the American brig suddenly opened fire with six 3-pounders, driving the British off temporarily.

Meanwhile, the patriot guard three miles away at Cape May saw what was happening and sped word of the stranded *Nancy* to Captain Wickes aboard the *Reprisal*. He in turn alerted Captain Barry in the *Lexington* and Captain John Bauldwin in the schooner *Wasp*. Wickes then tried to sail out of Delaware Bay to aid the *Nancy*, but light winds and tricky currents held him back. Anchoring just inside the Delaware capes, he sent his brother Richard in the *Reprisal*'s barge to help the *Nancy*. Darkness soon overtook the barge, and Richard had to wait until daylight. In the morning, with the British men-of-war firing at him, Richard and his men boarded the *Nancy*, cut her cable, and ran her ashore in hopes of moving the gunpowder inland before the British overtook them. When the patriots reached shore, they were joined by Captain Barry in one of his longboats from the *Lexington*.

By this time, the *Kingsfisher* had maneuvered closer to the *Nancy*. With her shot whizzing over their heads, Captain Barry, Richard Wickes, and their men managed to unload 260 barrels of powder from the beached brig. While they did, five barges from the *Kingsfisher* rowed toward the *Nancy*. When the first of them reached her, its entire crew leaped aboard, arriving just as the powder left behind by the fleeing patriots blew up. Horrified, the other four of the *Kingsfisher's* boats turned and ran. Five minutes before the action ended, Richard Wickes was shot through the arm and body by a cannon and died. Later "eleven dead British bodies [drifted] on shore with two gold-laced hats and a leg with a white spatter dash."

When Captain Wickes and passenger William Bingham finally stood out from Delaware Bay for Martinique, they convoyed a group of merchantmen part of the way south and later took three prizes. Then, on July 27, while Wickes was still en route to Martinique, the British 16-gun sloop-of-war *Shark* attacked the *Reprisal*, but Wickes managed to beat her off and landed Bingham safely.

On November 1, 1776, when the Delaware River was becoming a key battleground, Wickes and the *Reprisal* were again mindlessly sent off, this time to carry Benjamin Franklin and his grandsons to Paris. Any number of private vessels could have done the job just as well, but the Marine Committee routinely employed a scarce Continental warship, since it was a common British practice to transport important diplomats to their stations in men-of-war.

Of all the talented officers in the Continental Navy, John Manley had perhaps the most frustrating year. Washington had been so impressed with Manley that in January 1776 he had appointed him commodore of his tiny fleet in Boston. But on April 17, Manley received a captain's commission in the Continental Navy, taking him away from Washington at a critical moment. Manley then spent the remainder of the year in Boston and Newburyport as his new frigate *Hancock* was built and equipped, a process that went on month after frustrating month, preventing him from participating in the great battles of 1776. (Manley was not alone in his frustration with the frigate *Hancock*; none of the thirteen new Continental frigates got to sea in 1776.) Lieutenant Colonel Benjamin Tupper tried to fill in for Manley in New York but lacked his talent and experience. The British, meanwhile, were happy to see Manley out of action. Impressed by his exploits in Washington's navy in Boston, they considered him the most formidable American officer afloat.

While the Marine Committee was sending its best captains and scarce warships out to raid British commerce or on other inconsequential assignments, hundreds of American privateers were boldly setting sail for the British Isles, the West Indies, and any other place where they saw a potential for profit. According to Samuel Eliot Morison, "privateering . . . was probably the greatest contribution of seaboard Massachusetts to the common cause. Six-hundred and twenty-six letters of marque were issued to Massachusetts vessels by the Continental Congress, and some thousand more by the General Court." Morison points out that "privateers were of little use in naval operations . . . but they were of very greatest service in preying on the enemy's commerce, intercepting his communications with America, carrying terror and destruction into the very chops of the Channel, and supplying the patriot army with munitions, stores, and clothing at John Bull's expense."

In a burst of enthusiasm James Warren wrote to John Adams, "[The promise of privateers is so great] it will be in the power of the Congress another year to command the American Sea." It has been estimated that Massachusetts sent out half of the privateers deployed during the Revolution.

Though deprived of help from the Continental Navy, Washington still had to defend Manhattan. As in Boston, he had to concoct marine defense on his own. While he was in Philadelphia in May, he'd had a good chance to observe some.

Unlike Charleston, New York, Boston, Virginia, Savannah, Falmouth, and Rhode Island, Pennsylvania had paid serious attention to defending Philadelphia (then the largest city in America) against the Royal Navy. Preparations had begun the previous year under

Franklin and the Committee of Public Safety, and by May 1776, naval defenses along the Delaware River were well advanced. Washington was favorably impressed and was inspired to adapt them to New York. But the Hudson and the Delaware were very different rivers. Moreover, the Delaware defenses themselves were wrongheaded, a fact that Washington, having no naval experience, did not appreciate. In constructing the naval defense of New York, he was about to repeat the same mistakes being made in Pennsylvania. But in New York the mistakes were magnified because the Hudson was even more ill suited to the type of defenses used on the Delaware than the Delaware itself was.

The one element of Philadelphia's arrangements that held some promise was the Pennsylvania navy's fleet of row-galleys that Franklin and his associates had built and deployed during the summer of 1775. These gunboats were fifty feet long, thirteen feet wide, and four and a half feet deep with flat bottoms, and they each carried a single heavy cannon of between eighteen and thirty-two pounds in the prow. As unglamorous as they appeared, they were ideal for fighting in the confined waters of the Delaware with its strong currents, shallow waters, and shifting sands. Powered by twenty oars and two lateen sails, they could maneuver in places where mammoth British warships couldn't follow. Every boat could inflict a telling blow. When scattered, they could attack from different angles simultaneously, presenting even the largest man-of-war with serious problems.

In building the gunboats Franklin had received critical help from the city's shipyards like Wharton & Humphreys, the same yards that were now stretched to the limit building the ships of the Continental Navy as well as Philadelphia's armada of privateers. Unfortunately, the Pennsylvania Committee of Public Safety, failing to grasp the real value of the row-galleys, built only thirteen of them, when dozens were needed.

Although defending the Hudson River had been discussed for months, nothing was actually done about it until Washington arrived in New York City on April 13, 1776. The burden of defending the river fell entirely on him. The Hudson should have been the Continental Navy's first priority, but it stayed far away. John Hancock wrote bitterly to Washington about "the shameful inactivity of our fleet for some time past; [and] the frequent neglect or disobedience of orders in Commodore Hopkins." Of course, even if Hopkins had been making every effort to support Washington, the ships at his command were so unsuited to a battle with Admiral Howe they would have been quickly captured or destroyed.

Washington was disgusted with Hopkins for another reason. As Washington told Hancock, he had not even received the cannon and other armament captured in the Bahamas raid. Hopkins had kept control of nearly all of the weaponry in New London, Connecticut, and Providence, Rhode Island. Washington had hoped to work with the "admiral" on the defense of New York, but Hopkins, using a variety of pretexts, remained safely tucked away in Providence. Infuriated, Hancock ordered him to Philadelphia in June to account for his behavior, but even he failed to move Hopkins. On August 16, 1776, Congress officially censured Hopkins, erasing what little credibility he had left.

The unenviable task of directing Washington's navy in New York fell mainly on General Putnam, who had many other pressing duties. Putnam's modest objectives were "[preventing] the King's ships being supplied with fresh provisions by the enemies of America, [distressing] those bound here with stores from Great Britain and West Indian islands . . . and [protecting] the vessels bound here with ammunition [for the American army]."

Organizing a fleet of row-galleys and whaleboats to attack British warships was beyond Putnam's imagination. Assisting him was the resourceful Benjamin Tupper, promoted to lieutenant colonel for his work in Boston harbor the previous summer. Putnam assigned Tupper to command the sloop *Hester* and a small number of whaleboats, with the mission to patrol the western shore of New York harbor from Amboy to Sandy Hook. Tupper expressed the hope that he might work in concert with Admiral Hopkins, but that never happened. Eventually Tupper found himself in command of all the various armed vessels operating under Washington and Putnam around New York. But no matter how courageously he performed, he was never supplied with remotely enough row-galleys, whaleboats, men, or armament to do an effective job.

Washington might have urged Congress to provide him with a naval arm to help defend the city. But he had no appreciation of how a fleet of small vessels could be of real use against the British navy. He placed all his faith in land batteries and river obstructions, neither of which were effective.

Besides Tupper in the *Hester*, Putnam had the armed schooner *Mifflin*, with four whaleboats, to watch over Barren Island and Hog Island Inlet near Rockaway; the armed sloop *General Schuyler*, with two whaleboats, to attend the inlet at Fire Island; and Captain Thomas Cregier in the armed schooner *General Putnam*, ranging from Sandy Hook to Egg Harbor. This pathetic fleet would have had difficulty accomplishing much of anything. Had Washington and the Continental Navy appointed a commander with the abilities of Benedict Arnold, John Manley, John Barry, John Paul Jones, Nicholas Biddle, or even Colonel Tupper, and concentrated on building dozens of row-galleys and gathering hundreds of whaleboats to operate in all weather, hiding in shallow water and creeks, they would have had a force that could seriously challenge Admiral Howe on New York's waterways. Organizing this kind of guerrilla fleet—precisely the kind that Admiral Graves had feared—would have given the lie to General Lee's bleak assessment of the patriots' prospects on the water.

The model for such a Continental fleet had been displayed on May 8, 1776, in Delaware Bay, where all thirteen row-galleys of the Pennsylvania state navy engaged in a battle with Snape Hamond's 44-gun heavy frigate *Roebuck* and her companion, Henry Bellew's 20-gun *Liverpool*. Hamond was sailing up Delaware Bay in company with Bellew and their tenders to test Philadelphia's defenses. At two o'clock in the afternoon, Captain Henry Dougherty, taking advantage of a favorable wind and tide, sailed down from Marcus Hook with his tiny fleet of row-galleys and challenged the surprised frigates. Dougherty was leading in the 104-foot row-galley *Washington*, with a 32-pounder in her prow.

Seeing this odd assortment of small craft approaching must have caused some amusement on the British quarterdecks; Dougherty had only thirteen cannon—one on each galley—whereas the British had sixty-four. Moreover, the British had experienced gunners; Dougherty's crews were mostly landsmen who had never been in combat. Nevertheless, Dougherty bravely pressed the attack, wondering if his pitiful flotilla would be in splinters before three o'clock.

Looks can be deceiving on the water, though, and Dougherty's row-galleys had a decided advantage that afternoon. At two o'clock the incoming tide was running fast, but Dougherty had the weather gauge: with the wind at his back, he could engage or not as he chose. The initiative was his. Snape Hamond noted that he was "obliged to engage them at the distance they chose to fix on, which was scarcely within point blank shot," as he would have preferred.

When Dougherty was a mile or so from the frigates, he held fast and lobbed cannonballs at them. The British gunners fired back at a rapid rate—enough to blow Dougherty out of the water instantly. But the row-galleys sat low in the water and were hard to hit from that distance. "It was with some difficulty," Hamond reported, "that we could strike them." The downwind frigates, on the other hand, sitting up high, were far easier targets.

This unlikely David-and-Goliath duel lasted for two and a half hours. Toward the end, the frustrated Hamond, while attempting to reach the galleys, ran the *Roebuck* aground at Kearney's Point on the Jersey shore, where she stuck fast in soft mud as the tide turned. Just at that moment the galleys ran out of powder and shot—Pennsylvania always kept them on short rations—and broke off the engagement.

Given an unexpected reprieve, Hamond worked furiously to break free, but to no avail. Seeing his plight, Captain Bellew bore up in the *Liverpool* and anchored close by to offer help and protection.

Through the night, the two warships remained trapped on the Jersey shore. The fog was so thick that an attack by patriots from the land might have gone undetected. But no such force approached, for Captain Dougherty, and indeed the whole Pennsylvania navy, were organized for defense, not offense. Had Dougherty mounted a land attack during the night using row-galleys and whaleboats filled with armed men, he could have overwhelmed the *Roebuck* and the *Liverpool* and captured them both. Captain Hamond wrote later that "if the commanders of the galleys had acted with as much judgment as they did courage, they would have taken or destroyed [the] ship."

There was at least one patriot capture that day, however. While the fight between the galleys and the frigates raged, Captain Charles Alexander in the Continental schooner *Wasp* slipped out of his hiding place in Wilmington Creek, where the two British frigates had driven him the previous day, and captured the *Roebuck*'s tender *Betsey*.

During the early morning of the following day Alexander and his first officer, Master's Mate Joshua Barney, discovered the *Roebuck*'s plight. Using the thick fog as a screen, they tried to approach her. Hamond, however, had already worked his ship free. At eight o'clock, the fog suddenly lifted. The *Roebuck* was revealed close by the *Wasp* with the row-galleys in the distance. The wind was blowing upriver. Hamond and Bellew now raced after the *Wasp*, firing as they went. Alexander retreated, staying ahead of the frigates until he reached the row-galleys. Then they all made upriver before the wind. A couple of hours later, with his own wind dropping and the tide ebbing against him, Hamond gave up the chase.

Captain Alexander was impressed with Joshua Barney and recommended him for promotion. Robert Morris of the Marine Committee took up Barney's cause, and soon Barney found himself in Morris's office in Philadelphia. Barney recalled later that "Mr. Morris, after asking my name, put his hand in his pocket and pulled out a paper which was a commission as lieutenant in the navy."

At seventeen, Barney was mature for his age and already an experienced captain. Before the war, he had been skipper of the merchant vessel *Sidney*, sailing between Baltimore and Europe. When the *Sidney*'s first lieutenant left the ship in a huff and her captain died en route to Nice, France, Barney had taken command and completed an adventure-filled voyage before bringing the *Sidney* home to Baltimore, to the great delight of her owner. Young Barney could have had a promising career as a merchant

captain or a privateer, but he wanted to serve in the Continental
Navy. He traveled from Baltimore to Philadelphia, and when
William Hallock, captain of the 10-gun Continental sloop *Hornet*,
was looking for a second in command he chose Barney. Hallock,
however, turned out to be an inept commander unwilling to fight,
and Barney looked for another ship. He eagerly transferred to the
Wasp, under Charles Alexander.

Apart from Alexander's action, the Continental Navy took no part
in the important fight with the *Roebuck* and the *Liverpool*, even
though two of its best captains, John Barry and Lambert Wickes,
were in Philadelphia at the time. Barry had his *Lexington* in port for
repairs, and Wickes was readying the *Reprisal* for sea. Both were
asked to contribute men for the row-galleys, which they did. Other
than that, they were not called upon.

The patriots had gained an important naval triumph, but in
doing so lost a chance to capture two great men-of-war. The significance of Dougherty's victory escaped the Marine Committee, which continued to put its faith in costly new frigates and
sail of the line. Washington obtained half a dozen row-galleys for
New York's defenses, but that was far too few to be effective. And
when it came to defending the Hudson, instead of organizing
row-galleys and whaleboats, Congress directed Washington to
physically block the river, using the same techniques that
Franklin and his Committee of Public Safety had developed for
the Delaware.

It was not until the beginning of July 1776, as the first troops of
General Howe's invasion army were settling on Staten Island, that
work actually began on the Hudson River defenses. The patriots
built artillery batteries on both sides of the river at the site of what is
now the George Washington Bridge, where the river was only a
thousand yards wide. Below that they built Fort Washington. Directly
across the river, they built Fort Lee, named after the supposed victor
of Charleston, whose reputation was growing by the day.

Between the two forts the Hudson was thirty-three hundred feet
wide, and the navigable channel about twenty-four hundred. The

current ran swiftly enough to make the longevity of any obstructions problematic, but the patriots nonetheless sank hulks of ships, and in between, chevaux-de-frise, as had been done in the Delaware. Together the forts and obstructions were expected to stop any warship from passing up the Hudson. Meanwhile, Washington was busy placing batteries all around lower Manhattan (and on Governor's Island and the New Jersey shore) as protection against a direct assault, and to play upon any ship sailing up the Hudson or the East River. This is where he put his major effort, as well as on Brooklyn Heights, which commanded the East River and the city.

As a result of all this activity, Washington had left himself practically defenseless on the water, so that when on June 25, General Howe finally arrived off New York aboard the frigate *Greyhound*, accompanied by Admiral Shuldham in the *Chatham*, he was able to drop anchor inside Sandy Hook uncontested. There were no patriot vessels to salute him—no fleet of whaleboats loaded with patriot fighters or row-galleys with heavy cannon in their prows. As if thumbing his nose at the patriots, Howe anchored in comfort off the Hook for the next four days, until the rest of his imposing fleet of 130 warships and transports arrived from Halifax. They began appearing on the 29th, and in the next few days, while the divided Congress debated the wording of the Declaration of Independence, ninety-three hundred well-trained, well-fed regulars disembarked on Staten Island with their draft horses and equipment. By all accounts, the populace welcomed them.

Curiously, on July 2, while the fleet was unloading, some of the transports, fighting a contrary wind and tide, were thrown into confusion and drifted dangerously close to Long Island—no more than seven or eight hundred yards from the shore. "Lucky for us," one British observer wrote, "the rebels [onshore who were firing muskets] had no cannon . . . or we must have suffered a great deal."

Ten days later, on the evening of July 12, Admiral Lord Richard Howe and his armada arrived. The admiral entered the harbor grandly in his magnificent flagship, HMS *Eagle*, to the accompaniment of loud cheers and the booming of cannon. With the arrival of Lord Howe the British now had something they didn't have before, a genuine joint command. The army and navy were actually working together. The Americans, doing their poor imitation of the British, still had an entirely separate army and navy.

The morning before Lord Howe's arrival, Admiral Shuldham (still the naval commander in North America) ordered Captain Hyde Parker Jr., in the 44-gun *Phoenix*, and Captain James Wallace, in the 20-gun frigate *Rose*, with three tenders, to sail up the Hudson and take the measure of the river's defenses. As the warships approached the lower end of Manhattan, batteries on the New York and New Jersey shores shot at them, but with a southerly wind and a strong incoming tidal current, the frigates passed without difficulty. When they came to the vaunted obstructions between Forts Washington and Lee, they blew through them as if they were so many cobwebs. They then proceeded north for thirty-six miles to Haverstraw Bay, where they dropped anchor. The alarm went out to the highlands. Colonel George Clinton called out the militias, and the patriots responded in strength, ready to counter whatever the warships had in mind.

Although this foray demonstrated the ease with which the Royal Navy could breach the Hudson's defenses, it also revealed how difficult it would be for the British to actually control the river. Once the frigates and tenders anchored, they were separated from the rest of the fleet. Thus isolated, they could not be easily supplied, nor could they withstand an assault by large numbers of row-galleys and whaleboats.

On August 3, Lieutenant Colonel Tupper attacked the two frigates in Haverstraw Bay with five row-galleys he had assembled at Spuyten Duyvil Creek. With his flag hoisted on the *Washington*, which sported a 32-pounder in her bow, Colonel Tupper struck "at ¼ past one on the afternoon of the 3rd." As Tupper recorded later, all five galleys were employed. They engaged the warships for "an hour & a half" before being forced to retreat to Dobbs Ferry, about four miles downriver. Had Tupper possessed three dozen row-galleys rather than just five, he might have captured or sunk both British warships. On the 16th, Tupper again attacked the frigates with row-galleys. He never had more than six, however, so he could bring only six heavy guns to bear. Though his assaults inflicted serious damage, he was forced to retreat on both occasions.

Tupper was not the only one harassing the frigates. In Haverstraw Bay they were subjected to repeated attacks from shore, although never of a size sufficient to sink or capture them. Two days after Tupper's final attack, the *Phoenix* and *Rose* had had enough. Fearing that the patriot assaults might eventually succeed, they took advantage of a favorable wind and tide, weighed anchor, and scurried back downriver. In doing so, they had to pass once more through the river obstructions and run the gauntlet of the two forts, Washington and Lee, before they reached the safety of the fleet in New York harbor. They had been upriver for a month, and during that time the patriots had sunk even more hulks and chevaux-de-frise in the Hudson. But once again the British warships sailed right through them. This time they sustained more damage from the forts, but they still got through handily. Of course, Captains Parker and Wallace called their retreat a victory, but if Tupper had had the wherewithal, they never would have made it back to the fleet.

The long-awaited battle for New York began in earnest at daybreak on August 22, 1776. Admiral Howe, aboard the 44-gun *Phoenix*, supported by the 28-gun *Greyhound*, the 20-gun *Rose*, and the bomb ketches *Thunder* and *Carcass*, stationed himself in Gravesend Bay off the western tip of Long Island. At the same time the 44-gun *Rainbow* quietly slipped into the narrows off Denyse Point and dropped anchor. Then a steady procession of flatboats and bateaux, loaded with infantrymen and their battle gear, crawled back and forth between the British base on Staten Island and the flat Long Island shore near Gravesend. For three hours the parade continued until fifteen thousand of His Majesty's finest were ashore with their German allies. Ambrose Serle, one of Admiral Howe's secretaries, described the stunning panorama: "A fleet of 300 ships and vessels with their sails spread open to dry, the sun shining clear upon them, the green hills and meadows after the rain, and the calm surface of the water upon the contiguous

sea and up the Sound, exhibited one of the finest and most pictur-
esque scenes that the imagination can fancy or the eye behold."

When the landings were completed, Admiral Howe kept his
warships active during the rest of the morning, sailing toward
Manhattan and then back, to make it appear that a direct move on
the city was imminent.

Reports of the British movements came immediately to Washington, who was uncertain whether General Howe's main thrust
would be at Brooklyn Heights on Long Island or at lower Manhattan—or, conceivably, farther up the Hudson, near King's Bridge, to
seize control of the Harlem River and trap the weaker patriot army
on Manhattan. All three were possibilities, and none would be easy
to defend. In fact, with at best two-thirds of the men General
Howe had and no navy to speak of, Washington's position on Manhattan was, as it had always been, indefensible. Adjutant General of
the Army Joseph Reed, the commander in chief's closest confidant, advised him to retire from the city and burn it before the
patriots lost both their army and the war. But the Congress and
Washington deemed New York so vital that they were determined
to hold it, come what may.

Contemplating Howe's opening gambit, Washington ordered
eighteen hundred more men across the East River to reinforce
Brooklyn Heights, which commanded lower Manhattan. If Brooklyn fell, the patriots would have to evacuate New York. It would
have been logical for General Howe to make Brooklyn his primary
target, but Washington couldn't be sure. If the British planned to
seize Brooklyn, why hadn't Admiral Howe established naval control
of the East River? He had twenty-eight men-of-war available: two
64s, the flagship *Eagle* and the *Asia*; six 50-gun ships; three 44-gun
heavy frigates; five 32-gun frigates; four smaller frigates; four
sloops-of-war; two bomb ketches; one brig; and a fire ship—more
than enough to successfully contest any river crossing. Why hadn't
Howe stopped him from moving thousands of men, horses, and
equipment across the rivers around New York at will? Could it be
that the admiral was willing to let him remove troops from Manhattan because the city itself was his real objective? Or was this

simply an oversight born of arrogance? It was hard to believe that the admiral's moves weren't carefully calculated.

Lord Howe was a man to be reckoned with, as unlike Admiral Graves as two leaders in the same service could be. The most capable flag officer in the Royal Navy, Howe was as good as any in British history, including Horatio Nelson, and would be the only officer of the first rank, in either the army or the navy, to serve the king during the entire war. While he was in New York, however, and later in Philadelphia, his role was to support his brother, General Howe, a man of far less ability.

As Washington assessed the Howes' opening moves, he kept his already weak army divided between Brooklyn and Manhattan, courting defeat in both places. His uncertainty was heightened when the Howes, after landing on Long Island, let four days pass without making a move.

Finally, on the night of the 26th, General Howe struck, orchestrating an undetected flanking movement against the patriots' outer defenses on the heights of Guan. Washington was caught off guard. Four columns, amounting to about twenty thousand redcoats and Hessians, sent twenty-eight hundred patriots fleeing wildly back to the protection of the tight inner defenses around Brooklyn Heights. There, with no more than seven thousand dispirited soldiers, Washington awaited Howe's final thrust, expecting it to come on the afternoon of the 27th. Defeat appeared certain.

But then General Howe paused unexpectedly. Not wishing to take any chances and laboring under an inflated idea of the actual numbers behind the patriot barricades, he stopped to regroup, saving his enemy from disaster. From the beginning of their campaign, the British had overestimated the strength of the American army, believing it to be about thirty thousand men. Washington had assiduously cultivated this misconception. Despite a surfeit of Tory spies in the city, he had concealed his dreadful weakness from the Howes. Undoubtedly the debacle at Breed's Hill the previous year also haunted Howe, who felt no need to risk another massacre. Still, with the Royal Navy in command of the water, Washington appeared trapped on the heights.

Actually, at that moment the Royal Navy wasn't in the East River at all. It was confined to the lower bay, the narrows, and the upper bay. On the same morning of the Howes' pause, Sir Peter Parker, with a squadron of one 64, two 50s, and two frigates, tried to work his way toward the entrance to the East River and Brooklyn Heights, but wind and tide checked his progress three miles short of the river. The following day a northeaster struck with cold, heavy rain and wind, making further progress impossible.

Even so, General Howe was certain that Washington wasn't going anywhere. If the Royal Navy couldn't work its way up the river, neither could Washington cross it. Knowing he could afford to take his time, Howe broke ground methodically, creating the trenches for making regular approaches toward the patriots' defenses.

Washington, meanwhile, ferried more troops over from Manhattan, bringing his total in Brooklyn to ninety-five hundred—more than half his army. He apparently intended to make a final stand here, although his position was nearly hopeless. He had been working for months constructing forts, redoubts, and entrenchments along every foot of ground on the heights. His defenses stretched across the entire small peninsula between Gowanus Bay and Wallabout Bay. But Howe had more than twice the number of troops, and as he systematically approached, his force looked overwhelming.

Howe's slow-motion advance, however, gave the resourceful American commander invaluable time. On August 29 a thick early-morning fog hung over the battlefield. General Mifflin, Adjutant General Reed, and Colonel Grayson of Virginia were reconnoitering when a breeze lifted the fog somewhat, revealing the British fleet engaged in strenuous activity. Worried that as soon as the weather eased, men-of-war would move into the East River and cut off the patriots' only line of retreat, the trio hastened to warn Washington. Reed urged him to evacuate Brooklyn immediately. After a council of war, Washington proceeded to do so. He ordered General Heath to gather every boat he could find. Heath in turn dispatched Colonel Hughes to round up every small craft between Spuyten Duyvil Creek on the Hudson and Hell Gate at the entrance to Long Island Sound.

Hughes was told to exercise the utmost secrecy and have the boats in place by nightfall—hardly an easy assignment.

Colonel Hughes had an assortment of small boats in place by eight o'clock that evening. Somehow the British failed to notice the commotion. At this point Colonel John Glover of Marblehead, Massachusetts (the same John Glover who had helped Washington organize his tiny navy in Boston), and his regiment of Marblehead sailors took charge. Having crossed the river from Manhattan to Brooklyn with General Mifflin earlier that morning, they were still fresh. But the weather remained severe, and they were charged with the nearly impossible job of ferrying an entire army at night across an unfamiliar, stormy, mile-wide river. There weren't enough boats to take everyone at once, so the rowers, even if they made it across the first time, had to go back again at great hazard. Washington himself was at the embarkation point directing the whole proceeding. In spite of all the hubbub, General Howe remained unaware of what was afoot.

The tide turned during the night while a strong northeast wind continued to blow, making the going even tougher for Glover's men. There were times when the boats, under oar and sail, were making no headway at all. Even Admiral Howe's veterans could not maneuver their heavy warships up the river in these conditions. For the Marblehead sailors to row across in small craft they had never handled before required exceptional courage and skill.

Mercifully, the northeaster let up while it was still dark, calming the waters enough to allow the boats to be loaded to the gunwales. The patriots were now making considerable progress, but as morning arrived on the 30th the evacuation was still incomplete. A providential fog, however, hung as densely as ever over the entire area, allowing the retreat to continue unabated. In the end, Washington was able to bring his entire army—horses, supplies, military equipment, and all—across the river to Manhattan without the loss of a single life and without the enemy knowing its supposedly trapped prey had escaped.

British sea power allegedly controlled the waters around New York, but obviously that was not the case. The patriots' ability to operate on the water in small craft, undetected in dirty weather, demonstrated that Admiral Howe's vaunted fleet was itself vulnerable. On many occasions bad weather could have covered American operations, allowing whaleboats and row-galleys to attack his warships. Of course, nothing of the kind was ever attempted or even contemplated. Had the Continental Navy been structured differently, it could have given the admiral plenty of trouble. Admiral Howe, like Admiral Graves before him, was well aware of the possibility. To counter it, he kept his fleet anchored where the tides protected it and ran guard boats continually every night.

Washington's brilliant retreat from Brooklyn still left his army in continuing peril. Admiral Howe moved the bulk of his fleet close to Governor's Island, bringing lower Manhattan within cannon range. Meanwhile, General Howe's troops, buoyed by an easy victory and overflowing with confidence, stood poised on Brooklyn Heights, expecting to surge across the East River and finish off the rebels while they had them on the run.

Washington watched in dismay as his demoralized army shrank by the hour. "Our situation is truly distressing," he wrote to John Hancock. "Great numbers . . . have gone off; in some instances by whole regiments, by half ones, and by companies at a time." Washington expected the Howes to exploit their advantage and attack Manhattan at any moment. With command of the water, they could land at a number of different points, and his diminishing army would be overwhelmed.

But to everyone's surprise, General Howe halted once again and waited mysteriously on Brooklyn Heights. Maneuvers were detected on the water at night—suspicious, unnerving movements. On September 3, for instance, the frigate *Rose* convoyed thirty boats up the East River during the evening and anchored near Wallabout Bay. But nothing further happened; there was no general movement. Howe's army remained stationary.

The reason for the general's puzzling delay soon became evident: Admiral Howe wanted talks with the Congress before more blood was shed. The king had appointed the brothers as dual peace commissioners, authorizing them not to negotiate but to accept the surrender of the rebels and to grant pardons to all except their top leaders. The admiral, however, intended to bend these instructions to get the rebels talking, and out of that perhaps reach an agreement that would satisfy both sides and keep America in the empire. He hoped that the demonstration of British power on Long Island would induce the Congress to talk, despite the recent declaration of independence. Even before the battle of Brooklyn, when the *Eagle* first arrived in July, the admiral had tried to open discussions with Washington, thinking that the dazzling display of British might in New York harbor would be enough to get negotiations started, but Washington had declined.

The admiral now sent patriot Major General John Sullivan, who had been captured in the fight for Brooklyn, to Philadelphia to arrange a meeting, and Congress had reluctantly agreed. A committee of three—John Adams, Edward Rutledge, and Benjamin Franklin—was sent on September 11 to meet with Howe in a two-story, gray stone house on Staten Island that had been built nearly a century before by Captain Christopher Billopp of the Royal Navy. According to Adams, it "had been the habitation of military guards, and was as dirty as a stable." The admiral had prettied up one of the larger rooms where the meeting was held, but nothing came of the discussion. Howe had no real power. That much was apparent from the outset, when he said that he could not negotiate on the basis of American independence.

The three patriots made it clear that independence was the only basis for a serious parley. On July 20, in response to a query from Howe, Benjamin Franklin had already explained to him why separation was inevitable. "Were it possible for *us* to forget and forgive," Franklin wrote, ". . . it is not possible for you (I mean the British nation) to forgive the people you have so heavily injured. You can never confide again in those as fellow-subjects, and permit them to enjoy equal freedom, to whom you know you have given such just cause of lasting enmity. And this must impel you, were we again under your government, to endeavor the breaking of our spirit by the severest tyranny, and obstructing, by every means in your power, our growing strength and prosperity."

The destruction of Charlestown, Massachusetts, during the battle of Bunker Hill; the incineration of Falmouth, Maine; the senseless burning of Norfolk, Virginia—all of these atrocities stuck in Franklin's craw, as did the depraved treatment of American prisoners in Boston, New York, and elsewhere. The ugly side of His Majesty's policies convinced Franklin that following a British victory America would experience not the idyllic peace of Admiral Howe's imagination but the nightmare in Ireland, where Irish Catholics—some two-thirds of the population—had been brutally and relentlessly suppressed.

The depredations of Hessian and British troops gave further evidence of what "Parliamentary supremacy" really meant for America. The pillage and rape practiced by the Howes' men, far more than the admiral's conciliatory words, indicated what was in store for the patriots should they lose. Even Ambrose Serle, the admiral's anti-American secretary, was appalled at the wanton behavior of the troops and how it harmed the king's cause. Serle wrote in his journal that he was "mortified" by "the accounts of plunder, etc, committed on the poor inhabitants by the army and the navy. . . . The Hessians are more infamous and cruel than any. It is a misfortune we ever had such a dirty, cowardly set of contemptible miscreants." Congress called them "barbarous ravagers."

The admiral's peace initiative granted the beleaguered Washington time to regroup. It was obvious to him that if negotiations failed, General Howe planned to trap the entire American army on Manhattan. Nevertheless, after a council of war on September 7, Washington divided his army again and, worse, kept it on the island. He placed five thousand men under General Putnam in lower Manhattan, and nine thousand under Heath to hold the upper portion of the island from Harlem Heights to King's Bridge. He sent five brigades of militiamen under General Greene to guard the East River in the vicinity of Kip's Bay and Turtle Bay (today's Midtown).

Greene, who had fallen ill before the battle of Brooklyn and was now recovering, disagreed with this nonsensical arrangement. He wanted to withdraw from Manhattan altogether. Believing that two-thirds of the city's inhabitants were Tories, he advised burning it to deprive the British of a safe, comfortable base and barracks for the winter. Adjutant General Reed agreed.

But Washington remained on the island. The following day he wrote John Hancock a remarkable letter. Using all the hard lessons he had learned so far in the war, he outlined what he thought would be an effective long-term strategy. "We should on all occasions," he wrote, "avoid a general action, or put anything to the risqué, unless compelled by a necessity, into which we ought never to be drawn."

Joseph Reed had suggested an identical strategy back in July when he urged Washington to abandon Manhattan before the British struck. Charles Carroll of Carrollton had made a similar point more than a year before, telling Charles Carroll Jr., "It is certainly in our interest to protract the war, never to engage but with manifest advantage." Washington was now seeing the wisdom of avoiding a showdown. Yet by remaining on Manhattan and continuing to divide the army, he was once again putting everything "to the risqué."

In the same letter to Hancock, Washington reaffirmed his belief in the value of obstructing the Hudson River. "I am fully of the opinion," he wrote, "that by establishing strong posts at Fort Washington on the upper part of this island and on the Jersey side opposite to it, with the assistance of the obstructions already made and which may be improved in the water, that not only the navigation of Hudson River but an easier and better communication, may be effectively secured between the northern and southern states."

Two days later Congress voted to leave it up to Washington whether or not to evacuate New York. In another council of war on September 13, more of his generals, though not all, announced they were now in favor of withdrawal, except from Fort Washington, which everyone believed could be held.

In this dark hour there appeared on the scene thirty-four-year-old David Bushnell and his remarkable submarine. Resembling two huge tortoiseshells spliced together, Bushnell's invention could carry one man underwater for a considerable distance with an explosive device that contained a large quantity of gunpowder and a clock for a timing mechanism. It could be fastened to the bottom of a ship in the night without fear of detection while the operator retreated a safe distance and waited for the explosion. Bushnell's creation was not only a workable one-man submarine but also a "torpedo," an underwater explosive with enough power to sink the largest British man-of-war. Surface boats, even canoes or rafts, could have carried the explosives as well, but for the moment Bushnell was concentrating on delivering the blow by submarine.

Patriot leaders had known of his invention since the summer of 1775. On August 7 of that year, Benjamin Gale of Yale University had written a letter to Benjamin Franklin describing the amazing invention that one of his older students, who was about to graduate, had developed. Gale told Franklin that Bushnell had created a complete operative system that was relatively inexpensive to produce and offered great potential. Fascinated, Franklin carried the idea to Boston for meetings with General Washington in October, but the lateness of the season and the urgency of other matters delayed a demonstration.

It wasn't until September 1776 that an attempt was made on a British warship. During that time the Continental Navy had been born, but no thought was ever given to David Bushnell's novel submarine. If Congress failed to see the potential for whaleboats and row-galleys, they certainly were not about to build a fleet of newfangled submarines.

Washington, however, approved a demonstration, and on the night of September 6, Bushnell's *Turtle* very nearly blew a hole in the underwater side of HMS *Eagle*, Admiral Howe's 64-gun flagship. With fifty such contraptions, the Continental Navy could have driven Howe's fleet into the Atlantic, for the submarine and its torpedo worked well that night, and it was only the inexperience of the operator that spoiled the trial run. Until that time David's brother Ezra had operated the machine, but he became ill at the last moment, and on short notice Bushnell had been forced to employ Ezra Lee, a Connecticut army sergeant. Lee reach the *Eagle* undetected, but when he attempted to attach the explosive to the hull, the projecting point struck what he thought was a bolt, but was probably the copper sheathing. He quickly backed off and aborted the mission. Had David's brother been at the controls, the *Turtle* might well have sent the mighty flagship to Davy Jones.

On September 13, four frigates (the 44-gun *Phoenix*, the 44-gun *Roebuck*, the 32-gun *Orpheus*, and the 28-gun *Carysfort*) passed up the East River without firing a gun. They were joined the following day by another warship and six transports, presumably to support the large force General Howe already had on Long Island. Washington watched, waiting for the next onslaught.

Early in the morning of the 15th, Admiral Howe dispatched four warships up the Hudson with their guns run out: the 50-gun *Renown*, the 32-gun *Repulse*, the 32-gun *Pearl*, and the armed schooner *Tryal*. When they opened fire on the patriot batteries along the tip of Manhattan, they provoked a furious response. But they got through and anchored at Bloomingdale (today's Upper West Side).

Washington wondered why Admiral Howe was sending warships up the Hudson. It might be in preparation for a troop landing in his rear above King's Bridge, or it might be a distraction. That same morning, at eleven o'clock, the four men-of-war that had sped up the East River two days earlier now appeared in Kip's Bay and unleashed a massive bombardment, creating, Ambrose Serle wrote, "so terrible and so incessant a roar [the like of which] few even in the army and navy had ever heard before."

Shortly thereafter, the Royal Navy ferried four thousand redcoats in barges from Long Island across the East River and landed them on the beach at Kip's Bay. At the approach of an advance guard of only fifty regulars, the inexperienced patriot militiamen onshore threw down their arms and fled. General Howe planned to quickly reinforce this initial landing party until it reached nine thousand, at which point he intended to cut west across the middle of Manhattan Island to the Hudson, trapping General Putnam's five thousand men—nearly a third of Washington's army—in lower Manhattan.

But Admiral Howe failed to provide enough small craft to move the remaining troops across the East River in a timely fashion. He had dozens of small, flat-bottomed boats available to ferry soldiers in shallow waters, but there were not enough at Kip's Bay to successfully exploit the initial victory. Hours went by before General Howe had all the troops he needed in place.

Reacting to General Howe's successful thrust, Washington sent an express to General Putnam alerting him to the danger of being cut off. Putnam reacted by abandoning his precious military equipment and fleeing north on the west side of Manhattan, taking a trail known to his aide Aaron Burr. Some of Putnam's men, in a panic, missed the general retreat and fled in small boats to Paulus Hook in New Jersey. Admiral Howe made no attempt to stop them.

At Bloomingdale, Putnam's army passed so close to the Hudson that the warships Admiral Howe had placed there in the morning fired on the retreating patriots. Fortunately, the shots were wide of the mark. Putnam escaped without the loss of a man, but he had nearly been trapped, which might have been the end for Washington. The inability of the Howes to coordinate their amphibious assault saved Putnam.

The patriot army had once again survived, but New York City was now undefended. Late in the afternoon of September 15 a brigade of Howe's army broke off from the main body and marched down to the city, taking possession of it without firing a shot. Ambrose Serle reported that the inhabitants, "like overjoyed Bedlamites," greeted the British soldiers as liberators. At the same time Admiral Howe sent a party of marines ashore and positioned the 24-gun *Mercury* and the 20-gun *Fowey* "close to the town, to prevent [the men of] the transport boats from going on shore and plundering, which many of them appeared very ready to do."

At three o'clock on the morning of the 16th, Washington sent four fireships against the three British men-of-war still anchored at Bloomingdale. The blaze of the patriot ships was so bright that the officer of the watch aboard the *Eagle*, some four or five miles away, warned his skipper, Captain Duncan, that they might be headed for the flagship. By daybreak Duncan could see that the fireships were moving toward the *Renown*, *Repulse*, and *Pearl*, not the *Eagle*. Reacting swiftly, the British warships "towed [the fireships] off and left [them] to consume upon the shore." Only one of the fireships got close enough to cause concern.

At this point Washington's main army was still on Manhattan with perhaps sixteen thousand effectives, strongly fortified at Harlem Heights. Other elements were stationed near King's Bridge and Fort Washington. As the patriots were doing reconnaissance of Howe's positions on the morning of September 16, one day after their humiliating defeat at Kip's Bay, a skirmish developed between the two armies. This time the patriots held their own for two hours before retiring to their stronghold. During the action Colonel Thomas Knowlton, a hero of Bunker Hill and one of the most respected of Washington's officers, was killed.

The affair became known as the battle of Harlem Heights. Although it was much less than a battle, and even though Washington's position on Manhattan remained precarious, it lifted patriot morale.

When Admiral Howe, accompanied by Ambrose Serle, had a chance to examine Washington's abandoned fortifications in lower Manhattan on September 16, he was amazed. "They have formed breastworks and embrasures at the end of every street or avenue leading to the town," Serle wrote. "Redoubts, forts, and lines of communication everywhere round about it. The infinite pains and labor, which they must have bestowed . . . [should] have inclined them to make some sort of a stand." Had Washington put as much effort and treasure into a strong fleet of row-galleys as he did into these static land defenses, he would have been far better served.

Five days later, on the 21st of September, Manhattan was suddenly engulfed by a massive fire that consumed hundreds of buildings. A third of the city was left in ashes. General Howe thought the conflagration had been carefully planned. "Matches and combustibles," he wrote to Germain, ". . . had been prepared with great art and ingenuity. Many were detected in the fact, and some killed upon the spot by the enraged troops in garrison; and had it not been for the exertions of Major-General Robertson, the officers under his command in the town and the brigade of guards detached from the camp, the whole must infallibly have been consumed, as the night was extremely windy."

Washington refused to acknowledge any responsibility for what happened, but he was certainly pleased. He was saddened, however, to learn that after the fire Nathan Hale, an intrepid Connecticut schoolteacher who had been spying for Colonel Knowlton, was captured and hanged. Enraged by the burning of the city, Howe had dealt summarily with Hale.

Meanwhile, the patriot army remained on the top of Manhattan Island, tempting fate. Expecting Howe to attack at any moment, Washington redoubled his efforts to block the Hudson. He ordered General Putnam to add to the obstructions between Forts Washington and Lee by sinking two new ships filled with stones, and to set more and better chevaux-de-frise. Colonel Tupper was stationed above the obstructions with six row-galleys—a hopelessly inadequate squadron borrowed from Connecticut and Rhode Island. Bushnell's submarine, a Putnam favorite, was on hand as well, loaded in a sloop. But what a single submarine armed with one torpedo was supposed to accomplish wasn't clear.

On October 9 Admiral Howe decided to test the patriots' improved Hudson defenses, sending Hyde Parker in the 44-gun *Phoenix*, accompanied by Snape Hamond in the 44-gun *Roebuck*, and Captain Cornthwaite Ommanney in the 28-gun *Tartar*, along with their tenders, to break through the obstructions between Forts Lee and Washington and travel up the Hudson to the Tappan Zee. When they came to the barrier, the warships once again breezed right through it, while both forts fired at them as they passed. Lord Howe reported to the Admiralty that the frigates were banged up in the masts and rigging, sustaining seven deaths and eighteen wounded. But they broke through the barricade nonetheless and easily scattered the American galleys behind them. The British salvaged two of the galleys after their crews abandoned them on the shore, just above Dobbs Ferry. As for Bushnell's famous *Turtle*, the schooner carrying it was sunk by a well-aimed shot, though he later retrieved the submarine.

Once past the obstructions, Hyde Parker led his squadron upstream, unopposed all the way to the Tappan Zee. Ambrose Serle recorded in his diary, "The North River is now in full possession of His Majesty's fleet, and the retreat of the rebels entirely cut off." This was, however, a gross exaggeration.

Meanwhile General Howe was preparing his next thrust at Washington, who was still on Manhattan. Leaving Lord Percy behind with only three brigades to protect the city, Howe launched an encircling movement on October 12, aimed at getting in back of Washington. The first wave of four thousand regulars landed at Throg's Neck, but the terrain proved unsuitable. Howe waited for six days while reinforcements were brought up before moving to nearby Pell's Point.

The delay gave Washington time to react. He held an important council of war on October 16 and finally decided to evacuate New York. Only Fort Washington was to be held, partly because Congress wanted the Hudson River barrier defended and partly because General Greene believed that it could be defended. This was the same General Greene who had earlier advised Washington to exit Manhattan. General Lee also participated in the council; he had rejoined the army to great acclaim two days earlier.

Leaving fifteen hundred men under Colonel Robert Magaw at Fort Washington on October 18 and two thousand more under General Greene at Fort Lee, Washington at long last began moving his main army from Harlem Heights to White Plains, where he arrived on the 23rd with 14,500 men.

Howe might have attacked the patriots' thinly stretched line on the 19th. King's Bridge, where Washington's army was crossing over to the mainland, was only six miles from Howe on Pell's Point. By then the British force had swollen to twenty thousand. Such a move could well have brought on the general battle that Howe sought, and on advantageous terms. But again he let the moment pass, allowing Washington to establish himself at White Plains.

On the 24th Howe attacked him there, but the battle was inconclusive. Washington then gathered his army and two nights later moved it to a stronger position in the hills at North Castle. This time, Howe did not attack. Instead, beginning on the night of November 4 and for three successive days, he quietly withdrew his entire force from White Plains and marched it back toward the Hudson.

Upon learning that Howe had withdrawn—possibly to Dobbs Ferry—Washington held a council of war on the 6th. The state of his disintegrating army was growing more desperate by the hour. It seemed to him that General Howe's move might threaten both Fort Washington and New Jersey. Sitting isolated on Manhattan, the fort was obviously vulnerable, but the council did not consider evacuating it. Instead, Washington decided to divide his army into four parts. Seven thousand men would remain at North Castle under General Lee, in the unlikely event that Howe suddenly turned and pushed into New England; General Heath was given four thousand to guard the highlands and its passes; General Greene would keep thirty-five hundred, divided between the two forts, Washington and Lee; and Washington himself kept two thousand, which he intended to take to New Jersey in case Howe was headed there. Washington expected his tiny force to be strengthened by men from the Flying Camp in New Jersey and by the state's militiamen. However, the Jerseymen went home and stayed there awaiting developments, as patriot prospects continued to diminish.

While Washington was barely coping with his problems around New York, he received unexpected news from Lake Champlain. The message arrived on November 12, as he was reconnoitering the highlands near Peekskill. Twelve days earlier, General Gates had dispatched scouts from Fort Ticonderoga to reconnoiter Crown Point and had discovered, to his surprise and enormous relief, that General Carleton had disappeared, apparently having retreated north for the winter. In fact, Carleton had withdrawn his army all the way to Canada, relieving Washington of anxiety about an invasion from that quarter and even permitting him to draw reinforcements from the Northern Army—a change he would have thought impossible the day before.

Occupying Albany had always been seen in London as a key to winning the war. Although the king and his circle had no knowledge of the brutal realities of the North American frontier, they were convinced that converging on Albany would sever all communications between New England and the southern colonies, killing the rebellion. Their strategic vision was badly flawed, however. If Carleton's small army ever reached its objective, it would be far removed from supply bases in both Canada and New York City. Albany was 150 miles from Manhattan. Since Carleton was unlikely to find a supportive population in the vast area between Canada and Manhattan, he would be isolated and trapped. Lord George Germain and the king expected to remedy this difficulty by having the Howes push up the Hudson from Manhattan and supply Carleton with a lifeline to the sea.

Yet at no time did Admiral Howe have the resources to control the Hudson sufficiently to establish such a link. The most he could do was convoy supplies through a hostile countryside in all weather, and such an effort would occupy nearly his entire fleet. His supply transports would be subject to attack along the entire route by patriot militia and the main Continental Army. At the same time, Carleton would be cut off from Canada; in a hostile environment, the Royal Navy had no way of succoring him from that quarter.

Regardless of the difficulties involved, London was so determined to send a Canadian army to Albany that Carleton had been obliged to proceed. Before he could do so, he had to spend time at St. Jean assembling a navy superior to Benedict Arnold's, and that had taken him until October. Having access to far better personnel and equipment, he was able to fashion a squadron that, on paper at least, was far superior to Arnold's. The strongest part of it was the 18-gun, square-rigged *Inflexible,* under Lieutenant John Schank. When combined with a sufficient number of row-galleys, her battery of 12-pounders would make her the most powerful force on Lake Champlain. In addition, Carleton had the armed schooner *Maria,* mounting fourteen 6-pounders; the armed schooner *Carleton,* under Lieutenant James R. Dacres, with twelve 6-pounders; and twenty row-galleys or gunboats with a single cannon in each of their bows, ranging in size from 9- to 24-pounders. The British recognized the usefulness of Philadelphia-style row-galleys, even if the Continental Navy did not.

Carleton also had the *Loyal Convert,* a gondola with seven 9-pounders, and the *Thunderer,* a huge floating raft with three hundred men, carrying six 24-pounders, six 12-pounders, and two howitzers. These last two, however, were too clumsy to use. Carleton's fleet had roughly twice the strength of Arnold's but potentially far more, since the officers and men came from British naval vessels stationed in the St. Lawrence, and, unlike Arnold's men, they were well trained.

The weeks Carleton spent organizing a fleet gave Arnold desperately needed time to improve his own. And Arnold made the most of it. By August 20 he had ready not only the schooners *Royal Savage* and *Revenge,* and the sloops *Enterprise* and *Liberty,* but also the row-galleys *Congress, Trumbull,* and *Washington;* the gondolas *Boston, New Haven, Providence, New York, Connecticut, Spitfire, Jersey,* and *Success;* and the cutter (a small row-galley) *Lee.*

Arnold's row-galleys were twice the size of those built in Philadelphia, seventy to eighty feet long with eighteen-foot beams, round bottoms, and quarterdecks with cabins. For their size they were heavily armed, each carrying a 12-pounder and an 18-pounder in the bow, two 9-pound stern chasers, and four to six 6-pounders in their sides. They were powered by thirty-six oars and lateen sails on two masts. And they had room for a crew of eighty, although finding that many able seamen was impossible.

The gondolas were flat-bottomed with keels, about forty-five feet long, one mast with two square sails and a complement of forty-five men. Each carrying one 12-pounder, two 9-pounders, and swivel guns like the other vessels, they could sail before the wind but not go to windward like the row-galleys.

Arnold lined his galleys and gondolas with fascines against boarding and small arms fire. With no help from the Continental Navy, he put together crews of varying abilities, their total being around eight hundred. It was a remarkable achievement in such a short period of time.

As it turned out, Arnold was ready before Carleton. In searching for a place to fight, he settled on an anchorage off Valcour Island on September 23. There, concealed in a cove on the west side of the island, he awaited the British fleet, which began sailing south slowly from St. Jean on October 4, coming to anchor near Grand Island on the 10th.

The following morning a patriot lookout saw the fleet approaching Valcour Island. Since Carleton's force was so superior, patriot General Waterbury urged retreat. But Arnold thought it best to stay put. He arranged his vessels in a half-moon-shaped line in the channel between the island and the mainland. The galley *Congress* was his flagship, and he located it (as any admiral anticipating a fleet action would) in the center of the line. General Waterbury was in the *Washington*, commanding the right, and Colonel Wigglesworth of Massachusetts, the left, in the *Trumbull*.

Not knowing precisely where Arnold was, the British sailed past Valcour Island. Not until they were two miles beyond the southern tip did Arnold's fleet come into view. The squadron commander, Captain Thomas Pringle, had to beat back with great difficulty against the wind to get into position. He was unable to begin his attack until eleven o'clock.

With hardly any real seamen or gunners, but with the wind at his back, Arnold decided to meet the British coming up. He ordered the *Royal Savage*, his strongest ship, and four galleys underway, while keeping his other two schooners and eight gondolas anchored. Captain Hawley in the *Royal Savage* ran to leeward of the British and came within distant range of their entire fleet, including the *Inflexible*. Using their 12-pounders to good effect, her marksmen cut up Hawley badly, forcing him to run the *Royal Savage* aground to save his crew. The men managed to escape. Eventually the British set the ship on fire, and she blew up.

Carleton now turned on Arnold, but "the wind was so unfavorable," as Captain Pringle of the *Inflexible* reported, "that for a considerable time nothing could be brought into action with them but the gunboats; the *Carleton* schooner, commanded by Mr. Dacres, by much perseverance at last got to their assistance." Around twelve-thirty, Lieutenant Dacres was able to bring the *Carleton* to within 350 yards of Arnold, who now had to contend with the schooner as well as the seventeen row-galleys. "We suffered," Arnold reported later, "for want of seamen and gunners; I was obliged myself to point most of the guns on board the *Congress*."

Arnold concentrated his fire on the *Carleton*, managing to knock out Dacres and wound another officer. Nineteen-year-old midshipman Edward Pellew, as competent a young gentleman as the Royal Navy had, assumed command. But as he did, the spring on the *Carleton's* cable was shot away, and she swung bow forward to Arnold, who raked her mercilessly. Pellew kept his head, however, and bravely worked to get her towed away, as Captain Pringle had ordered.

This vicious exchange continued until five o'clock, when Pringle called back all his boats—which were being mauled—and ordered the *Inflexible* brought into position. Until then, he had kept her and the *Maria* out of the action. Both Pringle and General Carleton were aboard the *Maria*. In short order, the powerful *Inflexible* pointed her guns at the already battered American fleet. With five well-aimed broadsides she silenced Arnold's guns and then withdrew, leaving the patriots' gallant vessels badly damaged but still afloat. The *Philadelphia*, however, sank within the hour, and the *Congress* and the *Washington*, although able to sail, were in terrible condition. Arnold had lost sixty killed or wounded and had expended three-fourths of his ammunition.

As darkness fell, General Carleton from aboard the *Maria* ordered his remaining fleet to form a line across the southern passage between Valcour and the mainland, blocking the patriots' escape route. But Arnold refused to surrender and instead executed a brilliant escape. In the dark and fog he formed his remaining boats in a single line and hitched lanterns to each stern, carefully arranging them so that they remained invisible to the slumbering enemy. In this way Arnold slipped his wounded squadron through the British line undetected. Once past, he used his oars to put some distance between himself and Carleton.

The next morning, enraged at being outwitted, Carleton went after Arnold but did not catch him until October 13, allowing Arnold a brief respite to make temporary repairs before the next onslaught. Two of his gondolas, however, were beyond repair and had to be sunk.

When Carleton caught the retreating Americans, he reached the *Washington* first, and after a two-and-a-half-hour fight with the *Inflexible* and the *Maria*, General Waterbury surrendered. Captain Pringle then went after the rest of the patriot fleet, but Arnold, in spite of the damage he'd suffered, managed to run the *Congress* and four gondolas aground in a small creek ten miles from Crown Point. He burned them and got his men away safely, eventually making his way to Crown Point and then Ticonderoga. In the end Arnold lost all his vessels except the *Enterprise* and the *Liberty*, a galley, a schooner, and a gondola—eleven out of sixteen, and eighty men.

Carleton was now supreme on the lake, and he immediately moved to occupy undefended Crown Point. He then proceeded to Ticonderoga where he found General Gates well situated with a reinvigorated army of five thousand, reasonably well equipped with weapons that Henry Knox had thoughtfully left behind the previous December.

Gates had taken the shattered American army in June, and with steady reinforcements from New England militiamen beginning in July, he had built a strong position at the old fort. The change in circumstances gave Carleton pause. Conquering Ticonderoga now, if he conquered it at all, would take time and would significantly weaken his army. Even if he succeeded, he would have to leave a substantial force behind to defend the fort, further depleting his army. So, given the lateness of the season, he thought better of it and returned to Canada, much to the annoyance of General Burgoyne, who was second in command. Burgoyne advocated attacking the fort anyway and marching on to Albany. But Carleton did not think there was an urgency. The following spring, in his view, would be a far better time to mount an invasion.

Admiral Mahan, like nearly all historians, credited Arnold with frustrating British invasion plans that year. "Valcour Island was no defeat, therefore," Mahan insisted. "It was the American cause that was saved that day." A new invasion by the British from Canada would now have to be postponed until late in the spring of 1777, giving the Americans indispensable time to prepare. Christopher Ward maintained that "the capitulation of Saratoga [the following year], was due to the invaluable year of delay secured to them in 1776 by their little navy on Lake Champlain."

Although Arnold is given his due, Gates's critical contribution at Fort Ticonderoga has been discounted. The time Carleton had taken to create a fleet to deal with Arnold had also allowed Gates to rebuild the army at the old fort. This augmented force was what stopped Carleton's advance.

The absence of the Continental Navy has been overlooked altogether. It, not the army, should have been charged with the defense of the lake. And there was every reason to expect it to have constructed enough row-galleys and other vessels at Skenesboro by the summer of 1776 to keep the British at bay.

While there was good news in the north that November, Washington's situation in New York continued to deteriorate. On the 5th Admiral Howe sent the frigate HMS *Pearl* and two tenders, *Joseph* and *British Queen*, up the Hudson to join the *Roebuck*, *Phoenix*, and *Tartar*. Congress had ordered the river barriers reinforced yet again, but the *Pearl* and her tenders easily broke through them once more. The forts fired on the warships with some success and men aboard were killed, but the warships sailed through handily, finally convincing Washington that the forts and the obstructions were useless and should be abandoned. On November 8, he wrote to Greene, "The late passage of the three vessels up the North (Hudson) River . . . is so plain a proof of the inefficacy of all the obstructions . . . it will fully justify a change in the disposition which has been made."

The commander in chief left the critical decision to abandon Forts Washington and Lee to the inexperienced Greene, who knew that Congress had ordered the forts and river obstructions held, and was certain he could carry out their orders. Washington, although doubtful of the wisdom of this decision, deferred to Greene.

Washington remained at White Plains until November 10, when he left for New Jersey with two thousand troops, mostly Virginians and Marylanders. He arrived on the 13th to meet with Greene. Once there, Washington discovered that Jersey militiamen were unlikely to reinforce him, and that Greene hadn't changed his mind about holding the forts, even though it was clear by then that Howe, with his greatly superior army, intended to attack Fort Washington.

General Lee and seven thousand men remained at White Plains with orders from Washington to cross the Hudson to New Jersey if it became clear that Howe was going there. General Heath was already in the highlands with four thousand, and Greene had thirty-five hundred. Washington decided to leave these arrangements in place for the moment.

The most pressing problem for Washington was what to do about Fort Washington, still isolated on Manhattan and threatened with an immediate attack. Patriot Colonel Robert Magaw was in command; a resourceful, brave leader, he intended to put up a stiff fight. Joseph Reed pleaded with Washington to evacuate the fort and remove the men to New Jersey, but Washington hesitated. On the 16th, before he could decide what to do, Howe struck, overwhelming the valiant Magaw. The Americans fought heroically, but the odds were too great. In the end Magaw was forced to surrender 2,818 officers and men. After being robbed by the Hessians, the captives were dragged off to New York and thrown into wretched improvised prisons. Only eight hundred survived.

Washington did not hold himself responsible for this unnecessary tragedy. He wrote to his brother Augustine that Fort Washington had been held contrary to his opinion. A full council of officers had

determined on it, and "a resolution of Congress having been received, strongly expressive of their desire that the channel of the
river, which we had been laboring to stop for a long time at that
place, might be obstructed, if possible; and knowing that this could
not be done unless there were batteries to protect the obstructions,
I did not care to give an absolute order for withdrawing the garrison till I could get round and see the situation of things; and then it
became too late, as the place was invested."

Whether he was responsible or not, Washington received the
blame, further tarnishing his diminishing reputation and threatening
his capacity to lead. Throughout the country people were losing
faith in him, including Joseph Reed, who wrote to General Lee,
"All circumstance considered, we are in a very awful and alarming
state." Not knowing what had really happened at Charleston, Reed
had developed an admiration for Lee and looked to him as a possible replacement for the struggling commander in chief.

Washington told his brother of the desperate situation he was
facing. "In ten days from this date (November 6)," he wrote, "there
will not be above two thousand men, if that number, of the fixed
established regiments on this side of Hudson River to oppose
Howe's whole army; and very little more on the other. . . . I am
wearied almost to death with the retrograde motion of things. . . .
it is impossible, under such a variety of distressing circumstances, to
conduct matters agreeably to public expectations."

In spite of his myriad problems and mistakes, however, Washington held himself and his crippled army together and carried on.

With the fate of the Revolution resting on the survival of Washington and his army, Congress took this inopportune moment to
increase the frigate program, and even made plans to build ships of
the line. On November 20, it voted to construct three 74-gun battleships, five 32-gun frigates, an 18-gun brig, and a packet boat. The
big-navy men in Congress had learned nothing from the failures of
the Continental Navy during the past year. Nor had they learned
anything from the accomplishments of Captain Dougherty on the
Delaware, Lieutenant Colonel Tupper in New York, or Benedict

Arnold on Lake Champlain. Some in Congress, like Richard Henry Lee of Virginia, even criticized Arnold for losing two battles and most of his fleet.

In the end only one frigate, the *Alliance*, and two sloops-of-war, the *General Gates* and the *Saratoga,* were ever built. Robert Morris, one of the strongest supporters of the big frigate program, wrote to Silas Deane, "You will doubtless be surprised that our navy is not farther advanced, because you are not acquainted with many difficulties which have retarded its progress, particularly the want of sea coal for our anchor smiths, the disappointments in our first attempts to cast cannon, and above all the frequent calling out of our militia in a manner which would not permit an exemption of the necessary workmen." In spite of the difficulties and growing expense, Morris wanted even more large warships. In the same letter he wrote approvingly, "It has . . . been lately determined by Congress to build some line of battle ships; and at all events to push forward and pay the utmost attention to an American Navy."

At the same time that it was approving these big warships, Congress voted to reorganize the administration of the navy. The permanent Marine Committee, which had assumed the responsibilities of the old ad hoc Naval Committee in January 1776, was to conduct its business through a Navy Board of three members, "well-skilled in maritime affairs." This reorganization, however, did nothing to improve the fleet's performance.

After his dramatic victory at Fort Washington, General Howe, instead of pausing as he had in the past, went straight after Washington in New Jersey, hoping to strike a fatal blow. During the night of November 19, General Cornwallis, using two hundred boats, crossed the Hudson five miles above Fort Lee with a six-thousand-man column. Luckily, one of General Greene's officers riding patrol that night spotted Cornwallis's movements and raced to alert Greene. In a panic, Greene now moved to evacuate Fort Lee—a retreat Washington should have ordered days before. It was an ugly sight, as the patriots fled in disorder toward Washington's main camp on the Hackensack River, six miles away. Cornwallis's fast-moving column managed to capture some of Greene's critical supplies but not his gunpowder, which Greene had removed two days earlier. Worried about just such an attack, he had protected his ammunition, light artillery, and the better part of his stores. Still, he was caught by surprise when Cornwallis captured 105 of his men and killed 10.

Meanwhile, Washington's forces remained divided. General Lee, still at North Castle with fifty-five hundred effectives, showed no signs of coming to Washington's aid; General Heath remained at Peekskill with thirty-two hundred; and Washington himself had fifty-four hundred, including Greene's men. Rather than join Washington's bedraggled force, the New Jersey militias stayed at home. Robert Morris wrote indignantly to Silas Deane, "No Jersey militia turned out to oppose the enemy's march through the heart of their country, and it was not without much difficulty that the Associators of this city [Philadelphia] were prevailed upon to march and join the General." To make matters worse, Washington's men were deserting and enlistments were expiring.

General Lee might have helped, but instead of marching to strengthen Washington, he tried to replace him, accusing his chief of being indecisive. Washington had given Lee explicit orders to hasten to New Jersey if Howe headed there. But Lee disobeyed him—in spite of repeated pleas from Washington—and remained in North Castle. Now, with no more than three thousand men, Washington raced across New Jersey with Cornwallis at his heels, leaving Hackensack and marching west, crossing the Passaic River and moving to Newark, where he remained in danger for five days, seeking reinforcements from the New Jersey militias and urging the recalcitrant Lee to get moving.

Lee did not cross the Hudson River until early December. He already considered the patriot cause beyond hope. On December 13 he wrote to his close friend General Gates that "unless something, which I do not expect, turns up we are lost." On that very day, as if in fulfillment of his prediction, Banastre Tarleton captured Lee, who was temporarily separated from his troops for no good reason. The British eventually moved him to Manhattan.

General Howe might have trapped Washington at this point by sending troops from Staten Island to Amboy, crushing the now miniscule American army between himself and Cornwallis, but Howe failed to react fast enough and lost yet another opportunity to finish off Washington.

Instead of concentrating all his forces on the American army in New Jersey, Howe picked this moment to send General Clinton and seven thousand men to seize Newport and Providence, Rhode Island. Admiral Howe wanted a secure winter anchorage, which Newport and Narragansett Bay afforded. With Lord Percy as second in command, the expedition left New York on November 29. Admiral Sir Peter Parker, whom Clinton still blamed for the fiasco at Charleston, was the naval commander, and Admiral Howe assigned him fifteen warships—half the fleet. Parker sailed by way of Sandy Hook and the Atlantic, while Commodore William Hotham took three warships and convoyed the troop transports through Hell Gate and Long Island Sound. The entire force entered Narragansett Bay on December 7, led by the 50-gun *Experiment* under her new captain, James Wallace (formerly of the *Rose*), and anchored in Weaver's Cove. The following morning, in bitter cold, the British troops occupied Newport. The city surrendered without a fight.

Commodore Esek Hopkins had a powerful squadron in the Providence River at the time, which he kept well away from the British fleet. He had the new frigate *Warren*, which he had made his flagship, and the new frigate *Providence* under Captain Whipple. With them were the *Columbus* under Captain Olney, the *Blaze Castle*, and the sloop *Providence*, along with an assortment of privateers large and small, one of them the 20-gun *Jane* commanded by Captain William Cox.

"Admiral" Hopkins, the old privateer, avoided any fighting. On January 2, 1777, he was presented with an excellent opportunity to capture the British frigate *Diamond* when it ran aground on Warwick Neck near the mouth of the Providence River. Even though he had a powerful fleet to work with, he made no effort to take her. Hopkins probably would have destroyed his fleet if General Howe's orders to capture Providence had been carried out, but Clinton made no move in that direction.

Clinton's seeming reluctance irritated Howe, who expected results at Providence similar to those at Newport. This time, however, it was not caution but ferociously bad weather that prevented Clinton and Percy from moving beyond Newport. Dismissing this excuse, Howe criticized both leaders, causing a rift with Lord Percy, the ablest of the British generals and the heir to a dukedom. In a fit of anger Percy resigned and went home.

To counter Clinton's foray into Rhode Island, Washington sent one man, Benedict Arnold, who, after his triumph on Lake Champlain, was greeted as a hero throughout New England. But Clinton had no intention, nor did Howe, of invading the interior with only seven thousand men. They remembered only too well what had happened to General Gage the previous year when he ventured into the countryside outside Boston. With General Arnold to lead them, the country people were now likely to be even more difficult.

Meanwhile, on November 28, Washington left Newark, narrowly avoiding the oncoming Cornwallis. He moved his miniscule army to New Brunswick, New Jersey; from there, as he wrote to Congress on the 1st of December, he intended to retreat to the west side of the Delaware River. The following day, racing to avoid capture, his bedraggled men staggered into Trenton. Washington had previously collected all the boats on the Delaware for seventy miles. He now set about moving what was left of his troops across the river.

When Cornwallis reached New Brunswick, he halted beside the Raritan River for four days and waited for Howe, who had belatedly decided to bring up the main army. The short delay gave Washington essential breathing room. Howe finally arrived at New Brunswick on the 6th and Cornwallis resumed the chase, pushing on through Princeton to Trenton on the 7th, reaching it just as the last of Washington's boats left for Pennsylvania.

Howe's troops ranged up and down the New Jersey side of the river but made no attempt to cross, all the boats being on the other side. He had seriously considered crossing the Delaware and taking Philadelphia, but because he did not have control of the river, he decided not to. Then, on December 13, he closed the campaign for the season, announcing the suspension of military operations until spring. Philadelphia would fall easily enough then, he thought. The main British army would spend the winter in New York. New Jersey would be held by a few outposts, supplied by the cowed populace.

Many historians, Christopher Ward among them, believe that "the river was no substantial barrier." Although Washington had commandeered all the boats and moved them to the Pennsylvania side, Ward contends, Howe could have built more than enough from lumber at hand in local yards or by tearing down houses. In fact, if Howe had wanted to, he might have used the small craft Cornwallis had employed crossing the Hudson.

Whatever his reasoning, Howe decided against a Philadelphia campaign because he did consider the river to be a substantial barrier. Thanks to the row-galleys of the Pennsylvania navy, the patriots maintained naval supremacy there and were ready to fight Howe on the water. Before considering taking the capital, then, he, like Carleton on Lake Champlain, would have had to establish naval supremacy, which would not have been easy. As early as November 9, the Pennsylvania Committee of Public Safety had moved "to get things in forwardness to make a defense, in consequence of intelligence received that part of Howe's army was making a move toward Philadelphia."

The committee worried that Admiral Howe might send a fleet up the Delaware and attack the city with his brother. But the admiral made no move in that direction. Perhaps it was the memory of what the row-galleys had done to his close friend Snape Hamond in May, or the onset of winter; but for whatever reason, the admiral considered establishing naval supremacy at this time of year too big an undertaking. He had already sent half his fleet to Newport, so obviously he wasn't contemplating opening up the Delaware. And without control of the river, General Howe could not survive in Philadelphia. Unlike his superiors, he fully appreciated that fact. Without a logistical lifeline to the sea, his army would be isolated, just as Carleton's would have been in Albany.

Still, Washington worried that Howe might attack Philadelphia when the river froze. Morris agreed. "[Howe] doubtless means to attack [Philadelphia] whenever [he] can cross the [Delaware] on ice," he wrote to Silas Deane, "and have only been kept from it by our having sent up the [row-galleys] and brought off or destroyed all the boats along the Jersey shore." Meanwhile, Congress, unable to appreciate the naval situation, had fled Philadelphia unnecessarily, contributing to the general impression that the Revolution was collapsing. By the time General Howe had reached Burlington, New Jersey, twenty miles from the capital, Generals Putnam and Mifflin urged Congress to move to Baltimore, which it did on December 12, conferring temporary dictatorial powers on Washington before leaving. But the move was unnecessary. The patriots maintained naval supremacy on the Delaware, and the Howes were not prepared to challenge it.

At the time, four Continental frigates—*Delaware, Randolph, Effingham,* and *Washington*—were in Philadelphia in various states of completion, along with the sloop *Hornet*. Robert Morris, the only member of Congress still in the city, worked hard to save them. The *Randolph* was actually ready to sail under Captain Nicholas Biddle. Morris wanted her put to sea to avoid capture. He wrote to John Hancock on December 13, "As soon as I saw this authentic account of the enemy's design to cross the Delaware above the falls, I waited on General Putnam and proposed that the frigate *Randolph* and sloop *Hornet* should be sent to sea immediately as it was plain to me they would be of no use here, and I had received certain advice that there was not any British men-of-war in our Bay."

Morris was one of the great merchant princes of Philadelphia and an active member of the Marine Committee, but he could not appreciate how the patriots might successfully defend the Delaware against the mighty Royal Navy. He never grasped the importance of Captain Dougherty's victory in May.

Captain Biddle wanted to stay and fight. He thought that sending the *Randolph* and the *Hornet* away from the Delaware at this critical moment was the opposite of what Morris should have been doing, demonstrating to the Howes that the patriots intended to fight for the river.

Nevertheless, Biddle and the *Randolph* were sent away, as was the *Hornet*, and they escaped, although Biddle did not actually leave until the end of January 1777. In giving orders to Biddle for the Marine Committee, Morris told him that once the immediate crisis had passed, he should cruise the coast to intercept British "provision vessels or store ships," demonstrating again that the Marine Committee had no idea what to do with the fleet they were building. Commerce raiding would have been far better left to the hundreds of privateers sailing from every seaport on the Atlantic coast. It was this fleet that created problems for the British, not the patriots' few Continental warships.

Washington's wretched army had been strengthened somewhat in December by additions from General Sullivan, who had been exchanged. He brought what was left of Lee's force—two thousand distressed soldiers—into camp. General Gates arrived from the north with five hundred more, and an additional thousand associators (militiamen) came from Philadelphia. By the third week of December Washington had six thousand men, nearly all of them with enlistments expiring on the 31st.

On the 17th he wrote to his brother, Lund Washington, "Hitherto, by our destruction of the boats, and vigilance in watching the fords of the river above the falls (which are now rather high), we have prevented them from crossing, but . . . they are still hovering about the river." In the same letter Washington noted with dismay the "disaffection" of New Jerseymen and Pennsylvanians. "Our only dependence now," he wrote, "is upon the speedy enlistment of a new army. If this fails, I think the game will be pretty well up, as, from disaffection and want of spirit and fortitude, the inhabitants, instead of resistance, are offering submission and taking protection from General Howe in Jersey."

Alarmed at how low the patriots' fortunes had sunk, Joseph Reed wrote to Washington on the 22nd, "Something must be attempted to revive our expiring credit, give our cause some degree of reputation, and prevent a total depreciation of the Continental money, which is coming on very fast; that even a failure cannot be more fatal than to remain in our present situation; in short, some enterprise must be undertaken in our present circumstances or we must give up the cause. . . . In a little time the Continental Army will be dissolved. . . . The scattered, divided state of the enemy affords us a fair opportunity." Reed advocated an action of some sort around Trenton.

Washington wrote back the next day, "Our numbers, sorry am I to say, being less than I had any conception of: but of necessity, dire necessity, will, nay must, justify an attempt."

The attempt began at six o'clock on Christmas night, as twenty-four hundred patriots marched from their evening parade to McKonkey's Ferry on the Delaware, nine miles above Trenton. The river was only a thousand feet wide at the ferryway, and Washington once again called on Colonel Glover and his Marblehead mariners to ferry the troops across. It was a horrendous task. A blizzard was blowing snow and freezing rain, and large blocks of ice were flowing downriver. Henry Knox recalled that the men "passed the river . . . with almost infinite difficulty, with eighteen field pieces. The floating ice . . . made the labor almost incredible. . . . The night was cold and stormy; it hailed with great violence."

Glover's men had to operate unfamiliar Durham boats, river craft designed to move bulky loads up and down the fast-moving Delaware. Open, forty to sixty feet long, with eight-foot beams and shallow drafts, they were ideal for transporting troops and heavy equipment. A steering sweep, which could be placed at either end, guided the boat while pole men on both sides pushed it forward. In spite of never having managed such vessels before, Glover's patriots, as they had done on the East River in August, performed brilliantly.

At daylight the army gathered on the Jersey side of the river, and Washington went up and down the ranks. "Soldiers, keep by your officers," he shouted. "For God's sake, keep by your officers!" And they did. Trudging through snow and ice, many of them with bleeding feet, they surprised fourteen hundred Hessians under Colonel Johann

Rall at Trenton, routing them and winning the critical victory that kept the Revolution alive. They took nearly nine hundred prisoners, six cannon, and more than a thousand muskets. Forty Hessians died, while the patriots suffered only two dead and three wounded. About four hundred Hessians escaped. Colonel Rall was mortally wounded, and as he was dying, he pleaded with Washington to be kind to his men. With mixed feelings, Washington agreed to do so, and he faithfully carried out his promise, treating the Germans much differently from the way they and their British masters dealt with Americans who fell into their hands.

After the victory Washington crossed back over the Delaware on the flat-bottomed Durham boats with his Hessian prisoners. "Ice continually stuck to the boats, driving them downstream," a Connecticut soldier, Elisha Bostwick, recalled. "The boatmen endeavoring to clear off the ice pounded the boat, and stamping with their feet, [beckoning] to the prisoners to do the same, and they all set to jumping at once with their cues flying up and down, soon shook off the ice from the boats, and the next day re-crossed the Delaware again."

On December 29 and 30 Washington returned to unoccupied Trenton with fifteen hundred men, hoping to use the town as a base to harass Howe's other posts in New Jersey. But Howe, seeking to reverse the disaster at Trenton, had ordered Cornwallis, who had been about to leave for England, back to New Jersey. When he arrived, he assumed command from General Grant and marched eight thousand men to Princeton.

Patriot General Mifflin and Colonel Cadwalader had contributed reinforcements to Washington, bringing his force up to five thousand. But that wasn't enough to cope with Cornwallis, who, after leaving twelve hundred men at Princeton, reached Trenton in time to trap Washington there on January 2.

The patriot army appeared doomed. But Cornwallis, believing that Washington had nowhere to go, just as Howe had assumed at Brooklyn Heights, failed to administer the coup de grâce. He confidently waited overnight to bag his prey. That night Washington, although nearly surrounded, made another brilliant escape, moving his entire force around the British without alerting them and driving toward Princeton, where he won another impressive victory the next day.

Afterward, Washington marched toward New Brunswick, planning to build on his victories at Trenton and Princeton with another stunning triumph. The British had an enormous war chest of 70,000 pounds sterling stashed in New Brunswick and only a small contingent defending it. Although Washington didn't know the exact amount of the money, he knew it was there and dearly wanted to seize it along with the town. But at the moment he didn't have enough fresh troops, so he reluctantly turned his weary men away from New Brunswick toward the relative safety of Morristown.

On January 5 he wrote from Plukamin, New Jersey, "My original intention when I set out from Trenton was to have pushed on to Brunswick, but the harassed state of our own troops (many of them having no rest for two nights and a day) and the danger of losing the advantage we had gained by aiming at too much, induced me, by the advice of my officers, to relinquish the attempt, but in my judgment six or eight hundred fresh troops upon a forced march would have destroyed all their stores and magazines; taken (as we have since learnt) their military chest containing 70,000 [pounds] and put an end to the war."

The patriot successes at Trenton and Princeton revived the cause. Renewed hope for victory surged in the army, the country, the Congress, and in Paris. Washington's leadership was now unquestioned, his prestige immense. As his soldiers marched into Morristown, they may have been poorly clothed and few in number, but their hearts were filled with a new optimism.

4

SARATOGA
AND PHILADELPHIA

January 1777–January 1778

Captain James Wallace and the 50-gun *Experiment* reached London on February 12, 1777, with astonishing news of the Hessian surrender at Trenton. The king was expecting to be told of Washington's demise, not this, the first defeat for the Howes. Two weeks later, Admiral Shuldham arrived in the *Chatham* with even more disturbing reports directly from General Howe, giving details not only of the disaster at Trenton but of Cornwallis's subsequent failures, followed by the withdrawal of Howe's troops from their posts in western New Jersey.

His Majesty's hopes for winning the war in a single season had suddenly vanished. The Herculean effort of putting all those armies and fleets in the field three thousand miles away had come to naught. And now General Howe was requesting fifteen thousand additional troops, while Admiral Howe was asking for ten more sail of the line. It was a bitter pill for the king to swallow, but he was determined to fight on. After all, the Howes had come very close to winning; surely they would succeed the following year.

The compliant British cabinet voted to approve five additional sail of the line for the admiral, and Lord Germain did what he could to satisfy General Howe's request, although organizing more troops on the scale the general wanted would be extremely difficult. Britain had already made a supreme effort in 1776; to solicit even more troops was asking a great deal. But Germain, convinced that victory would inevitably come in 1777, did his best to find them.

Meanwhile, First Lord of the Admiralty Sandwich, an inveterate foe of Admiral Howe, quietly worked to frustrate the cabinet's wishes. He opposed additional battleships for Howe, being more concerned with making the Channel Fleet strong enough to defend the home islands against a combined Franco-Spanish attack; the French naval buildup posed a real threat. Sandwich thought Admiral Howe already had enough warships to do his job. Lord North, however, with uncharacteristic firmness, insisted that Sandwich release the ships and eventually he relented.

General Howe received few of the reinforcements he sought. That would have required a level of commitment from the country that the king dared not ask; the war simply wasn't popular enough. Howe's army was still far superior to Washington's, and the king expected him to win with it.

His Majesty wanted Howe to begin the new spring campaign by drawing Washington into a general engagement in which Howe's superior numbers, weapons, and leadership would prevail. While doing that, Howe was to cooperate with General Burgoyne, who would be bringing another army down from Canada via Lake Champlain to Albany, as the king thought Carleton should have done the previous year. New York City was already in British hands, and the Royal Navy controlled the waters around Manhattan and Lake Champlain. So it was expected to be an easy matter for Howe to reach Albany and connect with Burgoyne, dividing the colonies and driving a stake into the heart of the rebellion. More than likely, Washington would contend with Howe for the Hudson, entangling himself in the great battle that would finally end the cursed war. So the strategy for 1777 was much the same as it was in 1776. The only difference was in the south. Howe would deal with that later; the king still thought it would be the easiest part of the country to subdue.

Admiral Howe's fleet of more than seventy warships of all kinds was assigned a number of tasks, the most important being support for the army's spring campaign. In addition, he was ordered to raid seacoast towns, as Admiral Graves had done in Falmouth, Maine. The strategy was intended to create a diversion, destroy rebel privateers and warships, and force militiamen to remain at home. Howe was also expected to blockade the entire Atlantic coast from Florida to Newfoundland, perform convoy duty, and keep an eye on the Continental Navy.

Of course, he could not begin to accomplish all these tasks, even with five times the number of warships he had. Moreover, his men-of-war, like all wooden vessels in those days, required constant repair and refitting, so that some were always in port and not on station, leaving his fleet weaker than it appeared.

Admiral Howe had to set priorities. The first was support for his brother's campaign, which would occupy the bulk of the fleet. He quietly rejected the idea of attacking defenseless seaports, believing these tactics to be counterproductive, but did what he could to blockade the American coast during the winter, assigning thirty of his scarce warships to the task. In the first six months of 1777 the number of captured vessels increased from twenty-five per month the previous year to forty-six. Seeing the parade of prizes arriving in New York, many loyalists concluded that the blockade alone would bring the rebels to their knees.

But the admiral knew that despite these captures his blockade was porous and would remain so, no matter what he did. In New England alone, recurring fog and adverse winds made a tight blockade impossible, even in Boston. This fundamental reality had been demonstrated at the beginning of the war when John Derby in the *Quero* had sped past HMS *Lively* in Salem Bay during a dark night, bringing the news of Lexington and Concord to London. Even in places like the Delaware capes, merchantmen and privateers came and went with remarkable ease. To be sure, the British caught some of them, but American privateers by the hundreds continued to range up and down the Atlantic coast, the West Indies, the English Channel, and all of England's trade routes. Lord Howe freely admitted that he could not begin to stop them.

While juggling his various assignments, the admiral also kept an eye on the Continental Navy, such as it was. He was particularly concerned about John Manley, whose 32-gun frigate *Hancock* was finally ready to sail in May 1777. Following orders he had received from the Marine Committee back in October, Manley put to sea as soon as he could, setting out on May 21 with enough warships to represent a problem for Howe. Manley's squadron consisted of the 24-gun Continental frigate *Boston*, under Captain Hector McNeill, and nine privateers. They had slipped out of Boston, passed the ineffective British blockade, and appeared powerful enough to threaten any of Howe's warships doing blockade duty along the Atlantic seaboard. The admiral feared that the astute Manley might defeat the entire blockading fleet one by one, attaining local superiority at each point. Howe's other men-of-war were concentrated at New York to support his brother's spring campaign. None could be spared to chase Manley.

Howe's concerns were overblown; the Continental Navy had not progressed enough to carry out a fleet operation. Manley did not have command of his squadron, and his captains did not act as parts of a single unit. Britain's famed Admiral Horatio Nelson always attributed his famous victories, such as that at the Nile, to a team effort. An admiral's first duty, he maintained, was to inspire his captains to fight as integral parts of a single entity, and yet be prepared to take bold individual action in support of the fleet's objective. If Manley was aware of these imperatives, he was unsuccessful in achieving them. Once at sea all the privateers deserted him, and Captain McNeill was actually hostile. Manley wasn't the only one who faced this problem. No leader of the Continental Navy ever had a cohesive squadron of the kind Admiral Nelson required.

Furthermore, the Marine Committee was incapable of thinking strategically in the way Admiral Howe instinctively did. Manley was directed to go after the *Milford* and the few other British cruisers prowling New England's waters. The committee never dreamed of attacking the entire blockading fleet.

When Admiral Howe heard that Manley's squadron had departed Boston, he took his few blockading ships off the New England coast and sent them after him. In spite of these sea hounds, the desertion of the privateers, and the contrariness of Captain McNeill, Manley's early results were spectacular, and they drew the Admiralty's attention. Once the privateers had disappeared, Manley sailed with the reluctant *Boston* to Newfoundland's Grand Banks, and on June 7 the *Hancock* alone (with the *Boston* watching from a safe distance) captured British Captain Patrick Fotheringham's 28-gun frigate HMS *Fox*. Putting a crew aboard her, the two American warships continued on patrol with their prize. For a brief time Manley enjoyed naval supremacy in the area as Admiral Howe's chasers were nowhere to be seen.

On June 11, Admiral John Montagu, British commander on the Newfoundland station, wrote to the Admiralty that he feared for Newfoundland's seaports and for the fishing fleet on the Grand Banks. By this time, Admiral Howe was too preoccupied with his brother's spring campaign to spare any more ships to chase Manley. When news of the *Fox*'s surrender reached London, the Admiralty dispatched Captain John Macbride in HMS *Bienfaisant*, a 74-gun ship of the line, to hunt Manley down.

The *Bienfaisant* was unsuccessful. But on July 6 two other British warships out of Halifax, the 44-gun *Rainbow*, under Sir George Collier, and the 10-gun brig *Victor*, under Lieutenant Michael Hyndman, happened upon Manley east of Cape Sable at the southeastern tip of Nova Scotia. It was one o'clock in the afternoon. A lookout at the *Rainbow*'s masthead shouted down to the quarterdeck that three strange ships were in the distance. Collier immediately made sail and gave chase. By eight o'clock, he could make out three large warships with a smaller sloop in company. He suspected they were "rebel frigates" and followed them with all the canvas he could crowd on. By dawn on July 7 Collier had managed to approach to within five miles of the strangers and recognized Manley's *Hancock*. "One of the gentlemen of my quarterdeck," Collier reported to the Admiralty, "had been a prisoner lately at Boston, and [he] knew her to be the *Hancock* on board of whom Manley commanded, the sea officer in whom the Congress place all their confidence and reliance and who is the second in rank in their navy."

Manley believed the *Rainbow* to be the much larger battleship *Bienfaisant*, so he set fire to the prize sloop he had been towing and cut her loose. He then set every sail that could be of use, including top gallant royals, and tried to outdistance the *Rainbow*. At the same time, the *Boston* went off in a different direction, so that Collier could chase only one of them. Naturally he picked the larger *Hancock*.

Shortly afterward, at six o'clock in the morning, while Manley and Collier were concentrating on each other, another British warship, the 32-gun frigate *Flora*, under Captain John Brisbane, appeared suddenly on the scene. At first Collier thought she was another rebel warship. Brisbane hoisted the English red ensign and fired two guns to leeward so that Collier would know he was British. Manley was in no doubt about who she was.

Brisbane ignored the *Rainbow*, *Hancock*, and *Boston* and drove the *Flora* straight for the *Fox*. When he fired on her, Collier knew for sure that the *Flora* was British. After a brief fight, the *Fox* surrendered.

Collier, meanwhile, kept after the *Hancock*. Manley altered the trim of his ship and desperately tried to escape, still thinking he was being hounded by a 74-gun battleship. Try as he might, however, he could not shake Collier.

Using a night glass, Collier kept sight of Manley until dawn; by that time the *Rainbow* was only a mile from the *Hancock*. Collier opened fire with his bow chasers while Manley continued trying to get away. The *Rainbow* poured broadsides into him, and finally, still thinking his antagonist was a battleship, Manley struck his colors without attempting to fight.

Meanwhile, Captain McNeill escaped to Wiscasset on the Sheepscot River in the Maine district of Massachusetts, undoubtedly glad to have rival Manley humiliated. But McNeill himself was dismissed from the service for his conduct. Had he supported Manley and had Manley identified his adversary, they might have defeated Collier's squadron. They might then have recaptured the *Fox* and even taken the *Flora*. Thus strengthened, Manley would have presented an even more interesting problem for Lord Howe and the Admiralty. As it was, Manley became a prisoner of war and the *Hancock* was taken into the Royal Navy. She was renamed HMS *Iris* and used repeatedly against the Americans before being captured by the French.

Ambrose Serle noted in his diary how pleased Admiral Howe was to have Manley put out of action. His capture ranked as high with the Howe brothers as that of General Lee. Admiral Howe did not need to worry about the rest of the Continental fleet. The American warships were either in port or on senseless individual missions that could have no effect on the war. The frigates *Warren* and *Providence* were being held in the Providence River by Commodore Hopkins, along with the *Columbus*, the *Hampden*, and the sloop *Providence*.

When Congress suspended Hopkins from command in March 1777, the sloop *Providence* ran the blockade at Newport and put to sea for more commerce raiding. The other warships, including the two frigates, remained in Providence—for no apparent reason—the rest of the year.

The frigate *Trumbull* remained stuck in the Connecticut River, unable to clear the bar. The *Cabot* went commerce raiding out of Boston; it was captured and taken into the Royal Navy. The *Virginia*, under Captain James Nicholson, remained in Baltimore for the entire year. The *Raleigh* stayed in Portsmouth, New Hampshire, until August, when she sailed to France with the *Alfred* on an uncertain mission. The *Randolph* was forced to remain in Charleston for most of the year. John Paul Jones and the *Ranger* were in Portsmouth getting ready for sea; Jones left for France at the end of the year. The frigates *Congress* and *Montgomery* were still in the Hudson, unfinished, and the *Delaware*, *Washington*, and *Effingham* were in the Delaware River in the same condition.

The ships of the Continental Navy posed no threat to the British. Without a strategy that promised any hope of success, they remained dispersed, unready, and disorganized. Having built the wrong kind of fleet, Congress was unable to deploy it effectively against the Royal Navy.

While the British were planning their spring offensive, Washington was trying desperately to rebuild his army. During the winter at Morristown it had nearly disappeared. Despite his unremitting efforts to increase its size, by the middle of March his total force barely exceeded three thousand men—most being militiamen whose enlistments were about to expire. He did everything he could to conceal his true state from British spies, but that was hardly necessary, since General Howe was not contemplating a winter attack. Eighteenth-century armies fought during spring, summer, and fall, but nearly always remained in camp during the winter. General Howe was content to remain in icy New York City with his charming mistress, Mrs. Loring, confident that he would deal with Washington in the spring.

Howe did manage to orchestrate two successful amphibious raids against patriot storage depots, trying to destroy what he could before the approaching campaign. The first was an attack by five hundred men and ten vessels on Peekskill in March. The second, a much larger one, was against Danbury, Connecticut. Howe had ordered Major General William Tryon, the royal governor of New York, to capture or destroy a sizable cache of arms at the Danbury military depot. Three men-of-war and a few empty transports had sailed up the Hudson River as a diversion, while a fleet of fourteen transports with five regiments proceeded up the East River through Hell Gate into Long Island Sound on April 23. Two days later, they landed unopposed at night in Norwalk Bay near the mouth of the Saugatuck River. The following day Tryon marched to Danbury and destroyed not only the military stores but an unconscionably large number of nearby houses and barns.

Connecticut patriots remained inactive until Benedict Arnold arrived from New Haven with Generals Wooster and Stillman. Arnold brought five hundred militia and one hundred Continentals with him. As word got around that he was leading the charge, more patriots joined his ranks. Anxious to keep the British marauders from getting away, Arnold, with characteristic skill and bravery, attacked Tryon's much larger force as it made its way back to the vessels on Long Island Sound. A violent struggle developed. Arnold's horse was shot out from under him, and Tryon barely managed to stagger back to his ships, suffering on the way two hundred killed and many more wounded.

In May, Howe sent another foraging party to Sag Harbor, Long Island, but patriots in whaleboats led by Colonel Jonathan Meigs of Guilford, Connecticut, conducted a surprise attack the evening of the 23rd. They managed to capture or kill the entire Tory contingent, burn twelve of their vessels, and seize an armed schooner before returning to Guilford. Congress applauded with Colonel Meigs, a veteran of Arnold's assault on Quebec. Washington praised him too, but neither he nor the Congress fully appreciated how Meigs's methods might be employed elsewhere.

Back in Morristown, Washington was searching for recruits, and his efforts were bearing fruit. After failing to raise so much as a company of New Jersey fighters in the fall, he was pleasantly surprised at having his ranks swollen by so many Jersey militiamen that he could contemplate taking the offensive. The British and Hessian soldiers who had run riot after conquering New Jersey, molesting Tories as well as patriots, had so outraged the inhabitants that they now turned out in droves to fight. "Nothing could exceed the spirit shown on this occasion," Henry Knox wrote, "by the much injured people of the Jerseys. Not an atom of the lethargic spirit that possessed them last winter— all fire, all revenge. . . . This . . . fully proves that no people or country can be permanently conquered where the inhabitants are unanimous in opposition." In just two months the sad, three-thousand-man force of March had grown into a respectable army of nearly nine thousand.

On May 29, Washington moved his forces twenty miles south to Middlebrook, New Jersey, establishing himself in a strong defensive position at the foothills of the Watchung Mountains, eight miles from New Brunswick. General Sullivan, meanwhile, stationed a smaller force at Princeton. From his new camp Washington could respond to any attempt by Howe to make an overland dash to Philadelphia or move up the Hudson.

A short time later General Howe finally left the comforts of New York and set up headquarters at New Brunswick, New Jersey, with around eighteen thousand troops, confirming Washington's belief that Philadelphia was still a target. Capturing the rebel capital, however, was not part of the king's original plan for the spring campaign. Howe was supposed to move up the Hudson and cooperate with Burgoyne, who had already landed his new army in Canada. Philadelphia appeared to be an unnecessary diversion. Nonetheless, Howe obtained Lord Germain's approval for taking Philadelphia first and then attending to Albany. Ever optimistic, Germain believed that Howe could do both.

But first Howe tried to lure Washington into a general engagement. On June 13, as New Jersey's moist summer heat began to oppress the British and Hessian troops, Howe sallied forth from New Brunswick in force, hoping Washington would come out from his stronghold and meet him. Judging himself not yet strong enough, Washington wouldn't oblige.

Howe didn't give up. He retreated to New Brunswick on the 19th, making it appear that he was preparing a retrograde movement to Amboy. This time Washington was taken in; he followed the retreating British, and on the 26th at one o'clock in the morning Howe turned abruptly and raced to cut the American army off from the passes leading back to Middlebrook, forcing it to fight in the open. At the last moment, realizing Howe's gambit, Washington raced back to the safety of his mountain stronghold.

At this point Howe gave up and withdrew first to Amboy and then, to everyone's surprise, all the way to Staten Island. By the end of June no British or Hessian troops remained in New Jersey, to the consternation of the still loyal Tories. They had come out during the previous campaign to support Howe and were now subject to patriot reprisals.

By this time Howe had settled on attacking Philadelphia by sea. After testing the strength of the rebels in New Jersey, he concluded that marching overland was too dangerous. Doing so would inevitably mean crossing the Delaware River, which was still an enormous handicap in his mind. Brigadier General Arnold defended a portion

of it; after Arnold's fight at Danbury, Connecticut, Washington had assigned him to defend the fords above the falls at Trenton. And below
the falls, the Pennsylvania navy and its row-galleys were active. So
Howe concluded that approaching Philadelphia by sea was a better
alternative. Of course, attacking the city made no strategic sense, unless the American army could be lured into a decisive battle.

Although Philadelphia might still be Howe's objective, Washington
thought it more likely that the British general would leave sufficient
force behind to guard New York City and then sail up the Hudson to
meet Burgoyne at Albany. By May 6 Burgoyne had already reached
Quebec, and with General Carleton's unstinting help, he had moved
his army of eight thousand with impressive speed down the St.
Lawrence, then down the Richelieu River and onto the shores of
Lake Champlain, arriving there on June 20, just six weeks later. Since
the British had command of the lake, Burgoyne's thrust south could
proceed unchecked.

Washington moved his army back to Morristown, preparing to
counter a British drive either up the Hudson or on Philadelphia.
Whichever way Howe went, Washington would need naval support, and he knew he wasn't going to get any from the Continental
Navy. While these major moves and countermoves of the armies
were going on, the Continental Navy continued to perform unnecessary missions that took their best captains away from the main
theaters of action.

In the most egregious example of the Marine Committee's misguided strategy, it encouraged the American commissioners in Paris
to develop a branch of the navy in France to prey on British shipping, terrorize coastal towns, and capture British seamen to trade
for their American counterparts held in English prisons. With
Philadelphia in grave danger of attack, two of America's premier
fighting captains, Lambert Wickes and Gustavus Conyngham—
both Philadelphians—were in Europe, operating under the command of the American commissioners. Their mission was to carry
the war to British waters, and their commerce raiding was so successful it caused a diplomatic crisis between Paris and London.
Lord North was threatening war, though probably not in earnest,

and Vergennes, the French foreign minister, was angry at being forced into war before the French fleet was ready.

In reality, it was the hundreds of American privateers who were carrying the war to British waters, and they were doing an outstanding job of it; Wickes and Conyngham, although played up in the British press, added little. Their talents could have been better employed in Philadelphia, where one of the decisive naval battles of the war was about to be fought with a puny American naval force under poor leadership. Tragically, on Wickes's voyage home from France, his *Reprisal* was caught in a violent autumn storm three days' sail past the Newfoundland Banks; according to her cook, Nathan Jaquays, the only survivor, she "pooped with three heavy seas, which carried her down."

Nicholas Biddle, another superb Philadelphia fighter, was also kept far from the center of the action. The Marine Committee sent him out in the *Randolph* to do commerce raiding, and while he did manage to capture four Jamaicamen, he spent most of 1777 in Charleston harbor. On October 24, while the battle for the Delaware River raged, Biddle was ordered to sail the *Randolph* to France and place himself at the disposal of the commissioners. He dutifully arrived in December, only to turn around and sail back to Charleston because of British protests.

The *Raleigh* and *Alfred* were also sent to France at about the same time, along with the Continental sloop *Independence*, under Captain Young, and the new American sloop-of-war *Ranger*, under Captain John Paul Jones, all for use by the American commissioners, and all far from the real action in America. Jones had wasted most of the year waiting for the *Ranger* to be completed in Portsmouth, New Hampshire. On November 1, 1777, he stood out from the Piscataqua River and set sail for France, arriving in Nantes a month later. The following year he went on a spectacular but unnecessary cruise around the British Isles. He too should have been in the thick of the fight for Philadelphia.

Washington was still watching and waiting for General Howe to indicate where he was going, when an express from General Schuyler arrived at headquarters in Morristown on the morning of July 10, 1777, with the shocking news that on the 6th, Burgoyne had forced patriot General Arthur St. Clair and thirty-five hundred men to flee Fort Ticonderoga. Washington was dumbfounded. He and the Congress had been under the impression that Ticonderoga was nearly impregnable. General Schuyler had thought there was a good chance Burgoyne might not assail the fortress but instead place a force before it and, with the remainder of his army, cut across to the Connecticut River and wreak havoc on New England.

Following St. Clair's surrender, Washington wrote to encourage Schuyler but did not dare weaken his own army by sending reinforcements. He did allow Colonel John Nixon to take six hundred Continentals from Peekskill to Schuyler, and he sent Generals Benedict Arnold and Benjamin Lincoln to help with the New England troops; they had become so disenchanted with Schuyler and St. Clair that some of them swore the two were traitors.

After more disasters at Hubbardton and Skenesboro, General St. Clair retreated with the remnants of his army to Fort Edward on the Hudson, fifty-five miles above Albany. He arrived exhausted on July 12. Burgoyne was right behind him, only twenty-three miles away at Skenesboro, but then stopped, satisfied with the progress he was making. Schuyler now had time to rush up from Albany to Fort Edward and set about reinforcing the natural obstacles that stood in the way of Burgoyne's moving his army through the wilderness to Fort Edward.

Schuyler's obstructive tactics were successful. Burgoyne did not reach the fort until July 29 (seventeen days after St. Clair arrived), badly in need of supplies and horses. He was now deep in enemy territory, far from the Royal Navy. He had ignored the well-established principle that no British army could operate in America for long without ready access to the sea, something General Howe never forgot.

Meanwhile, British Lieutenant Colonel Barry St. Leger was advancing with a second column of eighteen hundred regulars, Tories, and Indians down Lake Ontario to Oswego, New York, planning to march through the Mohawk Valley for a rendezvous with Burgoyne and Howe at Albany. Like Burgoyne, St. Leger had an easy time of it to begin with, moving down the Oswego River to Lake Oneida, then to Wood Creek, and after that to Fort Stanwix (now Rome), arriving on August 2. Situated at the headwaters of the Mohawk River, the fort was only 110 miles from Albany. Once past it, the way to Albany was clear.

Twenty-eight-year-old patriot Colonel Peter Gansevoort was defending the fort with about 750 Continentals. He refused St. Leger's demand to surrender. In the meantime, patriot General Nicholas Herkimer had called out the Tryon county militia, and was marching to Fort Stanwix with eight hundred men to bolster Gansevoort. On hearing of Herkimer's movements, St. Leger sent Mohawk war chief Joseph Brandt and his braves with a few Tories to intercept him. The chief set an ambush at Oriskany, and on August 6 a fierce hand-to-hand fight developed. Herkimer died from his wounds and only half his men escaped alive, but the Indians and Tories, having suffered severe casualties themselves, withdrew.

Alarmed by St. Leger's progress, General Schuyler dispatched General Arnold with nine hundred New Englanders to reinforce Fort Stanwix and protect the Mohawk Valley. Schuyler did this when Burgoyne was one day's forced march away, and Schuyler had only forty-five hundred men to oppose him.

Arnold gathered his men and began marching on August 23. He soon discovered that a ruse he employed had worked. He had captured a British spy named Hon Yost Schuyler, a relative of the general. To secure his release and keep his considerable estate, Hon Yost agreed to return to the British camp and tell the Indians, with whom he had considerable influence, that Arnold's force was gargantuan. Hon Yost performed his part to perfection and thoroughly frightened the Indians, who then left camp en masse—eight hundred of them. Deserted by his Indian allies and confronted by Gansevoort's strong defense, St. Leger was forced to retreat to Canada without a fight, clipping the right wing of Burgoyne's attack.

While Generals Schuyler and Arnold were resisting Burgoyne in the north, on July 8 General Howe began loading eighteen thousand troops onto sea transports in New York harbor. Instead of sailing immediately, however, he left his foot soldiers and cavalry to swelter in summer heat while he waited, for no apparent reason. Six days later, upon receiving news of the fall of Ticonderoga, he prepared to sail, confident that Burgoyne would succeed without his help. Howe wrote to him on the 17th, "My intention is for Pennsylvania, where I expect to meet Washington, but if he goes to the northward contrary to my expectations, and you can keep him at bay, be assured I shall soon be after him to relieve you." In the same letter Howe pointed out, "Sir Henry Clinton remains in control here and will act as occurrences direct."

Howe was leaving Clinton in Manhattan with four thousand regulars and three thousand Tories of uncertain ability. Supporting him would be Commodore William Hotham. His force consisted of one 64, two 50s, one 32, two 20s, two bomb vessels, three row-galleys, and a sloop—an inviting prospect for assault by the Continental Navy. The patriots, however, gave no thought to attacking Hotham.

Reinforcements from London were expected to arrive in New York at any moment. If need be, Howe thought, Clinton could use them to move up the Hudson and cooperate with Burgoyne. But at the time, that appeared unnecessary. As far as Howe knew, Burgoyne was doing just fine on his own. And by putting to sea, Howe was confusing Washington about his destination, freezing him in place, and preventing him from coming to aid the patriots' Northern Army.

On July 23, after waiting several days for favorable winds, Admiral Howe and his fleet of 260 vessels—including five sail of the line and ten additional warships—stood out from Sandy Hook.

Washington was still uncertain of their destination. It looked as if General Howe, having satisfied himself that Burgoyne was doing well, was sailing to Philadelphia. Washington responded by moving his army closer to the Delaware River. But by the time he arrived, Howe's armada had not yet been spotted by patriot lookouts stationed at the Delaware capes, so Washington held his men on the New Jersey side of the river in case Howe had tricked him and circled back to New York, planning to go up the Hudson after all.

Patriot lookout Henry Fisher was at his post at Lewes, Delaware. On the 29th he spotted Howe's fleet struggling in high winds and rough seas off the Delaware capes, confirming that Philadelphia was indeed his objective. But three days later Fisher sent word that Howe had disappeared and had not entered Delaware Bay after all. Fisher also reported that Captain Snape Hamond of HMS *Roebuck* had met with the Howes on the 30th for a daylong conference.

Notwithstanding his experience with Captain Dougherty and the Pennsylvania navy, Hamond had recommended that in spite of its geography, tides, and defense, the Delaware was a more suitable approach to Philadelphia than Chesapeake Bay was. Nevertheless, General Howe decided to go by way of the Chesapeake. Hamond might not have been intimidated by the Delaware's defenses, but Howe certainly was. He feared that Washington could make landing the British troops there too dangerous.

By choosing the roundabout Chesapeake Bay route, Howe was ruling out a meeting with Burgoyne in Albany, negating the very heart of the king's grand strategy. Thus Captain Dougherty's fight with Snape Hamond the previous year became one of the more significant naval battles of the war. It did not influence Hamond but undoubtedly swayed General Howe.

Ambrose Serle thought the decision wrongheaded. He had heard stories of how terribly humid and hot Chesapeake Bay was, how filled with dangerous fevers. "The worst climate in America at this worst season of the year," he moaned. General Howe thought the Chesapeake might be preferable because possession of it could possibly sever Washington's communication with the south and make Virginia, North Carolina, South Carolina, and Georgia easier to subdue later.

While speculating about Howe's ultimate destination, Washington gave serious thought to attacking New York City. It was even possible, he realized, that Howe was drawing attention away from Manhattan so that General Clinton could strike the New York highlands and cooperate with Burgoyne. If that were the case, the city would be an even more inviting target. Had the Continental Navy been strong enough, he likely would have carried out such an attack, but without naval support he was at too great a disadvantage.

The patriots did conduct raids at King's Bridge and eastern Long Island, but they were weak, and the British easily thwarted them. General Sullivan made a more serious attack on August 22 against Staten Island, but it too was repulsed. Had Sullivan been successful, Howe would have been forced to rush troops back to New York, which at the time would not have been easy. In any event, these raids increased Henry Clinton's doubts about the wisdom of moving up the Hudson to help Burgoyne.

All conjecture about where the Howes were heading ended on August 16, when Washington received intelligence that the British armada, having been detained by adverse winds, had appeared in Chesapeake Bay and anchored at Swan's Point, more than two hundred miles beyond the entrance. General Howe would now certainly attack Philadelphia.

While waiting for the British to arrive, Washington decided to parade his entire army of sixteen thousand through Philadelphia. On August 25, riding at the head of his troops with the Marquis de Lafayette at his side, the commander in chief sought to give heart to patriots in the capital and pause to the loyalists. He also wanted to make it clear that he would fight for the city.

John Adams watched the parade and came away with mixed feelings. He wrote, "The Army . . . I find to be extremely well armed, pretty well clothed, and tolerably disciplined . . . Much remains yet to be done. Our soldiers have not yet quite the air of soldiers. They don't step exactly in time. They don't hold their heads up quite erect, nor turn out their toes exactly as they ought. They don't all of them cock their hats; and such as do, don't all wear them the same way." Afterward, Washington placed his entire force between Howe and Philadelphia, risking the general battle he had long hoped to avoid.

On the day of the parade Washington heard encouraging news from the north.

Burgoyne had reached abandoned Fort Edward in need of provisions and horses. Tory Colonel Philip Skene then told him that the rebels had horses, wagons, and military stores at Bennington in the New Hampshire Grants (now Vermont). And, Skene added, the loyalists in the area outnumbered the Whigs five to one. They would rally behind Burgoyne, Skene assured him, once an army was around to encourage them.

Despite contrary advice from his close friend Brigadier General Simon Fraser and German Major General Baron von Riedesel, Burgoyne dispatched seven hundred men under Lieutenant Colonel Friedrich Baum to secure the horses and whatever else he could find at Bennington and scour the countryside for food and supplies. When Baum ran into trouble and sent for reinforcements, Burgoyne dispatched an additional 650 men under Lieutenant Colonel Breymann. They weren't enough. Patriot General John Stark—a hero of Bunker Hill—administered a crushing defeat at Bennington. Two hundred British soldiers were killed and seven hundred captured—men Burgoyne would have great difficulty replacing.

Washington had predicted that Burgoyne's early successes might precipitate his ruin, writing to Schuyler, "[The British] can never think of advancing without securing their rear, and the force with which they can act against you will be greatly reduced by detachments necessary for that purpose." Now it looked as if Washington's prediction might be coming true.

Though General Schuyler was making significant progress against Burgoyne, his detractors in Congress were intent on getting rid of him. Dissatisfaction over the fall of Ticonderoga and the subsequent patriot retreat was pervasive. The Adamses, among others, were promoting General Gates to replace Schuyler, on the grounds that Gates could work more easily with the New England militias who were critical to stopping Burgoyne. So, despite Washington's support for Schuyler, on August 4 Congress appointed Gates and gave him almost dictatorial powers in the Northern Department.

Gates dawdled so long on the way from Philadelphia to Albany that he did not arrive until August 19; by then the tide of battle had already turned. When he finally got down to business, Gates pointedly ignored Schuyler, keeping him out of councils, ignoring the inevitable discord this would sow in an already divided camp. Schuyler was angry that Gates would not rely on his intimate knowledge of the terrain and the circumstances. Bitterly disappointed, he went home to Albany alone and thence to Philadelphia to defend himself before Congress.

Meanwhile, Burgoyne had moved south from Fort Edward to Fort Miller, still on the eastern side of the Hudson, forty-seven miles from Albany. The battle of Bennington had been a severe blow, and now he had to wait for provisions and men from the north. Bennington had cost him nine hundred of his best troops, his Indian allies were leaving him, and the Tories he had counted on so heavily to flock to his banner never materialized. Instead of loyalists Burgoyne found patriots. "Wherever the King's forces point," he wrote to Germain, "militia, to the amount of three or four thousand, assemble in twenty-four hours; they bring with them their subsistence, etc., and, the alarm over, they return to their farms."

While Burgoyne's difficulties mounted, Admiral Howe was bringing his huge fleet laboriously up Chesapeake Bay. As Ambrose Serle had anticipated, the passage was long, grim, and dull. The Continental Navy gave the admiral a wide berth—no American naval forces shot out from hidden creeks at night, in fog, or in dirty weather to pick off a straggling transport or two. The bay's novel landscape, however, provided Serle with some points of interest. This was the first time he'd seen slaves on American plantations, and he had an excellent view of them working hard on fertile lands that came down to the water's edge. Most of America's 500,000 slaves at the time toiled in the Chesapeake Bay area, tending the tobacco fields. "Scarce a white person was to be seen," Serle wrote in his diary, "but Negroes appeared in great abundance. These live in huts or hovels near the houses of their owners, and are treated as a better kind of cattle, being bought or sold according to fancy or interest, having no property, not even in their wives or children. Such is the practice or sentiment of Americans while they are bawling about the rights of human nature and oppose the freest government and most liberal system of polity known upon the face of the earth!" Serle was apparently unaware of Britain's role in the slave trade and the merciless treatment slaves received on British plantations in the West Indies.

Admiral Howe finally reached the head of Chesapeake Bay on August 25, dropping anchor off the Elk River a month after leaving New York. It had been an unexpectedly rough voyage, and many horses had died. The disembarking soldiers, having waited for two weeks aboard ship in stifling heat, even before leaving New York harbor, were now sick and exhausted. But Washington did not, as Howe had feared, challenge the landing, allowing the British time to recover. "This morning," Serle wrote, "the troops landed, without the least opposition, about seven miles from Turkey Point on the Western shore of the River Elk. We anchored near the Place of Landing. Two men were hanged, and 5 severely whipped, for plundering. If this had been done a year ago, we would have found its advantages."

Just as General Howe was landing, he received news of the patriot victory at Bennington. Burgoyne was obviously in trouble, but there was nothing Howe could do about that now. He had to make certain, especially if Burgoyne was defeated, that he succeeded in Philadelphia. The king's cause could not withstand two such calamities.

The provisions, military stores, and baggage necessary for Howe's army were not fully unloaded until September 7. The two armies finally met on September 11 at Chad's Ford on Brandywine Creek, engaging in the great battle the British craved. General Howe began his attack at eight o'clock in the morning, outfoxing Washington once again with a clever flanking movement and gaining an impressive victory. But as night fell, Howe's men were too tired to administer the coup de grâce. One more hour of daylight, he estimated, would have permitted him to deal the patriots the crushing defeat he had long sought.

Washington's army fled the battlefield, running wildly for twelve miles to the bridge at Chester Creek. The night both protected and confused them. At the bridge General Lafayette, who had been wounded in the fighting, stopped the headlong retreat and tried, with some success, to restore order. Soon Washington, accompanied by Greene, arrived on the scene and quieted the men. Totally exhausted, they camped at Chester for the night.

Howe did not chase them; his troops were spent as well. After sending a detachment to take Wilmington, he rested on the Chad's Ford battlefield for the night. The following morning Washington moved to the falls of the Schuylkill River and camped near Germantown, still keeping his ragged army between Howe and Philadelphia. Two days later on September 14, Washington marched west to guard Swede's Ford over the Schuylkill, where he thought Howe might attempt to cross.

On the 16th Howe finally roused himself and left Chad's Ford, marching toward Washington and hoping to engage him in a final battle. Washington, whose army had recovered its balance and was in remarkably good spirits, considering what it had just been through, planned to challenge him. The two armies met that day and were poised to fight again, when a deluge of biblical proportions struck. Severe rain and wind swept the battlefield, soaking the weapons on both sides, making them impossible to fire.

With the storm finally over on September 18, Washington marched to Reading Furnace, a big supply depot, to find replacements for the arms destroyed by the storm. He then returned to Swede's Ford and Richardson's Ford, camping along Perkiomen Creek, still on the east side of the Schuylkill between Howe and Philadelphia.

As Howe's supply lines stretched farther from the Royal Navy warships on the Elk River, Washington decided to send General Anthony Wayne with fifteen hundred men to sit on Howe's rear. But this deployment was reported by local Tories, and Major General Grey, using bayonets, surprised Wayne on the 20th at Paoli, killing as many as three hundred patriots while suffering only three dead.

The next day, Howe moved his army to Valley Forge, encamping along the Schuylkill. Washington, fearing that Howe would outflank him again, marched north to meet him. He worried too that the British would reach Reading Furnace and seize the patriots' stores there. But Washington was fooled again when his troops got too far ahead of the British. Howe whirled, turned south, and raced for Philadelphia, arriving at Fatland Ford and Gordon's Ford during the night, scattering the few defenders. The whole British army then crossed at Fatland Ford without opposition. Washington was twenty miles away.

With the British getting closer, Philadelphians frantically carried all the munitions they could out of the city. On September 25 the unfinished Continental frigates, the *Effingham*, under Captain John Barry, and the *Washington*, under Captain Thomas Read, together with the packet *Mercury*, were floated up the Delaware River, accompanied by an armada of smaller boats filled with military stores, as well as the private belongings of well-to-do people fleeing the city. Thus preoccupied, Barry and Read, two of the best fighting officers in the Continental Navy, were away when the critical naval battle for Philadelphia was fought two days later.

On the 26th Lord Cornwallis, at the head of a small detachment with ten guns, marched into the open city and took possession of it, cheered by the many loyalists who had remained. Immediately he threw up batteries along the waterfront to defend against seaborne attacks by patriot row-galleys and other vessels. This was a prescient move, for the patriots were determined to dispute control of the waterfront and organized a naval force under Commodore John Hazelwood of the Pennsylvania state navy to attack Cornwallis.

Captain Alexander in the Continental frigate *Delaware* took the lead, accompanied by the Continental sloop *Fly*, four row-galleys, and the Pennsylvania state ship *Montgomery*, which had sixteen 9-pounders. This patriot force should have been far larger, but even so, it could have presented the British with much greater problems than it did. Its leaders were bickering and indecisive. Neither Hazelwood nor Alexander had thought of preventing Cornwallis from erecting batteries on the city's riverfront before attacking him on September 27.

The results were disastrous for the patriots. When the makeshift American fleet approached, the newly installed British guns opened fire. A sharp exchange followed for a half hour until the *Delaware* ran aground and Captain Alexander struck his colors. The British swarmed aboard, taking the crew prisoner and dousing a few fires. They now possessed the most powerful American warship on the Delaware River. The *Fly* was also damaged, but it went aground on the Jersey side, where the patriots salvaged her. Admiral Howe promptly ordered an experienced crew aboard the *Delaware*, and she became an important part of the Royal Navy's drive to gain control of the river.

The British had also captured dozens of small craft moored about the city in creeks and inlets. In a twinkling, General Howe had gained naval supremacy on that part of the river. The rest of the Delaware to the south, however, remained in patriot hands. Howe's position in the city would not be secure until he had command of the entire river.

While these critical land and sea battles were being waged in and around Philadelphia, Burgoyne, with a diminished army and against all reason, kept pressing on toward Albany. He had crossed over to the west bank of the Hudson on September 13 and 14. His army was now reduced to seventy-seven hundred, and he had in front of him a steadily expanding American army on well-fortified high ground at Bemis Heights near Saratoga. Behind him, increasing numbers of patriots were attacking his supply lines. The defeat of St. Leger and the losses at Bennington, combined with Burgoyne's inability to garner strong support from Tories or keep his Indian allies from deserting, had badly weakened him. It was now unlikely he'd ever reach Albany or even be able to save his army. Still, he kept doggedly moving forward. On the 18th he camped three miles from Bemis Heights. Since his Indian scouts had left, he knew little about the patriot force facing him.

Meanwhile, General Gates's Northern Army had grown to around nine thousand and was increasing, while Burgoyne's was steadily diminishing. On the following day Burgoyne, undeterred by his losses, divided his army into three columns—left, center, and right—and attacked the Americans at Freeman's Farm, just north of

Bemis Heights. Burgoyne led the center himself. He met spirited resistance from Morgan's riflemen, Benedict Arnold, John Glover, Henry Dearborn, Enoch Poor, Ebenezer Learned, and William Hull. At the end of a bloody day the British remained on the battlefield while the Americans retired, but the redcoats and Hessians had sustained losses of 524 men killed and 42 missing—a crushing blow. The Americans had suffered about half those losses. It was, as a British lieutenant admitted, "a dear-bought victory."

Burgoyne, however, was certain he had won an important battle. "We have had a smart and very honorable action," he wrote, "and we are now encamped in front of the field, which must demonstrate our victory beyond the power of even an American news writer to explain away."

Thus, in spite of his shrinking, dispirited army, Burgoyne was planning another attack when he received a message from General Clinton in Manhattan that caused him to delay. It was dated September 12 but arrived on the 20th. Clinton wrote that he was expecting reinforcements any day, and when they arrived he would consider attacking Fort Montgomery in the highlands, forty miles up the Hudson from Manhattan, with about two thousand men. From there, if all went well, he might move farther north. If, however, his flanks were threatened, he would return to New York.

Grasping at this thin straw, Burgoyne dug in and waited for Clinton's help. Burgoyne thought that Gates, being an inexperienced battlefield general, would panic and send part of his growing army south to confront Clinton. In any event, Burgoyne recognized that his situation was desperate enough that he had to rely on Clinton.

Luckily for Burgoyne, Gates was willing to wait and not attack. The Americans were low on ammunition, and Gates decided more was needed before he could make a move. So both armies, in close proximity, entered into an undeclared truce for a time.

On September 28, reports of Burgoyne's predicament reached Washington. Howe heard the news at about the same time, making it even more imperative that he succeed. The next day, he began his campaign for the Delaware River.

Washington, however, had a surprise for him.

When Cornwallis had marched into Philadelphia on the 26th, Howe encamped the bulk of his force—roughly nine thousand men—outside the city at Germantown. Unknown to Howe, Washington's army was growing and now numbered about twelve thousand.

On October 4 a heavy fog concealed the patriots as Washington attacked the British lines at Germantown.

The experienced redcoats did not panic; Howe rushed reinforcements from the city under Cornwallis and counterattacked, causing the still-green American troops to flee. Patriot losses were twice those of the British—approximately eleven hundred to five hundred dead, wounded, or captured—and the redcoats held the battleground when the fighting ended. But Washington, his officers, and his men did not feel in the least like a defeated army. With all their disadvantages, the Americans had stood up to the British and might well have carried the day, had they been more experienced and had Washington's plan of attack not been so complicated. They had come very close to succeeding, and Washington knew that if they had, the war would have ended right there.

Meanwhile, patriot spies from New York City had reported to General Putnam, the commander in the highlands, that British reinforcements had arrived, and General Clinton was preparing to move a large contingent up the Hudson to aid Burgoyne. Putnam had feared this for months and repeatedly warned Washington of the danger. Nevertheless, Washington had depleted Putnam's force, moving troops from the highlands to fight for Philadelphia and support Gates in the north. Putnam had only fifteen hundred men left.

Clinton began his move on October 3. On the 5th he landed three thousand men just below Peekskill on the east side of the Hudson, forcing Putnam to retreat. Putnam assumed that Clinton was about to attack him directly, since this was what he had been predicting for months.

But Clinton was only feigning. The following morning, taking advantage of the fog, he led two thousand men across the river to the western side and attacked the two highland forts, Clinton and Montgomery, which were defended by a brave but woefully inadequate force under Governor George Clinton and his brother, Brigadier General James Clinton. The patriot Clintons and their men fought valiantly but were overwhelmed; they made their escape as best they could.

A strong naval contingent, led by Commodore William Hotham and Captain James Wallace, had accompanied General Clinton. It included Admiral Graves's old flagship, the 50-gun *Preston*, along with the 20-gun *Mercury*, under Captain Graeme, and the 28-gun *Tartar*, under Captain Ommanney, accompanied by row-galleys. During the fighting on the 6th, Commodore Hotham had moved close enough to fire on the forts. He was also within firing range of American warships stationed on the other side of two obstructing chains stretching across the Hudson between Forts Clinton and Montgomery on the west side and Anthony's Nose on the east side.

The American fleet facing Commodore Hotham included two unfinished Continental frigates, the 28-gun *Congress*, under Captain Thomas Grennell, and the 24-gun *Montgomery*, under Captain John Hodge, both seeing their first action with undermanned, inexperienced crews. Accompanying them were the row-galleys *Lady Washington* and *Shark*, and the 10-gun privateer sloop *Camden*. Governor George Clinton had placed Captain Hodge in overall command of this makeshift fleet and ordered him to defend the chains.

Hodge's squadron fired on Hotham from above the barriers and the British shot back, initiating an hour of long-distance exchanges between five and six o'clock in the afternoon. While Hodge's ship fired, she drifted downriver with the ebbing tide closer and closer to the chains. Having no anchors to secure her, she eventually fell hard against the nearest chain, leaving her stranded in the middle of the Hudson. In the meantime, Forts Clinton and Montgomery had both fallen. Fearing capture by the British, Captain Hodge ordered his trapped frigate burned as he and the crew escaped. The flames eventually reached her magazine, and the brand-new *Montgomery* blew up, with thunderous echoes reverberating through the rocky mountain passes.

The *Congress*, meanwhile, had fled north toward Fort Constitution but went aground along the way and was burned to prevent her from falling into British hands. The *Shark* and the *Lady Washington* were also burned and the *Camden* captured. After the Americans fled, Commodore Hotham cut through the chain obstructions, and by October 7 the Hudson was open to the British.

With a small collection of survivors, Governor Clinton and General Putnam watched, prepared to shadow the British along both sides of the Hudson should they move north.

General Clinton now had to decide whether or not he would proceed north. Meanwhile, Burgoyne waited anxiously. A German officer wrote that "at no time did the Jews await the coming of their Messiah with greater expectancy than we awaited the coming of General Clinton." But Clinton did not come, and after two weeks, with food running out, Burgoyne was forced to act. By now his army had shrunk to less than six thousand effectives. Many of his men had deserted to the patriots or disappeared into the woods.

General von Riedesel counseled retreat, but falling back was unthinkable to Burgoyne. He decided to move forward, developing an ill-considered plan to attack Gates again at Bemis Heights near Saratoga. A major battle developed on October 7. By then the American army had swollen to over eleven thousand. Inspired by the incomparable battlefield leadership of Benedict Arnold and the great skill of Morgan's riflemen, the patriots crushed the British and their German allies. Burgoyne began a pitiful retreat but found no way out, and he formally surrendered on October 17.

Unaccountably, General Gates accepted the defeated Burgoyne's own terms of surrender in order to facilitate a quick end to the fighting. Gates agreed to let Burgoyne march his army to Boston and embark all of it to England, on condition that the men not serve in America again during the war. The American general, who had remained far from the action during both battles (unlike Burgoyne who had been in the thick of the fighting), evidently was frightened by Clinton's foray into the highlands. Gates wanted Burgoyne out of the way in case he had to deal with a large army coming up from Manhattan.

General Clinton's success in the highlands on October 6 emboldened him to think of doing more than he had originally planned, perhaps even marching all the way to Albany. But it was already too late. Had he done so, he would have fallen into the jaws of Gates's huge army, of which Clinton was still unaware. Ignorant of the real situation, on October 13 Clinton dispatched two thousand men under General Vaughan, supported by a naval contingent under Captain Wallace, to probe north of the highlands in the hope of aiding Burgoyne. Two days later Vaughan reached Esopus (now Kingston), the seat of the New York legislature and the third largest town in the state, mercilessly reducing it to ashes; not a house was left standing. Despite reports of Burgoyne's surrender, Vaughan continued north from Esopus to Livingston Manor, where, to his dismay, he saw thousands of armed patriots gathering on both sides of the Hudson ahead of him, making continued movement north out of the question.

On the same day, Clinton received dispatches from General Howe (his first since the end of August) ordering him to send four thousand troops immediately to Philadelphia. Fearing that Howe might be in trouble, Clinton responded quickly, bringing Vaughan and Wallace back to Manhattan, abandoning the hard-won highlands.

General Howe needed Clinton's men to help clear the Delaware River and protect Philadelphia from Washington, whose army was very much intact. After the attack on Germantown, Washington had moved to White Marsh, fourteen miles from Philadelphia, hoping to trap Howe by preventing provisions from reaching the city. Detachments of American militiamen scoured the countryside looking for supplies, while Washington strengthened the river defenses below Philadelphia. There were limits to how many troops he could spare, however; he didn't want to weaken his main army and invite a surprise attack.

The Delaware's defense rested on three elements: forts, chevaux-de-frise and other obstructions placed in the river, and a tiny force of row-galleys, warships, floating batteries, and fire ships under Commodore Hazelwood. "If the river's defenses can be maintained," Washington wrote, "General Howe's situation will not be the most agreeable; for if his supplies can be stopped by water, it may easily be done by land . . . the acquisition of Philadelphia may, instead of his good fortune, prove his ruin."

Immediately after hearing of his brother's victory at Brandywine Creek, Admiral Howe had his fleet on the move down Chesapeake Bay from the Elk River to the Virginia capes, where the weather forced him to tarry until September 23 before standing out into the Atlantic. Once at sea he met with more heavy storms and reached Chester on the Delaware on October 6, determined to secure control of the entire river.

Snape Hamond and an advance party of four frigates were already at nearby Billingsport, working with General Howe to remove a double line of chevaux-de-frise strung between Billingsport and Billingsport Island. A small fort overlooked the double line, but when the general put up a brief show of force, the patriots abandoned it. However, on the row-galleys, fire rafts, and other assorted craft defending the river obstructions, they fought with such fierce determination that it took Hamond until the 15th to break through them.

The Howes still had a long way to go; far more difficult patriot defenses lay closer to Philadelphia. Just below the mouth of the Schuylkill River two forts, Mercer and Mifflin, anchored obstructions that blocked the main channel from Chester to the city. Fort Mercer was at Red Bank, where the river's main channel ran along the east bank near the Jersey shore. Opposite it was Fort Mifflin on Mud Island. Between the two forts was a triple line of chevaux-de-frise that blocked the channel. The American fleet, such as it was, stood behind the obstructions. Philadelphia should have been defended by more than this miniscule, untested squadron, but, as in New York and all the other ports along the coast, the capital's waterborne defense had been neglected by the Continental Navy.

General Howe ordered batteries placed on the western side of the river to play upon Fort Mifflin; he organized a force of Hessians and artillery to deal with Fort Mercer. Admiral Howe was to support these attacks with his warships. The converted Indiaman *Vigilant*, a floating battery carrying twenty-four 32-pounders, was to aid in the destruction of Fort Mifflin, while seven other warships in the main channel were to act as a diversion in support of the attack on Fort Mercer. These included Hamond's four frigates of the advance party; the 64-gun *Augusta*, under Captain Francis Reynolds; the 50-gun *Isis*, under Captain William Cornwallis; and the 16-gun sloop-of-war *Merlin*, under Captain Samuel Reeve.

In the meantime, Washington dispatched Colonel Christopher Greene and four hundred Rhode Island Continentals to defend Fort Mercer at Red Bank, telling Greene his mission was "of the utmost importance to America." Regardless of his concern, Washington could spare only this small contingent. His calls for support from Jersey militiamen had gone unanswered.

On October 19 General Howe pulled his army back from Germantown to tighter defensive positions around Philadelphia, and then sent Admiral Howe's warships and Colonel von Donop with twelve hundred Hessians and artillery to attack Forts Mifflin and Mercer. The fighting began late in the afternoon of the 22nd when Colonel Donop and his Hessians suddenly appeared out of the woods and rushed toward Fort Mercer, expecting to overwhelm the defenders. Colonel Greene, however, was prepared. He had fourteen guns and help from a talented young French engineer, the Chevalier de Maudit du Plessis, who had thrown up some clever fortifications. The row-galleys and floating batteries in the river were also a help.

While Donop was advancing, Captain Reynolds and the British squadron made their diversion on the water. But the extensive patriot obstructions in the river had altered its natural course, and both the *Augusta* and *Merlin* went aground well short of the fort. Their crews worked frantically to free the big warships, but they failed to float them on the next flood tide. The rest of the British warships advanced, receiving fire from the patriot row-galleys and other vessels. With night approaching, the British observed, to their utter amazement, that Colonel Greene's small force was slaughtering the Hessians. Despite what was happening ashore, the warships on both sides maintained their duel and did not cease firing until darkness fell. The stubborn British warships remained in place through the night, refusing to retreat. Neither did the Americans.

The following morning the patriots discovered the state of the *Augusta* and *Merlin*. Greene fired on them from Fort Mercer while the American row-galleys and floating batteries struck them from the water. Commodore Hazelwood even floated four fireships toward the *Augusta*, but they were towed down the channel by British boats and harmlessly burned themselves out. Captain Reynolds, aboard the *Augusta*, continued working hard to free her, but a fire broke out abaft that spread rapidly and could not be contained. Reynolds abandoned ship just in the nick of time, as she became a giant fireball and blew up with an earsplitting roar. Admiral Howe now decided to withdraw Hamond's frigates and destroy the stranded *Merlin*. Because of adverse winds the *Vigilant* never got into action against Fort Mifflin.

One would think that the defense of Philadelphia would have been foremost in the minds of the Marine Committee, which could have placed dozens of row-galleys on the river with the Continental Navy's finest officers in command. As it was, the pathetically inadequate forces under Commodore Hazelwood and Colonel Greene, against overwhelming odds, had inflicted a galling defeat on the British.

The Howes regrouped and focused their attention on Fort Mifflin, a much less formidable target than Fort Mercer. They brought six 24-pounders from the *Eagle* and four 32-pounders from the

Somerset and placed them on Province Island to play upon Fort Mifflin's weak northern side. At the same time, the *Vigilant* and a floating battery carrying three 18-pounders were brought through the channel around Hog Island to cooperate with the cannon on Province Island and fire on the fort from the Pennsylvania side. On November 10 these powerful cannons opened fire and on succeeding days softened up the fort considerably.

Aided by the row-galleys, the undermanned defenders fought back doggedly. Their commander, Lieutenant Colonel Smith, was severely wounded during the cannonade and had to be evacuated to Red Bank. Rhode Islander Major Simeon Thayer took his place, and the outgunned Americans held on for five more torturous days.

On the 15th Admiral Howe moved the 64-gun *Somerset* and 50-gun *Isis* up the eastern channel of the Delaware to bombard the front of the fort. The 44-gun *Roebuck*, 32-gun *Pearl*, and 28-gun *Liverpool* frigates, with the *Cornwallis* galley and some smaller armed vessels, came up to destroy the new patriot battery erected near Manto Creek. In combination with the *Vigilant*, the floating battery, and the guns on Province Island, they obliterated Fort Mifflin, forcing the gallant Thayer to evacuate his survivors at night to Red Bank. The British ships now turned all their fire on Fort Mercer, and Colonel Greene, seeing that his position was hopeless, wisely evacuated. The Howes now controlled the Delaware. On November 23 the first British supply ship pulled in to the Philadelphia waterfront.

Had Commodore John Hazelwood of the Pennsylvania state navy had dozens of row-galleys to command, or had the Marine Committee organized the Continental Navy so that it could put up a respectable defense of the capital, Fort Mifflin would likely have been saved and the Delaware held. Patriot Major Thayer maintained that had the *Vigilant* been put out of commission by attacking her with row-galleys, he could have held the fort. Commodore Hazelwood did order such an attack, but his order wasn't carried out.

Once Admiral Howe had broken through the river barriers, the remaining patriot vessels were caught between his powerful fleet and HMS *Delaware*, formerly of the Continental Navy, and its supporting ships. All the patriot vessels were either captured, destroyed by the British, or burned by their own crews.

General Howe now turned on Washington, sending his redcoats to confront the patriot army at White Marsh on December 4. But Howe found Washington too strongly entrenched to attack, occupying two commanding hills secured by a strong advance post. After four days of fruitless marching and skirmishing, Howe gave up trying to lure Washington out and returned to Philadelphia. Although there had been no battle as such, this encounter became known as the battle of White Marsh.

Shortly afterward, on December 12, in cold and snow, Washington took his entire army across the Schuylkill, his soldiers fatigued from lack of proper food and clothing, particularly shoes. The following day they moved to Valley Forge for the winter. Incredibly, Howe never attempted to attack them there. He had already tendered his resignation in October. Apart from foraging parties, he planned to winter as comfortably as possible in Philadelphia while awaiting a decision from London as to his future.

At this time David Bushnell reappeared with another invention of great potential that had been available, but ignored, since 1775—floating mines. As Bushnell explained to Thomas Jefferson many years later, in December 1777 he had "fixed several kegs underwater, charged with powder, to explode upon touching anything, as they floated along with the tide: I set them afloat," he wrote, "above the English shipping in the Delaware." But Bushnell was "unacquainted with the river," and the season was so inhospitable to the enterprise that it failed. A premature explosion alerted the British, and they fired at the floating devices, exploding them before they reached the shipping. But they did give the British a fright, and the incident became known as the Battle of the Kegs. Why this experiment was not followed by others remains inexplicable.

5

THE FRENCH ALLIANCE

January 1778–September 1779

News of the patriot victory at Saratoga and near victory at German-town reached London and Paris during the first week of December, prompting sweeping policy changes in both capitals. Racing to head off a Franco-American alliance, Lord North dispatched the arch-spy Paul Wentworth to Paris to inform Benjamin Franklin and Silas Deane of the far-reaching concessions London was now willing to make. Wentworth did not approach the other American envoy in Paris, the Virginian Arthur Lee. Wentworth's boss, the young English spymaster William Eden, considered the acerbic Lee too anti-British. Franklin, of course, wasn't any more amenable to North's overtures than Lee would have been, and he used Wentworth's presence to prod the French, who hardly needed prodding. They were so intent on humiliating their hated rival that they couldn't wait to openly ally themselves with the Americans.

King Louis XVI would have preferred to act in concert with Bourbon Spain, but the dons wanted the war to continue at the same pace, bleeding both sides. Until now, France, and to a much lesser extent Spain, had supplied the Americans with enough money and arms to keep the pot boiling, which Spain found agreeable. But an alliance was out of the question. Madrid feared that a strong republic might emerge from the war, threatening her own American colonies, which she had been mercilessly exploiting since the days of Christopher Columbus nearly three hundred years before.

Vergennes, the powerful French foreign minister, had no such fears. He was confident that thirteen squabbling states would emerge from the war. The Americans had shown ample evidence of their inability to work together. Even though Congress had announced the Declaration of Independence in 1776, it had been unable to agree on terms of confederation until November 1777, and then only under the extreme pressure of events. The Articles of Confederation established a weak central government, with real power continuing to reside in the states. Even so, there was no certainty that the states would approve the Articles. In addition, the Americans had refused to tax themselves; they were paying for the war by printing money, issuing a bewildering array of domestic debt, and begging for loans all over Europe. Vergennes was not about to pass up an opportunity to drive a lance into the lion's heart merely because one day the Americans might become too strong. He was ready to fight now, even if it meant doing so without the dons.

On February 6, 1778, he signed the Treaty of Alliance with the Americans, and on the same day the Treaty of Amity and Commerce. On March 13 Paris formally announced these agreements, and on March 20 King Louis XVI received the American commissioners. A week earlier the French ambassador in London, the Marquis de Noailles, had informed the North ministry of the new arrangements, and London and Paris had both withdrawn their ambassadors. Without a formal declaration, a state of war now existed between civilization's two greatest powers, transforming a colonial dispute into a world war. Their quarrel stemmed mainly from France's desire to avenge its defeat in the Seven Years War. Vergennes also believed that humiliating Britain would restore the balance of power in Europe.

For his part, Lord North was shamelessly changing course, desperately seeking to return America to her allegiance. His policy reversal was revealed to the House on February 17, and, according to Horace Walpole, shocked supporters and opponents alike. The government was saying, in effect, that the principles on which Britain had sent abroad the largest expeditionary force in her history were to be thrown over in an instant on receipt of adverse news.

North was obviously trying to wean the Americans away from France, but everyone in Parliament knew that an alliance had already been formed and that North's overtures would not placate the Americans. The king still refused to concede independence, the sine qua non of patriot demands. So the costly war, which was becoming more and more unpopular in Britain, would continue.

Paradoxically, the British ministry needed French involvement to obtain continuing public support for the war. After watching the king raise enormous armies and having heard extravagant promises of a quick victory, the British were fast losing their enthusiasm for fighting the Americans. The French were another matter. Britain's animus toward France, never far from the surface, surged, giving His Majesty essential new support. The recriminations that would have ordinarily followed the disasters of 1777 were muted by a burst of patriotism.

Major changes in strategy, of course, were inevitable. The king's main focus now was on distressing France while defending the home islands, the West Indies, and Canada. The war in America would be a lesser priority, although it was unclear exactly what that meant. The king still intended to crush the rebellion, albeit with a reduced force.

The burden of reconciling the irreconcilable fell on the new commander in chief, Sir Henry Clinton, and the various naval commanders assigned to the North American station—Admirals Howe, Gambier, Byron, Arbuthnot, Graves, and Digby. Not even men of great ability, like the Duke of Wellington or Admiral Nelson, could have coped with this impossible assignment, and General Clinton was a man of limited capacity, as were the admirals who served beside him, with the exception of Lord Howe.

Before inviting Clinton to assume command, the king had offered the post to Sir Jeffery Amherst, the old hero of the French and Indian War. But Amherst had turned him down. Without the necessary resources, Amherst saw more failure ahead. He estimated that seventy-five thousand troops would be necessary to accomplish the king's objectives. Just maintaining the territory Britain already occupied would require stationing forty-five thousand regulars in America indefinitely. In Amherst's view, making America a secondary theater guaranteed defeat.

The Howes agreed with Amherst, which is why they had submitted their resignations during the third week of October 1777, even before receiving news of Burgoyne's final surrender. In their view, the government had never given them adequate tools to do the job, and now Germain and Sandwich were intent on making them scapegoats for the ministry's own failures.

At that point, the king had turned to Sir Henry Clinton, almost by default. Clinton had been in London the previous winter, and Germain had more or less promised him the command should General Howe falter. Fixated on blaming the Howes for Britain's failure to achieve a quick victory in America, Germain gave little attention to Clinton's abysmal war record, particularly his inability to work with the navy. Clinton's father had been an admiral, and as a youth, Clinton had spent considerable time aboard warships, even in New York, when Admiral Clinton was stationed there. Still, General Clinton found it impossible to work in harness with his naval counterparts.

The king presented Clinton with new orders in March, directing him to prosecute the war with "the utmost vigor" but with fewer resources. Clinton was ordered to evacuate Philadelphia and move to New York. His Majesty insisted that holding the American capital would require troops needed elsewhere. Of course, abandoning Philadelphia and leaving the Tories in the lurch would incur heavy political costs. Ambrose Serle bitterly opposed the idea, as did his close friend, Joseph Galloway. For Serle, giving up the rebel capital meant the end of the war. Trust in the British would be forever forfeited.

Once established in New York, Clinton was to attempt what General Howe had been directed to do earlier: bring "Mr. Washington to a general and decisive action." But if that failed, Clinton was to "relinquish . . . offensive operations against the rebels within the land . . . [and carry out attacks on] ports [along] the coast from New York to Nova Scotia." Except for raids on coastal towns, operations in the north would cease, and attention would be directed to the south.

The king assumed that Clinton would base himself in New York; if this proved impossible, he was to use Newport or even Halifax. Come what may, His Majesty intended to hold Canada. He promised to reinforce Halifax with twenty-seven hundred additional men.

Lord Germain estimated that "operations on the sea coasts of the northern provinces" would be completed by the end of September, in which case, "it is the King's intention," he told Clinton, "that an attack should be made upon the Southern colonies with a view to the conquest and possession of Georgia and South Carolina . . . [where] a general disposition to return to their allegiance" prevailed. Clinton was directed to start with Savannah, where only two thousand men, Germain assured him, would be "fully sufficient to take and keep possession of it." The attack would be coordinated with General Prevost, marching into Georgia from St. Augustine, Florida, and with John Stuart, British superintendent of Indian affairs for the Southern Department, who would be leading "a large body of Indians" to help take Augusta, Georgia.

Having secured Georgia, Clinton would then attack Charleston with five thousand troops. After that he would use forces collected in Georgia to move into the Carolina backcountry, where loyalists would flock to his banner. At the same time, Clinton would send a small force to occupy the Cape Fear River and make "every diversion" on Virginia and Maryland.

In the king's plan, the West Indies took precedence over both Canada and America. On March 21 His Majesty ordered Clinton to dispatch five thousand men to support Rear Admiral Samuel Barrington in an attack on the island of St. Lucia, hoping to place a check on the large French naval base at nearby Martinique. Barrington had been ordered to capture and garrison St. Lucia as soon as possible. In the same letter, the king ordered Clinton to send three thousand men to St. Augustine and Pensacola to defend the Floridas—British territory since the end of the Seven Years War.

Clinton's new orders disclosed a new strategy to achieve the old objectives. The king clung to the belief that victory in America was possible and that the south was the key. Capturing it, he believed, could be done with a minimum of effort. And "once restored to its allegiance," Germain wrote, it would be "easily maintained." If the south fell, he reasoned, the north would inevitably follow, since attacks on its seacoast towns, coupled with a tight blockade, would create the utmost distress.

Meanwhile, on March 22, the Admiralty notified Lord Howe that the object of the war had changed and the contest in America was now a "secondary consideration." Their Lordships had accepted Howe's resignation in February and were preparing to send a replacement, but in the meantime Howe was to cooperate with the king's new policies, particularly in regard to the West Indies.

Unlike Clinton, who dutifully attempted to execute the king's instructions, however unrealistic, Admiral Howe carried out his orders selectively. He had too high an appreciation of the ludicrous contradiction between trying to negotiate a settlement short of independence and at the same time incinerating defenseless coastal towns. Furthermore, he refused to become a member of Lord North's new peace commission, considering its objective futile. As for the rest of his assignment, he continued to muddle through, first assisting Clinton and then carrying out blockade and convoy duty, destroying as many privateers as he could and keeping an eye on the shrinking Continental Navy. Of course, if a French fleet appeared in North American waters, his first priority was to destroy it.

As for the Continental Navy, key parts of it had already been captured or destroyed, while others were unable or unwilling to put to sea. The few warships available were dispersed on inconsequential missions. On a bitterly cold night in February, for example, forty-two-year-old John Adams and his son John Quincy secretly boarded the 24-gun frigate *Boston*, anchored off Braintree on the Massachusetts coast. In a small boat, the captain, Samuel Tucker, and a midshipman had picked them up from the beach and rowed to the warship. Tucker had orders to deliver Adams to Bordeaux, whence he would travel by coach to Paris and help negotiate a treaty of alliance that, unknown to Congress, had already been signed.

Adams was as responsible as anyone for the shape and direction of the Continental Navy, but he had never been to sea. A private vessel could have taken the new envoy to France just as easily as the *Boston*, but Adams saw nothing wrong with traveling on one of America's few frigates at a critical time in the war. He was, after all, an important person traveling on a critical mission; it seemed logical to have the navy take him.

Captain Tucker hailed from Marblehead, Massachusetts. At thirty years of age, he was already one of the Continental Navy's stars. As fearless as he was experienced, Tucker delivered Adams unharmed, although during the long voyage the *Boston* was chased by British frigates and encountered mighty winter storms. To Adams's delight, Tucker even took a prize before landing his distinguished passenger safely at Bordeaux.

Twenty-seven-year-old Captain Nicholas Biddle did not have the same luck. On March 7, 1778, Biddle, in the *Randolph*, was sixty leagues east of Barbados on a commerce raiding mission, sailing in company with five other vessels: the *General Moultrie*, an 18-gun South Carolina privateer; the *Notre Dame*, an 18-gun South Carolina navy brigantine; the *Polly*, a 14-gun South Carolina privateer brigantine; the *Fair American*, a 14-gun South Carolina brigantine; and a prize schooner. At one o'clock in the afternoon, while Adams and the *Boston* were at sea, a lookout at the *Randolph's* main masthead spotted a strange sail standing toward them.

Three hours later a British deserter aboard the 32-gun *Randolph* identified the ship to windward as HMS *Yarmouth*, a 64-gun two-decker under Captain Nicholas Vincent. Biddle immediately signaled his fleet to make sail and endeavor to escape, but Captain Philip Sullivan in the *General Moultrie* did not respond, causing Biddle to delay. This allowed the *Yarmouth* to sail past the privateer and come up with the *Randolph* so speedily that Biddle was forced to engage. His men were superbly trained and he held his own, trading broadsides with the larger ship.

Early in the exchange, as Biddle stood by the quarterdeck guns, a shot grazed his thigh and he called for a chair. As a surgeon's mate dressed his wound, he continued directing the battle, telling his men his leg was only scratched. Suddenly, while Biddle was in his chair and the surgeon's mate still tending his wound, the *Randolph* blew up, scattering debris over the *Yarmouth*, no more than three or four ship lengths away. All but four members of the *Randolph*'s 315-man crew were killed. Horrified, Biddle's companion vessels fled. The surprisingly fast *Yarmouth* clapped on all sail in pursuit, but the Americans split up, each sailing a different course, forcing Captain Vincent eventually to give up the chase.

Meanwhile, the four survivors from the *Randolph* had somehow found each other and had fashioned a makeshift raft from the debris scattered about. Five days later, on March 12, a lookout at HMS *Yarmouth*'s main masthead called down to the officer of the watch on the quarterdeck that something was floating in the sea abaft the starboard beam. Thinking the object could be survivors from a shipwreck, Captain Vincent hauled his wind and saw with his spyglass that it was four men who appeared to be standing in the water. No raft was visible.

In two hours the great warship was alongside them, turned into the wind. When Captain Vincent ordered them hauled aboard, he was flabbergasted to find they were from the *Randolph*, and had spent five days floating on the warm water. Luckily, they were all good swimmers (most seamen were not), and after being thrown overboard had stayed afloat long enough to piece together a raft out of broken spars and bits of frayed rope. They had then shaped a blanket into a reservoir to catch the rain. Captain Vincent found the young men in remarkably good condition. After a basin of tea and a few hours of rest in hammocks, they were fully restored, their only complaint being swollen feet from the lengthy immersion in saltwater.

Two days later the British 20-gun small frigate HMS *Ariadne*, under Captain Thomas Pringle, was sailing on patrol north of Barbados in company with the 16-gun sloop-of-war *Ceres*, under Lieutenant James R. Dacres, the same intrepid officer who had commanded the *Carleton* during the battle of Valcour Island on Lake Champlain the previous year. They happened upon two American warships from France employed in commerce raiding in the Caribbean—the *Alfred*, carrying twenty 9-pounders, under Captain Elisha Hinman, and the 32-gun *Raleigh*, under Captain Thomas Thompson. Despite their inferior force, the British warships chased the Americans. The copper-bottomed *Ariadne* quickly caught the slower *Alfred*, and after exchanging a few broadsides, Captain Hinman struck his colors. The *Raleigh* stood by and watched, and when the *Alfred* surrendered, Captain Thompson fled. While the *Ceres* tended to the *Alfred,* the *Ariadne* went after the American frigate. In spite of being a far more powerful ship, the *Raleigh* shamelessly ran, Captain Thompson tossing overboard whatever he could to lighten his load. The *Ariadne* pursued, but even though she had a copper bottom, the *Raleigh* outdistanced her, and eventually the British frigate gave up the chase.

The *Ceres* took the *Alfred* into Barbados, and it became part of the Royal Navy. The *Raleigh* eventually reached Portsmouth, New Hampshire, where the navy relieved Captain Thompson of command and dismissed him from the service. He had given evidence of similar cowardice the previous year on a voyage to France in company with the *Alfred*, but the navy had overlooked it and permitted him to remain captain of one of America's finest warships. The episode with the *Ariadne*, however, could not be ignored.

While these events were unfolding, the Continental vessels supposedly trapped in Rhode Island's Providence River made a run for it. As long as Commodore Hopkins remained in command, he kept these warships hiding safely in the river. But after he had been cashiered out of the service in January 1778, a new spirit had begun to arise in the fleet.

Taking advantage of favorable winds during a foul night, the commodore's nephew, Captain John B. Hopkins, ran the 32-gun *Warren* past the small British squadron at Newport and into the Atlantic, reaching Boston on March 23. Next, the frigate *Providence* under Captain Abraham Whipple succeeded in getting to sea, something Whipple could have done earlier had he wanted to. The Marine Committee ordered him to sail to France and place the *Providence* under the direction of the commissioners in Paris. A third vessel, the *Columbus*, under Captain Hoysted Hacker, did not have similar luck. In trying to escape, she ran aground on Point Judith. While Hacker and his crew fled, the British burned the grounded vessel. Hacker was later given command of the 12-gun sloop *Providence*, John Paul Jones's old ship.

The 28-gun *Virginia*, under Captain James Nicholson, had even worse luck. In March 1778 she was finally launched in Maryland, but in making her way to sea for the first time, she became stranded on Middle Ground shoal at the mouth of Chesapeake Bay. HMS *Emerald* happened by and easily captured her. The Royal Navy welcomed the new frigate into the fleet, renaming her HMS *Virginia*. Nicholson was later acquitted of all charges.

Meanwhile, John Paul Jones had sailed the 18-gun *Ranger* to France, and now that the alliance was settled, he received full cooperation from the French government in what was to become one of his most famous cruises. Jones's notion of a proper strategy for the Continental Navy was "to surprise and spread alarm, with fast sailing ships." "When we grow stronger," he wrote, "we can meet their fleet and dispute with them the Sovereignty of the ocean." Jones never lacked for ambition.

He began his voyage in the *Ranger* during the first week of April, leaving Brest and returning a hero twenty-eight days later with the British warship *Drake*, mounting twenty 6-pounders, in tow. He had captured several prizes in addition to the *Drake* and had taken two hundred prisoners, raiding the British coast in retaliation for similar British forays in America.

While the French applauded his success, the British public worried about the security of their seaport towns, and their newspapers played on this fear. Actually, Jones's exploits had little effect on the outcome of the war. As far as the Admiralty was concerned he was just one more privateer, though perhaps the most famous one. It was the cumulative effects of hundreds of Yankee privateers that worried London. Lloyd's reported 733 merchantmen taken by American privateers from May 1777 to January 1778.

While the Continental vessels were thus employed far from where they were most needed, on May 7, British Major John Maitland led a devastating raid against the remaining patriot naval vessels on the Delaware River above Philadelphia. Using flat-bottomed boats and captured row-galleys, the soldiers of the Second Light Infantry, encountering no opposition, torched forty-four scarce American boats and storehouses between Bristol and Bordentown. Privateers were burned along with many other vessels, including the two unfinished frigates, the 32-gun *Washington* and the 28-gun *Effingham,* laden with military equipment and stores. Neither ship had yet received its armament. Washington had warned the Marine Committee repeatedly that these ships might be destroyed. He had wanted them sunk and thereby saved. Now they were lost to the British.

Just before Major Maitland delivered his blow, Washington received the stunning news of the Franco-American alliance. Like the rest of the country, he was now convinced that deliverance was at hand. "I believe no event was ever received with more heartfelt joy," he told Congress.

Indeed help was on the way. Immediately after the Treaty of Alliance was signed in March, Vice Admiral Charles-Henri, Comte d'Estaing, left Paris and traveled to the French naval base at Toulon in the Mediterranean, where five frigates and twelve sail of the line, including the magnificent 90-gun flagship *Languedoc,* were fitting out for the long voyage to America.

A neighbor and close friend of Franklin's in the fashionable Paris suburb of Passy, d'Estaing had discussed strategy with John Paul

Jones at Franklin's apartments in the Hotel de Valentinois. Jones had suggested that d'Estaing trap Admiral Howe's fleet in the Delaware, and this eventually became the Frenchman's objective. Paris wanted a quick victory and sought to achieve it by putting a fleet superior to Howe's on the American coast, trapping him in Delaware Bay, and leaving General Clinton's army caught between Washington and d'Estaing.

On paper at least, d'Estaing's force was far stronger than Howe's. Although there had been no formal declaration of war (it would not be made until July 10), the French assumed that an alliance with the Americans was its equivalent and proceeded accordingly. D'Estaing stood out from Toulon on April 13 and reached the Straits of Gibraltar on May 16. Five weeks was an inordinately long time for a trip that should have taken a few days. In any case, once he reached Gibraltar, the admiral had clear sailing for North America.

Comte d'Estaing's ultimate destination was intensely debated in London. He might be sailing to America or making for Brest and a rendezvous with the main French fleet of twenty-five sail of the line under Admiral d'Orvilliers, threatening the British Channel Fleet. Or he might join the Spanish squadron at Cadiz or attack British positions in the West Indies, Nova Scotia, Newfoundland, or Canada. Whatever d'Estaing intended, he would be obliged to pass through the Straits of Gibraltar, where the Royal Navy might have engaged him. But no British squadron blocked his way. Admiralty spies had reported all of d'Estaing's movements, but their Lordships made no attempt to bottle him up in the Mediterranean.

Lord Germain, who did not get along with Sandwich, argued for blockading d'Estaing in the Mediterranean, but Sandwich insisted there weren't enough warships available to prevent d'Estaing from entering the Atlantic and protect the home islands against the French fleet at Brest, or a possible Franco-Spanish task force.

Three British sail of the line were in the Mediterranean at the time, but Sandwich did not want to augment that number. Instead of dispatching a fleet, he sent Captain Evelyn Sutton in the frigate *Prosperine* to shadow d'Estaing and attempt to learn his destination.

Sutton and the *Prosperine* returned to Falmouth, England, on June 2 to report that d'Estaing was indeed sailing to America—most likely the West Indies. The following day the frigate *Enterprise* of the Mediterranean squadron sailed into Plymouth with similar intelligence. Three days later the cabinet dispatched a strong fleet of thirteen sail of the line and one frigate, under Vice Admiral John Byron with Rear Admiral Hyde Parker as second, to chase d'Estaing.

Byron's battleships included one of 90 guns, eleven of 74, and one of 64. When added to Admiral Howe's fleet, they would greatly outnumber d'Estaing's. Paris was aware of the possibility but decided not to reinforce d'Estaing.

On June 12, six days after Byron's departure, British Admiral Keppel, commander of the Channel Fleet, put to sea with twenty-one sail of the line and orders to cruise the Bay of Biscay, close enough to Brest to prevent a juncture of the Brest and Toulon squadrons, should that be d'Estaing's destination. Admiralty spies had reported twenty-one French battleships at Brest and twelve at Toulon. From documents found on captured French warships, however, Keppel judged that the fleet at Brest was far larger than at first thought, and on June 25 he returned to St. Helens on the Isle of Wight for reinforcements. By then it was clear that d'Estaing was bound for North America.

While d'Estaing plowed his way toward the American coast, Washington made plans to cooperate with him in delivering a crushing blow to the British. In May he had discovered that they planned to evacuate Philadelphia. He assumed they would leave the way they had come—by sea. If the French squadron arrived in time, it might trap Howe and Clinton in the Delaware River, destroy the British fleet, and end the war.

Weeks went by, however, with no sign of the French. While he waited, Washington learned that General Clinton did not have enough transports to evacuate by sea all the Philadelphia loyalists who wished to go with him. He would have to give up his troop ships to the civilians and march to New York. While Washington continued to hope that the French fleet would appear, Clinton's army, guarded by Howe's warships, began crossing the Delaware south of Philadelphia to Gloucester Point in New Jersey. At three o'clock on the morning of June 18, the last British troops had left the city, and still there was no sign of the French. Through all this, Washington watched and waited, feeling too weak to challenge the evacuation.

When the patriots reentered Philadelphia, they found that General Howe had used the State House (where Congress met) as a hospital, and had left it in a condition to give the utmost offense to the returning delegates. According to Henry Laurens of South Carolina, the new president of Congress (following John Hancock's resignation in November 1777), "they had opened a large square pit near the House, a receptacle for filth, into which they had cast dead horses and the bodies of men who by the mercy of death had escaped from their further cruelties. . . . a curse on their savage practices."

While Washington kept a close watch on Clinton and looked for signs of the French fleet, he had to consider whether to wait for d'Estaing or attack Clinton while he was in New Jersey, cut off from the Royal Navy. A decisive victory over Clinton would end the war. Despite the torments of the first months at Valley Forge, the American army had emerged from its winter encampment much stronger, and Clinton presented a tempting target. Washington judged that the armies were roughly equal, but he hesitated to risk all in a decisive battle when the French were about to arrive.

Clinton's army stretched for twelve miles and was divided in two, half in front of a long wagon train and the rest behind. In addition to the necessary baggage and provisions for the soldiers, the wagons and packhorses had to carry all the personal accoutrements of the British officers. Bridges and causeways that Washington had destroyed also needed to be reconstructed.

Clinton's march slowed to a crawl. Seeing this, Washington decided to attack his rear; if that went well, he would commit his entire army to a general battle. What came of this plan was the battle of Monmouth Courthouse on June 28.

The day was exceptionally hot, and by nightfall both armies were exhausted. Washington expected the battle to resume the next morning and had his men sleep on their arms. He slept on the battlefield

under a tree—as Clinton stole silently away. With the patriots unable
to stop him, he reached Sandy Hook three days later on July 1.

The day after Clinton evacuated Philadelphia, Admiral Howe, understanding the urgency of the situation, weighed anchor and began
moving his fleet down the Delaware. Alternately encountering
strong headwinds and none at all, he did not enter the Atlantic until
June 28, the day of the battle at Monmouth Courthouse. The following morning, now off the Jersey coast, Howe met the *Grantham*,
a fast packet with dispatches from London containing the first detailed intelligence of d'Estaing's movements. Howe hurried on to
New York. With fair winds, he had his entire fleet safely within the
bar at Sandy Hook on July 1, just in time to meet General Clinton's
troops from New Jersey. Howe immediately set about ferrying them
across the Hudson to Manhattan, and by July 5 the entire force was
secure in the city.

Six days later, Snape Hamond arrived in New York harbor from
Delaware Bay in the *Roebuck* and reported that the frigate *Mermaid*
and the sloop-of-war *Haerlem* had sighted d'Estaing off the coast of
Virginia on the 5th. The following day the *Haerlem* sailed into New
York harbor and reported that d'Estaing was off the Delaware
capes.

On the afternoon of the 11th the entire French fleet hove into
view off Sandy Hook, where d'Estaing dropped anchor. He had
missed trapping Howe in the Delaware by only a few days. "Had a
passage of even ordinary length taken place," Washington wrote
later, "Lord Howe with the British ships of war and all the transports in the river Delaware must inevitably have fallen; and Sir
Henry Clinton must have had better luck than is commonly dis-
pensed to men of his profession under such circumstances, if he
and his troops had not shared at least the fate of Burgoyne."

D'Estaing now had the inferior British fleet trapped in New
York. Howe had six 64-gun battleships, three of 50-guns, two 44-
gun heavy frigates, five smaller frigates, and a few smaller vessels,
while d'Estaing had one 90-gun ship, one 80, six 74s, three 64s, and
one 50, as well as five frigates.

Before seeing d'Estaing off Sandy Hook, Howe thought it likely the Frenchman would attack Newport, which was much easier to approach, and he assisted Clinton in sending reinforcements there. When d'Estaing instead appeared off New York harbor, Howe immediately went into action, placing one 50-gun ship, supported by two smaller vessels and four row-galleys, to contest d'Estaing's entrance over the bar. With fair winds helping him, Howe arranged his weaker fleet so that as the French came into the harbor single file—as they would be forced to do—they would have to sail through the narrow channel that ran past the Hook, over the bar, and into the lower bay, exposing each man-of-war in turn to the fire of all the British warships.

Howe's arrangement gave d'Estaing pause. If he burst into the harbor and fought it out, he stood a good chance of being trapped, his ships badly cut up and unable to put back out to sea. Coming in over the bar was difficult enough, but returning could prove impossible because wind and tide would have to be perfect. Undoubtedly Howe's fleet would have been damaged as well, but d'Estaing knew that Byron was about to reinforce him, while he had no one coming to his aid. If Byron appeared before d'Estaing defeated Howe, the French fleet might be crushed, perhaps putting an end to the war. At a minimum, the West Indies and the rest of the American coast would be left undefended.

Howe held the better hand, and he ardently wished that d'Estaing would challenge him. But the cautious French admiral remained off Sandy Hook, pondering what to do. He studied the problem for eleven days, capturing twenty British supply ships in the meantime.

On the evening of July 22, the entire French fleet disappeared over the horizon. Howe was uncertain where it had gone. Newport seemed the most likely place, in which case he would be needed there to assist Major General Sir Robert Pigot, who had fought so bravely at Bunker Hill and was now in command at Newport with a substantial army of six thousand. But with Byron expected at any moment, Howe did not want to risk his inferior fleet in a premature engagement with d'Estaing. He decided to sail to Newport anyway and put himself in a position to aid Pigot without hazarding his ships unnecessarily, although how he would do that remained unclear.

Howe was right about Newport. Finding New York impossible to attack with any probability of success, d'Estaing and Washington had turned their attention there. On July 17 Washington warned General Sullivan, who had been in command on Rhode Island since March, to be prepared with troops and boats. Sullivan immediately sent out a call for militiamen from Connecticut, Rhode Island, and Massachusetts. The response was all Sullivan or Washington could have wished for. Men and provisions poured into Sullivan's camp outside Newport, and expectations ran high as the New England militiamen prepared for battle, many of them remembering the heady days of Lexington and Concord back in April 1775.

From July 15 through July 20, Washington moved his entire army across the Hudson at King's Ferry and camped at White Plains. From there he sent Lafayette with two brigades under Generals Varnum and Glover to strengthen Sullivan. In addition, Washington temporarily relieved General Greene of his duties as quartermaster general of the army and assigned him to Sullivan, hoping Greene's influence in Rhode Island would be helpful. Washington then ordered Sullivan to divide his army into two divisions, one under Lafayette and the other under Greene.

D'Estaing arrived at Newport on the 29th, dropping anchor off Point Judith seven miles from the entrance to Narragansett Bay. By then General Sullivan's ranks had swollen to eighty-one hundred, seven thousand of whom were militiamen. D'Estaing had four thousand soldiers aboard his ships, making the combined allied force more than enough to defeat Pigot. Greene boarded d'Estaing's flagship to coordinate plans, which, because of the admiral's insistence on etiquette and protocol, wasn't easy. But with Lafayette helping, communications went forward, and a sound plan of attack evolved. Unfortunately the allies did not execute it immediately.

On July 30, the day after d'Estaing arrived, he sent two sail of the line under Bailly de Suffren, the most heralded French naval officer of the day, to anchor in Narragansett Bay on the western side of

Rhode Island at the southern end of Conanicut Island, in the main channel facing Newport. At the same time, two French frigates and a smaller corvette took up positions in Seakonnet Passage on the eastern side of Rhode Island. Seeing them caused General Pigot to burn the 16-gun sloop-of-war *Kingsfisher* and some row-galleys to prevent capture. On August 5 de Suffren moved his two warships closer to town while two more entered the bay, persuading Pigot to remove the guns and crews from five frigates and another sloop-of-war before scuttling them. Three days later d'Estaing brought the rest of his fleet into Newport harbor's main channel and positioned them between Conanicut and Goat islands, where they exchanged fire with Pigot's shore batteries without results.

Meanwhile Lord Howe's fleet had been reinforced in New York by the 64-gun *Raisonable* and the 50-gun *Centurian*, both from Halifax; the 50-gun *Renown* from the West Indies; and the 74-gun *Cornwall*, the first of Byron's storm-tossed fleet to arrive. Howe had been unable to confirm that d'Estaing was making for Newport until July 27, and, hampered by adverse winds, he was unable to leave New York until August 6. He arrived off Point Judith on the 9th, shortly after d'Estaing had disembarked his four thousand troops on Conanicut Island in preparation for the combined attack on Newport the following day.

When he arrived on the scene, Howe had a fair wind to enter Narragansett Bay. Had he chosen to, he might have caught the French, who, between Pigot's shore batteries and the British fleet, would have had difficulty maneuvering. But Howe chose not to. His squadron was still inferior to d'Estaing's, and if he were beaten and Byron did not appear, the French fleet would then command the North American coast and the West Indies. Howe decided not to risk a major battle. He waited cautiously outside Narragansett Bay for reinforcements, while General Clinton was busy assembling four thousand troops in New York to rescue Pigot.

Although Howe hesitated, d'Estaing did not. When he saw the British fleet, he recalled his troops and prepared for battle, assuming a defensive posture for the night. The following morning at seven o'clock, with a favorable northeasterly wind, he cut his cables and

178 IF BY SEA

sortied from Narragansett Bay. He might have instead ignored Howe and continued the assault on Newport with Sullivan, for the wind wasn't favorable for Howe to enter the bay that morning. But, worried about Byron appearing, d'Estaing decided to deal with Howe first, before a combined British fleet could overwhelm him. In two hours he was in the open ocean steering toward the British fleet.

Suddenly deprived of d'Estaing's troops without being consulted, General Sullivan called off his planned attack. And so, merely by arriving, Howe accomplished his immediate objective of relieving Newport. He now turned his attention to the powerful French fleet that had abandoned its strong position in Narragansett Bay and was approaching. Spirits in the British warships soared. Admiral Howe, the master tactician, was in his element, his captains and crews supremely confident that he would prevail.

Howe did not immediately engage, as many of his officers had expected. Instead, he played on d'Estaing's sense of urgency and withdrew south, aiming to gain the weather gauge when the wind turned back to its normal seasonal direction—southeast. The northeast wind, however, continued to strengthen, and the first day ended without shots being exchanged. The following morning, Howe continued to exploit d'Estaing's impatience by retreating and methodically maneuvering to obtain the weather gauge.

Frustrated by Howe's reluctance to fight and conscious of Byron and of the need to return to Narragansett Bay to support Sullivan, d'Estaing permitted Howe to gain the weather gauge, hoping to bring him to battle. As the fleets drew closer, however, the weather grew dirtier. Only two miles separated the two fleets, with Lord Howe almost in position to engage, when the northeaster reached such intensity that both combatants were forced to break off and secure their ships. The storm continued unabated for two days through August 13, scattering the warships.

Colonel Paul Revere, in Newport at the time with his Massachusetts regiment of artillery under Major General John Hancock, wrote to his wife Rachel, "We have had the most severe N. East Storm I ever knew, but thank Heaven, after 48 hours it is over." In fact, it was the storm of the century—the worst in memory. It would still be talked about a hundred years later.

Meanwhile, General Sullivan, enraged by d'Estaing's sudden departure, decided to attack Pigot without French help. Lafayette, who commanded the left wing, urged him to wait for d'Estaing's return. But Sullivan was not to be dissuaded. On the morning of the 11th, before the storm struck, he had prepared to attack. But the severe weather forced him to abandon his plans.

While Sullivan waited for the storm to abate, the French fleet was being torn apart. The mighty flagship *Languedoc* was dismasted. "The bowsprit broke," d'Estaing reported, "then the foremast, then the maintop, then the mizzenmast, [and] finally the mainmast. Our rudder broke next. . . . We were now only a floating mass with nothing to steady us and nothing to guide us." With the *Languedoc* in this condition, the 50-gun British warship HMS *Renown* happened on the scene and attacked. With great difficulty the *Languedoc* managed to bring her stern chasers to bear and drove the *Renown* away. On the same evening, the 50-gun *Preston* came across the badly torn-up 80-gun *Marseilles*, but the British captain decided to wait until morning to attack, and by that time other French warships had appeared, forcing him to retire.

Eventually the battered French fleet gathered off the Delaware capes. One 74 was missing and, in addition to the flagship, the *Marseilles* and the 74-gun *Tonnant* were badly damaged. Not wanting to risk a meeting with Byron in this condition, d'Estaing decided to sail for Boston to make repairs.

Meanwhile, Sullivan and what remained of the besiegers anxiously awaited d'Estaing's return. As the days passed without word of the French, Sullivan grew increasingly nervous, frustrated, and angry.

Finally, on August 20, the French fleet hove back into view off Newport. The patriots exulted, but d'Estaing and his officers, anxious for their ships, were in no mood to fight. D'Estaing offered to help Sullivan retreat, but that was all.

Sullivan felt betrayed. He urged d'Estaing at least to leave his land forces behind. Lafayette strongly supported this idea. He went aboard the flagship with General Greene to argue that all they needed to carry Newport was two days. Moved by Lafayette's plea, d'Estaing wavered. But his principal officers insisted that the admiral follow the letter of his orders, which required him not to hazard the fleet. In case of misfortune, he had been directed to repair to Boston, which he proceeded to do on the 22nd, arriving on the 28th. When the French left, Sullivan's men, foreseeing a slaughter, began a wholesale desertion, two or three thousand leaving in a single day.

Admiral Howe survived the storm in far better shape than d'Estaing; he had gathered his scattered fleet back at Sandy Hook by the 17th and found that only two frigates were beyond immediate repair; the rest could still sail and fight. While they prepared to put to sea, the 64-gun *Monmouth*—the second of Byron's squadron to arrive—joined them. Howe hoped to catch d'Estaing before he reached the safety of Boston, but he was a shade too late. When Howe's fleet reached Newport, d'Estaing had already left. Howe then went after him, neglecting Rhode Island and failing to coordinate with Clinton, who was still planning to trap Sullivan's disintegrating army. Howe could have held the patriots on Rhode Island long enough for Clinton and Pigot to destroy them, but all he could think about was chasing d'Estaing.

Clinton's transports finally managed to leave New York on the 27th with four thousand men aboard but were delayed by fierce headwinds. Warned by Washington, Sullivan began to retreat on the 28th. General Pigot, supported by the sloops-of-war *Vigilant* and *Sphynx*, the *Spitfire* galley, and the brig *Privateer*, was close behind. A heated battle developed between the retreating patriots and Pigot's men, but during the night Sullivan quietly slipped away from his pursuers, reaching Tiverton and the safety of the mainland the following morning.

Although Sullivan had escaped, the entire episode was a huge disappointment for the patriots, who had relied heavily on the French. To his brother John Augustine, Washington wrote, "An unfortunate storm, and some measures taken in consequence of it by the French admiral, blasted in one moment the fairest hopes that ever were conceived; and, from a moral certainty of success, rendered it a matter of rejoicing to get our own troops safe off the island. If the garrison of that place, consisting of nearly six thousand men, had been captured, as there was, in appearance at least, a hundred to one in favor of it, it would have given the finishing blow to British pretensions of sovereignty over this country; and would, I am persuaded, have hastened the departure of the troops in New York, as fast as their canvas wings would carry them."

The day after Sullivan reached Tiverton, Clinton suddenly appeared in Narragansett Bay with seventy vessels and five thousand soldiers—eight regiments of infantry, a battalion of grenadiers, a battalion of light infantry, and two brigades of artillery. He would have crushed Sullivan, but he was too late.

On the same day, Howe arrived off Boston and found his prey well fortified within the confines of the harbor. The French had thrown up a strong new battery at Hull. Faced with the regular Boston defenses and the still-potent guns of the French fleet, the British squadron would have been badly cut up if Howe had tried to enter. He wisely backed off, leaving some frigates to watch d'Estaing while he repaired again to Newport, where he hoped to meet Byron and turn over his command.

At this point, frustrated by missing Sullivan and what would have been a brilliant victory, Clinton angrily carried out the king's orders of March and unleashed Major General Charles Grey to ravage the Massachusetts coast. Grey was the same sanguinary officer who had massacred Anthony Wayne's men at Paoli a year earlier during General Howe's campaign against Philadelphia. Grey relished his assignment. Supported by Admiral Gambier, he conducted a series of gruesome raids on New Bedford and Martha's Vineyard. More than seventy patriot vessels were destroyed on the Acushnet River alone.

Seeking to retaliate and make some sort of statement after the Newport fiasco, Silas Talbot, then a major in the patriot army, with sixty men in the sloop *Hawke* (owned by Governor Nicholas Cooke of Rhode Island), planned to attack the much larger *Pigot*, a two-hundred-ton British schooner armed with eight 12-pounders.

In combination with shore batteries, the *Pigot* dominated the eastern passage of Narragansett Bay, known as the Sekonnet River. During the night of October 28 Talbot, making himself less visible by drifting downriver under bare poles, managed to slip past the British shore batteries undetected and drew close to the *Pigot*. When her marines saw him, they started shooting but Talbot did not reply. Instead, he rammed his jib-boom through the *Pigot*'s fore shrouds, and as he did, his men fired a vicious volley, causing the schooner's crew to scamper below, whereupon Talbot's men boarded and took the ship. Talbot then boldly sailed her out of Narragansett Bay to safety at Stonington, Connecticut. This was the kind of guerrilla operation that should have been the hallmark of the Continental Navy.

Talbot next set his sights on the 50-gun *Renown*, a warship Washington had unsuccessfully attacked with fireships in New York two years before. Talbot's tactics were the kind Admiral Graves had feared—boarding and overwhelming the warship's crew with numbers. Instead of whaleboats, Talbot planned to use a four-hundred-ton merchantman to run alongside the unsuspecting *Renown*. But the merchantman was rendered helpless by ice that formed around and imprisoned her, aborting Talbot's raid.

While this naval activity took place along the southern coast of New England, Captain John Barry was cooling his heels in Boston. Although he lost the *Effingham* without a fight, he performed important services for Washington on the Delaware River during the bleak winter at Valley Forge and maintained an excellent reputation. Barry, a Philadelphian, was sent by the Marine Committee on May 30 to Boston to replace the discredited Captain Thompson and take command of the *Raleigh*. Barry arrived on June 24 and spent many frustrating weeks trying to get to sea. All through the eventful summer, while the critical battle for Newport raged, he remained in Boston repairing his ship.

The frigate *Warren* and Captain Hopkins were also in Boston at the time. Barry hoped the two frigates could be of use to d'Estaing at Newport, but no vessel of the Continental Navy ever worked with the French admiral. Barry saw d'Estaing when his battered ships limped into Boston in late August and then watched as d'Estaing managed to do what Barry could not—repair and provision his ships in a remarkably short time, putting them into good enough shape to sail to the West Indies. Thanks to New England's huge privateer fleet, Boston had the necessary materials to repair and outfit the huge French force. D'Estaing's hard currency ensured Boston's maximum effort, even though its citizens were deeply disappointed by the admiral's inability to produce a decisive victory at Newport.

Captain Barry and the *Raleigh* finally stood out from Boston on September 25, with orders to cruise off the Carolina coast. He set sail at six o'clock in the morning, and at noon spotted two strange sails fifteen miles to leeward. Suspecting them to be powerful British warships, he abandoned his planned trip to the Carolinas, crowded on sail, and fled north away from the strangers. They immediately gave chase, but Barry kept his distance until nightfall, when he lost sight of them. His men remained at their guns through the tense night, and in the morning a thick fog hid his ship. By noon the sky cleared enough to reveal the two warships still following. Soon fog enveloped the entire area again, and night came on without an engagement.

The next morning, the two warships reappeared, and they went after the *Raleigh*. At five o'clock in the afternoon the 28-gun British frigate *Unicorn*, under Captain John Ford, overtook Barry in Penobscot Bay off the Maine coast, and a running battle began. The *Unicorn's* second broadside carried away the *Raleigh's* fore topmast and mizzen topgallant. The wreckage came tumbling down on the deck. Barry's crew worked tirelessly to clear the debris over the side and fired the cannon at the same time. Both captains fought frantically, with Barry ever conscious that the larger British warship, the fearsome 50-gun *Experiment*, under Captain James Wallace, was still coming on. Eventually Wallace drew close enough to cause Barry to stop skirmishing and run for shore, firing at the pursuing *Unicorn*. As darkness fell, Barry reached land, intending to burn the *Raleigh* when he had his men ashore. But the British drew too close, and while Barry was on land with some of his men, one of his remaining officers aboard the *Raleigh* surrendered the ship. Barry was forced to abandon her and flee with his men. The British retrieved the American frigate and later welcomed her into the Royal Navy.

Barry and what remained of his crew made their way through the Maine wilderness back to Boston, arriving in mid-December. By that time d'Estaing had departed, but the port was jammed with privateers, merchantmen, and what was left of the Continental fleet—the *Warren, Providence, Boston, Ranger,* the 32-gun *Deane* and the 28-gun *Queen of France,* both made in France, and the brand-new 32-gun *Alliance,* pride of the fleet, built in Salisbury, Massachusetts, on the Merrimack River. During the year, the Continental Navy had lost the *Washington, Effingham, Randolph, Virginia,* and *Raleigh.* The year before, it had lost the *Congress, Montgomery, Delaware,* and *Hancock.* A new frigate, the *Confederacy,* was being built in Norwich, Connecticut, under the supervision of Captain Seth Harding, but she was far from ready.

With the exception of the *Warren,* all the Continental warships in Boston had been in France during the better part of the year, engaged in nonessential missions. By August all had left Europe, arriving in Boston by the middle of October and remaining there for the rest of the year.

Having frustrated d'Estaing's and Washington's drive for a conclusive victory, Admiral Howe officially turned over his command on September 11 and sailed home in the *Eagle* to battle for his reputation against Germain and Sandwich. Admiral Byron was happy to take over, but he was unable to reassemble his fleet in New York until October 19. He then stood out from Sandy Hook to blockade d'Estaing in Boston harbor or engage him if he attempted to leave. Bad weather, however, continued to plague "Foul Weather Jack Byron." When he reached Boston on the 1st of November, another savage northeaster struck, scattering his fleet once more and forcing him to seek refuge in Newport to refit. While he was there, d'Estaing slipped out of Boston on November 4, bound for the West Indies, to defend the French island of St. Lucia from the British in nearby Barbados.

The Admiralty had long been concerned about growing French strength in the Caribbean. By the time Admiral Howe resigned, France had established a strong presence on four adjacent large islands—Guadeloupe, Dominica, Martinique, and St. Lucia. A force from Martinique, the principal French island, had seized Dominica, a heavily fortified island with a major naval base at Fort Royal. The commander of the British Windward Islands station in Barbados, Rear Admiral Samuel Barrington, one of the better officers in the Royal Navy, had been charged with capturing St. Lucia, but his force was too small. He had only two sail of the line: the 74-gun *Prince of Wales* and the 70-gun *Boyne*. He needed help from the naval and land forces stationed at New York, and he was about to get it. Back in March the king had ordered General Clinton to send Barrington five thousand men.

On November 3, the day before d'Estaing left Boston, British General Grant, with five thousand troops, escorted by two 64-gun sail of the line, three 50-gun warships, and three smaller vessels under Commodore William Hotham, left New York, bound for Barbados. D'Estaing's fleet ran parallel to Hotham's part of the way. The two fleets were unaware of each other until November 25, when one of Hotham's ships fell into d'Estaing's hands. He then learned of the reinforcements being sent to the West Indies, no doubt to be followed by Byron, when he finished repairs at Newport. D'Estaing did not learn precisely where Hotham and Grant were going but knew their likely destination was Antigua or Barbados.

When the British reinforcements arrived in Carlisle Bay, Barbados, on December 10, the resourceful Admiral Barrington was ready to move. Hoping to reach St. Lucia before a French fleet arrived, he set sail only two days later for the island, seventy miles away. By the 14th Barrington, with help from Grant, gained control of two key points of land on the island's western side: the Grand Cul de Sac and La Vigie Point, which overlooked the best anchorages on the island at Port Castries and the Cul de Sac inlet. Barrington set about strengthening both positions against a possible attack from d'Estaing's much stronger force, which arrived later that day.

Barrington's initiative proved decisive. D'Estaing showed his usual impatience and ineptitude by first attempting to attack Barrington's smaller but well-positioned fleet in the Cul de Sac on the 15th. When adverse winds prevented him, he landed seven thousand men and personally led a mindless frontal assault on Grant. The smaller but well-entrenched British force decimated the Frenchmen. D'Estaing withdrew his fleet, only to bring himself into a position to attack Barrington again on the 24th. But Barrington had further fortified his position, and d'Estaing withdrew on the 29th, leaving the British in control of this strategically important island.

Meanwhile, Admiral Byron, having mended his ships, rushed off to the Caribbean to fight d'Estaing, arriving at St. Lucia on January 6, 1779, with ten sail of the line, relieving Barrington of command. For one reason or another, however, Byron and d'Estaing did not get around to doing battle for six months, and when they did engage off Grenada on July 6, only an indecisive skirmish resulted.

While these events were transpiring in the West Indies, General Clinton began carrying out the king's plan for subduing the south, beginning with Savannah, Georgia. On November 27, 1778, Lieutenant Colonel Archibald Campbell left New York with Commodore Hyde Parker and thirty-five hundred men aboard twenty-seven transports and warships. Twenty-six days later, they anchored off Tybee Island at the mouth of the Savannah River, fifteen miles from the city. Commodore Parker noted, "The defense of this province must greatly depend on the naval force upon the different inland creeks. I am therefore forming some galleys covered from musketry, which I believe will have a good effect." He recognized the value of a fleet of row-galleys in lowland waterways, even if the patriots did not.

Opposing the British was a weak force of 850 Continentals and a few militia under General Robert Howe, commander of the Southern Department. Of course, there was no navy to speak of. At the moment, Howe was entangled in a thicket of local politics. The rebel governments of Georgia and South Carolina had all but deserted him. Patriot Governor John Houstoun and militia

Colonel George Walton of Georgia considered Howe an outsider and refused to work with him.

When informed of the patriot weaknesses, Colonel Campbell attacked Savannah immediately. First he secured the river, which was guarded by only two Georgia row-galleys. The man-of-war *Vigilant*, the galley *Comet*, the armed brig *Keppel*, and the sloop-of-war *Greenwich* easily dispatched them. A single shot sent them scurrying. Had there been a large patriot force of row-galleys on the Savannah led by an able commander coordinating with General Howe, they might have mounted a stout defense.

Instead of meeting opposition from the Continental Navy, Campbell sailed up the Savannah unopposed, landing three miles below the city at Girardeau's Plantation, adjacent to the main road into town. Howe stationed his weak force on the road before Campbell, but a slave showed the British how to get around the Americans undetected. Sir James Baird took that route while Campbell waited with the main body facing Howe. Baird struck the patriot infantry from the rear, and Campbell struck from the front, crushing Howe. Eighty-three of his men were killed and 453 taken prisoner. The remainder fled upriver. On December 29, 1778, Campbell marched into Savannah, while Howe and about 250 survivors retreated deep into South Carolina, leaving Georgia to the British.

Coordinating with Campbell, General Augustine Prevost, the British commander in east Florida, moved from his headquarters at St. Augustine into Georgia with two thousand men, planning to join Campbell for the attack on Savannah. But with the patriots so obviously weak, Campbell went ahead without him. Prevost then turned on January 10 and captured Howe's old garrison at Sunbury, a coastal town thirty miles south of Savannah. Later in the month Campbell easily took Augusta, and with a wisdom and maturity rare among British commanders, treated the Georgians with generosity. They flocked to his banner. Georgia's former royal governor, James Wright, returned, and Georgia became a British colony again.

Meanwhile, patriot Major General Benjamin Lincoln was making his way toward Savannah to bolster Howe and take command. Congress had appointed him to replace Howe as head of the

Southern Department back on September 25, 1778, but he had been delayed. Recommended by Washington, who usually had an eye for talent and character, Lincoln was a poor choice, a northerner with an undeserved reputation as a combat leader.

Lincoln had arrived in Charleston on December 7. While he was navigating the shoal-ridden waters of southern politics, trying to organize an army to protect Georgia, Campbell had taken Savannah. Lincoln now had to retake it. He managed to encamp a mixed body of about twenty-five hundred Continentals and militias at Purysburg, South Carolina, on the muddy Savannah, thirty miles from its mouth and fifteen from the city. British General Prevost was on the opposite bank with about three thousand men and the Royal Navy, in control of the river. He moved a small body of infantrymen across the Savannah and took Port Royal Island, thirty miles behind Lincoln. But patriot General Moultrie, who had been in Beaufort, South Carolina, since the first week of February, engaged and forced Prevost back to his former position by the river.

While Lincoln was at Purysburg, fighting between rival militias erupted in the backcountry. On February 14, 1779, patriot Colonel Andrew Pickens of South Carolina, aided by Georgians John Dooly and Elijah Clarke with about three hundred men, defeated seven hundred Tories at Kettle Creek, Georgia.

Heartened by the victories of Moultrie and Pickens, patriots flocked to Lincoln's camp at Purysburg, increasing it to five thousand, inspiring him to cross the Savannah and reclaim Georgia. General Prevost, however, outmaneuvered him and on March 3 devastated a patriot detachment of fourteen hundred under General John Ashe at Briar Creek, fifty miles above Savannah. Lincoln was sent reeling back into South Carolina to regroup.

On April 23 Lincoln again moved into Georgia with about five thousand men. Prevost countered by marching on Charleston, and on May 12 he was outside the city with twenty-five hundred troops demanding its surrender. Lincoln, who had just occupied Augusta (after Campbell had abandoned it), now reversed course and made a forced march on Charleston. To avoid being caught between General Moultrie in Charleston and the oncoming Lincoln, Prevost retreated to nearby James Island and later to Johns Island. He crossed the Ashley River and its adjacent creeks without naval opposition, there being none to defend Charleston, a busy port for privateers. Like many coastal towns, Charleston had ignored its defenses. Even a modest number of row-galleys would have been useful.

On June 16 General Prevost withdrew to Savannah in small boats without opposition, leaving Lieutenant Colonel Maitland with nine hundred men to defend the fortifications at Stono Ferry and Johns Island. Maitland was the same officer who had destroyed all the patriots' shipping, including the Continental frigates *Washington* and *Effingham*, on the Delaware River above Philadelphia in May 1778.

With more than six thousand men, Lincoln and Moultrie planned to attack Maitland, but for some unexplained reason, they deployed only fifteen hundred of them. On June 20 they were easily repulsed. Using small boats, Maitland then withdrew to Beaufort, South Carolina, on Port Royal Island between Savannah and Charleston. He was lucky to have only Lincoln and no patriot row-galleys to oppose him. There matters rested for the remainder of the hot, humid summer of 1779. Either Washington or the Congress might have reacted to Lincoln's inept performance by relieving him, but neither did.

The easy reestablishment of British rule in Georgia in early 1779 was welcome news in London. The king's southern strategy was apparently vindicated; he now had real hope of winning the war. The next step in his grand plan was for General Clinton to take Charleston. Clinton relished the assignment. He hoped to redeem himself for the disaster at Sullivan's Island in 1776, which he continued to blame on Admiral Parker. But the cautious Clinton insisted on being reinforced and having Admiral Gambier recalled before he would move from New York.

A politically potent incompetent, Gambier had arrived in June 1778. Admiral Howe had him relegated to the position of port admiral for New York, where he could do the least harm. Clinton described him as "in every respect a horrid performer." The cabinet agreed and ordered Gambier home on November 11,

1778. But with Admiral Howe retired in England and Byron in the West Indies, Gambier remained commander of the North American fleet through the winter of 1779. He did not finally sail for England until April 5, 1779.

His replacement, sixty-eight-year-old Vice Admiral Marriot Arbuthnot, was hardly an improvement. Blind in one eye and nearly blind in the other, the ailing Arbuthnot was chiefly interested in lining his pockets before retiring and had no interest in fighting. He did not leave England until June 4, 1779, arriving in New York on August 25. In the interim, the energetic, rabidly anti-American Commodore Sir George Collier assumed temporary command. He had considerable military ability and, oddly enough, worked tolerably well with the temperamental Clinton.

Admiral Arbuthnot was transporting the additional troops Clinton required before attacking Charleston. Germain had promised sixty-six hundred to replace those Clinton had sent to the West Indies and Florida. Clinton had asked to be either reinforced or permitted to resign, but after such encouraging news from the south, the king would not let him go. When Arbuthnot arrived in New York he had only thirty-eight hundred troops, a bit more than half the number Clinton had expected, and they were ridden with disease. Confined aboard transports for weeks, the infantrymen had contracted the usual shipboard maladies, which they passed to the troops in New York. Despite the setback, Clinton did not abandon plans to attack Charleston.

While waiting for Arbuthnot to arrive, Clinton turned to raiding, as the king had instructed him to do the previous March. On May 5, 1779, Commodore Collier sailed from New York for Chesapeake Bay with a squadron of warships and eighteen hundred soldiers under Major General Edward Matthews. They arrived on May 10 in the Elizabeth River near Portsmouth, Virginia, taking possession of the town without opposition and staying two weeks, ravaging nearby Norfolk and then Suffolk, Gosport, Kemp's Landing, and other towns, plundering and destroying large caches of military stores. They met so little resistance that Collier wanted to remain and hold Portsmouth, whose inhabitants were unexpectedly friendly. But

General Matthews, fearing rebel militias in the countryside, opposed him. So Collier reluctantly departed on May 24, returning to New York in triumph. Clinton was happy with the limited results. He did not want to establish a permanent post in Portsmouth at this time.

Immediately after Collier's return, Clinton moved up the Hudson with six thousand men to King's Ferry, Washington's main crossing point between New England and the mid-Atlantic. On May 30, Clinton attacked the small fort known as Fort Lafayette, at Verplank's Point on the east side of the river, and the unfinished works at Stony Point on the west side. When the British approached, the patriots at the tiny garrison at Stony Point fled, and the few men in Fort Lafayette surrendered.

Instead of engaging Clinton, Washington withdrew his army from its winter camp at Middlebrook farther up the Hudson to West Point, his major defensive position on the Hudson. Clinton did not feel strong enough to attack that fortress and returned to New York, leaving a substantial force at Verplank and at Stony Point to complete work on the forts.

Clinton turned next to making bloody raids on the Connecticut coast. On July 3 General William Tryon embarked from New York with twenty-six hundred regulars and attacked defenseless New Haven, Fairfield, and Norwalk. Tryon deemed these attacks great victories—just what Germain and the king wanted—but Clinton considered them counterproductive, enraging the inhabitants and strengthening the rebellion.

Washington countered the Connecticut forays with a surprise attack on Stony Point on the night of July 15. The British garrison, although large, was reduced because Tryon had diverted so many troops to Connecticut. Patriot General Anthony Wayne led the charge, his men using only bayonets. After half an hour of hand-to-hand fighting, Wayne's tough veterans overwhelmed the defenders, killing sixty-three, wounding seventy, and capturing an astounding 543. Even so, Washington withdrew, persuaded that holding the fort would require more troops than he could spare.

Clinton reacted to Wayne's surprise attack by bringing Tryon's troops back to New York and retaking Stony Point, rebuilding it, and stationing a larger garrison there. A few weeks later, on August 19, patriot Major Henry "Light-Horse Harry" Lee Jr. attacked Paulus Hook in New Jersey opposite Manhattan and briefly occupied the British post before withdrawing. Clinton then reoccupied it.

In early June, while these minor skirmishes were taking place around New York and Connecticut, British General Francis MacLean and seven hundred Scottish Highlanders set out from Halifax to capture Castine (then Bagaduce) in the Maine district of Massachusetts. Captain Henry Mowat, the man who had incinerated Falmouth, supported MacLean with a small naval escort consisting of Mowat's flagship, the 16-gun sloop-of-war *Albany*, the miniature frigate *Nautilus* of 14 guns, under Captain John Collins, and the 10-gun armed sloop *North*. Mowat's orders were to establish a naval base at Castine. From there, he could attack American and French privateers, provide a safe haven for loyalists driven from their homes, and most importantly, protect the white-pine mast traffic moving between Penobscot Bay and Halifax. Without these huge trees, the British North American fleet would have to send many more of its damaged men-of-war back to England for repairs.

Alert to the danger, the Massachusetts General Court on June 26 began organizing an expedition to dislodge MacLean and Mowat. It gave Brigadier General Solomon Lovell of the Massachusetts state militia command of twelve hundred militiamen, including Lieutenant Colonel Paul Revere's artillerymen. It secured permission to use Continental vessels and organized a mixed fleet under Captain Dudley Saltonstall of the Continental Navy to support Lovell. Saltonstall's force consisted of three Continental warships: the 12-gun sloop *Providence* under Captain Hoysted Hacker, Saltonstall's 32-gun frigate *Warren*, and Captain Brown's 14-gun swift brig *Diligent*, formerly a British warship that Hacker had captured earlier that spring. The entire Massachusetts navy of two armed vessels, the brigantines *Active* and *Tyrannicide*, was included, as was New Hampshire's single state warship, *Hampden*. Sixteen Massachusetts privateers, ranging from sixteen to twenty guns, were also pressed into service, along with twenty-one transports. The warships carried eight hundred marines. Expecting an easy victory, the Massachusetts General Court made no effort to inform General Washington, much less coordinate with him.

Captain Saltonstall had replaced Captain John Hopkins as commander of the 32-gun *Warren*. Hopkins had fallen into disfavor for using the navy for personal gain, as his uncle Esek Hopkins had done.

Lovell and Saltonstall shared command. They left Boston on July 18, arriving off Castine on the 25th. Noting the size of the patriot force, the British commander, MacLean, who occupied a small, half-completed fort overlooking Castine harbor, sent to New York and Halifax for reinforcements. Captain Mowat, meanwhile, waited at the mouth of the harbor with a miniscule fleet of three warships and four transports rigged as fireships. Instead of attacking Mowat immediately, Commodore Saltonstall engaged in a meaningless long-range exchange of fire, which did little damage to either fleet, then ceased for the night. The next day, the patriots captured Banks Island at the entrance to the harbor, strengthening their position. Saltonstall, however, did not press the attack, as his Continental officers, the commanders of the privateers, and the captains of the state warships were urging. Instead, he waited until the following day and engaged in another pointless long-range duel with Mowat.

Meanwhile, General Lovell landed his troops on the mainland. He placed the fort at St. George under siege but did not assault it, giving the defenders more time to prepare. But Saltonstall and Lovell argued endlessly over tactics. Lovell wanted Saltonstall to attack, but even with his overwhelmingly superior numbers, Saltonstall didn't want to make a move until the cannon at Fort George were silenced.

While the patriot commanders haggled, the British rushed reinforcements to the scene. On August 13 Commodore George Collier appeared suddenly from New York with the 64-gun *Raisonable*; frigates *Blonde*, *Virginia*, *Greyhound*; and three sloops-of-war, *Camilla*, *Galatea*, and *Otter*. He attacked the patriots without hesitation, and pandemonium broke loose. The captains of the American warships, having lost all faith in Saltonstall, ran for the nearby Penobscot River, as did Saltonstall, who didn't waste any time showing his heels. It was every man for himself. Saltonstall eventually blew up the *Warren*. In all, twenty-eight scarce patriot warships were either captured or destroyed.

When the patriot militiamen heard of the approaching British, they ran for their transports and sailed for the Penobscot River. As General Lovell later described the scene, "four [British warships] pursued seventeen [patriot] armed vessels, nine of which were stout ships. Transports on fire, men-of-war blowing up every kind of stores on shore, throwing about, and as much confusion as can possibly be believed."

Collier had won an easy victory, but in doing so he left New York unguarded against Admiral d'Estaing, whose fleet, then in the West Indies, might have been sailing for North America, as it had the previous year. Even before Collier left New York for Castine, General Clinton had been anxious about the French fleet, but Collier had convinced him the danger was slight. Admiral Arbuthnot was also sailing for New York, which he reached during the third week of August. For a brief period, however, New York was left undefended. And even when Collier and Arbuthnot were both there, the threat from d'Estaing remained. His West Indian fleet contained thirty-three warships, more than enough to dominate the waters around New York and Newport. Only two weeks after the Castine debacle and before Arbuthnot arrived, d'Estaing's entire fleet turned up suddenly off the coast of Georgia at Savannah. Had he been more astute, d'Estaing might have appeared before New York or Newport, giving Washington an opportunity to deliver a crushing blow to Clinton.

For his bizarre, cowardly behavior, Saltonstall was dismissed from the service. But no one questioned why the Continental Navy's best officers were not in command. Had John Paul Jones been leading, the battle for Castine would have gone quite differently. When Commodore Collier happened on the scene, he would have met with a much different reception, and the battle for Castine might have been won by the patriots.

Actually, John Paul Jones was in Europe at the time, hoping to play an important part in the grand Franco-Spanish invasion of England, planned for the summer of 1779. King Louis, urged on by Vergennes, had decided to join with Spain and attack Britain directly across the English Channel. The king did not aim to conquer the British, which would have been impossible, but to capture an important port such as Portsmouth and force a negotiation, which might result in American independence, Spain's regaining Gibraltar, and above all, Britain's humiliation.

When d'Estaing failed to win a quick victory in America, Foreign Minister Vergennes had considered it urgent for France to ally herself with Madrid. He thought he needed help from the dons in order to succeed against England, particularly at sea.

The Spanish monarch, Charles III, insisted on a joint Franco-Spanish invasion of England, which he thought would end the war quickly. This was necessary, in his view, to protect Spain's colonial empire in the Caribbean and in North America. Above all, he wanted Gibraltar and Minorca. He had already tried to obtain them from Britain as the price of his neutrality. But London would never part with Gibraltar, and so Charles chose France and war, signing a secret treaty with Paris at Aranjuez near Madrid on April 12, 1779.

The French minister of marine, Sartine, preoccupied with the invasion of England, found a role for John Paul Jones to play in it. His *Ranger* had sailed home the previous year, while Jones remained in France looking for a larger ship and a more glorious mission. His cruise in the *Ranger* had thrilled Paris, and Sartine was anxious to employ him. He thought Jones might act as a distraction while the larger Franco-Spanish fleets battled for control of the English Channel.

Jones's small command consisted of the 40-gun *Bonhomme Richard*, the 36-gun American frigate *Alliance,* the 26-gun French frigate *Pallas*, the 12-gun brig *Vengeance*, the 18-gun cutter *Cerf,* and two privateers, *Monsieur* and *Grandville*. Sartine expected Jones to do what he had done so successfully in the *Ranger*—circle the British Isles, take what prizes came his way, perform what mischief he could, visit any port he might choose to terrorize, and create enough alarm to cause the Admiralty to divert some of its larger warships to go after him. Dr. Franklin warned Jones, "Although the English have wantonly burned many defenseless towns in America, you are not to follow this example."

By the time Jones set out from Groix Roadstead off L'Orient on August 14, however, the Franco-Spanish invasion had already collapsed. French Admiral d'Ovilliers did not formally call off the attack and enter Brest with the Spanish fleet until September 10, but the invasion threat was over by the middle of August. The main fleets never engaged. The French and Spanish found it so difficult to coordinate their navies that delays had allowed scurvy, typhus, and smallpox to ravage the French warships. By August they bore a greater resemblance to floating morgues and hospitals than to a fighting fleet. D'Ovilliers had no choice but to return to port.

While the invasion of England had failed, Jones, in the most trying circumstances, had succeeded brilliantly. At the outset of his mission, he had been unable to gain the cooperation of his squadron captains. Landais of the *Alliance*, who was French, refused to work with him and went his own way. Captain Cottineau of the *Pallas* and Lieutenant de Vaisseau Ricot of the *Vengeance* cooperated only when they pleased. The *Cerf*, under Ensign de Vaisseau Varage, disappeared early in the voyage along with the two French privateers. Even though Jones could not control his squadron, he obtained an unusual degree of loyalty and cohesiveness aboard the *Richard*.

After a voyage plagued with difficulties, Jones and his squadron were cruising in the North Sea off the east coast of England near Flamborough Head on the afternoon of September 23 when lookouts spied forty-one sail bearing north-northeast. This was the huge British Baltic convoy of merchantmen, and it was guarded by the 50-gun heavy frigate HMS *Serapis* and the 20-gun small frigate *Countess of Scarborough*. Mounting twenty 18-pounders, twenty 9s, and ten 6s, the *Serapis* was a formidable fighting machine. With a copper bottom, an experienced captain, and a well-trained crew, she was much stronger and more maneuverable than the *Richard*.

The merchant vessels hoisted all sail and scurried for cover as the two British warships steered toward Jones. It was what he had been waiting for, and he "crowded every possible sail" to join the battle. But his squadron deserted him. *Alliance* ignored Jones's signals and refused to fight. *Vengeance* stood by and watched. Only the *Pallas* engaged. She took on the *Countess of Scarborough* while Jones dealt with *Serapis*.

After being deserted by *Alliance* and *Vengeance,* Jones would have been justified in avoiding combat. Instead, he eagerly sought a fight. What ensued was one of the most famous battles in American naval history. At seven in the evening the action between the *Bonhomme Richard* and *Serapis* began "with unremitting fury," Jones reported. The two ships were within pistol shot of each other. Jones knew from the start that his only chance was to close with the *Serapis* and neutralize her speed, agility, and firepower. "As I had to deal with an enemy of greatly superior force," he wrote in his narrative, "I was under the necessity of closing with him, to prevent the advantage which he had over me in point of maneuver." Miraculously, Jones succeeded. In the course of the battle, "the ships [eventually] lay square alongside of each other, the yards being entangled, and the cannon of each ship touching the opponents side."

By eight o'clock, all of the *Richard*'s 12-pounders under stalwart First Lieutenant Richard Dale had been silenced. Jones's 18-pounders had been out of action from the beginning when two of them exploded, and Jones had ordered all of them to cease firing. Only four 9-pounders were serviceable, and they were on the *Richard*'s quarterdeck. Jones managed to get three of them operating and commanded them himself, playing on the mainmast of the *Serapis*. He also had the three tops heavily armed with swivels, coehorns, muskets, and grenades. Twenty men were in the maintop, fourteen in the foretop, and nine in the mizzen top, led by midshipmen, one of whom was Nathaniel Fanning. They won the battle of the tops during the first hour, managing to clear the *Serapis*'s main deck. She continued firing 18-pounders from her lower gun deck, however, pouring fire into the *Richard*'s hull and tearing her guts out.

The battle raged on, with Jones refusing to give up, continuing to pound away, and Captain Pearson of the *Serapis* doing the same. Midshipman Fanning's men crossed over to the *Serapis*'s tops and threw grenades down on her deck. One of them tumbled down the steps to a lower deck, igniting, according to Captain Pearson, "a cartridge of powder . . . the flames of which running from cartridge to cartridge all the way aft, blew up the whole of the people and officers quartered abaft the main mast, from which unfortunate circumstance all those guns were rendered useless for the remainder of the action."

At nine-thirty the *Alliance* appeared unexpectedly in the moonlight and plunged into the fray, firing at both combatants. Shocked, Jones frantically signaled her to stop, but she kept blasting away, giving the *Richard* a full broadside. Landais then stopped firing and sailed away out of sight. But in half an hour he returned and delivered another broadside into both combatants, before disappearing into the darkness once more. Landais later claimed that he was aiming at the *Serapis* and hit the *Richard* by mistake.

The exhausted combatants fought on. The "scene was dreadful beyond the reach of language," Jones later recalled. Nearly four hundred men on both sides, about half their complements, were either killed or wounded. Finally, at ten-thirty, Captain Pearson struck his colors. Getting himself entwined with the *Richard* was the tactical error that robbed him of his advantages and caused his defeat.

Jones had achieved an improbable victory over one of England's finest warships. The *Alliance* and *Vengeance* saw the American flag flying over both combatants, as did the *Pallas*, which had defeated the *Countess of Scarborough*. All three then rejoined Jones. The unstable Captain Landais in the *Alliance* hated Jones but reluctantly followed his orders, awaiting his next chance to destroy him. Jones transferred his command to the wounded but still serviceable *Serapis* and tried to save the battered *Richard*, but she was too far gone. A few days later he let her sink. He then led his squadron in a zigzag route toward neutral Holland. Continuous bad weather in the North Sea slowed his progress, but also concealed him from the pack of hunters the Admiralty had looking for him. Ten days later the *Serapis* and the others limped into the Dutch port of Texel Island, securing Jones's triumph.

This battle had no strategic effect on the outcome of the war, but it had a huge political impact in France, America, and England. The Admiralty received more hysterical letters over its inability to deal with Jones than it had for any other matter in British history. The French were ecstatic and made Jones an even bigger hero than he already was. In America his brave actions would make him the most celebrated hero in the Continental Navy.

6

DENOUEMENT

September 1779–September 1783

While John Paul Jones was giving his virtuoso performance and the invasion of England was collapsing, the Franco-American allies were suffering another defeat at Savannah, Georgia. On the 1st of September 1779, when Admiral d'Estaing had appeared unexpectedly off Tybee Island at the mouth of the Savannah River, he had his entire West Indian fleet of twenty sail of the line, two 50-gun ships, eleven frigates, and supporting transports carrying six thousand troops. It was the height of the hurricane season, something he worried about constantly.

Washington had been waiting since spring for d'Estaing to pay his annual visit to North America, expecting to organize a joint attack on New York or Newport, and was making plans accordingly. If d'Estaing came north, Washington anticipated raising an army of twenty-five thousand. By September 29, however, it was clear to him that d'Estaing was concentrating on Savannah. South Carolina Governor John Rutledge and General Moultrie had sent messages to d'Estaing pleading with him to attack Savannah, and he was responding to them. Nonetheless, Washington continued to hope that if d'Estaing succeeded in Savannah, he would then sail north.

When the French fleet arrived, General Lincoln was in Charleston, surprised by its sudden appearance. There had been no previous communication from d'Estaing, but Lincoln hurriedly put a force together and marched to Savannah, expecting to conduct a joint operation.

British General Prevost was defending Savannah with a small force of twelve hundred, but as soon as he became aware of the danger, he moved quickly to increase his strength, hoping the patriots would delay and allow him time to prepare. They did, and his force grew to thirty-two hundred, largely because he was able to move Colonel Maitland's 850 troops from Beaufort to Savannah. Had patriot row-galleys been patrolling the network of waterways Maitland had to cross, he could have been stopped and Savannah liberated.

Lincoln finally managed to connect with d'Estaing on September 16. With France's entire West Indian fleet sitting exposed in the Atlantic, the admiral continued to worry about hurricanes. After seeing how strong Prevost had become, d'Estaing thought seriously of leaving.

Lincoln and his men were having greater difficulty working with the Frenchman than Sullivan had at Newport. He eventually prevailed on d'Estaing to remain and fight, but the allies did not bombard Savannah until October 3, more than a month after d'Estaing's arrival. After an intense five-day attack, Prevost refused to surrender. Finally, at four in the morning, the combined Franco-American force made a frontal assault on the town and suffered a severe repulse. D'Estaing gave up and prepared to leave, anxious as ever for his fleet. He departed the coast on October 19, regretting the outcome of the battle but feeling lucky that no hurricane had struck during that time. He sailed home to Europe, sending part of his fleet back to the West Indies in two divisions under de Grasse and La Motte-Picquet by participating in d'Estaing's venture. Admiral de Grasse thus gained the experience of bringing an entire fleet to the American coast; he would use that knowledge to great effect in 1781.

Prevost now held Savannah securely, making a later attack on Charleston more feasible. Lincoln then returned to South Carolina, leaving Georgia in British hands.

When General Clinton in New York had been informed of d'Estaing's appearance, he feared an attack on Manhattan. Now he was pleased that the French fleet was aiming at Savannah. But after that, what? Clinton prepared by withdrawing his troops from Kings Ferry on October 7 and from Newport a few days later, bringing his army in Manhattan up to twenty-five thousand. He was greatly relieved when d'Estaing sailed home.

The victory at Savannah could now be followed by an attack on Charleston, just as the king had ordered. Clinton wrote to Eden, "I think this is the greatest event that has happened the whole war." With the number of troops he had in Manhattan, Clinton could leave a substantial force to protect it from Washington and attack Charleston at the same time. By the end of December he was ready. Leaving General Knyphausen in command in New York, Clinton boarded his personal warship on Christmas Day, joining the rest of the fleet under Admiral Arbuthnot at Sandy Hook. The winter was one of the coldest on record. Seven troop transports had already been damaged by floating ice. The following day Clinton went to sea with eighty-five hundred freezing soldiers, their horses, and equipage.

The gigantic fleet of 106 ships included five battleships—*Europe, Robust, Raisonable, Russell,* and *Defiance*—a 50-gun ship, and seven frigates. The first of a series of potent winter storms struck the very next day. Savannah was the rendezvous point, and normally it took ten days to reach there from New York; it took Clinton and Arbuthnot five weeks. The battered fleet was unable to regroup off Tybee Island at the mouth of the Savannah River until January 30, 1780, and not until February 11 did Clinton enter North Edisto inlet and land on Johns Island, thirty miles south of Charleston.

After Clinton disembarked on Johns Island, Admiral Arbuthnot began a blockade of Charleston harbor, stationing his warships outside the bar. Clinton then dallied before seizing Stono Ferry, which connected Johns Island to James Island. On March 6 he took Fort Johnson on James Island, and the next day crossed over to the mainland. But exercising his usual caution, he did not cross the Ashley River onto Charleston's peninsula until the 29th.

Clinton's snail's pace was no help to the patriots. Even though General Prevost's maneuvers earlier should have ignited a burst of energy to improve their land defenses, Charlestonians had neglected them. They only began to tend to them when they saw Clinton, and by that time it was too late. The Continental Navy, however, was on the scene and ready to help. Having gotten wind of Clinton's plan to attack Charleston months before he left New York, the Marine Committee ordered Commodore Abraham Whipple of Rhode Island there with a powerful fleet. Whipple left Nantasket Roads off Boston on November 23 with the Continental frigates *Boston* of 24 guns, the 28-gun *Providence*, the 28-gun *Queen of France*, and John Paul Jones's old sloop-of-war, the 18-gun *Ranger*. When he arrived in Charleston on December 23, 1779, Whipple found the *Bricole*, 44, the *Truite*, 26, the *General Moultrie*, 20, the *Notre Dame*, 16, the *L'Aventure*, 26, and the polacre, *Zephyr*, 18, of the South Carolina navy. Whipple's force might have been even larger, but three French frigates that had planned to winter in Charleston left when they received word that a British fleet was coming.

Before Whipple arrived in Charleston, the failed Marine Committee of Congress, which had run the navy since succeeding the ad hoc Naval Committee in December 1775, had been replaced by the five-member Board of Admiralty on October 28, 1779. The new administrative body was composed of two members of Congress and three commissioners. But it kept making the same old mistakes, and the navy continued to deteriorate.

Appointing Commodore Whipple to command the fleet at Charleston was yet another example of the inability to position the best leaders where they were most needed. For the first time, the Continental fleet was being tested in a major battle. Commodore Whipple had never commanded such a force or participated in a fleet action, nor had he ever shown any stomach for it. He had no conception of how to employ his forces and gave no thought to challenging Clinton as he crossed Stono Creek, Wappoo Cut, and the Ashley River, nor to disputing Arbuthnot's crossing of the bar, when the British fleet would be most vulnerable. He might have organized swarms of gunboats and whaleboats to challenge Arbuthnot at that point, but he did not.

Instead, on February 27, Whipple informed General Lincoln, who had overall command of Charleston, that he was unable to oppose Arbuthnot as his warships crossed the notoriously difficult bar because there was no satisfactory anchorage for the patriot fleet. Whipple argued that his ships could best be employed by coordinating with Fort Moultrie on Sullivan's Island to create a crossfire that would attack the British fleet as it entered the harbor.

On March 14 Colonel John Laurens, Washington's aide on the scene, wrote his estimate of the situation to the commander in chief. "The Commodore and all his officers renounce the idea of defending the passage over the bar; they declare it impracticable for the frigates to lie in a proper position for that purpose. The government has neglected to provide floating batteries, which might have been stationed there, so that it has been agreed, as the next best plan, to form a line of battle in such a manner as to make a crossfire with Fort Moultrie, a shoal called the Middle Grounds being on the right of the ships, and the fort advanced on the left. As it would be the enemies policy, with a leading wind and tide, to pass the fire of the fort and run aboard of our ships, the Commodore is contriving an obstruction which he thinks will obstruct their progress and allow time for the full effect of our fire.

"The impracticality of defending the bar, in the first instance appears to me a great diminution of our means of defense. . . . The Commodore has destroyed one set of the enemy's buoys, and I hope he will cut away such as may have been since put down, and order the galleys to give all possible annoyance to the enemy's ships in the act of entering."

Actually, when the time came to fight, Whipple not only failed to dispute Arbuthnot's entrance over the bar but put up no defense at all, allowing Arbuthnot to approach the harbor's entrance. And then, as the British fleet prepared to engage, Whipple ran. In his report to the Admiralty, Arbuthnot wrote, "[After seeing to the landing of the army], preparations were next made for passing the squadron over the Charleston bar, where at high water spring tides there is only 19 feet of water. The guns, provisions, and water were taken out of the *Renown, Roebuck,* and *Romulus* to lighten them, and we lay in that situation on the open coast in the winter season of the year, exposed to the insults of the enemy for sixteen days, before an opportunity offered of going into the harbor, which was effected without any accident on the 20th of March, notwithstanding the enemy's galleys continually attempted to prevent our boats from sounding the channel. . . . The enemy naval force . . . made an appearance of disputing the passage up the river at the narrow pass between Sullivan's Island and the Middle Ground, having moored their ships and galleys in a position to make a raking fire as we approached Fort Moultrie, but on the squadron arriving near the bar and anchoring on the inside, they abandoned that idea, retired to the town and changed their plan of defense."

Arbuthnot brought only nine warships and three transports into the harbor. He left his large battleships outside and never even considered floating them over the bar, even at high spring tide. There were only four left now; *Defiance* had been lost to the weather. Arbuthnot worried that a large French fleet might appear at any moment, as had happened the previous two years, and overpower his relatively small squadron. But, worried or not, he had to press on, and he made his way unopposed over the bar, past Fort Moultrie, and then into the harbor. One of the transports caught fire coming in and had to be destroyed, but other than that he made it in with no trouble.

Instead of fighting this by no means overwhelming force, Commodore Whipple withdrew his fleet up the Cooper River to the channel between the town and Shute's Folly, an island, where he sank four patriot frigates and some merchant vessels as part of a log-and-chain obstruction strung across the river. Whipple stationed his remaining warships behind the barrier, but except for the *Ranger* and *Queen of France*, he removed all their guns and men to the town to strengthen its defenses.

After seeing Whipple retreat, the irascible, unpredictable Arbuthnot anchored in the upper harbor for the rest of the battle. He refused to cooperate with Clinton by attacking Whipple, removing the obstructions on the Cooper, and cutting off the American army's last avenue of escape. Clinton urged the admiral to secure the Cooper River and thereby seal General Lincoln in the town, but Arbuthnot refused, saying it wasn't safe for his frigates because of possible artillery fire from the land.

Clinton was furious, but he could not make Arbuthnot budge and had to devise other means of trapping Lincoln. On April 14 Clinton sent Tarleton's Legion and Major Patrick Ferguson's Tory volunteer riflemen, a total of fifteen hundred men, to seize control of the far side of the river. Tarleton moved swiftly, surprising patriot General Isaac Huger at Monck's Corners and defeating him. That opened the way for Clinton to close off Lincoln's last way out of Charleston.

General Lachlan McIntosh, an important political figure in Georgia whom Washington had sent south to aid Lincoln, had urged him to evacuate over the Cooper when he still had the chance, but, typically, Lincoln hesitated until it was too late.

Meanwhile, Clinton took his time approaching Charleston, drawing additional men from New York and Georgia until his army had swollen to ten thousand. His methodical advance was slowed because he insisted on establishing secure posts as he moved forward, protecting his line of retreat to the fleet, as Howe had always done.

Pressured by Congress and nearly all of Charleston's patriot leadership, including Governor Rutledge, Christopher Gadsden, and Charles Cotesworth Pinckney, General Lincoln decided to remain in the city with his entire army of fifty-five hundred and defend the Charleston peninsula to the last, even though he was outnumbered by two to one. The only patriot leader to urge retreat was General McIntosh. Lincoln himself believed that Charleston could be held with a force half the size of Clinton's. With no way to evacuate, he was risking the patriots' entire Southern Army.

On April 13 Clinton began an intense bombardment of the town from lines that stretched across the peninsula from the Ashley to the Cooper River. His approach was conventional and careful, as had been his entire operation. By early May, Lincoln's outer defenses collapsed, and on the 6th, Fort Moultrie surrendered to a land party of British marines. On the 12th Lincoln surrendered his entire force, suffering the worst patriot debacle of the war.

Commodore Whipple never got into the fight. If he had fought as he had originally proposed in cooperation with Fort Moultrie, where Colonel Pinkney had twenty guns, he might well have stopped Arbuthnot and changed the course of the battle. Arbuthnot's small fleet never saw action either. The two naval commanders had merely observed.

Every vessel in Commodore Whipple's fleet was either destroyed or captured, and he was taken prisoner, as were Lincoln, Gadsden, Pinkney, and McIntosh. The *Providence* 28, *Queen of France* 28, *Boston* 24, *Ranger* 18, and a few smaller vessels fell into enemy hands. The *Providence, Boston,* and *Ranger* were eventually taken into the Royal Navy. All that now remained of the Continental Navy were the 32-gun *Alliance,* the 32-gun *Hague* (formerly the *Deane*), the 32-gun *Confederacy,* the 28-gun *Trumbull,* and a ship or two bought or borrowed in Europe. Because no funds were available, Congress did not attempt to add to this number, and its naval reliance on France became total. Whipple's bad judgment and cowardice had, to all intents and purposes, ruined what was left of the Continental Navy.

The defeat at Charleston stunned America, emboldened the king, and had a sobering effect on the Comte de Vergennes. Less than a month later, word came of a French fleet en route to America, and on June 8, Clinton and Arbuthnot rushed back to defend New York, leaving Lord Cornwallis with an army of eight thousand to subdue the rest of South Carolina and then North Carolina. Clinton wanted Cornwallis to proceed slowly, as he had done at Charleston, securing all "liberated" territory as he went. Neither Clinton nor Cornwallis was cautious about dividing the army between north and south, leaving both forces vulnerable. They assumed that Cornwallis would win the south easily, and that Clinton had more than enough men to handle Washington's weak army. They were confident as well that the

Royal Navy would maintain naval supremacy, making a combined Franco-American land and sea attack impossible.

Arriving in New York on June 18, Clinton discovered that a French fleet was indeed on the way, its destination Rhode Island. His intelligence came from Benedict Arnold, who had been feeding him information from time to time during the year—nearly all of it accurate. The size of the fleet, though, was unknown. Clinton pressured Arbuthnot to secure Newport before the French arrived but Arbuthnot refused, wanting confirmation they were actually coming and, more importantly, reinforcements. It was now clear that Clinton and Arbuthnot, whose relationship had never been amicable, could no longer work together. Not only had Arbuthnot performed dreadfully at Charleston, but he and Clinton argued endlessly over the spoils of victory. Their quarrel would last for years.

While Arbuthnot and Clinton dithered, on July 11 French Admiral de Ternay and seven ships of the line, convoying General Rochambeau and an army of six thousand men, slipped into Newport unmolested. Before leaving Brest on May 1, Rochambeau's men had spent twenty-seven days aboard ship and then endured another sixty-six at sea. When they landed, a third of them were suffering from scurvy. Clinton urged Arbuthnot to attack this weakened force immediately, but the admiral had no desire to risk his ships or cooperate with Clinton. Even with clear naval superiority, he claimed he needed reinforcements.

They arrived on July 13 when Rear Admiral of the Blue Thomas Graves, a younger cousin of Admiral Samuel Graves, sailed into New York harbor with six battleships, all with copper bottoms, which made them faster than any French sail of the line. The Admiralty had dispatched Graves to intercept de Ternay, and he had departed England on May 17.

This would have been the perfect time to attack Newport, but Clinton and Arbuthnot, continuing to feud, let this opportunity slip away. And the longer they waited, the stronger the French became, until attacking them would have meant a major fight. Thus they permitted a large French force to settle in the best harbor on the east coast within striking distance of New York.

Meanwhile, on June 13 the Congress, horrified by what had happened to General Lincoln and Charleston, gave command of the Southern Army to the victor of Saratoga, Horatio Gates, without consulting Washington, who had recommended Lincoln.

Gates left his Virginia plantation and arrived in North Carolina on July 25, 1780, to take command of a small patriot army of three thousand assembled at Coxe's Mill on the Deep River, commanded by Baron de Kalb, a Bavarian. Two-thirds of the Americans were raw militiamen, but Gates ignored their inexperience and immediately attacked the British post at Camden, South Carolina. There on August 16 he ran into Lord Cornwallis and twenty-two hundred regulars. The British veterans crushed Gates, who fled the battlefield like a raw recruit and left the Continentals and the brave de Kalb to fend for themselves. He did not rest until he had ridden all the way to Hillsboro, North Carolina, 180 miles from Camden.

Gates's defeat and flight from the battlefield surprised and sickened the already dispirited Congress. Patriot morale plummeted further. General Rochambeau had written his first dispatch to Vergennes on July 16, describing a desperate situation for Washington, who had only three to four thousand men and a plummeting currency. After receiving a halfhearted welcome at Newport, Rochambeau reported that the patriots were weary and depressed. No one was on the streets to greet him; apprehensive faces peered from every window. Nevertheless Rochambeau remained optimistic, believing that the country could still summon the energy to support a successful war. Gates's defeat, however, caused dismay in Paris.

London, of course, was elated. Cornwallis's standing with the king soared as His Majesty compared him favorably to his inactive commander in chief, Clinton, in New York. Despite the king's impatience, Clinton allowed the rest of the summer to pass without taking action against Newport. He was planning a far bigger victory than Cornwallis's at Camden, one that would finally break the backs of the reeling patriots: a surprise capture of West Point.

Washington, although disappointed by Gates's defeat, was encouraged by the promise that a French force equal to Rochambeau's was on its way. On August 25, however, Rochambeau informed him that the second contingent of French troops was blockaded at Brest. This shocking announcement was followed by worse news. On September 14 ten British battleships arrived unexpectedly in New York from the West Indies. Washington was flabbergasted; he had expected a French fleet, not a British one. And leading it was a celebrated fighter, Sir George Brydges Rodney, Admiral of the White, commander in chief of the Leeward Islands station. He was not an incompetent like Arbuthnot or Gambier, Samuel Graves or Thomas Graves, but one of the most talented warriors in the Royal Navy. He may not have been the equal of Lord Howe, but he was far better than the fourth-rate admirals Lord Sandwich had been sending.

During the first months of 1780 Admiral Comte de Guichen, having replaced d'Estaing as commander of the French West Indian squadron, had been dueling Rodney in the Caribbean. In July he arrived at Cap François, the major French base in Saint-Domingue, where he found letters from Lafayette and the French minister to America, La Luzerne, urging him to bring his fleet to the American coast, as d'Estaing had done, for a decisive move against the British. De Guichen had twenty-nine sail of the line but declined their urgent request. Leaving ten battleships at Cap François, he sailed home with the rest, claiming, truthfully, that he had no orders to sail to America. Thus 1780 passed without a French fleet appearing off the American coast to work with Washington.

Rodney, however, believed that de Guichen was sailing to New York and rushed to counter him. Of course Rodney was coming north to avoid the Caribbean storms, but he also hoped to strengthen the king's cause in America. Once he arrived, the British had overwhelming naval superiority and could have crushed the French fleet at Newport and retaken the city. De Ternay and Rochambeau, along with Washington, expected Rodney and Clinton to do just that.

Rodney urged an immediate attack on Newport and Admiral Graves supported him, but Arbuthnot did not. He had been outraged when Rodney appeared out of the blue to assume command

and with it, all the money Arbuthnot thought was his as commander of the station. Clinton sided with Arbuthnot, considering the combined American-French land force at Newport too strong to attack. He thought Washington might assemble a huge army and inflict a crushing defeat. Rodney disagreed but, new to the scene, he bowed to Clinton's superior knowledge.

Rather than fighting an uncertain battle for Newport, Clinton was more interested in acquiring West Point bloodlessly from Benedict Arnold. While he was military governor of Philadelphia, Clinton had maintained a secret correspondence with Arnold, who passed him important and accurate intelligence. To be of real use, however, Arnold had to leave Philadelphia and obtain a vital post. He convinced Washington to give him command of West Point and then made a bargain with Clinton to turn over the fortress in return for a general's commission and £20,000 if he succeeded in handing over the fort, and £6,000 if he failed.

Clinton was convinced that capturing the fortress would end the war. So, although Rodney's fleet gave him the opportunity to take Newport and West Point and to set up a post in Chesapeake Bay to aid Cornwallis as well, he demurred. Rodney advocated attacking all three places; in his judgment, the combined actions would really end the war. But he was forced to go along with Clinton.

Conquering the New York highlands had been a fixation of Clinton's ever since 1777. He abandoned that ambition only when General Howe insisted on reinforcements for Philadelphia. Clinton remained determined to prove that the Hudson was the key to victory in America, and he was certain that West Point's commander, Arnold, would hand it over to him with minimal resistance.

After Rodney arrived in New York, Washington rushed to prepare for a combined land and sea assault on West Point and Newport. On September 17 he met with General Arnold at King's Ferry, where he ordered him to be ready. Arnold assured him that he would be. At the same time, Arnold planned to have Washington captured at the meeting, and narrowly missed doing so.

Unaware of the close call, Washington rode on to Hartford, Connecticut, for talks with Rochambeau, de Ternay, and their officers—their first face-to-face meeting. This time Washington was not leaving it to subordinates to deal with the French. With Lafayette acting as interpreter, the talks went well. But without the certainty of a large fleet appearing, nothing substantial could be decided; everything depended on Admiral de Guichen. But shortly afterward, the frigate *Gentille* sailed into Newport from Cap François with news that de Guichen had returned to Europe.

Washington then left Hartford and rode to West Point. Lafayette, Knox, Hamilton, and their entourage accompanied him. Washington wanted to inspect the fort to make certain it could withstand an attack from Clinton and Rodney. On the morning of August 25, just before Washington arrived, Arnold received news that incriminating documents found on Major John Andre had been forwarded to Washington. Arnold left immediately, telling an aide he had to go to the fort to prepare for Washington's visit. He then made his escape to Manhattan aboard the 16-gun British sloop-of-war *Vulture*, anchored in Haverstraw Bay.

When Washington arrived at Arnold's headquarters, he proceeded to inspect the fort and was distressed to find it in poor condition. As he finished his inspection, the papers incriminating Arnold caught up with him. Washington was thunderstruck. Under one pretext or another Arnold had dispersed the fort's defenders and given Major Andre, the adjutant general of the British army and one of General Clinton's closest confidants, full plans of the fortress, the grounds that commanded it, the approaches, and every detail necessary for taking it.

Washington immediately ordered the fort strengthened and put his army on alert for an imminent attack. But with Arnold's treachery exposed and no easy victory assured, Clinton, even with Rodney to support him, decided against assaulting West Point. The attack that Washington feared never came. He described the patriots' good fortune as "a most providential interposition."

Uncovering Arnold's treason and thwarting Clinton's plan were tonic for the beleaguered commander in chief. Soon afterward, there was even more encouraging news from the south. Flush with optimism from his easy victory over Horatio Gates at Camden, Cornwallis left there on September 7 and pushed confidently into North Carolina. He marched to Charlotte, expecting Tories to flock to his banner. At the same time he sent Major Patrick Ferguson to organize loyalists in the backcountry and bring recalcitrant Whigs into the king's camp.

Ferguson's efforts, however, produced an opposite result. On October 7, a force of frontiersmen from the mountains of Tennessee, South Carolina, and North Carolina annihilated his troops at King's Mountain on the border near Blacksburg, South Carolina. Ferguson's men were all partisans, but so were the patriots. Southern sympathies were deeply divided, and both sides were ready to fight.

Ferguson's dramatic failure shocked Cornwallis, who withdrew to a point south of Camden at Winnsboro, South Carolina, where he remained for the next three months.

While Cornwallis regrouped, Congress, on Washington's recommendation, appointed General Nathanael Greene to replace Gates as commander of the Southern Department. Greene reached the patriot camp at Charlotte on December 4 and was greeted by General Daniel Morgan, Light-Horse Harry Lee, and fifteen hundred men, a third of them militiamen. Acting quickly, Greene divided his small army and sent Morgan to strike at Cornwallis's supply lines.

Gates's defeat had also shocked Governor Thomas Jefferson of Virginia. He now feared an invasion of his state either by Cornwallis or by a naval force coming into Chesapeake Bay from New York. Ferguson's subsequent defeat at King's Mountain and Cornwallis's retreat to South Carolina gave him some relief, but Jefferson still worried about an amphibious invasion. He thought Virginia lacked the men, forces, and equipment to resist even a minor British foray. Until now Chesapeake Bay had not been a major battleground, but the governor didn't expect the inactivity there to continue.

Jefferson had been the wartime governor since June 1, 1779, and would remain so until the end of May 1781. Virginia's new constitution severely limited the governor's powers, but being the most visible state official, Jefferson was expected to lead the state's war effort. As Dumas Malone notes, "No one so weakly armed with authority could have been expected to cope with the situation in which the British invasion of Virginia placed him." Jefferson also had to contend with runaway inflation, which made supporting an army nearly impossible.

On October 20, 1780, Governor Jefferson's fears of invasion were confirmed. Taking advantage of Admiral Rodney and his fleet, General Clinton reinforced Cornwallis, sending twenty-five hundred regulars under Major General Alexander Leslie to Chesapeake Bay with orders to create a diversion in Virginia. Clinton thought this would take the pressure off Cornwallis in the Carolinas. Clinton also directed Leslie to establish a post on the Chesapeake so that the British would have a secure southern naval base nearer to New York than Charleston was.

Leslie's appearance should not have come as a surprise, but Virginia was woefully unprepared, particularly on the water. Leslie established himself without opposition in Portsmouth at the mouth of the James River and allowed his troops to pillage ruthlessly. He remained in Portsmouth undisturbed for a month before leaving, much to the relief of Governor Jefferson. Leslie traveled south and Virginia was spared for a time, although the governor was increasingly anxious about Cornwallis marching overland from North Carolina.

Contrary to Clinton's wishes, Cornwallis had ordered Leslie to bring his entire contingent to the Cape Fear River in North Carolina. On further orders from Cornwallis, Leslie moved them to Charleston. Clinton had wanted Leslie to operate on the James River, but Cornwallis, having rested for nearly ninety days, was in a mood to take the offensive again, so he ordered Leslie to leave Charleston and join him in North Carolina. With Cornwallis having appropriated Leslie's force, Clinton now sent Brigadier General Benedict Arnold with sixteen hundred men to establish the post at Portsmouth. Arnold arrived at the mouth of the James on December 30, a little over ninety days after deserting. By the time he landed, he had only twelve hundred men. Heavy gales had taken the lives of four hundred regulars.

Jefferson and Virginia, despite the arrival of Leslie and warnings from Washington, were still unprepared. Arnold took immediate advantage of the state's weakness. Disembarking his troops into small vessels seized from the Virginians, and guarded by the armed vessels *Hope* and *Swift*, he sailed one hundred miles along the James River to Richmond unopposed, destroying what he pleased. Although Virginia had a state navy, no naval force attempted to stop him.

Jefferson's call for the militia met with so weak a response that Arnold, with only twelve hundred men, entered the new state capital in Richmond without resistance on January 5, 1781. Arnold gathered whatever weapons and military stores he found, as well as tobacco and other products lying open on the river and surrounding warehouses. He then set fire to the capital before returning, again unopposed, to Portsmouth, where he established a post for the winter. Had there been a slave uprising, perhaps the governor and the militia would have acted with more energy. Their lack of defense allowed Arnold to make a nice show for his new British masters. A fleet of row-galleys could have stopped him—a fact not lost on Jefferson.

While Arnold attacked Virginia, Cornwallis dueled Greene and Morgan, neither of whom he took seriously at first. When Morgan moved southwest to hearten patriot partisans in the backcountry and disrupt British supply lines, Cornwallis dispatched Tarleton's Legion of one thousand cavalry to go after him, expecting an easy victory. On January 16, Tarleton caught up with Morgan at Cowpens, South Carolina, where he suffered a crushing defeat, losing at least six hundred men, killed, captured, or wounded, and nearly being taken himself.

Outraged, Cornwallis chased Morgan, burning his own luggage, supplies, tents, spare clothing, and even rum to gain speed. But the resourceful American was impossible to catch. He reunited with Greene, and together they retreated over the Dan River to Virginia.

After being reinforced, Greene marched back into North Carolina and crossed swords with Cornwallis at Guilford Courthouse on March 15. At the end of the day Cornwallis held the battlefield, but his men and supplies had been so reduced that he was forced to withdraw 175 miles to Wilmington, North Carolina, at the mouth of the Cape Fear River, where he could be resupplied by the Royal Navy. Thus ended his attempt to subdue North Carolina. Banastre Tarleton later said that the earl's "victory had every consequence of a defeat."

Washington, meanwhile, had watched Benedict Arnold's movements in Virginia with growing anger and was determined to crush him. To this end he sought help from the French fleet at Newport. The Chevalier de la Luzerne, the French minister to the United States in Philadelphia, supported him, and he asked Admiral Destouches, the fleet commander in Newport (succeeding de Ternay, who had died in December), to send a few ships and attack Arnold.

Heretofore Destouches had been blockaded by Admiral Arbuthnot from an anchorage at Gardiner's Bay, Long Island. But on January 22, 1781, a severe winter storm scattered the British fleet, leaving an opening for Destouches. He took advantage of it and dispatched the 64-gun battleship *Eville*, under Le Gardeur de Tilly, and two frigates to Chesapeake Bay, but by the time they arrived, Arnold had withdrawn his vessels up the shallow Elizabeth River at Portsmouth. The much larger French warships could not get at him, so they returned to Newport, arriving on February 24.

Considering Arnold's destruction of the first importance, Washington rode to Newport and urged the French to use their entire squadron to attack the traitor. Washington hoped to trap Arnold between the French fleet and a land force composed of Virginia militiamen and Continentals under Lafayette. He had already dispatched Lafayette with twelve hundred New England and New Jersey Continentals to Virginia on February 20. Arriving at Head of Elk on March 3, Lafayette lost no time gathering a squadron of small boats to move his men and equipment to Annapolis. Captain James Nicholson of the Continental Navy took command of Lafayette's tiny fleet and guided it safely to Annapolis, arriving on the 12th.

At Newport, General Rochambeau received Washington with great ceremony and agreed to his plan. On March 8, 1781, Commodore Destouches sortied from Narragansett Bay and sailed for the

Chesapeake with eight battleships and the 44-gun British heavy frigate *Romulus*, which he had captured in January. Aboard Destouches's warships were eleven hundred grenadiers and chasseurs under Baron de Viomenil, Rochambeau's second in command. If this powerful force could get into Chesapeake Bay, Arnold's fate would be sealed.

Admiral Rodney had returned to the West Indies with his fleet in November, and Admiral Arbuthnot was back in charge. Showing uncharacteristic energy, he gathered what was left of his warships after the great storm of the previous month and went after Destouches, leaving Gardiner's Bay on March 10, trailing the French fleet to the Chesapeake.

Arbuthnot's force was slightly larger and much faster, since all his capital ships had copper bottoms, whereas only half of Destouches's did. Arbuthnot caught the French on March 16 before they could enter the bay, and the two fleets engaged for a brief hour off Cape Henry. The weather was foggy, and a high sea was running. Although Arbuthnot's force was superior, Destouches bloodied him enough to feel that he had won the encounter. But instead of occupying Chesapeake Bay, he sailed back to Newport, while Arbuthnot moved his squadron into the bay and anchored in Lynnhaven Roads. Destouches explained later that Arbuthnot's ships were so much faster than his that he had no chance to beat him into the Chesapeake. Lafayette was forced to forget about Arnold for the moment.

Arbuthnot was now in position to resupply Arnold and guard the twenty-six hundred regulars and their supply transports that Clinton planned to send from New York. They began arriving at Portsmouth on March 26, under the command of Major General William Phillips. He now assumed command of all His Majesty's troops in Virginia, with Arnold as his second. The British did not really trust the patriot traitor, so, despite Arnold's success, Clinton put Phillips in charge and eventually brought Arnold back to New York for a lesser assignment.

Phillips had been Burgoyne's second in command at Saratoga. After the defeat, he had been sent to Virginia as a prisoner of war, traveling from Boston with the four thousand captured British and Hessian soldiers. Because they were housed near Monticello and were splendid company, Jefferson formed a congenial relationship with Phillips as well as the Hessian general, Baron Frederick von Riedesel, and his diminutive, brilliant wife, Frederika. Now Phillips, having been exchanged for General Benjamin Lincoln, was in Virginia, threatening his old host.

On April 18 Arnold led twenty-five hundred regulars in a probe along the James River with a view to occupying Petersburg, across the river from the village of Richmond. Governor Jefferson had weeks, indeed months, to prepare, but he could not find the resources to counter this small thrust. He looked to the French at Newport to supply ships and arms, and he beseeched Washington for help. In the past Jefferson had contributed as much as he could to the common cause, often against the advice of those in Virginia who wanted to keep their Continentals close to home. In the winter of 1780, Washington had detached Virginia's line from his army and had sent it to General Lincoln at Charleston. When the city fell, the Virginians had all been captured. Many in the state felt their best soldiers had been wasted.

Encountering little opposition on land or water, Arnold advanced to Petersburg. A mile east of the town he easily dispatched a thousand Virginia militiamen under General Muhlenberg. Afterward, Arnold burned four thousand hogsheads of tobacco and some small boats.

Encouraged by Arnold's success, Philips sent him on April 27 to the small village of Osborne, fifteen miles below Richmond, where the Virginia navy had gathered. It consisted of the 20-gun *Tempest*, the 26-gun *Renown*, the 14-gun brig *Jefferson*, and some smaller armed ships and brigantines. Three hundred militiamen supported them. Arnold set two 6- and two 3-pound brass field pieces on a bluff overlooking the river within a hundred yards of the ships and then opened fire with his artillery and sharpshooters. The crews on the warships panicked. They abandoned their guns and tried to scuttle or set fire to their vessels, before escaping from Arnold's deadly fire in small boats. Seeing this debacle, the militiamen fled as well. Arnold tried to salvage as many vessels as he could. He wrote to General Clinton, "Two ships, three brigantines, five sloops, and two schooners loaded with tobacco, cordage, flour, etc. fell into our hands. Four ships, five brigantines, and a number of small vessels were sunk and burned—we had not a man killed or wounded."

Before making any further moves, Phillips awaited direction from Lord Cornwallis, who was still in Wilmington, North Carolina. On April 10 a letter from him arrived. "Here I am," Cornwallis wrote, "getting rid of my wounded and refitting my troops . . . Now, my dear friend, what is our plan? Without one we cannot succeed, and I assure you that I am quite tired of marching about the country in quest of adventure. If we mean an offensive war in America we must abandon New York and bring our whole force into Virginia, then we have a state to fight for, and a successful battle may give us America." On the same day he wrote to Clinton, "Until Virginia is in a manner subdued our hold on the Carolinas must be difficult if not precarious."

Focusing on Virginia in this manner was not what Clinton had in mind, although the king looked favorably on the idea. Clinton wanted only to establish a post in the Portsmouth area. He expected Cornwallis to keep control of Charleston and pacify South Carolina and North Carolina before attempting Virginia. Without previously subduing the Carolinas, Clinton felt, substantial reinforcements from New York would be necessary to conquer Virginia. But he did not want to weaken his army in Manhattan to that extent, for fear of inviting Washington to attack.

Clinton was far more aware than Cornwallis of the need for the Royal Navy to maintain superiority at sea. Cornwallis seemed to take it for granted. Yet only unquestioned naval supremacy would allow Clinton the luxury of splitting the army between New York and the south, or allow Cornwallis to concentrate Britain's North American army for an all-out attack on Virginia. As Clinton was all too aware, in 1778 and the following year, the French had placed a fleet on the American coast that had momentarily deprived the British of naval superiority.

On April 25 Cornwallis, instead of sailing to Charleston and securing South Carolina, as Clinton wanted, marched out of

Wilmington with his entire force and traveled north to join Phillips and Arnold at Petersburg, arriving on May 20 with fifteen hundred men, including Tarleton's Legion. Five days before, General Phillips had died of a fever, leaving Arnold in temporary command. Cornwallis had been close to Phillips, and the loss affected him deeply.

Cornwallis's move to Virginia surprised Clinton, but he did not order his nominal subordinate to return to Charleston and the Carolinas. Instead, he went along with Cornwallis, without any definite idea of where the operation was headed. "My wonder at this move of Lord Cornwallis," he wrote, "will never cease. But he has made it, and we shall say no more but make the best of it."

Opposing Phillips and Cornwallis was Lafayette, who was on the other side of the James River at Richmond with an army less than half the size of theirs. He had raced to counter the British invasion, arriving at Richmond on April 29. By an odd coincidence, Phillips was the British officer Lafayette blamed for killing his father at the battle of Minden during the Seven Years War. The young Frenchman dearly wanted to engage him, but his force was too small.

Cornwallis's army was soon reinforced by seventeen hundred Germans from New York and now numbered seventy-two hundred, while Lafayette had three thousand. On May 24, Cornwallis crossed the James River to attack "the boy," as he liked to call his opponent. But Lafayette, wanting neither to engage nor disengage, conducted a masterful retreat, staying just out of reach until reinforcements could arrive. He knew General Anthony Wayne was marching from York, Pennsylvania, with eight hundred Continentals, and he hoped for help from Governor Jefferson; very little came.

While contending with Lafayette, Cornwallis attempted to destroy the Virginia government, which by this time was in full retreat from Richmond to Charlottesville and then to Staunton. Jefferson had fled to Monticello, intent on retiring from office. He refused to continue as governor, no matter what the emergency. He officially left the government on June 1 and was nearly captured a few days later. On the 4th Colonel Tarleton, riding at the head of 180 dragoons and

70 mounted infantry, galloped toward Charlottesville with impressive speed, reaching Monticello just as Jefferson made his escape.

Jefferson was thirty-six years old when he first took office and had no prior military experience, nor any taste for it. His trials as governor made a profound impression on him. He developed the firm conviction that war was an unmitigated evil that should never be resorted to until all other measures had been tried. When he left office, he had seen enough fighting to last a lifetime and wanted nothing more to do with it.

Cornwallis eventually decided that chasing Lafayette was fruitless and gave it up, marching south toward Portsmouth to organize a naval base, as Clinton had directed. Lafayette followed and at one point presented the earl with an opportunity to destroy him, but Cornwallis let it pass. Communications between Clinton and Cornwallis, already poor, deteriorated further. Tension between them grew, as Cornwallis remained committed to the idea of making Virginia the focal point of British strategy, while Clinton wanted to establish a base there and retrieve as much of Cornwallis's force as possible for use in the north. At one point Cornwallis got angry enough to request permission to send his entire force to New York while he returned to Charleston, leaving Virginia altogether. Exasperated, Clinton responded by issuing a direct order to move to Williamsburg Neck immediately and establish a post. Portsmouth was unsuitable because it was too difficult to defend. Cornwallis obeyed, and after rejecting Old Point Comfort, he settled on Yorktown and repaired there, arriving on August 1. He was not entirely satisfied with the place but believed it would do.

Meanwhile, Washington and Rochambeau were trying to exploit the division in British ranks in the north and achieve the major victory that had eluded the allies for nearly four years. A signal triumph now seemed a dire necessity, just as the attack on Trenton had been on Christmas 1776. The patriots were desperate for something "to revive expiring hopes and languid exertions," Washington would recall later. Their cause, he said, was "in the most ruinous train imaginable."

On May 1 he wrote in his journal, "instead of having everything in readiness to take the field, we have nothing, and instead of having the prospect of a glorious offensive campaign before us, we have a bewildered, and gloomy defensive one, unless we should receive a powerful aid of ships, land troops and money from our generous allies." The allies, however, had themselves grown weary. If Washington did not achieve a great victory soon, Vergennes would more than likely abandon the Americans and make a separate agreement with the British, leaving the patriots to suffer the consequences. "Why need I run into the detail," Washington wrote, "when it may be declared in a word that we are at the end of our tether, and that now or never our deliverance must come."

On May 6, 1781, the French frigate *Concorde* arrived in Boston with news that a huge fleet under Rear Admiral Francis Joseph Paul, Comte de Grasse, had left Brest on March 22 with orders to cooperate with Washington on any enterprise in North America. De Grasse, however, was sailing first to the West Indies, where Admiral Rodney maintained a strong fleet that might prevent the French admiral from ever reaching America.

En route to the Caribbean, de Grasse had dispatched the 50-gun *Sagittare* and 660 soldiers to Newport. On board the *Sagittare* was a letter from de Grasse to Rochambeau notifying him of his plans. "It will not be until July 15th, at the earliest," he wrote, "that I shall be on the North American coast." De Grasse also indicated that because of prior agreements with the Spanish he could only remain until October.

When Rochambeau received the news, he immediately sought a meeting with Washington, which was held at Wethersfield, Connecticut, on May 22–23. Unaccountably, Rochambeau did not tell Washington at that time of de Grasse's firm intention to sail to North America. Washington had long since been convinced that only a substantial French naval force appearing in a timely fashion offered him any chance of success. As he had written to Franklin in December, "Naval superiority [is] the pivot upon which everything [turns]."

At Wethersfield, Washington and Rochambeau decided that if a French fleet did appear, they would concentrate their attack on New York. But if that became impracticable, they would move south "as circumstances and a naval superiority might render more necessary and eligible." In any event, Washington would not attempt anything unless he was certain of success. "The failure of an attempt against the posts of the enemy," he recalled later, "could, in no other possible situation during the war, have been so fatal to our cause."

From this point forward until August 14, Washington, in overall command of the allied forces (the French king had ordered Rochambeau to place himself under Washington's orders), concentrated on attacking New York. The tepid support given him by the state governors, including John Hancock of Massachusetts, continued to impede his plans. But whether or not the governors gave him support, he was still dependent on the arrival of de Grasse's fleet. In keeping his attention on New York, Washington was also holding General Clinton there, making it unlikely he would strengthen British forces in Virginia.

Washington gave no thought to wether the Continental Navy might be a resource; it had never been in the past, and in fact it had almost disappeared. At the beginning of the year all that was left were the frigates *Trumbull*, *Alliance*, *Confederacy*, and *Deane*, and the sloop-of-war *Saratoga*. During the first half of the year the *Trumbull* was kept in Philadelphia, fitting out, while the *Alliance* took Colonel John Laurens and Thomas Paine to France.

John Barry was in command of the 36-gun *Alliance*. He left Nantasket Roads off Boston on February 13, 1781, with Laurens and Paine aboard. They arrived at L'Orient off the Brittany coast on March 9 after a remarkably short voyage. Congress had sent Laurens to secure more aid from the king. Success was critical; without additional resources, Congress could not carry on the war. But sending Laurens was a foolish mistake. It was meant as a calculated snub to Franklin; but since Laurens was unskilled in diplomacy and knew nothing of the intricacy of French politics, he managed to step on enough French toes to be a burden to

Franklin. In any event, Franklin had already secured the money before Laurens arrived.

In spite of a troublesome crew, Barry had his ship ready to return to Boston in three weeks, and on March 30 he departed L'Orient for home. On May 28, off the coast of Newfoundland, he observed two British warships off the weather bow standing directly for him. They were the 16-gun sloop-of-war *Atalanta* and the 14-gun brig *Trespassy*. Since it was dusk, both Barry and the captain of the *Atalanta*, Sampson Edwards, decided to wait until morning before engaging.

At first light the sea was dead calm, and the three warships found themselves a league apart. With no wind, the *Alliance* floated like a powerless log on the flat surface. Seeing his opportunity, Captain Edwards raised British colors and beat to quarters. The sound of the marine drums carried clearly over the morning water. Using sweeps (long oars) to propel the *Atalanta* and the *Trespassy*, Edwards closed with the *Alliance*. Since Barry had no sweeps and could not make steerageway, he could only watch helplessly as the British stationed themselves off his quarters and began blasting away at eleven o'clock. Barry could bring only a few guns to bear. Three punishing hours later he was severely wounded by grapeshot and had to be carried below. Hoysted Hacker, the first officer and one of the more capable men in the Continental service, assumed command. At three o'clock, a small breeze arose, and Hacker maneuvered just enough to pour a full broadside into *Atalanta* and then *Trespassy*. Captain Edwards lowered his colors. The grueling battle lasted four hours and cost the British two ships, eleven dead, including the *Trespassy*'s captain, and twenty-five wounded.

While Barry and the *Alliance* were winning laurels, the *Deane*, *Saratoga*, and *Confederacy* were sent on another meaningless commerce-destroying mission to the West Indies in March. On their return the *Deane* reached Boston, but the *Saratoga* was lost at sea and the *Confederacy* captured, surrendering without a fight on April 15 to the 44-gun *Roebuck* and the 32-gun *Orpheus*. She was taken into the Royal Navy and rechristened the *Confederate*.

When the *Alliance* docked in Boston, she passed the summer receiving copper sheathing. On August 8, the *Trumbull*, under Captain James Nicholson, finally left Philadelphia and put to sea, but almost immediately lost her fore topmast and main topgallant in a storm. In this condition she encountered HMS *Iris*, formerly the 32-gun Continental frigate *Hancock*, escorted by the *General Monk*, formerly the American privateer *General Washington*. After a ninety-minute struggle in which most of the *Trumbull's* crew refused to fight, Nicholson struck his colors. The *Trumbull* was such a wreck that the Royal Navy declined to take her.

By the summer of 1781 only the *Alliance* and the *Deane* were still afloat. Nonetheless, Congress chose once more to reorganize its dying navy, terminating the failed Board of Admiralty and replacing it with a single Agent of Marine, Robert Morris. He ordered the last two ships not to aid Washington, but to sail on another commerce-destroying mission to the West Indies. The battle of Yorktown intervened, however, and the mission was canceled.

While the Continental Navy was withering, America's fleet of privateers was growing and prospering. It was now larger than it had ever been, numbering in the hundreds. And numbers alone did not tell the story, for the ships themselves had become larger and faster, often double the size of vessels in the early stages of the war. Their guns were more powerful too. Instead of 4s and 6s, there were now 9s and 12s. The crews consisted of experienced seamen rather than the amateurs of earlier years. And their captains and officers were veterans of many encounters with British men-of-war, privateers, and armed merchantmen.

The frigate *Concorde* left Boston on June 20, arriving in Saint-Domingue on July 26 with dispatches for de Grasse, informing him of Washington's intention to attack either New York or Cornwallis's post in Chesapeake Bay, depending on de Grasse's pleasure. The *Concorde* also delivered thirty American pilots for de Grasse's use. Remembering d'Estaing's difficulties crossing the treacherous bar at New York in 1778, de Grasse, supported by his officers, chose Virginia.

Rochambeau marched his army out of Newport on June 10 to join Washington at Peekskill, New York, on July 6. Each had about five thousand effectives, a total of ten thousand, while Clinton had about fourteen thousand in Manhattan. With Rochambeau away, Admiral de Barras, who had replaced Destouches, was now at risk in Newport. Washington suggested that he move his fleet to Boston, but de Barras ignored the suggestion. In one bold stroke, Clinton could have thwarted Washington's plans by crushing de Barras and capturing Newport again, but he did nothing. Arbuthnot was still in command, and Clinton preferred to remain idle rather than conduct another joint operation with him.

When Arbuthnot left on July 4, Clinton thought seriously about attacking Newport, and Admiral Graves (Arbuthnot's replacement) supported him. But Clinton decided he had to have reinforcements before moving, which would come either from home or from Cornwallis's army after he secured a base in the Chesapeake. But Cornwallis was not willing to part with any men, and reinforcements from England were not immediately at hand. So for the moment Clinton did nothing.

Reinforcing his lethargy was the conviction that the Franco-American war effort was near collapse. Captured enemy documents suggested that all he had to do was survive without a major defeat, and the American war effort would disintegrate. The French were tired of supporting it and would soon turn away, leaving Washington with a smattering of troops, one or two warships, and no money.

By the end of July Washington and Rochambeau had agreed not to attack New York, leaving Virginia as the alternative. De Grasse confirmed this choice when he wrote back on July 28 via the *Concorde*, giving preference to the Chesapeake. His letter arrived on August 12, and Rochambeau informed Washington of its contents on the 14th. Focusing now on a decisive battle in the Chesapeake, Washington sent an express to Lafayette the next day, ordering him to prevent Cornwallis from retreating to North Carolina. Six days later Washington and Rochambeau marched south, leaving twenty-five hundred men under General Heath to defend the highlands.

Taking nearly his entire army to Virginia was another of Washington's great gambles.

Meanwhile, twenty-five hundred Hessians had reinforced Clinton, bringing his total in Manhattan to around 16,500. He could have taken Newport and the New York highlands, but Washington held him in place by continuing to threaten an attack on Manhattan.

Washington put out word that de Grasse's West Indian fleet was headed for New York and a joint operation planned there. He then ordered the troops he was taking to Virginia to assemble in New Jersey as if they were organized for an attack on Staten Island. Inquiries were made about boats to ferry the troops. Pontoons to create a span for them to reach the island were openly displayed. A huge bread oven was constructed to make it appear that it was the first of many to support an attack on New York. Spies faithfully reported all this activity to Clinton. He wasn't aware until September 2 that the bulk of Washington's army was marching south. And by that time de Grasse had already arrived in Chesapeake Bay, appearing on August 31.

De Grasse had with him twenty-eight sail of the line—the entire French West Indian fleet. He left the important French merchant convoy at Cap François in Saint-Domingue and the rest of the Caribbean unprotected while he raced for the Chesapeake. He was taking an enormous risk—so great, in fact, that it completely fooled both the Admiralty and Rodney. De Grasse hoped to link de Barras's eight sail of the line with his own; he would then have a combined fleet of thirty-six battleships.

The Admiralty had blundered badly in permitting de Grasse to leave Brest in the first place, and then in not providing enough reinforcements for the North American station to counter him. Rodney had likewise fallen short. He knew the French fleet was coming to the West Indies, and although he had fewer warships, he had enough to challenge de Grasse. But he had chosen not to. Had he done so, de Grasse might not have come to America in such strength, or at all.

Clinton and Cornwallis were depending on Rodney to check de Grasse, as Rodney had done the previous year when he raced to New York to get ahead of Admiral de Guichen, who never came.

Germain had warned Clinton in April that de Grasse might sail north during the hurricane season, but the French fleets in the past had been so ineffective that Clinton wasn't overly concerned.

By the end of June Clinton knew positively that de Grasse was coming, and he wrote to Rodney urging him to rush to New York. Rodney was aware of the danger, but he never anticipated that de Grasse would bring his entire fleet north. To complicate matters, Rodney was sick. On August 1 he sailed home to recover, taking three much needed battleships with him when a frigate could have transported him just as well. Admiral Sir Samuel Hood was left in charge of the West Indian fleet, with orders to sail a portion of it to New York. At the same time Rodney warned Admiral Graves in Manhattan to be on the lookout for de Grasse. Graves was Hood's superior and would be in overall command when Hood arrived. Graves, however, did not have Hood's ability.

Meanwhile, the summer dragged on. In the middle of July Admiral Graves, as if unaware of the larger strategic picture, took all seven of his sail of the line out of New York to search for a French supply convoy in the Atlantic, leaving the city open to a seaborne attack. Graves never found the convoy and returned to New York in mid-August. While he was away de Barras might have sailed his Newport fleet to New York, or he might have met de Grasse and the combined fleets could have attacked New York. Or they could have simply captured Graves off New York when he was returning.

On August 28 Admiral Hood appeared off Sandy Hook with fourteen line-of-battle ships. On the way, he had looked into Chesapeake Bay and, seeing no French warships there, moved on to New York, even though he knew there was a strong possibility that the Chesapeake was de Grasse's destination. Rodney had intelligence indicating that de Grasse was definitely headed to the Chesapeake, but he never communicated it to either Hood or Admiral Graves. If Hood had known for certain, he could have entered the bay before de Grasse arrived and remained there, stationed between the French fleet and Cornwallis, while sending to New York for reinforcements. Moreover, had de Grasse seen him there when he arrived, he might have chosen not to risk having a good part of his fleet torn up and sailed back to Saint-Domingue. De Grasse had already rejected the idea of going to New York; it was unlikely he would sail there as an alternative.

When Hood left the Chesapeake area and raced to New York, he expected to combine his fleet with Graves's and return to the Chesapeake with a force at least equal to the French. He was still under the impression that de Grasse would bring only a portion of his fleet north, perhaps as few as twelve battleships. When Hood reached New York, however, he was aghast at Graves's apparent lack of strategic understanding. Even at this late hour Graves suggested that Hood move his fleet inside the bar while Graves prepared his ships, the work of a week or two. Hood was appalled. He urged Graves to race to Chesapeake Bay and arrive before de Barras or de Grasse. De Barras had already sailed from Newport with his eight battleships on August 25, three days before Hood arrived off Sandy Hook.

Responding to Hood's appeal, Graves set sail for the Chesapeake on the 31st with nineteen sail of the line, expecting to have a superior fleet should he meet de Grasse. Graves's sojourn to Boston Bay in July to look for the French convoy had cost him two battleships, the *Robust* and the *Prudent*. They had been weakened in the brief encounter between Arbuthnot and Destouches in March, and the trip in July had put them out of action. Thus Graves had nineteen sail of the line rather than twenty-one, but he expected this number to be sufficient. With his copper-bottomed ships he made excellent time, arriving off the Chesapeake capes the morning of September 5, only to discover that de Grasse had already established himself inside the bay with an eye-popping twenty-eight sail of the line, the largest fleet ever to operate on the American coast.

Nonetheless, Graves pressed forward with a fair wind and tide to enter the bay. The mouth of the Chesapeake between Cape Charles in the north and Cape Henry in the south was ten miles wide, with the main channel between Cape Henry and Middle Ground shoal, three miles wide. One of de Grasse's frigates on picket duty off Cape Charles, Virginia, spotted the British fleet and signaled that the enemy was in sight. De Grasse was at anchor, unloading troops for

Lafayette, but he reacted swiftly. Instead of taking up a defensive position, he ordered twenty-four sail of the line to be ready by noon to beat out of the Chesapeake and meet the British in the open Atlantic. De Grasse wanted to deal with Graves in a manner that would allow de Barras, when he arrived from Newport, to enter the bay without finding Graves blocking the entrance.

De Grasse waited until noon for the tide to turn before beginning his exit. He left four battleships in the bay and arranged the remaining twenty-four in the traditional three divisions: van, middle, and rear. De Monteil commanded the van, de Grasse the middle, and de Bougainville the rear. As the tide began to ebb, the wind remained contrary, and the French ships were forced to make several tacks before they could maneuver beyond Cape Henry into the Atlantic. Struggling against the wind proved difficult. As they clawed their way out of the Chesapeake to form a line of battle, adverse winds forced a dangerous separation between the van of eight ships and the center and rear, giving Graves an excellent opportunity to attack and perhaps even the odds between the two fleets, or even defeat the French outright.

By the time de Grasse's van had worked up to Cape Henry, it was close enough to the British fleet for Graves to exert his entire force on it. Not yet having weathered the cape, de Grasse's van was trapped for a time against a lee shore. Under similar circumstances Admiral Rodney, as well as Hood, almost certainly would have attacked, but Graves ignored his advantage and sailed in line ahead straight for the bay, taking no account of de Grasse's difficulties.

Graves kept proceeding west, his ships continuing in line toward the bay until his van approached the Middle Ground shoal. He then signaled the fleet to wear together, which the ships did with precision and then sailed east close-hauled, out to sea. Meanwhile, the French van was also moving east, still struggling to weather Cape Henry. Graves saw that his fleet was ahead of de Grasse's, and, as if his maneuvers were being scripted by the French admiral, he hove to for a time until the enemy caught up with him.

Graves's line was also arranged in the traditional manner—van, center, and rear—with Graves directing from the center. Admiral

Sir Francis Drake was in command of the van, and Admiral Sir Samuel Hood the rear. With his vessels thus strung out, one behind the other in the traditional line-of-battle formation, Graves allowed de Grasse to come abreast of his fleet and run nearly parallel to it. Of course, with five more ships than Graves, de Grasse's line extended farther. Graves now signaled his lead ship, *Shrewsbury*, to steer toward the French van, and with the rest of the British line following this lead, it inclined toward de Grasse's ships. The British line was no longer running parallel to the French but at an angle, with the van closer than the rear.

By four in the afternoon, when the battleships in both vans were a cable's length apart, they each began blasting away at an enemy ship in the opposite line. The firing then extended down both lines to the center. But Graves's rear squadron under Hood did not fully engage, since it had not gotten close enough to the French line. The captain of the *Citoyen* noticed that "although master of the wind, [Hood] only engaged from far off and simply in order to be able to say they had fought. In that part of the line it was not at all the way it was in the vans of the two fleets, where one could see only fire and smoke billowing on both sides."

Hood later claimed that signals from the flagship were confusing, even though he could see perfectly well that the two fleets were fighting. Signals or no signals, it was his duty to join in. As Admiral Nelson wrote to his commanders just before the battle of Trafalgar, "In case signals can neither be seen or perfectly understood, no captain can do very wrong if he places his ship alongside that of an enemy."

The heavy fighting continued until six-thirty, when the sun set and firing ceased. Graves expected to resume in the morning. During the night he discovered that his damages were far greater than he had thought. The British van under Admiral Francis Drake had been badly mauled, as had the first ships of the center, *Europe* and *Montagu*, both of 64 guns. De Grasse had also received a pounding, though less severe than the British sustained.

The following day the two fleets remained in sight of each other, repairing damages. Graves watched from aboard his flagship

London as de Grasse stood off fixing his ships. A feeble north wind continued for most of the day until late in the afternoon when it shifted to the southwest. De Grasse then moved toward Graves, but darkness overtook him and the two fleets did not engage. The following day de Grasse made an attempt to engage, but Graves stayed out of reach repairing his ships. Then variable winds and storms kept the fleets apart. On the 8th de Grasse maneuvered to obtain the weather gauge and keep Graves from entering the bay before de Barras arrived. There was no engagement, however, and the fleets spent the day observing each other. During the night the wind fell, and on the 9th the fleets remained in sight of each other. But again no fighting developed.

On the evening of the 9th, with a north-northeast breeze, de Grasse drifted steadily southward, and on the morning of the 10th he disappeared. On the same day, de Barras anchored safely in the bay. He carried the indispensable French siege guns for Washington's attack on Cornwallis, as well as fifteen hundred tons of salt beef for the patriots. The next day, September 11, de Grasse reappeared in Chesapeake Bay. The combined French fleet now numbered thirty-six sail of the line.

Graves, meanwhile, had done nothing to get into the Chesapeake ahead of de Grasse, despite urging by Hood to do so. On the 10th Graves burned the 74-gun *Terrible*, which was beyond repair, and waited until the 13th to reconnoiter the bay, where he discovered that de Barras and de Grasse had placed their ships inside Horseshoe shoal in a great crescent, blocking the entrance to the York River. Thoroughly outmaneuvered and with ten ships needing extensive repairs, Graves sailed for New York, arriving on September 20. Three days later his replacement, Admiral Digby, appeared in New York, but he had only three sail of the line to add to the fleet. He also brought the Prince of Wales, the future William IV. The young prince improved everyone's morale, but he could not make up for the deficiency in battleships. Digby did not immediately assume command but left Graves in charge until the crisis had been resolved.

On the 24th Clinton wrote to Cornwallis urging him to hold out for as long as possible, and that reinforcements were on the way. "If you cannot relieve me very soon," Cornwallis replied, "you must be prepared to hear the worst."

While these events were taking place, Clinton dispatched Benedict Arnold to attack New London, Connecticut, on the Thames River—twelve miles south of the port of Norwich, birthplace of the infamous traitor. On September 6, in the most senseless act of barbarism in this gruesome war, Arnold set fire to New London and murdered the garrison at Fort Griswold on the opposite side of the river, seeking to win favor with not only Clinton but also Lord Germain and the king. Arnold knew this massacre would please the hard-liners in London, who, from the very beginning of the war, had wanted such raids conducted against coastal towns. Arnold's unbridled cruelty was of a piece with that of Admiral Samuel Graves when he burned Charlestown and Falmouth back in 1775.

On September 28, 1781, Washington's combined Franco-American army appeared before Yorktown and formed a line six miles long between the York River and Wormley Creek and began a formal siege. Washington had about nine thousand troops, and the French about eight thousand. Cornwallis had about seventy-two hundred, now with no naval support.

On the 30th Cornwallis abandoned his exterior works and withdrew his troops into tighter lines around Yorktown, where conditions among his men worsened. Hundreds were in the hospital, and food for the troops and forage for horses were getting scarce.

Meanwhile, Washington had been digging trenches and moving closer by regular approaches. Late in the afternoon of October 9, he opened fire on the British lines with heavy guns. The bombardment continued with increasing intensity day after day. On the 16th, in one last desperate gamble, Cornwallis tried to row his army across the York River to Gloucester and attempt a breakout, but a storm forced him back into Yorktown. Early the next morning Washington opened fire again with all his heavy guns, persuading Cornwallis at ten o'clock to beat a parley for settlement of conditions for surrender.

Two days later he accepted Washington's final terms, and the battle was over.

What remained of the Continental Navy had no part in these momentous proceedings. Nothing illustrates its failures more vividly than what happened to John Paul Jones, its most celebrated captain, during the critical months leading up to Yorktown.

Jones had left France in the *Ariel* on October 7, 1780, and arrived back in Philadelphia on February 18, 1781. He wrote to Washington in April, hoping to be "instrumental to put the naval force that remains on a more useful footing." But Washington had nothing for him to do; the commander in chief of the American army had never been permitted to lead the navy. The British may have had trouble coordinating their army and navy, but the Americans never even attempted it. None of the congressional leaders who built and ran the navy had the slightest idea of how to employ it effectively with the army.

Instead of using Jones in the Yorktown campaign, the Marine Board ordered him to repair to Portsmouth, New Hampshire, where he was to assume command of the first American sail of the line, the 74-gun *America*. Congress had authorized her construction late in 1776, but she was still far from ready.

On August 12, two weeks before the decisive naval battle between Graves and de Grasse, Jones left Philadelphia and traveled overland to Portsmouth. On the way he stopped at White Plains, New York, to meet Washington and Rochambeau, who were discussing the great campaign to follow. Without other orders, Jones rode on to Portsmouth and months of frustration. He never did command the *America*. When she was finally finished, she was given to the French.

Jones himself commented on the painful irrelevancy of the Continental Navy: "It has upon the whole done nothing for the cause and less for the flag. The public has been put to a great expense, yet the poor seamen have, almost in every instance, been *cheated,* while the public has reaped neither honor nor profit; and the whole result . . . only appears to have augmented the purses of the agents, besides enabling a few of the actors, perhaps not the first in merit or ability, to purchase farms &c."

Jones had also written to Washington. "Our navy has been badly conducted," he lamented; "it has ever been without a head and is now almost entirely lost." Of course, Washington didn't need to be told of this. John Adams wrote, "Looking over the long list of vessels belonging to the United States taken and destroyed, and recollecting the whole history of the rise and progress of our navy, it is very difficult to avoid tears."

Jones's opinions were widely shared, but neither he nor his correspondents understood *why* the Continental Navy had failed—neither the Adamses, nor Franklin, nor Robert Morris, nor any of those who had trumpeted the need for an American "naval power." Most just shrugged their shoulders and assumed the Royal Navy was just too strong. Starting from scratch in the midst of a war, the United States could not hope to compete against it. Actually, as the record shows, the real problem was not that the patriots could not produce an effective navy, but that they created the wrong kind. They squandered their limited resources building a fleet that was of little use and bound to fail. With those same resources, and even fewer, they might have created a navy that would have served Washington well in every critical battle of the war.

Not knowing if the defeat at Yorktown would move London to the peace table, Washington hoped to follow with a joint attack on Charleston, feeling that another victory "would destroy the last hope which induces [the King] to continue the war." He wrote to de Grasse with his plan and also offered a substitute: Wilmington, North Carolina, which the British still occupied. Lafayette carried Washington's two proposals to de Grasse, who considered them seriously but was anxious to return to the West Indies. In the middle of November Admiral Hood stood south from New York with eighteen sail of the line, apparently making for the Caribbean, and de Grasse had no choice but to follow. If the French fleet had stopped at Charleston on the way south, General Greene, whose troops were well positioned outside the city, felt certain he could have forced a surrender.

News of the shocking defeat at Yorktown arrived in London on November 25, 1781, and the country was stunned. By now, Lord North, the Parliament, and the people were thoroughly sick of the war and ready to end it, but they weren't expecting to be defeated and humiliated. Neither was the king, who dug in his heels as he had on previous occasions, and prepared to fight on. In his speech at the opening of Parliament he continued to call for members to be "firm . . . [against] the designs of our enemies, equally prejudicial to the real interests of America and to those of Great Britain."

Despite Yorktown, His Majesty was fulsome in his praise of Lord Cornwallis. The opposition was as well, refusing to criticize the earl while placing the entire onus for defeat on the Royal Navy. Charles James Fox, a leading critic of the government throughout the war, rose in Parliament and declared, "The whole conduct of Lord Cornwallis was great and distinguished . . . when prudence became necessary, he took up a station, which in any former period in our history, would have been a perfect asylum, and planted himself at the edge of the sea. In former wars the sea was regarded as the country of an English commander, to which he could retire with safety, if not with fame. There he was invincible, whatever might be his strength on shore; and there Lord Cornwallis stationed his army, in the hope of preserving his communication with New York—nay with the city and port of London. But even this was denied him, for the ocean was no longer the country of an Englishman; and the noble Lord was blocked up, though planted on the borders of the sea."

Germain and Sandwich wanted to continue the war as much as the king did. Their delusions were encouraged by Benedict Arnold when he arrived in London on January 22, 1782. He had departed New York on December 15 on HMS *Robuste* with Lord Cornwallis, who was on parole. They were part of a large fleet of a hundred sail. Eleven days out a severe storm had struck and almost sank the *Robuste*. She sailed to the West Indies for repairs while Arnold continued to England in the *Edward* and Cornwallis in the *Greyhound*. Arnold had plans to continue the fight, and he produced a paper for the king outlining a new strategy. Eager for ideas, the king read Arnold's "Thoughts on America" with great interest.

Regardless of the king's zeal to fight on, the opposition was now in the ascendancy, and the war with America was over. It took until September 3, 1783, for a final peace treaty to be signed, but Britain had given up the idea of subjugating America by force. Diplomacy was moved to center stage, and here the Americans fared better than they had on the battlefield, negotiating a peace so favorable that it remains the greatest diplomatic triumph in American history. When an armistice and preliminary terms were agreed to by all the combatants, John Adams wrote to Abigail, "Thus drops the curtain upon this mighty tragedy, it has unraveled itself happily for us—and heaven be praised."

John Derby of Salem, Massachusetts, who had carried the first news of the battle of Lexington and Concord to London in 1775, now brought back to America from Paris the first reports of the armistice and preliminary peace terms. At the end of December 1782, Derby, a successful privateer during the war, had sailed to France in his fast armed schooner *Astrea*, making the trip to Nantes in a remarkable eighteen days. He began his return voyage on March 12, reaching Salem only twenty-two days later.

The last two naval battles between American and British warships were waged by Joshua Barney and John Barry. After escaping from England's Old Mill prison, twenty-two-year-old Barney made his way back to Philadelphia, arriving in March 1782. Several merchants, anxious to protect their ships from British marauders, arranged for him to take command of the merchantman *Hyder-Ally*. In a month Barney had her converted into a warship with sixteen 6-pounders, and she was taken into the Pennsylvania state navy.

In April, while escorting a convoy of seven merchantmen down Delaware Bay, Barney spotted the frigate HMS *Quebec*, the 20-gun ship HMS *General Monk*, and several loyalist privateers. As Barney attempted to reverse course and shepherd his convoy upriver to

avoid this powerful squadron, *General Monk* and the loyalist privateer *Fair American* bore down on him. The *Fair American* reached
Barney first and fired two successful broadsides. But instead of finishing the job, the privateer left Barney and raced after the fleeing
convoy. In her haste she went aground on Egg Island flats, while
the merchantmen escaped.

Barney now had to face the oncoming *General Monk*. He held
his fire, keeping his gunports closed to lure the larger ship in close,
instructing his helmsman to steer in the opposite direction from
what was called out. When Barney ordered the helm to port, *General Monk's* captain, Josiah Rogers, shouted the same command. But
Hyder-Ally's helmsman turned to starboard, causing *General Monk*
to become entangled with Barney's ship. Barney lashed the two
vessels in a position that enabled *Hyder-Ally's* starboard guns to rake
General Monk, rendering her deck a shambles, wounding her captain, and killing most of her officers. Barney's men then cut *General
Monk's* rigging, making her unmanageable. The last British officer
on his feet, a midshipman, struck *General Monk's* colors.

Almost a year later, on March 10, 1783, John Barry and the *Alliance*
fought the final naval battle of the war off the southern coast of
Florida with HMS *Sybil*, a 32-gun British frigate captained by James
Vashon. Barry was sailing in company with a 20-gun sloop-of-war,
the *Duc de Lauzon*, which was carrying seventy-two thousand desperately needed Spanish silver dollars to Robert Morris's Bank of
North America in Philadelphia. Congress had chartered the bank on
December 31, 1781. The Continental warships had departed Havana,
Cuba, on March 6, and two days later, after seeing how slow the *Duc
de Lauzon* was, Barry transferred all the money to the *Alliance*, one of
the fastest warships afloat, able to attain speeds of fourteen knots.

On the morning of the 10th Barry sighted three large British warships, HMS *Alarm*, a 32-gun frigate, HMS *Sybil*, and HMS *Tobago*, an
18-gun sloop-of-war. They were coming on fast and Barry wanted
to flee, but the *Duc de Lauzon* was a sluggish sailer and the British
ships were getting closer. Barry decided to abandon the sloop and
advised her skipper, Captain Green, to throw his guns overboard,
lighten the ship, and escape as best he could. By this time the *Sybil*

was within gunshot of the *Alliance*, with her two companions not far behind. In order to give the *Duc de Lauzon* a chance to get away, Barry engaged the *Sybil* for forty-five minutes in a punishing gun battle that severely damaged the British ship while leaving the *Alliance* relatively unscathed. After receiving this thrashing from Barry, the *Sybil* broke off the engagement and fled, her companions not coming to her aid. They had spotted a 60-gun French battleship on the horizon and did not want to take on both the Frenchman and the *Alliance*. When the *Sybil* caught up with them, they all fled.

Barry and the *Duc de Lauzon* then made sail for Philadelphia, but on March 18 they became separated off the Delaware capes. The following morning Barry encountered two British warships that chased him. In the meantime, the *Duc de Lauzon* slipped into Delaware Bay, arriving in Philadelphia unharmed. Barry outdistanced his pursuers and put into Newport, Rhode Island, on March 20 with Robert Morris's Spanish silver.

A pantheon of authentic naval heroes emerged from the Revolution, as did talented young officers such as Thomas Truxtun and Edward Preble and experienced seamen from hundreds of privateers and from the Continental and state navies. The patriots also gained a valuable body of technical expertise in the construction and management of warships and their crews, and a rudimentary understanding of how a navy should be organized and employed.

When the war ended, the universal hope among patriots was peace. No one wanted to repeat the horrors of the past eight years. Washington believed the two great goals of the country going forward should be keeping the states together and avoiding entrapment in Europe's wars. In his mind, building a successful republic and a prosperous economy required peace. He thought that in time an American navy would be built and would play a critical role in keeping the country out of war. To be sure, the record of the Continental Navy was not encouraging, but at least it was a beginning. That mistakes were made—large, glaring, fundamental errors—there can be no doubt, but when the time came for the nation to build a new navy, it would not be starting from scratch. It now had the beginnings of a naval tradition.

7

A NEW REPUBLIC

September 1783–March 1793

When the War of Independence ended, America was exhausted, divided, loaded with debt, and faced with an uncertain future. She desperately needed time to recover, away from Europe's incessant quarrels. Fortunately Britain and France also required healing, and from the Treaty of Paris in 1783 until the outbreak of the wars of the French Revolution in 1792, relative peace reigned in Europe, granting the United States ten years to recuperate and reform.

For the only time in her history America had no fighting force on the high seas. What was left of the Continental Navy was sold, and there was no clamor to replace it. In 1784 Robert Morris, the Agent of Marine, citing a shortage of funds, had urged Congress to sell at auction the navy's last two warships, *General Washington* and *Alliance*. There had been little opposition. The *General Washington* was quickly disposed of, and on August 5, 1785, a group of investors led by Morris gathered at Merchant's Coffee House near Philadelphia's waterfront and bought the 32-gun *Alliance*—the pride of the fleet—for $26,000. A few critics grumbled that the historic man-of-war should be preserved in memory of the Revolution's heroic sea warriors, but most people were indifferent.

Operating under the Articles of Confederation, Congress had no taxing power and consequently was unable to build a successor fleet. Until the states could rise above slavish ties to local interests, America would remain impotent, the plaything of Europe, unable to achieve either peace or prosperity. She desperately needed to unite, but doing so appeared nearly impossible.

Had it not been for the public's unlimited admiration of George Washington, the thirteen states might never have transferred sovereign power to a national government. Trusted by all parties, he was the symbol of unity, looked to by citizens high and low for disinterested leadership. In July 1783, even before the Treaty of Paris was signed, he wrote, "It now rests with the [states] by the line of conduct they mean to adopt, to make this country great, happy, and respectable; or to sink into littleness; worse perhaps, into anarchy and confusion; for certain I am, that unless adequate powers are given to Congress for the *general* purposes of the federal union that we shall soon molder into dust and become contemptible in the eyes of Europe, if we are not made the sport of their politics; to suppose that the general concern of this country can be directed by thirteen heads, or one head without competent powers, is a solecism, the bad effects of which every man who has the practical knowledge to judge from, that I have, is fully convinced of; tho' none perhaps has felt them in so forceful, and distressing a degree."

The Barbary States—Morocco, Tunis, Algiers, and Tripoli—regularly administered stark reminders of America's weakness under the Articles of Confederation by seizing Yankee merchantmen. The Revolution had interrupted colonial America's profitable trade in the Mediterranean. About a sixth of the country's wheat and flour exports had been shipped there in the past. Thomas Jefferson estimated that between eighty and a hundred American vessels had visited the Mediterranean each year, employing twelve hundred seamen.

When the Revolution ended, Yankee schooners and brigs began reappearing, but without the protection of the Royal Navy. The

Barbary States discovered they could prey on the Americans with impunity while leaving Britain's ships alone in return for a modest subsidy. Viewing the United States as a serious commercial rival, London was content to let this state of affairs continue. Benjamin Franklin, still in Paris, declared, "If there were no Algiers it would be worth England's while to build one."

The Americans soon learned that neither the French nor the Dutch would protect them, either. England's Lord Sheffield observed with satisfaction that "the American States will have a very free trade in the Mediterranean; it will not be in the interest of any of the great maritime powers to protect them there from the Barbary States. . . . The Americans cannot protect themselves from the latter, they cannot pretend to a navy."

On October 11, 1784, as the *Alliance* was about to be put on the auction block, the Moroccans captured the small merchant vessel *Betsey*. Being better disposed toward the United States than the other pirate states were, Morocco released the *Betsey* and her crew after the countries signed a treaty of friendship in January 1787; the agreement did not include the payment of tribute.

The other Barbary powers were not so accommodating. In 1785 Algiers was temporarily allowed to send its warships into the Atlantic. Normally Spain and Portugal prohibited such activity. On July 25, 1785, an Algerian corsair captured the Boston trading schooner *Maria*, under Captain Isaac Stevens, near Gibraltar, and on July 30 the Algerians took the merchant ship *Dauphin*, under Captain Richard O'Brien, 150 miles west of Lisbon, enslaving twenty-one seamen. Seizing ships and crews and holding them for ransom was the principal source of income for the Dey of Algiers. "If I were to make peace with everybody," he once said, "what should I do with my corsairs? What should I do with my soldiers? They would take off my head for the want of other prizes, not being able to live on their miserable allowance."

Congress formed a commission composed of John Adams, Thomas Jefferson, and Benjamin Franklin to negotiate with the Barbary States, but it did not appropriate enough money for the commissioners to meet Algeria's demands. Unable either to pay the ransom or to send men-of-war to free the prisoners, Congress accepted humiliation until a unified government could be empowered to raise revenue. In the meantime the American captives remained enslaved in Algiers.

On January 12, 1785, Jefferson, who was about to replace Dr. Franklin as the American ambassador in Paris, wrote to General Nathanael Greene that he was "suspended between indignation and impotence." Jefferson thought a naval force was needed. "We ought to begin a naval power," he wrote to James Monroe, "if we mean to carry on our own commerce. Can we begin it on a more honorable occasion, or with a weaker foe? I am of the opinion Paul Jones with half a dozen frigates would totally destroy their commerce . . . by constant cruising and cutting them to pieces by piecemeal." Jefferson's recommendation was ignored, as was that of John Jay, the secretary of foreign affairs for the Continental Congress, who proposed building five 40-gun frigates. John Adams, who would become America's new ambassador to Britain in June 1785, agreed with Jefferson. Nevertheless, since he saw no prospect of an American navy being built, he recommended paying whatever bribes were required, although he knew Congress would never approve that much tribute. "Neither force nor money will be applied," he predicted.

During the critical summer of 1787, when the Constitutional Convention was meeting in Philadelphia, delegates paid scant attention to the problem of the Barbary pirates. Neither in their formal sessions at the State House (now Independence Hall) nor in the taverns and lodging houses where they liked to congregate did they seriously discuss creating a navy. Those who voted for the final document agreed that Congress should have the power to "provide and maintain a navy," and most thought the country would eventually have one, but not until her financial house was in order. Maintaining a permanent sea force would require substantial taxes in a country notoriously allergic to them. Unless a broadly recognized national emergency existed, the public was unlikely to agree to make the sacrifices necessary to support a strong navy. In the meantime, America's protection would have to lie in the oceans and European rivalries.

Yet many delegates, including Washington, agreed with Alexander Hamilton that an American navy was needed. "If we mean to be a commercial people," Hamilton wrote, "or even to be secure on our side of the Atlantic, we must endeavor, as soon as possible, to have a navy." He took it for granted that, under the new Constitution, America would soon be able to afford a respectable fleet. "There can be no doubt," he wrote, "that the continuance of the union under an efficient government would put it in our power, at a period not very distant, to create a navy which, if it could not vie with those of the great maritime powers, would be at least of respectable weight if thrown into the scale of either of two contending parties. This would be more particularly the case in relation to the West Indies. A few ships of the line, sent opportunely to the reinforcement of either side, would often be sufficient to decide the fate of a campaign . . . By a steady adherence to the Union, we may hope, erelong, to become the arbiter of Europe in America and to combine the balance of European competition in this part of the world as our interest may dictate."

James Madison, who would later oppose the creation of a navy, agreed with Hamilton. "[America's] maritime strength," he wrote, ". . . will be a principal source of her security against danger from abroad." He added, "[naval guns] can never be turned by a perfidious government against our liberties."

Although no voices were raised in opposition to a navy at the Constitutional Convention, several were heard at the state ratifying conventions. Patrick Henry of Virginia was perhaps the best known of these, although there were many others, including George Mason, William Grayson, Melancthon Smith, James Monroe, and Peyton Randolph of Virginia; Rawlins Lowndes of South Carolina; and Governor Clinton of New York. Henry argued that America could not afford a navy of any real consequence. A small sea force of the kind produced during the War of Independence would be of no use against European nations, he argued, yet it would have the capacity to embroil America in their quarrels, provoking the very wars it was meant to avoid. Henry was convinced that those who wanted America to be a naval power respectable in the eyes of Europe were also bent on making the national government so powerful it would threaten the rights of its citizens. He was more interested in making liberty secure than in having a prestigious army and navy. And the burden of paying for a navy, he thought, would fall disproportionately on the south and west, while profiting the commercial interests of the northeast. Three thousand miles of blue water was protection enough for him.

More importantly, Henry did not want Congress to be powerful enough to abolish slavery. "Among ten thousand implied powers which they may assume," he proclaimed, "they may, if we be engaged in war, liberate every one of your slaves if they please. . . . Did we not see a little of this last war? We were not so hard pushed, as to make emancipation general. But acts of Assembly passed, that every slave who would go to the army should be free." Henry claimed that he would like to emancipate the state's 236,000 slaves but now wasn't the time; it would cause too many problems. "Manumission," he said, "is incompatible with the felicity of the country."

James Madison, the most effective advocate for the Constitution at the Virginia ratifying convention, answered Henry by pointing out the safeguards for slavery written into the document. Under the Constitution, he argued, slaves would not be able to gain their freedom by escaping to a free state whose laws emancipated them, whereas now they could.

Virginia narrowly ratified the Constitution, but many of its white citizens remained worried that the federal government would become powerful enough to liberate the slaves, who comprised half of the state's population. Madison and Jefferson shared their concerns, but they believed the central government's powers would be so limited that it would not pose a threat to slavery. Even so, they held that any military force, including a navy, had to be limited in size and strictly controlled. Henry was right, they believed, when he observed that war was a threat to slavery and must be avoided. Although they denounced slavery as evil on many occasions, as Henry did, Madison and Jefferson shared the views of the great majority of Virginians who wanted to preserve their comfortable tyranny. All of the state's politicians, including

Madison and Jefferson, recognized that the minute they tried to abolish the institution they claimed to abhor, they would be signing their political death warrants.

Washington, particularly after 1785, supported gradual emancipation, although he kept his views private. Hamilton was a member of the New York Manumission Society and advocated the abolition of slavery, although he owned slaves for most of his life. Jefferson and Madison, on the other hand, by their actions, not their words, considered slaves inferior human beings not capable of managing freedom. They believed that if the ideals of the Declaration of Independence were applied to slaves, a suicidal race war would result.

During Washington's first term (March 1789 to March 1793), no European threat caused the country to rush into a naval program, except for a brief moment in 1790. When a crisis developed between Britain and Spain over Nootka Sound, off present-day Vancouver Island, British Columbia, Europe's quarrels might have intruded on America's peace, forcing Washington to divert scarce resources to national defense before the new republic's fragile institutions were established.

Early in 1790 Lord Dorchester (formerly Sir Guy Carleton), the governor general of Canada, had dispatched his aide-de-camp, Major Beckwith, to New York to determine if President Washington would permit British troops to march across American territory and attack Spain in Louisiana. In the Treaty of Paris, Britain had ceded West and East Florida back to Spain, while Madrid had retained New Orleans and Louisiana. The nightmare of Britain gaining control of Spain's North American possessions haunted Washington. He far preferred having a weak Spain as a southern neighbor. Of course, America had unresolved problems with Spain as well as with Britain, the most important being free navigation of the Mississippi, which Washington considered essential to holding the union together. The southern boundaries of the United States were also in dispute, as was Madrid's continuous fomenting of Indian unrest. But Spain's weak fighting capacity posed only a minimal threat. The crisis passed when British Prime Minister William Pitt took firm action against Spain. Ever conscious of their military weakness, the dons backed down.

Washington's first priority in foreign affairs was to keep Europe's never-ending power struggles from interfering with America's new republican government. He was determined to observe strict neutrality. "Separated as we are by a world of water from other nations," he explained, "if we are wise, we shall surely avoid being drawn into the labyrinth of their politics and involved in their destructive wars." By relying on the protection of the oceans, keeping enthusiasm for one European country over another contained, and abstaining from great ambitions such as conquering Canada, Louisiana, Florida, Texas, or Mexico, Washington believed America could remain neutral without building a permanent navy for the time being. In the event of an emergency, he recommended arming merchant vessels. But clearly that would be insufficient, and he hoped the occasion would never arise.

When he first came into office, Washington judged that relations with Britain were most likely to drag America into the war he so desperately wanted to avoid. Like the rest of Europe, with the exception of France, Britain had treated the United States with contempt while she was governed by the Articles of Confederation, refusing to carry out important provisions of the peace treaty and ignoring requests for a more equitable trading relationship.

No two people felt British disdain more than John Adams, the American minister plenipotentiary in London from 1785 to 1788, and his close friend, Thomas Jefferson, the U.S. ambassador to France. Adams was hoping to negotiate a treaty of commerce, as Ambassador Jefferson had negotiated with the French in 1788, but Pitt ignored him. The degrading treatment accorded Adams was markedly different from what Jefferson was experiencing in Paris. "I found the [French] government entirely disposed to befriend us on all occasions," Jefferson wrote, "and to yield us every indulgence not absolutely injurious to themselves." As for the British, Jefferson characterized them as "the only nation on earth who wishes us ill from the bottom of their souls."

His opinion was reinforced when he visited London in 1786 and attended the king and queen at their levees. "It was impossible for anything to be more ungracious than their notice of Mr. Adams and myself," he wrote in his autobiography. "I saw at once that the ulcerations in the narrow mind of that mulish being left nothing to be expected on the subject of my attendance; and on the first conference with the Marquis of Caermarthen, his Minister of Foreign Affairs, the distance and disinclination which he betrayed in his conversation, the vagueness and evasions of his answers to us, confirmed me in the belief of their aversion to have anything to do with us."

Later he would complain to Madison, "[France] has engaged herself in a ruinous war for us, has spent her blood and money to save us, has opened her bosom to us in peace, and received us almost on the footing of her own citizens, while . . . [Britain] has moved heaven, earth, and hell to exterminate us in war, has insulted us in all her councils in peace, shut her doors to us in every port where her interests would admit it, libeled us in foreign nations, [and] endeavored to poison them against the reception of our most precious commodities."

John Adams, while irate, was less upset than his colleague. But there was no denying Britain's sour attitude. Galled by defeat, she had maintained an active dislike of her former colonies since the war. George III was particularly aggravated, as were England's upper classes. The king exhibited the same animus toward America that he had since the Intolerable Acts of 1774, indeed, since the Stamp Act crisis of 1765.

Britain's hauteur was encouraged by her emergence from the American war in a far stronger position than the nominal victor, France, who had bled herself white. France's irrational hatred of England and equally illogical generosity toward America had wrecked her already precarious financial system. Nothing similar had happened in Britain. The disasters to the empire that the king and his circle had predicted would follow American independence never materialized. Despite her defeat, Britain remained the most powerful country in the world. Of course, she had enormous war costs to pay, her navy needed to be restored, and her political system needed to be reformed. But she was fortunate in having a gifted new leader, William Pitt. He became prime minister in December 1783, at the age of twenty-four, and would dominate English politics for most of the next twenty-two years.

Although it did not appear so at the time, Pitt had a strong hand to play when he first took office. Even with all its problems, the Royal Navy remained dominant on the oceans, which alone made Britain formidable. But what made her so resilient was her unrivaled position at the forefront of the Industrial Revolution. The ingenious application of newly invented technology to manufacturing had gathered momentum in England throughout the eighteenth century; by the 1780s she was producing an impressive array of merchandise for trading. A high percentage of these goods moved through London. Many of the raw materials that fueled Britain's new factories passed through the city as well, making it preeminent in the world's commerce. Essential partners of her manufacturers and traders, London's great merchant banking houses were also growing at a dizzying pace, adding to the country's opulence and power.

The timely reform of her political system was another key to Britain's growing strength. Pitt's years as prime minister witnessed the diminution of the king's power and the rise of the modern cabinet system, which allowed Britain to meet the challenges of recovery from the American war, the wars of the French Revolution, and the war with Napoleon. The Parliament of place hunters and borough mongers that the king had managed gave way to a partially reformed institution led by a prime minister ultimately responsible to Parliament rather than to the king.

During the brief Rockingham ministry in 1782, the Economy Bill, the exclusion of contractors from Parliament, and the exclusion of revenue officers from the franchise had provided small but sufficient reforms to limit the power of the king. Pitt then used his great skill to revise the entire system. The king's reduced role also resulted from his own sensible restraint after defeat in the American war and from Pitt's personal independence. Gradually a cabinet system developed that evolved into the modern British system.

His Majesty, however, retained a good deal of power, especially in Pitt's earlier years. A source of strength for him was the people's memory of how he quelled the Lord George Gordon riots of June

2–9, 1780. London's streets had been taken over by a savage mob that ran riot, frightening the country and threatening the stability of the government. The king was the hero of the hour, and the memory of his swift action lasted into the era of the French Revolution.

Despite his residual strength, the king's political wings had been clipped. Pitt was now responsible to a majority in Parliament. To be sure, the House remained an oligarchy. But it did respond to the general sentiments of the country, particularly the squirearchy. At war's end, the country gentlemen were in no mood to be generous to America, nor were they throughout the 1780s.

Regardless of English prejudice, Washington hoped that the strength derived from the new Constitution would move London to settle the myriad problems left over from the Revolution. In the spring of 1790 he sent Gouverneur Morris to England as a special emissary. Washington intended to find out if the British would negotiate a commercial treaty and withdraw from the forts in the northwest that they still occupied in violation of the peace treaty. Morris was already in Paris on private business, and when he arrived in London he received a chilly reception. Prime Minister Pitt and his foreign secretary, Lord Grenville, behaved toward him with the same studied condescension that Pitt and Caermarthen had administered to Adams and Jefferson earlier. The prime minister felt no need to adjust the policies he had been successfully pursuing since 1783. Nor, in his view, was America strong enough, even under the new Constitution, to force a change.

Some historians have argued that Pitt rebuffed Washington because relations with the United States were unimportant to him. Although he was at great pains to avoid showing it, America had always been important to him because she was inexorably linked to the restoration of the Royal Navy—his first priority.

During the tenure of Lord Sandwich at the Admiralty in the 1770s and early 1780s, Britain's wooden walls had suffered grievously. Corruption wracked the navy and left its shipyards grossly mismanaged. Sir Charles Middleton, comptroller of the navy, wrote to Pitt, "The principle of our dockyards at present is a total disregard to public economy in all its branches."

Burdened by greed and incompetence during the American war and humiliated by the French at Chesapeake Bay, the Royal Navy was sorely in need of restoration when Pitt took office. Some of its prestige had been restored by Admiral Rodney's victory and subsequent capture of de Grasse and his flagship, the *Ville de Paris*, at the battle of the Saintes on April 12, 1782, but much remained to be done before the service could return to its former glory. Such was Pitt's main concern, and before the end of the decade he had accomplished his goal. Between 1783 and 1790, Britain produced twenty-four line-of-battle ships. By the time the crisis with Spain over Nootka Sound arose in 1790, the Royal Navy had ninety-three capital ships ready for battle and a prime minister eager to use them, which is why the dons had rushed to negotiate a settlement.

In the minds of the British mercantilists who dominated Parliament, the navy's strength was linked inextricably with the question of American trade. Immediately after the Revolutionary War, Britain had a strong desire to resume the profitable trading relationship with America that had ceased under wartime prohibitions. This generally agreed goal, however, was seen by the leading mercantilists, William Eden, later Lord Auckland, and John Holyroyd, Lord Sheffield, as a potential threat to the Royal Navy. An overly generous trade policy, they warned, could have the unintended consequence of undermining Britain's shipping industry and her carrying trade, which was "the great nursery for seamen" essential to a strong navy. Since the United States had an abundance of cheap raw materials, she could build merchantmen at a much lower cost than Britain. Thus the question of trade with America was of great concern to Pitt.

His policies were always guided by the preponderance of opinion in Parliament, and the mercantilists had the ear of the House. Although doubting the validity of Sheffield's arguments and preferring those of Adam Smith, the prime minister allowed Sheffield's views to dominate British policy for more than a decade out of political necessity. Protecting British shipping from American competition while at the same time enjoying the benefits of American trade became the cornerstone of Pitt's policy.

The mercantilists insisted that Britain had the power to shape relations with the United States as she pleased. Regardless of the Revolution, America was still considered an economic appendage of the mother country. Lord Sheffield argued in Parliament and in his popular pamphlet, *Observations on the Commerce of the United States*, published in 1783, that there was no need to offer the Americans any inducements to resume trade; their commerce was so tied to Britain's that they had no alternative. London, he felt, needn't worry that the Americans would shift their business to the Continent. American produce would always find the British market more suitable than any other.

In the summer of 1783—months before Pitt took office—when Lord Shelburne's government was replaced by the short-lived Fox-North ministry, Charles Fox had set about restoring the strong trading relationship with America that the War of Independence had interrupted. He repealed the wartime prohibitions against trade and moved to admit American raw materials to British markets as if the war had never happened.

In a series of orders in council (executive decrees) beginning on July 2, 1783, American raw materials were admitted directly to Britain at duty rates below those of other countries, giving the United States a substantial incentive to resume prewar trading patterns. English credit was critical to the process, and this was plentiful. Neither French nor Dutch lenders cared to compete; too many of them had bad experiences with American merchants. Meanwhile a flood of English imports were welcomed into the United States, demonstrating that the American desire for English manufactured goods was greater than ever. American exports carried in British ships to the West Indies and Canada also resumed at a brisk pace.

Shipments of goods in American bottoms to Britain's colonies in the West Indies, however, were strictly prohibited. Shipments could be made only in British bottoms or colonial bottoms, not American. Subsequent orders in council extended the West Indian prohibitions to Nova Scotia, New Brunswick, Newfoundland, Prince Edward Island, Cape Breton, the coast of Labrador, and the islands bordering the St. Lawrence.

American merchants were furious at these restrictions and did everything they could to circumvent them. And they were partially successful. British edicts did nothing to curb the appetite for cod in the West Indies or rum in New England, and American captains, nearly all of whom had experience as privateers during the Revolution and as smugglers before that, had no trouble outsmarting or bribing British officials to land their goods. As Samuel Eliot Morison points out, "A Massachusetts vessel putting into a British port 'in distress' was likely to obtain an official permit to land its cargo and relieve the 'starving population.'"

While Yankee merchantmen reestablished old avenues of trade, they also opened new ones, traveling the globe in search of profit, going around the Horn, into the Pacific, up the western coast of South and North America, out to the Pacific islands, and up the Pearl River to Canton in China. Despite this burgeoning world trade, however, Britain remained by far the most important U.S. trading partner, and when America came out of her postwar economic depression in the late 1780s, British trade was seen by Yankee merchants as, in good part, responsible for it.

When Pitt took office, he strengthened the mercantilist policies of his predecessors. This tough approach toward America extended beyond matters of trade and shipping. For years the prime minister declined to send an ambassador to the United States; none was appointed until George Hammond arrived at the end of October 1791. Pitt refused to withdraw from the western forts that the British had agreed (in the Treaty of Paris) to evacuate "with all convenient speed," using the excuse that the United States had not carried out its obligations to loyalists and English creditors under the peace agreement.

When the treaty was signed, Britain held eight strategic forts around the Great Lakes: Fort Michilimackinac at the western end of Lake Huron, a fort at Detroit (the western end of Lake Erie), Fort Erie at the eastern end of Lake Erie, Fort Niagara at the western end of Lake Ontario, a fort at Oswego on the southeastern shore of Lake Ontario, and forts at Dutchman's Point and Pointe au Fer at the outlet of Lake Champlain.

Only Fort Erie was on Canadian soil; the rest were within American territory. The British clung to the forts for a number of reasons: unhappiness with the generous terms of the treaty, a desire to unilaterally redraw the boundary with Canada, a determination to keep ministering to their Indian allies in order to protect the hugely profitable fur trade that had flourished between Europe and the Indians for nearly two centuries, and a desire to limit American westward expansion. London even dreamed of splitting the western and eastern parts of the United States.

The British entered into arrangements with the Allen brothers of Vermont, offering them important trading advantages that would link Vermont with Canada. They tried to induce Tennessee and Kentucky to split off from the union, and they worked to separate the entire Northwest Territory (composed of the present states of Ohio, Indiana, Illinois, Michigan, and Wisconsin) from the United States, with a view to establishing a British-dominated Indian buffer state between the Ohio River and Canada.

Having been excluded from the negotiations, the Indian nations of the Northwest Territory did not accept the Treaty of Paris. They refused to recognize the sovereignty of the United States over their lands. In spite of their willingness to fight for what was rightfully theirs, however, their small numbers made successful resistance impossible without British support.

At the time of the Treaty of Paris the Indians in the Northwest Territory probably numbered between 100,000 and 200,000. There were even fewer Americans, but their numbers were increasing fast. Ohio, for instance, had a few thousand settlers, but by the start of the War of 1812 its population had grown to over 250,000. Indiana, Illinois, Michigan, and Wisconsin had similar increases. South of the Ohio River the population explosion was even more pronounced. In 1783, Kentucky contained perhaps 12,000 settlers; by 1812 it had 400,000. Because their numbers were so small, the Indians had no way to successfully fight this massive appropriation of their lands.

Despite their weakness, the Indian nations fought back tenaciously, causing Indian affairs to trouble Washington throughout his presidency. Unlike the British, who had sold out the Indians at the

Treaty of Paris by giving away their lands without consulting them, Washington was driven to find a more humane way of dealing with them than simply killing them and stealing their territory. He concluded that they could only save themselves by giving up their ancient culture and becoming part of America as simple farmers, as other immigrants had done. But the Indians would never give up their way of life, nor did Washington really expect them to.

War debts owed to British creditors were also at issue between the two countries, as was restoration of property confiscated from loyalists and the collection of debts due to loyalists before the war. Slaves too were a problem. Under the terms of the treaty the British agreed not to carry "away any Negroes" when they withdrew from American soil. But feeling an obligation to the former slaves who had joined their ranks, the departing British took many with them. Their southern owners demanded compensation, and they made this an important issue—a test of how much northern politicians such as Hamilton, who wanted to free the slaves, would protect southern interests.

While reaching a settlement with Britain was of great importance, Washington's main task during his first term was turning the brave words of the Constitution into a workable republican government. Nothing like it had ever been attempted over so wide an expanse of territory. Aristocratic Europe, especially Britain, assumed that America would fail. Many in London even thought that once the republican experiment had collapsed, America would return to the empire.

Essential to the success of the new government was maintaining unity. To Washington it was self-evident that republican government could only succeed if the country held together. His first priority thus was strengthening the country's centripetal forces. In this he had the support of congressional leaders, but the task was formidable. In its first session Congress passed the Bill of Rights, established a federal judiciary, organized the executive departments, and built a strong fiscal underpinning for the federal government. A new American force on the high seas would have to wait until these more pressing matters were settled.

Anxious to appease anti-Federalists such as Patrick Henry, James Madison, the leader in the new House of Representatives, moved adroitly in the first Congress to enact the Bill of Rights. With its passage the Constitution's opponents faded away as a political force. Congress also passed the Judiciary Act and set up four executive departments—Treasury, State, War, and Attorney General—allowing the president, not the Congress, to remove their heads. In addition, Congress began to address the government's fiscal health.

These far-reaching measures were necessary second steps in laying a solid foundation for the new republic. The first had already been taken by the unanimous election of Washington as president. On April 23, 1789, when the new chief executive arrived in New York City to assume office, thirty-one-year-old Fisher Ames, a newly elected congressman from Massachusetts, spoke for his countrymen when he said, "When I saw Washington, I felt very strong emotions. I believe that no man *ever* had so fair a claim to veneration as he." John Quincy Adams wrote later, expressing sentiments he felt at the time, "Washington's character would to all ages be a model of human virtue untarnished by a single vice. . . . [His was] one of the greatest names that ever appeared upon the earth for the pride and consolation of the human race. I feel it as an inestimable happiness to have been the contemporary and countryman of that man."

Even before the Bill of Rights was approved, Madison began the complicated task of putting the country's fiscal affairs in order. He arrived in New York in mid-March 1789 and made creating a permanent revenue stream his first order of business. Establishing a tax base was necessary for all subsequent financial reforms and, indeed, for the experiment in republican government to succeed. When the House of Representatives managed its initial quorum on April 1, he introduced a bill that placed a general tariff on foreign imports, with specific duties on molasses, rum, wine, liquor, tea, cocoa, sugar, and coffee. A tariff on imports, he thought, would be the least intrusive way of exacting revenue. At the same time duties would protect America's fledgling industries, particularly shipping.

Madison's proposal received broad support in Congress. To be sure, pulling and hauling occurred over specific duties such as that on molasses. Fisher Ames, the most eloquent of New England's representatives, claimed molasses was essential to the economy of his region and a duty on it should be kept to a minimum. Others argued on behalf of their own states and regions, but the dire need for a dependable revenue was so generally recognized that the differences were soon resolved.

Young Ames gave this impression of Madison: "A man of sense, reading, address and integrity . . . He speaks low, his person is little and ordinary. He speaks decently, as to manner, and no more. His language is very pure, perspicuous and to the point. Pardon me if I add that I think him a little too much of a book politician and too timid in his politics. . . . He is not a little of a Virginian and thinks that state the land of promise, but is afraid of their state politics and of his popularity there more than I think he should be. . . . He is our first man."

Madison also introduced a bill to collect duties on every vessel entering an American port based on its carrying capacity in tons. He made a distinction between American-owned and -built ships and foreign-owned in order to discriminate in favor of American shipping. Tonnage duties and a modest assist to American shipping had wide support in Congress. Madison also proposed that foreign-owned vessels from countries having a commercial treaty with the United States, such as France, pay a duty of thirty cents per ton, while those from other countries, such as Great Britain, pay fifty cents. Discriminating against the British in favor of the French introduced a complicated and controversial issue. Congress was deeply divided on the matter. Without France, America would not have won the Revolution, and French benevolence had continued throughout the 1780s, but Britain was the nation's chief trading partner, the source of the federal government's revenue. Ninety percent of American trade was with Great Britain. Under the going arrangements America was experiencing a pleasant prosperity that many did not want to disrupt, no matter how annoying the British were.

During the War of Independence the patriots and the French hoped their alliance would shift American commerce away from Britain to France. Trade with the French at the time was negligible, but Foreign Minister Vergennes expected that to change. His hopes, however, never materialized. Madison and Jefferson wanted to revive Vergennes's old dream by enacting economic sanctions against the British. They believed such sanctions would radically alter trading patterns in favor of the French. They were also convinced that if Britain's trade were seriously threatened, she would settle her outstanding differences with America.

Hardheaded members of Congress from both north and south did not share the Virginians' dream. Shipping interests in the northeast did not see any likelihood that business would shift to France. They preferred to rely, as they always had, on English trade and English credit. The south wasn't enthusiastic either. Since most of its products were carried in British bottoms, excessive tonnage duties would make shippers pay more and in so doing aid the northeast without any profit to themselves. In the end the House of Representatives passed Madison's bill, but the Senate, reflecting the views of the country, refused, eventually approving it without Madison's tonnage duties.

After creating a permanent revenue stream, the House agreed to take up the far more difficult matter of establishing the credit of the United States. It directed the thirty-three-year-old Treasury secretary, Alexander Hamilton, to submit a plan that would solve the nation's debt crisis. The task was daunting. The country had been living on expedients since 1775; the Continental Congress had more creditors than any other regime in the world and no means of payment. When Hamilton totaled how much the country owed, it was staggering: foreign debt alone amounted to $11 million, plus $1.6 million in interest. Of this total the French king had loaned $4.4 million, Dutch bankers $1.8 million guaranteed by France, Dutch bankers $3.6 million without a French guarantee, and Spain $175,000. The United States was in arrears on both interest and principal. All the revenue generated by Madison's new taxes would be consumed by servicing the foreign debt and making scheduled principal payments of $1.4 million a year.

The domestic debt was even more complicated. It consisted of a bewildering variety of obligations taken on by the Continental Congress and state governments during the Revolution. The debts acquired by the Continental Congress amounted to $40 million, and Hamilton estimated the combined debt of the various state governments at around $25 million.

To establish public credit Hamilton had to refinance this entire debt—foreign, national, and state—on more favorable terms and obtain additional revenue. He had given years of thought to the problem and had a clear idea of how to proceed. On January 9, 1790, he presented to Congress a bold, far-reaching program entitled *Report on the Public Credit* designed to turn America's debt problem into a source of strength. Hamilton proposed that the federal government assume responsibility for all of the country's old obligations and guarantee that interest would be paid automatically and would not depend on annual appropriations. Accomplishing this required an annual revenue, which Hamilton proposed to create by lowering interest payments in a manner acceptable to foreign credit holders and raising taxes. He advocated additional duties on coffee, tea, and alcoholic beverages, and an excise tax on spirits made domestically.

Hamilton proposed leaving the principal intact to be funded, that is, not paid immediately but managed by the government so as to provide stability and capital for a growing economy, and to serve as a foundation for a sound currency. The principal would eventually be paid slowly by a sinking fund, similar to the one Pitt had used to retire Britain's massive debt from the American war.

As he did with all cabinet officers, Washington oversaw Hamilton's work in detail. The president was not a financial expert, but what the secretary proposed made sense to him and he gave Hamilton his critical support.

The fate of any future navy depended on getting the national debt right. Before the country could consider building adequate defenses, it had to put its finances on a sound footing. Washington felt this basic need deeply from his experiences during the Revolution, when only timely gifts and loans from France had allowed his ragged army to continue the fight.

Hamilton's far-reaching program provoked fierce opposition, led by Madison and supported behind the scenes by the new secretary of state, Thomas Jefferson. Their basic complaint was that Hamilton's scheme represented an unconstitutional accumulation of power in the federal government, endangering individual liberties and states' rights.

Madison's stance surprised Hamilton, just as the Virginian's proposal of discriminatory tonnage duties had the previous year. Madison was Hamilton's friend and had collaborated on the *Federalist Papers,* which helped the Constitution pass the state ratifying conventions. Hamilton found it difficult to believe that Madison would oppose his fiscal program, which he saw as strengthening the federal government and binding the diverse elements of the country together—Washington's fundamental objectives. In addition to opposing Hamilton's program of establishing public credit, Madison would oppose nearly every measure Hamilton proposed for the country's fiscal health. And in this he was supported at every step by Jefferson. The differences between Hamilton and the Virginians would eventually become so extensive they would spawn two political parties, the Federalists and the Republicans.

The precocious John Quincy Adams, observing the fight over Hamilton's proposals, wrote to his father on April 5, 1790. "The seeds of two contending factions appear to be plentifully sown," he said. "The names Federalist and Anti-federalist are no longer expressive of the sentiments which they so lately supposed to contain, and I expect soon to hear a couple of new names, which will designate the respective friends of the national and particular systems. The people are evidently dividing into these two parties."

Madison's biographer, Irving Brant, notes, "A new day began on January 14, 1790, when Secretary Hamilton submitted his *Report on Public Credit.* With it new battles began, new alignments were formed and political parties began to take shape in the United States."

Despite Madison's skillful opposition Hamilton was able to carry his entire program in the Congress except for the assumption of state debts; this point was resolved by a compromise organized by

Hamilton, Jefferson, and Madison, whereby the Virginians would accept Hamilton's debt assumption arrangement in return for establishing the new seat of government on the Potomac. Thanks to the efforts of Senator Robert Morris, Philadelphia would be the capital for ten years while the new capital was being built, and then the government would move south to the Potomac. Washington approved the compromise. He wanted Hamilton's debt scheme passed, and he couldn't help but be pleased that the new capital would be close to Mount Vernon.

On March 16, 1790, in the middle of the argument over the assumption of state debts, Benjamin Franklin, in his last significant public act as head of the Pennsylvania Abolition Society, presented a proposal to abolish slavery, which he considered America's greatest unresolved constitutional issue. For Franklin and his associates slavery was an abomination that made a mockery of every principle America stood for. It was a cancer eating away at the foundation of the republic. If the United States were to achieve the greatness he foresaw, slavery had to be eradicated. The shameful compromises made at the Constitutional Convention to protect it had to be undone.

Franklin's plan provoked a hysterical reaction among some southern members of Congress, led by William Loughton Smith of South Carolina, who vehemently denied that all men are created equal. Black Africans, he said, are inferior human beings who could not be emancipated without damage to themselves and to southern society. He made it clear that the southern states would withdraw from the union rather than give up slavery, an integral part of their cherished way of life. He threatened civil war over any attempt to forcibly abolish human bondage. "We took each other with our mutual bad habits and respective evils," he shouted, "for better for worse; the Northern States adopted us with our slaves, and we adopted them with their Quakers." Many who knew Smith well thought he was "a selfish, coldhearted, unscrupulous little Tory." He had never served with the patriots during the Revolution, remaining in England the entire time, where he exhibited no sympathy for the rebel cause.

Madison was embarrassed by Smith's crude assertion of these racist principles. When Madison was not in Virginia, where he had to support slavery or retire from politics, he liked to acknowledge "the imbecility ever attendant on a country filled with slaves." But for some reason or another, it was never the right time to actually do anything about the problem. On this occasion he quietly buried the issue, pointing to the constitutional prohibitions against removing slavery. He protested that although in theory he was opposed to slavery, this particular proposal was premature, liable only to incite the south and destroy the unity of the republic, perhaps even provoke a civil war.

Washington quietly supported Madison. In his view, this was not the time to tear the country apart over slavery. Unity was more important. Eliminating slavery would have to wait. Washington agreed with Franklin's purpose; he too was deeply troubled by the contradiction between the ideals of the Revolution and the reality of slavery. He wanted to emancipate the slaves gradually, but the necessity of holding the country together stayed his hand. His ultimate solution was gradual emancipation by the state legislatures, although, after listening to William Smith and his colleagues, this goal seemed a long way off.

Having passed Hamilton's debt program intact, the Congress adjourned on August 12, 1790, assigning him the additional task of proposing a program for new taxes, a national bank, and a mint. Hamilton returned with plans to establish a bank that would service the federal government's need for short-term capital, facilitate tax collection, serve as a depository for government funds, create a stable, expanding currency, and establish a pool of capital widely available for regular business and economic development. The bank would be privately owned and run for the benefit of its shareholders, something Hamilton hoped would bind the business community to the national government.

Madison and Jefferson supported the mint and an excise tax, but they opposed the national bank. After Congress had approved the measure, Washington, responding to Madison's argument that the bank was unconstitutional, reconsidered it. The president had great respect for Madison's acumen, especially when it came to interpreting the Constitution. He listened carefully to Madison's arguments but in the end rejected his line of reasoning and signed the bill in February 1791.

The divide between Hamilton and the Virginians widened in 1791, as Jefferson and Madison became convinced that Hamilton posed an increasing threat to republican institutions. Jefferson described Hamilton and his supporters as monocrats, claiming they were creating a moneyed aristocracy that would lead to either a military dictatorship or something akin to a British-style monarchy. Hamilton's open admiration for Britain was particularly alarming; it implied a permanent dependence on her. The Virginians wanted America to draw herself as closely as possible to France, whether she became a constitutional monarchy or a republic. Hamilton, on the other hand, held that since Britain was the source of the federal government's revenue and no immediate alternative existed, it was the height of folly to destroy this partnership. A friendly relationship with Great Britain seemed to him wise, even inevitable.

The French Revolution broadened the gulf of suspicion among the three men. The Virginians' love of France and hatred for Britain colored all their thinking. The revolution that began in Paris during the summer of 1789 had thrilled them. At the time, Jefferson was still the American ambassador in Paris and knew many of its liberal leaders intimately. He became convinced that the French government would reform itself peacefully, gradually turning into a constitutional monarchy based on the Declaration of the Rights of Man. When the new National Assembly passed the declaration on August 26, 1789, Jefferson's enthusiasm soared. "Men are born and remain free and equal in rights," declared Article I, in words reminiscent of Jefferson's own in the Declaration of Independence. He saw the French Revolution, following America's own, as a sure indication of the direction of history.

Jefferson would have liked France to evolve into a republic, but given the circumstances, he thought a limited monarchy was the most that could be achieved for the time being. Moving beyond that might trigger a violent reaction from France's unreconstructed aristocrats, which could make peaceful evolution impossible. He was pleased that reform appeared to be advancing peacefully during the early period of the Revolution, and as time passed he became more sanguine. When he returned to the United States in 1789 to become secretary of state, he came with high expectations for France, and for spreading French and American political ideals throughout aristocratic Europe, changing the nature of their societies and transforming international life. He also hoped that French ideals would strengthen America's.

Madison's view of the French Revolution was the same as Jefferson's. In the spring of 1791 he wrote, "France seems likely to carry through the great work in which she has been laboring. The Austrian Netherlands have caught the flame and with arms in their hands have renounced the government of the [Austrian] emperor forever. Even the lethargy of Spain begins to wake at the voice of liberty summoning her neighbors to her standard. All Europe must by degrees be aroused to the recollection and assertion of the rights of human nature. . . . the light which is chasing darkness and despotism from the Old World is but an emanation from that which has procured and succeeded the establishment of liberty in the new."

Washington was less optimistic. "The revolution which has been effected in France," he wrote to Gouverneur Morris, "is of so wonderful a nature that the mind can hardly realize the fact. If it ends as our last accounts to the first of August [1789] predict that nation will be the most powerful and happy in Europe; but I fear though it has gone triumphantly through the first paroxysm, it is not the last it has to encounter before matters are finally settled."

Hamilton had an even more skeptical view. In writing to Lafayette he expressed apprehension, fear, and dread for the Revolution's ultimate fate. "Your philosophic politicians," he warned, "may aim at more refinement than suits either human nature or the composition of your nation."

John Adams, with his long experience in France, also had deep misgivings about the Revolution from the very beginning. Although he hoped for the best, he feared the worst from the unicameral, all-powerful legislature that had sprung up. To Sam Adams he wrote, "Everything will be pulled down. So much seems certain, but what will be built up? Are there principles of political architecture? . . . Will the struggle in Europe be anything other than a change in imposters?" He feared not.

Seeing the rift in his cabinet between Hamilton and Jefferson as a threat to the unity he prized, Washington tried to mend it. He had a high regard for both men and urged them to reconcile, but the divide between them had become too wide. Like Hamilton, Jefferson was a fiscal conservative, but his view of the economic and political landscape was so utterly different from that of his rival that compromise was impossible. In addition, Jefferson ascribed the worst motives to Hamilton, accusing him of trying to undermine the Constitution and install a monarchy.

The president and Gouverneur Morris thought Jefferson's contention that Federalist oligarchs were intent on establishing a monarchy absurd. The secretary of state, Washington felt, was exaggerating Hamilton's views beyond all recognition. The Federalists supported a strong union, sound credit, and a hierarchical social order, and they were suspicious of mobs and anything that smacked of democracy, but they were not trying to install a monarchy. For one thing, as Morris pointed out, oligarchs and kings were normally engaged in a perpetual contest for power. Washington "did not believe that there were ten men in the United States whose opinions were worth attention, who entertained such a thought [as monarchy]."

The schism in the administration had important consequences for the navy. Wrangling over fiscal policy extended to other subjects, including building a respectable sea force. Changing their minds from what they had proposed the previous decade, Jefferson and Madison now opposed a navy, seeing it as contributing further to the alarming growth of federal power. Until a groundswell of public opinion supported the taxes necessary to pay for a new fleet, their opposition made the development of a successor to the Continental Navy impossible.

The president had wanted to begin building a navy earlier, in December 1790 advocating use of a sea force to stop Algerian attacks on American ships. A committee of the Senate on January 6, 1791, proposed starting a navy "as soon as the state of the public finances will permit." Strong opposition, however, killed the idea. As a loyal member of the administration, Jefferson had publicly supported the new program. He had always advocated using warships against the Barbary States, and he had not changed his mind. But if a naval force were built, he wanted it strictly limited, never large enough to be a factor in relations with Europe.

As a substitute for a deep-water fleet Madison and Jefferson proposed economic coercion. The heart of their approach to defense policy was to avoid war with any European power unless the United States were actually invaded. Even then, they did not want a standing army or navy to be ready ahead of time. In an emergency, they favored calling up militias and authorizing privateers. Jefferson abhorred armed conflict; in his view, peaceful means of settling disputes were always preferable. He was fond of pointing out that the Revolutionary War had been enough armed combat for him. Jefferson had also been impressed by how successful economic pressure had been before the Revolution in persuading Britain to change her policies, particularly during the fight over the Townsend duties in 1768. Madison's views on defense policy were identical.

Peace and unity had been the central themes of Washington's first term. Without them, he believed, the nation had little hope of establishing a viable republic. The future of the Constitution, in his view, rested on America's ability to hold together and to remain uncommitted to the French Revolution and to the countries that opposed it. He thought that a respectable naval force would serve the country well in accomplishing both objectives. He had little faith that the economic measures favored by Madison and Jefferson would achieve either goal.

John Barry.
"John Barry," artist unknown.
Courtesy of the
Naval Historical Center.

The Continental Navy Ship *Alfred*. "Alfred," by W. Nawland Van Powell. Courtesy of the Naval Historical Center.

Bonhomme Richard. "Bonhomme Richard, ex Dux de Duras, 1778," by Edward Tuffnell. Courtesy of the Naval Historical Foundation.

Bonhomme Richard versus *Serapis.* "The Action Between Serapis and Countess of Scarborough, and John Paul Jones's Squadron, 23 September, 1779," by Richard Paton. Courtesy of the Naval Historical Center.

Battle of the Virgina Capes. "Battle of the Virginia Capes," by V. Zveg. Courtesy of the Navy Art Collection.

Benjamin Stoddart. "Benjamin Stoddart," by E.F. Andrews. Courtesy of the Department of the Navy.

John Barry during the
Quasi-War. "John Barry,"
by Gilbert Stuart.
Courtesy of Navy Art Collection.

Thomas Truxtun.
"Commodore Thomas Truxtun,"
artist unknown. Courtesy of the
Navy Historical Center.

Stephen Decatur.
"Stephen Decatur,"
by John Wesley Jarvis.
Courtesy of the
Navy Art Collection.

John Rogers.
"Commodore John Rogers,"
artist unknown.
Courtesy of the
Navy Art Collection.

Isaac Hull.
"Commodore Isaac Hull,
USN (1773–1843),"
by Samuel L. Waldo.
Courtesy of the
Naval Academy Museum.

Oliver Hazard Perry.
"Commodore Oliver
Hazard Perry, USN," by
Orland S. Lagman.
Courtesy of the
Navy Art Collection.

United States versus *Macedonian*. "USS United States versus HMS Macedonian, 25 October 1812," by Edward Tuffnell. Courtesy of the Naval Historical Foundation.

Constitution versus *Java*. "USS Constitution Sighting HMS Java, December, 1812," by Edward Tuffnell. Courtesy of the Naval Historical Foundation.

John Paul Jones. "John Paul Jones," by Antoine Houdon.
Courtesy of the Library of Congress.

Shannon versus *Chesapeake*. "Chesapeake-Shannon," by J.C. Schetky, Esquire. Courtesy
of the Naval Academy Museum.

8

WASHINGTON AND
THE FEDERAL NAVY

March 1793–March 1797

By the end of Washington's first term in 1792 the gulf of suspicion between Hamilton and Jefferson so disturbed him that he changed his mind about retirement. He had planned to return to Mount Vernon after his first term, but the bothersome divisions in the country as reflected in the cabinet caused him to reluctantly stand for reelection. Since he was the essential force for unity in the country and his own cabinet threatened it, he felt compelled to remain. Once again, as he had been during the Revolution, at the Constitutional Convention, and as the first president, he was the indispensable man.

Interestingly, both Hamilton and Jefferson, sensing that matters could indeed spin out of control, urged the president to stay. And as things turned out, it was good that he did, for beginning in the spring of 1793 the maelstrom of the French Revolution reached America's shores, severely testing the new Constitution. Had it not been for Washington holding the center, the centrifugal forces unleashed by the new European war might well have torn the country apart.

By the fall of 1792, events in France took an ominous turn as reason gave way to passion. Since the hopeful days of 1789, the France that Jefferson and Madison so admired had undergone profound change. On the night of August 10, 1792, a second revolution occurred. The Parisian mob stormed the Tuileries, deposed and imprisoned King Louis XVI, dispersed the National Assembly, and convoked the National Convention to determine France's republican future. When it met, the convention called for a national election, which took place a month later. The election produced a new National Convention, which ruled France for the next three years with no constitutional restraints. Unlike America, where power was divided, in France all authority resided in the National Convention. It had no more checks on it than had the French kings, and perhaps fewer. In September 1792, after drumhead trials, eleven hundred assorted "enemies of the republic" were executed. Some estimates of the number murdered were as high as six thousand.

Secretary of State Jefferson knew of the bloody massacres, and, although he wished they hadn't happened, he was willing to overlook them. Ambassador Gouverneur Morris in Paris and William Short, the former American chargé d'affaires in France, now observing from The Hague, reported accurately on what transpired. But Jefferson objected to their interpretation of events. He wrote to Short, reprimanding him. "The liberty of the whole earth was depending on the issue of the contest," Jefferson said, "and was ever such a prize won with so little blood? My own affections have been deeply wounded by some of the martyrs to this cause, but rather than it should have failed, I would have seen half the earth desolated. Were there but an Adam and Eve left in every country, and left free, it would be better than it now is."

French armies under General Charles-François Dumouriez unexpectly won victories at Valmy on September 20, 1792, and at Jemappes on November 6, 1792, and easily conquered the Austrian Netherlands (now Belgium). The liberated Belgians had welcomed the French at first, and French revolutionaries began thinking that people all over Europe would welcome them as liberators. On November 19, 1792, the ideologically aggressive convention declared its intention to "grant fraternity and assistance to all people who wish to recover their liberty." Brissot de Warville, one of Jefferson's friends and a fiery leader of the convention, urged overthrowing the ancien régime in every European country, declaring "a war of the human race against its oppressors . . . a war of all peoples against all kings."

In December 1792, Louis XVI was convicted of high treason and decapitated on January 21, 1793. In a powerful speech to the convention, Danton spoke for the regicides. "Let us fling down to the Kings the head of a King as gauge of battle," he shouted.

On February 1, 1793, France declared war on Britain and then on Holland and Spain, making the fighting in Europe general. War had already begun the previous spring and summer against Austria and Prussia. The convention assumed that its brother republic, the United States, would be a staunch ally, and Jefferson and Madison hoped that it would.

Washington, however, did not. He received the news of war between Britain and France on April 12, 1793, just as his second term was beginning. An express rider from Philadelphia galloped up the drive at Mount Vernon and handed him the shocking report. His immediate instinct was to keep the country from being sucked into another European conflict. Ten days later, he wrote to the Earl of Buchan, "[We want] to have nothing to do with the political intrigues, or the squabbles of European nations; but on the contrary, to exchange commodities and live in peace and amity with all the inhabitants of the earth."

Even though Americans were overwhelmingly pro-French, and though it was not clear that the president had the authority to proclaim neutrality, Washington intended to do so as soon as possible. Congress was in recess and would not meet until December 3. A special session would take at least two months to assemble, and Washington didn't think he could wait that long. Events might spin out of control and the country could find itself allied with France whether it wanted to or not. At the moment, the French cause was wildly popular and Britain was still hated. Privateers were waiting to dash into the Atlantic to begin their lucrative trade.

Although he was usually scrupulous about observing congressional prerogatives, Washington rushed back to Philadelphia and on April 22 issued on his own authority what became known as the Proclamation of Neutrality. In it he demanded that the country be "friendly and impartial towards belligerent powers" and prohibited American citizens from "aiding or abetting hostilities or otherwise engaging in unnatural acts within the jurisdiction of the United States." He obtained the full backing of his four-member cabinet, including Secretary of State Jefferson, who made it clear that while the correct posture for the government might be neutrality, his sympathies were with France.

Privately Jefferson opposed neutrality. He thought that since Congress had the sole right to declare war, it also had exclusive power to declare neutrality. Madison felt the same. Jefferson proposed that America at least obtain concessions from the belligerents—particularly Britain—for remaining neutral, but Washington rejected the idea.

Jefferson was more ambitious politically than he admitted, and it was not lost on him that his "private" stance was popular in much of the country, particularly in the south and west. He made his views widely known through a steady stream of correspondence.

On April 8, 1793, four days before Washington received news of the outbreak of war, France's new ambassador to the United States, Edmund Charles Genet, had arrived in Charleston, South Carolina, aboard the frigate *Embuscade.* He had brought an ambitious program, aimed at negotiating a new treaty with the United States that would establish "an intimate concert to foster in every way the extension of the Empire of Liberty, to guarantee the sovereignty of peoples, and to punish those powers with exclusive colonial and commercial systems by declaring that their vessels should not be received within the ports of the two contracting nations."

Genet took it for granted that under Article 17 of the Treaty of Commerce of 1778, France had the right to sail warships and privateers into American ports, repair and victual them, outfit and man privateers, bring in captured vessels, dispose of prizes without having to sail to France and be subject to interception by the Royal Navy, and establish independent French courts to condemn those prizes. Article 22, in effect, also prohibited Britain, if at war with France, from fitting out privateers in American ports. Ambassador Genet carried with him hundreds of blank commissions for privateers, and it was precisely to prevent them from setting out under French flags that Washington had declared neutrality.

Genet also had instructions to obtain advance payment of the American debt to purchase grain for France and for Saint-Domingue. And he was ordered to encourage independence movements in Canada, Louisiana, and the Floridas. Bourbon Spain was Britain's ally at the time. In short, Genet intended to involve the United States in France's war with Britain whether the American president wanted it or not.

The French ambassador represented the Girondin faction in the National Convention. From August 1792 until June 1793, the Girondin ruled France, maintaining an ideologically aggressive foreign policy. Its leaders felt that if the governments of the world did not support France, their people would. Genet's instructions reflected this messianic sentiment. But on May 31, 1793, Jacobin zealots, supported by the Parisian mob, overthrew the Gironde and guillotined its leaders. The same fate would await Genet when he returned home. Unaware of his changed circumstances, however, he continued his clumsy attempts to align the United States with France.

Threatened internally and externally, the French convention had fallen more and more into the hands of its radicals, who concentrated power in the Committee on Public Safety, composed of twelve people. The police remained under the control of the Committee on General Security, but otherwise, a single committee now ruled France, dominated by a puritanical genius, Maximilien Robespierre, and a few cohorts.

Robespierre imposed an efficient dictatorship on France. Blood flowed freely as he dealt ruthlessly with any opposition, real or imagined. His Reign of Terror took the lives of as many as forty thousand citizens, until Robespierre himself was brought down and executed in July 1794. By that time the country had been in the grip of mindless violence for a year and a half. Hamilton and the Federalists were horrified and drew closer to Britain, while Jefferson, Madison, and the Republicans overlooked the killing and the dictatorship and continued to support France, believing that in time the republic of their dreams would be instituted.

Normally a new minister entering the country would present his credentials to the president at the seat of government in Philadelphia, so it was a surprise when Citizen Genet chose Charleston as his port of entry. Nevertheless, Governor Moultrie of South Carolina greeted him warmly. Genet expected as much; since France and America were fellow republics and allies under the treaties of 1778, the ambassador expected to be received with open arms. Immediately he began outfitting American ships as French privateers in Charleston and manning them with local sailors. Governor Moultrie allowed him to send out four privateers and make plans for more. The *Republican*, *Anti-George*, *Sans-Culotte*, and *Citizen Genet* put to sea and were soon sending captured British prizes into Charleston, where Genet had established prize courts administered by the French consul, Michel Ange Mangourit. Genet also entrusted Mangourit with organizing a clandestine army to invade Spanish Florida. Governor Moultrie assisted with the Army of Florida. Genet also started a Democratic Society in Charleston—an American version of the Jacobin Clubs in France. Similar organizations had been springing up all over the country since the beginning of the year.

Having set all this in motion in only eleven days, the energetic new minister traveled to Philadelphia not in the *Embuscade* but overland, speaking in perfect English to enthusiastic crowds who gave him the impression that overwhelming numbers of Americans supported the new French republic. When he arrived in Richmond, Genet learned of Washington's neutrality proclamation and was surprised, since it was so at variance with what he had experienced on his triumphal journey north. Genet concluded that the

American people would support the French cause despite their misguided president. Because in France all power resided in the legislative body, Genet was confident that he could appeal to Congress, and that it would countermand Washington's proclamation.

On May 2, while Genet was on the road to Philadelphia, the *Embuscade*, under Captain Bompard, sailed into Philadelphia with two British merchantmen in tow as prizes. One of them, the *Grange*, had been taken in Delaware Bay in American territorial waters—a direct violation of Washington's neutrality proclamation. The *Embuscade* had already captured two other British prizes and had brought them into Charleston. Hundreds of well-wishers crowded the wharves in Philadelphia, cheering the frigate as she approached the waterfront. Jefferson described the scene to Monroe: "The *yeomanry* of the city crowded and covered the wharves. Never before was such a crowd seen there, and when the British colors were seen *reversed* and the French flying above them they burst into peals of exultation."

When Genet arrived in Philadelphia on May 16, enthusiastic crowds greeted him there as well. So did Secretary Jefferson. "All America," Genet reported home, "has risen up to recognize me the Minister of the French Republic: the voice of the people continues to neutralize President Washington's declaration of neutrality. I live here amid perpetual feasts." For weeks Philadelphians feted Genet, their guests unaware of events in France that would soon make it impossible for him to return home without being led forthwith to the national razor. The Democratic Society of Philadelphia was just forming as he arrived, providing him more evidence of the enthusiasm for the French cause in America.

On May 18, Ambassador Genet belatedly presented his credentials to President Washington, who received him correctly but coolly, expressing no interest in a crusade to liberate North America from British or Spanish rule and replace it with an "Empire of Liberty." Undeterred, Genet kept on with his activities, which were directly at odds with Washington's policy of neutrality.

Hamilton kept the British ambassador, George Hammond, informed of the rift between Genet and the administration. The British were pleased that, without their having to alter their harsh policies toward the United States, a new Franco-American alliance was not in the cards. In fact, Genet's ill-conceived maneuvers allowed the British to become even tougher on neutral trade and impressment.

Meanwhile, in July Genet directly challenged Washington by arming and outfitting the brigantine *La Petite Democrate* as a French privateer right in Philadelphia. She had been the British merchantman *Little Sarah*, taken as a prize by the *Embuscade* and sent into Philadelphia to have her armament strengthened from four to fourteen guns. She had a crew of 120, some of whom were Americans. Genet planned to use her to help liberate Louisiana from Spanish tyranny. Genet himself directed the projected invasion from Philadelphia. He was aided by George Rogers Clark, a hero of the Revolution, and Clark's partner, Dr. James O'Fallon. At the same time that Genet had his eye on Louisiana he was also pursuing the old French dream of taking Canada back from the British.

All of these projects were a direct challenge to Washington. But when Pennsylvania authorities and Secretary Jefferson warned Genet that he was defying a presidential order, the ambassador threatened to fight any effort to stop *La Petite Democrate* from sailing. Genet's outburst angered Jefferson, who finally realized that the Frenchman was doing more harm than good. On the night of the interview, he wrote to Madison, "Never in my opinion [has] so calamitous an appointment [been] made as that of the present Minister of France here. Hot headed, all imagination, no judgment, passionate, disrespectful and even indecent to the [President] in his written as well as his verbal communications. . . . He renders my position immensely difficult."

Albert Gallatin, who originally had high hopes for Genet's mission, now described the minister: "Violent and conceited, he has hurt the cause of his country here more than all of her enemies could have done. . . . He is totally unfit for the place he fills."

On July 9 *La Petite Democrate* left Philadelphia and dropped down the Delaware to Chester, where she anchored. Two days later Washington arrived in Philadelphia from Mount Vernon, furious at Genet's effrontery and at the inability of the United States to do anything about it. A few days later, in defiance of the president, *La Petite Democrate* sailed down the Delaware and into the Atlantic. There was no American navy to stop her; not a single warship was flying the American flag. Secretary of War Knox had tried to set up a battery on Mud Island but was too late.

When Washington issued formal protests, Genet took vehement exception. On August 12, Washington demanded his recall and France, now securely in the hands of Robespierre and the Committee of Public Safety, agreed. The French needed American food, and Robespierre wanted to maintain friendly relations. He did not like Washington's neutrality, but until a change of presidents brought someone like Jefferson or Madison or Monroe to power, he was willing to work with the present administration. He did, however, link Genet's recall to that of Gouverneur Morris, the Federalist minister in Paris, who never had any use for the Revolution and certainly not for its most recent incarnation. To appease Robespierre, Washington replaced Morris with the pro-French Monroe.

Official word of Genet's recall did not reach America until the end of the year, and in the meantime Genet continued his fanciful projects. His ambition had soared during the second week of July 1793, when a French fleet commanded by Vice Admiral Cambis and Vice Admiral Sercey arrived on the American coast from Saint-Domingue in poor condition and put into New York for refitting. The fleet consisted of seven warships, two of them 74s. Genet had high hopes of employing them against Florida, Louisiana, and Canada, but the admirals had other ideas. They kept the fleet in New York until October 5 and then sailed home, taking Genet's dreams with them. In the end he succeeded in commissioning only twelve privateers in the United States, and they captured eighty British merchantmen.

Genet's replacement, Jean Fauchet, presented his credentials to Washington on February 22, 1794. He requested the arrest of Genet, intending to send him back to France and the guillotine. Fauchet also relieved every consul who had armed privateers and withdrew support for Genet's plan against Spanish Louisiana. As Fauchet confirmed, Robespierre intended to support Washington's neutrality.

Chastened, Genet sought asylum in the United States, which Washington generously granted. He had done the same for Genet's predecessor, Jean-Baptiste Ternant. Politically identified with Lafayette, Ternant was scheduled to return home when the Gironde was in power and any *Fayettiste* who showed his face in Paris would have been murdered.

The need for an American navy had become more apparent than ever to Washington. Genet's mischief had made it obvious that the time had come for the United States to begin the long process of building a respectable fleet. But a large body of opinion, led by Jefferson and Madison, still opposed the president, making his task exceptionally difficult.

While Washington was having trouble maintaining neutrality toward France, he was having an even more difficult time with Britain. War with France had led to the seizure of American ships by the Royal Navy and the impressment of America seamen. Despite London's manifest interest in keeping the United States neutral, Pitt was pushing Washington so hard that, regardless of Genet's bungling, America was being forced into the war on France's side. Pitt felt that the war would be over in a few months, and he could put up with the displeasure of the United States until then. Americans were outraged, not only by Britain's reckless tactics on the high seas but by her activities in the Northwest Territory as well. Talk of a second war of independence was widespread.

By the order in council of June 8, 1793, British captains had been instructed to stop all cargoes of corn, flour, and meal from reaching France, thus declaring food contraband. The American ambassador in London, Thomas Pinckney, protested immediately to Lord Grenville, the foreign minister, telling him that starving France into submission was impossible. Grenville responded by saying that starving France could bring peace. Washington insisted on the rights of neutral commerce, and Secretary Jefferson instructed Pinckney to keep protesting that free ships make free goods.

Pitt ignored Washington; British warships continued to stop American merchantmen, capturing them and impressing men as they pleased. Charles James Fox, the opposition leader in Parliament, thought it was folly for Pitt to pick a quarrel with the United States at this moment. Had it not been for Washington's preoccupation with Genet's intrigues, the reaction of the United States might have been far stronger.

Meanwhile, the Committee of Public Safety had ordered French men-of-war to seize neutral ships carrying British goods, but the state of the French navy was such that the order was merely an irritant.

The order in council of November 6, 1793, was worse than any that had preceded it. Under this decree British captains were allowed to seize any American vessel sailing to any French port or carrying any French goods. The order was kept secret for three months while dozens and then hundreds of unsuspecting American ships fell into British hands. Traders flying the flag of the United States were everywhere in the Caribbean, and British men-of-war captured them under any pretext, claiming they were carrying French goods or goods bound for French ports, whether they were or not. Royal Navy captains put the burden of proof on the American ship's captain to prove the goods in his hold were not going to France or her colonies. Since that was impossible, the merchantman would then be taken into a British port and confiscated, the crew given the choice of a British prison hulk or impressment. More than three hundred vessels were captured in the West Indies before the Americans realized what was happening.

While Pitt was pressing Washington hard on the high seas, he was also refusing to give up the forts in the northwest or cease encouraging the Indians against the Americans. Settlers in the Northwest Territory attributed the continuing hostility of the Indian nations north of the Ohio to British machinations. Lord Dorchester, the royal governor of Canada, upset by Genet's attempts to foment insurrection in Canada, thought war with the United States was imminent and on February 10, 1794, delivered a bellicose speech to the six Iroquois nations. He told them they would soon be at war with the Americans and promised British support to drive the "long knives" south of the Ohio once and for all. In response, Washington ordered intelligence collected to learn just how many troops Britain had in Canada.

Adding to the resentment against England was an agreement between Portugal and Algeria. Since 1786 the Portuguese navy had kept the Algerine corsairs confined to the Mediterranean. Portugal was the only European country that used force instead of bribery to contain the pirate states. In October 1793, Colonel David Humphreys, the American minister resident in Lisbon, wrote to Secretary Jefferson that Portugal had concluded a year's truce with Algeria and Algerian ships were now free to roam the Atlantic. On October 8, immediately after the truce had been signed, Algerian pirates seized the American merchantmen *Dispatch*, *Hope*, and *Thomas*, enslaving their crews and giving every indication of capturing more. Within two months Algeria had taken thirteen American vessels. In a separate letter to Washington, Humphreys insisted that this was the work of the British.

The U.S. consul in Lisbon, Edward Church, reinforced Humphreys's opinion. On October 12 he wrote to Jefferson, "The conduct of the British in this business leaves no room to doubt or mistake their object which was evidently aimed at us, and proves that their envy, jealousy, and hatred, will never be appeased, and that they will leave nothing unstamped to effect our ruin."

News of the Algerian attacks reached Philadelphia on December 12, 1793, throwing the country into an uproar. Americans saw Algeria as a British surrogate. On December 16 Washington laid Church's communications before Congress. Foreign Secretary Grenville denied that Britain was using Portugal's truce with Algeria as a weapon against the United States. He told Ambassador Pinckney that the truce was designed to free the Portuguese fleet for duty against France, not to unleash Algeria for attacks on American shipping. Few in the United States believed him.

At the opening of Congress in December 1793, the frustrated Washington gave vent to sentiments he had long held. "There is a rank due to the United States among nations," he said, "which will be withheld, if not absolutely lost by a reputation for weakness. If we desire to avoid insult we must be able to repel it; if we desire to secure peace—one of the most powerful instruments of our prosperity—it must be known that we are, at all times, ready for war."

Reacting to the brazen behavior of Ambassador Genet, Prime Minister Pitt, and the dey of Algiers, and frustrated with American impotence in general, Congress secretly debated whether or not the time had finally come to start a navy. On January 2, 1794, the House of Representatives voted narrowly, 46 to 44, to create a fleet adequate to protect American commerce from the Barbary corsairs and appointed a committee to determine its size. The select committee had estimates drawn up by Secretary Henry Knox in 1790, and by Samuel Hodgdon of Philadelphia in 1793. Hodgdon had been quartermaster general of the army and was now superintendent of military stores.

On January 20 the House select committee recommended building four 44-gun frigates and two of 20 guns at an estimated cost of $600,000, to be raised by additional customs duties. On February 6 the full House debated this proposal.

While they did, Secretary Knox invited naval architect Joshua Humphreys to his office. (At the time, the navy was part of the War Department.) Knox intended to get right to work on the frigates as soon as Congress passed a bill. Captain Richard Dale, the first lieutenant under John Paul Jones on the *Bonhomme Richard*, John Barry, and Thomas Truxtun had all written to Knox about the urgency of confronting the Barbary pirates. Knox wanted to push ahead with construction of a fleet while the political will existed in Congress to do it.

Madison led the opposition. Six warships, he thought, were only a beginning; supporters of a navy would want far more (as indeed they did). He decided to stop the momentum before it got started. He wrote to Jefferson, "You will understand the game behind the curtain too well not to perceive the old trick of turning every contingency into a resource for accumulating force in the Government."

Madison's allies maintained that bribing the Barbary pirates would be cheaper than building an expensive navy, which would expand the public debt. They pointed out that since the United States had no bases in the Mediterranean, a larger fleet would be required. And they contended that sending warships into a European war zone would provoke further hostilities. Britain, they argued, would aid the pirates, and the captives in Algeria would suffer rather than be saved. Abraham Clark of New Jersey warned that once construction of a fleet commenced "there would be no end of it. We must then have a secretary of the Navy and a swarm of other people in office, at a monstrous expense." In a similar vein, Senator William Maclay of Pennsylvania said, "It is the design of the Court party to have a fleet and an army. This is but the entering wedge of a new monarchy in America, after all the bloodshed and sufferings of a seven years' war to establish a republic. . . . eleven unfortunate men now in slavery in Algeria is the pretext for fitting out a fleet."

Madison assumed a building program would take a long time and, once completed, the warships, as had been the case with the Continental Navy, would be pitifully inadequate in any contest with Britain. A navy would necessitate high taxes that would grow as it embroiled the country in wars she could not win. A better way to deal with Britain, he argued, was through economic warfare, where America had substantial weapons and the British were vulnerable. He felt that England, with its heavy dependence on American business, would be forced to relent. He did not believe that economic sanctions would cause London to retaliate or declare war.

To Madison, Britain was at the root of America's problems. When the disputes with her were resolved, those with Algiers would be resolved as well. "It is all French that is spoken in favor [of Madison's measures]," Fisher Ames wrote. "I like the Yankee dialect better."

Led by Hamilton, the Federalists predicted that Madison's economic reprisals would provoke war at a time when the country was wholly unprepared. If the United States wanted to avoid both war and humiliation, they argued, she needed a respectable navy. They manifestly did not want war with Britain, but they did want a navy that could minimally protect the nation's rights and grow in the future. They insisted that six warships would be enough to handle Algeria.

The tide of anti-British feeling in the country was strong enough to give the Federalists the upper hand, and they pushed hard for approval of the proposed fleet. On March 7, 1794, news reached Philadelphia of the notorious British orders in council of November 6 and the unrestrained seizing of American vessels in the Caribbean. Even Hamilton was outraged. The feeling against England grew white hot. On March 25 the House enacted a thirty-day embargo against Britain, which the Senate approved the following day and Washington signed immediately. The law went into effect on March 28.

The Naval Act of 1794, having passed the House on March 10 by a vote of 50 to 39 and the Senate nine days later with no recorded vote, was signed by Washington on March 27. It authorized building four 44-gun frigates and two 36s, increasing the size of the latter from the earlier 20s. The bill also detailed the number, grades, and ratings of officers and men, even their pay and rations. The preamble stated that the law was meant to protect American commerce from the Barbary States. Left unsaid was the lawmakers' intention to make an impression on Britain and France as well. But the only impression they made was one of continued weakness, for the country was obviously divided, uncertain whether it wanted a navy or not. Six frigates, by any measure, was a pathetically small force. Weakening it further was the final section of the act, which read, "if a peace shall take place between the United States and the Regency of Algiers, that no farther proceeding be had under this act." In other words, when peace was secured with the dey, construction on an American fleet would cease. The Federalists in the House, led by South Carolinian William Loughton Smith, had included this provision to appease their opponents, but a more nonsensical compromise would be hard to imagine.

Pitt had maintained his tough policy toward the United States through 1793, expecting the war with France to be brief; in that case he could avoid altering his posture toward America. He had not anticipated the conflicting interests and gross incompetence

of his European allies or his own strategic misjudgments in attacking France in the West Indies and dividing his forces instead
of concentrating them directly against Paris. The war looked very
different to him and to the cabinet at the end of 1793 than it had
at the beginning. By year's end the French had grown far
stronger, and the war seemed likely to continue for some time.

France's strength came from her new radical government.
Robespierre and the Committee of Public Safety created the most
efficient (if not humane) regime France had known in the eighteenth century. Lazare Carnot took over direction of the army, and
by instituting conscription and ruthless efficiency, he created a
military force so large and powerful that it had the capacity to defeat the combined armies of all the European monarchs, including
Britain. The world had never seen such a force. Its sheer numbers
were overwhelming.

The French navy did not enjoy a similar renaissance. Prior to the
upheavals of 1789, the entire officer corps had been aristocrats—
officiers rouge. The Revolution drove nearly all of them out of the service. Mutinies occurred in every French port as crews rose against
their officers, who fled the country or were murdered. All French
admirals, including distinguished seamen like D'Albert de Rions,
were forced from the navy and either left France or were guillotined.
When the government tried to resuscitate the navy, it had to replace
the entire officer corps. Some deserving petty officers—*officiers bleu*—
were promoted from the ranks and performed well, although for the
most part men who lacked the training and experience to command
ships of war were installed. The chaotic state of the French navy
allowed the British a nearly uninterrupted string of victories at sea.

On January 8, 1794, as war fever spread in the United States, Ambassador Pinckney wrote from London that Pitt had reversed course and
revoked the noxious order in council of November 6, 1793. Food
bound for France, however, was still to be interdicted. Disturbed by
the drift toward war, Washington welcomed the news when it
reached him on April 4. Prior to Pinckney's message, the president
thought that Britain might be deliberately provoking hostilities. To

him, war was an unmitigated evil that profited no one. If peace could be honorably obtained, it was infinitely preferable.

Hamilton supported the president. Although he was dismayed by British behavior and demanded indemnification for losses, he also urged a pacific resolution of the crisis on revenue grounds. As Britain and America raced toward war, he wrote to Washington pointing out that should British imports be cut off, the consequences would be catastrophic. A stoppage would give a "sudden and violent blow to our revenue which cannot easily, if at all, be repaired from other sources," he argued. "It will be such a great interruption to commerce as may very possibly interfere with the payment of duties which have hitherto accrued, and bring the Treasury to an absolute stoppage of payments—an event which would cut up credit by the roots."

Hamilton and several others, including Edmund Randolph (Jefferson's successor as secretary of state), Robert Morris, Rufus King, George Cabot, Oliver Ellsworth, Caleb Strong, and John Jay, urged Washington to dispatch a special envoy to London. The president, reluctant to offend Ambassador Pinckney, eventually agreed. After rejecting Hamilton for the assignment, he chose Chief Justice Jay.

Washington wrote later to his secretary, Tobias Lear, "The order of his Britannic Majesty in Council of the 8th of June last, respecting neutral vessels had given much discontent in the United States, and that of the 6th of November, and its results had thrown them into a flame. . . . The subsequent order of the 8th of January has, in a degree, allayed the violence of the heat, but will by no means satisfy them without reparations for the spoliations on our trade, and the injuries we sustain from the non-performance of the Treaty of Peace. To effect these, if possible, by temperate means, by fair and firm negotiation, an envoy extraordinary is appointed."

The Senate confirmed Jay on April 19, 1794, by a vote of 20 to 8. One of those opposed was Senator James Monroe of Virginia, who declared Jay biased in favor of Britain and therefore "not a suitable character."

Jay avoided consulting with the Senate before leaving, for fear that it would put restrictions on his freedom to negotiate; senators would get the finished treaty to approve or not later. Jay sailed on

May 12 and arrived on June 8 with instructions that gave him wide latitude. He was, however, specifically prohibited from entering into an agreement contrary to the treaties the United States had with France, and he was not to approve any treaty of commerce that forbade American trade with British colonies in the West Indies. Apart from these two stipulations, he was left to his own devices.

While Washington was pursuing peace he was also arming. On June 5 he appointed six captains to oversee construction of the new frigates, assigning each captain a warship to superintend. The frigates would be built in six different cities, spreading the work around and thus strengthening political support for the navy, even though using separate sites would add substantially to costs. Philadelphia, Portsmouth, Boston, New York, Baltimore, and Norfolk were chosen, and the captains, in order of seniority, were John Barry, Samuel Nicholson, Silas Talbot, Joshua Barney, Richard Dale, and Thomas Truxtun—all veterans of the Revolutionary War. Barney, however, didn't like the arrangement; he insisted he was senior to Talbot, and when Secretary Knox informed him, none too tactfully, that he was not, Barney refused to serve. Not lacking for senior officers, Knox replaced him with James Sever. Barney was an exceptional leader, and Knox's unnecessarily harsh treatment of him deprived the service of perhaps the country's finest fighting sailor.

Washington expected the design of the frigates to answer the critics' argument that they would be useless against the British. Although they would certainly be inferior in numbers, Washington intended them to be, ship for ship, superior to any frigate in the Royal Navy. Secretary Knox considered a number of designers and finally settled on Philadelphian Joshua Humphreys, generally recognized as America's foremost naval architect. In May 1794, Knox appointed him "Constructor of the Navy of the United States." Humphreys had played a key role in designing and constructing the first ships of the Continental Navy when he was a young man in his twenties. Now in his early forties, he had many years of experience behind him. The father of eleven children, Humphreys lived in Haverford, Pennsylvania, a western suburb of Philadelphia, and he was eager for the assignment. A year before Congress passed the Navy Act of 1794 he had already developed plans for the frigates, consulting with many people, including Philadelphia's famous Captain John Barry and Senator Robert Morris, the most influential member of Congress on naval matters. Both Barry and Morris were strong supporters of the plans. Humphreys also had assistance from Josiah Fox, an Englishman with experience building British warships, and Thomas Doughty, a talented young naval architect.

Humphreys envisioned warships that were faster and more powerful than their European counterparts, able to fight or run, depending on the circumstances. Heavily influenced by French designers, who had "cut down several of their 74s to make heavy frigates," he "expected the commanders of [the American frigates to] have it in their power to engage, or not, any ship, as they may think proper; and no ship under 64-guns now afloat but must submit to them." Their largest guns were to be 24-pounders rather than the 12- and 18-pounders common on British frigates, and they were to be built with the best materials available: Georgia live oak, red cedar, pitch pine, locust, and Maine white pine.

Resembling small battleships, Humphreys's frigates could carry more than 50 guns, but he could not classify them as sail of the line without raising hackles in Congress. He devised planking and rigging similar to sail of the line, with tumble home (incurving) sides to handle greater weight on the top deck, wide beams that gave the masts more stability, and gun decks nine feet above the waterline, making a better platform for cannon and providing enhanced safety in dirty weather. In addition, Humphreys's frigates, because of the design of their hulls and sail plans, would be exceptionally fast.

The British found the notion of American frigates as the fastest and most powerful ships afloat absurd. The Royal Navy's superiority had been demonstrated time and again against every European country that challenged it, especially France. Their belief in English dominance conveniently overlooked the fact that the officer corps of the French navy had been decimated by the egalitarian theology of the Revolution; winning encounter after encounter with it proved little. A better test would come later in ship-to-ship battles with the Americans during the War of 1812, when Humphreys's frigates would vindicate his claims.

As powerful as they were, Humphreys's ships carried less armament than their displacement would allow. He used the extra space to improve living quarters for the crew and enlarge the storage area for water and food. This was but one indication of the humane treatment American seamen were accorded. Well paid, well fed, and well cared for, with enlistments of two years or less, they were all volunteers; impressment was forbidden, in contrast to the Royal Navy, where crews included felons or landsmen captured by press gangs and condemned to serve for as long as the ship was afloat, which could be years. British tars were illiterate for the most part and had no benefits, except for pay, which they were regularly cheated out of. They were never permitted leave for fear they would desert, and for the same reason they received no remuneration until their ship was discharged.

The unfortunates who were caught by British press gangs were hauled aboard warships with nothing but the clothes on their backs and thrown into a filthy hell below. None of them would ever forget the stench. Suffocating fumes produced an odor that no landsman could even conceive of. Its sources were easily identifiable. The men slept in hammocks fourteen inches apart, in a ship that, like all wooden ships, continually leaked in fair weather and foul, producing a perpetual damp. The crew seldom changed clothes or even washed. With no fires permitted below, except in the galley forward, the tars lay in their wet clothing in the cold. Sweaty, clammy, close packed, lousy, flea infested, they breathed air that reeked from dirty water in the bilge, an accumulation of rotting refuse swept into the ballast, and the decaying carcasses of drowned rats and other vermin trapped in hidden crevices.

Horrendous punishment awaited deserters who were caught, yet conditions aboard were so bad that many risked it, creating a continuous problem of manning. Death from disease and accidents was far more common than death in combat. It's a wonder that these men ever fought, but when the time came, they did, making the Royal Navy the strongest in the world.

In June Washington ordered the six captains to take charge of building, outfitting, and manning the frigates. Copper sheathing was required, and this, along with other materials, such as some of the cannon, had to be imported from England. Paul Revere's rolled copper would not be available until after the turn of the century.

Washington visited Humphreys's shipyard at Southwark on the Delaware River and was pleased with what he saw. The president kept a close eye on the frigate program in Philadelphia. So did John Barry, leaving the city on October 5, 1794, to spend a month in Georgia examining the live oak operation on St. Simons and Hawkins islands. Barry found that obtaining the live oak was extraordinary difficult. The inhospitable climate, the way the trees grew, and dangers from snakes and fevers delayed the harvesting.

Nothing about constructing the warships was easy, and invariably compromises had to be made. The builders looked for suitable wood wherever they could find it. The *Constitution*, which was being built in Boston, used white pine masts and spars from Maine. Fortunately these were the finest in the world. The giant trees were over a hundred feet tall and two to three feet thick. It took three dozen oxen and their drivers, with axmen and other laborers—about fifty men in all—to fell a tree and drag it to the nearest river. Mainers usually cut in winter because the deep snow cushioned the tree's fall. They would chop out a road leading to the nearest tidal river and then trample it down with oxen. The tree's larger branches—used for bowsprits, yards, and topsails—were pulled over the roadway to firm the ground, and then the great trunk itself was dragged on sleds by teams of oxen—thirty in front and four to eight at the side—down to the water, where the great pine would be floated to a mast house for hewing. The Royal Navy had used the pines for 130 years before the Revolution. Henry Hudson, it was said, had cut the first one near Penobscot Bay as early as 1609, but it wasn't until the summer of 1634, when HMS *Hercules* sailed into Camden harbor with orders from the Navy Board to collect great white pines from the surrounding hills, that serious harvesting had begun.

Most of the great trees close to rivers had been cut, so many of the trees for the *Constitution* had to come from the town of Unity, Maine, which was somewhat inland. Still, Unity was not far from the towns of Waldoboro, Damariscotta, and Sheepscot, whose shipbuilders had been using local white pine for decades. Their shipyards were conveniently located on tidal rivers like the Medomac, Damariscotta, and Sheepscot. The trees from Unity were hauled down to them and towed behind packet boats to Boston.

On June 5 Washington signed a bill for the construction of ten row-galleys, modeled after those built during the Revolution. Jeremiah Wadsworth of Connecticut praised the galleys' utility, as did Thomas Fitzsimons of Pennsylvania. The proponents of the bill told how useful they had been in the war, wildly exaggerating their accomplishments. The truth was that no ambitious officer wanted to command them; frigates were always far more attractive. Building only ten, however, was a waste. To be useful, hundreds were needed.

In any event, the row-galleys were never built.

When Ambassador Jay landed in England, Foreign Secretary Grenville received him warmly, emphasizing that the cabinet wanted a friendly relationship with the United States. During his first two weeks Jay talked frequently with the foreign secretary and dined with the cabinet. Despite the goodwill on both sides, however, the issues that separated them were difficult. But Jay and Grenville persevered, both knowing that the alternative was war, which neither wanted. On August 5, 1794, Jay wrote to Washington that the ministry was prepared to settle.

While negotiating with Jay, Grenville kept a wary eye on the new American ambassador in Paris, James Monroe. Monroe had arrived in France on July 31 aboard the *Cincinnatus*, captained by Joshua Barney. Three days earlier the convention had executed Robespierre, putting an end to his Reign of Terror and ushering in a period of uncertainty. Despite its disorganized state, the convention received Monroe warmly, and he reciprocated, ignoring the bloodshed of recent months and expressing great goodwill toward the republic. Grenville was suspicious. He didn't want to abandon Britain's North American forts, reduce her troops in Canada, weaken her policies on neutral trade, and in general seek a rapprochement with the United States, only to find Washington on the side of the enemy.

Grenville complained to Jay in writing, knowing that Jay would be receptive. Jay had never been enthusiastic about the French Revolution. He wrote letters to Washington, Hamilton, and Secretary Randolph, criticizing Monroe's behavior. Somewhat mollified, Grenville went on with the negotiations, although Monroe's desire to ally the United States to France, despite Washington's policy of neutrality, continued to be a problem.

When the negotiations ended and Jay was sending the finished treaty home, he wrote, "I do not know how the negotiation could have been conducted, on their part, with more delicacy, friendliness, and propriety, than it has been from first to last."

In the same spirit Grenville wrote to Jay on November 19, the day they signed the treaty, "I cannot conclude this letter without repeating to you the very great satisfaction I have derived from the open and candid manner in which you have conducted . . . the whole of the difficult negotiation which we have now brought to a successful issue, and from the disposition which you have uniformly manifested to promote . . . lasting friendship, between our two countries."

From Jay's point of view, the virtue of the treaty was that it prevented war and established a more friendly relationship with Britain at a time when the United States was defenseless. For the British, the treaty reinforced American neutrality. Pitt agreed to evacuate the northwestern posts. He gave up the idea of pushing the United States south of the Ohio River and setting up a British-dominated Indian buffer state between the Ohio River and Canada. The thorny issues of spoliations by the Royal Navy, debts from the Revolution, the Maine–New Brunswick boundary, and other Canadian boundary questions were left to commissions.

In addition, Jay agreed that Britain's enemies would not be permitted to operate warships and privateers from American ports or

sell prizes there. He accepted Britain's Rule of 1756, which stipulated that trade with enemy colonies not permitted in peace would
not be allowed in war, and he accepted the British doctrine of *consolato del mare* concerning neutral goods. This traditional British
practice allowed the Royal Navy to take enemy goods from neutral
ships and was entirely at odds with the American principle of freedom for neutrals to trade in noncontraband goods.

With certain restrictions, Article 13 of the treaty granted trade
privileges in India, a little-recognized provision that eventually
proved to be of importance to the expansion of American commerce. Article 12 allowed American merchant vessels not exceeding
seventy tons to trade in the British West Indies; in return, American
bottoms were prohibited from carrying molasses, sugar, coffee, cocoa, and cotton "to any part of the world, except the United States."
This article naturally caused much consternation in America because
these items, particularly cotton, were of increasing importance to
American trade, and because seventy tons of cargo seemed much too
little.

But this was only theoretical. American bottoms, regardless of
the law or the Royal Navy, continued to trade in the Caribbean.
The British themselves specifically granted exceptions because
they could not supply the goods needed in the West Indies. Smuggling continued as before.

Jay agreed to a ten-year guarantee against tonnage and tariff
discrimination against British goods, and granted Britain most favored nation treatment. The treaty also contained language aimed
at mollifying France. Article 25 stipulated, "Nothing in this Treaty
contained shall however be construed or operate contrary to former and existing Public Treaties with other Sovereigns or States."

The British offered no compensation for the slaves they carried off
after the Revolution. At the conclusion of the war, American slaves
who had joined British forces were taken aboard their departing vessels. The more fortunate were delivered to the Canadian maritime
provinces or taken to England, but many were shipped to the West
Indies and sold into even more abominable slave societies. This was an
important matter for the south. Jay was a known abolitionist, and

southerners watched closely to see if he would protect the property rights of slaveholders. But since Jay considered these "rights" obscene, he did not oppose Grenville's refusal to compensate the slave owners.

No mention was made of the Royal Navy's impressments of American seamen. It was not yet the issue that it would become later, but it still rankled. At this stage of the war with France, the Admiralty needed fewer seamen than it would when the war with France intensified.

Impressment would not have been a problem at all if the Royal Navy had treated its seamen decently. The grim lot of British tars caused young men to avoid the service, making impressing necessary in wartime. For three hundred years England had employed this counterproductive method of manning her warships, and she refused to change. It was no wonder that whenever a British warship docked in an American port, some crew members looked to desert and hire aboard the first American vessel they found.

If given fair treatment, British seamen might have volunteered in adequate numbers. Generous enlistment bonuses, fair and timely pay, better food, improved treatment for the wounded, the right to leave, pensions for the permanently injured, and a more equitable distribution of prize money would have strengthened the seamen's underlying patriotism and attracted the men Britain needed. But the continued dominance of the ocean by British warships against France and all other European navies led the Admiralty to cling to its traditions.

The more enlightened officers of the Royal Navy recognized that the foul treatment of crews reduced their fighting capacity. Had the Admiralty employed more humane methods, its ships would have been more effective instruments. But the old ways were hard to change. Even the dramatic mutiny at Spithead on Easter Sunday, April 16, 1797, and that at the Nore on May 7 did not lead to fundamental change. The chief complaint of the mutineers at Spithead was pay; despite inflation, wages for seamen in the Royal Navy had not changed since 1652. The mutineers' demand was so obviously just that the Admiralty and Parliament reluctantly agreed to a modest increase. The other demands of the Spithead mutineers, such as a more rational bounty system, more and better food, and improved conditions for the injured, were so modest that they were eventually agreed to, although the changes were fitfully administered.

On March 7, 1795, four days after the close of the congressional session, Jay's Treaty arrived in Philadelphia. Jay himself followed on the 28th. His treaty was the first of importance completed under the new Constitution, and it would become one of the most famous and controversial in American history. Washington thought it favored the British too much, but he accepted it as the best obtainable under the circumstances. It was a way to avoid having to choose between war and humiliation.

Popular indignation, however, ran rampant wherever the Republicans were strong. South Carolina's Christopher Gadsden declared that he would "as soon send a favorite virgin to a brothel, as a man to England to make a treaty." Jefferson called Jay's work "infamous." The treaty's sole merit for him was that it averted war, but, in his view, wasn't worth the price. He branded it as "nothing more than a treaty of alliance between England and the Anglomen of this country against the legislature and people of the United States."

It was a tribute to Washington's broad tolerance for differences of opinion that he had put up with Jefferson's bizarre criticism, while he was secretary of state, for as long as he did. To suggest, as Jefferson did at every opportunity, that Hamilton was bent on establishing a British-style monarchy in the United States seemed to the president patent nonsense.

On June 8, 1795, Washington laid the treaty before the Senate, and on the 24th it passed by a close two-thirds vote, on condition that Article 12 be suspended. This did not end the controversy, however. Republicans wanted to use the treaty's unpopularity to strengthen Jefferson's run for the presidency in 1796. Even though the Senate had approved it and the president had ratified it, the treaty still needed funds for the mixed commissions it created to do their work. Led by Madison, Gallatin, Edward Livingston of New York, John Beckley of Pennsylvania, and William Giles of Virginia,

House Republicans attempted to use their control of spending to destroy the treaty.

Public opinion, however, had changed since the treaty had first arrived in the United States the previous year. The country was enjoying a general prosperity, and people were reluctant to put it at risk by warring with Britain. In addition, Spain was responding to the Anglo-American rapprochement by allowing free navigation of the Mississippi. And the provisions in Jay's Treaty with respect to the forts of the northwest, coupled with General Anthony Wayne's victory over the Indians at Fallen Timbers on the Maumee River (near present-day Toledo) on August 20, 1794, appeared to emasculate the Indians and open the Northwest Territory to exploitation.

The matter came before Congress on February 29, 1796. For their opening move, House Republicans asked the president to release all documents related to the treaty. Washington viewed their request as unconstitutional and refused. The disagreement was bitter. Madison wrote to Jefferson, "The progress of this business throughout has to me been the most worrying and vexatious that I ever encountered. . . . The people have been everywhere made to believe that the object of the House of Representatives in resisting the treaty was war, and have thence listened to the summons 'to follow where Washington leads.' . . . The New England states have been ready to rise in mass against the House of Representatives. Such have been the exertions and influence of Aristocracy, Anglicism, and Mercantilism, in that quarter, that Republicanism is perfectly overbalanced, even in the town of Boston."

The fight over the treaty did not end until April 30, 1796. Washington prevailed when the House voted 51 to 48 to appropriate the money necessary to carry the treaty into effect. John Adams wrote to Abigail, "Five months have been wasted upon a question whether national faith is binding on a nation."

To demonstrate Britain's change of heart, Lord Grenville offered to intercede with Algiers on America's behalf, and his intervention drew a positive response from the dey, who had no desire to offend the British. Until this point, negotiations between the

United States and Algeria, which had been going on for months, had achieved nothing. Now, concerned that Jay's Treaty signaled a new relationship between the English-speaking countries that might include a secret naval alliance, the dey agreed to a deal. On September 5, 1795, Joseph Donaldson Jr., the American consul for Tunis and Tripoli, signed a treaty with Algiers in which the United States agreed to pay $642,500 in a lump sum, plus $21,600 yearly in naval stores, and deliver a 36-gun frigate.

Under the terms of the Naval Act of 1794, the treaty with Algiers halted construction of the six frigates. Washington asked Congress to reconsider the old law, which it did. On April 20, 1796, Congress passed the Naval Act of 1796, a nonsensical compromise that authorized completing three of the six frigates but not equipping or manning them, and leaving it up to the president to decide which ones should be completed. Washington was chagrined at the result of this Byzantine tug-of-war between the pro- and anti-naval factions in Congress, but decided it was the best he could hope for and signed the legislation. He chose the 44-gun *Constitution* being built in Boston under Captain Nicholson, the 36-gun *Constellation* in Baltimore under Captain Truxtun, and the 44-gun *United States* in Philadelphia under Captain Barry.

The new relationship between Britain and America concerned Spain as much as it did the dey of Algiers. Madrid worried about a secret Anglo-American alliance directed against her, and about the United States, with British acquiescence, invading her colonial territory. Advised of Spain's new attitude, Washington announced to the Senate on November 21, 1794, that he planned to send Thomas Pinckney to negotiate a resolution of disputes with Madrid that had festered since the Revolution.

Except for Spain's adamant refusal to open her colonial ports to American ships and goods, Ambassador Pinckney achieved every one of his aims: permission to navigate the Mississippi through Spanish territory, the privilege of deposit at New Orleans for three years to be renewed there or at some other location, recognition of the thirty-first parallel as the boundary between Spanish Florida and the United States, and Spain's pledge to end her policy of stirring up the Indians along the southern border of the United States. Spain also agreed to the principle that free ships make free goods. On October 27, 1795, Pinckney signed the Treaty of San Lorenzo, and it was greeted with universal praise in America.

In the eventful summer and fall of 1794, Washington also had to contend with what became known as the Whiskey Rebellion in western Pennsylvania. This uprising had its origins in Hamilton's excise law of March 3, 1791, which placed a tax on domestic distilled spirits. Farmers in Pennsylvania had always objected to such a tax imposed by easterners who did not understand the role of whiskey. Farmers with almost no cash used it as currency. They turned their surplus corn into liquor because it was too difficult to transport as corn to eastern markets. A gallon of moonshine was worth a quarter in every store west of the Alleghenies.

By the summer of 1794 anger had reached such a high pitch that on July 17, armed farmers attacked two federal officers, U.S. Marshal David Lenox and General John Neville, destroying Neville's home. The two men fled to Philadelphia, barely escaping with their lives.

David Bradford, a Washington county attorney, emerged as the leader of the radicals who wanted to defy the federal government. Moderates like Albert Gallatin and Hugh H. Brackenridge, at considerable risk to themselves, fought hard in several acrimonious meetings to convince disaffected farmers to obey the law and settle their problems peacefully. Bradford and his followers, however, were bent on armed resistance.

Washington understood the farmers' complaints and wanted Congress to fashion a compromise, but he would not tolerate defiance of the law by demagogues. He held cabinet meetings on August 2 and 6, and decided to issue a proclamation ordering the rebels to disperse and all inhabitants to "prevent and suppress dangerous proceedings." He also sent commissioners to reach a settlement with the angry farmers, but he made it plain that he had the authority, and the intention, to call out the state militias to put down these disturbances if Bradford and his followers persisted. On August 7, he began calling out the militias from eastern Pennsylvania, Maryland, Virginia, and New Jersey.

Washington's tough stance did not dissuade Bradford, who continued to organize mass resistance. Albert Gallatin was his main political opponent, but despite Gallatin's efforts, the insurgency continued. Washington, his patience running out, issued a second proclamation on September 25, warning that he intended to put the rebellion down by force if necessary. He then left Philadelphia for Carlisle, Pennsylvania, where he took command of the assembled troops, who now amounted to an impressive fifteen thousand. The rebellion collapsed in the face of this show of force, and Washington achieved his goals without bloodshed.

While the president's methods were successful, they reminded Republicans of the potency of the federal government, and of the need to put firm restraints on its military capacity. They were particularly worried over the prominent role played by the hated Alexander Hamilton as the president's right-hand man. Jefferson, now in retirement, sympathized with the rebels, describing Hamilton's excise levy as an "infernal tax." Jefferson felt that Washington's military measures had been excessive and wrote to Madison that "an insurrection was announced and proclaimed and armed against, but could never be found."

The president blamed the democratic societies encouraged by Ambassador Genet for the disturbances. "The self-created societies which have spread themselves over this country," he wrote to John Jay, "have been laboring incessantly to sow the seeds of distrust . . . and discontent, thereby hoping to effect some revolution in the Government." The president intended to crush them before they became a larger problem.

From the beginning, Jay's mission to London had drawn the ire of France, and the final treaty threw her into a rage. Despite the provision in Article 25 stating that nothing in the document would be construed as incompatible with America's French treaties, the Directory, France's five-man ruling body, insisted that the treaty was a virtual alliance with Britain. In Paris Ambassador Monroe reported that, so far as the French were concerned, Jay's Treaty annulled the alliance with the United States created by the treaties of 1778. Although warned of France's probable reaction, Washington had not anticipated how strong it would be. He tried to assure Paris of America's continuing neutrality, but the divided, corrupt Directory would not be appeased.

On July 2, 1796, the Directory signaled its growing displeasure by issuing an enigmatic decree, stipulating that henceforth France would "treat neutral vessels, either as to confiscation, or searches, or capture, in the same manner as they shall suffer the English to treat them." To underscore its chagrin, the Directory simultaneously re-called Ambassador Adet, although he would not leave the United States until months later, long after the election of 1796 was over.

It was hard to say exactly what the July decree meant. The French were clearly upset by America's rapprochement with England, but what exactly would they do? It wasn't long before Washington found out. The July decree became a license for French warships and privateers to prey on American shipping. The French now conducted unrestricted attacks, seizing American ships under any pretext. The French directors, along with their hangers-on, personally profited from this wholesale attack. They assumed that America, divided between pro-French Republicans and pro-British Federalists, would not retaliate.

Their knowledge of American politics, however, was poor. They were unaware of the level of anger building in the United States. Ambassador Monroe failed to give them an accurate picture of American sentiment. He vehemently opposed the Jay Treaty and a British-American rapprochement. He viewed Britain as "the enemy of mankind" and looked forward to France defeating her and carving up the empire. He convinced the Directory that the coming election of 1796 would bring Jefferson to power, and that he would restore Franco-American friendship.

Not content to let matters play themselves out, the French ambassador, Pierre Adet, took the bold but unwise step of working openly for Jefferson in the election, and may well have cost him a victory.

Adet was accustomed to interfering in America's internal affairs. He had worked hard behind the scenes in the Senate and later in the House of Representatives to defeat the Jay Treaty. At the same time he was hoping to claim Louisiana for France, and, having learned nothing from Genet's debacle, he even had a scheme to detach the lands west of the Appalachians from the United States.

Jefferson's defeat in the election of 1796 was the final straw for the Directory. They now edged closer to open war with America, believing they had little to worry about from a divided, defenseless country.

Exasperated by his envoy, who seemed more intent on furthering French interests than on supporting neutrality, Washington recalled Ambassador Monroe in July 1796. The president thought that Monroe wished to kill the Jay Treaty and then apologize to the French "for having made it, and enquire of France what more she required."

Monroe received notification of his removal in November and on December 30 made a farewell speech in Paris. "I was a witness to a revolution in my own country," he said. "I was deeply penetrated with its principles, which are the same with those of your revolution. I saw too, its difficulties and remembering these, and the important services rendered us by France upon that occasion, I have partaken with you in all the perilous and trying situations in which you have been placed. It was my fortune to arrive among you in a moment of complicated danger from within and without; and it is with the most heartfelt satisfaction that in taking my leave, I behold victory and the dawn of prosperity upon the point of realizing all the great objects for which . . . you have . . . so nobly contended."

The Directory viewed Monroe's recall as yet another example of Washington's hostility toward France and partiality toward Britain. The members pointedly refused to receive the president's new ambassador, Charles Cotesworth Pinckney, an ardent Federalist.

French hostility began to cast doubt on Washington's retirement. Four years previously the president had wanted to retire, and Madison had written a farewell address for him. Now Madison assumed that Washington would finally retire to Mount Vernon, clearing the way for Jefferson's run for president. The country, in Madison's opinion, needed Jefferson. But as long as a third term for Washington was a possibility, Jefferson's candidacy was out of the question. The president kept his own counsel, however, and the country was left in doubt about his intentions until September 19, 1796, when his farewell address appeared in David Claypoole's *American Daily Advertiser* in Philadelphia. Within a fortnight, the entire country was reading the address in the local papers.

Washington retained much of what Madison had written four years before and allowed Hamilton and, to a lesser extent, Jay to make important contributions, but the essential ideas were Washington's. The still-revered president reminded his countrymen of the importance of unity. "It is of infinite moment," he wrote, "that you should properly estimate the immense value of your national union to your collective and individual happiness; that you should cherish a cordial, habitual, and immovable attachment to it as of the Palladium of your political safety and prosperity." He went on to stress again the importance of neutrality. "The great rule of conduct for us," he wrote, "in regard to foreign nations, is in extending our commercial relations, to have with them as little *Political* connection as possible. . . . Europe has a set of interests, which to us have none, or a very remote relation . . . therefore, it must be unwise in us to implicate ourselves . . . in the ordinary vicissitudes of her policies. . . .

"Our detached and distant situation invites and enables us to pursue a different course. If we remain one people under an efficient government, the period is not far off, when we may defy material injury from external annoyance; when we may take such an attitude as will cause the neutrality we may at any time resolve upon to be scrupulously respected. When belligerent nations, under the impossibility of making acquisitions upon us, will not lightly hazard the giving us provocation when we may choose peace or war, as our interest, guided by our justice, shall counsel."

The French were displeased with the farewell address and even more so with Washington's final message to Congress, delivered on December 7. After reporting on the state of affairs with Algeria, Tunis, and Tripoli, he turned to the need for a navy. "To an active external commerce," he said, "the protection of a naval force is indispensable. This is manifest with regard to wars in which a state itself is a party. But besides this, it is in our experience, that the most sincere neutrality is not a sufficient guard against the depredations of nations at war. To secure respect to our neutral flag requires a naval force organized and ready to vindicate it from insult or aggression. This may even prevent the necessity of going to war, by discouraging belligerent powers from committing such violations of the rights of the neutral party, as may first or last, leave no other option. From the best information I have been able to maintain, it would seem as if our trade to the Mediterranean, without a protecting force, will always be insecure; and our citizens exposed to the calamities from which a number of them have but just been relieved.

"These considerations invite the United States to look to the means, and to set about the gradual creation of a navy. The increasing progress of their navigation, promises them, at no distant period, the requisite supply of seamen; and their means, in other respects, favor the undertaking. It is an encouragement, likewise, that their particular situation, will give weight and influence to a moderate naval force in their hands. Will it not then be advisable to begin without delay to provide and lay up the materials for the building and equipping of ships of war, and to proceed in the work by degrees, in proportion as our resources shall render it practicable without inconvenience; so that a future war of Europe, may not find our commerce in the same unprotected state in which it was found by the present."

His urgent call for a respectable sea force was ignored, demonstrating again the power of the anti-navy forces led by Madison, Jefferson, and Gallatin.

9

JOHN ADAMS
BUILDS A NAVY

March 1797–June 1798

Washington's voluntary retirement and the peaceful transfer of power to John Adams were widely viewed as significant events in guaranteeing the success of republican government. But as desirable as a change might be, the country remained committed to Washington's centrist policies. By any measure his presidency had been a resounding success. A republican government had been established, public credit was put on a sound footing, a settlement was made with Britain, the Mississippi was opened, the western territories were readied for exploitation, neutrality was maintained, and a navy was begun. To make things even better, prosperity was widespread.

It was natural to assume that should Washington step down, his vice president, a distinguished statesman in his own right, would succeed him. But the thin margin of Adams's election suggested that he was on trial, the public uncertain about his suitability for the office. His margin of victory over Jefferson had been only three electoral votes. The final tally was 71 to 68. Thus, notwithstanding his annoyance at the hero worship of Washington, Adams made continuity his first priority as president. Adams, whose political antennae were vastly underrated, believed he could look with some "accuracy into the hearts of [his] fellow citizens," and what he saw was a mandate for keeping to the path his predecessor had laid out.

Adams was fortunate that Washington's good health and continued presence at Mount Vernon reassured the country that his successor would not veer too far off course. To emphasize the solid link between administrations, Adams adopted Washington's cabinet as his own. Had he felt politically stronger, he undoubtedly would have changed it. Not wanting to incite the bickering that would accompany dismissals and new appointments, he decided to leave well enough alone. Unfortunately Washington's later appointments were not the giants of the first cabinet, but a collection of lesser men—Timothy Pickering, secretary of state; James McHenry, secretary of war; Oliver Wolcott, secretary of the Treasury; and Charles Lee, attorney general. Lee would later distinguish himself as an attorney, but at the time he was untried and little known outside Virginia. Even worse, Pickering, Wolcott, and especially McHenry looked to Alexander Hamilton for leadership, not to the president. Though retired from government since January 1795, Hamilton, who was practicing law in New York, was the acknowledged leader of the incipient Federalist Party. He had taken an active part in the election and then maintained a steady correspondence with cabinet members, advising them on policy. Without Adams being aware of it, the former Treasury secretary had been admitted to the president's inner circle.

Hamilton's influence was even more anomalous since it was well known that he had done everything possible to prevent Adams's election, trying to replace him with Thomas Pinckney of South Carolina. A successful diplomat (he had negotiated the popular treaty with Spain), Pinckney was a relatively unknown political novice. The unintended result of Hamilton's ill-conceived scheme to have Pinckney elected had been to secure the vice presidency for the Federalists' archenemy, Thomas Jefferson.

Following in Washington's footsteps wasn't difficult for the new president, since he agreed with his predecessor's basic policies. Although bored and frustrated for eight years as vice president, he had always supported Washington publicly and privately. But the president rarely consulted him. By ignoring Adams, Washington deprived himself and the country of an important asset.

Like Washington, Adams was a man of the center who understood the overriding importance of unity as the new republic struggled to find its footing. Adams stood above the partisan fight between the pro-British Hamilton and the pro-French Jefferson. He was the intellectual equal of both, and his experience in international and domestic politics was vast. A man of unquestioned integrity, he was articulate, knowledgeable, and fearless. Adams, of course, had his faults, and they had been well publicized by his detractors. James Madison described him as "kindled into flame by every spark that lights on his passions." Benjamin Franklin's oft-quoted description of Adams as "always an honest man, often a wise one, but sometimes wholly out of his senses," appealed to both Madison and Jefferson. But Adams's strengths far outweighed his weaknesses. He could have been of service to Washington, particularly as partisan politics tore at his administration in the second term.

The distance Washington maintained from the vice president could perhaps be explained by his memories of the Adamses, particularly Sam Adams, attempting to replace him with Horatio Gates during the Revolution. Washington might have still distrusted Adams. Nevertheless, for official reasons, the president and vice president maintained a cordial relationship; they often dined together with their wives, and from time to time, particularly toward the end of Washington's second term, when it looked as if Adams might succeed him, they conferred in strict secrecy about important policy matters.

The loyalty Adams gave Washington, and their similarity of views, were in sharp contrast to Adams's relationship with Vice President Jefferson. Jefferson held an altogether different view of the world and felt no qualms about opposing the president, either openly or behind his back. For the only time in the nation's history, the vice president was the leader of the opposition, secretly positioning himself to become president in the next election. When Adams took the oath of office on March 4, 1797, France and the United States were moving closer to war, and Jefferson was the acknowledged leader of the French faction in the United States. He still believed, even after the Terror, the Thermidor reaction, the ascendancy of the five-man Directory, and the growing power of General Napoleon Bonaparte, that the original ideals of the French Revolution had not been lost; they may have dimmed, but they had not been extinguished. He continued to dream that France would bring the blessings of liberty to Great Britain and reactionary Europe.

Adams, on the other hand, was as committed to neutrality as Washington was. In theory Jefferson subscribed to it as well, but he also had a passion to rid the world of kings and noblemen. "Monarchy and aristocracy must be annihilated," he declared, expressing sentiments he had long held, "and the rights of the people firmly established."

On March 2, two days before Adams took office, the French Directory issued a decree formally abrogating the principle that free ships make free goods. The decree permitted French warships to capture neutral vessels carrying British goods. It also provided that Americans serving aboard an enemy flag, whether impressed or not, would be treated as pirates and hanged. And any American ship without a *rôle d'équipage*, correctly presented, would be regarded as a proper prize. (A *rôle d'équipage* was a list of the crew and passengers that American ships rarely carried.) This decree was the equivalent of a declaration of war.

Secretary Pickering reported later to the president and Congress that from October 1796 to June 1797, French raiders had seized 316 American vessels. On March 13, Adams received the portentous news that the Directory had refused to receive the new American ambassador, Charles Cotesworth Pinckney. Arriving in Paris in December 1796, Pinckney had been subjected to studied abuse by the Directory before being expelled from the country. He had then traveled to Amsterdam and was still there awaiting instructions.

Despite these provocations, Adams, with a high appreciation of America's military weakness, favored negotiating the country's differences with France, as Washington had with Britain and Spain. At the same time Adams was determined to improve the nation's nonexistent defenses, particularly her navy. He thus embarked on a two-pronged strategy, as his predecessor had, of talking and arming at the same time. All of this met with Hamilton's approval initially; he favored negotiating rather than rushing into a war unprepared.

To begin talks, Adams chose three commissioners, Pinckney, John Marshall of Virginia, and Elbridge Gerry of Massachusetts. The president had wanted to appoint Madison, who had retired from the House of Representatives and returned to Virginia. Madison was a well-known French sympathizer, and the president thought he would give political balance to the commission. But with Jefferson's approval, Madison declined.

On May 15, 1797, the president appeared before a special session of Congress to support strong defense measures and to announce his attempt at a peaceful resolution of differences with France. He pointed out that the French Directory had concluded America was so politically divided between pro-French and pro-British factions that she would not fight. He urged Congress to disabuse Paris of this dangerous idea. "We shall convince France and the world," he said, "that we are not a degraded people, humiliated under a colonial spirit of fear and a sense of inferiority, fitted to be the miserable instruments of foreign influence, and regardless of national honor, character, and interest." The country, he declared, must prepare to defend its commerce and its coasts against French depredations by building coastal defenses and a naval power. He also recommended the immediate arming of merchant vessels. America should stay out of Europe's quarrels, he said, but be prepared to defend its neutrality.

Hamilton and the Federalists applauded the president's speech, but the Republicans were disturbed. Jefferson thought it was impossible to negotiate and prepare for war at the same time. Granting the

French every benefit of the doubt, he viewed Adams's defense program as unnecessarily provocative.

Adams reacted angrily, calling the vice president's criticism "evidence of a mind, soured, yet seeking for popularity, and eaten to a honeycomb by ambition, yet weak, confused, uninformed and ignorant. I have long been convinced that this ambition is so inconsiderate as to be capable of going to great lengths."

Albert Gallatin, the new Republican leader in the House, was prepared to fight the president's defense program alongside the vice president. Swiss-born, speaking with a French accent, and presenting an unimposing physique, Gallatin was a formidable opponent. Smart, industrious, well educated, and unafraid, he made it a habit to be exceptionally well prepared before entering into any political fight. On the House floor his powerful, incisive speeches commanded the attention of friend and foe alike. When he began serving in the House in 1795, he quickly became the Jeffersonian Republicans' expert on financial matters and Hamilton's chief critic. Gallatin took the lead in creating the House Ways and Means Committee, which made it possible for Congress to become expert in financial matters and not depend on the Treasury, as in Hamilton's day. Gallatin opposed Hamilton's funding program and found that Treasury policies were increasing rather than reducing the public debt. He saw no reason for the kind of debt Hamilton thought essential for America's economic health.

Gallatin believed that defense matters ought to be subordinate to the federal budget. Adams's proposed navy was too expensive, in Gallatin's view, and would result in a burdensome debt. He opposed having any federal debt at all, believing it to be an unmitigated curse. He did not think the United States either needed a large military or could pay for one; a minimal defense force would suffice. Jefferson and Madison agreed with him.

Adams's call for a naval armament ignited a spirited debate in Congress that lasted for two months. At the end of it, on July 1, 1797, just before adjourning, Congress passed the Act Providing a Naval Armament, authorizing the president to complete, man, and deploy the frigates *Constitution, Constellation*, and *United States*. It also approved strengthening coastal defenses and using the Treasury Department's few revenue cutters as warships. The arming of merchantmen was forbidden, even though French depredations were increasing.

The weakness of the bill demonstrated once again the Republicans' capacity to keep American defenses to a bare minimum. Afraid of stumbling into a shooting war, they maintained strict limits on naval preparations, leaving Paris with the comfortable feeling that it had nothing to fear from the United States. Fisher Ames said that Republicans were "just such friends to liberty as they would be to the Bank if they forbid guards, locks, and keys for the safety of their vault."

On June 27, in the midst of the controversy over the president's proposed defense measures, former ambassador Monroe arrived home from Paris, miffed that he'd been recalled. In his view, Washington had sent him to placate the French, and placate them he had. Jefferson and the other Republicans shared his view. They thought his removal was an unnecessary slap in the face of the Directory. Seeking to make a point, on July 1 they organized a public banquet in Monroe's honor at Oeller's Hotel on Chestnut Street in Philadelphia near Congress Hall. Vice President Jefferson attended, as did Governor McKean of New Jersey and more than fifty Republican members of Congress, including Albert Gallatin.

Monroe's reception displayed again the country's deep political divisions, and how difficult it was for the president to obtain support for an expensive naval program. Thus the navy continued to languish. As had been the case in Washington's time, only a groundswell of public opinion could overcome Republican opposition and produce the taxes necessary for an adequate fleet.

John Marshall boarded the brig *Grace* in Philadelphia on July 20, 1797, and sailed for France to join Ambassador Pinckney. Three days later Elbridge Gerry sailed from Boston. The envoys were entrusted with negotiating an agreement that would avoid a war the United States refused to prepare for. The commissioners met in Paris on October 4 and four days later had a brief, informal audience with Foreign Minister Talleyrand. He told them he could not receive them officially until he had prepared a report on American affairs for the Directory.

Having lived as an exile in the United States for two years, Talleyrand considered himself an expert on the country, and he was convinced that Americans were British, not French. No Frenchman, he believed, could ever feel at home in the United States the way an Englishman could. In his view, the Jay Treaty revealed this American prejudice quite clearly. Yet it was obvious to him that, in spite of its bias, the United States had a vigorous pro-French party led by Vice President Jefferson. Talleyrand counted on the Republicans to keep America too divided to adequately arm herself. France, on the other hand, had become the greatest military power in Europe. Napoleon's defeat of Austria and the humiliating Treaty of Compo Formio signed on October 17, 1797, confirmed French dominance of Europe. Only Great Britain remained to be subdued, and Napoleon was about to invade her, with a strong possibility of success. The powerful, conscripted Armée d'Angleterre was assembled at Boulogne, poised to strike across the Channel. Britain's position looked precarious, particularly since her fleet had just endured an unprecedented mutiny involving 113 ships and as many as 50,000 seamen.

Jefferson hoped Napoleon would succeed. "Nothing," he wrote to Edmund Randolph, "can establish firmly the republican principles of our government but an establishment of them in England. France will be the apostle of all this." At the beginning of the summer the vice president urged the Directory to drag out negotiations with the American envoys until Napoleon had conquered Britain. At the same time, he advised the French to moderate their pressure on the United States.

Feeling he had the upper hand, Talleyrand ignored Jefferson's advice and delayed receiving the American commissioners officially. Instead, he sent three emissaries on separate occasions to extract an apology for President Adams's negative remarks about France in his May 16 address to Congress, and to solicit a bribe for the Directors (and for the foreign minister) before any business went forward.

The commissioners identified Talleyrand's agents as XYZ and were amazed at the amount of money they demanded: 1.2 million livres.

The commissioners refused to consider paying a bribe as a condition of even talking. They insisted on being received officially, but Talleyrand declined. The mission thus dragged on week after week without anything being accomplished. Marshall thought the French wanted to delay while their warships and privateers continued to attack American shipping at great personal profit to the Directory.

To sway the Americans, Talleyrand enlisted the help of Pierre Augustine Caron de Beaumarchais, who had been instrumental in providing General Washington with French arms during the American Revolution. Beaumarchais urged Marshall, with whom he had a personal relationship, to accept the Directors' terms, but Marshall refused. More time elapsed and eventually, feeling that no progress could be made, Marshall and Pinckney demanded their passports. Marshall left France on April 24, 1798, sailing out of Bordeaux on the *Alexander Hamilton*. Pinckney's daughter was sick with fever in the south of France, and he stayed with her until August before returning home. At Talleyrand's insistence, Gerry remained in Paris to facilitate any new initiative that might arise. If he left, Talleyrand predicted, there would be war.

On November 22, 1797, while waiting for word from his envoys, President Adams addressed the second session of the Fifth Congress, urging again, as he had in the spring, the need for a navy and an expanded army, and the taxes to support them. The president had heard nothing from the commissioners, and speculation was rife. "I deem it a duty," he told Congress, "deliberately and solemnly to declare my opinion that whether we negotiate with [France] or not, vigorous preparations for war will be alike indispensable. These alone will give to us an equal treaty and ensure its observance." Adams was a firm believer in Edmund Burke's dictum, "A great state . . . to be secure . . . must be respected."

Observing from Virginia, Madison was anxious about the drift toward war. He wrote to Monroe, "Those who tolerate at present the fashionable sentiments will soon be ready to embrace them. . . . Let us hope that the tide of evil is nearly at its flood."

The Federalists had a strong majority in the Senate, but the House Republicans under Gallatin were powerful enough to block the war measures they abhorred. Gallatin's objective was to prevent the Federalists and Adams from dragging the United States into an unnecessary war. France's continuing aggressive attacks on American shipping, however, complicated his task. On February 5, 1798, the French privateer *Veritude,* with only two 6-pounders and a few swivels, burst into Charleston harbor, captured and burned a British vessel, and then passed back over the bar and captured two American ships. This impudence shocked and angered the entire country.

In the winter of 1798 rumors that the American envoys had failed circulated in Philadelphia. Then, on March 4, their first dispatches arrived. The next day President Adams announced he had received them. They had been sent in January and were in five parts, four of them in code. Only the fifth was immediately available, and when Adams read it he was indignant. The Directory had refused to receive the commissioners; it had closed French ports to neutral shipping and decreed that vessels carrying anything manufactured or produced in Great Britain were subject to capture. John Marshall wrote that he saw no hope of the mission succeeding.

The remaining four dispatches outraged Adams even more than the first. The treatment accorded his envoys was entirely unacceptable. He was angry enough to ask for a declaration of war, but he didn't think the country was ready for so drastic a step. He pondered whether or not to send the reports to Congress and decided they were too incendiary. Instead, on March 19, he delivered a carefully worded message informing Congress that the mission had failed and the country's defenses needed to be put in a state of readiness. He reiterated his call for protecting American shipping, defending the coast, and revoking Washington's order prohibiting American merchantmen from sailing in an armed condition.

Hamilton agreed that a declaration of war was premature, although other Federalists, including Secretary Pickering, did not. They wanted war now. The Republicans, on the other hand, rejected Adams's call for defense measures. Jefferson found them "insane." He was not persuaded that the Directory knew anything about Talleyrand's maneuvers, but he did know that he opposed war and a dramatic increase in defense spending. Above all, Jefferson wanted to prevent America from fighting France, whom he still considered a natural ally.

After receiving Adams's message, House Republicans, always willing to think the worst of the president, believed he was manufacturing a crisis. They were certain that when the contents of all the dispatches were known, the French would appear in a better light. On April 2, the House, led by Gallatin, voted 65 to 27 to see the unedited version of the dispatches and the instructions given the envoys. Many Federalists voted for the measure, knowing that Adams's portrayal of events was, if anything, restrained.

The following day the president released the papers to the House. They made it clear that, far from exaggerating the Directory's duplicity, Adams had understated it. Members were stunned. Within days Americans were reading the commissioners' reports in their newspapers, and a wave of anti-French feeling swept the country. Political divisions disappeared as people united behind the president. Adams was suddenly hugely popular. The French cockade that citizens liked to sport about Philadelphia disappeared, and the cry "Millions for defense, not one cent for tribute" became popular. Abigail Adams wrote to her sister, "The publick opinion here is changing very fast, and the people begin to see who have been their firm unshaken friends. . . . The common people say that if Jefferson had been our president, and Madison and Burr our negotiators, we should have been sold to the French."

For the first time the president had the political energy to push his defense program through Congress. In this atmosphere the American navy was born anew. Except for the brief period in 1794, when anger at the British had reached a high pitch, the people had not been willing to endure the taxes necessary to create a respectable navy; now they were. How long their enthusiasm would last was another question. Adams was afraid it might be short-lived.

As war fever grew, simple defense measures that had been impossible to enact a short time before now sailed through both houses of

Congress. The Republicans' ability to block them disappeared. In April, May, June, and July the president and the Federalists enacted a series of twenty bills that put the United States on a war footing. Since the country's defenses were practically nonexistent, it was a prodigious undertaking. The army had only thirty-five hundred men; there was no navy, except for the three frigates authorized to be completed the previous year, and fifteen revenue cutters from the Treasury Department. The cutters were part of an unsung service, the forerunner of the Coast Guard, that had been formed in 1790 to help Secretary Hamilton collect customs duties.

In April and May Congress authorized the president to lease or purchase cannon foundries, arms, ammunition, and other munitions, and to buy, build, or rent twelve additional warships of not more than twenty-two guns. Congress also appropriated substantial sums to fortify harbors.

As had been done with the Continental Navy in 1775 and 1776, Adams immediately set about acquiring and converting merchantmen to create an instant fleet while awaiting construction of additional warships. Of inestimable help to him was Joshua Humphreys, the constructor of the navy. The first of the converted vessels to be completed was the *Ganges* in Philadelphia, under Captain Richard Dale of Revolutionary War fame. He had been John Paul Jones's first lieutenant aboard the *Bonhomme Richard*, and had been wounded in the historic battle with HMS *Serapis*. The *Ganges* was equipped with twenty 9-pounders, and she put to sea on May 24, 1798, with orders to patrol the coast from Cape Henry, Virginia, to Long Island, New York.

Congress also authorized the president to purchase or build ten row-galleys for defense along the coast, particularly in the south. Having learned nothing from the record of row-galleys in the Revolutionary War, the naval committees of Congress failed to realize that this pitifully small number would be of no use whatever.

On April 30, Adams signed a law creating a Navy Department. The vote was surprisingly close—47 to 41—indicating that opposition was still strong. Opponents such as Albert Gallatin felt that once a separate department was established, the navy would take on a life of its own and grow out of control.

Adams thought carefully about his choice for first secretary of the navy. The head of the new department would be a member of the president's cabinet and would participate in forming national policy. The new secretary had to be politically reliable, as well as experienced in managing a fleet of ships. Adams's first choice was Federalist George Cabot of Massachusetts. A former senator, Cabot was an influential politician and a substantial merchant; the president thought he had the stature to fill the position. Cabot, however, refused the appointment for health reasons. Adams then turned to forty-six-year-old Benjamin Stoddert, a Federalist merchant from Georgetown, Maryland. After hesitating because of his deteriorating finances, Stoddert accepted, seeing his patriotic duty as overriding other considerations. A veteran of the Revolutionary War, Stoddert had been wounded at Brandywine. Afterward, he had served as secretary of the board of war, becoming well acquainted with the problems of men, materials, and money necessary to fight a war.

Until Stoddert took over the new department, the navy, such as it was, had been run out of the War Department by Knox, then Pickering, followed by McHenry. None of them were skilled administrators. The construction of the three frigates, for instance, had been started under Knox and was always behind schedule, consuming far more money than anyone had imagined. Someone new at the helm was needed.

Adams swore in Stoddert on June 19. Charles Goldsborough, his brilliant clerk, wrote, "A more fortunate selection could not well have been made. To the most ardent patriotism, he united an inflexible integrity, a discriminating mind, great capacity for business, and the most persevering industry." In time Stoddert was to acquire "more of the confidence of the President than any officer of the government."

The vote to give the navy its own department had been carried largely on grounds of increasing the efficiency of the service and giving it prestige and muscle within the government. Its proponents did not worry about the strategic consequences of separating the services, since this was what the British did. Consciously or not, the big-navy men, Republican or Federalist, always had the Royal Navy as a model.

From his experiences with the Continental Navy, Adams had long ago concluded that the service had to be organized as a separate department, with a single head responsible to the president. He never considered that it might be better if the navy and army worked together under the same roof. He had no appreciation of the difficulties that being separated from a sea force had caused Washington during the Revolution, or how much more effective the Continental Navy might have been had it been directly under Washington. But since the Quasi-War became exclusively a naval matter, Adams's organization was never questioned.

On May 28 Congress had passed a law authorizing the president "to instruct and direct the commanders of our armed vessels to seize, take and bring into any port of the United States . . . any armed vessel of the Republic of France . . . which shall have committed, or which shall be found hovering on the coasts of the United States, for the purpose of committing depredations" and to retake any captured American ships. And on June 25 Congress finally permitted the arming of American merchantmen. By the time the war ended, one thousand of them were carrying cannon, some of them as many as thirty-four. When they sailed in a convoy they were a formidable force.

On June 30 Congress authorized the president to accept twenty-four armed vessels offered as gifts or on loan from private persons. Demonstrating how strong war fever was, Newburyport, Massachusetts, informed the president that it intended to build a 20-gun warship and loan it to the government. Other cities—Salem, Marblehead, Boston, Providence, New York, Philadelphia, Charleston, and Norfolk together with Richmond—did the same. Philadelphia told the president that she was building a 36-gun frigate. These cities launched a total of ten warships during the short Quasi-War. They were able to do so only because of the invaluable knowledge they had gained building warships and privateers during the Revolution. In the latter stages of the War of Independence, American shipyards were launching 20-gun privateers that could stand up to any British sloop-of-war or small frigate. Now the shipyards' experience with the Continental Navy was proving its value in building the federal navy.

On July 7, the president signed a law abrogating all treaties with France, and two days later Congress extended naval operations against France to the high seas, authorizing the navy to capture armed French vessels wherever it found them. An embargo was placed against France and all her dependencies, effective July 1, and all French ships were prohibited from entering American ports.

Hoping to raise $2 million, Congress, on July 9, approved the Evaluation Act, which placed a direct tax on landholdings, houses, and slaves at fifty cents a head. Two days later, it created the Marine Corps. Five days after that, it appropriated money to complete construction of the remaining three frigates—*Chesapeake*, *Congress*, and *President*—as authorized on March 27, 1794. American privateers did not play the role in the Quasi-War that they had during the Revolutionary War. Congress had prohibited attacks on unarmed merchantmen, restricting attacks to armed French vessels. But the Royal Navy had so decimated French commerce that pickings were slim.

On June 22, Congress had authorized a ten-thousand-man increase in the army, and fifty thousand additional troops for the provisional army, which would not actually come into being until a war was declared or until the president determined that a national emergency existed. Congress also authorized the president to call up eighty thousand militiamen. Since he considered a French invasion only a remote possibility, Adams was not eager to expand the army to this extent. The Federalists in Congress pushed through the increase without consulting the president. Hamilton played a key role; the Federalists hoped to use the new army as a vehicle for increasing Hamilton's power by putting him at its head. They envisaged the army as enforcing federal laws against states that opposed them or against any other type of internal subversion. It could also be used, in their view, to obtain the Floridas and Louisiana, and perhaps other

Spanish territory in America as well. The Federalist claim that a large army was needed to defend the country against a possible French invasion was merely a pretext. Adams opposed all of their reasoning and intended to emphasize the navy. The controversy between Adams and the Hamiltonians over this huge standing army deeply divided the Federalist Party.

On July 2 the president nominated George Washington to be commander in chief of the new army of 13,500. Washington reluctantly accepted on condition that Hamilton be his second. Adams, against his will, agreed. It was clear that Washington would be a figurehead; the real commander would be Hamilton, and Adams didn't trust him, feeling that his ambitions were too expansive. But Washington insisted, and the president saw no alternative but to go along with him.

The Republicans, led by Gallatin and Jefferson, opposed all these measures, calling them costly, dangerous, and unnecessary. Gallatin argued in a House speech that "both Great Britain and France had plundered [our merchantmen] in a most shameful manner . . . . Yet, notwithstanding these depredations . . . year after year our exports have increased in value . . . [proving that] commerce can be protected without a navy, whilst a nation preserves its neutrality. . . . No man can doubt," he said, "that if in 1793, we had had twelve ships-of-the-line, we should have been involved in the present war, on one side or the other, according to the fluctuations of public opinion. . . . [Navies were]," Gallatin argued, "great engines of war and conquest" and, as such, threats to the Constitution.

The war crisis produced not only an unprecedented burst of defense spending, but the Alien and Sedition Acts as well. Federalists believed that the French were an internal threat as well as an external one. Having no concept of a loyal opposition, they identified the Republicans as the French party and viewed them as dangerous traitors. On June 18, 1798, Congress approved the Naturalization Act, increasing from five to fifteen years the residency period required for citizenship. A week later it passed the Alien Act, authorizing the president to expel any foreigner by executive decree. And on July 14, Congress approved the Sedition Act, which forbade any speech or writing against the president or Congress with "the intent to defame" or to bring them "into contempt or disrepute."

Although President Adams did not author the acts, he approved them, as did Abigail Adams and even George Washington. Abigail was convinced "of the close connection between the infernals of France and those in our own bosom. And in any other country," she wrote, "Bache and all his papers would have been seized and ought to be here . . . the President [should be enabled] to seize suspicious persons and their papers."

These controversial laws were intended to give the government tools to deal with the thousands of French and Irish immigrants the Federalists imagined were working on behalf of the Directory. Catholics in Ireland traditionally looked to Catholic France for support, and they were always sympathetic to the French in any contest with England. Prime Minister Pitt had had a similar problem of internal subversion in Britain, and he had overreacted, as Adams and Washington did. There was never an internal threat in either country. The British people, when faced with their traditional enemy and an invasion, united behind the king and their political leaders. Americans did the same. A threat to overthrow the American government was a fantasy.

Jefferson, Madison, Gallatin, and the Republicans were infuriated by the laws and vowed to fight them. Gallatin warned the House that "under pretense of preventing imaginary ills, an attempt is made to establish the omnipotence of Congress and substantial despotism, on the ruins of our Constitution."

Madison secretly authored a resolution for the Virginia legislature that repudiated the laws, declaring the right of states to determine the constitutionality of federal legislation, rather than the Supreme Court. Jefferson surreptitiously wrote an even more strident resolution for Kentucky.

The Virginia and Kentucky resolutions were never put to the test but did indicate the level of opposition in the Republican areas of the country, which would serve Jefferson well in the next election.

Hamilton, writing to Theodore Sedgwick, a powerful Federalist senator from Massachusetts, called the Virginia and Kentucky resolutions "a regular conspiracy to overturn the government." If given half a chance, he would have liked to use the new army to enforce federal law in these states.

Other than a historic reminder of the need to limit federal power, even in wartime, the Alien and Sedition laws were of little importance. They quietly disappeared, most of the country realizing that Adams and the Federalist Congress had gone too far. The Sedition law never stopped the Republican press from attacking Adams and the Federalists. The Alien Act expired on June 25, 1800, the Sedition law on March 3, 1801; Jefferson repealed the Naturalization Act when he became president.

By the time the energetic Fifth Congress adjourned on July 19, the new American navy was already at sea. The *Ganges* had been patrolling since May and was joined by another converted merchantman, the 20-gun *Delaware*, under Captain Stephen Decatur Sr. After leaving Delaware Bay on July 6, Captain Decatur was put on the trail of a French privateer and sighted her off Egg Harbor, New Jersey. The next day, he captured the first prize of the war, the 12-gun *Croyable*. She was taken into the American service and renamed *Retaliation*, under the command of Lieutenant William Bainbridge. In November, however, while cruising off Guadeloupe in company with the 20-gun *Montezuma*, under Commodore Murray, and the 18-gun brig *Norfolk*, under Captain Williams, Bainbridge got separated from his companions and found himself trapped by two French frigates, the 40-gun *Insurgente* and the 44-gun *Volontaire*. He wisely surrendered without a fight.

Congress adjourned on July 19 to escape the yellow fever that plagued Philadelphia every summer. Six days later, as the dreaded disease took control of the capital, the Adamses set out for Quincy. The president made it a practice to leave the city during the annual outbreak of fever and run the government from his farm in Massachusetts until late fall. He saw no reason why he couldn't manage just as well from Quincy as from Philadelphia.

While Adams was away, Secretary Stoddert was hard at work in Philadelphia putting together the new navy. The president wanted the work to proceed as fast as possible, not only to impress the French but because he knew the public would support a large military establishment for only a limited time. The clamor for military preparations in 1798 was unique in his experience, with the possible exception of the brief moment in 1794 when the people were angry enough to approve Washington's limited naval program.

Stoddert had to build the Navy Department from scratch. At the time, this was viewed as a great handicap, and it might have been had Stoddert been a man of lesser ability. But given his talents and drive, he could operate unhindered by an entrenched bureaucracy or a long naval tradition.

Stoddert had a tiny staff consisting of a chief clerk and five subordinate clerks, one of whom was nineteen-year-old Charles Washington Goldsborough, an articulate, hardworking young man from a wealthy Maryland family. In addition, the accountant of the navy had seven clerks. Stoddert was forced to rely on naval agents in the six cities where frigates were being built, and on the captains of the warships under construction there. He also had the services of the talented constructor of the navy, Joshua Humphreys.

Besides his own ability and the strong backing of the president and Congress, Stoddert had the priceless body of knowledge gained during the Revolution by shipyards up and down the coast. It was during the critical summer of 1798 that the legacy of the Continental Navy became so important. If Stoddert had been obliged to start anew, as the builders of the Continental Navy had been forced to, he could not have accomplished the remarkable feat that he did. Thanks to their experience during the War of Independence, the nation's shipyards had the expertise to build and convert men-of-war in a remarkably short time. They were particularly adept at constructing vessels of roughly 20 guns, similar to the large privateers they had turned out by the dozens at the end of the Revolution. Building 20-gun warships, especially in New England ports like Salem, had become routine. These fast, powerful vessels were miniature frigates.

Stoddert also had available the officers and men who had served in the Continental Navy or whose fathers and uncles had, as well as those who had been on the over two thousand privateers during the Revolution. These seamen were far superior to the mix the Continental Navy had to draw from in 1775. Not that recruitment in the new federal navy was ever easy; it wasn't. But captains of American warships, unlike their British counterparts, always seemed to manage. Delays might occur, but rarely would lack of men stop an American warship from getting underway. Stoddert, a slaveholder, barred "Negroes or Mulattoes" from serving in the new navy, and the Marine Corps did the same. Given the need to fill out their crews, however, captains often took free blacks as crew members. Both free blacks and slaves had served in the Continental Navy, the state navies, and privateers during the Revolution, but that precedent had been forgotten.

Stoddert also had help from the British, who were anxious to support America's anti-French mood. They supplied critical items such as copper, cannon, and other materials.

Stephen Higginson, the influential naval agent in Boston and a friend of President Adams, warned Stoddert to be careful when selecting officers and men who had served in the Continental Navy. Higginson viewed them with a skeptical eye, disregarding the many authentic heroes and patriots who had served selflessly in the Revolutionary navy.

A successful privateer during the Revolution, Higginson had famously declared that the Continental Navy "was a bad school to educate good officers in." He had something of the privateer's contempt for the Continental Navy, believing that private vessels were far more useful in attacking British commerce. Truxtun shared some of these prejudices when he was a privateer during the Revolution.

Of course the Continental Navy had had a hard time recruiting; it offered individual seamen little compensation and had to compete with privateers. But it was also a service that had not existed before—a fact Higginson conveniently ignored. Any navy with a similar task was bound to have personnel who were less than desirable. But the Continental Navy did make a beginning. What was truly remarkable was how many good men it did attract.

Despite all the difficulties, Stoddert had the navy up and running in six months, exceeding even Adams's expectations. By the end of 1798, Stoddert had twenty-one warships in service, by the end of 1799, thirty-three, and by the end of 1800, fifty-four. His predecessors, Secretaries Pickering and McHenry, had three frigates to construct. Although they had been authorized in 1794, they were still not ready for sea in January 1798.

Not only did Stoddert send more than a score of warships into action in a matter of a few months; he also gave them strategic direction. His task was far simpler than the one confronting the Continental Navy. He had to contend with a French navy that had been decimated by the Revolution and was being checked by the Royal Navy. Few French warships escaped the British blockade, and those that did slipped out of blockaded ports singly, so that the small U.S. Navy was soon more powerful than the French along the American coast and in the West Indies.

As warships became available, Stoddert first used them to clear the nation's shores and then sent them to the Caribbean. On July 30, 1798, he wrote to the president, "Our first care certainly ought to be the security of our own coasts—the next, to avail ourselves of the commercial and perhaps political advantages which the present state of the West Indies and Spanish America is calculated to afford us." Stoddert proposed ignoring hurricane season in the Caribbean (August, September, and October). He insisted that the storms were not as bad as they were portrayed. By the end of 1798 nearly all of the navy's twenty-one warships were slated for the West Indies or had arrived. The major French base was at Guadeloupe, and the American fleet was concentrated there. Stoddert wrote to Adams, "By keeping up incessant attacks on the French cruisers on their own ground they will, in a degree at least, be prevented from coming on ours."

French warships and privateers disappeared from the American coast in a matter of weeks. The number of French men-of-war and privateers operating there was lower than originally imagined.

When the American fleet appeared, the French retreated permanently to their base at Guadeloupe, where Stoddert went after them. He assigned the fleet multiple tasks: convoy American merchantmen, raid French commerce, and most importantly, attack the few French warships they found, as well as the swarms of privateers and pirates. Stoddert also used the navy to transport important people and dispatches, as had been done during the Revolution.

The big American frigates *Constitution*, *United States*, and *Constellation* put to sea for the first time early in the summer of 1798. Captain Thomas Truxtun in the 36-gun *Constellation* was the first, standing out from Chesapeake Bay on June 23. John Barry, the navy's senior captain, put to sea in the *United States*, sailing from the Delaware capes on July 13, and the *Constitution*, under her controversial captain, Samuel Nicholson, left Boston on July 12. Truxtun and Nicholson had orders from Stoddert to patrol the American coastline—Truxtun from Cape Henry to the St. Marys River on the Georgia-Florida border, Nicholson to join *Ganges* and patrol between New York and Georges Bank. Barry was sent to the West Indies in company with Stephen Decatur Sr. in the *Delaware*. Barry was the opening wedge in Stoddert's plan to attack the French in the Caribbean.

While Stoddert was busy getting ships to sea and directing their movements, he was also thinking about the navy's future. Midshipmen were of particular interest to him. They were being trained not at a naval academy but in ships-of-war. Captain Truxtun, who took this responsibility seriously, maintained that a man-of-war was the best place to educate the young gentlemen. At the age of sixteen, Truxtun himself had received some rough training from the Royal Navy when a no-nonsense press gang had caught him in London and forced him to serve for a few months aboard HMS *Prudent*, a 64-gun battleship. When he was released he sailed back to America in the merchant vessel *London*, feeling none the worse for wear. He thought he had learned a great deal from the *Prudent*'s captain, who had taken a special interest in him.

Some midshipmen aboard Truxtun's *Constellation*, including David Porter, thought the captain's methods were too strict. But First Lieutenant John Rogers, who had extensive experience as a merchant captain, thought Truxtun was hard but fair and approved his methods. Truxtun never used physical punishment as some other captains did, notably Samuel Nicholson, skipper of the *Constitution*. Truxtun believed that the use of physical punishment showed an absence of leadership. He thought repeated whippings were bound to alienate an American crew; that was the case with Nicholson in all his commands, both in the Revolutionary War and in the Quasi-War. "It is at all times very unpleasant to flog men, if it can in any way be avoided," Truxtun cautioned his officers, "and in an infant and totally unorganized Navy, ways and means more mild, should be devised to correct inattention, neglect, and other faults."

Stoddert tried to keep promising young officers and midshipmen in the service by offering them attractive pay and pensions, as well as reasonable chances for advancement. His success was as remarkable as the number of warships he sent to sea. The famous lieutenants and captains who would fight wars against Tripoli and Great Britain in the next century—John Rogers, Stephen Decatur, Oliver Hazard Perry, Thomas MacDonough, Isaac Hull, James Lawrence, William Bainbridge, Charles Stewart, David Porter, and many others—received their training and first taste of battle as midshipmen and young lieutenants in the Quasi-War.

On November 23, 1798, Stoddert proposed to Congress building twelve ships of the line, twelve frigates, and twenty additional warships not to exceed 24 guns. Congress responded on February 25, 1799, by authorizing construction and deployment of six 74s and six sloops-of-war, purchasing two dockyards, and acquiring timber and other shipbuilding materials. The measure passed by a vote of 54 to 42. Stoddert hoped to construct a respectable fleet that would become a permanent fixture in the American government, led by young officers trained in the Quasi-War. His dream, however, was never realized because of the public's unwillingness to bear the taxes necessary to sustain such a navy, and later because of Presidents Jefferson and Madison, who believed that blue water navies did more harm than good. President Jefferson discontinued the work in 1801.

George Washington was a consistent supporter of Stoddert. He wrote to him, "I cannot entertain a doubt, but it will be the policy of this country to create such a navy as will protect our commerce from the insults and depredations to which it has been subject to of late, and to make it duly respected."

While concentrating on building a blue water fleet, Stoddert and the president placed little emphasis on smaller vessels, including gunboats. This made no difference during the Quasi-War, but in the wars that followed, the usefulness of smaller fighting boats would again become evident, revealing an important flaw in Stoddert's plans for the future fleet.

Stoddert and Adams strayed from their strategy of concentrating on the Caribbean only once in the spring of 1799, when they planned to send two heavy frigates, the *Constitution* and the *United States*, to the French coast with the vague purpose of showing the flag and picking up whatever prizes might come their way. Stoddert wrote to Adams, "Our very fine ships will be seen in Europe—it will be seen there too, that we are not afraid of provoking the French Nation, when they give us cause." Complications arose, however, and the venture was delayed and eventually cancelled. Adams thought it was just as well. "Although I am very solicitous to strike some strokes in Europe," he wrote to Stoddert, "for the reasons detailed in your letter proposing the expedition, yet I feel the whole force of the importance of deciding all things in the West Indies."

10

THE QUASI-WAR
WITH FRANCE

June 1798–March 1801

As Adams vigorously organized and deployed the new navy, he pursued diplomacy just as energetically. On June 12, 1798, he received a troubling dispatch from William Vans Murray, the new American ambassador at The Hague. (He replaced John Quincy Adams, who had been reassigned to Prussia.) Murray reported that when the other commissioners had left Paris, Elbridge Gerry remained behind. Adams had expected that all the special envoys would return, and he was furious that Gerry was treating with the French alone.

Five days later, in the midst of the nation's war hysteria, John Marshall sailed into New York unexpectedly. He went directly to Philadelphia, where he received a hero's welcome. The Federalists organized a splendid reception at Oeller's Hotel. Marshall reported to the president that in his opinion the French would not declare war; they expected to get what they wanted without one. They were intoxicated with success, according to Marshall. They assumed that America would be divided and overawed, and would cave in.

Marshall's assessment surprised Adams. He concluded that now wasn't the time for a declaration of war. Perhaps, he thought, America's strong reaction to Talleyrand's clumsy diplomacy would awaken the Directory to the fact that they were not going to get what they wanted without a fight. If what Marshall said was true and the French did not want a war, perhaps there was still hope for diplomacy to work.

When the president asked why Gerry hadn't returned, Marshall informed him that Gerry had remained in Paris because Talleyrand had insisted that if he left, war would follow. Gerry would only observe, Marshall explained; he would not conduct negotiations. Gerry was staying for the good of the country, despite knowing how badly he would be treated for doing so. Adams was reassured on that point; he had been wrong to doubt his old friend and was glad of it.

In spite of Marshall's analysis, the public was still annoyed with the French. Adams was angry as well, but he sensed that the country was not ready to undertake a war with a major power. Congress would certainly approve a declaration of war if Adams requested it. On June 21 he told Congress that he would "never send another Minister to France without assurance that he will be received, respected, and honored, as the representative of a great, free, powerful, and independent nation."

In the summer of 1798 Victor du Pont, the French envoy Adams had refused to recognize, returned to France with news of America's hysterical reaction to the XYZ Affair and the Directory's decrees. Talleyrand had heard similar reports, and he realized that his contemptuous treatment of the American diplomats had united the American people behind war measures directed at France. He now had to face a growing American fleet and army.

Like his predecessors, Talleyrand had visions of resuscitating France's North American empire by acquiring Canada and Louisiana, but a militarily potent America would be an insurmountable obstacle. The United States had to be neutralized, and the only way of doing that now was through negotiations. Shaken, the foreign minister reversed course and warned the Directory of the consequences of pushing America into England's arms. The Directory then revoked its decree ordering attacks on American commerce and released its American prisoners.

Word began filtering into Quincy during the late summer of 1798 confirming John Marshall's opinion that Talleyrand did not want war. John Quincy Adams wrote to his father that the Directory had changed its mind and now wanted talks.

In September Talleyrand sent Louis Pichon to The Hague to show Murray a letter dated September 28, 1798, in which Talleyrand pledged that France would receive with appropriate respect any envoy sent by President Adams for the purpose of reconciling the differences between the two countries. Talleyrand's letter to Pichon was meant to be shown to Adams. It read, "Every plenipotentiary whom the government of the United States will send to France, to terminate the differences which subsist between the two countries, will undoubtedly be received with the respect due to the representative of a free, independent, and powerful country."

Murray conveyed these assurances to the president, but before Adams would send another envoy he insisted on direct assurances in writing from Talleyrand. Adams believed that the resolute actions taken by the United States, particularly on the high seas, had forced Talleyrand and the Directory to come to their senses.

The threat of an alliance with Britain also had moved them, Adams thought, although as far as he was concerned the nation's policy of strict neutrality remained in place. America would stand on its own. Hamilton and the Federalists, like Timothy Pickering, wanted close cooperation, even an alliance with Britain, but Adams was determined to maintain American independence.

Hamilton and his Federalist supporters (known as High Federalists) did not want neutrality; they wanted war. They had dreams of a large army headed by General Hamilton defending the country against a French invasion, seizing the Floridas and Louisiana from Spain, and detaching South and Central America as well. Spain was now allied with France. The dons had switched sides in 1796 and on August 19, 1796, had signed an alliance with the Directory at San Ildefonso.

Furthermore, Hamilton's army could be used to put down a domestic rebellion, even against a state like Virginia. The High Federalists thought a war with France would bind the country to the Federalist administration and assure it the presidency in the next election.

Adams's views were decidedly different. He was disturbed that the new army seemed to be taking on a life of its own, with George Washington only nominally in charge. Adams and Washington both opposed invading Louisiana and the Floridas without a declaration of war, and Adams had no intention of asking for one now. Hamilton's bizarre plans gave Adams an important reason for seeking peace: without a war, there would be no need for Hamilton's outsize army.

Late in November 1798, news reached the president that Admiral Horatio Nelson had defeated the French Mediterranean fleet at Aboukir Bay east of Alexandria, Egypt, on August 1. Bonaparte had set aside plans to invade Britain directly and marched east, as he had always wanted to do, expecting an easy triumph. But Nelson's victory in what became known as the battle of the Nile cut off Napoleon's army in Egypt, blocking his ambition to establish a French empire in the Middle East and forcing a major change in his plans.

Nelson's victory established British naval supremacy in the Mediterranean and permanently injured the French navy. It now appeared that no French invasion of the United States would take place in the near future. Moreover, France would probably be unable to put a significant number of warships in the Caribbean, giving the fledgling American navy a decided advantage there.

When the president heard of Nelson's triumph, he understood its implications and was impressed. "The English," he said, "have exhibited an amazing example of skill and intrepidity, perseverance and firmness at sea. We are a chip off that block."

Without the prospect of a French invasion, the president could shrink the army to its prewar size and cut the ground out from under Hamilton. Adams was aware of growing discontent over the internal taxes imposed to fund the expanded army and his other military preparations; politically, he believed he was on firm ground.

Elbridge Gerry returned from France, arriving in Boston on October 1, 1778. Three days later he met with Adams at his farm in Quincy and confirmed what Marshall had told him: the French did not want war. Having remained in Paris, Gerry was able to give an account of how the French had reacted to America's outrage over the XYZ Affair. The city's newspapers had caused Talleyrand considerable discomfort for his inept diplomacy, Gerry reported. Talleyrand had little credit with the Directory to begin with and now he had to move fast to repair the damage.

Gerry reinforced Adams's view that a diplomatic solution to the crisis with France was possible. Adams received further encouragement from the dispatches of Ambassador Murray at The Hague; from Thomas Adams, the president's son, who returned from Europe in January 1799; and from John Quincy Adams, who was keeping his father abreast of events in Europe from his post in Berlin.

On February 1, 1799, Washington wrote to Adams that "the American people were very desirous of peace. . . . Peace was the ardent desire of all friends of this rising empire." On February 18, 1799, Adams nominated William Vans Murray to be the new U.S. minister plenipotentiary to France. His mission was to negotiate a peace agreement. He was to travel to Paris, however, only when the French government assured the president in writing that his minister would be received properly. Later, on advice from the Senate, the president added two additional envoys, Chief Justice Oliver Ellsworth and Governor William Davie of North Carolina.

The announcement that Adams was sending another peace mission to Paris shocked and angered the Hamiltonian Federalists. For some time they had known that Paris wanted to negotiate, but they preferred declaring war and deferring peace talks until after the election of 1800. George Cabot wrote that "the incidents of active war would every day interest the feelings of the community" and advance the prospects of the Federalist Party. The High Federalists planned to keep enlarging the army and navy, raising taxes and the national debt, suppressing dissent, and using federal troops, if necessary, to enforce tax collection.

Adams found their program absurd; it went entirely against the grain of public opinion and would ensure Jefferson's election in 1800. The patriotic fervor spawned by the XYZ Affair, Adams felt, had dissipated. His reelection looked doubtful unless he could achieve the peace that the country now wanted.

The Republicans were as bewildered by the president's announcement as the High Federalists. Jefferson, ever suspicious, gave his old friend Adams no credit for making the courageous peace effort the Republicans themselves had long urged. Jefferson refused to believe that Adams was genuinely interested in peace. He thought the president was engaged in some sort of game whereby he "would parry [Talleyrand's] overture [for peace] while . . . [appearing] to accede to it." Jefferson accused Adams of nominating William Vans Murray, expecting that the Senate would "take on their shoulders the odium of rejecting [the nomination]."

Adams had not consulted the cabinet, which was more under Hamilton's influence than ever. The president made the decision alone, while receiving critical support from Washington, John Jay, and Patrick Henry.

The country supported Adams's position as well. Contrary to Hamilton's prediction, the Federalists did well in the congressional elections of April 1799.

During the second week of March 1799, word reached Philadelphia of Captain Thomas Truxtun's meeting with the French frigate *L'Insurgente* off the island of Nevis in the Caribbean. Truxtun was not a famous Revolutionary hero like John Barry, Richard Dale, or Silas Talbot. He had been a privateer during the War of Independence and believed firmly that he had contributed more to victory than any captain in the Continental Navy, including John Paul Jones. He rejected the notion that privateers were only interested in profits. In his mind, he was a patriot, performing essential services for the cause. During the Revolution he had commanded the well-known privateers *Independence*, *Mars*, and *St. James*, operating mainly in British waters. Washington admired his work and in 1794 had appointed him captain in the new U.S. Navy. Truxtun superintended construction of the 36-gun *Constellation* in the Baltimore shipyard of David Stodder, using Joshua Humphreys's plans. Apart from the American 44-gun heavy frigates. Truxtun judged his to be the finest in the world. Her keel was 161 feet long, and her beam 40 feet wide. Her complement was 340 men. She could muster ten knots on a wind and twelve and a half running free. As she put to sea, she carried one hundred tons of ballast, thirty thousand gallons of water, and four months' worth of provisions.

At noon on February 9, 1799, Truxtun was cruising a few leagues east of Nevis, near British St. Kitts, when a strange sail appeared standing westward, perhaps fifteen miles away, looking like a large man-of-war. Truxtun gave chase. With a following wind the *Constellation* bore down on the stranger, and Truxtun hoisted the British private signal. He saw no answer and sent up the American recognition signal. When there was no proper response, he ordered all hands to quarters and prepared to chase what turned out to be the 40-gun French frigate, *L'Insurgente*—one of their best—under an experienced captain, Citizen Michel Pierre Barreaut.

Truxtun was confident of his crew. He had trained them hard, and they were ready. At two o'clock, as Truxtun continued after his prey, a tropical squall spiraled across the sea, catching *L'Insurgente* amidships, cracking her topmast, and sending it crashing to her deck. The crew struggled to free the tangled wreckage and heave it overboard.

Truxtun had managed to avoid the squall's whirling gray cloud, and he bore down on the Frenchman. At a quarter past three he ranged up on *L'Insurgente*'s lee quarter and, from a hundred yards, delivered a full broadside. *L'Insurgente* returned fire, aiming at the *Constellation*'s sails, masts, and rigging.

Meanwhile, Captain Barreaut maneuvered to grapple and board. Losing a topmast made his ship more difficult to maneuver, and if he did not hook on to the American and neutralize her advantage, she could attack him from whatever angle she chose. But Truxtun was too agile. He kept out of reach and then ran circles around *L' Insurgente*, delivering broadsides and raking her by the bow and then the stern for an hour and a quarter until Barreaut surrendered his smoldering wreck. He had suffered twenty-nine killed and forty-one wounded. Truxtun had four men injured, one of whom was James McDonough (Thomas's older brother), and two who died.

Truxtun sent his first lieutenant, John Rogers, and midshipman, David Porter, with a party of eleven seamen to take possession of the French ship. They tended to the dead and wounded, and then transferred more than four hundred prisoners to the *Constellation* in heavy seas. *L'Insurgente* then had to be put into condition to sail to St. Kitts for repairs, so that she could be brought to the United States in triumph. Three days later the two big frigates limped into the British base at Basseterre, St. Kitts, to sustained applause from a British audience that included the governor. If he didn't know before, Truxtun knew now that he was a hero.

The president was elated. Although he had begun a new round of diplomacy that looked promising, Adams intended to keep prosecuting the naval war in order to strengthen the hand of his envoys in Paris. Pursuing the war while talking, the president believed, was the only way to achieve an honorable peace. "Our operations and preparations by sea and by land," he wrote to Secretary Pickering, "are not to be relaxed in the smallest degree; on the contrary I wish them to be animated with fresh energy. St. Domingo and the Isle of France and all other parts of the French Dominions are to be treated in the same manner as if no negotiation were going on."

Later, on February 1, 1800, Truxtun would fight and defeat the 54-gun French frigate *La Vengeance*. This and his battle with *L'Insurgente* were the only major battles of the war. For most of the Quasi-War the French had only two or three frigates on station, and Truxtun defeated two of them.

The victory over *L'Insurgente* was but one illustration of how successful Stoddert's strategy had been. His principal objective was protecting American commerce by convoying merchantmen to and from the Caribbean, as well as hunting down the swarms of French privateers and pirates who infested the West Indies from the Windward Passage (the major entry and exit point between the Atlantic and the Caribbean) to the north coast of South America. To accomplish this, Stoddert divided the fleet into four squadrons. The largest, under Commodore Barry in the *United States*, was stationed at Prince Rupert's Bay in British-controlled Dominica. Its cruising grounds were the Lesser Antilles from St. Kitts to South America. Samuel Nicholson and the *Constitution* were with Barry. (Stoddert was dissatisfied with the volatile Nicholson and intended to replace him with Silas Talbot as soon as he could, but in the meantime he controlled him by placing him under Barry rather than giving him an independent command.) Barry also had the 24-gun *George Washington*, the 24-gun *Merrimack*, the 24-gun *Portsmouth*, the 18-gun *Herald*, the 14-gun revenue cutter *Pickering* commanded by Captain Edward Preble, the 14-gun *Eagle*, the 14-gun *Scammel*, and the 12-gun *Diligence*.

Commodore Truxtun and the *Constellation* commanded the second squadron based at St. Kitts. His cruising grounds were from St. Kitts north to Spanish Puerto Rico. With him were the *Baltimore*, the 18-gun brig *Richmond*, the brig *Norfolk*, and the 14-gun revenue cutter *Virginia*.

A third squadron, stationed in the Windward Passage between Haiti and Cuba, was under the command of Commodore Tingey. He was in the *Ganges* and had with him the 18-gun brig *Pinckney* and the 12-gun revenue cutter *South Carolina*.

A fourth squadron, under Stephen Decatur Sr. in the *Delaware*, patrolled off the north coast of Cuba with the 14-gun revenue cutter *Governor Jay* and the 10-gun revenue cutter *General Greene*.

The 20-gun *Montezuma* patrolled independently.

Although Stoddert was disappointed with the lack of aggressiveness of Commodore Barry, who at age fifty-three lacked the vigor and enthusiasm of his Revolutionary War days, the effectiveness of the American fleet was impressive. John Roche Jr., a seventeen-year-old midshipman aboard the *Constitution*, noted, "The American and British cruisers swarm in these seas, and nothing belonging to the enemy dares appear out except a few privateers who skulk out in the night and in again as soon as it is light."

Of course, Stoddert had many problems to deal with, among them how to keep his ships on station. Because of their obligation to perform convoy duty, they were coming to the United States and going back to the Caribbean all the time. While they were at home they could refit and replenish their stores, but America had no base in the West Indies; the ships there had to waste valuable time traveling great distances to American shipyards, reducing their numbers on the various stations to low levels. This was particularly true during the latter half of 1799, when nearly the entire fleet was back home for one reason or another. Stoddert eventually sorted this out, but keeping the maximum number of ships in the Caribbean was a constant problem.

At the end of March 1799, Adams left Philadelphia for his farm in Quincy and remained there until September. His long absences presented an opportunity for his opponents. Robert Troup, a close friend of Hamilton's from their days at King's College in New York, said, "All the measures of the government are retarded by this kind of abdication."

The president's supporters were concerned. As 1799 wore on, Stoddert became worried that Hamilton might try to fill the void created by the absent president and form a de facto government. In fact, Hamilton had written to McHenry, "If there was everywhere a disposition, without prejudice and nonsense, to concert a rational plan, I would cheerfully come to Philadelphia and assist in it; nor can I doubt that success may be assured."

On June 23, 1799, while away in Quincy, Adams lifted the trade embargo on Haiti, giving General Toussaint L'Ouverture important aid in his struggle to gain control of Hispaniola and assert his independence from France. The leader of the 408,000 black Africans—formerly slaves—who made up nine-tenths of Haiti's population, Toussaint was a superb fighting general and politician. He reached out to all segments of society, including whites, trying to unite them under his leadership. His drive for personal power was as great as his determination to rid the country of slavery.

Andre Rigaud, Toussaint's rival, led Haiti's *gens de couleur*, the island's thirty thousand free mulattoes. Unlike the slaves, they were citizens of France.

Before the black revolt in 1791, twenty-four thousand whites had ruled the island. They were divided into three groups: government officials, rich planters, and small property owners and artisans. By the time Adams decided to reopen trade, their ranks had been decimated by flight, warfare, and the murderous attacks of their former slaves. As whites departed, Toussaint and Rigaud fought for control.

Inspired by the rhetoric of the Declaration of the Rights of Man and by their natural hatred for the masters who had brutalized them, the slaves had been fighting for their freedom since 1791. In 1794 the French Convention under Robespierre had, with great reluctance, emancipated them in order to retain some control over the country. Prior to the French Revolution, Saint-Domingue (as Haiti was then known) had been the most lucrative French possession in the Caribbean. In fact, France had the majority of her overseas investments in the island. At the time, Hispaniola was divided between Spanish Santo Domingo in the east and French Saint-Domingue in the west.

Before the embargo, the United States, particularly New England, had participated in the rich trade with Saint-Domingue. Trade restrictions against the island, as against all French possessions, had been in place since the start of the Quasi-War; no American goods were entering the country legally. President Adams's desire to resume that lucrative trade figured in his decision to lift the embargo in the summer of 1799. Adams also had an interest in depriving the French of an important asset and enlisting Toussaint's help to prevent French privateers from using Haitian bases to attack American shipping.

The president's decision alarmed southern slaveholders, Thomas Jefferson among them. Fearing that rebellion in Haiti would inspire a slave revolt in the United States, they wanted white rule and slavery reestablished in Haiti as soon as possible. As early as September 1791, Governor Charles Pinckney of South Carolina had pointed out "how nearly similar the situation of the southern states and St.

Domingo [was]."When Adams lifted the embargo on Haiti, Jefferson wrote indignantly, "We may expect. . . black crews and . . . missionaries [advancing] into the Southern states. . . . If this combustion can be introduced among us under any veil whatever, we have to fear it." The president was aware of this heightened level of concern and certainly didn't want to precipitate a rebellion in the United States. He considered good relations with Toussaint as helping to prevent such an event, rather than precipitating it. Of course, he realized that he had no control over the spread of ideas.

Adams was determined to work closely with the British in Haiti. He told Secretary Pickering, "Harmony with the English, in all this business with St. Domingo, is the thing I have most at heart."

Until British Brigadier General Thomas Maitland arrived back on the scene in March 1798, British policy in Haiti had been a total failure. Four and a half years earlier, in September 1793, Prime Minister Pitt had decided to weaken France by attacking her West Indian empire. Haiti was an attractive target because of its size and economic importance, and because its slaves had conducted a successful revolt. Once he conquered Haiti, Pitt intended to reimpose slavery so that the contagion of independence would not lead to a revolt of England's West Indian slaves, especially the 300,000 in Jamaica, only three hundred miles away.

But Toussaint and his former slaves fought heroically against Pitt. Disease ravaged the British ranks, as Pitt became bogged down in nightmarish jungle warfare that claimed the lives of tens of thousands of his troops. By the time President Adams took office in March 1797, the British were still fighting and dying in Haiti, yet were farther than ever from Pitt's original goals. The next year Pitt gave up, retaining only the port of Mole Saint Nicolas, the Gibraltar of the West Indies, on the northwest coast opposite the Windward Passage; the port of Jeremie in the south; and Port-au-Prince.

The following year, the British turned the three ports over to Toussaint. By creating a working alliance with him instead of trying to defeat him militarily, General Maitland reversed Britain's fortunes. Adams chose to associate the United States with this new policy. Maitland went to Philadelphia and reached a tacit agreement with the administration, and a new American consul general, Dr. Edward Stevens, traveled to Cap François to implement it.

Toussaint, however, still had to deal with Andre Rigaud. In June 1799, a bloody civil war, the War of Knives, began in earnest, with the British and Americans providing critical help, including food and military aid, to Toussaint, who was in desperate need of both. The French Directory supported Rigaud but did not sever ties with Toussaint, supplying him aid as well, although in lesser amounts.

As part of his bargain with Adams and the British, Toussaint agreed to suppress French privateers to the extent he could; he also agreed to open the ports of Cap-Haïtien and Port-au-Prince to American and British trade. Toussaint could also grant a laissez-passer to French ships cooperating with him; this would prevent them from being captured by the Americans or the British. Furthermore, Toussaint agreed not to export his revolution to Jamaica or the United States.

In support of the president's new policy, a substantial American squadron now gathered off Haiti under the command of Commodore Silas Talbot, whose flagship was the *Constitution*. With him was William Roberts, a Jamaican slave he had owned for many years. (Stoddert had finally succeeded in putting Nicholson ashore in charge of building a ship of the line and substituting Talbot, who had lost none of his fighting capacity since the Revolution.) Talbot's squadron eventually included the 28-gun *Boston*, the 28-gun *General Greene*, the brig *Norfolk* commanded by William Bainbridge, the *Herald*, the schooner *Experiment*, and the brig *Augusta*.

On September 23, 1799, the frigate *General Greene*, under the Revolutionary War veteran Captain Christopher Perry (Oliver Hazard Perry's father), had sailed from Newport, Rhode Island, planning to join Talbot off Haiti. When the great showdown between Toussaint and Rigaud took place at Jacmel on March 10–11, 1800, Perry and the *General Greene* provided decisive naval support, stopping supplies being delivered to Rigaud by sea and, at a critical moment, bombarding the town's three forts from the water while

Toussaint attacked from the land. Rigaud was crushed in between, but he and part of his army escaped.

Toussaint had to rely on an American warship because Admiral Hyde Parker, who commanded the British naval forces in Haiti from his base in Port Royal, Jamaica, repudiated General Maitland's policy of cooperation with Toussaint. Parker refused to interdict supplies being delivered to Rigaud from France or aid Toussaint in the battle of Jacmel. Parker considered Toussaint a threat; he believed the Haitian leader was fomenting a slave rebellion in Jamaica.

After defeating Rigaud, Toussaint invaded the Spanish part of the island, establishing control there on January 28, 1801. He now ruled the entire island of Hispaniola, but by this time his British and American supporters had deserted him; without them, he was forced to remain nominally part of the French republic in something of a dominion status. In the meantime, Napoleon had seized power in France, and there was little doubt that he would eventually move to reassert control of Hispaniola and reinstitute slavery. At this juncture, Toussaint could no longer turn to America or Britain for help, since both had made their own peace with the French dictator (the United States in the Treaty of Mortefontaine, and Britain in the Treaty of Amiens).

On August 5, 1799, Adams received word in Quincy from Secretary Pickering that Talleyrand, in a letter dated May 12, had officially assured the president that the American envoys would be received properly. This was the letter Adams had been waiting for. Having regarded Talleyrand's earlier letter to Pichon as an inadequate substitute, Adams had refused to move until he received directly from the foreign minister "authentic, regular, official, diplomatic assurances."

On September 30, 1799, Adams left Quincy and traveled to Trenton, where the government was temporarily housed to escape the yellow fever decimating Philadelphia. Arriving on October 10, Adams was surprised to find General Alexander Hamilton waiting to see him.

Hamilton hoped to persuade the president to suspend the peace mission to France. In a lengthy meeting, Hamilton spoke warmly of the necessity of drawing close to Britain and waging war against the French. He expected that Britain would win the war with France and restore the Bourbons to power. He also believed that war would bind the United States together and ensure the electoral success of the pro-British, anti-French Federalist Party. He referred to Jefferson and the Republicans scornfully as democrats and Jacobins, and wanted to crush them permanently; there was no room in his universe for a loyal opposition. Hamilton also described his vision of attacking all the Spanish colonies in the Western Hemisphere, including Louisiana, the Floridas, Mexico, and Latin America.

Adams saw nothing new in Hamilton's ideas, which he found ridiculous. In fact, he thought Hamilton had taken leave of his senses. There appeared to be no limit to the general's ambition. Adams found Hamilton's analysis of European affairs uninformed, his dreams of conquest ludicrous, and his views on domestic politics laughable. America had no interest in seeing the Bourbons restored; nor did the people support an invasion of Spain's colonies, or a large standing army, or high taxes and loans to support it. "Never in my life," the president recalled, "did I hear a man talk more like a fool."

On October 15 Adams met with his cabinet in Trenton, where Pickering, Wolcott, and McHenry, following Hamilton's lead, urged postponing the peace mission. Secretary Stoddert advised continuing it. Adams stuck to his policy and ordered his envoys to proceed to Paris. On November 3, 1799, the *United States*, under Captain John Barry, left Newport, Rhode Island, for France, with Chief Justice Oliver Ellsworth and North Carolina Governor William Richardson aboard. When they reached France in January, they joined Ambassador Murray for the peace negotiations. By this time, a year had passed in which Adams could have moved the talks forward, if not completed them. Dragging out the negotiations meant that the all-important question of peace would go unresolved as the country entered the presidential election year of 1800.

Before the American diplomats were a week at sea, on November 9, 1799, thirty-three-year-old Napoleon Bonaparte overthrew the Directory and declared himself First Consul, casting great uncertainty over their mission. Word of the coup reached Philadelphia in February 1800. The president was not surprised; from the beginning he had predicted the French Revolution would fail and end in a military dictatorship. He was thankful that he had not let down his guard but had continued the naval war, since it was unclear what Napoleon's position would be with respect to the talks. But Adams was keenly aware of how much the negotiations meant for his political future. Americans wanted an end to the war and to the high taxes and high-interest government loans needed to sustain it. If the envoys came home with an acceptable peace, Adams thought he could win reelection.

On December 3, 1799, the president addressed the new Congress, stressing that the size of the army and navy had to be "commensurate with our resources and the situation of our country." Instead of emphasizing the need to build America's defenses, the president emphasized his desire for peace and an end to the Quasi-War. The mood of the country had changed dramatically since the spring and summer of 1798. Adams had been known as the war president; now he wanted to be known as the man who brought peace.

Eleven days later, on December 14, George Washington died. Abigail Adams wrote to her sister, Mary Cranch, "No man ever lived, more deservedly and beloved and respected. The praise, and I may say adulation, which followed his administration for several years, never made him forget that he was a man, subject to the same weakness and frailty attached to human nature. He . . . ever maintained a modest diffidence of his own talents. . . . Possessed of power, possessed of an extensive influence, he never used it but for the benefit of his country. . . . If we look through the whole tenor of his life, history will not produce to us a parallel. . . . Our mourning is sincere, in the midst of which, we ought not to lose sight of the blessings we have enjoyed . . . that he was spared to us, until he saw a successor filling his place, pursuing the same system which he had adopted, and that in times which have been equally dangerous and critical."

The election of 1800 was hotly contested all year. In keeping with the fashion of the times, Adams and Jefferson pretended to be above the fray, but they were absorbed in it. No two candidates in American history worked harder to get elected. Adams had his record to run on and his hopes for peace. Jefferson also had a long record. He had been in public life at the highest levels for two and a half decades, but much of his political activity had been conducted surreptitiously. His less than stellar performance as governor of Virginia was there to examine, but luckily for him, people had forgotten it. His basic approach to governing, however, was generally known. He expressed it succinctly in a letter to Elbridge Gerry:

"I am for preserving to the states the power not yielded by them to the Union, and to the legislature of the Union its constitutional share in the division of power; and I am not for transferring all the power of state to the general government, and all those of the government to the executive branch. I am for a government rigorously frugal and simple, applying all the possible savings of the public revenue to the discharge of the national debt; and not for a multiplication of officers and salaries merely to make partisans, and for increasing, by every device, the public debt, on the principle of its being a public blessing. I am for relying, for internal defense, on our militia solely, till actual invasion, and for such a naval force only as may protect our coasts and harbors from such depredations as we have experienced; and not for a standing army in time of peace, which may overawe the public sentiment; nor for a navy. Which, by its own expenses and the external wars in which it will implicate us, will grind us with public burdens, and sink us under them. I am for free commerce with all nations; political connection with none; and little or no diplomatic establishment. And I am not for implicating ourselves by new treaties with the quarrels of Europe, entering that field of slaughter to preserve their balance. Or joining in the confederacy of kings to war against the principles of liberty. I am for freedom of religion, and against all maneuvers to bring about a legal ascendancy of one sect over another: for freedom of the press, and against all violations of the constitution to silence by force and not by reason the complaints or criticisms, or just or unjust, of our citizens against the conduct of their agents."

Adams waited impatiently for word from France. After six months of negotiations, the Convention of Mortefontaine was finally signed on October 3, 1800. Word of it did not reach Washington until the first week of November—too late to win Adams the election. The treaty effectively sacrificed all American spoliation claims, in return for France agreeing to the cessation of hostilities. In addition, the old treaties of 1778 were effectively repealed, which pleased Adams greatly; they had threatened to drag the United States into every French war. The treaty also approved the principle of "free ships make free goods." Napoleon hoped to interest the United States in joining Russia, Sweden, Denmark, and Prussia in the anti-British armed neutrality that he was encouraging. Neither Adams nor Jefferson, however, was interested.

On February 3, 1801, the Senate passed the treaty with reservations. Adams wasn't satisfied with either the treaty or the reservations, but he consented to both because they meant peace, and on balance that was most important to him. The country wanted to end the fighting and return to its prewar prosperity. Above all, the people wanted internal taxes eliminated.

Adams attributed the successful negotiations to his dramatic naval buildup, a willingness to fight, and at the same time, a determination to talk. The U.S. Navy, he thought, had made an impression on not only the Directory but Bonaparte as well. The reasons for success, however, were quite different. Napoleon was using the peace settlement as part of his scheme to restore Louisiana to French rule. His overarching plan was the same as his predecessors', but it extended far beyond their dreams. He intended to establish a new French empire that included Haiti and the West Indies, Louisiana, Canada, the Floridas, and even the western part of the United States, Mexico, and South America.

The agreement at Mortefontaine was intended to lull the United States to sleep. Indeed, four months before signing it Napoleon had already begun the process of secretly acquiring Louisiana from the weak Spanish king. The day after signing a peace with America,

Napoleon completed the secret Treaty of San Ildefonso, by which Spain effectively ceded him all of Louisiana.

While negotiating with the United States and Spain, Bonaparte was also preparing a huge expeditionary force at Brest to invade Haiti and use it as a base from which to occupy New Orleans and Louisiana. By the time the Convention of Mortefontaine was signed, preparations were already far advanced. The threat of a French invasion, which Adams had dismissed only a short time before as wildly improbable, was now imminent.

On November 22, 1800, Adams delivered his annual message to the new Congress, meeting for the first time in the unfinished capital. He recommended, as Washington had before him, that the nation maintain reasonable measures of defense, even in peacetime. But Adams knew that the country would not support a large army or navy, and with the anti-navy Jefferson about to become president, the question for Adams was what he could hope to preserve of the defense establishment he had created. In his speech he lauded the navy. "The present Navy of the United States," he said, "called suddenly into existence by a great national emergency, has raised us in our esteem; and by the protection afforded to our commerce has effected to the extent of our expectations the objects for which it was created."

In fact, the navy's performance had been nothing short of remarkable. It had grown from no ships to fifty, including the *United States, Constitution, Constellation, President, Congress,* and *Chesapeake*—the original six frigates. And there were now almost five hundred officers, five thousand men, and eleven hundred marines.

The navy had continued to operate in the Caribbean during the peace negotiations, expanding its presence, convoying merchantmen, and attacking privateers. It did not eliminate French privateers or pirates, but it had success against them. American merchants felt safer sailing their ships into the Caribbean. The U.S. Navy took twice as many privateers in 1801 as it did in 1799, sending insurance rates down to prewar levels. Before the war the normal rate to ensure a merchantman sailing to the Caribbean was 6 percent of the estimated value of the ship and cargo. In the late summer of 1798 it had risen to 33 percent. By the end of 1800, it had fallen to 10 percent.

Stoddert had also reached out beyond the Caribbean by sending Captain Edward Preble and the frigate *Essex* to protect American trade against French marauders in the Sundra Strait that ran between Java and Sumatra in the Dutch East Indies. "The *Essex* is a good sea boat and sails remarkable fast," Preble said. "She went eleven miles per hour with topgallant sails set and six points of the wind." Built in Salem, Massachusetts, and paid for by the citizens of Essex County, the *Essex* was launched on September 30, 1799, and presented to the navy on December 17, 1799. She was to sail to the Far East in company with the *Congress*, under Captain James Sever, but on January 12, shortly after leaving Newport, Rhode Island, on the first leg of their journey, a violent gale struck. The winds dismasted the *Congress* and severely tested the *Essex*. Captain Sever struggled back to port for repairs, while Preble continued his mission, sailing to Cape Town at the southern tip of the Cape of Good Hope, and then to the Sundra Strait. There he gathered a group of merchantmen and convoyed them back to America, arriving in New York on November 28, 1800. The *Essex* was the first U.S. warship to round the Cape of Good Hope twice, although American merchantmen had been doing it routinely for many years.

In spite of the navy's performance and his wish to maintain a strong sea force, Adams, on March 3, 1800, a day before leaving office, signed the Peace Establishment Act. It reduced the navy to thirteen frigates, only six of which were to be kept on active duty. The numbers of smaller men-of-war were left to the discretion of the new president; he could keep whatever he pleased or do away with the lot. The bill also shrank the officer corps. Nine of twenty-eight captains were retained, 28 of 110 lieutenants, and 159 of 344 midshipmen.

In Adams's view, shrinking the navy, though painful, was inevitable. Taxpayers were unwilling to support a large fleet. The newly elected Jefferson would certainly follow public opinion and drastically reduce the navy, if not eliminate it. Adams decided to trim it himself, hoping that Jefferson would not go further. The rise of Napoleon Bonaparte and his disquieting ambitions, Britain's continued searches of American merchantmen and impressment of sailors, and trouble in the Mediterranean were all known to Adams. Yet he was not aware of the extent of Bonaparte's dreams, and he viewed Britain as a sometime ally whose transgressions during the Quasi-War he had purposefully overlooked. The Barbary pirates, although irritating, seemed of little consequence. So, distasteful as it was, Adams decided it was safe to cut the navy.

I I

THE NAVY
UNDER JEFFERSON

March 1801–March 1805

On March 4, 1801, newly elected President Thomas Jefferson, accompanied by a small entourage, strode from his lodgings at Conrad's Boardinghouse to the unfinished capital building, entering the Senate chamber—the only completed part—to deliver his first inaugural address. Nearly fifty-eight years old, he had spent most of his past twenty-five years in public life. As the principal author of the Declaration of Independence, he was a world-renowned figure. His immortal words had already inspired millions: "We hold these truths to be self-evident, that all men are created equal, that they are endowed by their Creator with certain unalienable Rights, that among these are Life, Liberty and the pursuit of Happiness. — That to secure these rights, Governments are instituted among Men, deriving their just powers from the consent of the governed."

The president gloried in the high ideals of the declaration and wished to spread them around the world. He habitually made

reference to those ideals being embodied in "this solitary republic . . . the only monument of human rights, and the sole depository of the sacred fire of freedom and self-government, from
hence it is to be lighted up in other regions of the earth, if other
regions of the earth shall ever become susceptible of its benign
influence."

He was not proposing to force these ideals on other nations
but rather inspire them by example. His idealism had not turned
into an aggressive ideology, as France's had. His noble words,
however, must have sounded hollow coming from a slaveholder.
While the new president was undeniably a leader in the struggle
for human rights, he was also part of a Virginia aristocracy that
presided over one of the more tyrannical slave societies in history. Jefferson didn't really mean that "all men" were created
equal. Clearly he did not consider the enslaved blacks who
labored in his fields and household his equals, although as a man
of scientific bent he was always open, he said, to the possibility
that slaves were not lesser creatures but people degraded by the
circumstances inflicted on them. Nevertheless, controlling
them—making certain they did not revolt—was as much of a
preoccupation as his determination to see the great principles of
the declaration fulfilled.

Much to Jefferson's embarrassment, during the election campaign of 1800, a major slave uprising occurred in Virginia. For a
time black revolutionaries, led by a slave known as Gabriel, threatened Virginia's new capital at Richmond. Organizing large numbers of artisans and mechanics in towns from the Chesapeake to
the Piedmont, the slaves fought to free themselves. Rumors spread
that Gabriel had help from Toussaint L'Ouverture.

Governor Monroe, one of Jefferson's more important political
supporters, called out the Virginia militia, while loyal household
slaves reported the revolutionaries' movements. As Gabriel's force
approached Richmond, an unusually violent thunderstorm im-
peded his attack, allowing Monroe to crush the insurrection and
capture its ringleaders, including Gabriel himself, who refused to

reveal any intelligence about what had happened. The governor hanged him along with three dozen of his lieutenants.

Monroe, who did everything he could to minimize the insurrection, was shaken by it. "This was unquestionably the most serious and formidable conspiracy we have ever known of the kind," he told Jefferson, "tho' indeed to call it so is to give no idea of the thing itself."

Jefferson worried how the revolt would look to the outside world. He warned Monroe, "The other states and the world at large will forever condemn us if we indulge a principle of revenge, or go one step beyond absolute necessity."

Even more embarrassing for the president was the manner of his election. He had always held majority rule to be the only way to confer political legitimacy, yet he had been elected not by a majority of free citizens but by virtue of the three-fifths rule in the Constitution. For purposes of establishing the number of members in the House of Representatives, each slave counted as three-fifths of a person. Each state's numbers in the House and Senate determined its representation in the Electoral College. Had the three-fifths rule not applied, John Adams would have been reelected. Of the seven southern states containing the preponderance of American slaves, six (Maryland, Virginia, South Carolina, Georgia, Kentucky, and Tennessee) voted exclusively for Jefferson. North Carolina was an exception; it gave Adams four votes, Charles Cotesworth Pinckney four, and Jefferson eight. The solid south thus gave its native son the election. Its aristocrats were not worried that the new president would threaten their way of life. Federalists in the north dubbed Jefferson the "Negro president."

As Jefferson stood in the Senate chamber to deliver his first inaugural address, neither the lofty ideals of self-government nor the infamy of slavery were on his mind. He was focused on healing the wounds from the recent election. The campaign had reached levels of vituperation that threatened to tear the country apart, and the struggle in the House of Representatives between Jefferson and Aaron Burr had cast doubt on whether the republic could peacefully transfer power a second time. "Let us, then, fellow-citizens, unite with one heart and one mind," urged the president. "Let us restore to social intercourse that harmony and affection without which liberty and even life itself are but dreary things. And let us reflect that, having banished from our land that religious intolerance under which mankind so long bled and suffered, we have yet gained little if we countenance a political intolerance as despotic, as wicked, and capable of as bitter and bloody persecutions." However hard they had fought, the president reminded his audience, they were bound together by fundamental constitutional principles.

Tolerance was something Jefferson had championed throughout his political life. He considered religious toleration the foundation of all individual rights. He was that rare partisan who exhibited forbearance for differing opinions. Jefferson had no love for his political opponents, only tolerance for their misguided beliefs. In a typical letter to Madison he referred to the Federalists as "patrons of usurpation and aristocracy." As much as he despised their beliefs, however, they had every right to voice them. Jefferson would rely on reason and the good sense of the people to counter noxious ideas, rather than sedition laws, and by doing so he broadened the essential foundation of the infant republic.

Though he preached unity and shared republican values, Jefferson intended to make far-reaching changes in the policies of his predecessors, amounting to what he and his followers considered a "revolution." The essence of the change, he said in his inaugural, was to create "a wise and frugal government, which shall restrain men from injuring one another, shall leave them otherwise free to regulate their own pursuits of industry and improvement, and shall not take from the mouth of labor the bread it has earned. This is the sum of good government, and this is necessary to close the circle of our felicities."

Jefferson thus stood for a strictly limited federal government, one contracted in its pursuits beyond what Washington and Adams had considered sensible. Such a national government would not threaten the liberties of its citizens or the powers of state governments, nor would it be strong enough to eliminate slavery.

Since Jefferson believed that "economy in the public expense" is the highest virtue of government, it is not surprising that, next to Secretary of State James Madison, Secretary of the Treasury Albert Gallatin became the most important member of his cabinet. Acknowledged as the Republican expert on financial matters, Gallatin knew the ins and outs of the federal budget better than anyone else. Debt reduction was an obsession with Jefferson, and Gallatin proposed eliminating the federal debt as soon as possible and simultaneously lowering taxes. He and the president were intent on eliminating internal taxation altogether. Gallatin planned to pay off the national debt in sixteen years; with receipts projected at $10.6 million, $7.3 million would be allocated each year for debt reduction, leaving the government to run on $2,650,000.

The navy consumed the largest part of the budget, so it was there the ax would fall. The tiny army of thirty-five hundred was needed to defend western settlers against the Indians. Jefferson, Madison, and Gallatin continued to maintain that a navy was not only unnecessary but dangerous. An American blue water fleet, they thought, would inevitably be gobbled up by the Royal Navy in the opening stages of a conflict, as it had been during the War of Independence. Jefferson believed that the United States should avoid, at all costs, a war with either Britain or France. On the other hand, at no time was he willing to spend the money necessary to protect the United States against an invasion by either power. He relied on state militias as well as harbor and river defenses using small boats. On the high seas, privateers were the only American warships he would allow in any numbers. During the Adams administration, naval expenditures had reached $3 million a year. Gallatin proposed cutting them to slightly under $1 million, with additional cuts to come later.

Jefferson intended to lay up the inactive frigates in ordinary (mothball them). "I shall really be chagrined," he wrote, "if the water in the Eastern Branch [of the Potomac] will not admit our laying up the whole seven [frigates] there in time of peace, because they would be under the immediate eye of the department, and would require but one set of plunderers to take care of them." Thus the president did not lay up all thirteen frigates; he kept six operational, as the law required.

Not surprisingly, Jefferson had trouble finding a replacement for Stoddert, who remained at his desk until March 31, 1801. The president acknowledged the navy as "the department I understand least, and therefore need a person whose complete competence will justify the most entire confidence and resignation." He had hoped to appoint Robert Morris, but he was confined in debtors' prison.

While the president searched for Stoddert's replacement, Representative Samuel Smith handled the department's affairs. A Revolutionary War veteran, Smith was a powerful Republican congressman from Maryland and a pro-navy merchant. After offering the permanent position to him and then to Robert R. Livingston, John Langdon, and William Jones, the president finally settled on Robert Smith, Samuel's brother, an ambitious Baltimore lawyer with no training or aptitude for the position. Smith took office on July 27 and remained through Jefferson's two terms.

During the election of 1800 Abigail Adams had wondered what "visionary system of government" Jefferson was likely to employ. Her answer came in the president's approach to defense policy. Jefferson had the novel idea that he could substitute economic coercion for an army and navy. He was not a pacifist; he intended to defend the country if attacked. But he was not going to spend public money building an expensive army and navy to advance the country's interests abroad or have it ready at home in case of war. In place of a standing military he wished to substitute commercial sanctions. "Our commerce," he wrote, "is so valuable to [foreign nations] that they will be glad to purchase it, when the only price we ask is to do us justice." As Henry Adams explained, "The new President found in the Constitutional power 'to regulate commerce with foreign nations' the machinery for doing away with navies, armies and wars." Jefferson told his ambassador to France, Robert R. Livingston, "[we mean to employ] peaceable coercions." In a letter to Thomas Paine the president wrote, "Determined as we are to avoid, if possible, wasting the energies of our people in war and destruction, we shall avoid implicating ourselves with the powers of Europe . . . We believe we can enforce [our] principle . . . by peaceable means."

Jefferson hoped to bring "collisions of interest to the umpirage of reason rather than of force," but failing that, he would play one power off against another, employing first the threat of economic sanctions and then ultimately, and very reluctantly, sanctions themselves.

Jefferson's experience as governor of Virginia during the Revolution had left him with an abhorrence of war. He had failed then as a leader and never wanted the nation engaged in combat again. "No one so weakly armed with authority could have been expected to cope with the situation which the British invasion of Virginia [in 1780–1781] placed him in," his sympathetic biographer Dumas Malone wrote. "That traumatic experience left an ineffaceable mark on his memory."

The president viewed war as the ultimate scourge of mankind and the biggest threat to republican institutions, not to mention its threat to slavery. He did not want to destroy the great principles of the Revolution or Virginia's slave society by becoming embroiled in unnecessary warfare. He believed that by building a "respectable" navy of the kind his predecessors preferred, the people of the United States would be cutting their own throats.

Washington and Adams wanted to avoid war as much as Jefferson did, and they had gone to great lengths to negotiate differences with the European powers. In a letter to Lord Buchan in the midst of the crisis with Britain in 1794, Washington had decried the wastefulness of war. "If, instead of the provocation to war, bloodshed, and desolation (often times unjustly given) the strife of nations and of individuals was to excel each other in acts of philanthropy, industry, and economy, in encouraging useful arts and manufactures, promoting thereby the comfort and happiness of our fellow men; and in exchanging on liberal terms the products of one country and clime for those of another," he wrote, "how much happier would mankind be."

John Adams felt the same way. Nonetheless, both he and Washington believed that to achieve peace, diplomacy had to be backed by military force. Jefferson, on the other hand, thought diplomacy could succeed without it. By playing one great power off against another and by employing economic sanctions, he was confident that he could achieve his objectives.

Five days after his inauguration, Jefferson convened the cabinet to consider the ongoing problem of the Barbary pirate states. Contrary to everything he said about peaceful coercion, he was determined to use the navy to force the Barbary powers to respect the American flag, something he had been advocating since 1785.

Trouble had been brewing in the Mediterranean for months. On April 18, 1800, James Cathcart, the American consul in Tripoli, had reported that Pasha Yusuf Karamanli was displeased with the amount of tribute he was receiving, compared to that given Algeria and Tunis. Since Washington's day, $2 million in bribes had been paid to the four pirate states of North Africa. The ruler of Tripoli was annoyed because he was receiving only $83,000 a year, far less than the dey of Algiers. As the weeks went by without a satisfactory response, Yusuf grew angrier and threatened war. Cathcart continued to report on the deteriorating situation. His latest warning arrived in Washington on March 13, 1801.

There were also problems with Algeria. In October and November 1800, Dey Bobba Mustafa delivered a humiliating blow to American prestige. He forced William Bainbridge, captain of the 24-gun small frigate *George Washington* (the first American warship to enter the Mediterranean), to lower the American flag, replace it with an Algerine ensign, and transport tribute to Constantinople, the capital of the Ottoman Empire, Algeria's nominal ruler. Bainbridge's mission was to deliver tribute to Algiers, but he acquiesced in the dey's demands.

When the *George Washington* reached Constantinople, Bainbridge was pleasantly surprised to find the grand sultan of the Ottoman Empire friendly toward him and annoyed with the dey. Returning to Algiers, Bainbridge conveyed the sultan's irritation to the dey.

The Algerian ruler immediately changed his tune, swearing undying friendship for the United States. Bainbridge then sailed home, reaching Philadelphia on April 19, 1801. He did not know how he was going to be received, but he feared the worst; his orders had not included lowering the American flag and traveling to Constantinople. Much to his relief, the president showered him with praise for handling his complicated task wisely.

Bainbridge was given command of the frigate *Essex*. She had only recently returned from the East Indies, under Captain Preble, and was now outfitting to become part of a squadron Jefferson was sending to the Mediterranean. Preble could not sail the *Essex* because of illness.

On May 15, 1801, the cabinet voted unanimously to send four warships to the Mediterranean. After Captain Truxtun refused Jefferson's offer to lead the squadron, the president selected Revolutionary War hero Richard Dale, ordering him to be on the alert for a possible war with one or more of the Barbary powers. James Fenimore Cooper described the commodore as "a man of singular modesty, great simplicity of character, and prudence."

Jefferson ordered Dale to use retaliatory force if attacked but not to engage in offensive operations, since that would require Congress to declare war. If one of the Barbary States declared war, however, Dale was to blockade it and attack its warships. The president forbade any land operations. Jefferson also directed Dale to protect American commerce, but told him his primary mission was to impress Tripoli, Algeria, Tunis, and Morocco with the sea power of the United States.

Four warships, however, were not enough to make an impression on one Barbary state, much less all of them. The president wanted to accomplish his objectives on the cheap and failed to give Dale enough warships to accomplish any part of his mission. Jefferson's parsimony guaranteed that the commodore would fail, the expense of the expedition would be wasted, and the Barbary States emboldened.

The day before Jefferson decided to dispatch Dale, the pasha of Tripoli had already declared war by chopping down the flagpole in front of the American consulate. When the news reached

Washington, Dale was already at sea. His task force consisted of the 44-gun *President*; the 44-gun *Philadelphia*, under Captain Samuel Barron; the 32-gun *Essex*, under William Bainbridge; and the 12-gun armed schooner *Enterprise*, under Lieutenant Andrew Sterrett. Captain Truxtun had turned over command of the *President* to Dale at Hampton Roads, declaring her to be "the finest frigate ever floated on the waters of this globe."

The squadron set sail for the Mediterranean on May 29, 1801, arriving in Gibraltar Bay during the last week of June. Commodore Dale learned that Tripoli had declared war, and he found the pasha's two largest warships, the *Meshuda* (the converted Boston merchant brig *Betsey*) and another brig, moored in the harbor. Since Gibraltar was a British port, Dale could not attack them. Instead, he left the *Philadelphia* to patrol offshore in an effort to prevent the Tripolitan warships from leaving the harbor. He then sent the *Essex* to Tunis, and later, on convoy duty, while he sailed the *President* and the *Enterprise,* to Tripoli to begin a blockade. When he arrived, Dale offered to negotiate, but Yusuf, viewing the puny force before his city, turned him down.

By the end of July Dale needed water and dispatched Sterrett and the *Enterprise* to Malta to obtain it. Sterrett had been the third lieutenant aboard Truxtun's *Constellation* in 1799 when she defeated the French frigate *L'Insurgente*; he was famous in the navy for having inflicted the only American fatality during that fight when he ran his sword through seaman Neal Harvey for fleeing his post. On the way to Malta, Sterrett encountered the 14-gun Tripolitan warship *Tripoli*. A gun battle raged for over three hours; the *Enterprise* destroyed her opponent while suffering no casualties.

Jefferson was as thrilled by Sterrett's triumph as Adams had been with Truxtun's victory over *L'Insurgente*. Unfortunately, Sterrett had to release his prize, since his orders did not allow him to take any. He continued on to Malta but could not carry enough water to supply the *President*. Dale was forced to weigh anchor and sail to Malta himself. He did not return until the end of August, leaving the *Enterprise* in the impossible position of having to blockade Tripoli alone.

Unable to obtain all the supplies he needed at Malta, Dale returned to Tripoli. By this time 152 crew members were sick from lack of fresh provisions, and Dale was forced to sail back to the United States. On the way he stopped again at Malta, where a pilot ran the *President* aground. In need of repairs, Dale then put into Toulon, the major French naval base in the Mediterranean, and he was still there on January 10, 1802, when the 32-gun frigate *Boston*, under Captain Daniel McNeill, arrived with the new American ambassador to France, Robert R. Livingston. The *Boston* now became part of the Mediterranean fleet.

Dale finally stood out from Toulon on February 10 and arrived at Gibraltar, where he ordered the *Philadelphia* to sail to Tripoli and then to winter at Syracuse. He directed the *Essex* to winter close to Gibraltar. After an uneventful voyage, Dale reached Hampton Roads on April 13, 1802, where he promptly resigned from the navy and retired to Philadelphia, his mission a failure.

Dale was convinced that he would have succeeded had Jefferson given him enough warships. He estimated that to protect American commerce in the Mediterranean, four to six frigates with smaller supporting vessels, such as gunboats and bomb ketches, would have to be stationed there permanently. Since the United States had no bases in or near the Mediterranean, and warships needed frequent servicing, doing what Dale suggested would take a much larger navy than the one Jefferson was fashioning. The president, not surprisingly, was unwilling to spend the money for a larger fleet, and the problem of the Barbary States continued unresolved.

While Jefferson's experiment with "peaceful coercion" did not apply to the Barbary pirates, it did to Napoleon Bonaparte, who was moving ahead stealthily with his plans to reestablish a French empire in America. "My intention," he wrote to his minister of marine, "is to take possession of Louisiana with the shortest delay, and that this expedition be made in the utmost secrecy, under the appearance of being directed on St. Domingo." Napoleon also had his heart set on having West and East Florida, but the Spanish king, Carlos IV, although willing to part with Louisiana, refused to budge on the Floridas. Napoleon backed off temporarily but maintained his determination to create an expansive French empire in the Americas.

Before Bonaparte could embark on his American adventure, he first had to deal with the Second Coalition in Europe, which, when he seized power on November 9, 1799, was doing quite well. Composed of Great Britain, Austria, and Russia, the coalition had cut off Napoleon's army in Egypt when Nelson won his great battle of the Nile. Russian armies had then pushed into Switzerland and northern Italy. During the negotiations with the American envoys over ending the Quasi-War, Napoleon had set out to smash the Second Coalition. He accomplished his objective with remarkable speed, culminating in a victory over the Austrians at Marengo on June 14, 1800. The stubborn Austrians, however, remained at war with Napoleon until a French army under Moreau defeated them on December 3, 1800, at Hohenlinden, north of the Alps.

To create an American empire Napoleon needed British acquiescence. The Royal Navy had already prevented him from sending an expedition to Haiti, convincing him that he needed peace with Britain. Aiding him was the interest both Britain and the United States had in restoring slavery to Haiti. Britain's new prime minister, Henry Addington, was eager for respite from war. On October 1, 1801, he signed preliminary articles for the Treaty of Amiens, clearing the way for Napoleon to send a fleet to the Caribbean.

In the summer of 1801 rumors of what the First Consul was up to had begun to circulate in Washington. Jefferson and Madison lost no time making it clear to the French that their taking Louisiana was unacceptable. Secretary of State Madison told French chargé d'affaires Louis Pichon that the United States could tolerate neither French nor English control of Louisiana. America could endure Spain, but not the others. If France were to occupy Louisiana, Madison warned Pichon, it would mean a British-American alliance and war. At the end of September, Madison advised Robert Livingston, before he left for his diplomatic post in Paris, that Louisiana had likely been transferred to France. Madison emphasized that such a transfer was anathema to Jefferson.

At the same time that he worried about Napoleon, Jefferson continued to be concerned that Toussaint L'Ouverture would inspire a slave revolt in the United States. Since Gabriel's insurrection the previous summer, the possibility of a rebellion in America had been on Jefferson's mind and on the mind of the south. White French refugees from Haiti had been spreading horrific tales of massacres in Haiti. They said that blood had been flowing freely since the beginning of the slave uprising in 1791.

The president's policy was to encourage the return of French rule in Haiti but not to countenance Napoleon's using it as a base from which to occupy Louisiana. Jefferson told Pichon in July 1801 that if Bonaparte made peace with Britain, the United States would help him reestablish French rule and slavery in Haiti. Nevertheless, when asked by Pichon to cease trading with Toussaint, Jefferson refused, telling the French diplomat that if Napoleon wanted the trade stopped, he would have to gain control of the island. Trade with Toussaint was important to the United States; Jefferson did not want to offend the Haitian dictator in the event that Napoleon failed to regain control of Haiti.

On November 24, 1801, word reached Washington that England and France were at peace. Napoleon was now free to attack Haiti. On February 2, 1802, General Leclerc, Napoleon's brother-in-law (and a superb general) arrived off Cap François with a huge fleet and twenty thousand soldiers. A month later Jefferson was informed of the invasion and grew increasingly alarmed about Napoleon's intentions with respect to Louisiana.

Jefferson warned the French repeatedly that possession of Louisiana would mean an American alliance with Britain and war. He insisted that Napoleon could never win a contest against British naval power and American militias. The United States could produce a 200,000-man army from the western states alone, Jefferson predicted, and he called attention to America's own naval potential.

On April 18, 1802, Jefferson wrote to Ambassador Livingston, "Of all nations of any consideration France is the one which hitherto has offered the fewest points on which we could have any conflict of right, and the most points of a communion of interests. From these causes we have ever looked to her as our *natural* friend, as one with which we never could have an occasion of difference. Her growth we therefore viewed as our own, her misfortunes ours. There is on the globe one single spot the possessor of which is our natural and habitual enemy. It is New Orleans, through which the produce of three-eighths of our territory must pass to market, and from its fertility it will ere long yield more than half of our whole produce and contain more than half our inhabitants . . . The day that France takes possession of New Orleans fixes the sentence which is to restrain her forever within her low water mark. It seals the union of two nations who in conjunction can maintain exclusive possession of the ocean. From that moment we must marry ourselves to the British fleet and nation. We must turn all our attentions to a maritime force, for which our resources place us in very high grounds. . . . If France considers Louisiana however as indispensable for her views she might perhaps be willing to look about for arrangements which might reconcile it to our interests. If anything could do this it would be the ceding to us the island of New Orleans and the Floridas."

Jefferson was anxious to buy New Orleans and West Florida. Sooner or later, he believed, the mouth of the Mississippi and Mobile Bay would be in American hands. Possession of them was essential to keeping the country united, her commerce strong, and her basic policy of neutrality intact. He was convinced that as long as a European power controlled New Orleans, the United States would be drawn into every European conflict.

Even as Jefferson was threatening Napoleon with military force, he was busy dismantling the navy and counting on notoriously unreliable state militias for defense against an actual invasion. He could not eliminate the navy entirely, however, because of the continuing war with Tripoli. In fact, Commodore Dale's experience showed Congress that the president needed more flexibility to expand the navy's presence in the Mediterranean. On February 6, 1802, the Act for the Protection of the Commerce and Seamen of the United

States against Tripolitan Cruisers received congressional approval. The law removed the restrictions on the navy imposed by the Peace Establishment Act, passed in the last days of the Adams administration. Congress gave the president latitude to expand the navy as he saw fit. But Jefferson continued with his program of keeping the navy and the army small, making any increases in the Mediterranean squadron minimal. In his annual message to Congress on December 15, he declared that no changes in the army and navy were necessary. He apologized that a small squadron was still required to deal with the Barbary States. He then urged Congress to construct a huge dry dock on the Potomac's eastern branch so that he could use it to lay up and preserve seven frigates to reduce their expense. Congress turned down the proposal.

Ignoring Jefferson's threats, Napoleon continued with his plan to use Haiti as a base for occupying Louisiana. He brushed aside the warnings of Louis Pichon that America's population was growing rapidly, and that she, not France, would inevitably dominate the continent. A French Louisiana, Pichon argued, would depend on the United States "in time of peace [and be] at their mercy in the first war with England."

Napoleon had badly compromised General Leclerc's small chance of success in the summer of 1802 by reinstituting slavery in the French Caribbean islands. Realizing the reaction this news would evoke in Haiti, Leclerc had begged him not to. When the general heard that Napoleon had done it anyway, he tried to keep it quiet, but word filtered into Haiti from Guadeloupe and then spread throughout the country, making Leclerc's task impossible. Toussaint's soldiers fought with a zeal that overwhelmed the French.

By the end of 1802, General Leclerc had died, and his army had been nearly annihilated. In just a few months, deadly fevers and guerrilla attacks had reduced Leclerc's force to four thousand and threatened to wipe it out. As more French soldiers arrived, his replacement, General Donatien de Rochambeau, kept fighting, and the soldiers kept dying, until the number of dead reached thirty thousand and then forty thousand. Rochambeau continued to request more, but the French army and nation began to balk. The wretched corpses of France's finest lying in the jungle began endangering Napoleon's political position at home. He had already suffered defeat in Egypt, with only one-third of his troops returning. This second disaster at the hands of former slaves could endanger his aura of invincibility.

Napoleon didn't waste a moment lamenting the fate of his armies; he had shown in Egypt that he would abandon them in an instant if it suited his purpose. His thoughts were entirely on the next scheme to divert people's attention away from the fiasco in the West Indies.

On March 12, 1803, Napoleon told the British ambassador, Lord Whitworth, in a public setting, "I must have Malta or war!" It was now clear where the First Consul would turn next. Word spread rapidly throughout France and Europe that the two great enemies would resume their combat soon, and the Haitian debacle was soon forgotten.

Aggravating Jefferson's problems, on October 18, 1802, in direct violation of the Pinckney Treaty of 1795, the Spanish intendant in New Orleans, Juan Ventura Morales, had withdrawn the right of deposit from American traders on the Mississippi. This came as a complete surprise and caused a violent reaction in the west. The Federalists called for swift military action. Many suspected that the French were behind the move, which would make it easier for Napoleon to close the Mississippi after he occupied Louisiana. Demands came from all over the United States for the president to do something. In order to deflect this rush to war, Jefferson made vigorous protests to Madrid and Paris, and in March 1803 he appointed James Monroe as a special envoy to negotiate with both France and Spain. The president talked as if willing to take military action but intended to do everything possible to obtain his objectives peacefully.

Wishing to avoid a military confrontation with the United States, the Spanish king, Carlos IV, gave in to Jefferson's threats. On

March 1, 1803, he restored the right of deposit, sending a fast mail boat to Washington with the news. Spain saw no reason to fight over New Orleans when Napoleon was about to take it over.

Monroe landed in France on April 8 and reached Paris with his family five days later. By sending him, Jefferson was following the example of Washington and Adams, giving diplomacy a last chance. There was a significant difference, however, between him and his predecessors. His threats of war were empty, while theirs were real. He had no intention of fighting unless the United States was actually invaded, and he was opposed to having regular military forces ready beforehand. He intended to call up state militias only when the invaders were on American soil. Washington and Adams carried sticks—not large ones, perhaps, but sticks nonetheless; Jefferson carried amorphous military threats and economic sanctions.

Regardless of what Jefferson said or did, Napoleon had already made up his mind to abandon his American adventure and sell all of Louisiana to the Americans for as much money as he could get. On April 11, 1803, before Monroe reached Paris, Talleyrand asked Ambassador Livingston what he would pay for the whole of Louisiana. Livingston was dumbfounded. Caught completely off guard, he reiterated that the United States was interested in buying only New Orleans and Florida. On second thought, he realized that the offer was an enormous opportunity, and he tried to conclude an agreement as fast as possible, even before Monroe became involved. It proved impossible, though, to exclude Monroe from the negotiations.

In spite of their rivalry, the two diplomats now focused on acquiring a tract of land that would more than double the size of the United States. Negotiations moved rapidly, and the Americans signed the treaty of cession with Napoleon on April 30, 1803, agreeing to pay 60 million francs for Louisiana and assuming 20 million francs owed to Americans for claims against France. Secretary Madison, in perhaps the greatest understatement ever written by an American secretary of state, allowed that "with respect to the terms on which the acquisition is made, there can be no doubt that the bargain will be regarded as on the whole highly advantageous."

The Louisiana Purchase was enormously popular in the United States. A breathtaking achievement, it would rank with the Treaty of Paris as the greatest diplomatic triumph in American history. "The world will ere see such an extent of country under a free and moderate government as it has never seen," Jefferson declared. To a French friend he wrote, "Your government has wisely removed what certainly endangered collision between us. I now see nothing which need ever interrupt the friendship between France and this country."

Despite its popularity, the Federalists opposed the Louisiana Purchase on the grounds that it was unconstitutional. The president, they claimed, had no authority to expend public funds for the purchase of additional land. The real reason they objected was fear that a territorial expansion of such magnitude would dilute their already diminished political strength and secure the Republicans in power forever.

Jefferson had achieved through peaceful means a foreign policy triumph that in the late 1790s the Federalists had only dreamed of doing with a large army, war with France, and an alliance with Britain. Without a war Jefferson had deprived France of a goal she had sought since at least 1793.

The president attributed success to his strategy of threatening to enter an alliance with Britain and dramatically expand the navy and army, while waiting patiently for the British and French to be at each other's throats again. Actually, what moved Bonaparte was the annihilation of Leclerc's army. Haiti's former slaves, fighting to keep their freedom, and tropical diseases were responsible for Jefferson's triumph. Bonaparte could have easily avoided renewing his war with Britain; Addington was certainly willing. But regaining control of Haiti appeared to require the expenditure of resources that even Napoleon shrank from. So he turned his restless ambition away from the Americas and back toward Europe, inflicting another decade of unimaginable suffering there instead of in the New World. How ironic it was for Jefferson to suppose that threats to expand the American navy and ally it with Britain's—policies he had consistently opposed—were what moved the French dictator.

With all of Louisiana suddenly American territory, Jefferson persisted in trying to acquire West Florida peacefully from Spain. During the twenty years following the Seven Years War, from 1763 to 1783, when Britain possessed Florida, it had divided the territory at the Apalachicola River, designating the eastern portion as East Florida, with its capital at St. Augustine, and West Florida, with its capital at Pensacola. Jefferson judged West Florida, particularly Mobile Bay, to be second only to New Orleans in importance to the south. Mobile Bay was the only good naval harbor on the Gulf coast. In addition, the president wanted to wipe out the fugitive slave encampments and smugglers that infested Florida.

Jefferson hoped to buy West Florida from the Spanish. If that failed, he planned to wait patiently, confident that eventually all of Florida would fall into American hands. He thought that with the renewal of war between France and Britain, Napoleon would pressure Spain to sell the Floridas to the United States rather than have them fall into British hands. Spain, after all, was too weak to defend them, while the United States would never permit a British occupation.

Madrid was afraid the southern president would march into West Florida and annex it. Her fears were heightened by Jefferson's claim that West Florida was part of the Louisiana Territory, although France had never claimed it, and all historical documents supported that view. Spain was further outraged by the Mobile Act passed by Congress in February 1804, which held, in effect, that the Mobile River and Bay were now American territory. Jefferson declared that Madrid misunderstood the law; but his hopes to acquire the territory peacefully were dashed and he had no intention of invading; the result, for the moment, was a standoff.

While Jefferson was acquiring Louisiana, the war with Tripoli dragged on. Unimpressed by Commodore Dale's show of force the previous year, the Sultan of Morocco declared war on the United States on June 22, 1802; Tunis appeared to be threatening as well. Navy Secretary Smith agreed with Dale that America should vigorously prosecute the war against Tripoli and Morocco. But Secretary Gallatin wanted to give "an annuity to Tripoli. I consider it no greater disgrace, to pay them than Algiers," he wrote Jefferson. "And, indeed, we share the dishonor of paying those barbarians with so many nations as powerful and interested as ourselves, that in our present situation, I consider it a matter of mere calculation whether the purchase of peace is not cheaper than the expense of a war, which shall not even give us the free use of the Mediterranean trade. . . . Eight years hence we shall, I trust, be able to assume a different tone; but our exertions at present consume the seeds of our greatness and retard to an indefinite time the epoch of our strength."

Although the president agreed with Gallatin's long-term fiscal goals, he still thought the problems in the Mediterranean should be dealt with by the navy. Secretary Smith agreed, but he urged a substantial expansion of the naval force and a far more vigorous prosecution of the war than Jefferson had in mind. The president decided to augment the Mediterranean fleet slightly (although much less than Smith wanted). When Truxtun turned the job down, he gave Commodore Richard Morris command, with orders similar to Dale's.

On April 27, 1802, Morris left Hampton Roads in the 36-gun frigate *Chesapeake*. His squadron, when gathered in the Mediterranean, included the 28-gun *Boston*, the 28-gun *John Adams*, the 36-gun *Constellation*, the 28-gun *Adams*, the 36-gun *New York*, and the armed schooner *Enterprise*. Unfortunately the commodore, although politically well connected, was ill suited to command and had an independent streak that often set him at odds with Jefferson. He was also lazy about communicating with Secretary Smith, a trait that particularly annoyed the president, who had given Morris wide latitude but wanted to keep track of his movements. As it turned out, the commodore was actually doing very little. He had brought his wife and family with him on the *Chesapeake* and was disporting himself as if he were on a pleasant cruise.

On arriving in the Mediterranean, Morris confronted new problems with Morocco, Tunis, and Algiers. His convoy duties kept his ships away from Tripoli, and his supplies had to come from far-away Gibraltar, taking more ships off blockade duty. He may not have been the most energetic commander, but even if he had been, he wouldn't have had enough warships to accomplish his mission. Like Commodore Dale, Morris had orders to blockade only, not to put men ashore for an attack on the city. Dale had recommended such an attack as the surest way to bring Tripoli to terms, but Jefferson had rejected it as too expensive.

In any event, the president placed all the blame for failure on Morris. Frustrated by the commodore's inactivity, on June 21, 1803, Jefferson removed him from command. Secretary Smith wrote to Captain John Rogers, who temporarily replaced Morris, "We have been for some time much displeased with the conduct of Captain Morris. He has not done anything which he ought to have done, and despairing of his doing anything, and also as a mark of our disapprobation, it has been determined to suspend him." After a court-martial, Jefferson dismissed Morris from the service.

The president now offered Commodore Dale the assignment again, but Dale turned him down. Then Jefferson turned to John Barry, but the old revolutionary, who had always answered his country's call, was dying at his home in Philadelphia. Next the president offered the job to Captain Edward Preble of Portland, Maine. Secretary Smith had already given Preble command of the *Constitution* in May. The frigate was then in Boston, moored in the Charles River, where she had been since the end of the Quasi-War. Preble would spend weeks getting her ready for sea, including sheathing her with copper from Paul Revere's mill. On July 13, 1803, Jefferson appointed Preble to lead the Mediterranean squadron. The new commodore could not have been more pleased.

Preble's orders required him to blockade Tripoli "during the season in which it may be safely done." The entire North African coast was a lee shore during winter, making it dangerous and ineffective to attempt a blockade. Preble was told to "annoy the enemy" and "keep a vigilant eye over all the movements of the other Barbary powers . . . and . . . protect our commerce by all means in your power against them."

Preble assumed that he'd be given enough force to do the job. Secretary Robert Smith continued to argue for a larger Mediterranean squadron. "Nothing but a formidable force," he wrote to the president, "will effect an honorable peace with Tripoli and repress the dispositions of the other Barbary powers to hostility." But, as with Dale and Morris, Jefferson failed to provide the new commodore with an adequate fleet.

At eight o'clock on the evening of August 13, 1803, the *Constitution* sailed past Boston Light on Little Brewster Island and stood out into the Atlantic bound for Gibraltar. Tobias Lear, the new American consul general for Algiers, was aboard, expecting to handle peace negotiations with Tripoli.

On September 10, while approaching Cádiz, Spain's principal naval base, Preble encountered a strange ship that had drawn uncomfortably close. It was dusk, and a haze hung around both ships. Preble called out through a speaking trumpet for the stranger to identify herself. Instead of answering, a voice demanded to know who Preble was. The notoriously short-tempered commodore shouted back that if the other ship refused to give a proper response, he'd fire a shot into her.

"If you fire a shot, I will return a broadside," came the insolent reply. "This is His Britannic Majesty's ship *Donegal*, 84 guns. Send your boat on board."

Without hesitating, Preble leaped onto a nearby shroud and hollered, "This is the United States ship *Constitution*, 44 guns, Commodore Edward Preble, who will be damned before he sends his boat." He paused and then shouted to his crew, "Blow your matches, boys."

Before Preble could shout another order, a boat pulled alongside, and a contrite British lieutenant climbed aboard. He explained to Preble that his ship was really the 32-gun frigate HMS *Maidstone*, smaller than the *Constitution*. The *Maidstone*'s captain, George Elliot, had simply been buying time for his crew to scramble to their battle stations. Preble accepted his explanation and the incident passed harmlessly, but Preble's crew would never forget the commodore's swift, courageous action.

On September 12, 1803, the *Constitution* put into Gibraltar Bay, where she was joined by six warships: the 36-gun *Philadelphia*, the

36-gun *New York*, the 28-gun *John Adams*, the 12-gun *Vixen*, and the 12-gun *Nautilus*. The *New York* and the *John Adams* were under the command of John Rogers, who was scheduled to take them home. Preble, however, prevailed on Rogers to remain for a while, for as soon as Preble dropped anchor at Gibraltar, Captain William Bainbridge of the *Philadelphia* had come aboard the *Constitution* and explained that Morocco was creating more trouble.

After declaring war on the United States the previous year, the sultan had reversed himself and announced that he wanted peace, but he was still acting as an ally of Tripoli. And he was seizing American ships when he could get away with it. After hearing Bainbridge's report, Preble decided to confront the sultan before traveling to Tripoli. He sent Bainbridge and the *Philadelphia* ahead with the *Vixen* to begin the blockade of Tripoli and ordered the *Nautilus* to do convoy duty, while he and Rogers took the rest of the squadron to Morocco.

Preble's show of force had the desired effect on the sultan, who signed a peace agreement on October 4. Preble sailed next to Algiers, where he deposited Tobias Lear and his family, and finally set sail for Tripoli. But he did so without the *New York* and *John Adams*. Following his orders, Rogers took them back to the United States, leaving Preble with a tiny fleet that was about to get even smaller.

On November 24, while on the way to Tripoli, Preble met the British frigate *Amazon* off the coast of Sardinia. Her captain told him that the *Philadelphia* had been captured three weeks before, on October 21, and that her crewmen were now prisoners. Preble was aghast. Apparently, while chasing a hostile schooner off Tripoli, Bainbridge had run aground. Frustrated and angry, he had worked feverishly to float her, lightening his load by throwing overboard everything he could, including most of her guns. But nothing helped, and when nine Tripolitan gunboats came out to investigate and saw the frigate stuck fast on a hidden shoal, they grew bolder, drawing closer with their guns ready. Bainbridge could not maneuver his ship. The few remaining guns were useless, and he was forced to strike his colors. A storm produced an unusually high tide that allowed the Tripolitans to free the frigate and bring her into

Tripoli, where they repaired her. The pasha now had 307 prisoners and an American frigate, which was reported to be for sale as Yusuf had trouble manning her.

Preble wondered why Bainbridge had not been able to scuttle his ship before it was taken, and he was somewhat bitter about it, since without the *Philadelphia* he had little prospect of bringing Tripoli to terms. Sailing on to the ancient city of Syracuse on the southeastern coast of Sicily, where he was basing his fleet, Preble decided that his first order of business would be to either retake the frigate or destroy her. After reaching Syracuse and getting settled, he sailed the *Constitution* to Tripoli in company with Stephen Decatur Jr., in the *Enterprise*, to reconnoiter. Preble waited offshore out of sight, while Decatur took the *Enterprise* and sailed close enough to the city to see the *Philadelphia* anchored close to land under the protection of the 115 big guns of the pasha's shore batteries. Added to them were the frigate's own heavy weapons, which made the pasha's defense formidable. The only way to get at the *Philadelphia*, Decatur concluded, was through trickery. Returning to Syracuse, he and Preble concocted a scheme that required an unusual amount of luck to succeed. Preble appointed Decatur to lead the attack.

The expedition secretly departed Syracuse harbor on February 2, 1804. Decatur was in the ketch *Intrepid*, a captured Tripolitan trader that provided perfect camouflage. Lieutenant Charles Stewart and the brig *Syren* accompanied him. The *Intrepid's* crew was composed of volunteers from Decatur's *Enterprise*, disguised as Arab sailors. Aboard were Lieutenant James Lawrence and Midshipmen Thomas Macdonough and John Rowe, men Decatur knew he could count on.

When the two small vessels arrived off Tripoli, the *Syren* waited offshore while the *Intrepid* slipped into the harbor without attracting any notice, indistinguishable from the other Arab traders plying those waters. Decatur himself stood next to the helmsman; both were in disguise. As they drew closer to the *Philadelphia*, her guards at first appeared to ignore them, but when they drew too near, they heard shouts, warning them to stay away. Salvator Catalono, a Sicilian whom Decatur had engaged, called back in Arabic that they needed help. He convinced the guards that he had lost his anchor, and they allowed him to hitch *Intrepid* to the big frigate. As he did so, the Tripolitans realized their mistake and started screaming hysterically. Decatur then led sixty well-drilled men aboard and overcame the crew, using only swords and tomahawks, never firing a pistol or a musket. Decatur's men then set the frigate on fire. Seeing what was happening, Tripolitan gunboats and shore batteries opened fire as Decatur and his crew scrambled back to the *Intrepid* and made their getaway, cannonballs splashing around them as they went. The whole action took only twenty minutes. When they were safely on their way, they looked back and saw a great ball of flame engulfing the frigate.

Admiral Nelson, commander of the British Mediterranean fleet, described Decatur's exploit as "the most bold and daring act of the age." The twenty-five-year-old Decatur was hailed at home for his gallantry. At Preble's urging, the president promoted him to the rank of captain—the youngest in the navy's history.

Despite this dazzling feat, Tripoli remained defiant, and Preble planned to use what ships he had to get the pasha to relent. In the spring and early summer of 1804 Preble used his only small warships—*Argus, Enterprise, Vixen, Scrounge,* and *Syren*—to blockade Tripoli while he tended to business elsewhere. At the same time he requested more warships from Jefferson and was promised the frigate *John Adams.* He thought he would get her, and perhaps more, but none came, not even the *John Adams.* Preble did obtain six gunboats and two mortar vessels from the King of Naples in May, but no reinforcements arrived from home.

Nonetheless, Preble was determined to fight with what he had, and on August 3, 1804, his small squadron, including the *Constitution,* six gunboats, two bomb ketches, and the five smaller American warships, appeared off Tripoli and began an attack.

The pasha had a strong fleet of nineteen gunboats, an armed brig, two armed schooners, and two galleys, as well as the 115 guns of his shore batteries. He had his captured Americans working on an additional battery when Preble's assault commenced. Decatur led three of Preble's gunboats and Lieutenant Richard Somers three others. They met Yusuf's nineteen coming out from the inner harbor. Fog and smoke obscured the two fleets as they came together. In vicious hand-to-hand fighting, Decatur dispatched the first boat he met, and then heard that his brother, Lieutenant James Decatur, had been killed in a melee on one of the larger Tripolitan gunboats. Enraged, with blood and tears in his eyes, Decatur tore after that gunboat, and somehow found her, boarded, and wildly slashed everyone in his path.

Trying desperately to stave off defeat, the Turkish captain pounced on Decatur and wrestled him to the bloody deck, where Decatur fired his pistol into the giant Turk just before being stabbed in the chest. With their captain dead, the gunboat's crew surrendered. Decatur and his men had killed seventeen and wounded four. Midshipman Macdonough was with Decatur the entire time, distinguishing himself in the close, grueling fight. Along with Decatur three others were wounded, but none were killed.

The overall battle ended in a draw, and Preble withdrew his boats toward the end of the afternoon.

At around nine o'clock that night, the American frigate *John Adams*, under Master Commandant Isaac Chauncey, suddenly appeared on the scene. Chauncey was carrying dispatches from Washington. The loss of the *Philadelphia* had finally moved Jefferson to send an adequate force to the Mediterranean. Secretary Smith advised Preble that he was dispatching four more frigates as reinforcements: the *President*, under Samuel Barron; the *Congress*, under John Rogers; the *Essex*, under James Barron; and the *Constellation*, under Hugh G. Campbell. Commodore Samuel Barron, the senior captain, would replace Preble as fleet commander.

The news that he was being removed galled Preble, but he carried on. He offered to negotiate with the pasha, but Yusuf refused. Preble attacked again on August 7, but Yusuf still would not come to terms. Further attacks in late August and early September also failed to move the pasha.

Commodore Samuel Barron eventually arrived in the *President* on September 9, and Preble took his leave. Secretary Smith had expected Preble to stay and work under Barron, but Preble declined and returned to the United States in the *John Adams*, which Barron had graciously provided him for the journey.

Before word of the disastrous capture of the *Philadelphia* reached Washington in March 1804, Jefferson and Gallatin were still trying to save money and hoping for the best from the small fleet in the Mediterranean. The president was determined to pay the interest on the Louisiana Purchase out of current revenues, which meant a tighter squeeze on the navy. Gallatin proposed cutting its budget from $900,000 to $600,000 and urged that the "fleet" be cut. Although Jefferson did not go along with such a drastic reduction, he did tell Congress on October 17, 1803, that expenses for the war in the Mediterranean would "sensibly lessen" in 1804. But news of the *Philadelphia*'s capture stunned the country in the middle of an election year.

Scrambling to put the best face on his failed wartime leadership, Jefferson suddenly dispatched the Mediterranean force he should have sent in 1801. For years Secretary Smith had been advocating stronger measures to settle the Barbary problem, but the president would never spare the money. Jefferson had been trying to achieve victory on the cheap, ignoring what it cost in American lives and prestige. His inability to bring even Tripoli to terms had not been lost on either Napoleon or Great Britain. Now Jefferson asked Congress for more money, and it increased naval appropriations by $1 million, imposing an additional import duty to pay for it. The money from the added tax was placed in a "Mediterranean fund." Congress also authorized the construction of more gunboats and two additional warships of not more than sixteen guns.

News of Decatur's burning of the *Philadelphia* and his other heroic deeds, along with Preble's bold attacks on Tripoli, took people's minds off the earlier *Philadelphia* debacle. Wishing to blunt Federalist criticism of his inept handling of the Barbary problem, Jefferson made sure these officers and events were well publicized.

On February 25, 1805, Preble sailed the *John Adams* into New York harbor. Although he had done his best with the tools he had been given, he was convinced that his command had been a failure. He had not brought the pasha to terms, nor had he liberated Captain Bainbridge and his crew. Preble certainly wasn't expecting applause. His mood changed abruptly, however, when he discovered that the entire country considered him a hero. New York celebrated his arrival, and everywhere he went he was hailed for his actions off Tripoli. The widespread publicity Jefferson had given his heroes had its desired effect. Preble welcomed the attention, feeling, with some justification, that he deserved it. In Washington he received a warm reception from Jefferson, Secretary Madison, and the secretary of the navy. Congress presented Preble with a gold medal. There was even talk of Preble replacing Smith, who was interested in becoming attorney general. That idea was soon forgotten, however, and Smith remained at his post.

As Jefferson worked to ensure his reelection and deal with Tripoli, he was keeping a watchful eye on the English Channel, where Napoleon had been gathering a huge army around Boulogne. Since announcing on May 23, 1803—less than a month after selling Louisiana—his decision to conquer Britain, Napoleon's Grand Army had expanded to 100,000 men, along with 700 barges. Jefferson told Congress, "We have seen with sincere concern the flames of war lighted up again in Europe, and nations with which we have the most friendly and useful relations engaged in mutual destruction."

With Britain under supreme threat, Parliament brought back William Pitt, who resumed leadership of the ministry on May 10, 1804, over three years after he had resigned as prime minister on February 4, 1801. Eight days after Pitt's return, Napoleon, having eliminated his rivals, including the celebrated General Moreau, declared himself emperor of the French.

Pitt did not have a large conscripted army—no *levée en masse* existed in Britain as it did in France. But the British people had closed ranks and were committed to defending their homeland. Pitt was already organizing the countryside. Judging that the most likely landing place for the French would be Romney Marsh, he took special pains to prepare it, aided by the strong volunteer movement in East Kent. Local boatmen at Deal and Walmer, showing the patriotism that was motivating the entire country, pledged to man fifty gunboats against the invaders.

Of course, England's principal defense was the Royal Navy. Napoleon would need to draw enough of the Channel Fleet away in order to create a three- or four-day opening for his troops to make the initial twenty-two-mile crossing. But even if he did manage to land a substantial army on British soil, he still would have to keep them supplied across the Channel. The sea was an element that Napoleon never understood. Although he was a brilliant general, he had no feel for naval tactics, nor did he have much of a navy.

As the showdown between the two powers drew closer, Jefferson appeared indifferent to the outcome. His hatred for Britain was well-known, although he had been at pains to deny it since becoming president, and Napoleon's seizure of power had devastated him. France had evolved not into the constitutional monarchy that he and Lafayette had hoped for in 1789, but into an aggressive imperial dictatorship with unlimited ambition. A Napoleonic victory over Britain, however improbable, would have been catastrophic for America, as the emperor almost certainly would have attempted to extend his empire to the New World.

Jefferson, however, considered Britain just as dangerous as France, "a tyrant," he wrote, "as unprincipled and as overwhelming, for the ocean, [as Napoleon was on land]." In Jefferson's view, Britain was worse than France. "Bonaparte," he explained, "will die, and his tyrannies with him. But a nation never dies. The English government and its piratical principles and practices, have no fixed term of duration."

The resumption of war in Europe and continuing war in the Mediterranean did not affect Jefferson's reelection in 1804. The Louisiana Purchase, the ending of internal taxation, and the dramatic reduction in the federal debt made the president overwhelmingly popular. The "visionary schemes" Abigail Adams had worried about appeared to be working. Jefferson had been victorious over a European power led by a ruthless dictator, using only diplomacy and empty threats. He also had little political opposition. The Federalist

Party continued to stand for rule by an aristocracy of wealth and talent in a country that was becoming increasingly democratic. Out of 176 electoral votes Jefferson received an astounding 162. In 1800 he had garnered 73 out of 138. In the congressional races Republicans crushed the Federalists, electing 27 of 34 senators and 116 of 141 congressmen.

As he delivered his second inaugural address, Jefferson had no inkling of just how different his second term would be from his first. He never mentioned Napoleon being at Britain's throat, or any other foreign policy matter. He did dwell on how proud he was of his fiscal stringency and the elimination of internal taxes. "What farmer, what mechanic, what laborer," he asked, "ever sees a tax-gatherer of the United States?"

12

PEACEFUL COERCION

March 1805–March 1809

While Bonaparte gathered his army along the English Channel, Pitt was busy organizing the Third Coalition with Austria and Russia to bring pressure on Napoleon from the east. The coalition was in place early in the summer of 1805, with Russian and Austrian armies on the march west. On August 27 Napoleon, feeling threatened, abandoned his plans to invade England, broke camp at Boulogne, and sent his army east to meet the Russians and Austrians on the upper Danube.

Almost immediately, Napoleon won a series of stunning victories with the Grand Army, securing his position in France and in Europe, making people forget about the bungled invasion of England and the disasters in Egypt and Haiti. On October 15, at Ulm in Bavaria, Napoleon's troops surrounded fifty thousand Austrians under General Mack and forced them to surrender without a fight. He then wheeled east to meet a combined Russian-Austrian army in Moravia; at Austerlitz on December 2, 1805, he defeated them decisively. The Russians retreated to Poland, and Austria signed a degrading peace at Pressburg.

In a matter of weeks, Napoleon had shown again that he was master of the Continent. But while he was doing so, England had reconfirmed that she was master of the sea at the battle of Trafalgar on October 21, 1805. A combined Franco-Spanish fleet under French Admiral Villeneuve had sortied from Cádiz harbor that day, heading not toward the English Channel but to the Mediterranean. Napoleon had already postponed his invasion of Britain.

Despite having superior numbers of battleships, Admiral Villeneuve was pessimistic about his chances against Admiral Horatio Nelson. Napoleon, who personally directed the movements of the fleet, had no feel for naval warfare; he had lost confidence in Villeneuve and the admiral knew it. In addition, the Spanish despised Napoleon and hated being part of a force loyal to him. Working with the Spanish in a fleet action, then, was not something that appealed to Villeneuve.

Waiting offshore for Villeneuve was an excellent British fleet under a gifted leader. Nelson's ships, Villeneuve knew, would be working as a unit, unlike his own, and thanks to the superiority of their crews and officers, they would have every advantage. Nelson knew this as well and waited impatiently for Villeneuve to leave the safety of Cádiz harbor.

Following Napoleon's orders, the dispirited Villenueve sortied and fell in with Nelson's fleet. The ensuing battle off Cape Trafalgar was even more of a disaster than Villeneuve had anticipated. Nelson decimated the Franco-Spanish force, capturing or destroying twenty-two enemy sail of the line while losing none of his own. Some individual French and Spanish ships fought well but were overwhelmed by the superiority of the English men-of-war. Nelson was mortally wounded, while Villeneuve was captured and taken to England.

Napoleon, however, had not given up his dream of defeating England's fleet. He had a plan to combine all the navies of the conquered European countries and turn them against her. The superiority in numbers that would be achieved, he thought, would give him the victory he had craved for so long.

The Prussians, belatedly realizing the danger from Napoleon's designs on Germany, declared war on France, but they fought alone and were crushed in October 1806 at Jena and Auerstadt. Napoleon then attacked the Russians in East Prussia and, after an indecisive battle at Eylau, defeated them at Friedland on June 14, 1807. Czar Alexander I made peace with Napoleon at Tilsit on June 25, 1807, neutralizing Russia.

Napoleon's dominance over Europe was now greater than ever. Among the great powers, only Britain stood outside his sphere of influence. He directed his attention back to her, still dreaming of strutting in London. "After Russia had joined my alliance," he wrote, "Prussia, as a matter of course, followed her example; Portugal, Sweden, and the Pope alone remained to be gained over, for we were well aware that Denmark would hasten to throw herself into our arms. If England refused the proffered mediation of Russia, the whole maritime forces of the continent were to be employed against her, and they could muster 180 sail of the line. In a few years this force could be raised to 250. With the aid of such a fleet, and my immense flotilla, it was by no means impossible to lead a European army to London. One hundred ships of the line employed against her colonies in the two hemispheres would have suffered to draw off a large portion of the British Navy; while eighty more assembled in the Channel, would have sufficed to assure the passage of the flotilla and avenge the outraged rights of nations. Such at bottom was my plan."

From his spies, British Foreign Secretary George Canning learned immediately of the Russian-French rapprochement at Tilsit and of Napoleon's plans for a new fleet. Canning urged the cabinet to counter the emperor's strategy. A squadron under Admiral Gambier and a military force under Sir Arthur Wellesley attacked Copenhagen, and on September 8, 1807, the crown prince surrendered. The British then brought the whole Danish fleet to England for the duration of the war. And before the year was over the prince regent of Portugal reluctantly turned over his fleet to the British, destroying Napoleon's invasion plans.

At the same time that Bonaparte was attempting to organize a colossal fleet, he was also waging economic warfare against the

British on a grand scale by shutting her out of European markets. His Continental system, he thought, would not only bring Britain to her knees but at the same time bind the European economy to France, making her the dominant economic power in the world. France, in effect, would take Britain's place in Europe.

With France and England at each other's throats, Jefferson still had the war with Tripoli to conclude. His appointment of Samuel Barron to succeed Preble was an inauspicious beginning, since Barron had far less ability than Preble. When the new commodore arrived off Tripoli on September 9, 1804, William Eaton, the former American consul in Tunis, accompanied him with a scheme to use the pasha's unreliable brother, Hamet Karamanli, to unseat him.

Not convinced that Eaton's plan would work, Barron gave him minimal support. The commodore hoped to use his warships to bring the pasha to terms without Eaton's help. Barron had under him the largest squadron yet assembled in the Mediterranean: the frigates *Constitution*, *President*, *Constellation*, *Congress*, and *Essex*; the brigs *Argus* and *Syren*; the sloop *Hornet*; the schooners *Enterprise*, *Vixen*, and *Nautilus*; the bomb vessels *Vengeance* and *Spitfire*; and ten gunboats—nearly the entire American navy. Barron would have to act fast, though, before winter arrived, when he would be forced to lift the blockade of Tripoli and wait until spring. In the end, despite having a strong fleet, Barron could manage neither a negotiation with the pasha nor an attack on him, and as bad weather approached, the commodore, suffering from liver disease, retired to Malta for the winter.

The attack on Tripoli resumed in April 1805. On the 28th, three warships from Barron's fleet—the *Argus* under Isaac Hull, the *Nautilus*, and the *Hornet*—arrived off Derna, a Tripolitan coastal fortress, five hundred miles from Alexandria, Egypt. They met a land force led by William Eaton, Hamet Karamanli, and Marine Lieutenant Neville Presley O'Bannon. Hull's warships, working in concert with Eaton and O'Bannon, routed the defenders in less than two hours. But Eaton could not advance any farther west. Going from Derna to Tripoli would require substantial reinforcements, and they were nowhere to be found.

The ailing Commodore Barron turned over command of the Mediterranean fleet on May 22 to Commodore John Rogers, who was in the *Constitution* off Tripoli. Itching for a chance to teach the Tripolitans a lesson, Rogers immediately put the American fleet to work, threatening an all-out attack.

The pasha sensed that this was no bluff. During the first week of June, Rogers's display allowed Tobias Lear to finally negotiate a settlement with Tripoli. Eaton's operations, which Lear had always opposed, played no part in the deliberations. Lear paid $60,000 in ransom for Bainbridge and his crew and $5,000 for the establishment of an American consulate in Tripoli, but no other money. The American prisoners were released and peace restored without Rogers having to fire a single cannon. Lear reported to Secretary of State Madison, "On June 6th at eleven o'clock in the morning the flagstaff was raised on the American House, and the flag of the United States displayed, which was immediately saluted with twenty-one guns from the castle and forts, and was returned by the *Constitution*." This could have been accomplished in 1801 had Jefferson applied enough force.

Rogers dispatched the frigate *Constellation* to Derna to pick up the few Americans who remained there and then moved his fleet to Tunis, arriving on July 31. Lear accompanied him and easily persuaded the bey of Tunis, Hamuda Bashaw Bey, to seek peace with the United States. An agreement was signed on August 12, 1805. Lear wrote to Madison, "The judicious and decided measures taken by Commodore Rogers made so powerful an impression on the mind of the Bashaw, that the negotiation afterwards became easy and unembarrassed."

After nearly five years, the war with Tripoli finally ended, as well as the troubles with Tunis, Algiers, and Morocco. The peace represented something of a triumph for Jefferson and the American navy. Under a Republican administration that theoretically opposed a deep water fleet, the navy had achieved success and made heroes of Preble, Decatur, Rogers, and Hull. Their exploits were celebrated throughout the country, and their growing esteem created a base in public opinion for the president to expand the navy if he wished.

But Jefferson had not changed his mind about the dangers and wastefulness of a blue water fleet. He ordered Rogers and most of the fleet home, leaving only the *Constitution, Enterprise,* and *Hornet* in the Mediterranean during 1806 to protect American interests. During the following year, they too would be brought back to the United States.

The continuing depredations of both France and Great Britain against America's neutral commerce, coupled with the increasing problem of British impressments, forced Jefferson to reexamine his defense policies. Dumas Malone noted that "at this juncture and during the months that followed (1805–1806), Jefferson . . . showed more concern for a well-balanced navy than at any other time in his presidency." Jefferson even contemplated building battleships, pointing out to Congress in his fifth annual message that materials for constructing 74s had already been gathered. On May 13, 1806, he wrote to his friend Jacob Crowninshield, a merchant prince of Salem, Massachusetts, "The building of some ships of the line instead of our most indifferent frigates is not to be lost sight of. That we should have a squadron properly composed to prevent the blockading of our ports is indispensable. The Atlantic frontier from numbers, wealth, and exposure to potent enemies have a proportionate right to be defended with the Western frontier, for whom we keep up 3,000 men." Jefferson, however, was just musing; he wasn't really serious.

Navy Secretary Smith recommended building more gunboats, putting all thirteen of the country's frigates in commission, and constructing twelve 74s. Gallatin opposed him. The Treasury secretary wanted no military buildup, and the president supported him. Jefferson was gratified that American trade was booming, but he was not going to acquire a blue water fleet to support it. He felt, as he had since the Revolution, that a seagoing force would be swept from the ocean in the opening stage of any war with Britain; thus building one would be a colossal waste of money. Britain's triumph at Trafalgar reinforced his thinking. He stuck to his old policies, eschewing sail of the line as well as frigates.

By the fall of 1806 most of Commodore Rogers's squadron was laid up in ordinary in Washington. The active fleet now consisted of one frigate and two smaller vessels in the Mediterranean and two bomb ketches at New Orleans. On April 21, 1806, the Republican Congress passed legislation drastically reducing the navy's manpower. The law stipulated that the service would be limited to 13 captains, 9 master commandants, 72 lieutenants, 150 midshipmen, and 925 seamen. Full pay was restricted to those actually in service.

The only thing Jefferson and the Republican Congress were willing to spend money on was gunboats. From 1803 to 1805, Congress had authorized 40; in 1806, 50; and in 1807, 188. By 1807 a total of sixty-nine had been built. Gunboats varied in size from forty-five to seventy-five feet. The smaller ones carried one cannon; the larger carried two. They were inexpensive to build and easily maintained and, most importantly, they were defensive in nature. Not one naval officer, however, supported a gunboat fleet. Only Preble had any tolerance for them, provided they were part of a well-balanced force.

Jefferson was well acquainted with the criticism. "I am not unaware," he wrote to Madison, "of the effect of the ridicule cast on this instrument of defense by those who wish for engines of offense. . . . I know, too, the prejudices of the gentlemen of the Navy, and that these are very natural. . . . But . . . it is impossible not to see, that all these vessels [i.e., seagoing warships] must be taken and added to the already overwhelming force of our enemy; that even while we keep them, they contribute nothing to our defense, and that so far as we are to be defended by anything on the water, it must be by such vessels as can sail under advantageous circumstances, and under adverse ones withdraw from the reach of the enemy. This, in shoally waters, is the humble, the ridiculed, but the formidable gun-boats."

Jefferson's approach to defense was increasingly tested when the Royal Navy resumed impressment of American seamen after the peace of Amiens collapsed. Britain had relaxed its impressment during the peace but resumed immediately after the war started up again. The Admiralty had seven hundred warships of all kinds at sea and another three hundred in shipyards under repair or being built.

With the renewal of the European war U.S. maritime trade expanded, creating a need for thousands of additional seamen. This put American merchantmen in direct competition with the Royal Navy for manpower. The British were always at a disadvantage because their inhumane treatment of seamen caused them to desert not only warships but merchantmen as well. The Royal Navy regularly impressed men from the British merchant fleet. Often, when an East Indiaman returned to an English port from a long voyage, its men, who desperately craved shore leave, were impressed before they set foot on land. They would then be brought aboard a warship to serve for an indefinite period with no possibility of leave.

Wages were higher on American ships and working conditions far better, so it was not surprising that thousands of British tars suffering under the lash fled to American merchantmen. The British accused the United States of draining off their finest sailors, posing a threat to their "nursery of seamen." The Royal Navy claimed the right to search American vessels on the high seas for deserters. Thousands of seamen on ships flying the flag of the United States were illegally impressed, some being killed in the process.

The humiliation felt in the United States was intense; emotions ran high. But they did so in England as well. Impressment became the most important issue dividing the two countries, one they could never resolve. Grievances accumulating over decades made the problem far larger than the numbers suggested. For America the dispute was over the insulting practice of searching; for the British it was about the loss of scarce seamen to a country that was profiting from a war that endangered their country, and indeed the world.

If the British could have set aside their anger at American money-grubbers, they might have realized that they could stop the searches and impressment with little injury to themselves. According to Britain's own figures, of the roughly 145,000 seamen manning British warships, only about 3,500 were impressed from American merchantmen. The U.S. figure was much higher—around 6,000; some observers had it as high as 15,000. Even so, the Royal Navy's need might have been far less than imagined.

Interference with neutral trade was another explosive issue between the two countries. Englishman James Stephen spoke for many of his countrymen when he wrote in his popular, semiofficial pamphlet, *War in Disguise; or the Frauds of Neutral Flags*, published in October 1805, that American merchants were aiding Napoleon under the guise of neutral rights.

It was generally recognized that Britain had the right to prevent contraband from reaching France and stop all goods if she were actually blockading a French port. Beyond that, Jefferson was unwilling to go. Britain, on the other hand, felt free to seize all enemy goods. She particularly wanted to stop the American practice of transporting cargo from French, Spanish, or Dutch colonies in the West Indies to Europe. An order in council of January 25, 1798, had prohibited American traders from sailing directly between an enemy West Indian port and Europe. Under the Jay Treaty such voyages had been allowed. But the order did permit American shippers to bring enemy goods to the United States, pay a duty, and then transport them to Europe. American merchants took full advantage of this "broken voyage" rule, and the business had grown important. American merchants also wanted to engage in Europe's intracoastal trade without British interference.

As the war in Europe dragged on and grew more intense, the issues of impressment and trade became more contentious and threatened to ignite a war. Then on July 23, 1805, the English Admiralty judge Sir William Scott in the *Essex* case decided to deny the broken voyage doctrine and uphold the Rule of 1756. The decision, in effect, prohibited all trade between enemy colonies in the West Indies and Europe. The Royal Navy vigorously enforced Judge Scott's ruling, creating a crisis.

It was hard not to conclude that Prime Minister Pitt was so vigorous in his enforcement precisely because Jefferson was so pusillanimous. The president's policy of peaceful coercion invited contempt. England's ambassador in Washington, Anthony Merry, disliked Jefferson and kept reminding London of America's weakness. "Both the American government and the American people," he reported, "so far from meaning to use force, were trembling lest Great Britain should declare war. . . . Should His Majesty's government . . . [send] a reinforcement to the British squadron on the American station sufficiently great to be noticed, [it would put a stop] to all the hostile proceedings of this government."

In spite of British provocation, Jefferson clung to his pacific system. On February 18, 1806, he wrote that Europe must be shown that the American government was not "entirely in Quaker principles." But he never found the means to do so.

Pitt died unexpectedly from exhaustion on January 23, 1806, and a new government, the All Talents Ministry, brought some hope that British-American relations might improve. The new prime minister, Lord Grenville, had negotiated the Jay Treaty, and the foreign minister, Charles James Fox, was an old friend of the United States. Jefferson saw a ray of hope.

In the summer he sent William Pinkney to assist Ambassador Monroe with negotiations. Monroe had replaced Rufus King as the American ambassador in London and had been presented to George III on August 17, 1803. After negotiating the Louisiana Purchase, Monroe had remained in Europe with his family. The two main issues he and Pinkney would wrestle with were impressment and reinstituting the broken voyage rule. Fox and Grenville were open to finding a satisfactory solution to both problems and reestablishing the friendly relations that had prevailed between the two countries immediately after the Jay Treaty and during the early phase of the Quasi-War with France.

Prior to opening talks, however, two events caused problems for the negotiators. On April 18, 1806, Congress passed the Non-Importation Act, forbidding importation of certain British products but not all. It was an ineffectual law that only irritated the new ministry and was suspended until November 1806 to give Monroe and Pinkney time to negotiate.

The second problem was far more serious. On April 25, 1806, the British frigate *Leander*, under Captain Whitby, provoked an international incident. Accustomed to sitting off Sandy Hook, stopping whatever merchantmen he pleased and impressing their sailors, Whitby was often stationed off New York with his sister warships, *Cambrian* and *Driver*. While these men-of-war waited menacingly offshore, they would send boats into New York for supplies, which were always forthcoming. President Jefferson never attempted to use the navy to drive these British pests away, for fear it could lead to a crisis.

On April 25 Captain Whitby was occupying his usual position off Sandy Hook when he spotted a merchantman and decided to search her for "deserters." He normally stopped a ship by firing a shot across her bow, which he did on this occasion. But his ball went beyond its mark, ricocheted off the water, and carried across the stern of a passing American sloop, the *Richard*, within a quarter mile of the beach. A seaman named John Pierce was at the sloop's helm, and the cannonball whizzed by so close to his head that it killed him instantly.

The *Richard*'s irate captain brought the young man's body into the city. A great cry of anguish arose from the citizenry, moving Jefferson on May 3 to order the ports and harbors of the United States closed forever to the *Leander* and her companion ships. The president also ordered Captain Whitby arrested and held for murder. But Jefferson did not send the navy to prevent further outrages. Instead, he hoped that Monroe and Pinkney would negotiate a treaty that solved the problem.

After Pinkney's arrival in June, serious talks began in London and went on through the summer. But Fox died in September and time was lost while new negotiators—Lord Auchland (the former William Eden) and Lord Holland, Fox's nephew—were brought in. When negotiations resumed, they went well on every issue (including the difficult problem of the broken voyage rule) except for impressment. At the urging of the Admiralty, the cabinet refused to make impressment part of a formal treaty. Informally, however, the British agreed to limit the practice to legitimate deserters from the

Royal Navy and stop impressing bona fide American citizens. Monroe and Pinkney were willing to accept this compromise.

Before the agreement could be signed, Napoleon unexpectedly issued his Berlin Decree on November 21, 1806. It declared a blockade of the British Isles and prohibited all British products from entering any port in Europe. Napoleon intended the decree to bring the "nation of shopkeepers" to its knees. But it was not enforced for a year, and so there was no immediate British response.

Monroe and Pinkney signed their agreement on December 31, 1806. But when it reached the United States, Jefferson rejected it out of hand, refusing to submit it to the Senate because it said nothing about impressment. He was not willing to rely on an informal understanding. Since the British cabinet refused to make impressment part of the treaty, the president assumed they would, sooner rather than later, resume their old practices.

Jefferson disliked the idea of giving up the weapon of nonimportation in return for an empty promise on impressment. He did not want to incur the wrath of France, as had happened after the Jay Treaty, for an agreement that gave the United States so little. Napoleon, the president thought, was still the key to obtaining Florida, which remained an important objective for Jefferson and the south.

With the failure of the rapprochement between England and America, impressment became an even bigger problem in 1807. A single incident nearly caused a war.

The British frigate *Melampus* was part of a British squadron blockading two French men-of-war in Chesapeake Bay. In February, five British seamen from the *Melampus* stole their captain's gig while a party was in progress and rowed to Norfolk, Virginia, where they enlisted in the U.S. Navy.

The frigate *Chesapeake*, which was outfitting and needed hands, took three of the deserters aboard. Britain's consul in Norfolk made a formal protest and asked for their return by name. When he was unsuccessful, the British minister in Washington inquired into the matter, and Secretary Smith asked Commodore James Barron to check on the status of the seamen in question. Barron declared that the three sailors were Americans whom the British had impressed, and he refused to release them. Furious about this decision, Admiral Sir George Canfield Berkeley, commander of the British North America station, issued a directive to his fleet commanders to recover the sailors from the *Chesapeake*.

Commodore Barron had orders to proceed to the Mediterranean in the *Chesapeake*, and he departed Norfolk on June 22, 1807. Barron wasn't expecting to find any trouble until he arrived at his station on the other side of the Atlantic. None of the *Chesapeake's* guns had their firing mechanisms fitted, and not all were on their carriages. Her decks were cluttered with the refuse from fitting out and the baggage of civilian passengers, as well as sick sailors in hammocks. About nine miles east-southeast of Cape Henry, Barron encountered the 50-gun British warship *Leopard*, under Captain Salisbury Pryce Humphreys. The *Leopard* had departed the bay earlier and was waiting for Barron. Presently, Humphreys drew close to the *Chesapeake*, hailed her, and signaled that he had a message for Commodore Barron. Barron replied through a speaking trumpet that he'd be happy to receive it.

As the ships drifted closer together, British Lieutenant John Meade arrived aboard the *Chesapeake* with a note from Captain Humphreys and a copy of Admiral Berkeley's order to search the frigate for deserters. Barron was taken aback. He wrote a reply to Humphreys denying there were deserters aboard his ship and insisting he would not agree to an inspection.

Lieutenant Meade returned to the *Leopard* and delivered Barron's message. Captain Humphreys now watched as the *Chesapeake's* crew began silently clearing for action. Deciding to confront Barron before he was ready to fight, he sent a single shot across the *Chesapeake's* bow. When no satisfactory response came, Humphreys unleashed a full broadside without warning. Confusion reigned on the *Chesapeake* as cannonballs crashed into her from point-blank range. Barron was astonished; he had not expected a surprise attack, and his ship was still far from ready. While his men continued to scramble to their battle stations, two more broadsides poured into the frigate in fifteen minutes, killing three and wounding eighteen. Feeling overwhelmed and having managed to get off just one shot, the discombobulated Barron struck his colors. Humphreys then sent Lieutenant Meade back with a boarding party to muster the *Chesapeake*'s crew and seize the men Admiral Berkeley wanted. When the *Chesapeake*'s men were mustered, Meade picked out four and returned with them to the *Leopard*. Three later turned out to be American citizens, but a fourth, Jenkin Ratford, was a British citizen, recently deserted from the 16-gun sloop-of-war *Halifax*—part of the British squadron lying within the Chesapeake capes. Having retrieved the four men, Humphreys refused to take the surrendered American frigate as a prize; he found the whole business distasteful and was only following orders. He sailed the *Leopard* back to Lynnhaven Bay within the Chesapeake capes, rejoining his squadron. Barron returned to port the next day. He was court-martialed the following year and found guilty—condemned, essentially, for not putting up a fight.

The incident caused an uproar in the United States. Madison wrote to Jefferson, "Having effected her lawless and bloody purpose, [the *Leopard*] returned immediately to anchor with her squadron within our jurisdiction. Hospitality under such circumstances ceases to be a duty; it becomes a degradation." Federalists as well as Republicans condemned the British action. Federalist John Rutledge of South Carolina wrote that "a war (even with Great Britain) would prove more honorable . . . than a state of peace in which a foreign nation is to exercise the right of searching our national ships. . . . we must kick against this and fight against it."

"This country has never been in such a state of excitement since Lexington and Concord," Jefferson declared, "a cord vibrates in every heart." The president could have used the tidal wave of public anger to obtain a declaration of war. At a minimum he would have found strong support for a military buildup, as had Washington in 1794 and Adams in 1798. But Jefferson, while musing about going to war—as he had in the past—refused to lead the country in that direction. Instead, he instructed Ambassador Monroe in London to demand from the British "a formal disavowal of the deed, and restoration of the four seamen to the ship from which they were taken." In addition, he directed Monroe to demand "the entire abolition of impressment." At the same time, Jefferson issued an edict excluding British warships from American waters and ordering those already present to leave.

Unknown to the public, the president was not terribly serious about his exclusion order. In September 1807, the British frigate *Jason* and the armed brig *Columbine* visited New York's waterfront. Commodore John Rogers, commanding the American squadron there, expected to be ordered to chase them out, but he was told by Gallatin that the president had no intention of using force to exclude the British from our coastal waters. Rogers was cautioned to keep away lest his movements "might have the appearance of menace."

Britain's notoriously anti-American foreign secretary, George Canning, responded to Jefferson's demands by disavowing the *Leopard*'s actions, recalling Admiral Berkeley, and indicating a willingness to pay reparations to the families of the victims. But that was all; he was not about to renounce impressment. London's *Morning Post* (Canning's mouthpiece) said, "America is not contented with striking at the vitals of our commercial existence; she must also, by humbling our naval greatness and disputing our supremacy, not only lessen us in our own estimation, but degrade us in the eyes of Europe and of the world. . . . It will never be permitted to be said that the 'Royal Sovereign' has struck her flag to a Yankee cockboat."

Canning was part of the Tory government that had come to power in March 1807, replacing the All Talents Ministry that had negotiated with Monroe and Pinkney the previous year. Canning considered the *Chesapeake-Leopard* affair of little importance; he was not moved by Jefferson's demands or hints of war. He was far more concerned with Napoleon.

A short time later, Canning and the Tory ministry, led by the Duke of Portland and Spencer Perceval, demonstrated again what little regard they had for Jefferson by issuing the notorious order in council of November 11, 1807, made in response to Napoleon's Berlin Decree of the previous year. London had waited twelve months because France did not begin enforcing the Berlin Decree until the fall of 1807. Under Britain's order, all neutral shipping was forbidden to sail directly to Europe. American merchantmen were required first to pass through a British port and obtain a license, and, if appropriate, pay a duty, before proceeding to a seaport controlled by Napoleon. The cabinet was trying to monopolize world trade to Europe, creating a situation whereby Napoleon could not obtain overseas goods more cheaply than from Britain. "Our orders," explained Perceval, the Chancellor of the Exchequer, ". . . say to the enemy, 'If you will not have *our* trade, as far as we can help it you shall have none.'" Thus all American trade with Europe had to stop en route at a British port.

On December 17, 1807, Napoleon retaliated by issuing the Milan Decree. It declared that any American vessel that had been visited by a British cruiser or sent into a British port, or had paid any tax to the British, was subject to seizure as British property. If an American merchantman stopped in England before coming to the Continent, she became lawful prize.

Jefferson responded to these decrees not by declaring war or seriously threatening one, but by enacting an embargo that imposed a complete ban on exports both by sea and by land from the United States to any part of the world. Under its terms, all American vessels were prohibited from sailing to foreign ports, and all foreign vessels were denied the right to pick up cargoes in American seaports. The president saw this as a historic experiment in "peaceful coercion," an alternative to either war or humiliation. It was based on the assumption that both combatants were so dependent on American trade they would soon rescind their noxious decrees.

The embargo law passed the Senate by 22 to 6 in one day, and was approved by the House three days later, 82 to 44. The president signed the bill on December 22, 1807. The "visionary system" that Abigail Adams had wondered (and worried) about when Jefferson first became president was now fully employed. The president explained that his object was "to keep our seamen and property from capture, and to starve the offending nations." In his eighth annual message to Congress (after the embargo had been in effect for months), he reported that it "has had the important effects of saving our mariners and our vast mercantile property, as well as affording time for prosecuting the defensive and provisional measures called for by the occasion. . . . and has thus frustrated those usurpations and spoliations which, if resisted, involve war; if submitted to, sacrifice a vital principle of our national independence."

As secretary of the Treasury, Gallatin was responsible for policing the embargo but had originally opposed it. "In every point of view: privations, sufferings, revenue, effect on the enemy, politics at home, I prefer war to a permanent embargo," he had written to the president. "As to the hope that it may . . . induce England to treat us better, I think it entirely groundless." Secretary Smith also opposed the embargo. After enactment, of course, Gallatin put aside his reservations and vigorously enforced the law.

The navy's principal mission became the enforcement of the embargo. Commodore John Rogers was put in command of a gunboat flotilla that was expected to guard the coast from Delaware Bay to the Canadian border. Commodore Decatur was ordered to use his fleet of gunboats at Norfolk to patrol from Chesapeake Bay to Florida.

Evasions were widespread. The embargo was not meant to interfere with intracoastal trade, but many American captains, after setting out on innocent-looking coastal voyages, found ingenious ways to make their way to Europe or the West Indies. Being blown off course was the most common ploy. Smuggling was rampant, particularly in New England, where the embargo hit the economy hard and was bitterly opposed. Maritime commerce was New England's lifeblood; giving it up meant severe hardship for shipbuilders, merchants, seamen, and farmers. Illegal trade with Canada flourished. New England goods that made their way overland across the border were then reshipped overseas.

As 1808 progressed, managing the embargo absorbed nearly all of Jefferson's time. But he never doubted the wisdom of his original decision. "The embargo law," he wrote to Gallatin, "is certainly the most embarrassing one we have ever had to execute. I did not expect a crop of so sudden and rank growth of fraud and opposition by force could have grown up in the United States. I am satisfied with you that if the orders and decrees are not repealed, and the continuance of the embargo is preferred to war (which sentiment is universal here), Congress should legalize all *means* which may be necessary to obtain its *end*."

Congress tried its best to do just that. When enforcement problems came to light, it passed additions to the original law, extending the president's powers. The last of the five embargo laws, the Enforcing Act, flew through the Republican Congress in January 1809. It granted a degree of power to the president beyond anything Washington or Adams had ever contemplated; boosting bonds on coastal traders; giving revenue collectors extensive, unconstitutional powers to seize property anywhere; and authorizing the president to use the army, navy, and militias to enforce the law. Jefferson's sympathetic biographer, Merrill D. Peterson, wrote that "over-all, so vast was the concentration of power in the President and in minor functionaries, the measure mocked every principle Jefferson held except the one principle, that of the embargo itself, which he believed the crisis of affairs had made a national imperative."

Samuel Eliot Morison scoffed at "Jefferson's theory that his embargo would be a perfect substitute for war. . . . Practically," Morison wrote, "the embargo proved the greatest failure of any political experiment ever tried in the United States—excepting prohibition. It protected ships, but destroyed commerce; it produced no effects on either belligerent, but threw the carrying trade into other hands; [and] it could be enforced only by measures which violated popular ideas of liberty."

Jefferson feared the embargo might interfere with his plan to have Madison succeed him as president. The Republicans nominated Madison in January 1808, before the effects of the law were known. But later in the year, while the controversy over the measure raged and Madison was elected by a comfortable margin, Jefferson was encouraged to think that perhaps the embargo had more support in the country than he had supposed.

Despite widespread resistance and evasion, the law was generally observed. The navy's gunboats, combined with Gallatin's revenue officers and revenue cutters, proved effective. Gradually the American economy slowed and government revenues diminished. As the months went by, economic stagnation grew widespread. But the effects on the British were minimal. Their world markets made up for the deficiency of goods coming from and going to America, particularly when Spain's colonial market opened as a result of the Spanish uprising against Napoleon in 1808 and the ensuing Peninsula War.

Napoleon reacted to the embargo by issuing the Bayonne Decree in April 1808. It declared that, since the embargo prohibited American merchantmen from leaving port, any American vessel entering a Continental port would be seized under the assumption that it was British in disguise.

Despite its obvious failure to move either London or Paris, the embargo continued in effect for fourteen months. Throughout that time, Jefferson remained confident it would work. The alternative, he thought, was war. As the weeks dragged on, however, and it became obvious that the country would not bear the burden of the embargo much longer, Jefferson grew increasingly frustrated. He had no wish to be a wartime president. But if the embargo did not work and war was not an alternative, what was left? He continued to dream that if he persisted just a while longer, the embargo would work.

A strange lethargy overtook Jefferson during the last five months of his presidency, which placed a heavy burden on Gallatin to manage the unpopular embargo and in effect run the country before Madison took office. Jefferson's weariness was reminiscent of his last weeks as the governor of Virginia during the Revolution. With his embargo experiment a failure, he wanted only to leave Washington and return to the peace of Monticello. "Never did a prisoner, released from his chains, feel such relief as I shall on shaking off the shackles of power," he wrote to a friend. "Nature intended me for the tranquil pursuits of science, by rendering them my supreme delight. But the enormities of the time in which I have lived, have forced me to take a part in resisting them, and to commit myself to the boisterous ocean of political passions. I thank God for the opportunity of retiring from them without censure, and carrying with me the most consoling proof of public approbation."

By the end of 1808, resistance to the embargo was strong enough to threaten civil war. The harsh terms of the Enforcement Act of

January 9, 1809, further heightened tension. With New England on the verge of open revolt, Congress hastily repealed the unpopular law. On March 1, 1809, Jefferson reluctantly signed the legislation.

On March 15, the embargo was replaced by the Non-Intercourse Act. It permitted American trade with all nations except Britain and France. Furthermore, it stipulated that if either country stopped its noxious trade practices, the United States would resume trading with it. This legislation favored Britain, since she controlled the seas, and American produce could reach her in any number of ways. Jefferson disliked the law. He judged that in another two months the embargo would have worked, and Britain, at least, would have given in.

At the same time Jefferson was applying his embargo, he had quietly taken precautions for the defense of the country. He planned with state governors for a fast call-up of militias in an emergency, and he strengthened harbor defenses, including continuing to build gunboats. But he resisted, as he always had, increasing the blue water navy. In doing so, he left the country defenseless, for the militias were notoriously unreliable. They were not, however much Jefferson wished they were, a substitute for a regular army; nor were gunboats, in and of themselves, a substitute for a blue water fleet that could be a force outside harbors, rivers, and the immediate coast. And even if gunboats were theoretically effective as defensive weapons against either Britain or France, Jefferson never built enough, nor did he organize them properly. The president thus passed on to his successor the conundrum of how to protect American rights against two powers of vastly superior strength.

Three days after Madison was sworn into office, Jefferson rode off to Monticello, never to return to Washington again.

13

WAR CLOUDS

March 1809–June 1812

Shortly after taking office, President Madison wrote to William Pinkney, the American ambassador in London, that the United States had to choose either making "fresh efforts to vindicate our rights or enforce our resentments." Madison had been elected with a handsome majority (122 electoral votes out of a total of 169), but what new policies might vindicate American rights on the high seas were unclear to him. The economic sanctions he favored were not working, and he had been unalterably opposed to war his entire political life. He had come to office as a champion of the embargo, supporting it even more strongly than Jefferson. He felt that with a little more time and better enforcement it would have succeeded. But he also recognized that politically the embargo was dead and could not be resuscitated.

Yet something had to replace it. No self-respecting country could accept impressment and Britain's abusive orders in council. But what "peaceful coercions" would work? None readily came to mind. War seemed the only alternative, but the country was woefully unprepared for one, and so was Madison. He had supported Jefferson and the Republicans in Congress in their neglect of the nation's military. "War," he believed, "contain[ed] so much folly, as well as wickedness," that all other measures should be tried before resorting to it. The last thing he wanted was to be a wartime president. But if matters were not resolved with Great Britain, that appeared to be his fate.

Like Jefferson, he preferred neither Britain nor France, viewing one as bad as the other. France was a great land power gone mad, and Britain a sea power bent on establishing sovereignty over the world's oceans. Madison had no interest in defeating Napoleon and reestablishing the balance of power in Europe. He saw his alternatives as either submitting to the oppression of both belligerents, war, or withdrawing America's commerce from the high seas.

His opponents believed that the most significant question before the United States was not impressment or neutral trading rights, but whether Europe would be ruled by Napoleon Bonaparte or have the balance of power restored. In their view, Britain, with all her faults, was the champion of the balance of power, and she was fighting a cruel war to prevent Napoleon from conquering Europe. They believed that the United States had a huge stake in the outcome of this titanic struggle. But Madison, like his predecessor, refused to acknowledge that Napoleon was the greater evil. He continued to insist that Britain and France were equally dangerous.

The British surprised Madison when he first took office by offering to rescind their trade restrictions on the United States. Toward the end of Jefferson's term, Gallatin had alerted David Erskine, England's likeable, pro-American ambassador in Washington, to the possibility that the new administration might be open to a negotiated settlement of their differences. While Madison was mired in indecision, Gallatin, anticipating his appointment as secretary of state, had spoken boldly to the ambassador about a new approach.

Erskine had notified Foreign Secretary Canning that an accord with the United States was possible, and Canning had written back on January 23, 1809, ordering Erskine to open negotiations. The ambassador received his instructions on April 7 and began talks with President Madison, Gallatin, and the new secretary of state, Robert Smith.

Gallatin's hopes of becoming secretary of state had been thwarted by congressional enemies; and so, much against his will, he remained at Treasury. The politically potent Smith clan of Maryland, as well as other Republicans such as William Branch Giles of Virginia, who also wanted to be secretary of state, had objected to Gallatin's appointment. Madison gave in to them, appointing Robert Smith, the former secretary of the navy, a man for whom he had no regard. As a result, the president acted as his own secretary of state.

Within six weeks Madison had reached an agreement with Erskine, and he was overjoyed. The president assumed that Jefferson's embargo and the pressures of the Napoleonic War had forced the cabinet to seek a reconciliation. Erskine agreed to withdraw the noxious orders in council, and Madison, under the terms of the Non-Intercourse Act, could now remove restrictions on trade with Britain. The thorny issues of impressment and reparations for the *Chesapeake-Leopard* affair were set aside to be negotiated later. The British had long ago disavowed the attack on the *Chesapeake* and had agreed to a settlement, although years had passed and nothing had actually been done.

In his euphoria Madison imagined that when Napoleon learned of the rapprochement he would remove his trade barriers as well. Ever since 1789 Madison, like Jefferson, had wanted to substitute economic sanctions for war. He believed that trade with the United States was so important to Britain and France that they would be forced to respect American interests. Economic coercion now appeared to have worked.

Jefferson was as elated as Madison. "The British ministry," he wrote to the president, "has been driven from its Algerine system. . . . [The agreement with Erskine is] the triumph of our forebearing and yet persevering system. . . . It will lighten your anxieties, take from cabal its most fertile ground of war, [and] will give us peace during your time."

Madison proclaimed June 10, 1809, as the day he would remove nonintercourse with the British. He thought he had achieved a real understanding with them. His joy lasted only until the end of July, however, when word reached Washington that the cabinet, at Canning's urging, had disavowed the Erskine Agreement, accusing Ambassador Erskine of having exceeded his instructions and recalling him. Madison was devastated, baffled by what had happened. He had offered to repair relations and enter into a quasi-alliance with Britain. Why would Canning refuse?

Erskine, it turned out, *had* exceeded his instructions. Canning had ordered the ambassador to require Madison to permit the Royal Navy to stop all private vessels of the United States in order to enforce Madison's own nonintercourse law against France. Under that legislation, when Britain withdrew its orders in council, Madison was required to discontinue nonintercourse against Britain but continue it with France. Canning was insisting that the British navy be allowed to enforce America's own law, since the U.S. Navy, in his opinion, could not.

Since Erskine knew that Madison would never agree to such an arrangement, he never brought it up. When Canning saw the final agreement without his stipulation, he angrily rejected it, and the cabinet supported him. To emphasize his displeasure, Canning replaced Erskine with an ambassador of a totally different stripe, Francis James Jackson, an envoy whose brusque, undiplomatic manner was legendary.

On August 9, the president restored nonintercourse with Great Britain. Increasingly, war appeared to be his only alternative, and he was angry enough to consider it. He yearned to retaliate against a country that for his entire political life had been an enemy. It was clear to him now that the hostile Tory government of Spencer Perceval, George Canning, the still anti-American (albeit insane) George III, as well as a hostile English press, made it a foregone conclusion that Erskine's approach would be rejected. America might be Britain's natural ally in the contest with Napoleon, but she made rapprochement impossible.

America, however, was unprepared for war and deeply divided politically. New England was suffering from the embargo and despised Jefferson and Madison; most Federalists of the northeast were sympathetic toward Great Britain; the Republican Party was divided into hostile factions. Uniting the country behind a war with Britain would require far greater political skills than Madison possessed.

Furthermore, America's armed forces were in a deplorable state. The navy had few warships other than Jefferson's gunboats, which were loathed by every officer of note. Rogers, Decatur, and their colleagues did not aspire to command a "mosquito fleet." Yet that had been their lot during the embargo. When it was repealed, Acting Navy Secretary Charles Goldsborough ordered 86 of the country's 165 gunboats laid up in ordinary. The New Orleans station was allowed to keep all twenty-six of its gunboats. The Navy Department then tried to reactivate what warships it could.

The naval commands along the eastern seaboard were divided between Commodore John Rogers in New York and Commodore Stephen Decatur at Norfolk, Virginia. Two additional small flotillas were maintained at Charleston, South Carolina, and New Orleans. Rogers had the better part of the navy's tiny operational fleet, consisting of his flagship, the 44-gun *President*; the 44-gun *Constitution*, under Captain Isaac Hull; the 32-gun *Essex*, under David Porter; the 18-gun brig *Argus*, under Lieutenant James Lawrence; and twenty gunboats. Decatur had the 44-gun *United States*, the 38-gun *Congress*, the 16-gun sloop-of-war *Wasp*, the 14-gun *Nautilus*, and fourteen gunboats. All told, the navy had sixteen warships of various kinds other than the gunboats: eight frigates, two sloops-of-war, and six smaller vessels. All the frigates had been built before Jefferson took office. Seven of the other eight ships had been built for the war with Tripoli. The warships not available to either Rogers or Decatur were in ordinary or were being overhauled.

The navy's few warships were manned by officers with extensive combat experience and all-volunteer crews. But how to use them against the overwhelming numbers of the Royal Navy wasn't clear. The new navy secretary, Paul Hamilton, had little conception of how to deploy the country's warships. No one quite knew why Madison had chosen him other than to balance the cabinet geographically. Hamilton had no obvious qualifications for the job. Now fifty years old, he had fought as a young man in the Revolutionary War under Francis Marion, had been elected governor of South Carolina, and was a rice planter. He also had a drinking problem; little would get done in the department after lunch. Hamilton's appointment indicated how important the president considered the position.

The new secretary was a staunch patriot with a belief in having a respectable blue water fleet of the kind that Washington and Adams had advocated. He had a poor opinion of Jefferson's gunboats and more or less ignored them. Before becoming secretary, he had been outraged by the *Chesapeake-Leopard* affair and by the general treatment Britain and France were according America. He ordered his commanders to observe strict neutrality and not initiate any action, but if the occasion arose, not to hesitate to use all the force at their command to uphold the honor of the United States. He used the small squadron stationed at Charleston under Captain Hugh C. Campbell to suppress the slave trade, which had been outlawed in 1808. The problem was so large, however, and the navy's resources so limited that Hamilton had little success.

The army was in even worse shape than the navy. The available force amounted to only six thousand inexperienced troops. Its leaders, equipment, and strategy were woefully inadequate. Brigadier General James Wilkinson, a political intriguer and an incompetent, was its ranking officer. Back in 1796, he had replaced General Anthony Wayne. Jefferson had inherited him and kept him on because of his help against Aaron Burr. Madison decided to retain Wilkinson as well. The secretary of war was Dr. William Eustis, whom Jefferson had appointed just before leaving office; Madison kept him because he was from Massachusetts and politically well connected. A former student of Dr. Joseph Warren's in Boston, Eustis had served in the Revolutionary War, had been a congressman for two terms, and was a loyal Republican, but he had no feel for his job as leader of the army. Many of his fellow Republicans wanted Madison to get rid of him.

The state of the two services moved Joshua Barney, who was running for Congress in 1810, to declare, "We are kicked by England, we are kicked by France . . . We have a population of more than seven millions; we could receive and repel the greatest force of any nation on earth at the point of the bayonet or the cannon's mouth. Yet our Congress, knowing the facts, has sat shivering or sleeping in the Capital at edicts and orders issued three thousand miles off."

When Congress assembled in November 1809, Madison warned that a crisis was at hand. "In the state which has been presented of our affairs," he said, "with the parties to a disastrous and protracted war, carried on in a mode equally injurious and unjust to the United States as a neutral nation, the wisdom of the national legislature will be again summoned to the important decision on the alternatives before them." The president offered no opinion on which alternative the Congress ought to select.

Although Madison was reluctant to lead, young Henry Clay, a newly elected senator from Kentucky, was not. "The conquest of Canada is in your power," he told the Senate. "I trust I shall not be deemed presumptuous when I state that I verily believe that the militia of Kentucky are alone competent to place Montreal and Upper Canada at your feet."

The assumption that Canada was there for the taking was widespread in the country, not just among Clay and his supporters. Using Canada's vulnerability to force the British to change her policies on the ocean was a strategy that had broad appeal. Even the president and his mentor Jefferson were taken with the idea.

Nonetheless, on April 16, 1810, the Republican Congress voted to reduce the army and the navy in order to save money. Nonintercourse with England had cut deeply into tax revenue. Congress refused to compensate for the losses by raising internal taxes to support even minimal preparations for war; instead, it authorized the government to obtain a loan of $5 million. And on May 1, 1810, it enacted Macon's Bill Number 2, which replaced the Non-Intercourse Act. The new law reopened trade with the world, including Britain and France, so that the revenue stream from British trade could start moving again and the moribund economy could revive. The bill also stipulated that if either country removed its restrictions on neutral trade, the United States would cease commerce with the other.

This provision intrigued Napoleon. On August 5, his foreign minister, the Duke de Cadore, notified the American ambassador in Paris, General John Armstrong, that France intended to revoke the Berlin and Milan decrees. But on the very same day, Napoleon, secretly pursuing a contrary policy, ordered all sequestered American ships and cargoes condemned. Publicly, he announced that after November 1, 1810, the Berlin and Milan decrees would be withdrawn under certain conditions. Those conditions remained vague enough for him to do whatever he pleased; in any case, he wanted to give Madison the impression that his policy toward American trade had fundamentally changed.

Though aware of the hollowness of Napoleon's revocation, Madison chose to act as if it were genuine; he was determined to send the arrogant British a warning. On November 2, he declared, "Whereas it has been officially made known to this government that the edicts of France violating the neutral commerce of the United States have been . . . revoked," nonintercourse with Britain would resume in three months unless the British rescinded the orders in council.

The British cabinet was not convinced that the French were doing what they claimed and refused to rescind the orders. John Quincy Adams, now the American ambassador to Russia, warned the president that Napoleon's bogus policy shift was "a trap to catch [America] into a war with England." Madison, however, was intent on ignoring the obvious; he wanted to punish the British. Meanwhile, American shipping in and out of French ports continued to be seized and confiscated. Madison ignored this inconvenient fact and on February 11, 1811, invoked the Macon Act, cutting off trade with Great Britain. At the same time, he warned London of the most serious consequences if the cabinet did not rescind the orders in council.

But the British were not listening, and the crisis Madison had dreaded for so long was now fast approaching. The Royal Navy continued to impress, to stop and seize American ships, and in general, to act as if the United States were impotent. Particularly provocative was Britain's renewed blockade of New York.

An incident off Sandy Hook in May 1811 illustrated just how provocative. While Commodore Rogers and the other ships in his squadron were away, the British frigate *Guerriere* and a companion, the *Melampus*, appeared off Sandy Hook and started seizing ships bound for France, impressing whatever seamen they chose. On the morning of May 1, the *Guerriere* chased the American brig *Spitfire*, bringing her to with a shot across her bow. Captain Dacres, the *Guerriere*'s skipper, then sent a search party on board the *Spitfire* and impressed John Diggio, a Maine man serving as an apprentice to the master.

The incident was highly publicized, and indignation became widespread. Secretary Hamilton ordered Commodore Rogers to hurry back to New York, reminding him "to vindicate the injured honor of our navy and revive the drooping spirits of the nation . . . to maintain and support at any risk and cost the honor" of the flag. At the time, Rogers was in Annapolis, and he immediately prepared the *President* and got underway. But with adverse winds delaying him, he did not stand out to sea until May 14. He had not traveled far when, around half past noon on May 16, he spied a strange sail forty-five miles northeast of Cape Henry. The stranger had all her sails spread and was coming directly down on him. As she drew closer, however, she suddenly turned and fled. Rogers tore after her, thinking that she might be the *Guerriere* and that he might be able to rescue the American seaman she had impressed, although it must have occurred to him that if she were the *Guerriere*, she probably wouldn't have reversed course.

The stranger turned out to be the 20-gun British sloop-of-war *Little Belt*, under Captain Arthur Bingham. By eight o'clock the two warships were drawing close to each other, with their crews at battle stations. By eight-thirty it was growing dark, and they were two hundred feet apart with their guns thrust out.

"What ship is that?" Rogers shouted through a speaking trumpet. As a reply he received a shot that struck his mainmast. Soon both ships were bombarding each other with full broadsides, and in ten minutes the *Little Belt's* guns fell silent. Rogers ordered his men to cease firing. Within a few minutes, however, the British sloop began shooting again, and Rogers, now thoroughly annoyed, unleashed a murderous broadside. Within five minutes Captain Bingham struck his colors.

The lateness of the hour made visibility so poor that Rogers wasn't sure just how big his opponent was until daylight. The *Little Belt* was a former Danish man-of-war the British had captured in the battle of Copenhagen, and she was a double-decked ship, which made her appear larger than she actually was. Shortly after sunrise Rogers sent over a boat to express regrets to Captain Bingham for the incident and to see if he could be of assistance. Bingham politely refused, and Rogers's boat returned with the news that *Little Belt* had been badly damaged, suffering thirteen dead and nineteen wounded. Rogers had only one boy injured.

The *Little Belt* limped back to Halifax while Rogers returned to New York in triumph. Secretary Hamilton and President Madison were delighted with the action and heaped praise on the commodore. Rogers was a hero everywhere but in New England, where people were not anxious to get into a fight with Britain.

A deeply divided Congress convened a month early, on November 4, 1811. Madison's annual message was opaque. He told the members that "the period has arrived [to put the country] into an armor and an attitude demanded by the crisis." He recommended expanding the army, preparing the militia, gathering munitions, and improving the navy. Madison had spent the summer conferring with Jefferson and Monroe, who was now secretary of state. (Robert Smith had been dismissed on April 2, 1811.) In the course of discussions the president had decided that if Britain would not relax her policy with respect to trade, he would ask for a declaration of war in the coming session of Congress. He wrote to Joel Barlow, the American plenipotentiary to

France, that "unless a change in the British system should arrest the career of events," war was likely.

Nonetheless, Madison was still hoping that Britain would relent and withdraw its orders in council before it was too late. The British ambassador, Augustus John Foster, however, continued to report that Madison and the Congress were not serious about going to war. Even after a ninety-day embargo was enacted during the first week of April 1812, Foster's reports remained the same. He felt that the new embargo would be ineffective, which it was.

Britain showed no willingness to bend until Prime Minister Spencer Perceval, an unswerving supporter of the orders, was shot to death by a deranged man on May 11. Hope for a change in British policy flickered briefly when the new prime minister, Lord Liverpool, assumed office. He had no desire to get into a war with the United States. He was far more concerned with fighting the war in Europe, which had grown increasingly dangerous for Britain. For months he had watched nervously as Bonaparte assembled a gargantuan army to invade Russia, and it looked as if the French dictator would easily crush the czar.

On June 23, as soon as Liverpool had formed a ministry, he announced the repeal of the orders in council, hoping this would calm the Americans. The repeal, however, was conditional and could be reinstated at any time. And Liverpool would not budge on impressment.

Meanwhile, the long-awaited sloop-of-war *Hornet* arrived in New York on May 19, carrying dispatches dated April 10, 1812, confirming Perceval's intention to maintain the orders in council. President Madison, without knowledge of Perceval's death and Lord Liverpool's actions, delivered his war message to Congress on June 1. Three days later the House voted 79 to 49 in favor of war. Not a single Federalist voted for the resolution. On June 17, the Senate approved the bill by the narrow margin of 19 to 13, and the following day the president signed the law. Madison was bringing a divided country into a war it was utterly unprepared to fight. The Federalist *Boston Gazette* asked, "Is there a . . . patriot in America, who conceives it his duty to shed his blood for Bonaparte, for

Madison or Jefferson, and that host of ruffians in Congress who have set their faces against the United States for years?"

Impressment was the first reason the president gave for declaring war. "American citizens," he said, ". . . have been torn from their country and everything dear to them; have been dragged on board ships of war of a foreign nation and exposed, under the severest of their discipline, to be exiled to the most distant and deadly climes, to risk their lives in the battles of their oppressors, and to be the melancholy instruments of taking away those of their own brethren." Second, he condemned "British cruisers . . . violating the rights and the peace of our coasts . . . plundering our commerce . . . the sweeping system of blockades, under the name of orders in council . . . [which have established a] monopoly . . . for her own commerce and navigation." Last, Madison cited the use of the Indians as evidence of British depravity.

The president was also outraged by the duplicity of France, but the prospect of going to war with both powers simultaneously was too much to contemplate; he chose war with the one he considered worse.

It was openly acknowledged in Congress that the United States was unprepared for combat, yet there was confidence among those who voted for the war that the country could prepare swiftly enough to win. Their strategy was to capture Canada and use it as a lever to force London to come to terms. Many believed America could keep Canada once it had been taken. All the United States needed to do, they thought, was threaten to cut off Canadian trade with Britain, particularly in timber and fur, for the cabinet to accede to American demands.

Those who advocated invading Canada assumed that the small British force of sixty-five hundred stationed there could be easily overpowered. Jefferson was one of them. "It is not ten years," he wrote, "since Great Britain began a series of insults and injuries which would have met with war in the threshold by any European power. . . . Our present enemy will have the sea to herself, while we shall be equally predominant at land, and shall strip her of all her possessions on this continent. . . . I hope we shall confine ourselves to the conquest of their possessions, and defense of our harbors, leaving the war on the oceans to our privateers. . . . Upon the whole, I have known no war entered into under more favorable auspices."

John Adams also supported Madison. "A more necessary war was never undertaken," he wrote. "It is necessary against England; necessary to convince France that we are something: and above all necessary to convince ourselves, that we are not nothing." Adams, however, did not support the policies that led up to the war. "I have never approved of non-importations, non-intercourses, or embargoes for more than six weeks," he told Jefferson. "I never have approved and never can approve of the repeal of taxes, the repeal of the Judiciary System, or the neglect of the Navy."

While supporters of the war were enthusiastic about American prospects in Canada, they did not believe money should be wasted attempting to build a sea force to challenge the Royal Navy. Thus Congress voted in favor of war but against expanding the navy. During the months leading up to the war, the most Congress would authorize was enough money to repair and man the old frigates *Chesapeake*, *Constellation*, and *Adams*, and to purchase timber for future use. Those who urged invading Canada expected privateers to conduct the naval war against Britain. On January 27, 1812, Langdon Cleaves of South Carolina, the chairman of the House Naval Committee, reported a bill to the full House that included authorization to build ten additional frigates. It was defeated by a vote of 62 to 59.

Napoleon's long-anticipated invasion of Russia coincided exactly with America's declaration of war against Great Britain. On June 24, 1812, the French dictator crossed the Neiman River (the Russian-Polish border) at the head of a multinational army of 612,000—the largest ever assembled—and struck deep into Russia, heading toward Smolensk, Borodino, and Moscow. "Before the month is out," Napoleon declared, "the Russians will be on their knees before me."

Czar Alexander had been preparing for Napoleon's onslaught for months, and he had developed a strategy that would take advantage of Russia's considerable strengths. Withdrawing as the invasion progressed, he sought to deprive Napoleon of supplies and food. Provisions for Bonaparte's troops and animals grew scarcer the farther he penetrated into the Russian vastness. Napoleon would never admit error and so, in spite of the horrendous difficulties his army was experiencing, he ignored its problems and single-mindedly drove forward. As he did, the Russians kept retreating, kept denying him the sustenance he needed.

On September 7 at Borodino, seventy miles west of Moscow, the Russians under Kutuzov finally stood and fought. After twelve hours of bloody combat, having lost tens of thousands of men, Kutuzov withdrew his army during the night in good order. Napoleon had suffered nearly as many casualties. Although the world had never seen such a slaughter, Napoleon considered himself victorious. The Russians, however, would not surrender.

On September 15 the French entered Moscow, the religious center of Russia. They tramped into the city expecting to find the food and fodder that had been denied them for weeks. All around them were magnificent buildings and churches but no people. Moscow was deserted, its 300,000 inhabitants having nearly all fled. Napoleon had anticipated negotiating a punitive peace with the czar, but instead, Moscow burst into flames. Napoleon soon found himself in an empty ruin, with his resources getting thinner by the day.

Kutuzov remained outside Moscow, strengthening his army and stubbornly refusing to parley. Weeks passed with Napoleon continuing to insist that the czar would give in and seek peace. On October 19, with winter rapidly approaching and supplies getting critical, Bonaparte could no longer wait. He evacuated Moscow and began a long, disastrous retreat. The Grand Army marched back over roughly the same barren landscape through which it had come. Winter arrived early, and provisions were nowhere to be found. With the Russian army harassing it the entire way, along with the harsh weather and the difficult terrain, what was left of the Grand Army disappeared. Over 400,000 died and perhaps 100,000 were captured; only 43,000 recrossed the Neiman.

As he had done in Egypt, Napoleon deserted his men. By sleigh and carriage he hastened back to Paris in December 1812. The trip took him two weeks. News of his defeat reached Washington in March 1813. Madison viewed it with some disappointment; he did not see it as a triumph over a dangerous dictator but as strengthening Britain's hand against America. Later in life Madison reflected on the situation. "Had the French emperor not been broken down," he wrote, "as he was to a degree at variance with all probability and which no human sagacity could anticipate, can it be doubted that Great Britain would have been constrained by her own situation and the demands of her allies to listen to our reasonable terms of reconciliation? The moment chosen for war would therefore have been well chosen, if chosen with a reference to the French expedition against Russia."

But, of course, the moment Madison decided to call for a declaration of war was not well chosen at all. Had he delayed and patiently waited for Napoleon's demise, the European conflict would have ended and the need for impressment and the orders in council would have disappeared. His mentor, Jefferson, held patience to be a critical virtue in a president. He liked to think that he had succeeded in obtaining Louisiana because he was willing to wait.

By June 1812, however, Madison felt he could wait no longer; the nation's honor required him to act. In his first annual message to Congress after it declared war, he said, "To have shrunk under such circumstances from manly resistance would have been a degradation blasting our best and proudest hopes; it would have struck us from the high rank where the virtuous struggle of our fathers had placed us, and have betrayed the magnificent legacy which we hold in trust for future generations. It would have acknowledged that on the element that forms three-fourths of the globe we inhabit, and where all independent nations have equal and common rights, the Americans were not independent people, but colonists and vassals."

Far more than manly resistance, however, was required to successfully war against the world's greatest sea power. Thanks in good part to the president's own policies, the nation was ill equipped to fight. Nor had the president exhibited the leadership skills to get the country prepared in a hurry. Rushing into a war with Britain appeared to be the height of folly.

14

THE NAVY SURPRISES

June 1812–August 1813

When war seemed inevitable, Secretary Hamilton searched for ideas on how to employ America's tiny fleet; he had no strategy of his own. Madison rejected out of hand the notion of keeping the nation's warships in port to defend her harbors and not allowing them to venture out on the high seas.

At the end of May 1812, Hamilton asked Commodore Rogers and Commodore Decatur their thoughts on strategy, particularly about how the navy could "annoy in the utmost extent, the trade of Great Britain while it least exposes it to the immense naval force of that Government." Rogers replied on June 3. "We have a dozen vessels in commission," he wrote, "and they have five hundred." Although it might be concluded that their commerce in the waters surrounding the coasts of England, Ireland, and Scotland was well protected by swarms of men-of-war, he asserted that "this . . . I well know by experience in my voyages when a youth, to be incorrect." Instead, he wrote, the British practice was to station their warships on the enemy's coast and keep the fighting away from their homeland. In view of this practice, Rogers advocated sending a squadron directly to the British Isles at the onset of hostilities, to cruise against their commerce, and in so doing, draw their available warships away from the American coast. He also advocated sending the navy's other warships to attack Britain's avenues of trade to and from the West and East Indies, Canada, Nova Scotia, and Newfoundland. And he encouraged the idea of watching the sea-lanes for British merchantmen traveling between the West Indies and Canada. It was of the utmost importance, he thought, for the American fleet to get to sea before the Royal Navy could blockade it in port.

In his reply to Hamilton, Decatur wrote that the fleet should be dispatched singly or "not more than two frigates in company" with "as large a supply of provisions as they can carry," without specific instructions. The navy ought to rely on the "enterprise of the officers," he argued, to harass British shipping wherever, in the officers' judgment, it was most vulnerable. "The advantage of distant cruising," he said, "would be to relieve our coasts by withdrawing from it a number of the hostile ships." Decatur pointed out that dispersing the fleet would prevent it from being destroyed in a single engagement.

When war broke out, neither Secretary Hamilton nor the president had decided between the divergent views of Rogers and Decatur. Although the administration had discussed the situation during the winter and spring and exchanged letters with the fleet commanders, it had adopted no overall strategy. Without saying so, Madison was pessimistic about the prospects of the minute American fleet. Developing a naval strategy was not a high priority for him, and he did not settle on one until hostilities had commenced. Privateers, the president felt, would do the bulk of commerce raiding, not the navy.

Rogers had prepared his squadron to depart New York at a moment's notice so that he could avoid being trapped by a superior British force coming down from Halifax. When he received word that war had been declared, he didn't let a lack of specific orders stop him from immediately putting to sea on June 21 with a good part of the American navy—the frigates *President* (his flagship), the *United States*, under Stephen Decatur, and the *Congress*, under John Smith; the sloop-of-war *Hornet*, under James Lawrence; and the brig *Argus*, under Arthur Sinclair. By Hamilton's order, Decatur had sailed his ships from Norfolk to join Rogers.

The frigate *Essex*, under David Porter, was also in New York, but she had just been laid up for repairs. All her masts had to be replaced, she needed caulking inside and out, her copper bottom required cleaning and repairing, and her ballast had to be replaced. Captain Isaac Chauncey, commandant of the New York navy yard, accomplished all this work in a remarkable three weeks.

On June 22 Hamilton directed Rogers and Decatur to employ a strategy contrary to the one they were following. He told them not to venture far from the American coast but keep their ships close to it, in order "to afford our commerce all possible protection."

At the time, dozens of American merchant ships were at sea, unaware of their jeopardy now that war had been declared. Madison wanted to get them safely into a home port before the British could seize them. Both Rogers and Decatur were alert to the danger, but they did not agree with the president on how to avoid it. They wanted to keep out to sea and draw the British away from the coast, not stay close to it, where they stood a good chance of being overwhelmed by a larger fleet. In any event, by the time Hamilton's new orders arrived, Rogers and Decatur were already at sea, charting their own course.

At the start of the war, British Vice Admiral Sawyer commanded the North American station at Halifax with one small ship of the line, the 64-gun *Africa*, which had fought at Trafalgar, seven frigates—*Acasta*, 40, *Shannon*, 38, *Guerriere*, 38, *Belvidera*, 36, *Aeolus*, 32, *Southampton*, 32, and *Minerva*, 32—and a number of smaller vessels. It was superior to Rogers's fleet, but if Sawyer divided his force, its parts might be vulnerable to the Americans.

Rogers was aware of Sawyer's limitations and hoped to take advantage of them before the Admiralty had time to send reinforcements. The initial phase of the war, Rogers believed, would last about six months, when the navy would have its best chance of "annoying" the enemy. Eventually, he thought, Britain's superior numbers would overwhelm the tiny American navy.

Jefferson's gunboats were not part of anyone's calculations. None had been built since 1810, and they were dispersed along the coast in various states of repair, with vague plans to be employed in harbor defense. Eight were at Portland, in the Maine district of Massachusetts; two in Boston; fifty-four in New York; ten at Baltimore; twenty at Philadelphia; four at Connecticut and Rhode Island; ten on the Potomac; eleven at St. Mary's, Georgia; four at Wilmington, North Carolina; two at Charleston, South Carolina; fourteen at Norfolk, Virginia; and twenty-six at New Orleans. Secretary Hamilton had no use for them, nor did any of his officers. The gunboats were orphans. Even if anyone had taken them seriously, there weren't enough of them to perform the defensive mission Jefferson had assigned to them.

They had been useful to David Porter, who was commanding the New Orleans station from 1808 to 1810. He had been charged with enforcing Jefferson's embargo and the new law against international slave trade. His gunboats patrolled the Mississippi, as well as the lakes and bayous of the area, attempting to hold the lid on illicit commerce. The pirates Pierre Lafitte and Jean Lafitte were active around the lower Mississippi and the Gulf, but as Porter's biographer David Long points out, "there is no evidence" he came in contact with them. In fact Jefferson's gunboats had performed limited service, but navy commanders dismissed them as ineffectual in a war with Britain.

The Great Lakes and Lake Champlain were of even less interest. Obviously the American army could not invade Canada without naval supremacy on the lakes, and at the moment the British dominated Lake Ontario and Lake Erie. The gunboats might have been of use in that theater if anyone had thought of it, but the navy's focus, at least in the beginning, was on the blue water fleet.

The British were far more worried about American privateers than they were about the United States Navy. Over 526 privately armed vessels put out during the War of 1812, and they created enormous problems for Britain's merchant fleet, including ships supplying the Duke of Wellington's army fighting in Spain. Many American privateers were the equivalent of 20-gun British frigates, and they were manned and officered by experienced seamen who could fight. Of course their primary object was profit and they wouldn't risk their necks if they could avoid it, but they could put up a good fight when forced.

The British assumed that the Royal Navy would sweep the American fleet from the seas in the first weeks of war. Britain's men-of-war could then destroy America's commerce by blockading her ports and seizing her merchant ships at sea. The Admiralty's only concern was privateers.

When Rogers left New York on June 21, he hoped to meet an enemy squadron out of Halifax or at least attract British attention so that their warships would pursue him rather than blockade American harbors. He hoped to occupy the Halifax fleet while the merchantmen were returning to port. In this he was successful; the merchants did reach home safely, even as the British searched in vain for Rogers.

Two days out of New York, on June 23, approximately one hundred miles southwest of Nantucket shoals, a lookout on the *President* spied a large sail in the northeast. It was six o'clock in the morning. Rogers immediately hoisted the signal for a general chase. His squadron made all sail as they pursued what turned out to be a British frigate. Rogers could not believe his good luck. The *President* was in the van, and by eleven o'clock Rogers had drawn close enough to his prey to clear the ship for action.

But then the wind changed direction and became lighter, preventing Rogers from getting any closer. A little after four o'clock he was again within shooting range and ordered his bow chasers readied. Meanwhile, the British warship, which turned out to be the 36-gun frigate HMS *Belvidera*, under Captain Richard Byron, had stern guns out, ready to fire at the oncoming *President*. Rogers gave the order to aim at the *Belvidera*'s spars and rigging, hoping to slow her down. Captain Byron replied with his stern guns. A hot exchange flared for ten minutes; then one of the *President*'s chase guns suddenly burst, killing or wounding sixteen men. Rogers himself was blown into the air, and in falling fractured a leg. The exploding gun damaged the forecastle and main decks near it, making the other chase gun on that side impossible to fire. Rogers, who remained in command in spite of his injury, put his helm to starboard and fired a broadside but inflicted no damage. He continued to run and shoot, stopping from time to time to deliver a broadside, but the British frigate kept just out of reach.

At six-thirty, Captain Byron began throwing overboard boats, anchors, water, and anything else he could spare to lighten his ship and gradually pulled away from the *President*. Rogers kept in pursuit for five more hours before giving up, bitterly disappointed.

Rogers then went in search of a large British West Indian convoy. He sailed north to the Grand Banks off Newfoundland. Seeing nothing, he sailed to within 150 miles of the Schilles, off England's southwestern coast. Previous statements of his suggested that he would then sail around the coasts of Ireland, Scotland, and England. Instead, he turned and headed home by way of Madeira. When he put into Boston on the last day of August, he had only seven insignificant prizes to show for his efforts. Rogers returned sooner than expected because of scurvy, three hundred men in the fleet having contracted the deadly disease. Even though measures to combat scurvy were well-known, Rogers and his captains had not utilized them.

Having failed to deliver Rogers his first set of orders in time, Secretary Hamilton had sent a fast brig, the 12-gun *Nautilus*, under Lieutenant William Crane, to deliver a second set, dated July 10: "there will be a strong British force on our coast in a few days—be upon your guard—we are anxious for your safe return into port." Crane was directed to put out from New York and find Rogers. He sailed on July 15, and on the following day, seventy-five miles off Sandy Hook at a quarter past four in the afternoon, he spotted five large sails off his weather beam. They were the 64-gun British battleship *Africa*, Captain John Bastard; the 38-gun *Guerriere*, Captain James R. Dacres; the *Belvidera*; the 32-gun *Aelus*, Captain Lord Townsend; and Commodore Broke's flagship, the 38-gun *Shannon*. Broke had swept down from the north, looking for Rogers's squadron.

Crane immediately wore ship and threw on all the sail his vessel could bear, while the five ships tore after him. A heavy swell came up, giving the advantage to the bigger ships in pursuit. Crane tried every maneuver in trimming his ship, but nothing worked. Finally he ordered the anchors cut from the bows and then threw over some water, half his guns, and part of his round shot. But nothing seemed to help. At midnight, the lead British ship, the *Shannon*, pulled within musket shot. Crane destroyed his signals books and the dispatches Hamilton had given him, and then surrendered. Broke put the officers and crew of the *Nautilus* in the *Africa*, except for Crane. He was kept aboard the *Nautilus* while a British prize crew sailed her to Halifax. Crane later wrote, "The treatment I received from Commodore Broke was polite and gentlemanly." The *Nautilus* was the first American warship captured in the war.

Rogers's squadron was supposed to have been strengthened by the *Constitution,* but when the commodore put to sea at the start of the war, Captain Isaac Hull had the old frigate berthed at Annapolis, Maryland, trying to acquire more crewmen. The *Constitution* had just been completely overhauled at Washington naval shipyard under the direction of Nathaniel "Jumping Billy" Haraden, her sailing master during the war with Tripoli. Haraden had recoppered her hull and reduced her ballast to give her more speed. Her officers thought he had breathed new life into her.

With his ship repaired, Hull had to round out her crew. Enlistments in the American navy were for two years, unlike those in Britain, where service was indeterminate, whether one volunteered or was dragooned by a press gang. A two-year enlistment made the American service more desirable, but it also necessitated having to part with able seamen at regular intervals, which could be especially difficult in wartime. Much of Hull's crew had signed on in 1810 and many had left at the end of their tour. Now he had to find replacements. The ship's complement was 440, and Hull soon had enough to get underway, but many of the newcomers were green. He wrote to Secretary Hamilton, "By Sunday next, the ship will be in tolerable order for sea but the crew you will readily conceive, must yet be unacquainted with a ship of war, as many of them have but lately joined us and never were in an armed ship before. We are doing all that we can to make them acquainted with [their] duty, and in a few days, we shall have nothing to fear from any single deck ship." Hull had been the *Constitution*'s captain for six years—an unusually long time. His first lieutenant was Charles Morris. As a midshipman during Decatur's famous attack on the *Philadelphia* in the war with Tripoli, Morris had been the first man to board the captured frigate.

Hull wanted to get to sea as fast as possible to avoid being shut up in Chesapeake Bay by a British blockade. He had orders to join Rogers, but he was unable to leave the Chesapeake for three weeks. At two o'clock in the afternoon on July 16, four days after departing the bay, Hull was off the coast of New Jersey, near what is now Atlantic City, when a lookout shouted from the main masthead that four sail were "to the northward." Hull thought they might be Rogers's squadron. A short time later, around four o'clock, the same lookout spotted another sail to the northeast, far from the others. Not knowing whether the ships were friends or foes, Hull steered toward the single ship, determined to "get near enough to make the night signal." As he got closer, Hull beat to quarters, in case this stranger turned out to be an enemy ship.

By ten o'clock the two ships were about seven miles apart. Hull made the private signal and kept it up for an hour. "But finding she would not answer it," he later reported, "I concluded that she and [the other four] ships were enemy." Hull now turned "southward and eastward" and tried to get away. The ship he had been chasing, the *Guerriere*, "hauled off after us," Hull wrote later, "showing a light, and occasionally making signals, supposed to be for the [other four] ships."

At dawn, Hull could see through the haze that all five ships were British. He had run into Commodore Broke's powerful Halifax squadron. Hull's only thought now was to escape. The four ships astern were no more than twelve miles away, while the *Guerriere* was only about "five or six miles." All the British ships had some wind and were in pursuit, but Hull reported that "the wind entirely left us and the ship would not steer." In desperation he hoisted out two cutters, and then six more of the ship's boats. He hauled two long 24-pounders to his cabin, where they protruded from the stern windows. Two other long cannon were taken to the spar deck and the taffrail cut so they could be used as stern guns.

At six o'clock, the *Shannon* opened fire from long distance with her bow chasers, but her round shot fell far short of its mark. The *Constitution*'s boats kept towing, while the British ships continued to gain. But when they came near Hull, they too lost their wind and started towing. At this point, Lieutenant Charles Morris suggested using kedge anchors to move the ship forward, and Hull immediately agreed. By seven o'clock the backbreaking task was well under way. It involved taking an anchor attached to a strong cable in a cutter and rowing it ahead some distance, dropping it, and using the *Constitution*'s capstan to draw the ship to the anchor. When the frigate came up to the first anchor, a second would be dropped and the ship brought up to it. In this manner the *Constitution* was moved forward.

By nine o'clock the *Belvidera*, the nearest British ship, fired her bow guns, and Hull shot back with his stern chasers, mounted in the cabin and quarterdeck. The *Belvidera*'s fire fell short, but Hull believed that some of his had hit home.

Shortly afterward, a breeze came up, and Hull took in two of his eight boats. A little later he pumped all of his fresh water overboard to lighten his load. Hour after hour, his men toiled at the oars and capstan bars, staying just ahead of the enemy. At eleven o'clock that night a light wind came up from the south. The *Constitution* overtook her boats, and Hull hoisted them in without losing any speed.

At daylight, Hull could see his pursuers still close behind. The wind had died and all eight of the *Constitution*'s boats were out again towing. In the evening, at about eleven o'clock, a wind came up, and the boats were hoisted in again. The breeze held during the rest of the night, and at daybreak, Hull was three miles ahead of his pursuers. By noon, the *Constitution* had increased its lead another mile. During the afternoon the gap widened. At six o'clock a squall temporarily hid the ship, and Hull managed to gain an additional mile. The following morning, July 19, he was twelve miles ahead of his pursuers and lengthening his lead. Hull then wetted his sails to make better use of the wind and gradually pulled away. At eight o'clock Commodore Broke gave up the chase.

Thinking that the British had probably blockaded New York by now and that Commodore Rogers had either left or become trapped, Hull sailed for Boston, reaching it on July 26. He loved the old city, but he was determined to get the *Constitution* to sea and engage the enemy. He had no orders, but if he had received any they probably would have directed him to remain in Boston and protect the harbor. Secretary Hamilton was leery of sending warships to sea only to be picked off by the British.

Fearing that a British squadron might show up at any time, Hull loaded what provisions he could while awaiting the first favorable wind, which arrived on August 2. At five-thirty in the morning he weighed anchor, leaving Boston on a southwest-by-south wind, planning to attack British shipping from the Gulf of St. Lawrence to Bermuda, and perhaps farther south.

During the next two weeks he took a few prizes and had a chance to drill his green crew every day. On the afternoon of August 19 at two o'clock, the *Constitution* was seven hundred miles east of Boston. The crew was about to begin afternoon drill, when a lookout spied a sail to the south. Hull viewed her through a telescope, thought she was interesting, and ordered all sail made to give chase. An hour later he could see that she was a full-rigged ship, making no attempt to get away. Half an hour later he knew he had run into a big English frigate—just what he had been hoping for.

Captain James Dacres, standing on HMS *Guerriere's* quarterdeck, also heard a lookout's cry that afternoon, describing a large sail to windward. Dacres, the son of the gallant commander of the *Carleton* during the famous battle of Valcour Island in 1776, hoped this stranger would be a heavy American frigate. He dearly wanted to fight one alone to prove they were overrated. He pulled a long telescope from a binnacle drawer, and as he surveyed the approaching ship, the outlines of a large enemy frigate became unmistakable. He was ecstatic and felt supremely confident. The British considered the *Guerriere* among the best in her class, and their frigates had been consistently victorious in individual fights with similar warships of every other European country, particularly those of France.

As the *Constitution* approached, Dacres backed his main topsail against the mast, stopping his ship and thereby delivering an invitation to battle.

Hull needed no invitation; he was eager for a fight, even though his opponent was a fearsome English warship with a veteran crew. At four-thirty Hull beat to quarters, and his men rushed to their battle stations. Working fast, he reorganized the ship's sails, taking down the royals, then hauling in the flying jib, staysails, and topgallants. The big courses were furled up and a second reef taken in the topsails. The crew appeared more eager than nervous and even gave three cheers. Hull was heartened by their enthusiasm.

At five o'clock, the two ships had drawn within two miles of each other, and Captain Dacres delivered two broadsides, but only a couple of balls thumped harmlessly against the *Constitution*'s thick hide. Dacres kept maneuvering and firing, but Hull did not reply. Instead, he closed steadily, holding his fire. Dacres also closed, impatient to start slugging it out toe-to-toe.

At six o'clock, when the *Constitution* was within "less than pistol shot" (twenty yards or so), Hull shouted, "Now, boys, hull her!" A lethal broadside of round shot and grape suddenly erupted from the *Constitution*, striking the *Guerriere* and staggering her. Broadsides then exploded from both ships. Dacres fired as rapidly as he could, and Hull did the same. But the *Constitution*'s shots were better directed than her opponent's. The *Guerriere*'s hull and sails were hit hard, and her mizzenmast was sent slumping over the starboard side. Dragging wreckage slowed the frigate and made her difficult to maneuver.

Dacres tried to compensate. In doing so he ran his bowsprit into the *Constitution*'s mizzenmast rigging. All the while, sharpshooters from the tops were raining musket balls down on the decks of both ships. Hull kept his stern guns active while Lieutenant Morris organized a boarding party. Before he could cross over, however, the *Constitution* lurched free, and as she did, the *Guerriere*'s fore- and mainmasts fell over the starboard side. As Dacres later described it, by then his ship was "a perfectly unmanageable wreck."

"In less than thirty minutes," Hull said in his report, "from the time we got alongside of the enemy (one of their finest frigates) she was left without a spar standing, and the hull cut to pieces, in such a manner as to make it difficult to keep her above water, and the *Constitution* in a state to be brought into action in two hours." Hull pulled off a slight distance to make repairs and waited to see if the *Guerriere*'s colors had been struck.

Recognizing that further fighting would be useless, Dacres wisely decided to fire a single gun to leeward, indicating that he had surrendered. His ship was dismasted, rolling like a log in the sea. Several of his big guns had torn loose and were traveling unimpeded around the deck, creating havoc. Dacres had thirteen killed and sixty-two wounded—a third of his men—while Hull had seven killed and seven wounded. The *Guerriere* was such a ruin that after Hull had removed her men and everything of use to him, he set her on fire. As the flames soared, they set off her guns intermittently. She was still burning when she slid below the surface, much of the surrounding debris being sucked down with her.

Hull now set his course for Boston, where he arrived on August 30. He anchored outside the harbor for the night at Nantasket Roads. In the morning he sailed into the inner harbor, where he received a hero's welcome. He passed Long Wharf and was saluted by a large concourse of people and all the merchant vessels in the harbor. After he set his hook near the navy yard, a joyful celebration commenced. Former President John Adams attended and could not have been more proud.

After the ceremonies and revelry, Hull unexpectedly requested appointment as commander of the Charlestown navy yard as his reward. Now that his father and brother were dead, he needed to be ashore to care for his extended family. Hull would never command another warship at sea. His friend William Bainbridge replaced him as the *Constitution*'s skipper. Commodore Rogers, having completed his seventy-day cruise, arrived with his squadron in Boston the day after Hull.

While Bostonians celebrated, the British, unwilling to acknowledge the superiority of American ships and crews, sought excuses. They were disturbed by how easily the *Constitution* had crushed the *Guerriere*. The defeat became a major political issue. As the *London Times* observed, "The loss of the *Guerriere* spread a degree of gloom through the town which it was painful to observe." The *London Evening Star* wrote, "Free ships make free goods. This is bold language to utter to a nation whose seamen have successively beaten every power in Europe into a confession of their superiority—a nation whose fleets have annihilated in succession, those of Spain, Holland, France, Russia and Denmark. Our maritime superiority is, in fact, part of the law of nations. . . . Is Great Britain to be driven from the proud eminence, which the blood and treasure of her sons have attained for her among the nations, by a piece of striped bunting flying at the mastheads of a few fir-built frigates, manned by a handful of bastards and outlaws?"

Parliament upbraided the Admiralty, which responded on November 18 by secretly ordering British frigates to avoid engaging "single-handed, the larger class of American ships." In Parliament, John Wilson Croker, secretary to the Admiralty, pointed out that the American frigates were "of a size . . . more resembling line-of-battle ships."

In the coming months, the Admiralty received more bad news, delivered by American men-of-war.

After completing repairs in New York, Captain David Porter headed out to sea in the 32-gun frigate *Essex*, bound for Florida. Finding no action there, he sailed north to Newfoundland and then turned south again. On July 11, he was off Bermuda when he ran into a seven-vessel British troop convoy, guarded by the 32-gun frigate *Minerva*. Porter challenged Captain Richard Hawkins, the *Minerva*'s skipper, to combat, but Hawkins refused and Porter did not attack him. Instead, he took one of his transports with two hundred soldiers aboard.

In the succeeding weeks, Porter captured seven more prizes, and on August 13, off the Newfoundland Grand Banks, he happened on HMS *Alert*, a 20-gun sloop-of-war. The British warship had disguised herself as a large, armed West Indiaman. Knowing that the *Essex* was an American frigate of superior strength, Captain L. P. Laugharne, the *Alert*'s skipper, thought he would surprise her, sail directly at her, deliver a well-directed broadside or two, gain an advantage, and then beat her into submission.

As the *Alert* drove toward the *Essex*, Porter watched her closely, giving the impression that he had been taken in by her disguise. But, while "concealing every appearance of preparation," he was ready for her attack. He allowed the *Alert* to approach to within pistol shot of his starboard quarter and then turned abruptly. As he did, the *Alert* got off a broadside, which, Porter reported, "did us no more injury than the cheers that accompanied it."

His initial gambit having failed, the *Alert*'s captain tried to flee, but Porter was on him. Hoisting a flag bearing the motto "Free Trade and Sailors' Rights," the *Essex* ranged up near the *Alert*'s starboard quarter, ready to unload a lethal broadside. Then, Porter recalled, "[Laugharne] avoided the dreadful consequences that [the *Essex*'s] broadside would in a few moments have produced by prudently striking his colors." The battle lasted eight minutes. The *Alert* was the first British warship taken by the United States in the war.

On his return voyage, Porter fell in with three British warships off Georges Bank, sixty miles east of Cape Cod. A chase began, but Porter eluded them. Afterward, judging that he was probably cut off from New York and Rhode Island, he put into Delaware Bay on September 7. During his cruise he had taken eight merchant vessels and one sloop-of-war, in addition to four hundred prisoners.

By the end of the first week of September the prospects for America's navy had brightened considerably. Bolstered by the *Constitution*'s escape from Commodore Broke and her unexpected trouncing of the *Guerriere*, as well as Porter's success with the *Alert*, Secretary Hamilton settled on a new strategy for his blue water fleet. In something of a compromise between the views of Rogers and Decatur, Hamilton divided the navy's large warships into three squadrons, consisting of "two frigates and a small brig" each. Commodore

Rogers in the *President* would lead the first group, Commodore Decatur in the *United States* the second, and Commodore Bainbridge in the *Constitution* the third. Hamilton ordered the three squadron commanders "to pursue that course, which to the commanding officer, may under all circumstances, appear the most expedient to afford protection to our trade and to annoy the enemy; returning into port, as speedily as circumstances will permit, consistently with the great objects in view."

Commodore Rogers was to command the *President*, the *Congress*, and the *Wasp*. Decatur was assigned the *United States*, *Chesapeake*, and *Argus*. Bainbridge had the *Constitution*, *Essex*, and *Hornet*. To complicate matters, not all the ships were in the same locales as the others in their squadron, nor in the same state of repair. When Rogers left Boston on October 8, 1812, he was accompanied only by the *Congress*, and by Decatur in the *United States* and the *Argus*. Rogers hoped to deceive the British as to American strategy by leaving port with Decatur. Four days later, they separated; Decatur and the *Argus* steered south while Rogers and the *Congress* continued eastward.

As Rogers and Decatur were carrying out Secretary Hamilton's vague orders, Captain Jacob Jones of Delaware, commander of the 18-gun sloop-of-war *Wasp*, was traveling north to join Rogers's squadron. Jones had been a midshipman under John Barry in the *United States* during the Quasi-War with France and had risen to the rank of master commandant. On the evening of October 17, he was off Cape Hatteras when he spied several sails in the distance. He decided to head toward the strangers, but it was so late that he "shortened sail and steered the remainder of the night the course [he] perceived them [to be] on." At daybreak on October 18, Jones discovered that he had been trailing seven large ships. He steered toward them and found they were six well-armed British merchantmen, escorted by a powerful sloop-of-war, the 22-gun *Frolic*, under Captain Thomas Whinyates. Without hesitating, Jones attacked.

When the two ships had closed to within fifty yards of each other, they ran parallel for a time, firing broadsides in a rough sea.

As the *Wasp* pitched and rolled, her gunners got off three shots to every two of the *Frolic's*. Within four minutes, the *Wasp* unleashed a broadside that cracked the *Frolic's* main topmast. With devastating accuracy, Jones decimated the enemy. The two antagonists then drew closer and became entangled. Jones's second in command, Lieutenant James Biddle of Philadelphia, led a boarding party, jumping onto the *Frolic's* forecastle. When he did, she immediately surrendered. So many of *Frolic's* crew had been killed or wounded in the exchange of broadsides that she could no longer resist. Jones's savage attack had killed thirty and wounded another fifty, among them Captain Whinyates. The *Wasp* had five killed and five wounded.

Jones immediately set about repairing battle damage to both ships in preparation for taking them home. Within hours, however, a British 74-gun line-of-battle ship, HMS *Poictiers*, under Captain John P. Beresford, happened on the scene. Jones endeavored to escape but he was in bad condition, and the *Poictiers* soon caught up with him. Jones was forced to strike his colors. He and his crew became prisoners of war and were taken to Bermuda. But they were soon exchanged as part of a larger prisoner swap, and Jones returned to New York a hero. Congress awarded the *Wasp's* officers and crew $25,000; Jones and Biddle received promotions.

After separating from Rogers on October 12, Decatur and the *United States* parted company with the *Argus*, and both ships cruised alone. On October 25, Decatur was standing on his quarterdeck in a heavy sea when the lookout at the main masthead shouted that a strange sail was to windward, bearing down hard. The *United States* was cruising midway between the Azores and the Cape Verde Islands. The stranger turned out to be the 38-gun frigate HMS *Macedonian*, under Captain John S. Carden, a man Decatur knew. When the ships had closed to within shooting range, Decatur stood off and fired his long 24-pounders. Carden replied, but the American crew was firing faster and more accurately. Decatur had trained his men well. When the *Macedonian* moved closer, she received a pounding from Decatur's carronades. In a little over two hours the British frigate, as her captain later explained, "[had her] mizzen mast shot away . . . topmasts shot away . . . main yard shot in pieces, [and] lower masts badly wounded, lower rigging cut to pieces, a small portion only of the foresail left to the foreyard, all the guns on the quarterdeck and forecastle disabled but two . . . two also on the main deck disabled, and several shot between wind and water, a very great proportion of the crew killed and wounded." Captain Carden struck his colors. Of his 301-man crew, thirty-six were dead and sixty-eight wounded. Decatur, with a crew of 478, had five killed and seven wounded.

After hurriedly making repairs, Decatur brought the captured *Macedonian* home. He intended to sail her into New London, Connecticut, but at the last moment the *United States* and her prize became separated in a fog. Decatur wound up sailing into New London alone on December 4, while the *Macedonian* made it into Newport, Rhode Island, where she received a tumultuous greeting. She was the only British frigate ever taken to an American port as a prize.

After the *Macedonian* was refitted, Madison took her into the U.S. Navy; in recognition of his victory over the *Frolic*, he appointed Captain Jacob Jones her skipper. Madison also held a gala in Washington to celebrate Decatur's victory. Secretary Hamilton attended and was so drunk he could barely stand up. The president was disgusted and soon replaced him with William Jones, a Philadelphia merchant and former congressman. Jefferson had offered to appoint Jones as secretary of the navy back in 1801, but Jones had turned him down. Now he was eager to take the job. The improvement in the Navy Department was immediately noticeable.

The third squadron that Secretary Hamilton had organized back in September was under the command of Commodore Bainbridge in the *Constitution*. He stood out from Boston on October 27, 1812, with the sloop-of-war *Hornet*, under Master Commandant James Lawrence, who had been Decatur's second in command when they burned the *Philadelphia* during the war with Tripoli. Bainbridge planned to rendezvous in the South Atlantic with the frigate *Essex*, which was refitting in Philadelphia, still under the command of David Porter. Porter had been Bainbridge's first lieutenant on the ill-fated *Philadelphia* when she was captured by the Tripolitans in 1803. Porter and Bainbridge had been prisoners in Tripoli together and were very close. Bainbridge had orders to cruise the northeast coast of Brazil and attack the extensive British commerce sailing past there on the way to India.

On December 13, Bainbridge and Lawrence arrived at the city of San Salvadore in the Brazilian state of Bahia, where they hoped to meet *Essex*. She wasn't there, but they did find a British sloop-of-war, *Bonne Citoyenne*, in the harbor. Since San Salvadore was a neutral Portuguese port, Bainbridge could not attack, so he departed but left Lawrence to try to lure the British captain out. Even though the ships were evenly matched, Lawrence was certain the *Hornet* could defeat the *Bonne Citoyenne*.

Lawrence challenged Captain Pitt Barnaby Greene, the *Bonne Citoyenne*'s skipper, to a duel outside the port, pledging that the *Constitution* would not interfere. To Lawrence's surprise, Greene turned him down and remained anchored. Greene was carrying 500,000 pounds in specie and did not want to risk it. Or he might have been worried that the *Constitution* was lurking offshore to trap him.

Bainbridge had indeed left, and while he was cruising along the Bahia coast on December 29, he spied the 38-gun British frigate HMS *Java*, under Captain Henry Lambert, who had a captured American merchantman with him. The *Java* was sailing close enough to shore for Bainbridge to see the coast. He watched as Lambert sent his prize into San Salvadore and then raced toward the *Constitution*. It was nine in the morning. At two o'clock the frigates had drawn within firing range. Bainbridge unleashed a broadside and Lambert did the same, killing and wounding several men on the *Constitution* with the first balls. Firing continued at a fast pace as the two ships drew closer. The *Java* was faster and more agile, and Captain Lambert tried to forereach on Bainbridge, cross the *Constitution*'s bow, and rake her. But when he did, Bainbridge wore his ship and the two ran off parallel. The combatants continued their fire, but the *Constitution*'s guns were faster and more accurate, and the blasts began to tell on the swifter *Java*. Bainbridge shot away the *Java*'s bowsprit and jib-boom, making her hard to maneuver. Bainbridge then poured a broadside into her stern, creating havoc as the deadly balls traveled the length of the ship.

Just after three o'clock, the *Java* was so damaged that Captain Lambert decided boarding the *Constitution* was his only hope. Before he could, Bainbridge raked him again, ruining his chance. The *Java*'s topmast was cut off, and her foremast gave way. The tangled wreckage fell partly on deck and partly over the side. The two ships now drew apart and continued to fire. Bainbridge raked the *Java* once more, and shortly after three o'clock, Captain Lambert was mortally wounded by a musket ball fired from the *Constitution*'s maintop. He was taken below, and Lieutenant Henry Chads, who was himself wounded, took his place. Although the ship was nearly disabled, Chads refused to strike his colors and continued to fight. A little after four o'clock, the *Java*'s guns fell silent.

Seeing that the *Java*'s colors were down in her main rigging and that she was "a complete wreck," Bainbridge supposed she had struck. He ceased firing, pulled off, and made some repairs to the *Constitution*'s rigging. At four-twenty the *Java*'s mainmast fell, and she was floating like a log in the sea. But to Bainbridge's amazement, Lieutenant Chads had still not struck. Bainbridge now maneuvered into position to rake the *Java* once more. Seeing how desperate his situation was, the valiant Chads finally struck his colors at five-twenty-five.

Two days later, after the *Java* had been cleared of men and whatever goods Bainbridge wanted, he set her on fire. In minutes a gigantic explosion scattered her wreckage over the ocean. In his report to the Admiralty Chads wrote, "I cannot conclude this letter without expressing my grateful acknowledgement thus publicly for the generous treatment Captain Lambert and his officers have experienced from our gallant enemy Commodore Bainbridge and his officers."

Bainbridge now decided to end his cruising. He returned to Boston to make repairs, tend the wounded, deliver his prisoners, and report the victory. He reached port on February 27, 1813. Lawrence and the *Hornet*, meanwhile, had sailed north separately and on the way fought the 18-gun British brig *Peacock* at the mouth of the Demara River in British Guyana, sinking her after a brief fight. Lawrence too went back to Massachusetts and landed at Martha's Vineyard with news of his victory, as well as £20,000 in gold and silver taken from the British packet *Resolution*.

The success of America's warships overshadowed the remarkable performance of her privateers. During the time the blue water navy was dazzling friend and foe, American privateers operating in Europe, the South Atlantic, the Indian Ocean, and the Far East had taken more than two hundred enemy merchantmen. The British had been concerned about privateers from the beginning of the war. Remembering their experience during the Revolution, Parliament passed the Convoy Act at the start of the war, requiring all merchantmen traveling to and from North America, Newfoundland, or the West Indies to be convoyed—with no exceptions.

In spite of this protection, privateers thrived. One of the more famous was the *America*, out of Salem, Massachusetts. She was heavily armed and exceptionally fast, which made her an excellent commerce raider. During the war she took forty-one prizes and made a fortune for her Yankee owners. Even more successful was the Baltimore privateer *Rossie*, skippered by Joshua Barney. On July 11, 1812, Barney left Chesapeake Bay and sailed north toward Nova Scotia, intending to hunt between there and Newfoundland. In the next six weeks he captured eighteen prizes before putting into Newport, Rhode Island, for supplies. Afterward, he sailed to the Caribbean, where he had even more luck, returning to Baltimore on October 22. In all, he took 3,698 tons of British shipping worth as much as $1.5 million.

Although single-ship actions of the Continental Navy had a negligible effect on the overall Revolutionary War, the victories of America's warships in the opening phase of the War of 1812 had a decided influence on events. The British blew the incidents way out of proportion, feeling that the reputation of the Royal Navy had been sullied and needed to be restored. Time and again the Americans demonstrated superior speed and accuracy in their gunnery. The Admiralty stopped reporting losses to the public and strengthened its gunnery practice. It also added substantially to the number and size of the fleet in American waters, until the Halifax station had ten 74s and one 50-gun ship. It planned to have thirty frigates and fifty sloops-of-war and gun brigs on station, but those figures were never quite realized. In addition, Newfoundland had one 50-gun ship, two frigates, and six smaller men-of-war. The Leeward Islands had one 74, four frigates, and eleven other vessels. And one 74, two frigates, and six smaller warships were off the Brazilian coast. By any measure, it was now a formidable force.

If the Admiralty had put this fleet into operation before the war, it might have prevented the stunning defeats it suffered. But London had always underestimated the Americans. Madison's declaration of war had come as a surprise, as had the performance of his warships. It was now obvious that the American men-of-war were superior to their British counterparts.

The Admiralty severely criticized Admiral Sir John Borlase Warren, whose command included not only the North American station but the Jamaican and Leeward Islands stations as well. When Warren replaced Admiral Sawyer in August 1812, he was expected to either destroy or blockade the American navy. The Admiralty never wanted another American warship active on the high seas. Warren was also directed to blockade the American coast south of New England and conduct hit-and-run raids, particularly in the Chesapeake Bay area. In regard to New England, he was to patrol offshore but not blockade it, since New Englanders opposed "Madison's War" and were actively helping the British in Canada. Warren was also tasked with preventing privateers from leaving port, or if they did, intercepting them. And he had convoy duty to perform, which occupied many of his smaller warships.

As the navy's victories were celebrated in the United States, the Republican Congress changed its attitude toward expenditures for the fleet. It had adjourned on July 6, 1812, without making any provision for enlarging the navy. At the end of November 1812, however, Congress considered legislation to dramatically expand the fleet, including the construction of 74-gun battleships. The arguments were spirited, but the public mood had changed, and the pro-navy forces had the upper hand. Their opponents directed their arguments at the 74-gun ships. They believed them to be too costly and worried about creating a permanent naval establishment, large enough to engage in foreign adventures after the war was over. In the final days of 1812, the Congress, in a series of votes, agreeed to build four sail of the line and six more frigates. The final vote on January 2, 1813, was 70 to 56. In March Congress approved six more sloops-of-war. This change was permanent; the old Jeffersonian strategy of dispensing with the blue water fleet and restricting the navy to defending rivers and harbors with gunboats and barges was jettisoned forever.

Ironically, the heavy frigates spurned by Madison and Jefferson were now supplying the political juice Madison needed to carry on the war. He and Jefferson had never built a frigate. Those in operation had all been constructed during the Washington and Adams administrations. Madison, Monroe, Jefferson, and their supporters had assumed that in any war with Britain the frigates would do as poorly as the warships of the Continental Navy had done. They took it for granted that American men-of-war were inferior. Now the despised frigates and sloops-of-war were not only building support for the war, even in New England, but were contributing to the president's bid for reelection in 1812.

Riding high on Madison's unpopularity in the northeast, De Witt Clinton of New York was making the election uncomfortably close. The morale-boosting naval victories were a factor in putting Madison over the top in Pennsylvania; he took twenty-five of its critical electoral votes for a narrow win, capturing 128 electoral votes to Clinton's 89.

The naval victories also compensated for the shock of defeats in Canada. Before the war, American prospects at sea against the Royal Navy seemed negligible, while in Canada they appeared to be excellent. Instead, early in the war there were continuous naval victories, but in Canada there was unrelieved failure.

Madison and Jefferson had little appreciation of the actual state of the army. It did not take them long, however, to learn how weak it was. General William Hull (Isaac's uncle), a sixty-year-old veteran of the Revolutionary War, had crossed the Detroit River and invaded Canada in mid-July, intending to capture Fort Malden (now Amherstburg), the headquarters for British forces in southwestern upper Canada. Because the British controlled Lake Erie and Lake Ontario, Hull had logistics problems, and he could not be supplied by water. His provisions had to travel overland and were subject to Indian attack.

As Hull proceeded toward Fort Malden, word came on July 17 that the British had captured Fort Michilimackinac on Michilimackinac Island in northern Lake Huron. Hull got nervous and retreated across the river to Fort Detroit, sending word to the commander at Fort Dearborn (now Chicago) to come to his aid. Indian fighters, however, wiped out the reinforcements and with British help took the fort. Hull had nightmarish visions of the aroused Indians descending on him from the west. Surprised at Hull's timidity, General Isaac Brock, the aggressive British commander at Fort Malden, boldly pursued him, even though he had a force only half the size of Hull's. Brock crossed the Detroit River and encamped before Fort Detroit, where he called for the Americans to surrender. Unaccountably, Hull did so without a fight. On August 16, 1812, he gave up four thousand men—a large part of the entire American army. The British now controlled the northwest, as well as Lake Ontario and Lake Erie.

Madison and the country were dumbfounded. So many Americans had settled in Canada near the border that Madison almost expected them to greet Hull as a liberator and hand that part of Canada over to him. General Hull had issued a call for support from these nominal Canadians, and even the Canadian authorities, including General Brock, anticipated that a good number of them would respond. When they didn't, Hull had to fight and proved utterly inept. A court-martial later ordered him shot, but Madison remanded the sentence.

While Hull was conducting his operation, the president received news in August that London had repealed the orders in council, but there was no word about impressment. He had made it plain, almost from the start of the war, that he was open to a negotiated settlement if the British would renounce impressment, but they refused. Madison felt he had no choice but to continue fighting.

Before the war started, Sir George Prevost, the governor-general of Canada, had assumed he would be on the defensive, with minimal support from England, as long as the war in Europe lasted. Even with the unexpected successes at Michilimackinac, Fort Dearborn, and Detroit, he would not consider taking the offensive. The victories allowed him to concentrate his tiny army near Montreal, where he thought the real battle for Canada would take place.

Beyond Hull's attack on Fort Malden to secure upper Canada and the northwest, the American plan for the Canadian invasion included a thrust in the Niagara area and another directly at Montreal via Lake Champlain. On October 13, U.S. Captain John E. Wool led a small force of regulars and attacked Queenston on the Canadian side of the Niagara River above the falls. He expected reinforcements from the New York militia under General Stephen Van Renssalaer, a political appointee with no qualifications for the job. Renssalaer's militiamen, however, refused to cross the Niagara River, claiming they were mustered to defend the United States, not invade Canada. The British then counterattacked. Led by General Brock, who had rushed from Detroit to the Niagara area, they crushed Wool and won the bloody battle of Queenston Heights. Brock was killed in the melee, depriving England of her best fighting general in Canada. American General Alexander Smyth, another incompetent given to making bombastic speeches, replaced Renssalaer but only managed to maintain a standoff along the Niagara frontier for the rest of 1812.

General Henry Dearborn, the former secretary of war and a Revolutionary War veteran, had charge of the Montreal campaign.

He was at Plattsburg on Lake Champlain with a sizable force, but it was ill equipped and unprepared, and winter had already arrived before he set out on November 20, 1812. His progress was painfully slow. As he approached the Canadian border, his militiamen refused to invade, claiming, as had the men serving under Renssalaer, that they had been mustered for defensive purposes only, not to attack another country. Dearborn was forced to return to Plattsburg for the winter.

The defeats in Canada shocked Madison. His strategy for winning the war had failed. "So wretched a succession of generals," Jefferson lamented, "never before destroyed the fairest expectations of a nation." But since Madison could think of no better plan, he decided to resume the invasion in the spring of 1813 and hope for the best.

The naval victories had been a welcome surprise, and the president was effusive in his praise. "Already," he told Congress, "the gallant exploits of our naval heroes proved to the world our inherent capacity to maintain our rights on one element." But while he was looking forward to more successes, the Admiralty was deploying so many additional warships on its American station that the U.S. Navy could not hope to continue its achievements. Madison's and Jefferson's neglect had left the service so truncated that the country's naval heroes could not carry on, at least not on the high seas. The lakes were a different matter; here the American navy was not at the disadvantage it was on the ocean. The Admiralty had put almost no resources into dominating the Great Lakes or Lake Champlain. Operating close to home, the American navy had a good chance to catch up and surpass British naval power on the lakes.

The new secretary of the navy, William Jones, took the oath of office on January 19, 1813. Unlike his predecessor, he understood the strategic importance of the Great Lakes and Lake Champlain. He was coming to office at a particularly inopportune moment, for although America's navy had done well up until now, its fortunes were bound to change as the British directed more resources to the American war. In a few weeks Washington would know what London already knew, that Napoleon had been defeated in Russia. It now appeared certain that Britain and her allies would finally crush him. With the European war no longer a distraction, the British could unleash their war machine on the United States.

Jones had little to work with. In a matter of months the Royal Navy could blockade America's chief ports, making it difficult for her few warships or her commerce to operate. The additions to the navy that Congress had voted were wrongheaded, as far as Jones was concerned. He thought smaller sloops-of-war, not 74s, were what was needed right now. Smaller warships could run the British blockade and, once out to sea, attack her trade. He also saw opportunity on the lakes, where the Royal Navy was weak.

As 1813 progressed, things got tougher and tougher for the American navy. The difficulties that a small sea force would inevitably encounter fighting the Royal Navy—which Jefferson and Madison had never tired of pointing out—became fully evident. By the end of the year, as Henry Adams wrote, "the American Navy had almost disappeared."

During the first part of the year, Commodore Stephen Decatur's *United States* and his trophy, the *Macedonian*, along with the sloop-of-war *Hornet*, found themselves trapped in New York by a powerful British squadron. In May 1813, Decatur attempted to run past the blockade, first by way of Sandy Hook and then, when that proved impossible, through Hell Gate and Long Island Sound.

In attempting to break out into the Atlantic from the sound, however, Decatur was nearly captured by a superior British force under the command of Sir Thomas Hardy, Nelson's favorite captain. Decatur barely escaped by turning back and running into the Thames River, where he anchored off New London. A short time later, thinking his ships too exposed, he moved five miles upriver to Gales Ferry, where he had much better protection. There the *United States* and the *Macedonian* remained for the rest of the war. The *Hornet* managed to slip past the British blockade off the mouth of the Thames in November 1813, only to slip back into New York, where she waited with the *President* and the sloop-of-war *Peacock* for a chance to get back to sea.

During 1813, John Rogers continued to cruise in the *President* with as little luck as he had on his first two cruises in 1812. His second cruise had lasted from October 8, 1812, to December 31. After sailing eleven thousand miles, he reentered Boston harbor at the end of the year, having seen only five other vessels, two of which he captured. Following these long journeys, the *President* needed repairs, which proceeded slowly during the severe winter. Rogers did not get back to sea again until April 30, 1813. The 38-gun *Congress*, under Captain John Smith, accompanied him, but they soon parted company, and Rogers sailed alone. Despite spending time patrolling around the British Isles with the Admiralty looking for him, Rogers captured only twelve insignificant prizes, putting back into Newport, Rhode Island, on September 27, 1813. He then went on a fourth cruise, evading the British blockade and sailing out of Newport on December 4, 1813. But he again accomplished little and put back into New York on February 18, 1814. The British blockade kept the *President* trapped there through the remainder of the year.

The *Constitution* was even less productive in 1813. Returning to Boston in March 1813 after her victory over the *Java*, she needed a complete overhaul. She was an old ship that had been in three wars. Repairs dragged on for the rest of the year under Captain Bainbridge and then under her new captain, Charles Stewart.

No new frigates were available to substitute for her. The navy even had to take supplies and men away from the Charlestown navy yard and send them to Oliver Hazard Perry on Lake Erie. Captain Stewart and the refurbished *Constitution* did not clear Boston Light and get back to sea again until December 31, 1813.

In 1813 the *Constellation* was unable to get past the British blockade at Norfolk, Virginia, and remained there for the rest of the war. The *John Adams* was laid up in New York harbor, while the 28-gun *Adams* remained trapped in Chesapeake Bay.

As 1813 progressed and the British blockade tightened, American commerce suffered a severe blow as well. On May 26, Admiral Warren declared "a strict and rigorous blockade of the ports and harbors of New York, Charleston, Port Royal, Savannah, and the river Mississippi." He also blockaded Delaware Bay and Long Island Sound off New London. By the end of the year, trade had dropped to 11 percent of what it had been in 1811. In addition, Warren conducted surprise raids along the coast at will, particularly in Chesapeake Bay. The rabidly anti-American Rear Admiral Sir George Cockburn led the attacks, striking Norfolk and the area around Lynnhaven Bay, and Havre de Grasse in Maryland, as well as Frederickton and Georgetown on Maryland's eastern shore.

The British were not blockading the coast of New England, but a large squadron was stationed off the Thames River in Connecticut. Their warships patrolled north and east of there, at times lurking near the principal ports, particularly in Massachusetts. Two British frigates, the *Shannon* and the *Tenedos*, had been patrolling off Boston on April 9, 1813, when the USS *Chesapeake* slipped past them into the harbor to replenish supplies and make repairs. Once there, Captain James Lawrence, who had been promoted for defeating the *Peacock,* was given command. Lawrence had been scheduled to replace Bainbridge in the *Constitution*, but she was laid up for extensive repairs, whereas the *Chesapeake* was nearly ready to go. Lawrence would have preferred the *Constitution*; the *Chesapeake* was considered an unlucky ship.

While Lawrence was preparing the *Chesapeake*, the *Tenedos* disappeared, leaving only the *Shannon* under Captain Philip Bowes Vere Broke. He challenged Lawrence to come out and fight him alone, even though the Admiralty had explicitly forbidden such duels. In fact, Broke had sent the *Tenedos* away to make his invitation more appealing.

Lawrence never received Broke's invitation, but he didn't need one. He was anxious to fight, and he came out on June 1 to confront the *Shannon*, which was provocatively stationed just off Boston Light. When Broke saw the *Chesapeake* approaching, he steered toward Cape Ann under easy sail so that the fight would be farther away from Boston, where small boats might come to assist Lawrence. Broke was confident of his crew. Most had been with him an unusually long time and were trained to a degree uncommon in the harried Royal Navy of the time. Lawrence, on the other hand, had just taken command of the *Chesapeake* and had no experience with his officers or crew.

When the two frigates were well off Cape Ann, Lawrence bore down on the *Shannon*. Broke waited patiently for him to get within hailing distance. Then the ships exchanged devastating broadsides. After a few minutes the *Chesapeake* pulled slightly ahead and presented her quarter to the *Shannon*. Broke fired into her, sweeping her quarterdeck while marksmen rained a hail of musket balls down on her. Captain Lawrence was mortally wounded and taken below. The first lieutenant and sailing master were killed; the *Chesapeake* was momentarily leaderless. Taking full advantage, Broke led boarders onto her quarterdeck and slashed his way to the forecastle, stepping over numerous bodies felled by marine marksmen from the *Shannon's* tops. Down below, Lawrence in a weak voice ordered, "Don't give up the ship." But it was too late. Broke had command of the upper deck, and Lawrence's men surrendered. Broke also was severely wounded, his head nearly cut off, but he survived.

News of the *Shannon's* triumph was greeted with wild enthusiasm in Britain, showing the country's deep feelings about the American victories in 1812. In the United States there was sorrow, but also pride at Lawrence's courage in his order not to give up the ship. His words would be taken up by the navy, soon becoming a permanent source of inspiration.

The American navy did achieve some successes on the high seas in 1813. An example was the 16-gun brig *Argus*, under Captain William Allen of Rhode Island. She was exactly the kind of warship Secretary Jones thought would be most effective against British commerce, which was where he thought the American blue water fleet ought to focus. Captain Allen was renowned in the navy as the first officer aboard the *United States* when she defeated the *Macedonian*. Commodore Decatur had praised Allen effusively, giving him credit for the victory. According to Decatur, Allen's outstanding gunnery had won the day: "My first Lieutenant William H. Allen, who has served with me upwards of five years and to his unmerited exertions in disciplining the crew is to be imputed the obvious superiority of our gunnery exhibited in the result of this contest." Decatur allowed Allen the honor of bringing the *Macedonian* into Newport.

On June 18, 1813, the agile, shallow-draft *Argus* slipped out of New York harbor past the British blockade and sailed to France with William H. Crawford, the new American ambassador to Paris, on board. Allen landed at L'Orient on July 11, deposited Crawford, and then cruised from the English Channel to the coast of Ireland for a month, collecting an astonishing twenty prizes, throwing London into an uproar and sending insurance rates soaring.

The Admiralty initiated an intensive search, and on August 13 Allen relaxed his guard enough to give the British hunters an opening. That day, he had captured a brig carrying a cargo of wine from Oporto and had allowed his crew to drink whatever they pleased, presumably doing the same himself. Afterward, as was his practice, he burned the prize. The flames soared high in the night, providing a perfect beacon for the British brig *Pelican*, which had been looking for the *Argus*. The *Pelican* raced after her prey and caught her at five o'clock the next morning. Allen saw the enemy approaching in plenty of time to escape, and since his orders called for him to engage in commerce raiding, he should have fled and resumed his remarkable career. He could not resist a duel with the oncoming brig, however, which appeared to be roughly the same size as the *Argus,* and so he chose to wait and fight.

The first shots were exchanged at six o'clock. Almost immediately Captain Allen's left leg was shot away, and he collapsed on the deck, mortally wounded. Shortly afterward, grapeshot wounded the first officer. The second officer fought the ship for another half hour but inflicted little damage, while the *Pelican* mercilessly pummeled the *Argus*, forcing her to surrender.

The British showed their respect for the brave Captain Allen by burying him with full military honors in Plymouth. Eight Royal Navy captains acted as pallbearers and two companies of marines as an honor guard. The surviving members of the *Argus* crew—officers and men—attended, as did the American vice consul and a number of ordinary local people.

Another exception to the dreary record of the American navy in 1813 was the duel between the USS *Enterprise* and the British brig *Boxer* near Portland, in the Maine district of Massachusetts. The *Enterprise* had been built in St. Michaels, Maryland, and completed in 1799, in time to serve with distinction in the Quasi-War with France and then in the war against Tripoli. She had undergone many changes in her career, and when she was on patrol in Maine she was a brig with fourteen 18-pound carronades and two long 9s. Old and slow, she had to hug the coast so that if a larger enemy cruiser appeared she could run into a shallow place for safety. Lieutenant William Burrows, her skipper, a Pennsylvanian, was just short of twenty-eight years of age. The navy had ordered him to curb the activities of smugglers, privateers, and pirates conducting illicit trade between New England and Halifax.

Sailing eastward on September 5, 1813, Captain Burrows saw a strange vessel lurking near Seguin Island at the mouth of the Kennebec River. On a clear day, Seguin was visible from Portland. Burrows investigated. The stranger turned out to be HMS *Boxer*, a brig carrying twelve 18-pound carronades and two long 6s. Although somewhat smaller than the *Enterprise*, she soon hoisted English colors and sailed laboriously against a light wind toward Burrows. Despite having the weather gauge, Burrows was content to let the *Boxer* struggle over to meet him.

Captain Samuel Blyth, the *Boxer*'s twenty-nine-year-old skipper, kept tacking, straining toward the *Enterprise*. Both ships held their fire until they were within half-pistol shot of each other—about ten yards. It was three-thirty in the afternoon. Suddenly cheers rang out from both vessels as they unleashed their first deadly broadsides. As acrid yellow-gray smoke curled around both brigs, stinging the eyes of crew members and making it difficult for them to see, both captains fell. An 18-pound ball had crashed through Blyth's body, killing him instantly. Meanwhile, grapeshot had pierced Burrows's thigh. He slumped to the deck, mortally wounded. Refusing to be taken below, he remained on deck, blood trickling from his wounds, as the battle raged on. *Enterprise* managed to surge ahead and rake the *Boxer* repeatedly by the bow, creating havoc along the entire length of the ship. The *Boxer* fought back gamely, but after forty-five minutes, with one-third of her men dead or injured, she surrendered. Captain Burrows was still alive and knew he had won the day.

Seven men were killed on the *Boxer* and thirteen injured, while four died on the *Enterprise* and eight were wounded. The *Enterprise* was not damaged nearly as much as her opponent, and she struggled into Portland with her prize. The city received her with open arms, organizing an elaborate ceremony to honor the two captains. Many dignitaries attended, including Isaac Hull, along with a large number of townspeople. Then, with the surviving officers and crews of both warships as mourners, Blyth and Burrows were buried side by side with full military honors in Portland's Eastern Cemetery near Henry Wadsworth Longfellow's home. He recalled the disturbing occasion in his poem "Lost Youth."

> *I remember the sea-fight far away,*
> *How it thundered o'er the tide!*
> *And the dead captains, as they lay*
> *In their graves, o'erlooking the tranquil bay*
> *Where they in battle died.*
> *And the sound of that mournful song*
> *Goes through me with a thrill:*
> *"A boy's will is the wind's will,*
> *And the thoughts of youth are long, long thoughts."*

The *Essex,* unlike the other frigates, was not stranded in port. She was in the Pacific, giving a good account of herself. Originally she was to have been part of the three-ship squadron under Commodore Bainbridge, but Captain Porter left the Delaware capes two days after Bainbridge sailed from Boston in the *Constitution,* and they never found each other. Porter stopped at every rendezvous point that he and Bainbridge had arranged, but without success. Porter was left alone in the South Atlantic to decide what to do.

Having discussed the possibility of the squadron sailing into the Pacific with Bainbridge, Porter chose to go there in search of glory. He promised his crew an exciting voyage. "The Pacific

Ocean affords us many friendly ports," he told them. "The unprotected British commerce on the coasts of Chile, Peru, and Mexico,
will give you an abundant supply of wealth; and the girls of the
Sandwich Islands [Hawaii], shall reward you for your sufferings
during the passage around Cape Horn."

The suffering Porter mentioned turned out to be greater than
he had imagined. In weathering Cape Horn the *Essex* was battered
by hurricane-force winds and mountainous seas that almost destroyed her. She barely survived. But with brilliant seamanship and
a good deal of luck, Porter reached Chile's Valparaiso harbor on
March 14, 1813. He didn't know what kind of reception he would
get, but he was in dire need of supplies and his men were desperate
for shore leave. He also required information about the British,
their warships in that part of the world, and their whalers.

To his surprise, Porter was greeted warmly by the revolutionary
Chilean government of Luis Carrera. Taking advantage of the hospitality, Porter put on board as much jerked beef and other provisions
as the *Essex* could conveniently stow, filled his water casks, and
headed down the Chilean coast to Peru in search of British whalers
and privateers. From there he sailed to the Galapagos Islands, five
hundred miles off the coast of Peru, where, he had been told, British
whalers congregated. The *Essex* cruised in the waters of the Galapagos from April 17 to October 3. The hilly islands, formed by erupting
volcanoes, teemed with exotic wildlife. Porter carefully recorded
what he saw—acres of enormous iguanas, huge sharks, sea lions,
seals, squid, penguins, pelicans and other birds, and giant tortoises,
weighing three hundred pounds, that his men ate with relish. Porter
found wood there but little water, and could only fill his casks with
excruciating difficulty.

During her time in the Galapagos the *Essex* captured twelve British vessels, most of them hunting spermaceti whales. All the ships
were armed, but none presented a problem for the frigate. Porter sent
three of them to Valparaiso and three more to America. He kept one
as a store ship for supplies from the other ships. The rest also stayed
with him. America now had a small fleet in the Pacific. The strongest
of the captures, the *Atlantic*, was converted into a 20-gun warship and

christened *Essex Junior*. First Lieutenant John Downes became her captain. Porter had a high regard for him. Porter dispatched *Essex Junior* with three prizes to Valparaiso, where Downes was told that British hunters had been sent by the Admiralty to destroy the *Essex*. Porter welcomed the attention; it was proof he was having an impact, and it held out the prospect of a fight with an English frigate, which he craved more than anything else.

Valparaiso seemed to Porter the most likely place to meet the British. He might have sailed back there immediately, but after being at sea for nearly a year, the *Essex* needed repairs and his men shore leave. He wanted the *Essex* to be at her fighting best when he tangled with the Royal Navy. And so, Porter sailed with his remaining prizes to distant Nooaheevah (Nuku Hiva) in the Marquesas Islands, twenty-five hundred miles southeast of Hawaii. At Nooaheevah, he had "the most friendly intercourse with the natives" and completely overhauled his ship, including fresh caulking and a new set of water casks. He spent seven weeks there, working, enjoying the hospitality of the local people, and becoming entangled in their wars with other tribes. With four months' provisions stowed in the big frigate, Porter left the islands and set a course for Chile on December 12. He left three of his ships under Marine Lieutenant John Gamble at Nooaheevah.

At this point, Porter might have returned to the United States. His voyage had been successful, and he had no need to confront a British squadron that was certain to be stronger than his. He later wrote of what he had accomplished, "I have completely broken up the British navigation in the Pacific, the vessels that were not captured by me were laid up and dared not venture out, I had afforded the most ample protection to our own vessels which on my arrival were very numerous and unprotected. The valuable British whale fishery is completely destroyed."

Perhaps as remarkable as anything else he achieved during his long voyage, only one crew member developed scurvy. This was no accident. Porter paid close attention to the health of his men, providing them with an antiscorbutic diet, including fresh food whenever it could be obtained and citrus juices, as well as cleanliness and as much ventilation as possible. He allowed his men to sleep in the fresh air instead of the suffocating quarters belowdecks. His reward was a healthy crew.

Still, Porter yearned for the glory of defeating a British frigate, as Isaac Hull, Stephen Decatur, and William Bainbridge had done. He wrote later, "I had done all the injury that could be done the British commerce in the Pacific, and still hoped to signalize my cruise by something more splendid before leaving that sea."

The *Essex* and *Essex Junior* arrived at Valparaiso on February 3, 1814. Porter didn't have to wait long for the British to arrive. In five days the frigate HMS *Phoebe* and her consort, the sloop-of-war *Cherub*, appeared. Porter had been expecting them. He had heard that they, and perhaps others, had been sent to find him, and he could not have been more pleased to be discovered. The *Phoebe*, under Captain James Hillyar, mounted 53 guns; the *Cherub*, under Captain Thomas T. Tucker, mounted 28. The *Essex* had 46 guns, the *Essex Junior* 20. For six weeks Hillyar stayed outside the neutral harbor, blockading Porter and awaiting reinforcements. Porter issued a challenge to Hillyar to fight him alone, but Hillyar declined. Porter believed the *Essex* to be so much faster than either British ship that he could escape anytime he wished.

On March 28 Porter took advantage of strong winds to sail boldly out of the harbor, intending to lure Hillyar away so that *Essex Junior* could escape. Porter had heard that more British warships were on the way, and he wanted to get into the open sea, where his speed would protect him. A sudden squall, however, carried away *Essex's* main topmast. The men aloft were thrown into a heavy sea and drowned. Porter was forced to turn back, but he could not regain the main harbor and had to anchor in a small bay on the eastern side "within pistol shot of the shore."

Hillyar had waited patiently for this moment, and he seized the opportunity to attack. That Porter was anchored in neutral territory did not seem to matter. Hillyar struck at four o'clock in the afternoon. He maneuvered to a position off Porter's stern and, using his long guns, pummeled him unmercifully. Porter was a sitting duck, but he and his men battled bravely. *Cherub* joined *Phoebe*, contributing to *Essex*'s misery. Porter managed to get three long guns employed out of his stern ports and inflicted enough damage on his tormentors that they pulled away for a time to make repairs. But Porter was stranded, and Hillyar came back and stationed the *Phoebe* and the *Cherub* on the *Essex*'s starboard quarter. Hillyar then commenced a blistering fire and Porter could not reply. He had to stay there and take it, or surrender, which he refused to do.

In desperation Porter cut away his anchor and used what little sail he had left to move slowly toward Hillyar. Hillyar, however, pulled back and kept a safe distance while continuing to pummel the *Essex*, mowing down Porter's men by the dozen. Porter now tried to run the *Essex* onshore, land his remaining men, and burn the ship. But just as he neared the beach, the wind turned against him and drove him back into Hillyar's withering fire. Porter still did not give in. But by twenty minutes after six, his ship and crew could stand no further punishment and he surrendered. The battle had lasted for two and a half grueling hours. Porter wrote bitterly, "We have been unfortunate but not disgraced." He suffered 155 casualties, 58 of whom were killed. The *Phoebe* had eleven men killed or wounded, the *Cherub* four.

Porter wrote later, "Commodore Hillyar [was] in violation of every principle of honor and generosity, and regardless of the rights of nations attacked the *Essex* in her crippled state within pistol shot of a neutral shore, when for six weeks I daily offered him fair and honorable combat terms greatly to his advantage; the blood of the slain must be on his head."

Essex Junior was not engaged in the fighting, except for receiving a pounding from the *Cherub* for a brief period. After the battle, Porter and what was left of his crew sailed home on parole in the *Essex Junior* with all her armament removed, and with a passport so that she would not be captured. On arrival in the United States, Porter and his men were to be exchanged for British prisoners of similar rank. Porter had a hard time arriving, however. When *Essex Junior* was off Sandy Hook a British frigate, HMS *Saturn*, stopped her. The frigate's captain made prisoners of Porter and his crew. Angry and determined to get home, Porter and some of his men escaped in one of the *Essex Junior's* boats and wound up rowing sixty miles to Long Island. The *Saturn's* captain then changed his mind and released *Essex Junior,* allowing her to finally make her way into New York harbor. Porter and his men received a tumultuous welcome from New Yorkers, and their exploits were celebrated throughout the country.

The pride Americans felt in the exploits of their naval heroes contributed to the growing consensus that the navy was critical to the nation's defense. The unexpected successes on the high seas were miraculous enough, but perhaps even more stunning was the navy's performance on the Great Lakes and Lake Champlain.

15

THE NAVY ESTABLISHED

August 1813–January 1815

Although the blue water fleet did poorly in 1813, a new freshwater hero emerged on Lake Erie. Madison had been hoping for a miracle in Canada that year. He claimed that the need to acquire naval supremacy on Lake Erie and Lake Ontario had always been "well understood." But if it had, nothing had been done about it prior to Hull's surrender of Fort Detroit. Even now, when Madison was counting so heavily on a victory, he sent a relatively junior officer to build a fleet from the stump in a matter of weeks.

Twenty-eight-year-old Master Commandant Oliver Hazard Perry arrived at Presque Isle (now Erie, Pennsylvania) early in 1813 and immediately set about constructing a fleet large enough to take naval supremacy away from the British. He reported to Captain Isaac Chauncey, who was in overall command of the lakes except Lake Champlain, where another young master commandant, Thomas Macdonough, was also attempting to build a respectable fleet from scratch. Both Perry and Macdonough had the critical backing of Secretary Jones. Requests for support from cities along the Atlantic coast were coming to Jones constantly, and he responded as best he could, but he always gave a high priority to the efforts on the lakes.

Perry was forced to haul cordage, sails, naval stores, cannon, and other supplies over the Allegheny Mountains to Pittsburgh and then take them by river and land portage to Lake Erie. He had crucial help from master lake mariner and shipwright Daniel Dobbins, as well as from Noah Brown, his brother Adam Brown, and their foreman Sidney Wright, New York shipbuilders of exceptional skill. In a few months, working with no more than two hundred men, Perry built a fleet of two 20-gun brigs, *Lawrence* and *Niagara*, and four armed schooners. The *Lawrence* was named after James Lawrence, and it would be Perry's flagship, flying a banner with the words "Don't Give Up the Ship."

Perry floated his two large warships over the shallow bar at Presque Isle, using a device Wright had invented, and by August 6, Perry had them out on the lake. He was joined by Commander Jesse D. Elliot, who brought two schooners from Buffalo and became his second in command.

Elliot was three years older than Perry and had served under Chauncey in the New York navy yard before becoming part of Chauncey's command on Lake Ontario in the fall of 1812. Although Perry was senior to Elliot on the navy list, Elliot thought he should have been awarded command on Lake Erie.

With Perry in the *Lawrence*, the fleet of nine sailed to the western end of the lake, anchoring at Put-in Bay. Perry's plan was to coax British Captain Robert H. Barclay, a wounded veteran of Trafalgar, to come out with his squadron—the only British force on the lake—and fight.

Barclay was headquartered at Fort Malden on the Detroit River, where it emptied into Lake Erie. Barclay would have preferred to wait before having a showdown with Perry, but he had no choice. The Royal Navy had neglected the Great Lakes, and he had had to construct a fleet much as Perry had, but with less support. He was at the end of a long, difficult supply line, and he knew he could not survive the winter with the provisions he had. Unless he decisively defeated Perry, he would have to either abandon his fleet or destroy it.

So Barclay accepted Perry's challenge and came out to meet him on September 10. The British squadron—two heavy ships of 20 guns each, the *Detroit* (Barclay's flagship) and the *Queen Charlotte*, three schooners, and a sloop—was smaller than Perry's. The battle began around noon. Perry arranged his squadron in a line, so that each member could fight her opposite number in the British line. Carronades were only devastating at short range, so Perry wanted to maneuver the *Lawrence* as close to the *Detroit* as possible in order to make his 32-pound carronades effective. Since Perry had the weather gauge, Barclay was forced to wait for Perry to approach instead of running at him and boarding him. The *Lawrence* was in the van of Perry's line, and as she approached the *Detroit*, Barclay fired his long guns at her to good effect. But Perry pressed on to within musket shot of the *Detroit* and delivered crushing blows of his own.

Perry expected Elliot in the *Niagara* to stay with him and take on the *Queen Charlotte*, but, for no obvious reason, Elliot hung back out of range to windward. It was a quarter past twelve when Perry and Barclay started pummeling each other at close quarters. Since Elliot was standing off, the *Queen Charlotte* and the schooner *Hunter* also fired at Perry.

The four ships fought it out for two hours while Elliot continued to remain apart. By two-thirty the *Lawrence* was a wreck. In one last desperate move, Perry left her and was rowed to the *Niagara* in the only boat that hadn't been smashed to pieces.

Perry took command of the *Niagara* and ordered Elliot off to direct the smaller schooners while Perry steered back to the *Detroit*. He was only a mile away; with a favorable wind he was able to reach her in fifteen minutes. He then pounded the *Detroit* and *Queen Charlotte*, which were already pretty well banged up.

At three o'clock Barclay struck his colors, surrendering his whole squadron—an act unprecedented in British history. Perry had twenty-nine killed and ninety-one wounded. The *Lawrence* suffered most of the casualties. Out of her crew of 110, twenty-two were killed and sixty-one wounded. The British squadron had forty-one killed and ninety-one wounded.

Despite the horrific carnage, it was a momentous victory. On the back of an old letter, Perry wrote to General William Henry Harrison, "We have met the enemy and they are ours." Perry now controlled Lake Erie, enabling Harrison to take back Fort Detroit and engage the new British commander, General Henry Proctor (Isaac Brock's replacement). With the lake in American hands, Proctor's supply lines were cut, and he evacuated Fort Malden, across the river from Fort Detroit, withdrawing east along the Thames River in southwestern Ontario. Harrison chased him and defeated him and his Indian allies on October 5, 1813, at the battle of the Thames in the center of the Ontario peninsula. During the fighting, the great Indian leader Tecumseh was killed and the Indian confederacy then dissolved. American supremacy was reestablished in the northwest. Madison was relieved.

The rest of the Canadian operation, however, had not gone so well. As the year began, the president believed that the reverses of 1812 could be redeemed. "If the reputation of our arms has been thrown under clouds," he told Congress, ". . . presaging flashes of heroic enterprise assure us that nothing is wanting to correspondent triumphs . . . but the discipline and habits which are in daily progress."

Apart from Perry's and Harrison's victories, however, the triumphs did not come. Concentrating American forces and attacking Montreal directly appeared to be the most obvious strategy, but the new secretary of war, General John Armstrong, rejected the idea. Instead, he proposed attacking three other areas before attempting Montreal. The first was Kingston, where the St. Lawrence River flowed into Lake Ontario. After taking Kingston the army would move west to York (now Toronto), the capital of upper Canada, and then to Fort George and Fort Erie at either end of the Niagara River. General Dearborn suggested changing the order and attacking York first and then the forts, followed by Kingston. Armstrong approved the new plan, and in April 1813 General Zebulon Pike, with the help of Captain Isaac Chauncey and his fleet, took York. Pike's troops rampaged through the town, burning the brick parliament houses, the governor's mansion, and other public buildings. Pike himself, along with three hundred of his men, was killed when a powder magazine exploded. A month later, General Dearborn attacked the forts at the western end of the lake and, in a series of failed encounters, managed to hold on precariously to Fort George and Fort Niagara at the northern end of the Niagara River.

Armstrong now replaced Dearborn with General James Wilkinson, still the ranking officer in the army. Wilkinson proposed bypassing Kingston and combining forces with General Wade Hampton at Plattsburg for an attack on Montreal. Armstrong approved the new plan, but Hampton and Wilkinson could not cooperate. Both were easily defeated in separate battles. General Wilkinson marched up the St. Lawrence from Sackett's Harbor on Lake Ontario, and General Hampton from Plattsburg, both heading for Montreal, but they were turned back at Chateauguay on October 26 and at Chrysler's Farm on November 11. Discouraged, Armstrong evacuated Fort George in December. Later the British retook Fort Niagara and even Buffalo. Except for the northwest, the stalemate along the Canadian border continued into the spring of 1814.

Meanwhile, the navy was locked in its own stalemate on Lake Ontario. Captain Chauncey had been at Sackett's Harbor since October 1812 and had done an impressive job of building a fleet to gain control of the lake. When he arrived, there was only one American warship on Lake Ontario, the 16-gun brig *Oneida*. In short order Chauncey purchased five schooners and converted them to warships, and then set about building two more warships. With the expert help of shipwright Henry Eckert, he launched the 24-gun *Madison* in November 1812. Before the year was out, he had a respectable little squadron.

The British trailed Chauncey in developing their lake fleet, and to make their situation worse, they divided their efforts between Kingston and York. Admiral Sir James Yeo was put in command of the Great Lakes and based himself at Kingston. Chauncey and Yeo engaged in an arms race, and initially Chauncey had the lead.

In the spring of 1813, after the ice had melted, Chauncey used his fleet to support General Henry Dearborn's attack on York. Chauncey had the *Madison*, the *Oneida*, the 10-gun schooner *Hamilton*, the 9-gun schooner *Scourge,* and nine other vessels. He transported General Dearborn's troops for their assault on York. While General Pike took the town, Chauncey captured the British warship *Gloucester* and destroyed a large warship that was being built. Chauncey also destroyed a large cache of naval stores. This proved of enormous importance to Oliver Hazard Perry in his arms race against Barclay on Lake Erie later in the year. Because it proved so valuable to Perry, Chauncey's raid was his most important accomplishment during the war.

Eventually both sides had built impressive fleets on Lake Ontario but they were well balanced, and neither Chauncey nor Yeo wished to risk them in a decisive fight. They sparred, but neither went for the jugular and risked all in the way that Perry did on Lake Erie. Neither Yeo nor Chauncey was ever able to destroy the other; the best they could do was a standoff, and it continued for the remainder of the war.

At the same time Madison learned of the victories on and around Lake Erie, word reached him that Britain and her allies had stopped their infighting and had defeated Bonaparte at the battle of Leipzig on October 18, 1813. Madison's opportunity to strike Canada while Britain was distracted was now gone. The British were free to bring their full weight to bear against the United States.

Madison and Jefferson theorized that perhaps the British, seeing the trade opportunities that peace would bring, might end the war with America on reasonable terms. From London, however, Gallatin reported the true feelings of the British public. "In the intoxication of an unexpected success, which they ascribe to themselves," he wrote, "the English people eagerly wish that their pride may be fully gratified by what they call the 'punishment of America.'"

The allied armies entered Paris on March 31, 1814, and Napoleon abdicated on April 6, freeing Britain to organize a major campaign against America. One would think that after two decades of fighting the British would have had enough, but their animus toward America was too great. They planned to invade at four points: the Niagara region, Lake Champlain, Chesapeake Bay, and New Orleans. The Royal Navy's blockade would continue, as would surprise coastal raids. The words used to describe America and its president in the English press were venomous. Henry Adams found "only extravagant enmity." The *London Times*, the *Morning Post*, and the *Courier*, which normally spoke for the government, were unrestrained in their attacks. Flush with victory in Europe, the British wanted revenge. They gave no thought to the difficulty of bringing a country as large as America to heel from a distance of three thousand miles, although they had tried once before, when the United States was half the size it was in 1814.

In the spring, the aggressive vice admiral, Sir Alexander Cochrane, was appointed to replace Warren as commander in chief of the American station, and he immediately extended the naval blockade north to include New England.

Before the British invasion of 1814 began in earnest, fighting along the Canadian border continued. In March, General Wilkinson trudged northward toward Montreal with four thousand troops but was easily thrown back by British artillery. In the Niagara area the army now had better leadership and performed well, but again the result was inconclusive. After American General Jacob Brown had boated five thousand men across the Niagara River on July 3, 1814, and captured Fort Erie, two battles were fought, one at Chippewa, near Niagara Falls, and the other at Lundy's Lane, just below the rapids. Brigadier General Winfield Scott carried the day for the Americans at Chippewa on July 5, but ten days later at Lundy's Lane the Americans, under Brown and Scott, and the British, under General Drummond and General Riall, fought a bloody battle to a draw, ending any hope for a successful American invasion of Canada before British troops arrived from Europe.

The American navy continued to have a difficult time on the ocean in 1814.

After departing Boston on the last day of December 1813, the *Constitution* went hunting. In February 1814, she captured three merchantmen and the 14-gun schooner *Pictou*. But she was then blockaded in Boston for eight months and did not get back to sea until December 18, 1814. On February 20, 1815, she defeated both the 34-gun British frigate *Cyane* and her consort the 18-gun *Levant*. The *Constitution's* captain, Charles Stewart, and his crew performed with consummate skill and bravery, but by then the war was over.

The 28-gun *Adams*, under Captain Charles Morris, slipped out of Chesapeake Bay in dirty weather on January 18, 1814. She had some success cruising off Newfoundland's Grand Banks, and when she was returning home at the end of August, Morris decided to put into Penobscot Bay, off the Maine coast, to avoid British patrols. He ran aground at Isle au Haut and decided to sail up the Penobscot River and find a place to make repairs. While he was there, he got caught in the British invasion of eastern Maine in late summer. He was forced to burn the *Adams* to prevent her from falling into British hands.

Three of the new sloops-of-war that Secretary Jones regarded so highly—*Frolic, Wasp,* and *Peacock*—saw action in 1814. The *Frolic,* under Master Commandant Joseph Bainbridge, departed Boston in February and captured two prizes, while also sinking a large privateer. But on April 20 she ran into the 36-gun British frigate *Orpheus,* accompanied by the 12-gun schooner *Shelburne.* Bainbridge endeavored to escape but was forced to surrender after a thirteen-hour chase.

The 22-gun *Wasp,* under Captain Johnston Blakeley, stood out from the Piscataqua River in Portsmouth, New Hampshire, on May 1, 1814, and sailed directly to the mouth of the English Channel, where she took five prizes. On May 28 she met the 10-gun British brig *Reindeer* and, after a blazing fifteen-minute battle, forced her to strike her colors. Blakeley put in to L'Orient, France, to refit, and the French welcomed him. After repairs, he put back out on August 27 and five days later encountered the 18-gun British sloop-of-war

Avon. After an hour's savage fighting at night, Blakeley forced her to surrender as well. Two other British warships were in the vicinity at the time, and one of them, the 18-gun *Castilian*, fired a broadside at the *Wasp* but then turned away to rescue the *Avon's* crew. Blakeley continued his cruise and on October 9 spoke a Swedish brig off the Cape Verde Islands. After that, the *Wasp* vanished without a trace. Blakeley had captured fourteen prizes and destroyed two warships in one of the most remarkable cruises of the war, but how he ended will never be known.

The third sloop-of-war, the *Peacock*, under Master Commandant Lewis Warrington, slipped out of New York in March 1814. On April 29, off the coast of Florida, near present-day Cocoa Beach, he ran into the 18-gun British brig *Epervier*. Although his ship was not as powerful as the *Peacock*, the *Epervier's* captain, Richard Wales, pulled close to her; for his trouble he was pulverized for three-quarters of an hour before surrendering.

After bringing the battered *Epervier* into Savannah, Warrington sailed the *Peacock* to the English Channel and took twelve prizes during July and August before returning home. He avoided the British blockade and sailed back into New York harbor on October 30, 1814.

The *Peacock* was now set to join the *Hornet*, under James Biddle, and the *President*, which would be blockaded in New York harbor until the end of the year. Stephen Decatur had taken command when John Rogers was ordered south, first to Philadelphia and then to Baltimore to participate in its defense. Decatur waited for his opportunity to escape into the Atlantic, which came on January 14, 1815. He put out in heavy weather and damaged his ship in exiting, which left him vulnerable to the British squadron blockading the port. Four warships closed in on him and eventually forced his surrender, but only after he had badly cut up one of them, the frigate *Endymion*, which was rated as a 40-gun ship but carried 50 guns. The *President* lost twenty-four killed and fifty-five wounded; the *Endymion,* eleven killed and fourteen wounded.

Warrington and Biddle put their ships to sea on January 22, 1815. The *Hornet* eventually fought and defeated the 10-gun British sloop *Penguin*. The two ships were relatively equal. The *Hornet* then met up with the *Peacock* and sailed to the Indian Ocean. They had originally planned to make this cruise in company with the *President*. The *Peacock* took four large East Indian merchantmen in the Indian Ocean and later defeated the 15-gun British cruiser *Nautilus* in the Sundra Straits. Although their endeavors were successful, they came after the war was over and therefore were of no consequence.

Thus, for the seagoing navy, 1814 was another inglorious year of frustration against an opponent of surpassing strength. The new sloops-of-war had performed better than even Secretary Jones had expected, but there had been only three of them, and two had been lost.

In the late summer of 1814, Britain finally began her great offensive to crush America's piddling army and impose a punitive peace. In August, General Sir George Prevost marched fifteen thousand of Wellington's battle-tested infantrymen across the Canadian frontier toward Plattsburg on Lake Champlain. He planned to take Albany and then march down the Hudson Valley to New York City. His red-coated, gray-trousered veterans included some of Wellington's finest soldiers. As soon as Napoleon abdicated, the "Iron Duke's" men were on the move from their camps in France to Canada. The blood-soaked flags of their storied regiments had been on display in America before—at places like Lexington and Concord, Bunker Hill, Saratoga, and Yorktown. Now, buoyed by their success in the Napoleonic Wars, they were coming back to win the second war of the American Revolution.

No comparable American force opposed them. Secretary of War John Armstrong had removed a respectable, well-entrenched army of four thousand that Major General Izard had painstakingly assembled at Plattsburg. On August 2, just as Prevost was about to march, Armstrong had ordered Izard to take the bulk of his men west to Sackett's Harbor at the eastern end of Lake Ontario, to defend against a possible attack from Kingston or reinforce Major General

Brown's army in the Niagara region. Major General Alexander Macomb was left at Plattsburg with fifteen hundred green recruits, convalescents, and poorly trained militiamen from New York and Vermont to stop the invasion.

General Prevost arrived at Plattsburg on September 6 for a combined land and sea attack. Accompanying him was a naval contingent under George Downie. Downie had taken command only four days before from Captain Peter Fisher, who had run afoul of his superior, Admiral Yeo. Despite Downie's lack of familiarity with his officers, men, and ships, Prevost expected him to seize control of Lake Champlain immediately and secure the British supply line from Canada.

Facing Downie was an American lake fleet under thirty-year-old Master Commandant Thomas Macdonough gathered in Plattsburg Bay. Ever cautious, Prevost expected Downie to crush Macdonough's squadron before he committed his army to combat. Although young, Macdonough was a savvy veteran, receiving his baptism by fire as a midshipman during the Quasi-War with France and serving under Preble and Decatur in the war against Tripoli. Congress had already awarded him a Silver Medal for his bravery.

Quick-witted and handy with a cutlass, the tall, commanding Macdonough had made it his business to study naval tactics, particularly Horatio Nelson's against Napoleon's fleet at the battle of the Nile in 1798. Macdonough would need all his experience and learning to fight Downie. The navy had given Macdonough command of Lake Champlain in 1812, and had required him to build his fleet from scratch, just as Oliver Hazard Perry had been ordered to do. But Perry had the cooperation of his superior; Macdonough, who had an independent command, did not. At times he even had to compete with Chauncey for men and equipment.

William Jones, the new navy secretary, understood the critical importance of defending Lake Champlain, and he gave Macdonough strong support, although it came late in the day. Jones made sure that Macdonough, like Perry, had the help of shipwrights Adam and Noah Brown, and their foreman, James Wright—after they had completed their work on Lake Erie. On April 11, 1814, only forty days after laying her keel, Macdonough and the Browns had launched the 26-gun *Saratoga*. They had also converted a steam vessel into the 14-gun schooner *Ticonderoga*, under Stephen Cassin. In addition, they had completed the 20-gun brig *Eagle*, under Robert Henley, and the sloop *Preble*, under Charles Budd, along with ten row-galleys.

At daylight on the morning of September 11, with the breeze blowing gently from the northeast, Downie's warships weighed anchor and sailed south to Plattsburg Bay. As they passed Cumberland Head, the small peninsula that forms the bay, they could see the white tops of Macdonough's fleet waiting for them. At seven o'clock they rounded Cumberland Head and hove into view of the enemy. Downie had the newly completed 36-gun frigate *Confiance*; the 16-gun brig *Linnet*, under Captain Daniel Pring; the 10-gun sloop *Chubb*, under Lieutenant James McGhie; the 10-gun sloop *Finch*, under Acting Lieutenant William Hicks; and twelve gunboats and row-galleys.

The entrance to the bay was a mile and a half wide between Crab Island in the west and Cumberland Head in the east. Macdonough had positioned his ships between the island and the peninsula, inviting Downie to approach him. On seeing this, Downie might not have obliged, since the wind at the moment was not in his favor. He might have waited for more favorable conditions, or until Prevost had secured a position inland from which to bombard the stationary American line. But Prevost had no intention of making a move until Downie had dealt with Macdonough. And because of the lateness of the season, Prevost was anxious to get on with the battle. He ordered Downie to attack as soon as possible. Prevost did not want his army caught in the wilds of New York in the middle of winter.

Macdonough had arranged his four large ships in a line from north to south. The southern end was protected by the shoals of Crab Island, and the head was close to Cumberland Head. All of Macdonough's ships had springs which allowed them to turn without setting sail. The two fleets were roughly equal, with the British slightly stronger. The 36-gun *Confiance*, the largest ship in the fight, was Downie's major weapon; the *Saratoga* was Macdonough's.

As Macdonough had anticipated, contrary winds forced Downie and the *Confiance* to stop two cable lengths short of the *Saratoga* and fire at a longer range than he would have liked. Downie had wanted to get close and lay his ship athwart hawse of the *Saratoga*—that is, across her bow—but the wind baffling prevented him. In Macdonough's line, the *Eagle* was first and the *Saratoga* second, both supported by four gunboats. The *Ticonderoga* was third, and the *Preble* last. Downie concentrated on the *Saratoga* while *Linnet* and *Chubb*, aided by three gunboats, took on the *Eagle*. The *Finch*, with the other British gunboats, took on the *Ticonderoga*, the *Preble*, and the remaining American gunboats.

While Downie was struggling to get into position, Macdonough fired the first shot himself, crying out to his crew, "Impressed seamen call on every man to do his duty." And with that, he put smoldering slow-match to a 24-pounder, igniting a bloody, two-hour-and-twenty-minute fight. "The firing was terrific," an eyewitness reported, "fairly shaking the ground, and so rapid that it seemed to be one continuous roar, intermingled with spiteful flashing from the mouths of guns."

Early in the exchange, the 10-gun *Chubb* had her cables, bowsprit, and main boom shot away. She drifted helplessly toward Macdonough's line, passed through it, and was forced to surrender. The 10-gun *Finch* received such a vicious pounding from the *Ticonderoga* that in the middle of the fight she lost control and drifted, going aground on a reef of rocks to the eastward of Crab Island. The 16-gun *Linnet* managed to get properly situated, although at a longer distance than Pring wanted, and she and the *Confiance* fought it out with Macdonough.

The *Saratoga*, with the *Eagle* and some gunboats, concentrated its fire on the *Confiance* and *Linnet*, while *Preble* and *Ticonderoga* attacked the gunboats that were firing at them. Captain Downie was killed in the first fifteen minutes of the fighting, while Macdonough, apart from being twice knocked unconscious—once by the head of a decapitated seaman smacking into his eye—remained in command throughout. At a decisive point in the battle, he was able to turn the *Saratoga* completely around and employ the remainder of his twenty-six guns, bringing deadly broadsides against the *Confiance* and the *Linnet*.

Lieutenant James Robertson, who had assumed command of the *Confiance*, tried to shift his broadside while taking a severe beating from Macdonough. Suddenly Robertson's crew refused to go on. "The ship's company," he reported, "declared they would stand no longer to their quarters, nor could the officers with their utmost exertions rally them. The ship was making water very fast. The rigging, spars and hull completely shattered; upwards of forty men killed, and the wind from that quarter as not to admit of the smallest prospect of escaping, had the ship been in condition."

In this disastrous state, Robertson struck his colors. It was eleven-twenty. All of Downie's ships were captured, destroyed, or scuttled, along with the gunboats that had not cut and run at the first shots. On the American side only the *Saratoga* was beyond repair with fifty-five round shot in her hull.

That night, the deeply religious Macdonough wrote to Secretary Jones, "The Almighty has been pleased to grant us a signal victory on Lake Champlain in the capture of one frigate, one brig, and two sloops of war of the enemy."

Immediately following the British surrender, Macdonough attended to all the injured on both sides. Captain Pring wrote to the Admiralty, "I have much satisfaction in making you acquainted with the humane treatment the wounded have received from Commodore Macdonough. They were immediately removed to his own hospital on Crab Island, and were furnished with every requisite. His generous and polite attention also to myself, the officers and men will ever hereafter be gratefully remembered."

Macdonough's stunning victory shocked Prevost. He had ordered Downie to attack under conditions that were favorable to Macdonough, and he paid a heavy price. Certain that control of Lake Champlain was essential, Prevost now lost heart, turned tail, and marched Wellington's proud veterans back to Canada.

News of Sir George Prevost's improbable failure reached London on October 17. The *London Times* declared, "This is a lamentable event to the civilized world." Among London's newspapers, the *Times* had been one of the more vociferous in denouncing Madison and America. On April 15, 1814, it had proclaimed, "There is no public feeling in the country stronger than that of indignation against the Americans . . . conduct so base, so loathsome, so hateful. . . . As we urged the principle, 'No peace with Bonaparte!' So we must maintain the doctrine of, 'No peace with Madison.'" On April 27 the *Times* had declared, "Mr. Madison's dirty, swindling maneuvers in respect to Louisiana and the Floridas remain to be punished."

While driving down from Canada early in August, the British were simultaneously conducting a major diversionary raid in Chesapeake Bay. Vice Admiral Cochrane and Major General Robert Ross, a veteran of Wellington's campaigns, led the attack. They intended to divert attention in favor of Prevost by conducting hit-and-run raids; they had no plan to penetrate inland or hold territory. The major invasions would come from Canada and later from New Orleans.

After consulting with Rear Admiral Sir George Cockburn, who had spent the summer marauding in the bay, Cochrane and Ross went after a small group of gunboats and barges under the command of Joshua Barney in the Patuxent River, north of the Potomac and southeast of Washington. While Cochrane, Ross, and their army of four thousand sailed up the bay, Barney and his contingent retreated up the Patuxent River. Cochrane dropped anchor at Benedict on the Patuxent, where Ross disembarked thirty-five hundred troops and marched along the southern banks of the river. At the same time, Cochrane sent a fleet of small boats under Admiral Cockburn after Barney, who decided to burn his few boats.

Ross now marched on Washington. The city had been left unfortified because General Armstrong thought it strategically unimportant; he had assumed the British would bypass it in favor of Baltimore. Concerned about British raids in the Chesapeake Bay area, Madison had ordered him to organize the defenses of the capital. But Armstrong had ignored him, and Madison had allowed the secretary to have his way. In a panic, the president now called out the militiamen that he and Jefferson relied on for such emergencies. Large numbers were in the immediate area, but few answered the call. Madison ignored Secretary Armstrong, who was proving himself useless in this crisis, and appointed General William H. Winder to lead those militiamen who did appear. Winder had served in the army since 1812 and had been captured on the Niagara frontier and exchanged in the spring of 1814. Winder now spent an extended time reconnoitering but failed to throw up any obstacles to an advance on Washington, not even blowing up bridges.

On August 24 at Bladensburg, a village five miles northeast of Washington on the eastern branch of the Potomac, Ross crushed Winder's militiamen, almost without a fight. About three thousand Americans were in the field, but of these only a thousand were regulars, assisted by four hundred sailors under Joshua Barney. The militiamen fled before the British, but Barney and his men fought valiantly, inflicting heavy casualties. "Board 'em! Board 'em!" the sailors cried as they delivered one blow after another to the sur-prised redcoats. But Ross's numbers were overwhelming. When he flanked Barney's men, they were forced to retreat, and the battle of Bladensburg was over. Barney was wounded and captured, but the British paid tribute to his bravery by treating him as one of their own, and he recovered. Barney later said that his captors gave him "the most marked attention, respect and politeness, as if I was a brother."

The way to Washington was now open. General Ross entered it that night with Admiral Cockburn and set fire to the White House. The next day they burned most of the public buildings, including the Capitol. It was thought this bit of savagery was in retaliation for the burning of York in Canada, but it is hard to imagine that the British commanders would have resisted destroying America's great capital buildings when they had the chance, no matter what had happened in Canada. Secretary Jones destroyed the Washington navy yard to prevent it from falling into British hands.

Madison and his wife Dolley barely escaped capture. To boost morale the president had stayed close to the fighting, but he had no idea how to cope with the situation. Well-drilled militias were supposed to turn out and send the redcoats scurrying back to their boats. But most of the militiamen did not heed the call, and those who did ran at the first sight of the enemy.

After leaving Washington, Admiral Cochrane turned his attention to Baltimore, which Secretary Armstrong had thought was the more likely target. Unlike Washington, Baltimore had an outstanding leader, General Samuel Smith, a political powerhouse in Maryland and Washington.

Admiral Cochrane had doubts about attacking Baltimore with his small force of four thousand, but after his success in Washington he went ahead with the raid on September 13. During Cockburn's raids in the Chesapeake the past two years, Baltimore, unlike Washington, had improved its defenses. It was the third largest city in America, a commercial and military center, and much less vulnerable to attack than Washington. Smith's militiamen were ready for the British when they appeared.

Ross's thirty-five hundred men landed at North Point, fifteen miles from the city. On the march to the center, they were met by militiamen. After heavy fighting the British broke through and continued on, but a rifleman shot and killed Ross while he was reconnoitering. Colonel Arthur Brooke took command of the redcoats, but he was soon stopped by the city's defenses, where thousands of militiamen, reinforced by a thousand sailors under Commodore John Rogers, manned well-constructed barriers.

Fort McHenry and Fort Covington guarded the harbor. They had been built to protect against British raids in 1794 during Washington's presidency. The defenders had sunk twenty-four ships to obstruct the harbor's entrance and stationed gunboats beyond the obstructions. Cochrane attacked the forts with guns from his fleet of sixteen warships, but to no avail. After twenty-four hours of bombardment the flag still flew over Fort McHenry, inspiring Francis Scott Key to later write "The Star-Spangled Banner." Recognizing that Baltimore's defenses were too difficult, Cochrane and Brooke withdrew from the immediate area on September 14, but they remained in Chesapeake Bay until October, when they sailed off to Jamaica to prepare for the attack on New Orleans.

The unexpected victories at Plattsburg and Baltimore had a decided impact on the peace negotiations, which had been going on since August 1814 in the old Flemish city of Ghent. As far back as September 1812, Czar Alexander had asked the British if he could mediate their conflict with the Americans. Napoleon's army was on his soil, and he did not want his British ally distracted by a war with America, a country whose trade the czar needed. Castlereagh, Britain's foreign minister, dragged his feet; he did not want Russia supporting America at a peace conference. Both were small-navy countries that had common interests in free trade.

In March 1813, the czar had informed Madison of his offer, which the president eagerly accepted. But the British continued to resist. Finally, in November 1813, Castlereagh formally declined the czar's offer and proposed direct negotiations with the United States instead. Madison, looking for any honorable way out of the war, quickly accepted. He appointed five negotiators: John Quincy Adams, ambassador to Russia; Federalist Senator James A. Bayard of Delaware; Albert Gallatin; Henry Clay; and Jonathan Russell.

Castlereagh, however, had no interest in starting the negotiations anytime soon. With Napoleon defeated, he had assumed that events on the battlefield in America would improve.

When talks finally did get under way in August, the British team, expecting success in New York and at New Orleans, took a hard line. Dictating terms as if they had already won the war, they demanded that a huge piece of the northwest be set aside as Indian territory under London's tutelage. The land would include one-third of the present-day state of Ohio, two-thirds of Indiana, and nearly all of Illinois, Wisconsin, and Michigan. The United States would be denied any military or naval contact with the Great Lakes, and Americans were to be excluded from the Newfoundland fisheries. A large portion of Maine would be ceded to Canada, and other Canadian boundary questions would be settled in Britain's favor. The British negotiators also intended to keep New Orleans and Louisiana.

But Plattsburg and Baltimore changed everything. A punitive peace was now out of the question, and the British lost interest in the war. They were ready to settle and so were the Americans. The parties reached an agreement on the basis of the status quo ante bellum. Nothing was mentioned about impressment or neutral trading rights or additional territory for Britain. The boundary disputes were to be settled later by commissions. The treaty was signed on December 24, 1814. "The causes for the war," Madison said, "have ceased to operate."

Complaints that the peace terms were too easy on the Americans appeared immediately in the British press. The *London Times* was particularly critical. The griping continued until March 1815, when the British public received news of two stunning events. Napoleon had escaped from exile in Elba and landed in France on March 1, 1815. He then declared himself emperor, and Frenchmen were flocking to his banner. Disillusioned with the reactionary government of the Bourbons and their aristocratic supporters, the French people were embracing Napoleon.

In days, a report reached England telling of a defeat at New Orleans. After hearing that more than two thousand casualties had been suffered in a single day and that Napoleon was again a threat, the British finally reconciled themselves to the Treaty of Ghent and the independence of the United States.

In his message to Congress recommending approval of the treaty, Madison presented the most important military lesson he had learned from the war: be prepared. Washington and Adams had expressed the same sentiment—that if the country were well equipped for war, it probably would not have to fight one. Madison now agreed and articulated a new American consensus on the navy, putting an end to the destructive bickering that had gone on since Washington's day. For the first time in the nation's history, the navy became an accepted part of the national government.

"The reduction of the public expenditures," Madison told Congress, "the demands of a peace establishment will doubtless engage the immediate attention of Congress. There are, however, important considerations which forbid a sudden and general revocation of the measures that have been produced by the war. Experience has taught us that neither the pacific dispositions of the American people nor the pacific character of their political institutions can altogether exempt them from that strife which appears beyond the ordinary lot of nations to be incident to the actual period of the world, and the same faithful monitor demonstrates that a certain degree of preparation for war is not only indispensable to avert disasters at the onset, but affords also the best security for the continuance of peace. The wisdom of Congress will therefore, I am confident, provide for the maintenance of an adequate regular force; for the gradual advancement of the naval establishment; for improving all the means of harbor defense; for adding discipline to the distinguished bravery of the militia, and for cultivating the military art in its essential branches, under the liberal patronage of the government."

The conclusion of the peace treaty did not stop the British invasion force heading to New Orleans. Knowing nothing of what had transpired, its leaders proceeded with their original plan to take Louisiana away from the United States. Sir Edward Pakenham, one of England's finest soldiers, was appointed to replace General Ross as the leader of the expedition. The dashing Pakenham was the Duke of Wellington's brother-in-law, and, at the age of thirty-eight, one of his best generals, having distinguished himself during the Peninsula Campaign in Spain. Pakenham appeared on the scene on December 25, the day after the Treaty of Ghent had been signed.

Before he arrived, Major General John Keene, another veteran of the Peninsula Campaign, had directed the army. Admiral Cochrane commanded the navy. By the first week of November, eight thousand British troops, mostly veterans of the Napoleonic Wars, had gathered at Negril Bay in Jamaica, along with fifty warships. The British goal was to gain command of the Mississippi and "rescue the whole province of Louisiana from the United States."

Andrew Jackson was in command of the American forces. Forty-eight years old and not in good health, he was committed to defeating the British. A veteran fighter whose experience went back to the Revolutionary War, he still harbored a deep anger toward Britain. He wrote to his wife in October, "The situation of our country require [that I be away from you] for who could brook a British tyranny, who would not prefer dying free, struggling for our liberty and religion, than live a British slave." In another letter he told Rachel, "I owe to Britain a debt of retaliatory vengeance. . . . Should our forces meet I trust I shall pay the debt—she is, in conjunction with Spain, arming the hostile Indians to butcher our women and children."

Jackson had already defeated the Creek Indians, whom the British were hoping to use against New Orleans. Admiral Cochrane had naively thought the Creeks would supply thousands of warriors to "liberate" Louisiana. Jackson had also frustrated British attempts to seize Mobile Bay in September by successfully defending Fort Bowyer, the key to the bay's defenses. He had strengthened the small force of regulars stationed there under Major William Lawrence, who then fought off a determined British attack on September 15. In October, Jackson occupied the town of Pensacola to further protect Mobile Bay and demonstrate to the Creeks the potency of American arms. Admiral Cochrane had considered marching a combined force of British regulars and Creek warriors overland from Mobile Bay to Baton Rouge and cutting off New Orleans from the north. That scheme, which probably would not have worked anyway, was now dead.

Tending to the Creeks, Mobile Bay, and Pensacola kept Jackson from reaching New Orleans until December 2. Secretary of War Monroe (he had replaced Armstrong) had repeatedly warned Jackson that the object of the British expeditionary force, which had been reported to Monroe by the negotiators at Ghent, was New Orleans. Monroe had wanted Jackson to go there immediately and prepare. But Jackson believed that the successful defense of New Orleans depended on securing Mobile Bay and Pensacola, and defeating the Creeks. When he finally arrived in the city, Jackson worked at full speed to prepare, hoping the British attack would be delayed.

Situated a hundred miles inland from the mouth of the Mississippi River, New Orleans had a population of around twenty-five thousand. It was the largest city in the western part of the United States, and of great strategic importance. Nearly all the goods traveling from west of the Appalachians to the eastern states and overseas passed down the Mississippi to New Orleans. The city was nearly surrounded by water—swamps, bayous, marshes, lakes, and the Mississippi itself. The easiest way of attacking New Orleans was by sailing directly up the Mississippi. The only obstacle was Fort St. Philip, located on the east bank of the river, some sixty-five miles south of New Orleans. The fort was in good repair; it was well defended and had twenty-eight serviceable 24-pounders. A single American gunboat was assigned to patrol in front of it. Farther upriver, eighteen miles south of New Orleans, was Fort St. Leon. It overlooked Edward Turn, a bend in the Mississippi that was notoriously difficult for sailing vessels to navigate. The fort, however, had fallen into disrepair and was of no use.

The American navy had no appreciable force stationed on the river, only the armed schooner *Carolina*, built in South Carolina in 1812, and the ship *Louisiana*, built in New Orleans in the same year. Nevertheless, Cochrane decided not to use the Mississippi as his main avenue of attack. Instead, he chose to approach the city from the east by way of Lake Borgne. Given the shallowness of the lake, Cochrane would be forced to anchor his fleet fifty miles from the western end and move all his equipment and soldiers in small craft to the battlefield. Having made that decision, he then had the choice of three different routes to travel from the lake to New Orleans. The first was from Lake Borgne to Lake Pontchartrain and then down Bayou St. John, bringing him to within two miles north of the city. The second was across the Plains of Gentilly, a narrow ridge of dry land between the lakes. Chef Menteur Road passed over it. The road ran from the Rigolets (the narrow bayou that connected Lake Borgne to Lake Pontchartrain) to within fifteen miles northeast of New Orleans. The third, and the one he selected, was a route that would land him south of the city. He would exit at the west end of Lake Borgne onto Bayou Bienvenue, and then onto Bayou Mazant, expecting to thread his way through the cypress swamp east of New Orleans to Villere's Plantation. The plantation was less than a dozen miles south of New Orleans on dry ground that ran down to the Mississippi.

Jackson originally thought the British would attack New Orleans by sailing their forces up the Mississippi. He speculated that if they didn't do that, the next most likely route would be across the Plains of Gentilly. Jackson thought the route Cochrane actually chose was the least probable, since it would give the Americans the most advantages.

Master Commandant Daniel Patterson, the American naval commander at New Orleans, had assigned five gunboats under twenty-four-year-old Lieutenant Thomas ap Catesby Jones to guard Lake Borgne. This pathetic force was all Patterson had; the navy had committed almost no resources to the New Orleans theater. On the morning of December 13, 1814, Jones sighted an armada of enemy small craft rowing under difficult conditions into the lake. They had come from Cochrane's invasion fleet, anchored nearly fifty miles away. Forty-five British barges armed with cannons in their prows eventually came into view. When Jones saw what he was up against, he retreated. The barges gave chase but did not catch him for another thirty-six hours. At noon on December 14 Jones's flagship came under heavy fire, but he fought back bravely, receiving a musket ball in the shoulder. The disparity of force, however, was too great for him, and he surrendered. The British then took Jones's boat and turned her guns on the others. By one o'clock they had all surrendered. Remarkably, Jones and his men had managed to kill nineteen British tars and wound seventy-five others, while suffering six killed and thirty-five injured. Jones and the other captured prisoners performed an additional service by telling their gullible captors that the American force under Jackson in New Orleans had risen to over twenty thousand—five times the actual number.

With Jones out of the way, Cochrane's invasion could proceed, but the difficult terrain proved a severe handicap. It was not until December 22 that an advance party of eighteen hundred exhausted regulars reached Villere's Plantation on the Mississippi River and encamped on the main road leading to New Orleans. General Jackson had no idea they were there, but when informed, he shouted, "By the eternal, they shall not sleep on our soil."

At seven-thirty the following evening, the American war schooner *Carolina*, under Commodore Patterson, began shelling the exposed British advance guard with grape- and round shot. The *Carolina* had one long 12-pounder and six 12-pound carronades for a broadside. Then, at eight o'clock, General Jackson and two thousand men, including two hundred free blacks, swooped down on the surprised British. The fighting raged for two hours. When British reinforcements arrived, Jackson withdrew. He posted his force two miles away behind Rodriguez Canal, a shallow, ten-foot-wide ditch that stretched three-quarters of a mile between the Mississippi and a cypress swamp.

Major General Keene, who had been taken in by Lieutenant Jones's story about the size of Jackson's army in New Orleans, did not pursue. Instead, he waited for the rest of the British contingent to arrive. While he did, Commodore Patterson in the *Carolina* and the 16-gun *Louisiana* shelled Keene's troops regularly. On December 25, when General Pakenham finally arrived in camp, he was aghast at the ground Admiral Cochrane had chosen to fight on. Pakenham thought the British fleet should have been brought directly into play by sailing up the Mississippi. He contemplated returning to the fleet and changing strategy but decided to remain where he was and fight from there.

The incessant fire from the American warships drew his immediate attention. He ordered artillery moved into place, and on the morning of December 27 he began shelling the *Carolina*. Flames soon shot up from her deck, causing Commodore Patterson and his crew to leap into the river. As they did, the flames sped to the schooner's magazine and she blew up with an earsplitting roar. The *Louisiana* pulled away just in the nick of time, sailing upriver out of range of the British artillery. Patterson and his men swam to shore; one was lost and six injured. They made their way to Jackson's camp, and he had them man the artillery.

The following day, December 28, Pakenham, driving from south of Rodriguez Canal, attacked Jackson's line in two columns but was driven back by the artillery and by fire from the *Louisiana*. Deciding that he needed additional firepower, Pakenham ordered more cannon brought from the fleet. Given the distances and the terrain, this was a horrendous and time-consuming task.

While Pakenham was adding to his artillery, Jackson worked overtime to strengthen his position behind the canal. He sent Commodore Patterson and his gunners across to the west bank of the river to set up batteries and ordered General David Morgan to support him. On the morning of New Year's Day, Pakenham began bombarding Jackson's line again. Jackson responded and an artillery duel developed. Commodore Patterson's veterans, from the other side of the Mississippi, were deadly accurate with their fire. By three o'clock in the afternoon Pakenham could see that he was getting nowhere and ceased firing.

Pakenham now decided to conduct a frontal assault on Jackson with his infantry. By this time, the British had discovered the true size of the American army. Pakenham assumed that his overwhelming numbers—probably two to one—would be more than enough to break through Jackson's line, scatter his men, and allow British regulars to drive straight to New Orleans. Reinforcements were due to arrive under Major General John Lambert, and Pakenham decided to wait for them before making his final push. In the meantime, he planned to send troops across the river to silence Commodore Patterson's battery of three 24-pounders and six 12-pounders. Pakenham hoped to then use the guns against Jackson at the Rodriguez Canal, catching him in a crossfire. But Pakenham had no boats and had to send back for them. He cursed the situation that Admiral Cochrane had placed him in. When Pakenham finally got the boats to the river and ferried his troops across on January 8, they defeated Morgan's men and captured Patterson's guns, but only after the commodore had spiked them and retreated. The British immediately set about repairing the cannon. Jackson later reported, "The enemy now occupied a position from which they might annoy us without hazard."

Meanwhile, at six o'clock on the same morning, while the British were achieving victory on the west bank of the Mississippi, Pakenham, on the east bank with eight thousand veterans, began his main thrust against the American line at Rodriguez Canal. General Gibbs and General Keane led the two main columns.

Four thousand confident American fighters waited behind a five-foot-high entrenchment. Jackson moved up and down the line, shouting words of encouragement, and then situated himself in the center of the line on slightly higher ground to direct the battle. The strength of his barricade and the accuracy of his twelve artillery pieces and three thousand riflemen would determine the outcome.

The British under Gibbs were close to the swamp, and as they approached, a withering fire from the American marksmen and artillery greeted them. They fell back in confusion. Gibbs was mortally wounded, and General Pakenham came up to rally the troops. He was struck by grapeshot three hundred yards from the canal and died instantly. General Keene's column fared somewhat better, but it too was eventually thrown back, and Keene himself was mortally wounded.

With three general officers dead or dying, command devolved on General Lambert. The sight of the dead and wounded around him was appalling and his men could not continue to fight. He called off the attack and ordered his troops on the west bank of the river to withdraw. British losses were staggering, amounting to 2,036 killed, wounded, or missing. Jackson had suffered only seventy-one casualties, of whom thirteen had been killed. After hurriedly arranging a truce to bury his dead, Lambert retreated to the protection of Cochrane's fleet.

Since the Battle of New Orleans took place after the Treaty of Ghent had been signed, there was a tendency to think it was unnecessary, but that was not the case. It performed an essential part in showing, once and for all, that America could not be conquered—that she was an independent country strong enough to withstand any foreign power.

The victory at New Orleans also helped convince the American people that they had won the second War of Independence. Their joy was unrestrained, and Madison became immensely popular. John Adams observed, "Notwithstanding a thousand faults and blunders, [Madison] has acquired more glory, and established more union; than all his three predecessors." Monroe was elected president in 1816, and a new era dawned for America. For the first time in her history, she was free to grow in her own way and pursue her own interests, without being embroiled in Europe's troubles.

The Europeans defeated Napoleon at Waterloo and preserved the wise peace they made at the Congress of Vienna. Prince Metternich, the brilliant, reactionary Austrian prime minister, wrote in his *Memoirs* that "the peace to be made with France could only be regarded from one of two standpoints. Either it would be dictated by the spirit of revenge or it would be inspired by the need to establish as perfect as possible a political equilibrium between the powers." The equilibrium that Metternich, Castlereagh, and their colleagues arranged laid the foundation for a century of peace.

Ending hostilities in Europe, however, did not lead to the dismantling of the United States Navy. Its usefulness in preserving peace had now been established. The arguments over the wisdom of having a respectable sea force—arguments that had gone on since the early 1790s—had been about how to avoid war. All the presidents since Washington had come away from the Revolution determined never to repeat that experience. The goal of each had been peace; their disagreements had been about how to achieve it. The War of 1812 now ended the argument in favor of Washington and Adams. It had shown that a permanent seagoing navy, if wisely managed, would be an indispensable tool in the endless struggle to prevent disagreements between nations from degenerating into war.

ACKNOWLEDGMENTS

In the years it took to complete this book I've accumulated many debts. My wife Kay, an artist and a discerning critic, offered advice and support to an often preoccupied mate. Her understanding of the torments, as well as the joys, of writing helped me through many tough patches. My agent, Rob McQuilkin of Lippincott Massie McQuilkin, a tireless, brilliant adviser, saw the merits of the project from the start and shepherded me through the long, difficult process of publication, spending many hours at every stage encouraging and teaching selflessly. Alexander (Sandy) Brook, the legendary Maine publisher, editor, and writer—a navy pilot during World War II—read and criticized the complete manuscript twice, providing critical insights and innumerable helpful suggestions. Lara Heimert, my patient, gifted editor at Basic Books, supported the project from beginning to end, offering sage advice continuously. Her assistant, Brandon Proia, rendered skillful assistance cheerfully in an often hectic environment. Alice Rosengard, whom Lara Heimert characterized as "wondrous," lived up to her billing. She edited the manuscript in its final stages, working long hours, seven days a week, expertly criticizing and polishing. I felt that I was getting a priceless lesson from a great pro. Chrisona Schmidt did an outstanding job copyediting, as did Kay Mariea, the director of editorial services, who oversaw the various stages of editorial production.

I am also indebted to my daughter Mary Daughan Sheft and her husband Mark Sheft for their advice and encouragement through many hard years. My nephew Michael Daughan, who knows the United States Navy intimately, gave advice and support when it was most needed, as did my brother William (Jerry) Daughan, another old navy hand.

In a work that encompasses forty years of American history the author is indebted to the work of innumerable scholars. They are listed in the endnotes and bibliography. Without them this book could never have been written. I would also like to thank my many colleagues and students over the years at Connecticut College, the Coast Guard Academy, and the Air Force Academy, as well as my teachers at the University of New Hampshire, Stanford University, and Harvard University, who helped me think about the great issues of war and peace which are at the heart of this book.

GLOSSARY

A

Abaft: to the rear of.
Aft: toward, or in, the stern of a vessel.
Astern: behind a vessel.

B

Ballast: any heavy substance used to maintain a vessel at its proper draft or trim, or its stability.
Beam: the breadth of a ship at its widest part.
Beam ends: a ship lying so far over on its side that the ends of her beams are touching the water and she is in danger of capsizing.
Beat to quarters: a marine drummer calling a crew to its battle stations.
Bilge: the lowest point of the hull, usually containing foul water.
Bomb vessel: a small ketch used to hold mortars for hurling bombs.
Boom: a long spar used to extend the foot or bottom of a specific sail.
Bow: the forward part of a ship.
Bowsprit: a spar extending forward from the bow or stem of a ship to carry sail forward and to support the masts by stays.
Brig: a two-masted, square-rigged vessel.
Broach to: to veer a ship's stern suddenly to windward so that her broadside is exposed to the wind and sea, putting her in danger of capsizing.
Bulkhead: a partition separating compartments on a vessel.

C

Cable's length: six hundred feet.
Capstan: a vertical cleated drum used for moving heavy weights powered by capstan bars pushed by hand.
Carronade: form of cannon used to throw heavy shot at close quarters.
Chasers: a chase gun.

Chevaux-de-frise: a piece of timber or an iron barrel traversed with iron-pointed spikes or spears or pointed poles, five or six feet long, hidden under water, and used to defend a passage.

Clew: a lower corner of a square sail or after lower corner of a fore-and-aft sail.

Clew garnets: one of the ropes by which the clews of the courses of a square-rigged ship are hauled up to the lower yards.

Clew lines: A rope by which the clew of an upper square sail is hauled up to its yard.

Clew up: to haul a sail by means of the clew garnets, clew lines, and so on, up to a yard or mast.

Close-hauled: sails pulled tight to allow a ship to sail close to the wind.

Collier: ship carrying coal.

Con: steer.

Consolato del mare: the right to take enemy goods from neutral ships.

Coppering a warship: sheathing with rolled copper.

Corvette: warship with flush deck, slightly smaller than a frigate.

Courses: the lowest sail on any square-rigged mast.

Cutter: a broad, square-sterned boat for carrying stores and passengers and either rowed or sailed.

F

Fall off: to steer to leeward, or away from the direction of the wind.

Fascines: a long bundle of wooden sticks bound together.

Fireship: a vessel carrying combustibles sent among enemy ships to set them on fire.

Fleches: a salient outwork of two faces with an open gorge.

Fore-and-aft rig: having not square sails attached to yards, but sails bent to gaffs or set on the masts or on stays in the midship line of the vessel.

Forecastle: that part of the upper deck of a ship forward of the foremast.

Foremast: the mast closest to the bow.

Forereach: to gain upon.

Frigate: a three-masted, square-rigged warship carrying a full battery of twenty to fifty guns on the main deck and having a raised quarterdeck and forecastle.

G

Gaff: the spar on which the head, or upper edge, of a fore-and-aft sail is extended.

Gallant: third highest sail on a square-rigged ship above the topsail and course.

Grapeshot: small iron balls held together by a canvas bag that act like shotgun pellets.

H

Halyards: a rope or tackle for hoisting and lowering sails, yards, flags, and so on.

Hawser: a large rope for towing, mooring, or securing a ship.

Heel: the lower end of a mast, a boom, the bowsprit, and so on.

Heel: to tilt or incline to one side.

J

Jib-boom: a spar that serves as an extension of the bowsprit.

Jibe: to shift a fore-and-aft sail or its boom suddenly and with force from one side of a ship to the other until the sail fills on the opposite side. A maneuver done when a vessel is running with the wind and changes direction.

K

Knot: a unit of speed equivalent to one nautical mile or 6,080.2 feet an hour.

L

Lateen sail: a triangular sail, extended by a long yard slung to the mast and usually low.

Lee: the side of a ship that is farthest from the point from which the wind blows, the sheltered side.

Lee shore: a shore on the lee side of a vessel, potentially dangerous in a storm.

Letter of marque: a license granted by a government to a private person to fit out an armed vessel to cruise as a privateer.

Line-of-battle ship. See sail of the line.

Luff: to turn the head of a vessel toward the wind.

M

Mainmast: the large center mast of a three-masted ship.

Maintop: the platform above the head of the mainmast in a square-rigged ship.

Main topmast: a mast next above the mainmast.

Merlon: one of the solid intervals between embrasures or openings of a battlement or parapet.

Mizzenmast: the aftermost mast in a two- or three-masted ship.

P

Palladium: champion.

Play upon: fire at.

Pounders: the weight of a cannonball.

Privateer: an armed private vessel operating under the commission of a government.

Prow: the bow of a vessel.

Q

Quarterdeck: that part of the upper deck abaft the mainmast reserved for officers.

R

Ratlines: one of the small traverse ropes attached to the shrouds and forming the steps of a rope ladder.

Redoubt: small enclosed work of varying size used to fortify hills and passes.

Reef: the part of a sail taken in or let out by means of the reef points, in order to regulate the size of a sail.

Reef point: one of the pieces of small rope used in reefing a sail.

Royal: a small sail immediately above the topgallant sail.

S

Sail of the line: largest of the warships, carrying from 50 to 120 guns, large enough to have a place in the line of battle. Most often a 74-gun ship with three decks. Also called ship of the line.

Scow: a large, flat-bottomed boat having broad, square ends.

Sheet: a rope that regulates the angle at which a sail is set in relation to the wind.

Slow match: a slow-burning fuse used to ignite the powder charge in a cannon.

Spring on her cable: a line led from a vessel's quarter to her cable so that by hauling in or slackening it she can be made to lie in any position.

Spring tide: a tide greater than usual, occurring at full moon and new moon.

Starboard: the right-hand side of a ship when facing toward the bow. The opposite of larboard or port.

Starboard tack: the course of a ship when the wind is coming over the starboard side.

Stern: the rear end of a vessel.

Stern sheets: the space at the stern not occupied by the thwarts of an open boat.

Swivel: a small gun fixed on a swivel on a stanchion so that it can be rotated. Usually shoots a one-pound ball.

T

Tack: change direction by bringing the head of a vessel into the wind and then shifting the sails so that she will come up into the wind and then fall off on the other side until she is sailing at about the same angle to the wind as before but on the opposite tack.

Taffrail: the rail around a ship's stern.

Tender: a vessel employed to attend larger ships, to supply them with provisions, and so on.

Topgallant: a mast or sail situated above the topmast and below the royal mast.

Topsail: the sail above the course.

Trim: to adjust sails and yards to get the best effect from the wind. Also, to arrange ballast, cargo, or passengers so that the ship will sail well.

V

Veer: to alter the course of a ship by turning away from the direction of the wind.

W

Warp: to move a ship by hauling on a line or warp.

Wear: to go about or change direction by turning the head of a vessel away from the wind.

Weather gauge: the position of a ship to the windward of another, giving an advantage in maneuvering.

Wherry: a long, light rowboat, sharp at both ends.

Windward: the point or side from which the wind blows.

Y

Yard: a long, narrow, cylindrical, tapered, wooden spar that supports and extends a sail.

Author's Note: The majority of the above definitions are based on *Merriam-Webster's Dictionary*.

SOURCE NOTES

ABBREVIATIONS

AHR   American Historical Review
LC   Library of Congress
MHS   Massachusetts Historical Society
NDAR   *Naval Documents of the American Revolution*
NDQW   *Naval Documents Related to the Quasi-War Between the United States and France*
NDWBP   *Naval Documents Related to the United States Wars with the Barbary Powers*
NDW1812   *The Naval War of 1812: A Documentary History*
PRO   Public Records Office, London

CHAPTER 1

5   *hidden around Concord:* Ester Forbes, *Paul Revere and the World He Lived In* (Boston: Houghton Mifflin, 1942), 241–247. The best of the extensive literature on Paul Revere and the battle of Lexington and Concord are Forbes, *Paul Revere and the World He Lived In*; John Galvin, *The Minutemen* (Washington, D.C.: Brassey's, 1996); Jayne E. Triber, *A True Republican: The Life of Paul Revere* (Amherst: University of Massachusetts Press, 1998); Allen French, *The First Year of the American Revolution* (Boston: Houghton Mifflin, 1934). Other accounts are included in the bibliography.

6   *they will submit:* King George III to Lord Sandwich, July 1, 1775, in G. R. Barnes and J. H. Owens, eds., *The Private Papers of John, Earl of Sandwich First Lord of the Admiralty, 1771–1782* (London, 1932), 1:63; William Bell Clark, ed., *Naval Documents of the American Revolution* (Washington, D.C.: U.S. Government Printing Office, 1964), 1:1306.

    to be subservient: George Otto Trevelyan, *The Early History of Charles James Fox* (New York: Harper, 1899), 70.

    set things to rights: Major John Pitcairn, R.M., to Lord Sandwich, March 4, 1775; in *NDAR*, 1:125.

7   *a fast horse waited:* Forbes, *Paul Revere*, 244–246.

8   *even hang them:* Paul Revere, letter to Dr. Belknap, *Proceedings of the Massachusetts Historical Society* 16 (1870): 370–376.

8   *requested Graves to do both:* PRO, Admiralty 51/906; *NDAR*, 1:199.

9   *a minute's notice:* Galvin, *Minutemen,* 51–98.

    a revolutionary army: The process by which the patriots organized is explained in two books: Robert A. Gross, *The Minutemen and Their World* (New York: Hill & Wang, 1976) for Concord; and Galvin, *Minutemen,* for Massachusetts as a whole.

11   *Percy in the dark:* Galvin, *Minutemen,* 99–231.

12   *possible to be:* John Barker, *The British in Boston: Being a Diary of Lt. John Barker* (Cambridge: Harvard University Press, 1924), 31–37; *NDAR*, 1:200–201.

    pouring in great numbers: Admiral Graves to Philip Stephens, July 24, 1775; in "Graves's Conduct," 1:153–156, MHS Transcript; *NDAR*, 1:961.

13   *head of the Massachusetts militia:* The Provincial Congress had appointed Jedediah Preble of Portland, Maine, to be major general and head of the patriot militia, but he declined because of age. Jedediah was the father of Edward Preble, who would later become a leader of the American navy during the Adams and Jefferson administrations.

    This glorious crisis: Samuel Adams to James Warren, June 10, 1775, in *Warren-Adams Letters*, MHS Collections, 72 (1917) and 73 (1925), 1:55. John Adams to James Warren, July 24, 1775, in *Warren-Adams Letters*, 1:88–89.

14   *the [English] Channel:* Minutes of the Massachusetts Committee of Safety, [Cambridge], April 27, 1775, *Massachusetts Archives,* vol. 140; *NDAR*, 1:229.

15   *had the news:* James Duncan Phillips, *Salem in the Eighteenth Century* (Salem, Mass.: Essex Institute, 1969), 366–369.

17   *supported in these colonies:* Dartmouth to Lords Commissioners of the British Admiralty, July 1, 1775, PRO Colonial Office, Class 5/121, LC Transcript; *NDAR*, 1:1307.

    the Taunton jail: "Diary of Dr. Ezra Stiles," May 23, 1775, Newport, Rhode Island; *NDAR*, 1:510.

18   *wasn't preparing any:* James S. Leamon, *Revolution Downeast* (Amherst, Mass.: University of Massachusetts Press, 1993), 63–67.

19   *Arnold reported: Massachusetts Archives,* vols. 193, 210, 211; *NDAR*, 1:364–366. *New England Chronicle,* May 18, 1775; *NDAR*, 1:751–752.

22   *took five prisoners: NDAR*, 1:523–524, 630.

    were limited: The four captured cannon, legend has it, would later be used at Bunker Hill.

26   *left her to rot:* Graves to Midshipman Moore, Graves to Gage, Graves to Jones, "Narrative of Graves," May 26, 1775, in "Graves's Conduct," 1:102, MHS Transcript; *NDAR*, 1:537–539; "Pilot Nathaniel Gadfrey's Report of Action Between the Schooner *Margaretta* and the Rebels at Machias," June 11, 1775; *NDAR*, 1:655–656; James Lyons to Massachusetts Provincial Congress, June 14, 1775; in *NDAR*, 1:676–677; Deposition of Jabez Cobb, June 26, 1775; in *NDAR*, 1:757–758; Deposition of Thomas Flinn, July 10, 1775; in *NDAR,* 1:848–849; also *NDAR*, 1:1059; *New England Chronicle,* June 24, 1775; *NDAR*, 1:745.

    lost on either side: Lt. John Knight to Graves, August 10, 1775, PRO; *NDAR*, 1:1108.

    the Lexington of the sea: James Fenimore Cooper, *The History of the Navy of the United States* (reprint; Annapolis: Naval Institute Press, 2000), 39.

27   *the threatened cord: NDAR,* 1:665, 721–722, 772, 774.

CHAPTER 2

29   *their enterprise:* Henry Steele Commager and Richard B. Morris, *The Spirit of Seventy-Six: The Story of the American Revolution as Told by Participants* (New York: Da Capo, 1995), 120–125.

30   *much about it:* Forbes, *Paul Revere*, 248.

      from the flagship: Journal of HMS Preston, PRO, Admiralty, 51/720; *NDAR*, 1:701.

      for four hours: Graves to Philip Stephens, June 22, 1775; in *NDAR*, 1:739–740.

31   *turned down:* William B. Willcox, *Portrait of a General: Sir Henry Clinton in the War of Independence* (New York: Alfred A. Knopf, 1964), 48–51.

      no manner of use: Barker, *Diary,* 61–62; in *NDAR*, 1:718.

32   *out of the action:* Thomas J. Fleming, *Now We Are Enemies* (New York: St. Martin's, 1960), 183.

33   *from musquettry:* General Howe to British Adjutant General, June 22 and 24, 1775; in Commager and Morris, *Spirit of Seventy-Six*, 131–133.

      was consumed: "Graves's Conduct," 1:117–118, MHS Transcript; *NDAR*, 1:704. Earlier in the year, Admiral Graves had seriously proposed burning nearby Cambridge, but General Gage overruled him.

      some days: Narrative of Vice Admiral Samuel Graves, "Graves's Conduct," 1:117–118, MHS Transcript; *NDAR*, 1:704.

34   *the fighting was over:* The best accounts of the battle are in Ketchum, *Decisive Day*; Fleming, *Now We Are Enemies*; and Harris, *America Rebels*, 167–224.

35   *inspired leadership:* John Adams to Josiah Quincy, July 29, 1775; in *NDAR*, 1:1004.

36   *time to succeed:* The king recalled Admiral Graves at the end of the summer; he was allowed to remain until January. Lord Sandwich to Graves, September 17, 1775, in Barnes and Owens, eds., *Sandwich Papers*, 1:73–74; *NDAR*, 2:721.

38   *suppress such rebellion:* Proclamation for Suppressing Rebellion and Sedition, August 23, 1775; in *NDAR*, 2:685.

39   *unworthy of the God:* Abigail to John, July 16, 1775, in L. H. Butterfield, Marc Friedlaender, and Mary-Jo Kline, eds., *The Book of Abigail and John: Selected Letters of the Adams Family, 1762–1784* (Cambridge: Harvard University Press, 1975), 100.

      dangerous situation: Washington's complete report to Hancock: Fitzpatrick, ed., *Writings of George Washington*, 3:320–329; *NDAR,* 1:850–851. Douglas Southall Freeman, *George Washington: Planter and Patriot* (New York: Scribner's, 1951), 3:492–494.

41   *nearby Braintree:* Narrative of Graves, July 31, 1775, "Graves's Conduct," MHS Transcript, 1:178. MHS Transcript; *NDAR*, 1:1022; Fitzpatrick, ed., *Writings of Washington*, 3:394; *NDAR*, 1:1058.

      couldn't be sure: Captain Broderick Hartwell to Graves, August 4, 1775; in *NDAR*, 1:1059–1060.

      around his warships: NDAR, 3:194.

42   *and Canada:* Washington to William Ramsay, December 8, 1775, in Fitzpatrick, ed., *Writings of Washington*, 4:200–202.

      unnecessary engagements: Washington to Captain Nicholson Broughton, September 2, 1775; in *NDAR*, 1:1287–1289.

      ever arrived: Richard M. Ketchum, *The Winter Soldiers* (New York: Doubleday, 1973), 189.

43   *lacking was gunpowder:* William Bell Clark, *George Washington's Navy* (Baton Rouge: Louisiana State University Press, 1960); *NDAR*, 3:69–72.

      the Nancy's Master: Lord Sandwich to Lord George Germain, December 28, 1775; in *NDAR*, 3:460.

44   *the progress of [this rebellion]:* Graves to Gage, September 1, 1775, "Graves's Conduct," MHS Transcript, 192–193; *NDAR*, 1:1281.

      in the harbors: Graves to Henry Mowat, October 6, 1775; in *NDAR,* 2:324–326.

45 *night undisturbed:* Lieutenant Henry Mowat to Graves, October 19, 1775; in *NDAR*, 3:1775, 513–516.

46 *must be conquered:* Wedderburn's speech in the Commons, October 26, 1775; Peter Force, *American Archives*, 4th series, 6:41–42, in Commager and Morris, *Spirit of Seventy-Six*, 260–261; French, *First Year of the American Revolution*, 562–563.
   at war: Hansard *Parliamentary History*, 18:992–994; *NDAR*, 3:378–379.

47 *the weapons he needed for such a move:* Freeman, *George Washington*, 3:530–539.
   troops to Newburyport: Gage to Lord Dartmouth, September 20, 1775; in *NDAR*, 2:160–161.

49 *limited resources:* William Bell Clark, "American Naval Policy, 1775–6," *American Neptune* 1 (1941). The tortuous path by which Congress enacted legislation creating what John Adams called "a naval power" is explained succinctly by Clark in this article. He emphasizes that a full offensive "against all the commerce of Great Britain" was not actually enacted until March 23, 1776. Legislation on that date authorized privateers, Continental war vessels, armed vessels of the various colonies, or detachments of the army to seize British commerce wherever found on the high seas. Adams saw this as another step on the road to independence. Neither Clark nor Adams considers this emphasis on commerce raiding by other than privateers misguided.
   tight civilian control: *Warren-Adams Letters*, January 7, 1776, MHS Collections, 72–73 (1917–1925), 1:197–198.
   done by halves: Franklin to Deane, August 27, 1775; in *NDAR*, 1:1244.

50 *be his model:* Adams to Gerry, June 7, 1775; in *NDAR*, 1:628–629.

51 *similar qualities:* L. H. Butterfield, ed., *Diary and Autobiography of John Adams* (New York: Atheneum, 1964), 3:350.

52 *in the next summer:* Benjamin Franklin to Charles William Frederick Dumas, December 12, 1775; in *NDAR*, 3:72.
   until it is ripe: Sam Adams to John Adams, December 22, 1775; in *NDAR*, 3:209.

53 *as many large ships as possible:* Francis Lightfoot Lee to Colonel Landon Carter, December 12, 1775; in *NDAR*, 3:75.
   their relationship unclear: William M. Fowler Jr., "Esek Hopkins: Commander-in-Chief of the Continental Navy," in James C. Bradford, ed., *Quarterdeck and Bridge: Two Centuries of American Naval Leaders* (Annapolis: Naval Institute Press, 1997), 7.

54 *first Captain:* L. H. Butterfield, ed., *Diary and Autobiography of John Adams* (New York: Atheneum, 1964), 3:350.
   officers and men: *NDAR*, 3:xv.

55 *much set upon:* Samuel Adams to James Warren, January 7, 1776; in *NDAR*, 3:670–671.

56 *from scattering:* Christopher Ward, *The War of the Revolution* (New York: Macmillan, 1952), 1:188–196.
   against General Howe: General Henry Knox to Washington, December 17, 1775; in *NDAR*, 3:138–139.

57 *take in Virginia:* Washington to Hancock, December 18, 1775; in *NDAR*, 3:147–148.
   means in your power: Naval Committee to Commodore Esek Hopkins, January 5, 1776; in *NDAR*, 3:637–638.
   capture all three: Continental Naval Committee to Commodore Esek Hopkins, January 18, 1776; in *NDAR*, 3:847.

58 *defeat the end:* Washington to Colonel Joseph Reed, January 4, 1776; in *NDAR*, 3:599.

60 *150 barrels:* Lieutenant John Paul Jones to Joseph Hewes, April 14, 1776; in *NDAR*, 4:815–817.

61   *cut to pieces:* Captain Tyringham Howe to Philip Stephens, April 27, 1776; in *NDAR*, 4:1281.

     severest censure: Captain Nicholas Biddle to Charles Biddle, May 2, 1776; in *NDAR*, 4:1378; William Bell Clark, *Captain Dauntless: The Story of Nicholas Biddle of the Continental Navy* (Baton Rouge: Louisiana State University Press, 1949), 102–113.

     British frigate: Hopkins's version is in Commodore Esek Hopkins to John Hancock, April 9, 1776; in *NDAR*, 4:735–736.

63   *at Poughkeepsie, New York:* Allan S. Everest, ed., *Mission to Canada: The 1776 Journal of Charles Carroll of Carollton* (New York: Champlain–Upper Hudson Bicentennial Committee, 1976).

CHAPTER 3

67   *in a few days:* Colonel William Moultrie, *Memoirs of the American Revolution* (reprint; New York: New York Times/Arno, 1968), 1:140; Ward, *War of the Revolution*, 2:667–668.

     subduing New York: The king wanted Parker's convoy to leave on December 1, but one delay after another kept it in Ireland.

     crushed and subdued: Lord Dartmouth to Governor Josiah Martin, November 7, 1775; in *NDAR*, 3:346–347.

68   *Moore's Creek bridge, North Carolina, in February:* Ignoring what had just happened at Great Bridge, Virginia, Governor Martin (who the year before had fled his splendid red brick "palace" in New Bern, North Carolina, to live in cramped quarters aboard the 14-gun sloop-of-war *Scorpion*) issued a call on January 10— even before Clinton had left Boston—for those who were strong in the king's cause to take back their colony. Many responded, most of them recent immigrants from the Scottish highlands still wearing kilts and sporting broadswords and dirks, and on February 27, 1776, one thousand of them, marching with high enthusiasm, had met a well-entrenched patriot force of roughly the same number under experienced leaders, Colonels Richard Caswell, John Lillington, and John Ashe, eighteen miles above Wilmington, at Moore's Creek bridge. The naive highlanders were badly mauled. The rebels captured 850 men and 30 officers, killing or wounding the rest. Only a handful escaped.

     That defeat ruined Governor Martin's plan to unite the Scots with General Clinton when he arrived off Cape Fear two weeks later. Even had the loyalists succeeded, however, Clinton, because of his firm orders to join General Howe in New York, would have been forced to leave them on their own, which, after Moore's Creek, would have been a death sentence.

     should he remain there: Lord George Germain to Governor Josiah Martin, December 23, 1775; Germain to Governor Robert Eden of Maryland, December 23, 1775; in *NDAR*, 3:445–446.

69   *after transports [and such]:* Robert Morris for the Committee of Secret Correspondence to Silas Deane, June 5, 1776; in *NDAR*, 5:383–385.

70   *helped guide him in:* Christopher Gadsden to Colonel William Moultrie, July 1, 1776; in Richard Walsh, ed., *The Writings of Christopher Gadsden* (Columbia: University of South Carolina Press, 1966), 115.

72   *severely injured:* Two years later Governor Campbell died from his wounds.

73   *to withdraw:* Journal of Captain Tobias Furneaux of HMS *Syren*; in *NDAR*, 5:798–799; PRO Admiralty 51/930.

73   *Moultrie's guns:* Commodore Parker's account of the battle is given in his report to the Admiralty, July 9, 1776. PRO, Admiralty 1/486; *NDAR,* 5:997–1002.

      worse situation: Moultrie's Memoirs, 1:174–181, in Commager and Morris, *Spirit of Seventy-Six,* 1068–1070.

74   *in this war:* Alfred Thayer Mahan, *The Major Operations of the Navies in the War of Independence* (reprint; Gloucestershire, U.K.: Nonesuch, 2006), 34.

75   *American cause alive:* Freeman, *George Washington,* 4:500.

      would ruin America: February 4, 1776; Boyd et al., eds., *Jefferson Papers,* 1:285–286; *NDAR,* 3:1127.

      the revolt: Freeman, *George Washington,* 4:369.

77   *the Franklin:* Major General Artemus Ward to George Washington, May 1776; in *NDAR,* 5:134–135.

78   *on New York:* A year earlier the Pennsylvania Committee on Public Safety, recognizing Biddle's talents, had made him captain of the row-galley *Franklin* and then promoted him to the Continental Navy's *Andrew Doria.* But Pennsylvania and the country would have been better off if he had remained commander of a row-galley and commodore of the Pennsylvania state navy. Since the Marine Committee was ignoring the need to bolster the defenses of the Delaware River with row-galleys, perhaps this would not have made any difference. But had they constructed a respectable fleet of row-galleys and placed Biddle in command on the Delaware, the British might not have taken Philadelphia in 1777.

      American prisoners: Lieutenant Colonel Archibald Campbell to Major General William Howe, June 19, 1776; in *NDAR,* 5:619–621.

80   *which he fir'd:* Captain John Paul Jones to the Continental Marine Committee, September 4, 1776; in *NDAR,* 6:684. The best depictions of Jones's sea battles are in Evan Thomas, *John Paul Jones: Sailor, Hero, Father of the American Navy* (New York: Simon & Schuster, 2003).

      the Marine Committee: Captain John Paul Jones to the Continental Marine Committee, September 30, 1776; in *NDAR,* 6:1047–1050.

      intentionally destroyed: Samuel Eliot Morison, *John Paul Jones: A Sailor's Biography* (Boston: Little, Brown, 1959), 62–66.

81   *he captured her:* Robert Morris to John Hancock, December 23, 1776; in *NDAR,* 7:574–577.

82   *renamed Sachem:* Autobiography of Joshua Barney, May 11 to July, 1776; in *NDAR,* 5:924.

83   *white spatter dash:* Lambert Wickes to Samuel Wickes, July 2, 1776; in *NDAR,* 5:882–884, 952.

      in men-of-war: Ironically, in July 1785, when Dr. Franklin left France at the end of his tenure, he hired another famous Philadelphia captain, thirty-year-old Thomas Truxtun, to transport him. Truxtun had made a reputation as a privateer during the Revolution, and he was then in command of the *London Packet,* a strong, elegant Philadelphia merchant ship built by Joshua Humphreys to carry cargo and passengers. It was a memorable voyage for Truxtun, who landed Franklin safely in Philadelphia on September 14. Truxtun could have just as easily brought Franklin to France in a privateer back in 1776.

84   *John Bull's expense:* Samuel Eliot Morison, *The Maritime History of Massachusetts* (Boston: Houghton Mifflin, 1921), 29.

      during the Revolution: Morison, *Maritime History of Massachusetts,* 27–40.

86   *Commodore Hopkins:* Hancock to Washington, June 14, 1776; in *NDAR,* 5:531; Hancock to Commodore Esek Hopkins, June 14, 1776; in *NDAR,* 5:528–530.

89   *destroyed the ship:* Various accounts of the battle are given in *NDAR*, 5:13–19.
      in the navy: "autobiography of Joshua Barney," May 11 to July 4, 1776, in *NDAR*, 5:924.
91   *and the city:* Lincoln Diamant, *Chaining the Hudson: The Fight for the River in the American Revolution* (New York: Fordham University Press, 2004), 36–67.
      a great deal: NDAR, 5:895–897.
      booming of cannon: Washington Irving, *Life of George Washington* (New York: P. F. Collier, 1904), 2:125.
92   *had in mind:* George Washington to John Hancock, July 12, 1776; in *NDAR*, 5:1040; Washington to Colonel James Clinton, July 12, 1776; in *NDAR*, 5:1040; Memoirs of Major General William Heath, July 12, 1776; in *NDAR*, 5:1041.
93   *on both occasions:* Lieutenant Colonel Benjamin Tupper to George Washington, August 3, 1776; Journal of HMS *Phoenix*; Journal of HMS *Rose*; in *NDAR*, 6:37–39.
94   *or the eye behold:* Ambrose Serle, *The American Journal of Ambrose Serle* (San Marino, Calif.: Huntington Library, 1940), 73–74.
      was imminent: Lord Howe to Commodore William Hotham, August 26, 1776; in *NDAR*, 6:309.
95   *appeared certain:* Ambrose Serle to Lord Dartmouth, September 5, 1776; in *NDAR*, 6:710–715.
97   *prey had escaped:* Ambrose Serle to Lord Dartmouth, September 5, 1776; in *NDAR*, 6:710–771; Minutes of the Council of War on the Evacuation of Long Island, August 29, 1776; Memoirs of General Heath, *NDAR*, 6:349–650.
98   *would be overwhelmed:* Washington to Hancock, September 8, 1776; in Commager, *Spirit of Seventy-Six*, 459–461.
100   *strength and prosperity:* Benjamin Franklin to Lord Howe, July 20, 1776; in Commager, *Spirit of Seventy-Six*, 449–450.
101   *never to be drawn:* Washington to Hancock, September 8, 1776; in Commager, *Spirit of Seventy-Six*, 459–461.
      to the risqué, Charles Carroll of Carrollton to Charles Carroll Jr., June 29, 1775; in Carroll Papers, Maryland Historical Society; *NDAR*, 1:779.
103   *to Davy Jones:* Diary of Captain Samuel Richards; in *NDAR*, 6:736; Dr. Benjamin Gale to Benjamin Franklin, August 4, 1775; in *NDAR*, 1:1088–1089.
      ever heard before: Serle, *American Journal*, September 15, 1776, 104.
104   *ready to do:* Serle, *American Journal,* September 15, 1776, 104.
105   *cause concern:* Journal of HMS *Renown,* Captain Francis Banks; in *NDAR*, 6:861.
      better served: Serle, *American Journal,* September 19, 1776, 109.
106   *was extremely windy:* General Howe to Lord George Germain, September 23, 1776; in Commager and Morris, *Spirit of Seventy-Six*, 474–475.
107   *gross exaggeration:* Serle, *American Journal*, September 9, 1776, 121.
110   *row-galley Lee: NDAR*, 6:96–98.
113   *eighty men:* The battle of Valcour Island is told in Mahan, *Major Operations*, 21–27; Brigadier General Benedict Arnold to Major General Horatio Gates, October 12, 1776; in *NDAR*, 6:1135.
115   *which has been made:* Washington to Greene, November 8, 1776; in *NDAR*, 7:88–89.
116   *the place was invested:* Washington to John Augustine Washington, November 6, 1776, in John Rhodehamel, ed., *George Washington: Writings* (New York: Library of America, 1997), 252–256.
      agreeably to public expectations: Rhodehamel, ed., *George Washington*, 252–256.
117   *were ever built:* One 74 was actually finished at Portsmouth, New Hampshire, after the battle of Yorktown had settled the war, but it was given to France and never became part of the American navy.

117   *an American navy:* Robert Morris to Silas Deane, December 20, 1776; in *NDAR*, 7:528–533.
118   *were expiring:* Morris to Deane, December 20, 1776; in *NDAR*, 7:528–533.
       we are lost: General Charles Lee to General Horatio Gates, December 13, 1776; in Commager and Morris, *Spirit of Seventy-Six*, 500.
121   *crossing the Hudson:* Ward, *War of the Revolution*, 1:285.
122   *the Jersey shore:* Morris to Deane, December 20, 1776; in *NDAR*, 7:528–533.
       in our Bay: Morris to Hancock, December 13, 1776; in *NDAR*, 7:475–476.
123   *few Continental warships:* Morris to Captain Nicholas Biddle, December 13, 1776; in *NDAR*, 7:476–477.
       in Jersey: Washington to Lund Washington, December 17, 1776; in Rhodehamel, ed., *George Washington*, 258–262.
124   *justify an attempt:* Reed to Washington, December 22, 1776; Washington to Reed, December 23, 1776; in Commager and Morris, *Spirit of Seventy-Six*, 510–511.
       with great violence: Henry Knox to his wife, December 28, 1776; in Commager and Morris, *Spirit of Seventy-Six*, 512–513.
125   *into their hands:* The best account of Washington's crossing and the battle of Trenton is in David Hackett Fischer, *Washington's Crossing* (New York: Oxford University Press, 2004).
       the Delaware again: Memoirs of Elisha Bostwick of the Seventh Connecticut Regiment; in Commager and Morris, *Spirit of Seventy-Six*, 511–512.
126   *an end to the war:* Washington to Hancock, January 5, 1776; in Rhodehamel, ed., *George Washington*, 268.

CHAPTER 4
127   *of the line:* Ira Gruber, *The Howe Brothers and the American Revolution* (Chapel Hill: University of North Carolina Press, 1972), 182.
128   *to find them:* Gruber, *Howe Brothers*, 174–175.
       eventually he relented: Gruber, *Howe Brothers*, 182.
130   *to stop them:* Vice Admiral Richard Lord Howe to Philip Stephens, March 31, 1777; in *NDAR*, 8:230–234.
132   *rank in their navy:* Captain Sir George Collier, R.N., to Philip Stephens, July 12, 1777; in *NDAR*, 9:270.
       attempting to fight: Benjamin Crowninshield's Journal, MHS; Collier's Journal, PRO, Admiralty 51/762; Hyndman's Journal, PRO, Admiralty 51/23; Jennison Diary, LC; Captain John Brisbane to Howe, July 9, 1777, PRO, Admiralty 1/487, 485–486, 497; Collier to Philip Stephens, July 12, 1777, PRO, Admiralty 1/1611, 61–63; *NDAR*, 9:226–230, 246–247, 269–273.
135   *many more wounded:* Lord Howe to Philip Stephens, May 18, 1777; in *NDAR*, 8:989–990; James Thomas Flexner, *George Washington in the American Revolution, 1775–1783* (Boston: Little, Brown, 1968), 210; Commager and Morris, *Spirit of Seventy-Six*, 532–536.
       employed elsewhere: Journal of Christopher Vail, May 23–25, 1777; in *NDAR*, 8:1028.
       unanimous in opposition: Colonel Henry Knox to Henry Jackson, June 21, 1777; in Commager and Morris, *Spirit of Seventy-Six*, 536–7.
136   *could do both:* Gruber, *Howe Brothers*, 239.
138   *the French fleet was ready:* Commager and Morris, *Spirit of Seventy-Six*, 939–941.
       carried her down: Jonathan Williams Jr. to the American Commissioners in France, November 29, 1777; in *NDAR*, 10:1050–1051.

138   *fight for Philadelphia:* Thomas, *John Paul Jones*, 128–134.

139   *to Fort Edward:* The best account of events leading up to what became known as the battle of Saratoga and the fighting is Richard M. Ketchum, *Saratoga: Turning Point of America's Revolutionary War* (New York: Henry Holt, 1997).

140   *Burgoyne's attack:* Ketchum, *Saratoga*, 332–335.

142   *swayed General Howe:* Gruber, *Howe Brothers*, 235.
       season of the year: Serle, *American Journal*, July 24 to August 14, 1777, 240–242.

143   *wear them the same way:* Quoted in Douglas Southall Freeman, *Washington,* abridged by Richard Harwell (New York: Scribner's, 1968), 348.

144   *difficulty replacing:* Commager and Morris, *Spirit of Seventy-Six*, 568–576.

145   *return to their farms:* Burgoyne to Germain, August 20, 1777; in Commager and Morris, *Spirit of Seventy-Six*, 577–579.

146   *face of the earth:* Serle, *American Journal*, September 8, 1777, 248–249.
       found its advantages: Serle, *American Journal*, August 25, 1777, 245–246.
       had long sought: Washington to the President of Congress (John Hancock), September 11, 1777; in Commager and Morris, *Spirit of Seventy-Six,* 616–617; Don Higginbotham, *The War of American Independence* (Boston: Northeastern University Press, 1983), 184–186.

149   *control of the river:* Journal of Captain John Montresor (British), September 27, 1777; and Diary of Captain Francis Downman, Royal Artillery, September 27, 1777; in *NDAR*, 9:972–974.

150   *dear-bought victory:* Ketchum, *Saratoga*, 369.
       to explain away: George F. Scheer and Hugh F. Rankin, *Rebels and Redcoats* (New York: Da Capo, 1957), 276.
       caused him to delay: Clinton's message is printed in Ketchum, *Saratoga*, 375.

151   *ended right there:* Washington to John Augustine Washington, October 18, 1777; in Rhodehamel, ed., *George Washington*, 276–279; Higginbotham, *War of American Independence*, 186–187.

153   *open to the British:* Governor George Clinton to Washington, October 9, 1777; in *NDAR*, 10:92–95; Clinton to Howe, October, 9, 1777; in *NDAR* 10:98–100; Commodore Hotham to Admiral Howe, October 9, 1777; in *NDAR*, 10:96–97; Major General Israel Putnam to George Washington, October 16, 1777; in *NDAR*, 10:185–186; George Clinton to George Washington, December 20, 1777; in *NDAR*, 10:762–763.
       coming of General Clinton: Ketchum, *Saratoga*, 382.
       formally surrendered: Ketchum, *Saratoga*, 420–425.

154   *out of the question:* Major General John Vaughan to Clinton, October 17, 1777; in *NDAR*, 10:192–193.

157   *defeat on the British:* Stephen R. Taaffe, *The Philadelphia Campaign, 1777–1778* (Lawrence: University Press of Kansas, 2003), 108–123; John W. Jackson, *The Pennsylvania Navy, 1775–1781* (New Brunswick: Rutgers University Press, 1974), 170–187. Colonel Baron D'Arendt to Washington, October 24, 1777; in *NDAR*, 10:263.

158   *Philadelphia waterfront:* Taaffe, *Philadelphia Campaign*, 123–141; Jackson, *Pennsylvania Navy*, 225–281; David Syrett, *Admiral Lord Howe: A Biography* (Annapolis: Naval Institute Press, 2006), 72–73; Diary of Johann Ewald, November 15, 1777; in *NDAR*, 10:500; Diary of Captain Francis Dowman (British), November 15, 1777, 501–502; Commodore John Hazelwood to Washington, November 15, 1777; in *NDAR*, 10:504–505.

159   *for the winter:* Washington to Henry Laurens, December 23, 1777; in Rhodehamel, ed., *George Washington,* 281–286.

159 *remains inexplicable:* "The Battle of the Kegs," Francis Hopkinson, 1778; in Commager and Morris, *Spirit of Seventy-Six*, 635–636; *NDAR*, 11:78–79; Gardner W. Allen, *A Naval History of the American Revolution* (1913; Cranbury, N.J.: Scholar's Bookshelf, 2005), 246–247.

CHAPTER 5

162 *adverse news:* Journal of Horace Walpole, February 17, 1778; in Commager and Morris, *Spirit of Seventy-Six*, 692–693.

163 *guaranteed defeat:* The king, unhappy with General Gage in Boston, had wanted Amherst to lead the effort in America as early as December 1774.

164 *Virginia and Maryland:* Germain to Clinton, March 8, 1778; in *NDAR*, 11:1069–1073.

165 *utmost distress:* Germain to Clinton, March 8, 1778; in *NDAR*, 11:1069–1073.
     the West Indies: Lords Commissioners of the Admiralty to Vice Admiral Viscount Howe, March 22, 1778; in *NDAR*, 11:1111–1112.

166 *safely at Bordeaux:* L. H. Butterfield, *The Adams Papers* (New York: Atheneum, 1965), 2:388–389.

168 *immersion in saltwater:* Clark, *Captain Dauntless*, 227–246; *NDAR*, 11:833; President Rawlins Lowndes to President of Congress, March 30, 1778; in *NDAR*, 11:837–838.
     could not be ignored: Journal of HMS *Ariadne* and Journal of HM Sloop *Ceres*, March 9, 1778; in *NDAR*, 11:575; Captain Thomas Pringle to Vice Admiral James Young, March 18, 1778; in *NDAR*, 11:708–709.

169 *of all charges:* Journal of HMS *Emerald*, Captain Benjamin Caldwell, March 31, 1778; in *NDAR*, 11:848–849.
     forays in America: Jones's Report to the American Commissioners, May 27, 1778; in Commager and Morris, *Spirit of Seventy-Six*, 945–946; Thomas, *John Paul Jones*, 128–136.

170 *to January 1778:* Gruber, *Howe Brothers*, 264.
     lost to the British: Gruber, *Howe Brothers*, 296; Taaffe, *Philadelphia Campaign*, 188.

172 *to chase d'Estaing:* Willcox, *Portrait of a General*, 213–218.

174 *the fate of Burgoyne:* Washington to Thomas Nelson, August 20, 1778; in Rhodehamel, ed., *George Washington*, 319–320.

175 *in the meantime:* Syrett, *Lord Howe*, 77–79; Gruber, *Howe Brothers*, 309.

176 *remained unclear:* Gruber, *Howe Brothers*, 311.

181 *would carry them:* Gruber, *Howe Brothers*, 315–316; Commager and Morris, *Spirit of Seventy-Six*, 715–720.

182 *Talbot's raid:* William M. Fowler Jr., *Silas Talbot: Captain of Old Ironsides* (Mystic, Conn.: Mystic Seaport Museum, 1995), 45–48. Talbot's raid, as Fowler points out, was originally Lafayette's idea.

184 *into the Royal Navy:* Allen, *Naval History of the American Revolution*, 315–319.

186 *skirmish resulted:* Mahan, *Major Operations*, 71–81.

187 *a British colony again:* Mahan, *Major Operations*, 81–82; Kenneth Coleman, *The American Revolution in Georgia, 1763–1789* (Athens: University of Georgia Press, 1958), 116–122; Higginbotham, *War of American Independence*, 354–355.

189 *but neither did:* David B. Mattern, *Benjamin Lincoln and the American Revolution* (Columbia: University of South Carolina Press, 1995), 62–75.

191 *at this time:* Washington to Governor Thomas Jefferson, June 29, 1780; in Commager and Morris, *Spirit of Seventy-Six*, 1195–1196; Willcox, *Portrait of a General*, 274–275.

192 *reoccupied it:* Journal of Commodore George Collier; in Commager and Morris, *Spirit of Seventy-Six*, 724–725; Christopher Ward, *The War of the Revolution* (New York: Macmillan, 1952), 2:596–610.

194   *be believed:* Willcox, *Portrait of a General*, 280–281; Allen, *Naval History of the American Revolution*, 423–437.

199   *securing Jones's triumph:* Nathaniel Fanning, *Fanning's Narrative* (1806; Bowie, Md.: Heritage Books, 2003), 21–53. Other excellent accounts of the battle are in Thomas, *John Paul Jones*, 178–198; Morison, *John Paul Jones*, 221–242; Thomas Schaeper, *John Paul Jones and the Battle off Flamborough Head* (New York: Peter Lang, 1989).

CHAPTER 6

201   *effect in 1781:* Scheer and Rankin, *Rebels and Redcoats,* 394–395; Mattern, *Benjamin Lincoln*, 76–87; Franklin B. Hough, *The Siege of Savannah* (Albany, N.Y.: Joel Munsell, 1866).

204   *in the act of entering:* Lieutenant Colonel John Laurens to George Washington, March 14, 1780; in Commager and Morris, *Spirit of Seventy-Six*, 1101–1103.

205   *plan of defense:* Arbuthnot's Report to the Admiralty, May 14, 1780, in Allen, *Naval History of the American Revolution*, 494–496.

206   *last way out of Charleston:* The best account of the battle of Charleston is in Carl P. Borick, *A Gallant Defense: The Siege of Charleston, 1780* (Columbia: University of South Carolina Press, 2003), 143–181.

        it was too late: Harvey H. Jackson, *Lachlan McIntosh and the Politics of Revolutionary Georgia* (Athens: University of Georgia Press, 1979), 104–110.

207   *merely observed:* Borick, *Gallant Defense*, 154–159.

209   *West Point:* Willcox, *Portrait of a General,* 339–341.

211   *if he failed:* Flexner, *George Washington in the American Revolution*, 375–395.

        with minimal resistance: Flexner, *George Washington in the American Revolution*, 375–395.

212   *a most providential interposition:* Freeman, *Washington*, 446.

215   *lost on Jefferson:* Dumas Malone, *Jefferson the Virginian* (Boston: Little, Brown, 1948), 336–341.

216   *of a defeat:* Willcox, *Portrait of a General*, 381.

        arriving on the 12th: Louis Gottschalk, *Lafayette and the Close of the American Revolution* (Chicago: University of Chicago Press, 1942), 189–208.

217   *for the moment:* Mahan, *Major Operations*, 119–122.

219   *killed or wounded:* Robert Armistead Stewart, *The History of Virginia's Navy of the Revolution* (Baltimore: Genealogical, 1934), 102.

        give us America: Willcox, *Portrait of a General*, 382–383.

        naval superiority: Willcox, *Portrait of a General*, 390.

220   *make the best of it:* Willcox, *Portrait of a General*, 390.

221   *for use in the north:* Willcox, *Portrait of a General*, 405.

        believed it would do: William Willcox, "The British Road to Yorktown: A Study in Divided Command," *American Historical Review* 52 (1946).

        in the most ruinous train imaginable: Washington to Noah Webster, July 31, 1788; in Rhodehamel, ed., *George Washington*, 690.

222   *our generous allies:* Journal of Yorktown Campaign; in Rhodehamel, ed., *George Washington*, 422.

        deliverance must come: Freeman, *Washington*, 464.

        the North American coast: Henri Doniol, *Histoire de la participation de la France à établissement Etats-Unis d'Amerique: Correspondence diplomatique et documents* (Paris, 1886–99), 5:466–468.

        everything turns: Washington to Franklin, December 20, 1780; in Rhodehamel, ed., *George Washington*, 402–403.

223   *necessary and eligible:* Journal of Yorktown Campaign; in Rhodehamel, ed., *George Washington,* 428.

　　　　fatal to our cause: Washington to Noah Webster, July 31, 1788; in Rhodehamel, ed., *George Washington,* 690.

224   *before Laurens arrived:* Edmund S. Morgan, *Benjamin Franklin* (New Haven: Yale University Press, 2002), 265–271.

　　　　twenty-five wounded: Allen, *Naval History of the American Revolution,* 548–554.

225   *mission was canceled:* Allen, *Naval History of the American Revolution,* 575–577.

226   *Clinton did nothing:* Willcox, *Portrait of a General,* 402.

　　　　warships, and no money: Willcox, *Portrait of a General,* 394.

227   *on August 31:* Willcox, *Portrait of a General,* 419.

228   *he was returning:* Willcox, *Portrait of a General,* 414.

229   *on the American coast:* Willcox, *Portrait of a General,* 420–421.

231   *on both sides:* French officer's observation of Hood during battle in Commager and Morris, *Spirit of Seventy-Six,* 1220–1221.

　　　　alongside that of an enemy: David Howarth, *Trafalgar* (New York: Atheneum, 1969), 73.

232   *had been resolved:* Mahan, *Major Operations,* 124–128; Michael Stephenson, *Patriot Battles: How the War of Independence Was Fought* (New York: HarperCollins, 2007), 341–347.

233   *to hear the worst:* Willcox, *Portrait of a General,* 432.

234   *the battle was over:* George Washington, Journal of the Yorktown Campaign; in Rhodehamel, ed., *George Washington,* 421–464. For an excellent account of the battle of Yorktown, see Richard M. Ketchum, *Victory at Yorktown: The Campaign That Won the Revolution* (New York: Henry Holt, 2004).

235   *purchase farms:* John Paul Jones to Captain McNeill; in Morison, *John Paul Jones,* 321.

　　　　almost entirely lost: Jones to Washington, May 7, 1781; in Allen, *Naval History of the American Revolution,* 577–578.

　　　　difficult to avoid tears: John Adams to the President of Congress, July 6, 1780; in William M. Fowler Jr., *Rebels Under Sail: The American Navy During the Revolution* (New York: Scribner's, 1976), 303.

236   *forced a surrender:* Flexner, *George Washington in the American Revolution,* 468–469.

　　　　to those of Great Britain: King's speech in J. Holland Rose, *Life of William Pitt* (London: G. Bell, 1923), 100.

　　　　borders of the sea: Sir George Otto Trevelyan, *George the Third and Charles Fox: The Concluding Part of the American Revolution* (London: Longmans, Green), 2:388.

237   *heaven be praised:* The United States and Britain signed a preliminary peace in November 1782, and on January 20, 1783, Britain, France, Spain, and Holland signed an armistice and preliminary peace. The terms were identical to those in the final peace treaty. Adams to Abigail Adams, January 22, 1783; in Butterfield, Friedlaender, and Kline, *Abigail and John: Selected Letters of the Adams Family, 1762-1784* (Cambridge: Harvard University Press, 1975), 337.

　　　　preliminary peace terms: James Duncan Philips, *Salem in the Eighteenth Century* (Salem, Mass.: Essex Institute, 1969), 442; Samuel Flagg Bemis, *The Diplomacy of the American Revolution* (Bloomington: Indiana University Press, 1957), 247.

239   *Spanish silver:* Account of John Kessler, mate on the *Alliance,* March 7, 1783; in Commager and Morris, *Spirit of Seventy-Six,* 962–963; Allen, *Naval History of the American Revolution,* 588–591, 605–608.

CHAPTER 7

241   *distressing a degree:* Washington to William Gordon, July 8, 1783; in Rhodehamel, ed., *George Washington,* 530–531.

241   *twelve hundred seamen:* Marshall Smelser, *The Congress Founds the Navy, 1787–1798* (South Bend: University of Notre Dame Press, 1959), 36.

242   *pretend to a navy:* James A. Field, *From Gibraltar to the Middle East: America and the Mediterranean World, 1776–1882* (Chicago: Imprint, 1991), 32.

243   *indignation and impotence:* Dumas Malone, *Jefferson and the Rights of Man* (Boston: Little, Brown, 1951), 27.

       by piecemeal: Malone, *Jefferson and the Rights of Man,* 27–28.

       will be applied: Jefferson to Adams, July 1, 1786; and Adams to Jefferson, July 31, 1786; in Dudley W. Knox, ed., *Naval Documents Related to the United States Wars with the Barbary Powers* (Washington, D.C.: U.S. Government Printing Office, 1939–1944), 1:10–12.

244   *to have a navy: The Federalist Papers,* no. 24 (New York: Penguin, 2003), 158.

       may dictate: Federalist Papers, no. 11, 81.

       against our liberties: Federalist Papers, no. 41, 247.

245   *enough for him:* Henry's speeches before the Virginia Ratifying Convention on June 5 and 7, 1788; in Ralph Ketcham, *The Anti-Federalist Papers* (New York: Penguin, 1986), 199–216.

       of the country: Quoted in Conor Cruise O'Brien, *The Long Affair* (Chicago: University of Chicago Press, 1976), 72.

246   *a minimal threat:* John C. Miller, *The Federalist Era* (New York: Harper & Row, 1960), 85.

247   *occasion would never arise:* James Thomas Flexner, *George Washington and the New Nation, 1783–1793* (Boston: Little, Brown, 1970), 145.

       injurious to themselves: Jefferson, Autobiography, in Merrill D. Peterson, ed., *Thomas Jefferson: Writings* (New York: Library of America, 1984), 58–59.

       of their souls: Malone, *Jefferson and the Rights of Man,* 185.

248   *anything to do with us:* Autobiography, in Peterson, ed., *Thomas Jefferson: Writings,* 57–58.

       precious commodities: Jefferson to Madison, August 28, 1789, in Paul A. Varg, *Foreign Policies of the Founding Fathers* (Baltimore, Md.: Penguin, 1970), 76.

250   *first priority:* Stanley Elkins and Eric McKitrick, *The Age of Federalism* (New York: Oxford University Press, 1793), 131.

       in all its branches: Middleton to Pitt, August 24, 1786; in Rose, *Life of William Pitt,* 210.

252   *than any other:* A. J. Burt, *The United States, Great Britain, and British North America: From the Revolution to the Establishment of Peace After the War of 1812* (New Haven: Yale University Press, 1940), 55–70; Charles R. Ritcheson, *Aftermath of Revolution: British Policy Toward the United States* (New York: Norton, 1969), 3–32.

253   *starving population:* Morison, *Maritime History of Massachusetts,* (Boston: Houghton Mifflin, 1921), 38.

255   *protect southern interests:* Donald L. Robinson, *Slavery in the Structure of American Politics, 1765–1820* (New York: Harcourt, 1971), 248–265.

       return to the empire: Roger H. Brown, *The Republic in Peril: 1812* (New York: Norton, 1971), 1–15.

256   *veneration as he:* Fisher Ames to William Tudor, N.Y., April 25–26, 1789, "Memoir of Tudor," MHS *Collections,* 2nd series, 8 (1819), 318; in Winfred E. A. Bernhard, *Fisher Ames: Federalist and Statesman, 1758–1808* (Chapel Hill: University of North Carolina Press, 1965).

       that man: Bemis, *John Quincy Adams,* 85.

257   *our first man:* Fisher Ames to G. R. Minot, May 3, 1789; in Irving Brant, *James Madison, Father of the Constitution: 1787–1800* (New York: Bobbs-Merrill, 1950), 248.

258   *1.4 million a year:* Forrest McDonald, *Alexander Hamilton* (New York: Norton, 1979), 147–148.

259   *made domestically:* McDonald, *Alexander Hamilton*, 148–149, 165–171.
260   *states' rights:* Drew R. McCoy, *The Elusive Republic: Political Economy in Jeffersonian America* (New York: Norton, 1982), 91–92.
      these two parties: Worthington C. Ford, ed., *The Writings of John Quincy Adams* (New York, 1913–1917), 1:50. Quoted in Bernhard, *Fisher Ames,* 145.
      in the United States: Irving Brant, *James Madison, Father of the Constitution: 1787–1800* (New York: Bobbs-Merrill, 1950), 289.
      compromise organized: On Jefferson's attitude toward this compromise, see McDonald, *Alexander Hamilton*, 184.
261   *with their Quakers:* George C. Rogers Jr., *Evolution of a Federalist:William Loughton Smith of Charleston, 1758–1812* (Columbia: University of South Carolina Press, 1962), 197.
      for the rebel cause: Leonard F. Guttridge and Jay D. Smith, *The Commodores* (New York: Harper & Row, 1969), 7.
262   *filled with slaves:* Brant, *James Madison*, 250.
      a civil war: Brant, *James Madison*, 308–309; Robinson, *Slavery in the Structure of American Politics*, 303–31; Ralph Ketcham, *Madison* (Charlottesville: University Press of Virginia, 1990), 315.
      a long way off: Don Higginbotham, *George Washington: Uniting a Nation* (Lanham, Md.: Rowman & Littlefield, 2002), 85.
264   *liberty in the new:* Brant, *James Madison*, 371.
      finally settled: Washington to Gouverneur Morris, October 13, 1789; in Rhodehamel, ed., *George Washington*, 746.
      of your nation: Hamilton to Lafayette, October 6, 1789; in O'Brien, *Long Affair*, 86.
265   *change in imposters:* David McCullough, *John Adams* (New York: Simon & Schuster, 2001), 418–421.
      a thought [as monarchy]: in John C. Miller, *The Federalist Era, 1789–1801* (New York: Harper, 1960), 95.
266   *relations with Europe:* Julia H. Macleod, "Jefferson and the Navy: A Defense," *Huntington Library Quarterly* (February 1945): 154–155.
      were identical: Stanley Elkins and Eric McKitrick, *The Age of Federalism* (New York: Oxford University Press, 1993), 209.

CHAPTER 8
268   *six thousand:* O'Brien, *Long Affair*, 151.
      than it now is: Jefferson to William Short, January 3, 1793; in Peterson, ed., *Thomas Jefferson: Writings*, 1004.
269   *against all kings:* in Rose, *Life of William Pitt*, 107.
      gage of battle, he shouted: Rose, *Life of William Pitt*, 112.
      of the earth: Washington to Earl of Buchan, April 22, 1793; in Rhodehamel, ed., *George Washington*, 838.
270   *lucrative trade:* Harry Ammon, *The Genet Mission* (New York: Norton, 1973).
      contracting nations: in Samuel Flagg Bemis, *Jay's Treaty* (New Haven: Yale University Press, 1962), 195.
271   *declared neutrality:* Charles R. Ritcheson, *Aftermath of Revolution* (New York: Norton, 1979), 284.
272   *invade Spanish Florida:* Ammon, *Genet Mission*, 44.
273   *peals of exultation:* Jefferson to Monroe, May 5, 1793; in O'Brien, *Long Affair*, 167.
      perpetual feasts: O'Brien, *Long Affair*, 163.

274   *from the British:* Frederick Jackson Turner, "The Origin of Genet's Projected Attack on Louisiana and the Floridas," *AHR* 3 (1897): 650–671.
       immensely difficult: Dumas Malone, *Jefferson and the Ordeal of Liberty* (Boston: Little, Brown, 1962), 114.
       the place he fills: In Raymond Walters Jr., *Albert Gallatin* (New York: Macmillan, 1957), 58.

275   *British merchantmen:* Miller, *Federalist Era*, 130–135.
       Washington's neutrality: O'Brien, *Long Affair*, 191.

276   *been murdered:* O'Brien, *Long Affair*, 153.

279   *ready for war:* Washington's Fifth Annual Message to Congress, December 3, 1793; in Rhodehamel, ed., *George Washington*, 848.
       military stores: Smelser, *Congress Founds the Navy*, 52–53.
       force in the Government: Elkins and McKitrick, *Age of Federalism,* 390.

280   *monstrous expense: Annals of Congress*, IV, 434 (February 6, 1794); Leonard D. White, *The Federalists* (New York: Macmillan, 1948), 156.
       fitting out a fleet: Thomas Wentworth Higginson, *Life and Times of Stephen Higgins* (Boston: Houghton Mifflin, 1907), 189.
       Yankee dialect better: Smelser, *Congress Founds the Navy*, 68.

281   *under this act:* U.S. Congress, *The Public Statutes at Large of the United States of America* (Boston, 1850-), 1:350–351.

282   *victories at sea:* Alfred Thayer Mahan, *The Influence of Sea Power upon the French Revolution and Empire, 1793–1812* (Boston: Little, Brown, 1897), 1:41–68.

283   *infinitely preferable:* Washington, letter to Buchan; in Elkins and McKitrick, *Age of Federalism*, 388–396.
       by the roots: Samuel Flagg Bemis, *Jay's Treaty: A Study in Commerce and Diplomacy* (New Haven: Yale University Press, 1962), 372.
       Chief Justice Jay: Elkins and McKitrick, *Age of Federalism*, 388–396.
       is appointed: Washington to Tobias Lear, May 6, 1794; in Rhodehamel, ed., *George Washington*, 866.
       suitable character: Walter Stahr, *John Jay*, 316.

284   *finest fighting sailor:* Hulbert Footner, *Sailor of Fortune: The Life and Adventures of Commodore Barney, U.S.N.* (New York: Harper, 1940), 193-194.
       America's foremost naval architect: For a different view of Humphreys, see Michael A. Palmer, *Stoddert's War* (Annapolis: Naval Institute Press, 1987), 27; and Howard I. Chapelle, *The History of the American Sailing Navy: The Ships and Their Development* (New York: Bonanza, 1949), 117–122.

285   *young naval architect:* Doughty would have a long career designing men-of-war for the navy.

286   *strongest in the world:* N. A. M. Rodger, *The Command of the Ocean: A Naval History of Britain, 1649–1815* (New York: Norton, 2005), 441–453; C. S. Forester, *The Age of Fighting Sail* (New York: Doubleday, 1956), 43–44.

287   *delayed the harvesting:* Virginia Steele Wood, *Live Oaking: Southern Timber for Tall Ships* (Annapolis: Naval Institute Press, 1981).

288   *were never built:* Smelser, *Congress Founds the Navy*, 76.

289   *first to last:* A. L. Burt, *The United States, Great Britain, and British North America from the Revolution to the Establishment of Peace After the War of 1812* (New Haven: Yale University Press, 1940), 156.
       our two countries: Burt, *United States,* 156.

290   *Sovereigns or States:* The full text of the treaty is conveniently printed in Bemis, *Jay's Treaty,* 453–488.

291   *slave owners:* Robinson, *Slavery.*

292   *fitfully administered:* For a different view, see Christopher Lloyd, *The British Seaman* (Rutherford, N.J.: Fairleigh Dickinson University Press), 1968; Michael Lewis, *A Social History of the Navy, 1793–1815* (London: Chatham, 1960), 116–127.

of the United States: Dumas Malone, *Jefferson and the Ordeal of Liberty* (Boston: Little, Brown, 1962), 3:249. Richard Walsh, ed., *The Writings of Christopher Gadsden* (Columbia: University of South Carolina Press, 1966), 265.

293   *Northwest Territory to exploitation:* Elkin and McKittrick, *Age of Federalism*, 431–441.

town of Boston: Quoted in Irving Brant, *James Madison: Father of the Constitution, 1787–1800* (New York: Bobbs-Merrill, 1950), 439.

on a nation: John Adams to Abigail, May 3, 1796; in Stephen G. Kurtz, *The Presidency of John Adams: The Collapse of Federalism, 1795–1800* (Philadelphia: University of Pennsylvania Press, 1957), 75. For the fight over the treaty in the House, see pages 19–77.

294   *36-gun frigate:* James A. Field Jr., *From Gibraltar to the Middle East: America and the Mediterranean World, 1776–1882* (Chicago: Imprint, 1991), 37–38.

295   *praise in America:* Samuel Flagg Bemis, *Pinckney's Treaty* (Baltimore: Johns Hopkins University Press, 1926).

dangerous proceedings: Freeman, *George Washington*, 652.

296   *could never be found:* Quoted in Malone, *Jefferson and the Ordeal of Liberty*, 189.

in the Government: Quoted in O'Brien, *Long Affair*, 211.

297   *to treat them:* Elkins and McKitrick, *Age of Federalism*, 537–538.

wholesale attack: Albert H. Bowman, *Struggle for Neutrality* (Knoxville: University of Tennessee Press, 1974) 234–235, 238.

the enemy of mankind: Miller, *Federalist Era*, 194.

298   *defeat the Jay Treaty:* Miller, *Federalist Era*, 192ff.

what more she required: Miller, *Federalist Era,* 194.

so nobly contended: Quoted in Harry Ammon, *James Monroe: The Quest for National Identity* (Charlottesville: University of Virginia Press, 1990), 155.

299   *shall counsel:* Washington's Farewell Address; in Rhodehamel, ed., *George Washington*, 962–977.

300   *by the present:* Rhodehamel, ed., *George Washington*, 980–981.

CHAPTER 9

302   *fellow citizens:* Quoted in Alexander Deconde, *The Quasi-War* (New York: Scribner's, 1966), 3.

his predecessor had laid out: Kurtz, *Presidency of John Adams*, 333.

303   *Madison and Jefferson:* Brant, *James Madison,* 455, 457.

policy matters: McCullough, *John Adams,* 415, 447–448, 459–460.

304   *firmly established:* *New York Journal* and *Patriotic Register*, April 6, 1793; quoted in McCullough, *John Adams,* 444.

seized 316 American vessels: *American State Papers*, 2:28–63; in Dudley W. Knox, ed., *Naval Documents Related to the Quasi-War Between the United States and France, February 1797–October 1798* (Washington, D.C.: U.S. Government Printing Office, 1935), 6.

305   *defend its neutrality:* Knox, ed., *NDQW*, 25.

306   *great lengths:* Adams to General Uriah Forrest of Georgetown, Maryland, June 20, 1797; quoted in Kurtz, *Presidency of John Adams*, 233.

307   *their vault:* Bernard, *Fisher Ames*, 291.

308   *apostle of all this:* Jefferson to Edmund Randolph, June 27, 1797; quoted in O'Brien, *Long Affair*, 244.

308   *conquered Britain:* McCullough, *John Adams*, 489.
309   *would be war:* Marvin R. Zahniser, *Charles Cotesworth Pinckney: Founding Father* (Chapel Hill: University of North Carolina Press, 1967), 136–195.
       must be respected: Page Smith, *John Adams* (New York: Doubleday, 1962), 2:987.
       at its flood: Madison to Monroe, December 17, 1797; in Kurtz, *Presidency of John Adams*, 291.
311   *sold to the French:* Abigail Adams to Mary (Smith) Cranch, April 13, 1798; Stewart Mitchell, ed., *New Letters of Abigail Adams, 1788–1801* (Boston: Houghton Mifflin, 1947), 156.
313   *the most persevering industry:* Quoted in Michael A. Palmer, *Stoddert's War: Naval Operations During the Quasi-War with France, 1798–1801* (Annapolis: Naval Institute Press, 2000), 10.
       of the government: This is Oliver Wolcott's estimate; Elkins and McKitrick, *Age of Federalism*, 634.
314   *during the short Quasi-War:* Frederick C. Leiner, *Millions for Defense: The Subscription Warships of 1798* (Annapolis: Naval Institute Press, 2000), 3.
315   *fifty cents a head:* Kurtz, *Presidency of John Adams,* 305.
316   *the Federalist Party:* Kurtz, *Presidency of John Adams*, 330–331.
       threats to the Constitution: Walters, *Gallatin*, 109.
317   *and their papers:* Abigail Adams to Mary (Smith) Cranch, June 19, 1798, Mitchell, ed., *New Letters of Abigail Adams, 1788–1801*, 193.
       ruins of our Constitution: Walters, *Gallatin*, 117.
318   *laws in these states:* Hamilton to Sedgwick, February 2, 1799; in Joanne B. Freeman, ed., *Alexander Hamilton: Writings* (New York: Library of America, 2001), 913.
       without a fight: Page Smith, *John Adams* (New York: Doubleday, 1962) 2:971.
320   *had been forgotten:* Bernard C. Nalty, *Long Passage to Korea: Black Sailors and the Integration of the U.S. Navy* (Washington, D.C.: U.S. Government Printing Office, 2003), 3.
       during the Revolution: Thomas Wentworth Higginson, *Life and Times of Stephen Higginson* (Boston: Houghton Mifflin, 1907), 198.
321   *coming on ours:* NDQW, 3:161–162.
322   *interest in him:* Eugene S. Ferguson, *Truxtun of the Constellation: The Life of Commodore Thomas Truxtun, U.S. Navy, 1755–1822* (Baltimore, Md.: Johns Hopkins University Press, 1956), 11–12.
323   *and other faults:* NDQW, 1:386.
324   *duly respected:* Washington to Stoddert, September 26, 1798; in *NDQW,* 455–457.
       things in the West Indies: NDQW, 3:29.

CHAPTER 10
326   *independent nation:* Quoted in Samuel Flagg Bemis, *John Quincy Adams* (New York: Knopf, 1950), 96.
327   *independent, and powerful country:* Bemis, *John Quincy Adams,* 99; Peter P. Hill, *William Vans Murray: Federalist Diplomat* (Syracuse: Syracuse University Press, 1971), 103–115.
330   *the odium of rejecting [the nomination]:* Quoted in Merrill D. Peterson, *Thomas Jefferson and the New Nation* (New York: Oxford University Press, 1970), 620.
       and Patrick Henry: Arthur Burr Darling, *Our Rising Empire, 1763–1803* (Hamden, Conn.: Archon, 1962), 34.

330   *April 1799:* Kurtz, *Presidency of John Adams*, 378–381.
331   *four months' worth of provisions:* Charles Oscar Paullin, *Commodore John Rogers* (1909; Annapolis: Naval Institute Press, 1967), 35.
332   *two who died:* NDQW, 2:326ff.
       he was a hero: Eugene S. Ferguson, *Truxtun of the Constellation* (Baltimore: Johns Hopkins University Press, 1956), 160–169.
       no negotiation were going on: Adams to Pickering, August 6, 1799; in NDQW, 3:33–34.
333   *patrolled independently:* Dudley W. Knox, *History of the United States Navy* (New York: Putnam, 1936), 47–48.
334   *this kind of abdication:* Quoted in Elkins and McKitrick, *Age of Federalism*, 638.
       success may be assured: John C. Miller, *Alexander Hamilton: Portrait in Paradox* (New York: Barnes & Noble Books, 1959), 501.
       nine-tenths of Haiti's population: These are estimates from the *London Times*, January 7, 1792. Given in Thomas O. Ott, *The Haitian Revolution, 1789–1804* (Knoxville: University of Tennessee Press, 1973).
335   *trade with Saint-Dominigue:* John H. Coatsworth, "American Trade with European Colonies in the Caribbean and South America, 1790–1812," *William and Mary Quarterly*, 3rd series, 24 (April 1967).
336   *we have to fear it:* McCullough, *John Adams*, 521.
       the thing I have most at heart: Smith, *John Adams*, 2:1008.
337   *owned for many years:* William Fowler Jr., *Silas Talbot: Captain of Old Ironsides* (Mystic, Conn.: Mystic Seaport Museum, 1995), 158.
338   *official, diplomatic assurances:* Peter P. Hill, *William Vans Murray* (Syracuse: Syracuse University Press, 1971), 128.
339   *loans to support it:* Miller, *Alexander Hamilton,* 495–505.
       more like a fool: Miller, *Alexander Hamilton,* 502.
340   *situation of our country:* McCullough, *John Adams,* 532.
       dangerous and critical: Mitchell, ed., *New Letters of Abigail Adams,* 222.
341   *conduct of their agents:* Jefferson to Gerry, January 26, 1799; in Peterson, ed., *Thomas Jefferson: Writings,* 1055–1061; Arthur M. Schlesinger Jr., ed., *The Coming to Power: Critical Presidential Elections in American* History (New York: McGraw-Hill, 1972), 50–51.
342   *was interested:* Elkins and McKitrick, *Age of Federalism*, 681–690.
343   *was created:* McCullough, *John Adams,* 554–555.
       eleven hundred marines: Dudley W. Knox, *A History of the United States Navy,* 55.
344   *to 10 percent:* Palmer, *Stoddert's War,* 235; Elkins and McKitrick, *Age of Federalism,* 891.
       six points of the wind: Christopher McKee, *Edward Preble* (Annapolis: Naval Institute Press, 1972), 68.
       on November 28, 1800: McKee, *Edward Preble*, 68–79.

CHAPTER 11

347   *susceptible of its benign influence:* Quoted in Noble E. Cunningham Jr., *In Pursuit of Reason: The Life of Thomas Jefferson* (Baton Rouge: Louisiana State University Press, 1787), 321; Margaret Smith and Gaillard Hunt, eds., *The First Forty Years of Washington Society* (New York: Scribner's, 1906), 59.
348   *the thing itself:* Noble E. Cunningham Jr., *Jefferson and Monroe* (Charlottesville: Thomas Jefferson Foundation, 2003), 32.
348   *beyond absolute necessity:* Cunningham, *Jefferson and Monroe,* 32.

Negro president: Gary Wills, *The Negro President: Jefferson and the Slave Power* (Boston: Houghton Mifflin, 2005) 2; William W. Freehling, *The Road to Disunion*, vol. 1 (New York: Oxford University Press, 1990); Leonard L. Richards, *The Slave Power* (Baton Rouge: Louisiana State University Press, 2000).

349   *fundamental constitutional principles:* First Inaugural Address, in Peterson, ed., *Thomas Jefferson: Writings*, 493.

our felicities: First Inaugural Address; in Peterson, ed., *Thomas Jefferson: Writings*, 494.

eliminate slavery: For a different view, see Malone, *Jefferson and the Ordeal of Power*, 207–213.

350   *Debt reduction was an obsession with Jefferson:* Dumas Malone, *Jefferson the President: Second Term, 1805–1809* (Boston: Little, Brown, 1974), 495.

additional cuts to come later: Leonard D. White, *The Jeffersonians: A Study in Administrative History, 1801–1829* (New York: Macmillan, 1956), 142; Merrill D. Peterson, *Thomas Jefferson and the New Nation* (New York: Oxford University Press, 1970), 687–689.

351   *take care of them:* Jefferson to S. Smith, April 17, 1801; in Henry Adams, *The History of the United States During the Administrations of Thomas Jefferson* (New York: Literary Classics of the United States, 1986), 151.

confidence and resignation: Adams, *History of the United States,* 151.

debtors' prison: Irving Brant, *James Madison: Secretary of State, 1800–1809* (New York: Bobbs-Merrill, 1953), 39.

likely to employ: Mitchell, ed., *New Letters of Abigail Adams*, 265.

navies, armies and wars: Adams, *History of the United States*, 144.

peaceable coercions: Jefferson to Robert R. Livingston, September 9, 1801; in Peterson, ed., *Thomas Jefferson: Writings*, 1093.

352   *peaceable means:* Peterson, *Thomas Jefferson and the New Nation*, 665.

rather than of force: Third Annual Message, October 17, 1803, in Peterson, ed., *Thomas Jefferson: Writings*, 516.

his memory: Dumas Malone, *Jefferson the President: First Term, 1801–1805* (Boston: Little, Brown, 1970), 51.

would mankind be: John C. Fitzpatrick, ed., *Writings of Washington* (Washington, D.C.: U.S. Government Printing Office, 1931–44), 33:382–383; James Thomas Flexner, *George Washington: Anguish and Farewell, 1793–1799* (Boston: Little, Brown, 1969), 135–136.

354   *task wisely:* Dudley W. Knox, ed., *Naval Documents Related to the United States Wars with the Barbary Powers* (Washington, D.C., 1939–1944), 1:378–379.

character, and prudence: Cooper, *History of the Navy*, 89.

355   *of this globe:* Ferguson, *Truxtun of the Constitution*, 217.

356   *continued unresolved:* Peterson, *Thomas Jefferson and the New Nation*, 664; Malone, *Jefferson the President: First Term, 1801–1805*, 98; *NDWBP,* 3:171–176.

directed on St. Domingo: June 4, 1802, quoted in Adams, *History of the United States*, 269.

357   *alliance and war:* Brant, *James Madison, Secretary of State*, 15.

359   *and the Floridas:* Jefferson to Ambassador Livingston, April 18, 1802; in Peterson, ed., *Thomas Jefferson: Writings*, 1104–1107.

360   *reduce their expense:* Adams, *History of the United States*, 288.

the proposal: Peterson, *Thomas Jefferson and the New Nation*, 836.

war with England: Brant, *James Madison: Secretary of State,* 117.

362   *threats and economic sanctions:* For a different view, see Alexander Deconde, *This Affair of Louisiana* (New York: Scribner's, 1976).

362   *highly advantageous:* Madison to Monroe and Livingston, October 6, 1803; in Robert A. Rutland, *James Madison: The Founding Father* (New York: Macmillan, 1987), 180.

363   *this country:* in Malone, *Jefferson the President: First Term, 1801–1805,* 295.

364   *a standoff:* Peterson, *Thomas Jefferson and the New Nation,* 797–798. President Madison seized a portion of West Florida in October 1810, and another in April 1813. The United States acquired the rest of Florida in the Adams-Onis Treaty on February 22, 1819.

365   *the epoch of our strength:* Henry Adams, *Albert Gallatin* (New York: Chelsea House, 1983), 211.

366   *too expensive:* Peterson, *Thomas Jefferson and the New Nation,* 664.
       suspend him: McKee, *Edward Preble,* 114.
       against them: McKee, *Edward Preble,* 130.

367   *powers to hostility:* Secretary Robert Smith to Jefferson, March 17, 1803; in McKee, *Edward Preble,* 128.
       courageous action: McKee, *Edward Preble,* 140–141; Tyrone G. Martin, *A Most Fortunate Ship* (Chester, Conn.: Globe Pequot, 1980), 47–48.

369   *115 big guns of the pasha's shore batteries:* McKee, *Edward Preble,* 269.

370   *engulfing the frigate:* McKee, *Edward Preble,* 194–199.

371   *move the pasha:* James T. De Kay, *A Rage for Glory: The Life of Commodore Stephen Decatur, Jr., USN* (New York: Free Press, 2004), 45–68; McKee, *Edward Preble,* 173–199, 247–277.

372   *"sensibly lessen" in 1804:* Third Annual Message, in Peterson, ed., *Thomas Jefferson: Writings,* 513.

373   *mutual destruction:* Jefferson's Third Annual Message to Congress, October 17, 1803; in Peterson, ed., *Thomas Jefferson: Writings,* 515.

374   *term of duration:* Jefferson to Madam de Stael, May 24 1813; in Peterson, ed., *Thomas Jefferson: Writings,* 1272.

375   *the United States:* Second Inaugural Address, March 4, 1805; in Peterson, ed., *Thomas Jefferson: Writings,* 519.

CHAPTER 12

377   *taken to England:* David Howarth, *Trafalgar: The Nelson Touch* (New York: Atheneum, 1969).

378   *my plan:* Sir Charles Petrie, *George Canning,* 2nd ed. (London: Eyre & Spottiswoode, 1946), 77–78.
       invasion plans: Peter Dixon, *George Canning: Politician and Statesman* (New York: Mason/Charter, 1976), 111–112.

380   *by the Constitution:* Lear to Secretary of State Madison, July 5, 1805; in *NDWBP,* 6:162.
       and unembarrassed: Lear to Madison, August 12, 1805; in *NDWBP,* 6:264–271.

381   *any other time in his presidency:* Dumas Malone, *Jefferson the President: Second Term* (Boston: Little, Brown, 1974), 496.
       3,000 men: Jefferson to Crowninshield, May 13, 1806; in Adams, *History of the United States,* 742.

382   *actually in service:* Statutes at Large, 2:402; William M. Fowler Jr., *Jack Tars and Commodores* (Boston: Houghton Mifflin, 1984), 142–143; Craig L. Symonds, *Navalists and Anti-Navalists: The Naval Policy Debate in the United States, 1785–1827* (Newark: University of Delaware Press, 1980).
       a well-balanced force: McKee, *Edward Preble,* 319–320.
       formidable gun-boats: Leonard D. White, *The Jeffersonians* (New York: Macmillan, 1956), 268.

384   *less than imagined:* Adams, *History of the United States,* 633.

385   *of this government:* Ambassador Merry to Lord Mulgrave, March 19, 1806; in Adams, *History of the United States,* 739–740.

386   *killed him instantly:* Adams, *History of the United States,* 740.

387   *the south:* Peterson, *Thomas Jefferson and the New Nation,* 860–865.

389   *a fight:* Log of U.S. Frigate *Chesapeake,* June 22–23, 1807; in *NW1812,* 26–28; Spencer C. Tucker and Frank T. Reuter, *Injured Honor: The Chesapeake-Leopard Affair, June 22, 1807* (Annapolis: Naval Institute Press, 1996).

    becomes a degradation: Robert A. Rutland, *James Madison: The Founding Father* (New York: Macmillan, 1987), 191.

    fight against it: Samuel Eliot Morison, *Harrison Gray Otis: The Urbane Federalist* (Boston: Houghton Mifflin, 1969), 281.

    every heart: Bradford Perkins, *Prologue to War* (Berkeley: University of California Press, 1961), 146.

    abolition of impressment: Perkins, *Prologue to War,* 146.

390   *appearance of menace:* Charles O. Paullin, *Commodore John Rogers* (Annapolis: United States Naval Institute, 1909), 190.

    Yankee cockboat: July 27, 1807; Henry Adams, *History of the United States of America,* 956.

391   *shall have none:* Peterson, *Thomas Jefferson and the New Nation,* 899.

    national independence: Eighth Annual Message to Congress, November 8, 1808; in Peterson, ed., *Thomas Jefferson: Writings,* 544.

392   *entirely groundless:* White, *The Jeffersonians,* 425.

    patrol from Chesapeake Bay to Florida: NDW1812, 1:38.

    obtain its end: Peterson, *Thomas Jefferson and the New Nation,* 907.

393   *national imperative:* Peterson, *Thomas Jefferson and the New Nation,* 913.

    ideas of liberty: Morison, *Harrison Gray Otis,* 298.

394   *public approbation:* Peterson, *Thomas Jefferson and the New Nation,* 920.

CHAPTER 13

396   *enforce our resentments:* Madison to Pinkney, March 17, 1809; Robert Rutland, *James Madison* (New York: Macmillan, 1987), 86.

397   *resorting to it:* Robert Allen Rutland, *The Presidency of James Madison* (Lawrence: University Press of Kansas, 1990), 43.

    to the ambassador: Burt, *The United States,* 269.

399   *was legendary:* Burt, *The United States,* 274–276; Bernard Mayo, ed., "Instructions to the British Ministers to the United States, 1791–1812," *AHR, Annual Report,* 1936, 3.

402   *three thousand miles off:* Hulbert Footner, *Sailor of Fortune: The Life and Adventures of Commodore Barney, U.S.N.* (New York: Harper, 1940), 246.

    alternatives before them: Madison's First Annual Message to Congress; Adams, *History of the United States of America During the Administrations of James Madison* (New York: Literary Classics of the United States, 1986), 125.

    at your feet: Adams, *History of the United States,* 134.

403   *orders in council:* Ralph Ketcham, *James Madison,* 503–504.

405   *Rogers had only one boy injured:* Commander Arthur Bingham, R.N., to Vice Admiral Herbert Sawyer, R.N., May 21, 1811; Commodore John Rogers to Secretary of the Navy Paul Hamilton, May 23, 1811, in *NDW1812,* 1:40–50.

    improving the navy: Ketcham, *James Madison,* 509–510.

406   *war was likely:* Ketcham, *James Madison,* 509–510.

    budge on impressment: Burt, *The United States,* 314.

407　*against the United States for years:* F. A. Updyke, *The Diplomacy of the War of 1812* (Baltimore: Johns Hopkins University Press, 1915), 134.

　　British depravity: Madison's War Message, June 1, 1812; in Jack N. Rakove, ed., *James Madison: Writings* (New York: Library Classics of the United States, 1999), 685.

408　*favorable auspices:* Jefferson to Kosciusko, June 28, 1812; in Peterson, ed., *Thomas Jefferson: Writings,* 1264–1265.

　　not nothing: Ketcham, *James Madison,* 565.

　　neglect of the Navy: Adams to Jefferson, May 1, 1812; in Lester J. Cappon, ed., *The Adams-Jefferson Letters: The Complete Correspondence* (Chapel Hill: University of North Carolina Press, 1959), 301.

　　vote of 62 to 59: John K. Mahon, *The War of 1812* (Gainesville: University Press of Florida, 1972), 5.

　　knees before me: Alan Schom, *Napoleon Bonaparte* (New York: HarperCollins, 1997), 593.

409　*recrossed the Neiman:* Schom, *Napoleon Bonaparte,* 628–644.

410　*expedition against Russia:* Madison to Wheaton, February 26, 1827; in Adams, *History of the United States,* 476–477.

　　colonists and vassals: Perkins, *Prologue to War,* 435.

CHAPTER 14

412　*in a single engagement:* Hamilton to Rogers, May 21, 1812; Rogers to Hamilton, June 3, 1812; Decatur to Hamilton, June 8, 1812; in *NDW1812,* 1:117–124.

414　*in contact with them:* David Long, *Nothing Too Daring: A Biography of Commodore David Porter, 1780–1843* (Annapolis: Naval Institute Press, 1970), 43.

416　*bitterly disappointed:* Commodore Rogers's Journal, June 23, 1812; Captain Richard Byron to Vice Admiral Sawyer, June 27, 1812; in *NDW1812,* 1:153–160.

417　*polite and gentlemanly:* *NDW1812,* 1:209–211.

418　*nothing to fear from any single deck ship:* Hull to Hamilton, July 2, 1812; in *NDW1812,* 1:160–161.

420　*Broke gave up the chase:* Captain Isaac Hull to Secretary Hamilton, July 21, 1812; in *NDW1812,* 1:161–165; Tyrone G. Martin, *A Most Fortunate Ship* (Chester, Conn.: Globe Pequot, 1980), 104–111.

422　*in two hours:* Hull to Secretary Hamilton, August 28, 1812; in *NDW1812,* 1:241.

　　sucked down with her: Martin, *A Most Fortunate Ship,* 114–121.

423　*painful to observe:* Adams, *History of the United States,* 623–625.

　　bastards and outlaws: Adams, *History of the United States,* 623–625.

　　line-of-battle ships: Adams, *History of the United States,* 623–625.

424　*four hundred prisoners:* Captain David Porter to Secretary Hamilton, September, 3, 1812; in *NDW1812,* 1:443–447; David Long, *Nothing Too Daring: A Biography of Commodore David Porter, 1780–1843* (Annapolis: Naval Institute Press, 1970), 64–69.

425　*with the great objects in view:* Secretary Hamilton to Commodore John Rogers, September 9, 1812; in *NDW1812,* 1:471.

426　*received promotions:* Master Commandant Jacob Jones to Secretary of the Navy Hamilton, November 24, 1812; in *NDW1812,* 1:580–588.

427　*Carden struck his colors:* Captain John S. Carden, R.N., to Secretary of the Admiralty John W. Croker, October 28, 1812; in *NDW1812,* 1:549–551; Commodore Stephen Decatur to Secretary of the Navy Hamilton, October 30, 1812, 552–553.

429　*wreckage over the ocean:* Journal of Commodore William Bainbridge, December 29, 1812; Lieutenant Henry D. Chads to Secretary of the Admiralty John W. Croker, December 31, 1812; in *NDW1812,* 1:640–648.

429 *Bainbridge and his officers:* NDW1812, 1:640–648.

430 *$1.5 million:* Joshua Barney, Journal of a Cruize on Board the Schooner *Rossie*; in NDW1812, 1:248–260.

431 *his smaller warships:* Lords Commissioners of the Admiralty to Admiral Sir John B. Warren, R.N., December 26, 1812; in *NDW1812,* 1:633–634.

432 *70 to 56:* For an analysis of the congressional fight over expanding the navy, see Craig L. Symonds, *Navalists and Antinavalists: The Naval Policy Debate in the United States, 1785–1827* (Newark: University of Delaware Press, 1980), 174–185.

435 *expectations of a nation:* Jefferson to Benjamin Rush, March 6, 1813; in Marshall Smelser, *The Democratic Republic, 1801–1815* (New York: Harper & Row, 1968), 251.
     rights on one element: James Madison, Second Inaugural Address; in *James Madison, Writings,* 696.

436 *almost disappeared:* Adams, *History of the United States,* 1033.
     back to sea: De Kay, *Rage for Glory,* 131–141.

437 *the remainder of the year:* Paullin, *Commodore John Rogers,* 264–277.

438 *eastern shore:* For the limits of the British blockade, see Wade G. Dudley, *Splintering the Wooden Wall: The British Blockade of the United States, 1812–1815* (Annapolis: Naval Institute Press, 2003).

439 *he survived:* C. S. Forester, *The Age of Fighting Sail* (New York: Doubleday, 1956), 160–165.
     victories in 1812: Forester, *Age of Fighting Sail,* 166.

440 *local people:* Forester, *Age of Fighting Sail,* 169–172; Adams, *History of the United States,* 830–833.

442 *Longfellow's home:* Adams, *History of the United States,* 815–817; Forester, *Age of Fighting Sail,* 189–193.

443 *around Cape Horn:* Quoted in Long, *Nothing Too Daring,* 81.

444 *whale fishery is completely destroyed:* Captain David Porter to Secretary of the Navy Jones, July 3, 1814; in NDW1812, 3:730–732.

446 *the Cherub four:* For the entire Porter voyage, see *NDW1812,* 3:707–767.
     on his head: NDW1812, 3:733–737.

447 *throughout the country:* Long, *None Too Daring,* 162–166.

CHAPTER 15

448 *well understood:* James Madison, *Writings,* 697.

450 *and ninety-one wounded:* For excellent accounts of the battle of Lake Erie, see Samuel Eliot Morison, *Old Bruin: Commodore Matthew C. Perry, 1794–1858* (Boston: Little, Brown, 1967), 41–49; and Theodore Roosevelt, *The Naval War of 1812* (New York: Modern Library, 1999), 141–156.

454 *in their attacks:* Adams, *History of the United States,* 1185.

455 *the war was over:* Martin, *A Most Fortunate Ship,* 153–168.
     into British hands: NDW1812, 3:339.
     forced to surrender: Adams, *History of the United States,* 1037–1038.

456 *never be known:* Adams, *History of the United States,* 1040–1045.
     on October 30, 1814: Adams, *History of the United States,* 1038–1039.
     fourteen wounded: De Kay, *Rage for Glory,* 143–152.

458 *to stop the invasion:* Major General Alexander Macomb to Acting Secretary of War Monroe, September 12, 1814; in *NDW1812,* 3:609.

459 *with ten row-galleys:* Secretary of the Navy Jones to Master Commandant Thomas Macdonough, February 22, 1814; in *NDW1812,* 3:396–397.

461 *the ship been in condition:* Lieutenant Robertson's Report; in *NDW1812,* 3:615.

in her hull: Roosevelt, *Naval War of 1812,* 207–218.

of the enemy: Macdonough to Jones, September 11, 1814; in *NDW1812,* 3:607.

gratefully remembered: Commander Daniel Pring, R.N., to Commodore Sir James L. Yeo, R.N., September 12, 1814; in *NDW1812,* 3:609–612.

463 *as if I was a brother:* Adams, *History of the United States,* 1012.

into British hands: Major General Robert Ross, British Army, to Secretary of State for War and the Colonies, Earl Bathurst, August 30, 1814; in *NDW1812,* 3:223–226.

465 *on New Orleans:* Scott S. Sheads, *The Rocket's Red Glare:The Maritime Defense of Baltimore in 1814* (Centerville, Md.: Tidewater, 1986); Roosevelt, *Naval War of 1812,* 177–178.

466 *ceased to operate:* James Madison, *Writings,* 708.

467 *of the government:* James Madison, *Writings,* 708.

468 *live a British slave:* Jackson to Rachel Jackson, October 21, 1814; in Reginald Horsman, *The War of 1812* (New York: Alfred A. Knopf, 1969), 234.

women and children: Jackson to Rachel Jackson, August 15, 1814; in Robert V. Remini, *The Life of Andrew Jackson* (New York: Penguin, 1990), 88.

471 *sleep on our soil:* Remini, *Life of Andrew Jackson,* 95.

472 *without hazard:* Adams, *History of the United States,* 1178.

473 *main columns:* A third column was to use the swamp to turn Jackson's left flank, but it had no success. Daniel Walker Howe, *What Hath God Wrought* (New York: Oxford, 2007), 8–18.

Cochrane's fleet: The best account of the battle of New Orleans is Robert V. Remini, *The Battle of New Orleans* (New York:Viking, 1999).

474 *all his three predecessors:* Lester J. Cappon, *Adams-Jefferson Letters* (Chapel Hill: University of North Carolina Press, 1987), 2:508.

equilibrium between the powers: Alan Palmer, *Metternich: A Biography* (New York: Harper & Row, 1972), 124.

Entire Book: See Henry Kissinger, *A World Restored: Metternich, Castlereagh, and the Problems of Peace, 1812–22* (Boston: Houghton Mifflin, 1973).

BIBLIOGRAPHY

DOCUMENTS

Abbot, W. W., et al., eds. *The Papers of George Washington*. Revolutionary War Series. Charlottesville: University of Virginia Press, 1985–.

Adams, Abigail. *New Letters*. Edited by Stuart Mitchell. Boston: Houghton Mifflin, 1947.

Adams, Henry, ed. *The Writings of Albert Gallatin*. 3 vols. Philadelphia, 1879.

Albion, Robert G. *Naval and Maritime History: An Annotated Bibliography*. Mystic, Conn.: Mystic Seaport Museum, 1972.

Allen, Gardner W., ed. *Commodore Hull: Papers of Isaac Hull, Commodore, United States Navy*. Boston: Atheneum, 1929.

American State Papers. 38 vols. Washington, 1832–1861.

Barker, John. *The British in Boston: Being a Diary of Lt. John Barker*. Cambridge: Harvard University Press, 1924.

Barnes, G. R., and J. H. Owens, eds. *The Private Papers of John, Earl of Sandwich First Lord of the Admiralty, 1771–1782*. London, 1932.

Baxter, James P., ed. *Documentary History of the State of Maine*. 24 vols. Portland: Maine Historical Society, 1869–1916.

Beck, Alverta S., ed. *The Correspondence of Esek Hopkins, Commander in Chief of the United States Navy*. Providence: Rhode Island Historical Society, 1933.

Biddle, Charles. *Autobiography of Charles Biddle*. Philadelphia: E. Claxton, 1883. Reprint, Whitefish, Mt.: Kessinger, 2006.

Boyd, Julian P., et al., eds. *The Papers of Thomas Jefferson*. Princeton: Princeton University Press, 1950–.

Brooks, G. S., ed. *James Durand: An Able Seaman of 1812*. New Haven: Yale University Press, 1926.

Butterfield, L. H., ed. *The Adams Papers*. Vol. 3, *Diary and Autobiography of John Adams*. New York: Atheneum, 1964.

Butterfield, L. H., Marc Friedlaender, and Mary-Jo Kline, eds. *The Book of Abigail and John: Selected Letters of the Adams Family, 1762–1784*. Cambridge: Harvard University Press, 1975.

Cappon, Lester J. *Adams-Jefferson Letters*. Chapel Hill: University of North Carolina Press, 1987.

Carter, Charles E., ed. *Correspondence of General Thomas Gage with the Secretaries of State . . . 1763–1775*. 2 vols. New Haven: Yale University Press, 1931–1933.

Chadwick, French Ensor, ed. *The Graves Papers and Other Documents Relating to the Naval Operations of the Yorktown Campaign, July to October, 1781*. New York: Naval History Society, 1916.

Chesnutt, David R., C. James Taylor, and Peggy J. Clark, eds. *The Papers of Henry Laurens*. 16 vols. Columbia: University of South Carolina Press, 1994–2002.

Clark, William B., and William James Morgan, eds. *Naval Documents of the American Revolution*. 11 vols. Washington, D.C.: U.S. Government Printing Office, 1964–.

Coletta, Paolo E. *A Bibliography of American Naval History*. Annapolis: Naval Institute, 1981.

Commager, Henry Steele, and Richard B. Morris. *The Spirit of Seventy-Six: The Story of the American Revolution as Told by Participants*. New York: Da Capo, 1995.

Cooper, James Fenimore. *Ned Meyers: Or, a Life Before the Mast*. 1843. New York: BiblioBazaar, 2006.

Davies, K. G., ed. *Documents of the American Revolution*. 21 vols. Shannon: Irish University Press, 1972–1981.

Department of the Navy. Naval History Division. *United States Naval History: A Bibliography*. Washington, D.C.: U.S. Government Printing Office, 1972.

Dudley, William S., and Michael J. Crawford, eds. *The Naval War of 1812: A Documentary History*. 3 vols. Washington, D.C.: U.S. Government Printing Office, 1985–.

Dunn, Susan. *Something That Will Surprise the World: The Essential Writings of the Founding Fathers*. New York: Basic, 2006.

Elliot, Jonathan, ed. *The Debates in the Several State Conventions on the Adoption of the Federal Constitution*. 5 vols. 2ed. Buffalo, N.Y.: William S. Hein, 1996.

Fanning, Nathaniel. *Fanning's Narrative: The Memoirs of Nathaniel Fanning. An Officer of the American Navy*. New York: Heritage, 2003.

Fitzpatrick, John C. *Writings of Washington*. 39 vols. Washington, D.C.: U.S. Government Printing Office, 1931–1944.

Force, Peter, ed. *American Archives: Fourth Series, Containing a Documentary History of the English Colonies in North America from the King's Message to Parliament of March 7, 1774, to the Declaration of Independence by the United States*. 6 vols. Washington, D.C., 1837–1846.

———. *American Archives: Fifth Series, Containing a Documentary History of the United States of America from the Declaration of Independence, July 4, 1776, to the Definitive Treaty of Paris with Great Britain, September 3, 1783*. 3 vols. Washington, D.C., 1848–1853.

Ford, Worthington C., ed. *The Writings of John Quincy Adams*. 7 vols. New York, 1913–1917.

Ford, Worthington C., et al., eds. *The Journals of the Continental Congress*. 34 vols. Washington, D.C.: U.S. Government Printing Office, 1904–1937.

Fredrikson, John C., ed. *War of 1812: Eyewitness Accounts: An Annotated Bibliography*. Westport, Conn.: Greenwood, 1997.

Gales, J., and W. Seaton. *Annals of the Congress, 1789–1824*. 42 vols. Washington, D.C., 1834–1856.

Goldsborough, Charles W. *The United States Naval Chronicle*. Washington, D.C., 1824.

Hamilton, Alexander. *The Papers of Alexander Hamilton*. Edited by Harold C. Syrett and Jacob E. Cooke. New York: Columbia University Press, 1961–.

———. *The Works of Alexander Hamilton*. 7 vols. Edited by John C. Hamilton. New York, 1851.

Hamilton, Alexander, James Madison, and John Jay. *The Federalist Papers.*

Kaminski, John P., and Gaspare J. Saladino, eds. *Documentary History of the Ratification of the Constitution.* Vol. 10. Madison: State Historical Society of Wisconsin, 1976.

Knox, Dudley W., ed. *Naval Documents Related to the United States Wars with the Barbary Powers.* 6 vols. Washington, D.C.: U.S. Government Printing Office, 1939–1944.

———. *Naval Documents Related to the Quasi-War Between the United States and France.* 7 vols. Washington, D.C.: U.S. Government Printing Office, 1935–1939.

Labaree, Leonard W., et al., eds. *The Papers of Benjamin Franklin.* New Haven: Yale University Press, 1959–.

Leech, Samuel. *Thirty Years from Home or a Voice from the Main Deck: Being the Experience of Samuel Leech, Who Was Six Years in the British and American Navies.* 1843. London: Chatham, 2003.

MacGregor, Morris J., Jr., and Bernard C. Nalty, eds. *Blacks in the United States Armed Forces: Basic Documents.* 13 vols. Wilmington, Del.: Scholarly Resources, 1977.

Mackensie, Frederick. *Diary of Frederick Mackensie.* Cambridge: Harvard University Press, 1930.

Mayo, Bernard, ed. "Instructions to the British Ministers to the United States, 1791–1812." *American Historical Association Annual Report* 3 (1936).

Moser, Harold, et al., eds. *The Papers of Andrew Jackson.* Vol. 3. Knoxville: University of Tennessee Press, 1991.

Moultrie, William. *Memoirs of the American Revolution.* 2 vols. Reprint. New York: New York Times/Arno Press, 1968.

The Naval Chronicle. 40 vols. London, 1799–1818.

Neeser, Robert W., ed. *Letters and Papers Related to the Cruises of Gustavus Cunningham.* New York: Associated Faculty Press, 1970.

———. *Statistical and Chronological History of the United States Navy, 1775–1907.* 2 vols. New York: Naval History Society, 1909.

Nevins, Alan, ed. *The Diary of John Quincy Adams, 1794–1845.* New York: Ungar, 1951.

Paullin, Charles Oscar, ed. *Out-Letters of the Continental Marine Committee and Board of Admiralty: August, 1776–September, 1780.* 2 vols. New York, 1914.

Porter, David Dixon. *Journal of a Cruise Made to the Pacific Ocean by Captain David Porter, in the United States Frigate Essex, in the Years 1812, 1813, and 1814, Containing Descriptions of the Cape de Verde Islands, Coasts of Brazil, Patagonia, Chile, and Peru, and of the Gallapagos Islands.* 2 vols. Philadelphia: Bradford & Inskip, 1815.

Public Statutes at Large of the United States of America. Washington, D.C.: U.S. Government Printing Office, 1845–.

Richardson, James D., ed. *Messages and Papers of the Presidents.* 10 vols. Washington, D.C., 1896.

Roche, John, Jr. "*Constitution* in the Quasi-War with France: The Letters of John Roche, Jr., 1798–1801." *American Neptune* 27 (1967).

Shea, J. G., ed. *The Operations of the French Fleet Under the Count de Grasse in 1781–2.* New York: Bradford, 1864.

Showman, Richard, et al., eds. *The Papers of Nathanael Greene.* 13 vols. Chapel Hill: University of North Carolina Press, 1976–2005.

Smith, Paul H., ed. *Letters of Delegates to Congress, 1774–1789.* 26 vols. Washington, D.C.: U.S. Government Printing Office, 1976–2000.

Taylor, Robert J., et al., eds. *Papers of John Adams.* Cambridge: Harvard University Press, 1977–1983.

Walsh, Richard, ed. *The Writings of Christopher Gadsden, 1764–1805*. Columbia: University of South Carolina Press, 1966.

Warren-Adams Letters. 2 vols. Collections of MHS. Vol. 72 (1917). Vol. 73 (1925).

Wharton, Francis, ed. *The Revolutionary Diplomatic Correspondence of the United States*. 6 vols. Washington, D.C.: U.S. Government Printing Office, 1889.

SECONDARY WORKS

Abbot, Willis J. *Blue Jackets of 1812*. New York: Dodd, Mead, 1887.

_____. *The Naval History of the United States*. New York: Dodd, Mead, 1896.

Adams, Henry. *Albert Gallatin*. New York: Chelsea House, 1983.

_____. *History of the United States of America During the Administrations of James Madison*. New York: Literary Classics of the United States, 1986.

_____. *History of the United States of America During the Administrations of Thomas Jefferson*. New York: Literary Classics of the United States, 1986.

Alden, John R. *The American Revolution*. New York: Harper & Row, 1954.

_____. *Charles Lee: Traitor or Patriot?* Baton Rouge: Louisiana State University Press, 1951.

_____. *General Gage in America*. Baton Rouge: Louisiana State University Press, 1948.

_____. *A History of the American Revolution*. New York: Knopf, 1969.

_____. *The South in the Revolution, 1763–1789*. 4th ed. Baton Rouge: Louisiana State University Press, 1981.

Alexander, John K. *Samuel Adams: America's Revolutionary Politician*. Lanham, Md.: Rowman & Littlefield, 2004.

Allen, Gardner W. *A Naval History of the American Revolution*. 2 vols. 1913. Cranbury, N.J.: Scholar's Bookshelf, 2005.

_____. *Our Navy and the Barbary Corsairs*. Boston, 1905.

_____. *Our Navy and the West Indian Pirates*. Salem, Mass.: Essex Institute, 1929.

Ambrose, Stephen. *Undaunted Courage*. New York: Simon & Schuster, 1996.

Ammon, Harry. *The Genet Mission*. New York: Norton, 1973.

Appleby, Joyce. *Inheriting the Revolution*. Cambridge: Harvard University Press, 2000.

_____. *Thomas Jefferson*. New York: Henry Holt, 2003.

Astor, Gerald. *The Right to Fight: A History of African Americans in the Military*. Novato, Calif.: Presidio, 1998.

Barney, Mary, ed. *A Biographical Memoir of the Late Commodore Joshua Barney*. Boston: Gray & Bowen, 1832.

Barrow, Clayton R. *America Spreads Her Sails: U.S. Sea Power in the Nineteenth Century*. Annapolis: Naval Institute Press, 1973.

Bell, Madison Smartt. *Toussaint L'Ouverture: A Biography*. New York: Pantheon, 2007.

Bemis, Samuel Flagg. *The Diplomacy of the American Revolution*. Bloomington: Indiana University Press, 1957.

_____. *Jay's Treaty: A Study in Commerce and Diplomacy*. New Haven: Yale University Press, 1962.

_____. *John Quincy Adams*. New York: Knopf, 1950.

Bernhard, Winfred E. A. *Fisher Ames: Federalist and Statesman, 1758-1808*. Chapel Hill: University of North Carolina Press, 1965.

Bierne, Francis F. *The War of 1812*. New York: Dutton, 1949.

Billias, George A. *General John Glover and His Marblehead Mariners*. New York: Holt, Rinehart & Winston, 1960.

_____. *George Washington's Generals*. New York: Morrow, 1964.

_____. *George Washington's Opponents*. New York: Morrow, 1969.

Birnbaum, Louis. *Red Dawn at Lexington*. Boston: Houghton Mifflin, 1986.

Black, Jeremy. *War for America: The Fight for Independence, 1775–1783*. New York: Palgrave Macmillan, 1991.

Bolster, W. Jeffrey. *Black Jacks: African American Seamen in the Age of Sail*. Cambridge: Harvard University Press, 1997.

Borick, Carl P. *A Gallant Defense: The Siege of Charleston, 1780*. Columbia: University of South Carolina Press, 2003.

Bowman, Albert H. *Struggle for Neutrality: Franco-American Diplomacy During the Federalist Era*. Knoxville: University of Tennessee Press, 1974.

Bradford, James C. *Quarterdeck and Bridge: Two Centuries of American Naval Leaders*. Annapolis: Naval Institute Press, 1997.

Brant, Irving. *James Madison, Father of the Constitution: 1787–1800*. New York: Bobbs-Merrill, 1950.

_____. *James Madison, Secretary of State: 1800–1809*. New York: Bobbs-Merrill, 1953.

_____. *James Madison, the President: 1809–1812*. New York: Bobbs-Merrill, 1956.

Brooks, George S., ed. *James Durant, an Able Seaman of 1812*. New Haven: Yale University Press, 1926.

Brown, Gerald Saxon. *The American Secretary: The Colonial Policy of Lord George Germain, 1775–1778*. Ann Arbor: University of Michigan Press, 1963.

Brown, Roger H. *The Republic in Peril: 1812*. New York: Norton, 1971.

Brown, Wilburt. *The Amphibious Campaign for West Florida and Louisiana*. Tuscaloosa: University of Alabama Press, 1969.

Bryson, Thomas A. *Tars, Turks, and Tankers: The Role of the United States Navy in the Middle East*. Metuchen, N.J.: Scarecrow, 1980.

Buel, Richard, Jr. *In Irons*. New Haven: Yale University Press, 1998.

Burstein, Andrew. *Jefferson's Secrets: Death and Desire at Monticello*. New York: Basic, 2006.

Burt, A. L. *The United States, Great Britain, and British North America from the Revolution to the Establishment of Peace After the War of 1812*. New Haven: Yale University Press, 1940.

Butler, Lindley S. *Pirates, Privateers, and Rebel Raiders of the Carolina Coast*. Chapel Hill: University of North Carolina Press, 2000.

Byrd, Harrison. *Navies in the Mountains: The Battles on the Waters of Lake Champlain and Lake George, 1606–1814*. New York: Oxford University Press, 1962.

Callahan, North. *Henry Knox: General Washington's General*. New York: Rinehart, 1958.

Carroll, John A., and Mary W. Ashworth. *George Washington: First in Peace*. New York: Scribner's, 1957.

Cary, John. *Joseph Warren: Physician, Politician, Patriot*. Urbana: University of Illinois Press, 1961.

Casto, William R. *Foreign Affairs and the Constitution in the Age of Fighting Sail*. Columbia: University of South Carolina Press, 2006.

Cecelski, David S. *The Waterman's Song: Slavery and Freedom in Maritime North Carolina*. Chapel Hill: University of North Carolina Press, 2001.

Chandler, David. *The Campaigns of Napoleon*. New York: Macmillan, 1966.

Chapelle, Howard I. *The History of the American Sailing Navy*. New York: Norton, 1949.

Clark, Thomas. *Naval History of the United States*. Exp. ed. 2 vols. Philadelphia: M. Carey, 1814.

Clark, William Bell. *Captain Dauntless: The Story of Nicholas Biddle of the Continental Navy*. Baton Rouge: Louisiana State University Press, 1949.

_____. *The First Saratoga: Being the Saga of John Young and His Sloop-of-War*. Baton Rouge: Louisiana State University Press, 1953.

_____. *Gallant John Barry, 1745–1803: The Story of a Naval Hero of Two Wars.* New York: Macmillan, 1938.

_____. *George Washington's Navy.* Baton Rouge: Lousiana State University Press, 1960.

_____. *Lambert Wickes, Sea Raider and Diplomat: The Story of a Naval Captain of the Revolution.* New Haven: Yale University Press, 1932.

Coburn, Frank Warren. *The Battle of April 19, 1775.* 2nd ed. Lexington, Mass.: Lexington Historical Society, 1922.

Coggins, Jack. *Ships and Seamen of the American Revolution.* Harrisburg, Pa.: Stackpole, 1969.

Cogliano, Francis D. *American Maritime Prisoners in the Revolutionary War: The Captivity of William Russell.* Annapolis: Naval Institute Press, 2001.

Coleman, Kenneth. *The American Revolution in Georgia, 1763–1789.* Athens: University of Georgia Press, 1958.

Coletta, Paolo E., ed. *American Secretaries of the Navy.* Vol. 1, *1775–1913.* Annapolis: Naval Institute Press, 1980.

Commager, Henry Steele, and Richard B. Morris. *The Spirit of Seventy-Six: The Story of the American Revolution as Told by Participants.* New York: Harper, 1975.

Cormack, William S. *Revolution and Political Conflict in the French Navy, 1789–1794.* New York: Cambridge University Press, 1995.

Countryman, Edward. *The American Revolution.* Rev. ed. New York: Hill & Wang, 2003.

Cox, Caroline. *A Proper Sense of Honor: Service and Sacrifice in George Washington's Army.* Chapel Hill: University of North Carolina Press, 2004.

Crow, Jeffrey, and Larry E. Tise. *The Southern Experience in the American Revolution.* Chapel Hill: University of North Carolina Press, 1978.

Crowhurst, Patrick. *The French War on Trade, 1793–1815.* Aldershot, U.K.: Scolar Press, 1989.

Cunningham, Noble E., Jr. *Jefferson and Monroe.* Charlottesville: Thomas Jefferson Foundation, 2003.

Dangerfield, George. *The Era of Good Feelings.* New York: Harcourt, Brace & World, 1952.

Darling, Arthur Burr. *Our Rising Empire, 1763–1803.* New Haven: Yale University Press, 1940.

Dauer, Manning J. *The Adams Federalists.* Baltimore: Johns Hopkins University Press, 1953.

Davis, Burke. *The Campaign That Won America: The Story of Yorktown.* New York: Dial, 1970.

Davis, David Brion. *Inhuman Bondage: The Rise and Fall of Slavery in the New World.* New York: Oxford University Press, 2006.

Dearborn, H. A. S. *The Life of William Bainbridge, Esq.* 1816. Princeton: Princeton University Press, 1931.

Deconde, Alexander. *This Affair of Louisiana.* New York: Scribner's, 1976.

_____. *The Quasi-War.* New York: Scribner's, 1966.

De Kay, James T. *A Rage for Glory: The Life of Commodore Stephen Decatur, Jr., USN.* New York: Free Press, 2004.

Diamant, Lincoln. *Chaining the Hudson: The Fight for the River in the American Revolution.* New York: Fordham University Press, 2004.

Dickerson, Oliver M. *The Navigation Acts and the American Revolution.* Philadelphia: University of Pennsylvania Press, 1951.

Dixon, Peter. *George Canning: Politician and Statesman.* New York: Mason/Charter, 1976.

Donovan, Frank. *The Tall Frigates.* New York: Dodd, Mead, 1962.

Douglas, W. A. B. *Gunfire on the Lakes: The Naval War on the Great Lakes and Lake Champlain.* Ottawa, Canada: National Museum of Man, 1977.

Drake, Francis Samuel. *Life and Correspondence of Henry Knox.* Boston: S. G. Drake, 1873.

Dudley, Wade, G. *Splintering the Wooden Wall: The British Blockade of the United States.* Annapolis: Naval Insitute Press.

Dull, Jonathan R. *A Diplomatic History of the American Revolution.* New Haven: Yale University Press, 1985.

_____. *The French Navy and American Independence: A Study of Arms and Diplomacy, 1774–1787.* Princeton: Princeton University Press, 1975.

Dupuy, R. Ernest, Gay Hammerman, and Grace P. Hayes. *The American Revolution: A Global War.* New York: David McKay, 1996.

Dupuy, Trevor Nevitt, and Grace R. Hayes. *The Military History of the Revolutionary War Naval Battles.* New York: Watts, 1970.

Dutton, Charles J. *Oliver Hazard Perry.* New York: Longmans, Green, 1935.

Dye, Ira. *The Fatal Cruise of the Argus: Two Captains in the War of 1812.* Annapolis: Naval Institute Press, 1994.

Eckert, Edward K. *The Navy Department in the War of 1812.* Social Sciences Monograph 48. Gainesville: University Press of Florida, 1973.

Ekins, Charles. *Naval Battles, from 1744 to the Peace of 1814.* London: Baldwin & Cradock, 1824.

Elkins, Stanley, and Eric McKitrick. *The Age of Federalism.* New York: Oxford University Press, 1993.

Eller, Ernest McNeill, ed. *Chesapeake Bay in the American Revolution.* Centerville, Md.: Tidewater, 1981.

Ellis, Joseph J. *American Creation: Triumphs and Tragedies at the Founding of the Republic.* New York: Knopf, 2007.

_____. *American Sphinx: The Character of Thomas Jefferson.* New York: Vintage, 1998.

_____. *Founding Brothers: The Revolutionary Generation.* New York: Vintage, 2000.

_____. *Passionate Sage: The Character and Legacy of John Adams.* New York: Norton, 1993.

Elting, John R. *Amateurs to Arms! A Military History of the War of 1812.* Chapel Hill, N.C.: Workman, 1991.

Everest, Allan S. *The War of 1812 in the Champlain Valley.* Syracuse: Syracuse University Press, 1981.

Fedorak, Charles John. *Henry Addington, Prime Minister, 1801–1804: Peace, War, and Parliamentary Politics.* Akron, Ohio: University of Akron Press, 2002.

Fehrenbacher, Don. *The Slaveholding Republic.* New York: Oxford University Press, 2001.

Ferguson, Eugene S. *Truxtun of the Constellation.* Baltimore, Md.: Johns Hopkins University Press, 1956.

Ferling, John. *Almost a Miracle.* New York: Oxford University Press, 2007.

Field, James A., Jr. *America and the Mediterranean World, 1776–1882.* Princeton: Princeton University Press, 1969.

Fischer, David Hackett. *Paul Revere's Ride.* New York: Oxford University Press, 1994.

_____. *Washington's Crossing.* New York: Oxford University Press, 2004.

Fitz-Enz, David G. *The Final Invasion: Plattsburgh, the War of 1812's Most Decisive Battle.* New York: Cooper Square, 2001.

Fleming, Thomas. *The First Stroke.* Washington, D.C.: National Park Service, 1978.

_____. *Now We Are Enemies: The Story of Bunker Hill.* New York: St. Martin's, 1960.

Foner, Jack D. *Blacks and the Military in American History: A New Perspective.* Reprint. New York: Praeger, 1974.

Footner, Hulbert. *Sailor of Fortune: The Life and Adventures of Commodore Barney, U.S.N.* New York: Harper, 1940.

Forbes, Ester. *Paul Revere and the World He Lived In.* Boston: Houghton Mifflin, 1942.

Ford, Worthington C. *George Washington.* 2 vols. New York, 1900.

Fowler, William M., Jr. *Jack Tars and Commodores: The American Navy, 1783–1815.* Boston: Houghton Mifflin, 1984.

_____. *Rebels Under Sail: The American Navy During the Revolution.* New York: Scribner's, 1976.

_____. *Silas Talbot: Captain of Old Ironsides.* Mystic, Conn.: Mystic Seaport Museum, 1995.

Freehling, William W. *The Road to Disunion.* Vol 1. New York: Oxford University Press, 1990.

Freeman, Douglas Southall. *George Washington: Planter and Patriot.* 7 vols. New York: Scribner's, 1951.

French, Allen. *The Day of Lexington and Concord.* Boston: Little, Brown, 1925.

_____. *The First Year of the American Revolution.* Boston: Houghton Mifflin, 1934.

_____. *General Gage's Informers.* Ann Arbor: University of Michigan Press, 1932.

Frey, Sylvia. *Water from the Rock: Black Resistance in a Revolutionary Age.* Princeton: Princeton University Press, 1993.

Frost, Holloway. *We Build a Navy.* Annapolis: Naval Institute Press, 1940.

Frothingham, Richard, Jr. *The History of Charlestown, Massachusetts.* Boston: Little, Brown, 1845.

_____. *History of the Siege of Boston.* Boston: Little Brown, 1851.

_____. *The Life and Times of Joseph Warren.* Boston: Little, Brown, 1866.

Galvin, John R. *The Minutemen.* Washington, D.C.: Brassey's, 1996.

Gardiner, Leslie. *The British Admiralty.* London: Blackwood, 1968.

Gardiner, Robert, ed. *Fleet Battle and Blockade: The French Revolutionary War, 1793–1797.* Claxton Editions, 2001.

_____. *Navies and the American Revolution.* Annapolis: Naval Institute Press, 1996.

Garitee, Jerome. *The Republic's Private Navy.* Middletown, Conn.: Wesleyan University Press, 1977.

Gilbert, Felix. *To the Farewell Address: Ideas of Early American Foreign Policy.* Princeton: Princeton University Press, 1961.

Gilkerson, William. *The Ships of John Paul Jones.* Annapolis: Naval Institute Press, 1987.

Gillmer, Thomas C. *Old Ironsides: The Rise, Decline, and Resurrection of the USS Constitution.* New York: McGraw-Hill, 1993.

Gottschalk, Louis. *Lafayette and the Close of the American Revolution.* Chicago: University of Chicago Press, 1942.

_____. *Lafayette Joins the American Army.* Chicago: University of Chicago Press, 1937.

Grant, Bruce. *Captain of Old Ironsides: The Life and Fighting Times of Isaac Hull.* New York: Pellegrini & Cudahy, 1947.

Greene, Lorenzo Johnston. *The Negro in Colonial New England, 1620–1776.* New York: Columbia University Press, 1942.

Greenwood, Isaac J. *Captain John Manley, Second in Rank in the United States Navy, 1776–1783.* Boston: Goodspeed, 1915.

Griffith, Samuel B., II. *In Defense of the Public Liberty: Britain, America, and the Struggle for Independence, from 1760 to the Surrender at Yorktown in 1783.* New York: Doubleday, 1976.

Gross, Robert. *The Minutemen and Their World.* New York: Hill & Wang, 1976.

Gruber, Ira. *The Howe Brothers and the American Revolution.* Chapel Hill: University of North Carolina Press, 1972.

Guttridge, Leonard F., and Jay D. Smith. *The Commodores.* New York: Harper & Row, 1969.

Hagan, Kenneth J. *In Peace and War: Interpretations of American Naval History, 1775–1984.* Westport: Conn.: Greenwood, 1984.

_____. *This People's Navy: The Making of American Sea Power.* New York: Free Press, 1991.

Haraszti, Zoltan. *John Adams and the Prophets of Progress.* Cambridge: Harvard University Press, 1952.

Harris, John. *America Rebels.* Boston: Boston Globe Newspaper Co., 1976.

Haw, James. *John and Edward Rutledge of South Carolina.* Athens: University of Georgia Press, 1997.

Hayward, Walter S. "The Penobscot Expedition." In *Essays in Modern English History in Honor of Wilbur Cortez Abbott*. Cambridge: Harvard University Press, 1941.

Hearn, Chester G. *George Washington's Schooners*. Annapolis: Naval Institute Press, 1995.

Heidler, David S., and Jeanne T. Heidler, eds. *Encyclopedia of the War of 1812*. Annapolis: Naval Institute Press, 1995.

Heimert, Alan. *Religion and the American Mind: From the Great Awakening to the Revolution*. Harvard: Harvard University Press, 1966.

Hibbert, Christopher. *Redcoats and Rebels: The American Revolution Through British Eyes*. New York: Grafton, 1990.

Hickey, Donald. *Don't Give Up the Ship: Myths of the War of 1812*. Urbana: University of Illinois Press, 2006.

_____. *The War of 1812*. Urbana: University of Illinois Press, 1989.

Higginbotham, Don. *George Washington: Uniting a Nation*. Lanham, Md.: Rowman & Littlefield, 2002.

_____. *The War of American Independence: Military Attitudes, Policies, and Practice, 1763–1789*. New York: Macmillan, 1971.

Higgins, Robert W., ed. *The Revolutionary War in the South: Power, Conflict, and Leadership*. Durham, N.C.: Duke University Press, 1979.

Higginson, Thomas Wentworth. *Life and Times of Stephen Higgins*. Boston: Houghton Mifflin, 1907.

Hill, Peter. *William Vans Murray, Federalist Diplomat: The Shaping of Peace with France, 1797–1801*. Syracuse: University of Syracuse Press, 1971.

Hoffman, Ronald, and Peter J. Albert. *Arms and Independence: The Military Character of the American Revolution*. Charlottesville: University of Virginia Press, 1984.

Holton, Woody. *Unruly Americans and the Origins of the Constitution*. New York: Hill & Wang, 2007.

Hough, Franklin B. *The Siege of Savannah*. Albany, N.Y.: Joel Munsell, 1866.

Howard, James L. *Seth Harding, Mariner: A Naval Picture of the Revolution*. New Haven: Yale University Press, 1930.

Howarth, David. *Trafalgar: The Nelson Touch*. New York: Atheneum, 1969.

_____. *Waterloo: A Near Run Thing*. London: Phoenix, 1997.

Howarth, Stephen. *To Shining Sea: A History of the United States Navy, 1775–1998*. Norman: University of Oklahoma Press, 1991.

Howe, Daniel Walker. *What Hath God Wrought*. New York: Oxford University Press, 2007.

Irwin, Ray W. *The Diplomatic Relations of the United States with the Barbary Powers, 1776–1816*. Chapel Hill: University of North Carolina Press, 1931.

Jackson, Harvey H. *Lachlan McIntosh and the Politics of Revolutionary Georgia*. Athens: University of Georgia Press, 1979.

Jackson, John W. *The Pennsylvania Navy, 1775–1781*. New Brunswick: Rutgers University Press, 1974.

James, William Milburne. *The British Navy in Adversity*. 1926. Cranbury, N.J.: Scholar's Bookshelf, 2005.

_____. *The Naval History of Great Britain During the French Revolutionary and Napoleonic Wars*. Vol. 6. Reprint. Harrisburg: Stackpole, 2003.

Jenkins, Ernest H. *A History of the French Navy*. London: Macdonald & Jane's, 1973.

Jensen, Merrill. *The Founding of a Nation: A History of the American Revolution, 1763–1776*. New York: Oxford University Press, 1968.

Jones, Thomas. *History of New York During the Revolutionary War*. Edited by Edward Floyd. 1879. New York: Arno, 1968.

Kaplan, Lawrence S. *Colonies into Nations: American Diplomacy, 1776–1801.* New York: Macmillan, 1974.

Kennett, Lee. *The French Forces in America, 1780–1783.* Westport, Conn.: Greenwood, 1977.

Ketcham, Ralph. *James Madison.* Charlottesville: University Press of Virginia, 1990.

Ketchum, Richard M. *Decisive Day: The Battle for Bunker Hill.* New York: Doubleday, 1962.

_____. *Saratoga: Turning Point of America's Revolutionary War.* New York: Henry Holt, 1997.

_____. *Victory at Yorktown: The Campaign That Won the Revolution.* New York: Henry Holt, 2004.

_____. *The Winter Soldiers.* New York: Doubleday, 1973.

Kite, Elizabeth S. *Beaumarchais and the War of American Independence.* 2 vols. Boston: Richard G. Badger, 1918.

Klein, Rachel N. *Unification of a Slave State: The Rise of the Planter Class in the South Carolina Backcountry, 1760–1808.* Chapel Hill: University of North Carolina Press, 1990.

Knox, Dudley W. *A History of the United States Navy.* New York: Putnam, 1936.

Kohn, Richard H. *Eagle and Sword.* New York: Free Press, 1975.

Kurtz, Stphen G., and James H. Hutson, eds. *Essays on the American Revolution.* Chapel Hill: University of North Carolina Press, 1973.

Labaree, Benjamin W. *Patriots and Partisans: The Merchants of Newburyport, 1764–1815.* Cambridge: Harvard University Press, 1962.

Larrabee, Harold A. *Decision at the Chesapeake.* New York: Clarkson N. Potter, 1964.

Larson, Edward J. *A Magnificent Catastrophe: The Tumultuous Election of 1800, America's First Presidential Campaign.* New York: Free Press, 2007.

Leiner, Frederick C. *Millions for Defense: The Subscription Warships of 1798.* Annapolis: Naval Institute Press, 2000.

Lewis, Charles L. *Admiral de Grasse and American Independence.* Annapolis: Naval Institute Press, 1945.

Lewis, Michael. *A Social History of the Navy, 1793–1815.* London: Chatham, 1960.

Link, Eugene P. *Democratic-Republican Societies, 1790–1800.* New York: Columbia University Press, 1942.

Lloyd, Christopher. *The British Seaman.* Rutherford, N.J.: Fairleigh Dickinson University Press, 1968.

_____. *The Navy and the Slave Trade.* London: Longmans, Green, 1949.

Logan, Rayford W. *The Diplomatic Relations of the United States with Haiti, 1776–1891.* Chapel Hill: University of North Carolina Press, 1941.

Long, David F. *Nothing Too Daring: A Biography of Commodore David Porter, 1780–1843.* Annapolis: Naval Institute Press, 1970.

_____. *Ready to Hazard: A Biography of Commodore William Bainbridge, 1774–1833.* Hanover, N.H.: University Press of New England, 1981.

Lord, Walter. *The Dawn's Early Light.* New York: Norton, 1972.

Lossing, Benson J. *Pictorial Field Book of the War of 1812.* New York: Harper, 1868.

Lovejoy, David S. *Rhode Island Politics and the American Revolution, 1760–1776.* Providence: Brown University Press, 1969.

McCoy, Drew R. *The Elusive Republic: Political Economy in Jeffersonian America.* Chapel Hill: University of North Carolina Press, 1980.

_____. *The Last of the Fathers: James Madison and the Republican Legacy.* Cambridge: Cambridge University Press, 1989.

McCusker, John J., Jr. *Alfred: The First Continental Flagship.* Washington, D.C.: Smithsonian, 1973.

McFarland, Philip. *The Brave Bostonians: Hutchinson, Quincy, Franklin, and the Coming of the American Revolution.* New York: Westview, 1998.

McKee, Christopher. *Edward Preble*. Annapolis: Naval Institute Press, 1972.

————. *A Gentlemanly and Honorable Profession: The Creation of the U.S. Naval Officer Corps, 1794–1815*. Annapolis: United States Naval Institute, 1991.

McManus, Edgar T. *Black Bondage in the North*. Syracuse: Syracuse University Press, 1973.

Mackesy, Piers. *The War for America, 1775–1783*. Cambridge: Harvard University Press, 1965.

Maclay, Edgar Stanton. *A History of American Privateers*. New York: Appleton, 1899.

Mahan, Alfred Thayer. *The Influence of Sea Power upon History, 1660–1783*. New York: Dover, 1987.

————. *The Influence of Sea Power upon the French Revolution and Empire, 1793–1812*. Boston: Little, Brown, 1897.

————. *The Life of Nelson: The Embodiment of the Sea Power of Great Britain*. Boston: Little, Brown, 1897.

Maier, Pauline. *The Old Revolutionaries: Political Lives in the Age of Samuel Adams*. New York: Knopf, 1980.

Malone, Dumas. *Jefferson and the Ordeal of Liberty*. Boston: Little, Brown, 1962.

————. *Jefferson the President: First Term, 1801–1805*. Boston: Little, Brown, 1970.

————. *Jefferson the President: Second Term, 1805–1809*. Boston: Little, Brown, 1974.

————. *Jefferson the Virginian*. Boston: Little, Brown, 1948.

Maloney, Linda M. *Captain from Connecticut: The Life and Times of Isaac Hull*. Boston: Northeastern University Press, 1986.

Marine, William M. *The British Invasion of Maryland, 1812–15*. Hatsboro, Pa.: Tradition, 1965.

Martin, Tyrone G. *A Most Fortunate Ship*. Chester, Conn.: Globe Pequot, 1980.

Massey, Gregory D. *John Laurens and the American Revolution*. Columbia: University of South Carolina Press, 2000.

Melville, Herman. *White Jacket*. New York: New American Library, 1979.

Meyer, Duane. *The Highland Scots of North Carolina*. Chapel Hill: University of North Carolina Press, 1961.

Middlekauff, Robert. *The Glorious Cause: The American Revolution, 1763–1789*. Rev. ed. New York: Oxford University Press, 2005.

Miller, John C. *Alexander Hamilton: Portrait in Paradox*. New York: Barnes & Noble Books, 1959.

————. *Crisis in Freedom: The Alien and Sedition Acts*. Boston: Little, Brown, 1951.

————. *The Federalist Era: 1789–1801*. New York: Harper Torchbooks, 1960.

Miller, Nathan. *Sea of Glory: The Continental Navy Fights for Independence, 1775–1783*. New York: David McKay, 1974.

Morgan, Edmund S. *Benjamin Franklin*. New Haven: Yale University Press, 2002.

Morgan, William James. *Captains to the Northward: Captains in the Continental Navy*. Barre, Mass.: Barre Gazette, 1959.

Morison, Samuel Eliot. *Harrison Gray Otis: The Urbane Federalist*. Boston: Houghton Mifflin, 1969.

————. *John Paul Jones: A Sailor's Biography*. Boston: Little, Brown, 1959.

————. *The Maritime History of Massachusetts*. Boston: Houghton Mifflin, 1921.

————. *Old Bruin: Commodore Matthew C. Perry, 1794–1858*. Boston: Little, Brown, 1967.

Muller, Charles G. *The Proudest Day: Macdonough on Lake Champlain*. New York: John Day, 1960.

Murdock, Harold. *Bunker Hill*. Boston: Riverside, 1927.

————. *The Nineteenth of April 1775*. Boston: Houghton Mifflin, 1923.

Nagel, Paul. *John Quincy Adams*. New York: Knopf, 1997.

Nalty, Bernard C. *Long Passage to Korea: Black Sailors and the Integration of the U.S. Navy*. Washington, D.C.: U.S. Government Printing Office, 2003.

_____. *Strength for the Fight: A History of Black Americans in the Military.* New York: Free Press, 1986.

Nevins, Allan. *American States During and After the American Revolution, 1775–1789.* New York: Macmillan, 1927.

Norton, Louis Arthur. *Joshua Barney: Hero of the Revolution and 1812.* Annapolis: Naval Institute Press, 2000.

Orieux, Jean. *Tallyrand: The Art of Survival.* Paris: Flammarion, 1970.

O'Shaughnessy, Andrew Jackson. *An Empire Divided: The American Revolution and the British Caribbean.* Philadelphia: University of Pennsylvania Press, 2000.

Ott, Thomas O. *The Haitian Revolution, 1789–1804.* Knoxville: University of Tennessee Press, 1973.

Pack, James. *The Man Who Burned the White House: Admiral Sir George Cockburn, 1772–1853.* Annapolis: Naval Institute Press, 1987.

Paine, Lincoln P. *Down East: Maritime History of Maine.* Gardiner, Me.: Tilbury, 2000.

Paine, Ralph D. *Joshua Barney: A Forgotten Hero of Blue Water.* New York: Century, 1924.

Palmer, Alan. *Metternich: A Biography.* New York: Harper & Row, 1972.

Palmer, Michael A. *Stoddert's War.* Annapolis: Naval Institute Press, 2000.

Palmer, Robert R. *World of the French Revolution.* New York: Harper & Row, 1971.

Paullin, Charles O. *Commodore John Rogers.* Reprint. Annapolis: United States Naval Institute, 1967.

_____. *The Navy of the American Revolution.* 1906. Chicago: Haskell House, 1971.

Perkins, Bradford. *Castlereagh and Adams: England and the United States, 1812–1823.* Berkeley: University of California Press, 1964.

_____. *The First Rapproachment: England and the United States, 1795–1805.* Berkeley: University of California Press, 1967.

_____. *Prologue to War.* Berkeley: University of California Press, 1961.

Peterson, Merrill D. *Thomas Jefferson and the New Nation.* New York: Oxford University Press, 1970.

Petrie, Sir Charles. *George Canning.* London: Eyre & Spottiswoode, 1930.

Philips, James Duncan. *Salem in the Eighteenth Century.* Salem, Mass.: Essex Institute, 1969.

Pitch, Anthony. *The Burning of Washington: The British Invasion of 1814.* Annapolis: Naval Institute Press, 1998.

Powell, William S. *North Carolina: A History.* Chapel Hill: University of North Carolina Press, 1977.

Puls, Mark. *Samuel Adams: Father of the American Revolution.* New York: Palgrave Macmillan, 2006.

Quimby, Robert S. *The U.S. Army in the War of 1812.* East Lansing: Michigan State University Press, 1997.

Rakove, Jack N. *The Beginnings of National Politics: An Interpretive History of the Continental Congress.* Baltimore: Johns Hopkins University Press, 1982.

Reilly, Robin. *The British at the Gates.* New York: Putnam, 1974.

Remini, Robert. *Andrew Jackson.* Vol. 1, *The Course of American Empire, 1767–1821.* New York: HarperCollins, 1982.

_____. *The Battle of New Orleans.* New York: Viking, 1999.

_____. *The Life of Andrew Jackson.* New York: Penguin, 1988. A one-volume abridgement of a three-volume biography.

Richards, Leonard L. *The Slave Power.* Baton Rouge: Louisiana State University Press, 2000.

Ritcheson, Charles R. *Aftermath of Revolution: British Policy Toward the United States, 1783–1795.* New York: Norton, 1971.

Robinson, Donald L. *Slavery in the Structure of American Politics, 1765–1820*. New York: Harcourt Brace Jovanovich, 1971.

Rodger, N. A. M. *The Command of the Ocean: A Naval History of Britain, 1649–1815*. New York: Norton, 2005.

Rogers, George C. *Evolution of a Federalist: William Loughton Smith of Charleston, 1758–1812*. Columbia: University of South Carolina Press, 1967.

Roosevelt, Theodore. *The Naval War of 1812*. New York: Modern Library, 1999.

Rose, J. Holland. *Life of William Pitt*. London: G. Bell, 1923.

_____. *A Short Life of William Pitt*. London: G. Bell, 1925.

Royster, Charles. *Light-Horse Harry Lee and the Legacy of the American Revolution*. New York: Knopf, 1981.

Rutland, Robert A. *James Madison: The Founding Father*. New York: Macmillan, 1987.

_____. *The Presidency of James Madison*. Lawrence: University Press of Kansas, 1990.

Schaeper, Thomas. *John Paul Jones and the Battle off Flamborough Head*. New York: Peter Lang, 1989.

Schama, Simon. *Rough Crossing: Britain, the Slaves, and the American Revolution*. New York: HarperCollins, 2006.

Scheer, George F., and Hugh F. Rankin. *Rebels and Redcoats*. New York: Da Capo, 1957.

Schlesinger, Arthur M., Jr., ed. *The Coming to Power: Critical Presidential Elections in American History*. New York: McGraw-Hill, 1972.

Schom, Alan. *Napoleon Bonaparte*. New York: HarperCollins, 1997.

Searcy, Condray. *The Georgia-Florida Contest in the American Revolution*. Tuscaloosa: University of Alabama Press, 1985.

Selby, John. *The Revolution in Virginia, 1775–1783*. Williamsburg, Va.: Colonial Williamsburg Foundation, 1988.

Sheads, Scott S. *The Rockets' Red Glare: The Maritime Defense of Baltimore in 1814*. Centerville, Md.: Tidewater, 1986.

Shy, John. *A People Numerous and Armed*. New York: Oxford University Press, 1976.

_____. *Toward Lexington*. Princeton: Princeton University Press, 1965.

Skaggs, David Curtis. *Thomas Macdonough: Master of Command in the Early U.S. Navy*. Annapolis: Naval Institute Press, 2003.

Smelser, Marshall. *The Congress Founds the Navy*. South Bend, Ind.: University of Notre Dame Press, 1959.

_____. *The Democratic Republic, 1801–1815*. New York: Harper & Row, 1968.

_____. *The Winning of Independence*. New York: New Viewpoints, 1973.

Smith, Charles R. *Marines in the Revolution: A History of the Continental Marines in the American Revolution, 1775–1783*. Washington, D.C.: U.S. Government Printing Office, 1975.

Smith, Ellen H. *Charles Carroll of Carrollton*. Cambridge: Harvard University Press, 1942.

Smith, Gene A. *Thomas Catesby Jones: Commodore of Manifest Destiny*. Annapolis: Naval Institute Press, 2000.

Smith, James Morton. *Freedom's Fetters*. Ithaca, N.Y.: Cornell University Press, 1956.

Smith, Page. *John Adams*. 2 vols. New York: Doubleday, 1962.

Smith, Paul H. *Loyalists and Redcoats: A Study in British Revolutionary Policy*. Chapel Hill: University of North Carolina Press, 1964.

Smith, Philip, and Chadwick Foster. *Fired by Manley Zeal: A Naval Fiasco of the American Revolution*. Salem, Mass.: Peabody Museum, 1977.

Snow, Elliot, and H. Allen Gosnell. *On the Decks of Old Ironsides*. New York: Macmillan, 1932.

Sprout, Harold, and Margaret Sprout. *The Rise of American Naval Power, 1776–1918*. Princeton: Princeton University Press, 1939.

Stagg, J. C. A. *Mr. Madison's War.* Princeton: Princeton University Press, 1985.

Stahr, Walter. *John Jay.* New York: Hambledon & London, 2005.

Stanley, Godbold E., and Robert H. Woody. *Christopher Gadsden and the American Revolution.* Knoxville: University of Tennessee Press, 1982.

Stephenson, Michael. *Patriot Battles: How the War of Independence Was Fought.* New York: HarperCollins, 2007.

Stewart, Robert Armistead. *The History of Virginia's Navy of the Revolution.* Baltimore: Genealogical, 1934.

Stinchcombe, William C. *The American Revolution and the French Alliance.* Syracuse: Syracuse University Press, 1969.

Stivers, Reuben Elmore. *Privateers and Volunteers.* Annapolis: Naval Institute Press, 1976.

Symonds, Craig. *Decision at Sea: Five Naval Battles That Shaped American History.* New York: Oxford University Press, 2005.

_____. *Navalists and Antinavalists: The Naval Policy Debate in the United States, 1785–1827.* Newark: University of Delaware Press, 1980.

_____. *New Aspects of Naval History.* Annapolis: Naval Institute Press, 1981.

Syrett, David. *Admiral Lord Howe: A Biography.* Annapolis: Naval Institute Press, 2006.

———. *American Shipping and the American War, 1775–1783.* London: Athlone, 1970.

Taaffe, Stephen R. *The Philadelphia Campaign, 1777-1778.* Lawrence: University of Kansas Press, 2003.

Tansill, Charles Callan. *The United States and Santo Domingo, 1798–1873: A Chapter in Caribbean Diplomacy.* Baltimore: Johns Hopkins University Press, 1938.

Thomas, Evan. *John Paul Jones: Sailor, Hero, Father of the American Navy.* New York: Simon & Schuster, 2003.

Tornquist, Karl G. *The Naval Campaigns of Count de Grasse.* Philadelphia: Swedish Colony Society, 1942.

Toutellot, Arthur B. *William Diamond's Drum.* New York: Doubleday, 1959.

Tregle, Joseph. *Louisiana in the Age of Jackson.* Baton Rouge: Louisiana State University Press, 1999.

Trevelyan, George Otto. *The American Revolution.* 6 vols. New York: Longmans, Green, 1899–1914.

_____. *The Early History of Charles James Fox.* New York: Harper, 1899.

Triber, Jayne E. *A True Republican: The Life of Paul Revere.* Amherst: University of Massachusetts Press, 1998.

Tucker, Glenn. *Dawn Like Thunder.* Indianapolis: Bobbs-Merrill, 1963.

Tucker, Robert W., and David Henderson. *Empire of Liberty: The Statecraft of Thomas Jefferson.* New York: Oxford University Press, 1990.

Tucker, Spencer C., and Frank T. Reuter. *Injured Honor: The Chesapeake-Leopard Affair.* Annapolis: Naval Institute Press, 1996.

Unger, Harlow Giles. *Lafayette.* Hoboken, N.J.: Wiley, 2002.

Updyke, F. A. *The Diplomacy of the War of 1812.* Baltimore: Johns Hopkins University Press, 1915.

Varg, Paul A. *Foreign Policies of the Founding Fathers.* East Lansing: University of Michigan Press, 1963.

Ver Steeg, Clarence L. *Robert Morris: Revolutionary Financier.* Philadelphia: University of Pennsylvania Press, 1954.

Vickers, Daniel. *Young Men and the Sea: Yankee Seafarers in the Age of Sail.* New Haven: Yale University Press, 2005.

Wagner, Frederick. *Submarine Fighter of the American Revolution.* New York: Dodd, Mead, 1963.

Ward, Christopher. *The War of the Revolution.* 2 vols. New York: Macmillan, 1952.

Wheelan, Joseph. *Jefferson's War: America's First War on Terror, 1801–1805*. New York: Carroll & Graf, 2003.

Wheeler, Richard. *In Pirate Waters*. New York: Crowell, 1969.

White, Leonard D. *The Federalists: A Study in Administrative History*. New York: Macmillan, 1948.

_____. *The Jeffersonians: A Study in Administrative History, 1801–1829*. New York: Macmillan, 1956.

Willcox, William B. *The American Rebellion: Sir Henry Clinton's Narrative of His Campaigns, 1775–1782*. New Haven: Yale University Press, 1954.

_____. *Portrait of a General: Sir Henry Clinton in the War of Independence*. New York: Knopf, 1964.

Wills, Garry. *The Negro President: Jefferson and the Slave Power*. Boston: Houghton Mifflin, 2005.

Wilson, David K. *The Southern Strategy: Britain's Conquest of South Carolina and Georgia, 1775–1780*. Columbia: University of South Carolina Press, 2005.

Wood, W. J. *Battles of the Revolutionary War, 1775–1781*. Chapel Hill: University of North Carolina Press, 1990.

Zahniser, Marvin R. *Charles Cotesworth Pinckney: Founding Father*. Chapel Hill: University of North Carolina Press, 1967.

Zilversmit, Arthur. *The First Emancipation: The Abolition of Slavery in the North*. Chicago: University of Chicago Press, 1967.

PERIODICAL ARTICLES

Adams, Mary P. "Jefferson's Reaction to the Treaty of San Ildefonso." *Journal of Southern History* (May 1955).

Alden, John R. "Why the March to Concord?" *American Historical Review* 49 (1944).

Allen, Gardner Weld. "Captain Hector McNeil, Continental Navy." *Massachusetts Historical Society Proceedings* 55 (1922).

Anderson, William G. "John Adams, the Navy, and the Quasi-War with France." *American Neptune* (April 1970).

Barnett, Richard C. "The View from Below Deck: The British Navy, 1777–1781." *American Neptune* (July 1978).

Bauer, K. Jack. "Naval Shipbuilding Programs, 1794–1860." *Military Affairs* (Spring 1965).

Baugh, Daniel A. "The Politics of British Naval Failure, 1775–1777." *American Neptune* (July 1982).

Bemis, Samuel. "British Secret Service." *American Historical Review* (April 1924).

Bolander, Louis H. "The Frigate *Alliance*, the Favorite Ship of the American Revolution." *U.S. Naval Institute Proceedings* (September 1927).

Breen, Kenneth. "Graves and Hood at the Chesapeake." *Mariners Mirror* 66 (1980).

Brewington, M.V. "American Naval Guns, 1775–1785." Pt. 1. *American Neptune* 3 (1943).

_____. "American Naval Guns, 1775–1785." Pt. 2. *American Neptune* 3 (1943).

Brown, Gerald S. "The Anglo-French Naval Crisis, 1778: A Study of Conflict in the North Cabinet." *William and Mary Quarterly*, 3rd series (January 1956).

Bulger, William T., ed. "Sir Henry Clinton's 'Journal of the Siege of Charleston, 1780.'" *South Carolina Historical Magazine*, 1965.

Carr, James A. "The Battle of New Orleans and the Treaty of Ghent." *Diplomatic History* 3 (1979).

Casto, William R. "'We Are Armed for the Defense of the Rights of Man': The French Revolution Comes to America." *American Neptune* 61, no. 3 (2001).

Clark, William Bell. "American Naval Policy." *American Neptune* 1 (1941).

Coatsworth, John H. "American Trade with European Colonies in the Caribbean and South America, 1790–1812." *William and Mary Quarterly*, 3rd series (April 1967).

Davidson, P. G. "Virginia and the Alien and Sedition Laws." *American Historical Review* 36 (1931).

Dudley, William S., and Michael A. Palmer. "No Mistake About It: A Response to Jonathan R. Dull." *American Neptune* (Fall 1985).

Eagan, Clifford L. "The United States, France, and West Florida, 1803–1807." *Florida Historical Quarterly* (January 1969).

Eckert, Edward K. "Early Reform in the Navy Department." *American Neptune* 33 (1973).

_____. "William Jones: Mr. Madison's Secretary of the Navy." *Pennsylvania Magazine of History and Biography*, April 1972.

Eller, Ernes M. "Sea Power in the American Revolution." *U.S. Naval Institute Proceedings* (June 1936).

Fowler, William M., Jr. "James Nicholson and the Continental Frigate Virginia." *American Neptune* (April 1973).

_____. "The Business of War: Boston as a Navy Base, 1776–1783." *American Neptune* 42 (1982).

Goodman, W. H. "The Origins of the War of 1812: A Survey of Changing Interpretations." *Mississippi Valley Historical Review* 28 (1941).

Griswold, A. Whitney. "The Agrarian Democracy of Thomas Jefferson." *American Political Science Review* 40 (1946).

Hayes, Frederic H. "John Adams and American Sea Power." *American Neptune* (January 1965).

Heaton, Herbert. "Non-Importation, 1806–1812." *Journal of Economic History* (November 9, 1941).

Jones, Robert F. "The Naval Thought and Policy of Benjamin Stoddert, First Secretary of the Navy, 1798–1801." *American Neptune* (January 1964).

Kaplan, Laurence S. "Jefferson, the Napoleonic Wars, and the Balance of Power." *William and Mary Quarterly* (April 1957).

Latimer, Margaret K. "South Carolina: A Protagonist of the War of 1812." *American Historical Review* 61 (1956).

Lemisch, Jesse. "Jack Tar in the Streets: Merchant Seamen in the Politics of Revolutionary America." *William and Mary Quarterly* (July 1968).

MacLeod, Julia. "Jefferson and the Navy: A Defense." *Huntington Library Quarterly* (February 1945).

Mayhew, Dean R. "Jefferson's Gunboats in the War of 1812." *American Neptune* (April 1982).

McCusker, John J., Jr. "The American Invasion of Nassau in the Bahamas." *American Neptune* 25 (1965).

Moomaw, W. H. "The Denouement of General Howe's Campaign of 1777." *English Historical Review* 74 (1964).

Morgan, William James. "American Privateering in America's War of Independence, 1775–1783." *American Neptune* (April 1976).

_____. "The Stormy Career of Captain Hector McNeil, Continental Navy." *Military Affairs* (Fall 1952).

Morison, Samuel Eliot. "Elbridge Gerry, Gentleman-Democrat." *New England Quarterly* (January 1929).

Norton, Louis Arthur. "The Continental Naval Brig Andrew (Andrea) Doria." *American Neptune* (Winter 2001).

Palmer, R. R. "The Dubious Democrat: Thomas Jefferson in Bourbon France." *Political Science Quarterly* 72 (1957).

Paullin, Charles Oscar. "Early Naval Administration Under the Constitution." *Proceedings of the United States Naval Institute* 32 (1906).

———. "Naval Administration Under Secretaries of the Navy Smith, Hamilton, and Jones, 1801–1814." *Proceedings of the United States Naval Institute* (December 1906).

Perkins, Bradford. "George Canning, Great Britain, and the United States, 1807–1809." *American Historical Review* (October 1957).

Quarles, Benjamin. "The Colonial Militia and Negro Manpower." *Mississippi Valley Historical Review* (March 1959).

Ritchie, Carson. "The Louisiana Campaign." *Louisiana Historical Review* 44 (1961).

Scott, Kenneth. "New Hampshire's Part in the Penobscot Expedition." *American Neptune* (July 1947).

Shaw, Henry I. "Penobscot Assault, 1779." *Military Affairs* (Summer 1953).

Smelser, Marshall. "George Washington and the Alien and Sedition Acts." *American Historical Review* (January 1954).

Smith, Abbot. "Mr. Madison's War: An Unsuccessful Experiment in the Conduct of National Policy." *Political Science Quarterly* 57 (1942).

Steel, A. "Impressment in the Monroe-Pinkney Negotiations, 1896–1807." *American Historical Review* 57 (1952).

Taylor, G. R. "Agrarian Discontent in the Mississippi Valley Preceding the War of 1812." *Journal of Political Economy* 39 (1931).

Turner, Frederick Jackson. "The Origin of Genet's Projected Attack on Louisiana and the Floridas." *American Historical Review* 3 (1897).

Willcox, William. "The British Road to Yorktown: A Study in Divided Command." *American Historical Review* 52 (1946).

INDEX